Praise for *Professional Excel Development*

"Think you know Microsoft Excel? Think again. This book covers intermediate (class modules, dictator applications, etc.) to advanced topics like XLLs, C APIs and Web Services. It offers plenty of easy to understand code listings that show exactly what the authors are trying to convey without forcing the readers to follow step-by-step."

Deepak Sharma, Sr. Systems Specialist, Tata Infotech Ltd.

"This book takes off where other Excel books stop. It covers Excel programming beyond VBA and looks at the professional issues—security, distribution, working with databases—using VB, VBA.NET and Windows API calls. The authors' depth and practical experience shows in the details. They explain complex issues clearly, describe best practices and point out traps to avoid."

Shauna Kelly, Microsoft Office MVP, www.ShaunaKelly.com

"The approach of following an application's development is very effective in developing the concepts as the chapters unfold. The practical, working examples used are relevant to many professional programmers."

Jan Karel Pieterse, JKP Application Development Services, www.jkp-ads.com

"This book stands out. While there are plenty of Excel books, I am not aware of any organized in this way. Information on .NET, and C, as well as other unique and useful chapters makes this a great offering."

Ken Bluttman, Author of Developing Microsoft Office Solutions

"This book explains difficult concepts in detail. The authors provide more than one method for complex development topics, along with the advantages and disadvantages of using the various methods described. They have my applause for the incorporation of development best practices."

Beth Melton, Microsoft Office MVP

Professional Excel Development

Professional Excel Development

The Definitive Guide to Developing Applications Using Microsoft Excel and VBA

Stephen Bullen, Rob Bovey, John Green

✦✦Addison-Wesley

Upper Saddle River, NJ • Boston • Indianapolis • San Francisco
New York • Toronto • Montreal • London • Munich • Paris • Madrid
Capetown • Sydney • Tokyo • Singapore • Mexico City

U. S. Corporate and Government Sales
(800) 382-3419
corpsales@pearsontechgroup.com

For sales outside the U. S., please contact:

International Sales
international@pearsoned.com

Visit us on the Web: www.awprofessional.com

Library of Congress Catalog Number: 2004114575

Pearson Education, Inc.
Rights and Contracts Department
One Lake Street
Upper Saddle River, NJ 07458

ISBN 0-321-26250-6
Text printed in the United States on recycled paper at R.R. Donnelley, Crawfordsville, IN.
Third printing, July, 2005

Contents

Chapter 24: Providing Help, Securing, Packaging and Distributing 863

Acknowledgments

First and foremost, this book would never have been written without the support of our partners and families, who have graciously put up with our insatiable computer habits and many late nights over the past year. Neither would it have been done without our dogs, who kept our feet warm while we worked and forced us to get out of the house at least once each day.

We all owe a debt of gratitude to the Excel group at Microsoft, past and present, for making Excel the amazing development platform it is today. It is their dedication and commitment to us that makes Excel application development possible and enjoyable. They have repeatedly demonstrated their willingness to listen to and implement our suggestions over the years.

There are many people we want to thank at Addison-Wesley Professional, particularly Amy Fleischer for bringing us together, Stephane Thomas, Ebony Haight and Joan Murray for their support while writing the book, Kristy Hart for steering us through the production process and Curt Johnson for getting it on the shelves.

The quality of a technical book depends as much on the reviewers as the authors, so we want to thank all our technical reviewers. Most of your suggestions were implemented. At the risk of offending the others, we would particularly like to thank Dick Kusleika and John Peltier for the quality and rigor of their reviews and Beth Melton for finding numerous errors nobody else spotted.

Lastly, we want to thank you for buying this book. Please tell us what you think about it, either by e-mail or by writing a review at Amazon.com.

Thank you,

Stephen Bullen
Rob Bovey
John Green

About the Authors

Stephen Bullen

stephen@oaltd.co.uk

Stephen Bullen lives in Woodford Green, London, England, with his partner Clare, daughter Becky and their dog, Fluffy. A graduate of Oxford University, Stephen has an MA in Engineering, Economics and Management, providing a unique blend of both business and technical skills.

He has been providing Excel consulting and application development services since 1994, originally as an employee of Price Waterhouse Management Consultants and since 1997 as an independent consultant trading under the name of Business Modelling Solutions Limited. In September 2004, BMS changed its name to Office Automation Limited. If you would like to make use of Stephen's services, please contact him at stephen@oaltd.co.uk.

The Office Automation Web site, www.oaltd.co.uk, provides a number of helpful and interesting utilities, examples, tips and techniques to help in your use of Excel and development of Excel applications.

Stephen contributed chapters to John Green's *Excel 2000 VBA Programmer's Reference* and co-authored the sequel, *Excel 2002 VBA Programmer's Reference* (both published by Wrox Press).

In addition to his consulting and writing assignments, Stephen actively supports the Excel user community in Microsoft's peer-to-peer support newsgroups. In recognition of his knowledge, skills and contributions, Microsoft has awarded him the title of Most Valuable Professional each year since 1996.

Rob Bovey

robbovey@appspro.com

Rob Bovey is president of Application Professionals, a software development company specializing in Microsoft Office, Visual Basic, and SQL Server applications. He brings many years' experience creating financial, accounting and executive information systems for corporate users to Application Professionals. You can visit the Application Professionals Web site at www.appspro.com.

Rob developed several add-ins shipped by Microsoft for Microsoft Excel, co-authored the *Microsoft Excel 97 Developers Kit* and contributed to the *Excel 2002 VBA Programmer's Reference*. He earned his Bachelor of Science degree from The Rochester Institute of Technology and his MBA from the University of North Carolina at Chapel Hill. He is a Microsoft Certified Systems Engineer (MCSE) and a Microsoft Certified Solution Developer (MCSD). Microsoft has awarded him the title of Most Valuable Professional each year since 1995. He currently resides in Edmonds, Washington, with his wife Michelle, and their two black labs, Jasper and Jade.

John Green

greenj@bigpond.net.au

John Green lives and works in Sydney, Australia, as an independent computer consultant, specializing in integrating Excel, Access, Word and Outlook using VBA. He has more than 30 years of computing experience, a Chemical Engineering degree and an MBA.

He wrote his first programs in FORTRAN, took a part in the evolution of specialized planning languages on mainframes and, in the early 1980s, became interested in spreadsheet systems, including 1-2-3 and Excel.

John established his company, Execuplan Consulting, in 1980, developing computer-based planning applications and training users and developers.

John has had regular columns in a number of Australian magazines and has contributed chapters to a number of books, including *Excel Expert Solutions* and *Using Visual Basic for Applications 5*, published by Que. He is the principal author of *Excel 2000 VBA Programmer's Reference* and its subsequent editions, published by Wrox Press.

Since 1995 he has been accorded the status of Most Valuable Professional by Microsoft for his contributions to the CompuServe Excel forum and MS Internet newsgroups.

CHAPTER 1

Introduction

About This Book

Microsoft Excel is much, much more than just a spreadsheet. Since the introduction of the Visual Basic Editor in Excel 97 and the improved stability of Excel 2000, it has become a respected development platform in its own right. Applications written using Excel are now often found alongside those written using Visual Basic, C++, Java, .NET and so on, as part of many corporations' core suite of business-critical applications. Indeed, Excel is often used for the client end of Web-based applications, made particularly easy with Excel 2003's XML import/export features.

Unfortunately, Excel is still all too often thought of as a hobbyist platform—that people develop spreadsheet-based applications in their spare time to help out with their day job. A brief look at the shelves of any bookstore seems to confirm that opinion. Although there are myriad titles explaining how to use Excel and numerous titles about Excel and VBA, none provide an overall explanation of how to develop professional-quality Excel-based applications. This is that book.

Whereas all the other major languages seem to have a de facto standard text that explains the commonly agreed best practices for architecting, designing and developing applications in that language, Excel does not. This book aims to fill that gap.

All three authors are professional Excel developers who run our own companies developing Excel-based applications for clients ranging from individuals to the largest multinational corporations. This book details the approaches we use when designing, developing, distributing and supporting the applications we write for our clients.

This is not a beginner-level book. We assume that the reader will have read and (mostly) understood our *Excel 2000/2002 VBA Programmer's Reference*, John Walkenbach's *Excel Power Programming*, or similar titles.

The Excel Developer

Excel developers can be divided into five general categories, based on their experience and knowledge of Excel and VBA. To varying degrees, this book has something to offer each of them, but with a focus on the more advanced topics. Putting yourself into one of these categories might help you decide whether this is the right book for you.

The basic ***Excel user*** probably doesn't think of himself as a developer at all. To basic users, Excel is no more than a tool to help them get on with their job. They start off using Excel worksheets as a handy place to store lists or perform simple repetitive calculations. As they discover more of Excel's functionality, their workbooks become more complex and start to include lots of worksheet functions, pivot tables and charts. There is little in this book for these people; although *Chapter 4 — Worksheet Design* details the best practices to use when designing and laying out a worksheet for data entry, *Chapter 14 — Data Manipulation Techniques* explains how to structure a worksheet and which functions and features to use to manipulate their lists, and *Chapter 15 — Advanced Charting Techniques*, explains how to get the most from Excel's chart engine. The techniques suggested in these chapters should help the basic Excel user avoid some of the pitfalls often encountered as their experience and the complexity of their spreadsheets increases.

The ***Excel power user*** has a wide understanding of Excel's functionality, knows which tool or function is best to use in a given situation, creates complex spreadsheets for his own use and is often called on to help develop colleagues' spreadsheets or to identify why colleagues' spreadsheets do not work as intended. Occasionally power users include small snippets of VBA they found on the Internet or created using the macro recorder, but struggle to adapt the code to their needs. As a result, they produce code that is untidy, slow and hard to maintain. Although this book is not a VBA tutorial, the power user has much to gain from following the best practices we suggest for both worksheets and code modules. Most of the chapters in the book are relevant to power users who have an interest in improving their Excel and VBA development skills.

The ***VBA developer*** makes extensive use of VBA code in his workbooks (often too much). VBA developers are typically either power users who have started to learn VBA too early or Visual Basic 6 developers who have switched to Excel VBA development. Although they might be very proficient at VBA, they believe every problem must have a VBA solution and lack sufficient knowledge of Excel to make the best use of its features. Their solutions are often cumbersome, slow and make poor use of Excel's object model. This book has much to offer VBA developers to improve their use of Excel itself, including explaining how to architect Excel-based applications, the best practices for designing worksheets and how to use Excel's features for their data entry, analysis and presentation. This book also seeks to improve their Excel VBA development skills by introducing advanced coding techniques, detailing VBA best practices and explaining how to improve their code's performance.

The ***Excel developer*** has realized the most efficient and maintainable applications are those that make the most of Excel's own functionality, augmented by VBA when appropriate. Excel developers are confident developing Excel-based applications for their colleagues to use or as part of an in-house development team. Their undoubted knowledge of Excel is put to good use in their applications, but it also constrains their designs, and they are reluctant to use other languages and applications to augment their Excel solutions. They have probably read John Walkenbach's *Excel Power Programming* and/or our own *Excel 2000/2002 VBA Programmer's Reference* and need a book to take them to the highest level of Excel application development—that of the professional developer. This is that book.

The ***professional Excel developer*** designs and develops Excel-based applications and utilities for clients or employers that are robust, fast, easy to use, maintainable and secure. Excel forms the core of their solutions, but they include any other applications and languages that are appropriate. For example, they might use third-party ActiveX controls; automate other applications; use Windows API calls; use ADO to connect to external databases, C/C++ for fast custom worksheet functions, VB6 or VB.Net for creating their own object models and securing their code; and XML for sharing data over the Internet. This book teaches all those skills. If you are already a professional Excel developer, you know that learning never stops and will appreciate the knowledge and best practices presented in this book by three of your peers.

Excel as an Application Development Platform

If we look at Excel as a development platform and not just a spreadsheet, we can break it down into five fundamental components we can use for our applications:

- The worksheet, charts and so on, used as a user interface and presentation layer for data entry and reporting

- The worksheet, used as a simple data store for lists, tables and other information used by our application
- VBA, Excel's programming language and forms engine
- The worksheet, used as a declarative programming language for high-performance numeric processing
- The Excel object model, allowing programmatic control of (nearly) all of Excel's functionality, from both within Excel and from outside it

The Worksheet as a Presentation Layer for Data Entry and Reporting

When most people think about Excel, they think in terms of typing numbers into cells, having some calculations update and seeing a result displayed in a different cell or on a chart. Without necessarily thinking in such terms, they are using the worksheet as a user interface for their data entry and reporting and are generally comfortable with these tasks. The in-cell editing, validation and formatting features built in to Excel provide an extremely rich and compelling data-entry experience, while the charting, cell formatting and drawing tools provide a presentation-quality reporting mechanism. It is hard to imagine the code that would be required if we tried to reproduce the experience using the form design tools available in most other development environments, yet it's there waiting for us to use in our Excel-based applications. The biggest problem we face is how to add some structure to the free-form grid of the worksheet, to present a simple and easy-to-use interface, while leveraging the rich functionality Excel provides. *Chapter 4 — Worksheet Design* introduces some techniques and best practices for developing worksheet-based data-entry forms, and *Chapter 15 — Advanced Charting Techniques* discusses using Excel's charting capabilities.

The Worksheet as a Simple Data Store

What is a worksheet when it is never intended to be shown to the end user? At its simplest, it is no more than a large grid of cells in which we can store just about anything we want to—numbers, text, lists, tables or pictures. Most applications use some amount of static data or textual or graphical resources; storing that information in a worksheet makes it both extremely easy to access using VBA and simple to maintain. Lists and tables in worksheets can directly feed Excel's data validation (as shown in *Chapter 4 — Worksheet Design*), greatly simplify the creation and maintenance of command bars (*Chapter 8 — Advanced Command Bar Handling*), and enable us to construct dynamic userforms (*Chapter 10 — Userform Design and Best Practices*).

VBA: Excel's Programming Language

We expect most readers of this book to have at least some familiarity with VBA. If not, we suggest you read either our *Excel 2000/2002 VBA Programmer's Reference* or John Walkenbach's *Excel Power Programming* before continuing much further. Many people see the *A* in VBA as meaning the language is somehow less than Visual Basic itself. In fact, both VB6 and Office 2000 and above use exactly the same DLL to provide the keywords, syntax and statements we program with. The only differences are the objects provided by the runtimes (the VB runtime vs. the Excel objects), the forms packages (VB's "Ruby" forms vs. Office UserForms) and that VB6 includes a compiler to create EXEs and DLLs, whereas VBA is always interpreted at runtime. Indeed, the Office Developer Edition (pre-Excel 2003) includes the same compiler VB6 uses, enabling us to compile (simple) DLLs from within the Office Visual Basic Editor.

Most beginner and intermediate VBA developers use VBA as a ***purely*** procedural language, with nearly all their code residing in standard modules. VBA also enables us to create applications using an object-oriented programming (OOP) approach, in which class modules are used to create our own objects. *Chapter 7 — Using Class Modules to Create Objects* and *Chapter 11 — Interfaces* explain how to use VBA in this manner, while basic OOP concepts (such as encapsulation) are used throughout the book.

Most of this book is dedicated to explaining advanced VBA techniques and a professional approach to application design and development that can put using VBA in Excel on a par with, and sometimes in front of, using VB6 or VB.Net for application development. We also show in *Chapter 20 — Combining Excel and Visual Basic 6* and *Chapter 22 — Using VB.NET and the Visual Studio Tools for Office* that the Excel developer can use the best of both worlds, by combining Excel, VB6 and/or VB.Net in a seamless application.

The Worksheet as a Declarative Programming Language

Consider the following code:

```
dSales = 1000
dPrice = 10.99
dRevenue = dSales * dPrice
```

This code could quite easily be a few lines of VBA. We give the variable dSales a value of 1000, the variable dPrice a value of 10.99 and then calculate the revenue as sales times price. If we change the names of the variables and adjust the spacing, the same code could also be written as follows:

```
D1     =1000
D2     =10.99
D3     =D1*D2
```

This preceding code looks much more like worksheet cell addresses and formulas than lines of VBA code, showing that a worksheet is in fact a programming language of its own, if we choose to think of it in those terms. The IF() worksheet function is directly equivalent to the If...Then...Else VBA statement, and the judicious use of circular references and iteration can be equivalent to either the For...Next or Do...Loop structures.

Instead of stating a set of **operations** that are executed line by line, we "program" in this language by stating a set of **declarations** (by typing formulas and values into worksheet cells), in any order we want to:

```
"D3 is the product of D1 and D2"
"D1 has the value 1000"
"D2 has the value 10.99"
```

To "run" this program, Excel first examines all the declarations and builds a "precedence tree" to identify which cells depend on the results of which other cells and thereby determine the most efficient order in which the cells must be calculated. The same precedence tree is also used to identify the minimum set of calculations that must be performed whenever the value in a cell is changed. The result is a calculation engine that is vastly more efficient than an equivalent VBA program, and one that should be used whenever complex numeric computations are required in our applications.

Microsoft Excel (and other spreadsheet programs) is unique among application development platforms in providing both a procedural (VBA) and a declarative (the worksheet) programming language. The most efficient Excel application is one that makes appropriate use of both these languages.

It is assumed the reader of this book has some knowledge of Excel and worksheet functions, so *Chapter 14 — Data Manipulation Techniques* focuses on using advanced worksheet functions (including best-practice suggestions for handling circular references) and Excel's other data-analysis features.

The Excel Object Model

Although the other four components of the Excel platform are invaluable in the development of applications, it is probably the richness of the Excel object model that provides the most compelling reason to base our application development on Excel. Almost everything that can be done through the user interface can also be done programmatically by using the objects in the Excel object model—accessing the list of number formats and applying a digital signature to a workbook are perhaps the most notable exceptions. The vast array of functionality exposed by these objects makes highly complex applications fairly simple to develop—it becomes more an issue of when and how to efficiently plug the functionality together than to develop the functionality from scratch. This book does not attempt to explore and document all the backwaters of the object model, but instead makes continual use of the objects in our application development.

Structure

Through the course of this book, we cover both the concepts and details of each topic and apply those concepts to a timesheet reporting and analysis application we build. The chapters are therefore arranged approximately in the order in which we would design and develop an Excel application:

- Chapter 2 discusses the different styles of application we might choose to create.
- Chapter 3 identifies some general best practices for working with Excel and VBA, which are followed throughout this book.
- Chapter 4 explains how to design and structure a worksheet for data entry.
- Chapters 5 and 6 introduce two specific types of application, the add-in and the dictator application, which form the basis of our timesheet reporting and analysis suite.
- Chapters 7 through 13 discuss advanced techniques for a range of VBA topics.

- Chapters 14 and 15 explain how to efficiently utilize Excel's features within an application to analyze data and present results.
- Chapters 16 and 17 discuss techniques for debugging and optimizing VBA code.
- Chapters 18 through 22 look outside of Excel, first by explaining how to automate other applications, and then by explaining how to interact with Excel using C, Visual Basic and VB.Net.
- Chapter 23 focuses on how Excel applications can make use of the Internet and XML.
- Chapter 24 completes the development by explaining how to provide help and how to secure, package and distribute the application.

Examples

Throughout the book, we illustrate the concepts and techniques we introduce by building a timesheet data-entry, consolidation, analysis and reporting application. This application comprises a data-entry template to be completed by each employee, with the data sent to a central location for consolidation, analysis and reporting. The end of each chapter presents a fully working example of both parts of the application included on the CD, which grows steadily more complex as the book progresses and therefore will be relevant to different types of companies.

In *Chapter 4 — Worksheet Design*, we start with a very simple data-entry workbook and the assumption that each employee would e-mail the completed file to a manager, who would analyze the results manually—a typical situation for a company with perhaps 10 to 20 employees.

By the end of the book, the data-entry workbook uses XML to upload the data to a Web service, where it is stored in a central database. The reporting application extracts the data from the database, performs various analyses and presents the results as reports in Excel worksheets and charts.

Along the way, we rewrite some of the parts of the application in a number of different ways, to show how easy it can be to include other languages and delivery mechanisms in our Excel-based applications.

Each chapter may also include specific examples to illustrate key points that it would be too artificial to include in our main application.

Supported Versions

When developing an Excel application for a client, their upgrade policy will usually determine which version of Excel we must use; very few clients will agree to upgrade their desktops just so we can develop using the latest version, unless there is a compelling business requirement that can only be satisfied by using features that the latest version introduces. There is so little difference between Excel 2000 and Excel 2003 that it is hard to imagine such a business requirement. An extremely unscientific poll (based on postings to the Microsoft support newsgroups) seems to indicate the following approximate usage for each version:

Excel 97	10%
Excel 2000	45%
Excel 2002	40%
Excel 2003	5%

There were a number of significant changes between Excel 97 and Excel 2000 for the application developer, including the switch from VBA5 to VBA6 and the introduction of modeless userforms, interfaces, COM Add-ins and support for ADO. We have therefore decided to use Excel 2000 as our lowest supported version and development platform, with our applications tested in the later versions. Most of the concepts detailed in this book apply equally to Excel 97, but our example timesheet application uses features Excel 97 does not support. Whenever we discuss a feature supported only in the later versions (such as XML import/export and VB.Net integration in Excel 2003), we state which version(s) can be used.

Typefaces

The following text styles are used in this book:

Menu items and dialog text will be shown as *Tools > Options > Calculation > Manual*, where the > indicates navigation to a submenu or dialog tab.

```
Sub SomeCode()
    'Code listings are shown like this
    'With new or changed lines highlighted like this
End Sub
```

Code within a paragraph is shown as `Application.Calculation = xlManual`.

Paths on the CD are shown as *Concepts\Ch11 - Interfaces*.

URLs are shown as `http://www.oaltd.co.uk`.

Important points or emphasized words are shown bold and italic, **_like this_**.

On the CD

Most of the code listings shown in this book are also included in example workbooks on the accompanying CD. For clarity, the code shown in the book uses shorter line lengths, a reduced indent setting, fewer in-code comments and less error handling than the corresponding code in the workbooks.

The CD has three main directories, containing the following files:

- *Tools* contains a number of tools and utilities developed by the authors that we have found to be invaluable during our application development. The MustHaveTools.htm file contains details about each of these tools and links to other third-party utilities.
- *Concepts* has separate subdirectories for each chapter, each one containing example files to support the text of the chapter. For best results, we suggest you have these workbooks open while reading through the corresponding chapter.
- *Application* has separate subdirectories for each chapter, each one containing a version of our timesheet example application suite. Beginning with *Chapter 4 — Worksheet Design*, most chapters end with a *Practical Example* section, explaining the changes that have been made to the timesheet application to implement some of the concepts introduced in the chapter.

Help and Support

Questions about the book itself (such as missing CDs, typos, errata and so on) should be directed to Addison-Wesley, at `http://www.awprofessional.com/contactus`.

Any errata and corrections will be posted to the Addison-Wesley Web site at `http://www.awprofessional.com/title/0321262506`.

By far the best place to go for help with any of your Excel development questions, whether related to this book or not, are the Microsoft support newsgroups' archives maintained by Google at `http://groups.google.com`. A quick search of the archives is almost certain to find a question similar to yours, already answered by one of the many professional developers who volunteer their time helping out in the newsgroups, including all three of this book's authors. On the rare occasions that the archives fail to answer your question, you are welcome to ask it directly in the newsgroups by connecting a news reader (such as Outlook Express) to `msnews.microsoft.com` and selecting an appropriate newsgroup, such as these:

- `microsoft.public.excel.programming` for VBA-related questions
- `microsoft.public.excel.worksheet.functions` for help with worksheet functions
- `microsoft.public.vsnet.vstools.office` for help with Excel/VB.Net integration issues
- `microsoft.public.excel.misc` for general Excel queries

A number of Web sites provide a great deal of information and free downloadable examples and utilities targeted toward the Excel developer, including the following:

`http://www.oaltd.co.uk`

`http://www.appspro.com`

`http://www.j-walk.com`

`http://www.cpearson.com`

`http://msdn.microsoft.com/office`

Feedback

We have tried very hard to present the information in this book in a clear and concise manner, explaining both the concepts and details needed to get things working and providing working examples of everything we cover. We have tried to provide sufficient information to enable you to apply these techniques in your own applications, but without getting bogged down in line-by-line explanations of entire code listings. We would like to think we have been successful in our attempt, but encourage you to let us know what you think. Constructive criticism is always welcome, as are suggestions for topics you think we may have overlooked. Please send an e-mail to one (or all) of the following:

Stephen Bullen: `stephen@oaltd.co.uk`
Rob Bovey: `robbovey@appspro.com`
John Green: `greenj@bigpond.net.au`

CHAPTER 2

Application Architectures

One of the first decisions to be made when starting a new project is how to structure the application. This chapter explains the alternative architectures we can use, the situations where each is most applicable, and the pros and cons of each choice.

Concepts

The choice of where to put the code for an Excel application is rarely straightforward. In anything but the simplest of situations, it is a considered trade-off between numerous factors, including the following:

- **Complexity**—How easy will the chosen architecture be to create?
- **Clarity**—How easy will it be for someone other than the author to understand the application?
- **Development**—How easy will it be to modify the code, particularly in a team environment?
- **Flexibility**—How easy is it to add new features?
- **Reliability**—Can the results be relied upon? How easily can calculation errors be introduced into the application?
- **Robustness**—How well will the application be able to handle application errors, invalid data, and so forth?
- **Security**—How easy will it be to prevent unauthorized changes to the application?
- **Deployment**—How easy will it be to distribute the application to the end user?
- **Updates**—How easy will it be to update the application after it has been distributed and started to be used? One of the most fundamental tenets of application design is that the "program" elements of the application must be physically separate from the "data" it works on.

Codeless Applications

The most basic application is one that only uses Excel's built-in functionality. Everybody creates this type of application without knowing it, simply by using Excel. They are typically created by beginning to intermediate Excel users who have not yet learned to use VBA. All the special formatting, validation, formulas and so on are placed directly on the same worksheet where data entry will be performed. There are some major issues with this approach, which together mean totally codeless applications are rarely a good choice.

Those who avoid using VBA may find that some of their worksheet functions and data-validation criteria get extremely complex and almost incomprehensible to anyone other than the author. The equivalent VBA will often be easier to understand.

The same worksheet is usually used for data entry, analysis, and presentation, often resulting in a cluttered appearance (usually with multitudes of differently colored cells to try to identify their purpose) that is difficult to understand, is unintuitive to use and is almost impossible for anyone except the author to modify reliably.

Such applications have to rely on Excel's cell protection and password-protecting the worksheet to prevent the users making unauthorized changes to the formulas, validation, formatting and so on. Worksheet passwords are notoriously easy to break, and a simple copy and paste will wipe out any data validation that has been set up. These applications are therefore neither secure nor robust.

Without any code, we are unable to provide much assistance to the user; we have to rely on them to do everything themselves—and do it correctly—instead of providing reliable helper routines that automate some of their tasks. The more complex the application, the less likely it is that all the tasks will be performed correctly.

If we consider a definition of what constitutes a "program" to be "anything that isn't the data," we see that all the conditional formatting, data validation, worksheet functions and so forth are really part of the "program," so these applications break the basic tenet of keeping the program and data physically separate. After the end users have started to enter data into their worksheet, it is very difficult to distribute an updated worksheet to them, without losing the data they have already entered. In addition to the new version of the worksheet, you would have to either provide clear instructions explaining how to copy their data across or write a conversion program that will copy their data from the old to the new workbook.

Codeless applications are ideal for simple situations where most of the following conditions apply:

- There will only be one copy of the workbook (so any changes can be done directly to that workbook), or each copy of the workbook will have a short lifetime, such as a survey or data-collection form that can be forgotten about after it has been completed and returned. In each case, the assumption is that the workbooks will not need updating after they have been deployed.
- The end users will be maintaining the workbook themselves (and don't know VBA), or the workbook will not require any maintenance at all.
- The workbook might be copied and updated on different machines (although only one at a time), such as when the workbook is taken home for the weekend—because it is self-contained, it can easily be copied to a floppy disk or e-mailed.
- There are relatively few routine or complex tasks to be performed to maintain or analyze the data.
- There are only a small number of end users, who can be well trained to ensure the application is used correctly and is not inadvertently broken.

A good example of a codeless application is a simple survey or data-collection form that requires the end user to fill in the details and e-mail the completed workbook to a central address for consolidation and analysis. The main benefit of a codeless application in such a situation is the avoidance of Excel's macro security warnings and the corresponding assurance that there is nothing malicious in the file.

Self-Automated Workbooks

A self-automated workbook is one in which the VBA code is physically contained within the workbook it acts upon. Probably the most common type of application, the automation code can be as simple as ensuring the workbook always opens with Sheet1 active or be as complex as an entire application. This is usually the first type of application a beginning VBA developer produces, built by adding numerous helper routines to the workbook that get progressively more complex (and usually cumbersome) over time.

After VBA is introduced to the workbook, we have much more flexibility in providing the required functionality and can make a considered choice whether to use Excel's built-in functions or write our own equivalents to avoid some of Excel's pitfalls. For example, Excel's data validation might not fire correctly when entries are made in multiple cells at the same time and is usually cleared when data is pasted onto the range. We can work around both these limitations by trapping the Worksheet_Change event and performing our own validation in code, making the worksheet more robust, reliable, and secure.

The workbook and worksheet code modules are provided for us by Excel to hook whichever events we want to use, and any ActiveX controls we add to the worksheet are automatically exposed in the same code module. This is the simplest architecture to create and probably the simplest to understand—most VBA developers will have written an application of this type and will therefore understand, for example, how the code within the worksheet code module is triggered.

The clearest advantage this style of application has over all the others is in the ease of deployment. There is only one file—the workbook—to distribute; there is no need to install or configure anything; and because the code is physically stored within the workbook, it is immediately available and working as soon as the workbook is opened.

Unfortunately, the self-automated workbook's clearest advantage is also its biggest problem. Because the code is physically inside the workbook, how do you issue updates to the code without affecting the data that has been entered on the worksheets? Although it is possible to write VBA that modifies the code within another workbook, the user has to specifically allow that to happen (in Excel 2002 and above), and it is only possible to unprotect and reprotect the VBA project using SendKeys, which cannot be relied on to work in foreign-language versions of Excel or if Excel does not have the focus. Even if the project could be unprotected and reprotected, saving the updated project would remove any digital signature that had been applied, resulting in macro virus warnings every time the workbook was subsequently opened. The only reliable way self-automated workbooks can be updated is to provide a completely new workbook with a routine (or instructions) to copy the data from the old workbook.

Self-automated workbooks are an ideal choice if the following conditions apply:

- The routines contained within the workbook provide specific functionality for that workbook (as opposed to general-purpose utilities).

- There will only be one copy of the workbook (so any changes can be done directly to that workbook), or

   The workbook will have a short lifetime and/or will be distributed to a large (and maybe unknown) audience, in which case the ease of deployment becomes a significant consideration, and there is no intention to distribute any updates, or

   The workbook does not contain any data that will need to be retained during an update, such as one that obtains its data from an external data source.

Codeless and self-automated workbooks are discussed in more detail in *Chapter 4 — Worksheet Design*.

Function and General-Purpose Add-ins

An ***add-in*** is a specific type of application, usually used to add features to Excel. The worksheets in an add-in are hidden from the user, so they never interact directly with the workbook. Instead, the add-in exposes its routines by adding items to Excel's menus and toolbars, hooking key combinations and/or exposing functions to be used within a worksheet. The routines in an add-in can also be executed by typing their fully qualified name (for example, MyAddin.xla!MyRoutine) in the *Tools > Macro > Macros* dialog, although they do not appear in the list of available macros.

The routines in a general-purpose add-in will always be available to the Excel user, so they are most appropriate when used for utility functions that are designed to work with any file, typically using the `ActiveWorkbook`, `ActiveSheet` or `Selection` objects to identify the items to operate on. Care should be taken to tidily handle "user error" issues, where the add-in's routines may be called from a context in which they will not work. For example, if your add-in changes the case of the text in the selected cell, you must check that there is a cell selected (and not a drawing object, for example), it isn't locked and it isn't the result of a formula. Similarly, if your code applies some custom formatting to the active worksheet, you must check that there is an active sheet (because there may be no workbooks open), it is a worksheet (and not a chart or macro sheet) and it is not protected.

An add-in is just a very hidden workbook, so it doesn't appear in the list of workbooks or the VBA `Workbooks` collection, and its macros are not listed in the *Tools > Macro > Macros* dialog. It is, however, just like any other workbook in almost every other way and should therefore be very easy for an intermediate Excel/VBA developer to understand and maintain. Indeed, you can toggle between having the workbook behave like an add-in or not by just changing the IsAddin property of the ThisWorkbook object in the VBE's Properties window.

Because add-ins never expose their worksheets to the user, all the user interaction is done through userforms (although VBA's InputBox and MsgBox functions can be used in simple situations). This gives us a high level of control over the user's entries, enabling us to create applications that are totally robust and reliable—assuming we include data-validation code and good error handling.

If the add-in needs to store any information, such as remembering a user's choices, that information should be kept separate from the add-in file, by storing it either in the registry (using SaveSetting/ GetSetting) or in a separate file (such as an INI file). If that is done, the add-in will never need to be saved by the end user and can be simply replaced by a new version if an update is required.

If you are willing to trust the end user to install the add-in correctly, it is also very easy to deploy—just send the XLA file with instructions to either copy it to their Library folder or to use the Browse button in the *Tools > Add-ins* dialog to locate the file. The alternative is to use an installation routine to write the required registry entries Excel uses to maintain its add-ins list, such that the add-in is automatically opened and installed when the client next starts Excel. These registry entries are covered in detail in *Chapter 24 — Proving Help, Securing, Packaging and Distributing*.

Structure of a Function or General-Purpose Add-in

Most general-purpose add-ins use the same structure:

- Code in an Auto_Open or Workbook_Open routine that adds the add-in's menu items and sets up the keyboard hooks. Each menu item has its OnAction property set to call the appropriate routine in the add-in file.
- Separate routines for each menu item, located in a standard module.
- Public functions, located in a standard module, exposed for use in worksheet formulas. Dedicated function add-ins often contain only functions and do not add menu items.

- Code in an Auto_Close or Workbook_Close routine that removes the add-in's menu items and clears the keyboard hooks.

Application-Specific Add-ins

As mentioned previously, the main problem with both codeless and self-automated workbooks is that the "program" is physically stored in the same file as the data the end user types in or otherwise works with. It is very difficult to reliably update the program part of those workbooks without affecting or in most cases destroying the end-user's work. The alternative is to structure the application such that all the code is contained within one workbook, with a separate workbook for the end user to use for data entry, analysis, and so forth. One such architecture is that of an application-specific add-in. These are very similar to normal add-ins, but instead of immediately setting up their menu items, keyboard hooks, and so on, they stay invisible until the user opens a workbook the add-in can identify as one for which it should make itself available.

Typically, the user would be supplied with at least two workbooks—the XLA add-in workbook and a template workbook to use for data entry. The template workbook(s) will contain some kind of indicator the add-in can use to identify it, usually either a hidden defined name or a custom document property.

The key benefit of using an application-specific add-in is that we can safely distribute updates to the code, knowing we will not be destroying the user's data. There is, however, a small price to pay for this convenience:

- Splitting the application into two (or more) workbooks makes it slightly harder to manage, because we have to keep the correct versions of both workbooks synchronized during the development process. Simple version control is discussed in more detail in *Chapter 3 — Excel and VBA Development Best Practices.*
- The application is slightly harder for other developers to understand—particularly if they are used to single-workbook applications or do not understand the technique of using class modules to hook application-level events, as explained in *Chapter 7 — Using Class Modules to Create Objects.*
- Deployment is more complicated because we need to distribute multiple files. Deployment strategies are discussed in *Chapter 24 — Providing Help, Securing, Packaging, and Distributing.*

Structure of an Application-Specific Add-in

Application-specific add-ins are very similar in structure to general-purpose add-ins, but with extra code to identify when to enable or disable the menu items:

- A class module used to trap the application-level events.
- Code in an Auto_Open or Workbook_Open routine adds the add-in's menu items. Each menu item has its OnAction property set to call the appropriate routine in the add-in file, but they are all initially either disabled or hidden. It then creates an instance of the class module and initializes application event hooks.
- Separate routines for each menu item, located in a standard module.
- (Optionally) Public functions, located in a standard module, exposed for use in worksheet functions.
- Code in the class module hooks the application-level Workbook-Activate event, checks whether the new workbook has the correct custom document property, and if so enables the menu items and sets up the keyboard hooks.
- Code in the class module hooks the application-level Workbook-Deactivate event, disables the menu items, and removes the keyboard hooks.
- Code in an Auto_Close or Workbook_Close routine removes the add-in's menu items.

General-purpose and Application-specific add-ins are discussed in more detail in *Chapter 5 — Function, General and Application-Specific Add-ins*.

Dictator Applications

All of the architectures we have considered so far have sought to enhance Excel in some way to improve the end user's experience when using our application. In contrast, ***dictator applications*** seek to completely take over the Excel user interface, replacing Excel's menus with their own and exercising a very high level of control over the user. In the ideal dictator application, users cannot tell they are inside Excel.

These applications are created in Excel to use the features Excel provides, but those features are entirely controlled by the application and rarely (if ever) exposed to the user. Instead, the user interface is made up of tightly controlled data-entry worksheets and/or userforms, designed to appear like any other Windows application. These applications typically require large amounts of code to be able to have that level of control, but that degree of control enables us to write full-scale, fully functional Windows applications, on a par with any that can be written in Visual Basic or other "mainstream" application-development platforms. Indeed, by building our application within Excel, we are immediately able to utilize the incredible amount of functionality Excel provides.

If there is a requirement for our dictator applications to work in Excel 97, we are not able to have userforms and menu items available at the same time, because userforms are always modal. We therefore have the choice to base our user interface on using worksheets and menus, using userforms with buttons to navigate between the forms or by building modeless forms using VB6. Excel 2000 introduced modeless userforms, enabling us to make both userforms and menus available and allowing us much more flexibility when deciding whether to use a form or worksheet for the user interface. For this reason, we recommend that, if possible, Excel 2000 should be set as the lowest-level version dictator applications are designed to work within.

As dictator applications get more and more complex, they will often start to use functionality that only exists in the most recent versions of Excel (such as the XML import/export introduced in Excel 2003), so you— as the designer of the application—need to decide what should happen if the application is opened in an older version. If the functionality being used is a core part of the application, it is unlikely the application will be usable at all in older versions. If the use of the new features can be limited to a small part of the application, it might make more sense to just disable that menu item, or provide separate routines for older versions to use. Making use of new Excel features will often result in compile errors if the workbook were to be opened in an older version, so many dictator applications use a "front-loader" workbook to do an initial version check, check whether all external dependencies (such as Outlook) are available, and then open and run the main application workbook if all the checks are okay. If the checks fail, we can provide meaningful error messages to the end user (such as "This application requires Excel 2000 or above and will not work in Excel 97").

There's no escaping the fact that dictator applications are much more complicated than either self-automated workbooks or application-specific add-ins and will require an intermediate to advanced-level Excel/VBA developer to create and maintain them. Although this type of architecture can get very complicated, the complexity can be mitigated by following the best-practices advice discussed in *Chapter 3 — Excel and VBA Development Best Practices* (general advice) and *Chapter 6 — Dictator Applications* (specific advice for dictator applications).

After the decision to build a dictator application has been made, we have an incredible amount of flexibility in terms of physically creating the application. The data could be stored in one or more separate workbooks, local databases (for example, Access databases), or a central database (for example, SQL Server). We could decide to include all the code in a single workbook or have a small "core" add-in, with numerous little applets that plug in to the core to provide the functionality, where each applet performs a single, specific task. The decision will probably be a trade-off between (at least) the following considerations:

- A single-workbook structure is easier for a single developer to maintain, because everything is in the one place.
- A multiple-workbook structure is easier for a team of developers to create, because each developer can work on his own applet without conflicting with another team member.
- If a multiple-workbook structure is built so each plug-in applet is not loaded until it is first used, the initial opening of the core add-in will be quicker than loading the full application of the single-workbook structure—although modern PCs might make that difference appear immaterial.
- A single-workbook structure must be updated in its entirety, but the applets of a multiple-workbook structure can be updated and deployed independently.
- The code required to implement a multiple-workbook plug-in architecture is quite complex, and might be too complex for the intermediate VBA developer to fully understand—although we explain it in *Chapter 11 — Interfaces*.

Requirements of a Dictator Application

To look and operate like a standalone Windows application, a dictator application needs to modify many `Application` properties, from turning on `IgnoreOtherApplications` (so double-clicking an XLS file in Explorer will not use our instance of Excel) to turning off `ShowWindowsInTaskBar` in Excel 2000 and above (because we may have multiple workbooks to be managed under program control), as well as hiding all the command bars. Unfortunately, Excel will remember many of those settings, to reuse them the next time Excel is started, so every dictator application must start by recording the existing state of all the settings that will be changed and restore them all when it closes. If the code to do this is written as two separate routines and assigned shortcut keys, they also provide an easy way to switch between the application's display and Excel's during development.

After a snapshot of the user's settings has been taken, the dictator application can set the application properties it requires; it then needs to lock down Excel to prevent users from doing things we do not want them to do, including the following:

- Hiding and disabling all the command bars (including the shortcut command bars), then setting up our own.
- Protecting our command bars and disabling access to the command bar customization dialog.
- Disabling all the shortcut key combinations that Excel provides, and then optionally re-enabling the few we want to be exposed to the user.
- Setting `Application.EnableCancelKey` to `xlDisabled` at the start of every entry point, to prevent users stopping the code.
- When using worksheets as data-entry forms, we don't want the user to be able to copy and paste entire cells, because that includes the formatting, data validation, and so on. Therefore we need to turn off drag and drop (which does a cut and paste); trap both Ctrl+X and Shift+Delete to do a copy rather than a cut; and trap Ctrl+V, Shift+Insert, and the Enter keys to ensure we only ever paste values.

Having locked down the Excel environment while our application is running, we need to provide a mechanism for the developers to access the code, to enable them to debug the application. One method is to set a global IsDevMode Boolean variable to True if a particular file exists in the application directory or (more securely) depending on the Windows username. This Boolean can then be used throughout the application to provide access points, such as enabling the Alt+F11 shortcut to switch to the VBE, adding a Reset menu item and/or shortcut key to switch back to the Excel environment and not setting the `EnableCancelKey` property, to allow the developer to break into the code. The Boolean can also be used within error handlers, to control whether to display a user- or developer-oriented error message.

Structure of a Dictator Application

A typical dictator application uses the following logical structure:

- A front-loader/startup routine to perform version and dependency checks and so on
- A main "core" set of routines, to do the following:

  Take a snapshot of the Excel environment settings and to restore those settings

  Configure and lock down the Excel application

  Create and remove the application's command bars

  Handle copying and pasting data within the worksheet templates

  Provide a library of common helper routines and classes

  (Optionally) Implement a plug-in architecture using class modules, as described in *Chapter 11 — Interfaces*

- A backdrop worksheet, to display within the Excel window while userforms are being shown, usually with some form of application-specific logo (if we are primarily using forms for the user interface)
- Multiple independent applets that provide the application's functionality
- Multiple template worksheets used by the applets, such as data-entry forms or preformatted report templates

Physically, all the elements that make up a typical dictator application can reside in a single workbook or can be distributed across multiple workbooks. Dictator applications are discussed in more detail in *Chapter 6 — Dictator Applications*.

Technical Implementations

In our discussion of the main types of application architecture, an underlying assumption is that the application will be written using VBA. That need not be the case, however, as we discuss in Chapters 19 through 22, where we examine how we can use the C API to create XLL add-ins and use Visual Basic 6 and/or VB.Net to support our VBA routines and create COM Add-ins.

Additionally, any of these architectures can be implemented using a traditional procedural design (where most of the functionality is implemented using helper routines in standard code modules) or an object-oriented approach (where the functionality is implemented as properties and methods of class modules), as discussed in *Chapter 7 — Using Class Modules to Create Objects*.

Conclusion

The five main types of application architecture have their pros and cons, and each is the most applicable for certain situations. The choice of architecture should be taken carefully, with appropriate consideration given to the ongoing maintenance (probably by a different person than the original author) as well as just the ease with which the application can be created initially.

Style	Pros	Cons	Applicable For
Codeless	No VBA requirement. No macro security issues. Easy to deploy.	Usually cluttered and hard to use. Neither robust nor reliable. Unable to provide much assistance to the user. Difficult to update.	Simple data-entry forms, surveys and so on.
Self-automated	Simple application, easy for a beginner VBA developer to understand. VBA can be used to improve robustness and reliability. Able to provide lots of extra functionality for the user. Easy to deploy.	If the VBA needs to be updated, it will be difficult or impossible to do so once deployed.	More complex data-entry forms, where the VBA can be used to improve the quality of the data being entered, but there is little data stored in the workbook long term.
General add-in	Designed to extend Excel's functionality. Simple application, only slightly more complex than an automated workbook. Easy to deploy (although not as simple as a workbook).	Must include robust context checks and error handling. Harder to deploy if it should be automatically ready for use.	Ideal for adding extra functionality to Excel, for use in any workbook.

Style	Pros	Cons	Applicable For
App-specific add-in	Separates the code from the data, so the code can be updated without affecting the user's work. Removing the code from the data workbooks makes them smaller and avoids the macro security warning.	Slightly more technically complex than the general add-in, requires an intermediate-level VBA developer. Slightly harder to deploy, because it requires at least two workbooks to be installed, sometimes to separate locations.	This is the recommended structure to use for an application that adds to Excel's menus.
Dictator application	Able to write fully functional applications that appear to be applications in their own right. High degree of control over the user interaction enables us to write very robust and reliable applications. Functionality can be split over multiple workbooks, making them easier for a team to develop and easier to deploy updates.	Much more complex than other architectures. Care must be taken to restore the user's Excel environment Harder to deploy, typically requiring an installation routine.	The ideal method for a Windows application that makes heavy use of the functionality that Excel provides.

CHAPTER 3

Excel and VBA Development Best Practices

This chapter appears early in the book because we want you to understand why we are doing certain things the way we are in later chapters. Unfortunately, this also means we must cover a few topics in this chapter that do not get full coverage until later. For best results, you might want to review this chapter after you have read the rest of the book.

As you read this chapter, keep in mind that even though the practices described here are generally accepted best practices, there will always be certain cases where the best thing to do is not follow the best practice. We try to point out the most common examples of this here and in the best practices discussions in the chapters that follow.

Naming Conventions

What Is a Naming Convention and Why Is It Important

The term *naming convention* refers to the system you use to name the various parts of your application. Whenever you declare a variable or create a userform, you give it a name. You implicitly name objects even when you do not give them a name directly by accepting the default name provided when you create a userform, for example. One of the hallmarks of good programming practice is the consistent use of a clearly defined naming convention for all parts of your VBA application.

Let's look at an example that may help demonstrate why naming conventions matter. In the following line of code, what do you know about x?

```
x = wksDataSheet.Range("A1").Value
```

From its usage you can reasonably assume it is a variable. But what data type is it designed to hold? Is its scope public, module level, or private? What is its purpose in the program? As it stands, you cannot answer any of these questions without spending some time searching through the rest of the code. A good naming convention conveys the answers to these questions with a simple visual inspection of the variable name. Here's a revised example. (We cover the specifics in detail in the next section.)

```
glListCount = wksDataSheet.Range("A1").Value
```

Now you know the scope of the variable (g stands for global or public scope), what data type it was designed to hold (l stands for the Long data type) and have a rough idea of the purpose of the variable (it holds the number of items in a list).

A naming convention helps you to immediately recognize the type and purpose of the building blocks used in an application. This enables you to concentrate on what the code is doing rather than having to figure out how the code is structured. Naming conventions also help make your code self-documenting, reducing the number of comments required to make the purpose of your code clear.

We present an example of a well-structured naming convention in the following section. However, the most important thing about naming conventions is that you pick one and use it consistently. As long as everyone involved in a project understands the naming convention, it doesn't really matter exactly what prefixes you use or how your names are capitalized. When it comes to naming conventions, consistency rules, both across projects and over time.

A Sample Naming Convention

A good naming convention applies not just to variables, but to all the elements of your application. The sample naming convention we present here covers all the elements in a typical Excel application. We begin with a discussion of variables, constants and related elements, because these are the most common elements in any application. Table 3-1 shows the general format of the naming convention. The specific elements of the naming convention and their purposes are described afterward.

Table 3-1 A Naming Convention for Variables, Constants, User-Defined Types and Enumerations

Element	Naming Convention
Variables	`<scope><array><data type>DescriptiveName`
Constants	`<scope><data type>DESCRIPTIVE_NAME`

User-defined types	`Type DESCRIPTIVE_NAME`
	`    <data type>DescriptiveName`
	`End Type`

Enumerations	`Enum <project prefix>GeneralDescr`
	`    <project prefix>GeneralDescrSpecificName1`
	`    <project prefix>GeneralDescrSpecificName2`
	`End Enum`

The Scope Specifier (`<scope>`)

g—Public
m—Module level
(nothing)—Procedure level

The Array Specifier (`<array>`)

a—Array
(nothing)—Not an array

The Data Type Specifier (`<data type>`)

There are so many data types that it's difficult to provide a comprehensive list of prefixes to represent them. The built-in types are easy. The most frequently used built-in types get the shortest prefixes. Problems arise when naming object variables that refer to objects from various applications. Some programmers use the prefix obj for all object names. This is not acceptable. However, devising consistent, unique and reasonably short prefixes for every object type you will ever use is also probably too much to ask. Try to find reasonably meaningful one- to three-letter prefixes for the object variables you use most frequently and reserve the obj prefix for objects that appear infrequently in your code.

Make your code clear, and above all, be consistent. Keep data type prefixes to three characters or fewer. Longer prefixes, in combination with scope and array specifiers, make for unwieldy variable names. Table 3-2 shows some suggested prefixes for the most commonly used data types.

Table 3-2 Suggested Naming Convention Prefixes

Prefix	Data Type	Prefix	Data Type	Prefix	Data Type
b	Boolean	cm	ADODB.Command	cbo	MSForms.ComboBox°
byt	Byte	cn	ADODB.Connection	chk	MSForms.CheckBox
cur	Currency	rs	ADODB.Recordset	cmd	MSForms. CommandButton
dte	Date			ddn	MSForms. ComboBox°°
dec	Decimal	cht	Excel.Chart	fra	MSForms.Frame
d	Double	rng	Excel.Range	lbl	MSForms.Label
i	Integer	wkb	Excel.Workbook	lst	MSForms.ListBox
l	Long	wks	Excel.Worksheet	mpg	MSForms.MultiPage
obj	Object			opt	MSForms. OptionButton
sng	Single	cbr	Office.CommandBar	spn	MSForms.SpinButton
s	String	ctl	Office. CommandBarControl	txt	MSForms.TextBox
u	User-defined type				
v	Variant	cls	User-defined class variable	ref	RefEdit Control
		frm	Userform variable	col	VBA.Collection

° Used for ComboBox controls with a DropDownCombo Style setting.
°° Used for ComboBox controls with a DropDownList Style setting.

Using Descriptive Names

VBA gives you up to 255 characters for each of your variable names. Use a few of them. Don't try to save yourself a little effort by making your variable names very short. Doing so will make your code difficult to understand in the long run, both for you and for anyone else who has to work on it.

The Visual Basic IDE provides an auto-complete feature for identifiers (all the names used in your application). You typically need to type only the first few characters to get the name you want. Enter the first few characters of the name and press Ctrl+Spacebar to activate an auto-complete list of all names that begin with those characters. As you type additional characters, the list will continue to narrow down. In Figure 3-1, the Ctrl+Spacebar shortcut has been used to display a list of message string constants available to add to a message box.

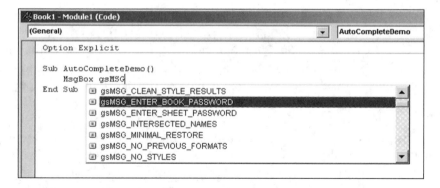

Figure 3-1 Using the Ctrl+Spacebar Shortcut to Auto-Complete Long Names

A Few Words About Enumerations

Enumerations are a special type of constant available in Excel 2000 and higher. They enable you to take a list of related values and package them up with similar, logical friendly names. VBA and the Excel object model make extensive use of enumerations. You can see these in the auto-complete list that VBA provides for the values of many properties. For example if you type:

```
Sheet1.PageSetup.PaperSize =
```

into a VBA module, you'll be prompted with a long list of XlPaperSize enumeration members that represent the paper sizes available to print on. Figure 3-2 shows this in action.

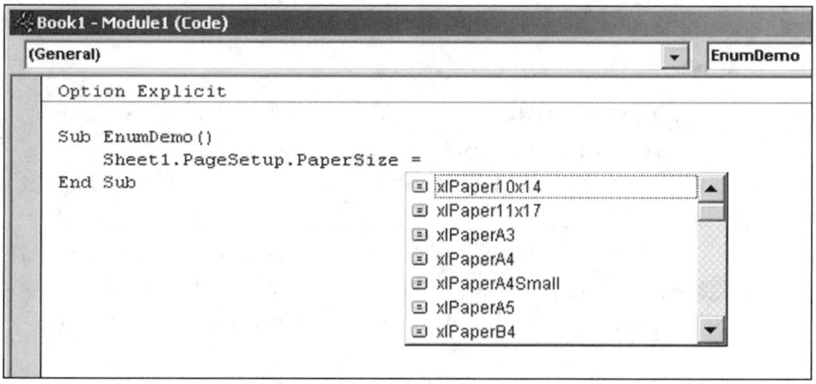

Figure 3-2 The Excel Paper Size Enumeration Member List

These names actually represent numeric constants whose values you can examine if you look them up in the Object Browser, discussed in *Chapter 16 — VBA Debugging*. Notice the structure of these enumeration names. First, they all begin with a prefix identifying the application they are associated with, in this case xl, which obviously stands for Excel. Second, the first part of their name is a descriptive term that ties them together visually as belonging to the same enumerated type, in this case Paper. The last part of each enumeration name is a unique string describing the specific value. For example, `xlPaper11x17` represents 11x17 paper and `xlPaperA4` represents A4 paper. This system for naming enumerated constants is very common and is the one we use in this book.

Naming Convention Examples

Naming convention descriptions in the abstract are difficult to connect to real-world names, so we show some real-world examples of our naming convention in this section. All of these examples are taken directly from commercial-quality applications written by the authors.

Variables

- **`gsErrMsg`**—A public variable with the data type String used to store an error message
- **`mauSettings()`**—A module-level array of user-defined type that holds a list of settings
- **`cbrMenu`**—A local variable with the data type CommandBar that holds a reference to a menu bar

Constants

- **`gbDEBUG_MODE`**—A public constant of type Boolean that indicates whether the project is in debug mode
- **`msCAPTION_FILE_OPEN`**—A module-level constant of data type String that holds the caption for a user-defined file open dialog (`Application.GetOpenFilename` in this instance)
- **`lOFFSET_START`**—A local constant of data type Long holding the point at which we begin offsetting from some Range object

User-Defined Types

The following is a public user-defined type that is used to store the dimensions and location of an object. It consists of four variables of data type Double that store the top, left, width and height of the object and a variable of data type Boolean used to indicate whether the settings have been saved.

```
Public Type DIMENSION_SETTINGS
    bSettingsSaved As Boolean
    dValTop As Double
    dValLeft As Double
    dValHeight As Double
    dValWidth As Double
End Type
```

The variables within a user-defined type definition are called ***member variables***. These can be declared in any order. However, our naming convention suggests you sort them alphabetically by data type unless there is a strong reason to group them in some other fashion.

Enumerations

The following is a module-level enumeration used to describe various types of days. The sch prefix in the name of the enumeration stands for the application name. This enumeration happens to come from an application called Scheduler. DayType in the enumeration name indicates the purpose of the enumeration and each of the individual enumeration members has a unique suffix that describes what it means.

```
Private Enum schDayType
    schDayTypeUnscheduled
    schDayTypeProduction
    schDayTypeDownTime
    schDayTypeHoliday
End Enum
```

If you don't indicate what values you want to give your enumeration members, VBA automatically assigns a value of zero to the first member in the list and increments that value by one for each additional member. You can easily override this behavior and assign a different starting point from which VBA will begin incrementing. For example, to make the enumeration above begin with one instead of zero, you would do the following:

```
Private Enum schDayType
    schDayTypeUnscheduled = 1
    schDayTypeProduction
    schDayTypeDownTime
    schDayTypeHoliday
End Enum
```

VBA will continue to increment by one for each member after the last member for which you've specified a value. You can override automatic assignment of values to all of your enumeration members by simply specifying values for all of them.

Figure 3-3 shows one of the primary advantages of using enumerations. VBA provides you with an auto-complete list of potential values for any variable declared as a specific enumeration.

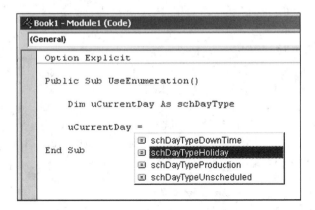

Figure 3-3 Even Custom Enumerations Get a VBA Auto-Complete Listing

Procedures

Subroutines and functions are grouped under the more general term *procedure*. Always give your procedures very descriptive names. Once again, you are allowed up to 255 characters for your procedure names, and procedure names appear in the Ctrl+Spacebar auto-complete list, so don't sacrifice a name that makes the purpose of a procedure obvious for one that's simply short.

It is not a common practice to do so, but we find that giving functions a prefix indicating the data type of their return value to be very helpful in understanding code. When calling a function, always place open and closed parenthesis after the function name to distinguish it from a variable or subroutine name, even if the function takes no arguments. Listing 3-1 shows a well-named Boolean function being used as the test for an If...Then statement.

Listing 3-1 An Example of Naming Conventions for Function Names

```
If bValidatePath("C:\Files") Then
    ' The If...Then block is executed
    ' if the specified path exists.
End If
```

Subroutines should be given a name that describes the task they perform. For example, a subroutine named ShutdownApplication leaves little doubt as to what it does. Functions should be given a name that describes the value they return. A function named sGetUnusedFilename() can reasonably be expected to return a filename.

The naming convention applied to procedure arguments is exactly the same as the naming convention for procedure-level variables. For example, the bValidatePath function shown in Listing 3-1 would be declared in the following manner:

```
Function bValidatePath(ByVal sPath As String) As Boolean
```

Modules, Classes and Userforms

In our sample naming convention, the names of standard code modules should be prefixed with an uppercase M, class modules with an uppercase C and userforms with an upper case F. This has the advantage of neatly sorting these objects in the VBE Project window if you don't care for the folder view, as shown in Figure 3-4.

This convention also makes code that uses classes and userform objects much clearer. In the following code sample, for example, this naming convention makes it very clear that you are declaring an object variable of a certain class type and then creating a new instance of that class:

```
Dim clsMyClass As CMyClass
Set clsMyClass = New CMyClass
```

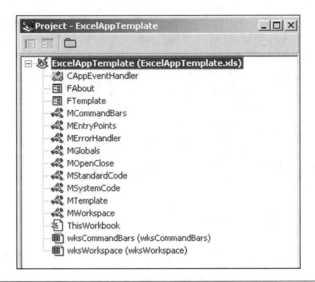

Figure 3-4 Class Modules, Userforms and Standard Modules Sorted in the Project Window

In each case, the name on the left is a class **variable**, and the object on the right is a **class**.

Worksheets and Chart Sheets

Because the CodeNames of worksheets and chart sheets in your project are treated by VBA as intrinsic object variables that reference those sheets, the CodeNames given to worksheets and chart sheets should follow variable naming conventions. Worksheet CodeNames are prefixed with wks to identify them in code as references to Worksheet objects. Similarly, chart sheets are prefixed with cht to identify them as references to Excel Chart objects.

For both types of sheets, the prefix should be followed by a descriptive term indicating the sheet's purpose in the application. Figure 3-4, for example, shows a wksCommandBars worksheet that contains a table defining the command bars created by the application. For sheets contained within an add-in or hidden in a workbook and not designed to be seen by the user, the sheet tab name should be identical to the CodeName. For sheets that are visible to the user, the sheet tab name should be a friendly name, and one that you should be prepared for the user to change. As discussed later, you should always rely on sheet CodeNames rather than sheet tab names within your VBA code.

The Visual Basic Project

Notice in Figure 3-4 that the Visual Basic Project has been given the same name as the workbook it's associated with. You should always give your VBProject a name that clearly identifies the application it belongs to. There's nothing worse than having a group of workbooks open in the VBE with all of them having the same default name VBAProject. If you plan on creating references between projects, you will be required to give them unique names.

Excel UI Naming Conventions

Excel user interface elements used in the creation of an application should also be named using a consistent and well-defined naming convention. We covered worksheets and chart sheets in a previous section. The three other major categories of Excel UI elements that can be named are shapes, embedded objects and defined names.

Shapes

The term **Shapes** refers to the generic collection that can contain the wide variety of objects you can place on top of a worksheet or chart sheet. Shapes can be broadly divided into three categories: controls, drawing objects and embedded objects. Shapes should be named similarly to object variables, which is to say they should be given a prefix that identifies what type of object they are followed by a descriptive name indicating what purpose they serve in the application.

Many controls that can be placed on userforms can be placed on worksheets as well. Worksheets can also host the old Forms toolbar controls, which are similar to the ActiveX MSForms controls but with their own unique advantages and disadvantages. *Chapter 4 — Worksheet Design* discusses these in more detail. Controls placed on worksheets should be named using exactly the same conventions you would use for controls placed on userforms.

Worksheets can also host a wide variety of drawing objects (technically known as Shapes) that are not strictly controls, although you can assign macros to all of them. These fall into the same naming convention category as the wide variety of objects that you can use in VBA. It would be very difficult to devise unique prefixes for all of them, so use well-defined prefixes for the most common drawing objects and use a generic prefix for the rest. Here are some sample prefixes for three of the most commonly used drawing objects:

pic	Picture
rec	Rectangle
txt	TextBox (not the ActiveX control)

Embedded Objects

The term *embedded object* is used here to refer to Excel objects such as PivotTables, QueryTables and ChartObjects, as well as objects created by applications other than Excel. Worksheets can host a variety of embedded objects. Common examples of non-Excel embedded objects would include equations created with the Equation Editor and WordArt drawings. Sample prefixes for embedded objects are shown here:

cht	ChartObject
eqn	Equation
qry	QueryTable
pvt	PivotTable
art	WordArt

Defined Names

Our naming convention for defined names is a bit different than for other program elements. In the case of defined names, the prefix should indicate the broad purpose of the defined name, as opposed to the data type it's expected to hold. This is because nontrivial Excel applications typically have many defined names that are much easier to work with if they are grouped together by purpose within the Define Name dialog. When a worksheet contains dozens or hundreds of defined names, there are significant efficiencies to be gained by having names with related functions grouped together by prefix in the defined name list.

The descriptive name portion of a defined name is used to specify exactly what purpose the name serves within its broader category. The following list shows some examples of purpose prefixes for defined names:

cht	Chart data range
con	Named constant
err	Error check
for	Named formula
inp	Input range
out	Output range
ptr	Specific cell location
rgn	Region
set	UI setting
tbl	Table

Exceptions—When Not to Apply the Naming Convention

You want to break the general rule and not apply your naming convention in two specific situations. The first is when you are dealing with elements related to Windows API calls. These elements have been named by Microsoft, and the names are well known within the programming community. The Windows API constants, user-defined types, procedure declarations and procedure arguments should appear in your code exactly as they appear in the Microsoft Platform SDK, which can be viewed on the MSDN Web site at:

```
http://msdn.microsoft.com/library/
en-us/winprog/winprog/windows_api_start_page.asp
```

Note that this reference is provided in C/C++ format only.

The second situation where you want to avoid applying your own naming conventions is when you use "plug-in" code from an outside source to perform a specific task. If you modify the names used in this code and refer to those modified names from code elsewhere in your application, you make it very difficult to upgrade the plug-in code when a newer version becomes available.

Best Practices for Application Structure and Organization

Application Structure

The One-Workbook vs. the N-Workbook Application

The number of workbooks used in an Excel application is driven primarily by two factors: the complexity of the application itself and the limitations imposed by application distribution issues. Simple applications and those for which you cannot impose a formal installation sequence demand the fewest number of workbooks. Complex applications and those over which you have complete control of the installation process allow division into multiple workbooks or other file types such as DLLs. *Chapter 2 — Application Architectures* discusses the various types of Excel applications and the structure suited to each.

When you have the liberty to divide your application across multiple files, there are a number of good reasons to do so. These include separation of the logical tiers in your application, separation of code from data, separation of user-interface elements from code elements, encapsulating functional elements of the application and managing change conflicts in a team development environment.

Separation of Logical Tiers

Almost every nontrivial Excel application has three distinct logical tiers or sections:

- **The user-interface tier**—The user-interface tier consists of all the code and visible elements required for your application to interact with the user. In an Excel application, the user-interface tier consists of visible elements such as worksheets, charts, command bars, user-forms and the code required to directly manage those visible elements. The user-interface tier is the only logical tier that contains elements visible to the user.
- **The business logic or application tier**—The business logic tier is completely code based. Its code performs the core operations the application was designed to accomplish. The business logic tier accepts input from the user-interface tier and returns output to the user-interface tier. For long-running operations, the business logic tier may transmit periodic updates to the user-interface tier in the form of status bar messages or progress bar updates.

- The **data access and storage tier**—The data access and storage tier is responsible for the storage and retrieval of data required by the application. This can be as simple as reading from and writing data to cells on a local, hidden worksheet or as complex as executing stored procedures in a SQL Server database across a network. The data access and storage tier communicates directly only with the business logic tier.

As Figure 3-5 shows, all three tiers are necessary for a complete application, but they must not be inextricably linked. The three tiers of your application should be loosely coupled, such that a significant change in one tier does not require significant changes to the other two. Strongly coupled application tiers inevitably lead to maintenance and upgrade difficulties.

Figure 3-5 The Relationships Among the Three Tiers of an Excel Application

For example, if your data access and storage tier needs to move from using an Access database for storage to using a SQL Server database for storage, you want the changes required to be isolated within the data access and storage tier. In a well-designed application, neither of the other two tiers would be affected in any way by such a change. Ideally, data should be transferred between the business logic tier and the data access and storage tier in the form of user-defined types. These provide the best trade-off between efficiency and loose coupling. Alternatively, ADO Recordset objects can be used, but these introduce subtle linkage issues that it would be better if the business logic layer didn't rely on, such as the order of fields returned from the database.

Similarly, if you need to provide an alternate Web-based presentation interface for your application, loose coupling between the user-interface tier and the business logic tier will make it much easier to accomplish. This is because there will be no implicit assumptions built in to the business logic tier regarding how the user interface is constructed. Elements that accept data input from the user should be completely self-contained. The business logic tier should pass the user-interface tier the data it requires for initialization as simple data type properties. The user-interface tier should collect the user input and pass it back to the business logic tier as simple data type properties or as a UDT for more complex interfaces. Because the business logic tier should have no intrinsic knowledge of how the user-interface is constructed, referencing controls on a userform directly from a business logic tier procedure is expressly forbidden.

Separation of Data/UI from Code

Within the user-interface tier of many Excel applications lie two unique subtiers. These consist of the workbook and sheet elements used to construct the user-interface and the code supporting those elements. The concept of separation should be applied rigorously to these subtiers. A workbook-based interface should contain no code, and the UI code that controls a workbook-based interface should reside in an add-in completely separated from the workbook it controls.

The reasoning for this separation is the same as the reasoning described above for separating the main application tiers, isolating the effects of change. Of all the application tiers, the user-interface tier undergoes the most frequent changes. Therefore it's not sufficient just to isolate user interface changes to the user interface tier; you should also isolate changes to the visible elements of the user interface from the code that controls the user interface.

We provide real-world examples of application tier separation in the chapters that follow, so don't be concerned if what is discussed here is not totally obvious to you at this point.

Application Organization for Procedural Programming

Procedural programming is the programming methodology most developers are familiar with. It involves dividing an application into multiple procedures, each of which is designed to perform a specific task within the application. An entire application can be written in procedural fashion, procedural elements can be combined with object-oriented elements or an entire application can be written in object-oriented fashion. This section focuses on best practices for procedural programming. We discuss object-oriented programming techniques in *Chapter 7 — Using Class Modules to Create Objects*.

Organizing Code into Modules by Function/Category

The primary purpose of separating code into modules is to improve the comprehensibility and maintainability of the application. In a procedural application, procedures should be organized into separate code modules in a logical fashion. The best way to do this is to group procedures that perform similar functions into the same code module.

TIP: VBA has an undocumented "soft limit" on the maximum size of any single standard code module. A standard code module should not exceed 64KB as measured by its text file size when exported from the project. (The VBETools utility included on the CD will report module sizes for you automatically.) Your project will not crash immediately upon a single module exceeding this 64KB limit, but consistently exceeding this limit will almost invariably lead to an unstable application.

Functional Decomposition

Functional decomposition refers to the process of breaking your application into separate procedures such that each procedure is responsible for a single task. In theory, you could write many applications as one huge, monolithic procedure. However, doing so would make your application extremely difficult to debug and maintain. By using functional decomposition, you design your application such that it consists of multiple procedures that are each responsible for a well-defined task that is easy to understand, validate, document and maintain.

Best Practices for Creating Procedures

A comprehensive set of guidelines for creating good procedures could easily fill a chapter of its own. We cover the most important guidelines in the following list:

- **Encapsulation**—Whenever possible, a procedure should be designed to completely encapsulate the logical operation it performs. Ideally, your procedures should have no linkages to anything outside of them. This means, for example, that a properly encapsulated procedure can be copied into a completely different project and work just as well there as it did in the project where it originated. Encapsulation promotes code reuse and simplifies debugging by isolating different logical operations from each other.

- **Elimination of duplicate code**—When writing a nontrivial Excel application, you will frequently discover you are writing code to perform the same operation in multiple places. When this occurs, you should factor this duplicated code out into a separate procedure. Doing so reduces the number of places where that particular operation needs to be validated or modified to one. The common procedure can also be optimized in one place, and the benefits will be felt throughout your application. All of this leads to a significant improvement in code quality. It also serves a second important purpose, making your code more reusable. As you factor common operations into dedicated procedures, you will discover that you can often reuse these procedures in other applications. This type of code forms the basis of a code library that you can use to increase your productivity when writing new applications. The more logical operations you have available as complete, fully tested library procedures, the less time it will take for you to develop a new application.

- **Isolation of complex operations**—In many real-world applications, you will find that some sections of the business logic are both complex and very specific to the application for which they were designed (that is, not reusable). These sections of business logic should be isolated into separate procedures for ease of debugging and maintenance.

- **Procedure size reduction**—Procedures that are overly long are difficult to understand, debug and maintain, even for the programmer who wrote them. If you discover a procedure containing more than 150 to 200 lines of code, it is probably trying to accomplish multiple goals and therefore should be factored into multiple single-purpose procedures.

- **Limiting the number of procedure arguments**—The more arguments a procedure accepts, the more difficult it will be to understand and the less efficient it will be to execute. In general, you should limit the number of procedure arguments to five or fewer. And don't simply replace procedure arguments with public or module-level variables. If you find yourself requiring more than five procedure arguments, it's probably a good sign that your procedure, or your application logic, needs to be redesigned.

General Application Development Best Practices

This section covers best development practices common to all application development areas. Most of the other chapters in this book recommend further best practices related specifically to the subject of that chapter.

Code Commenting

Good code commenting is one of the most important practices in Excel application development. Your code comments should provide a clear and complete description of how your code is organized, how each object and procedure should be used and what you are trying to accomplish with your code. Comments also provide a means of tracking changes to your code over time, a subject we cover later in this chapter.

Code comments are important to both you and to other developers who may need to work on your code. The utility of code comments to other developers should be self-evident. What you might not realize until the cruel fist of experience has pounded it into you is that your comments are very important to you as well. It is very common for a developer to write an initial version of an application and then be asked to revise it substantially after a long period of time has passed. You would be surprised at how foreign even your own code looks to you after it has been out of sight and out of mind for a long period of time. Code comments help solve this problem.

Comments should be applied at all three major levels of your application's code: the module level, the procedure level and to individual sections or lines of code. We discuss the types of commenting appropriate to each of these levels below.

Module-Level Comments

If you have used the module naming conventions described previously in this chapter, then anyone examining your code will have a rough idea of the purpose of the code contained within each module. You should supplement this with a brief comment at the top of each module that provides a more detailed description of the purpose of the module.

NOTE: For the purposes of code commenting, when we use the term *module*, we mean it to include standard modules, class modules and the code modules behind userforms.

A good module-level comment should be located at the very top of the module and look something like the example shown in Listing 3-2.

Listing 3-2 A Sample Module-Level Comment

```
'
' Description:    A brief description of the purpose of the
'                 code in this module.
'

Option Explicit
```

Procedure-Level Comments

Procedure-level comments are typically the most detailed comments in your application. In a procedure-level comment block, you describe the purpose of the procedure, usage notes, a detailed list of arguments and their purposes and a description of expected return values in the case of functions.

Procedure-level comments can also serve a rudimentary change-tracking purpose by providing a place to add dates and descriptions of changes made to the procedure. A good procedure-level comment such as the one shown in Listing 3-3 would be placed directly above the first line of the procedure. The procedure-level comment in Listing 3-3 is designed for a function. The only difference between a comment block for a function and a comment block for a subroutine is the subroutine comment block does not contain a Returns section, obviously because subroutines do not return a value.

Listing 3-3 A Sample Procedure-Level Comment

```
'''''''''''''''''''''''''''''''''''''''''''''''''''''''''''''''''''
' Comments:     Locates the chart to be operated on or asks
'               the user to select a chart if multiple charts
'               are located.
'
' Arguments:    chtChart      Returned by this function. An
'                             object reference to the chart to
'                             be operated on, or Nothing on user
'                             cancel.
'
' Returns:      Boolean       True on success, False on error
'                             or user cancel.
```

```
'
' Date          Developer     Action
' ---------------------------------------------------------
' 07/04/02      Rob Bovey     Created
' 10/14/03      Rob Bovey     Error trap for charts with no
'                             series
' 11/18/03      Rob Bovey     Error trap for no active workbook
'
```

Internal Comments

Internal comments are comments that appear within the body of the code itself. These comments should be used to describe the purpose of any code where the purpose is not self-evident. Internal comments should describe the **intent** of the code rather than the **operation** of the code. The distinction between intent and operation is not always clear, so Listing 3-4 and Listing 3-5 show two examples of the same code, one with a bad comment and the other with a good comment.

Listing 3-4 Example of a Bad Internal Code Comment

```
' Loop the asInputFiles array.
For lIndex = LBound(asInputFiles) To UBound(asInputFiles)
    '...
Next lIndex
```

The comment in Listing 3-4 is monumentally unhelpful. First of all, it describes only the line of code directly below it, giving you no clue about the purpose of the loop structure as a whole. Second, the comment is simply an exact written description of that line of code. This information is easy enough to determine by just looking at the line of code. If you removed the comment shown in Listing 3-4, you would not lose any information at all.

Listing 3-5 Example of a Good Internal Code Comment

```
' Import the specified list of input files into the working area
' of our data sheet.
For lIndex = LBound(asInputFiles) To UBound(asInputFiles)
    '...
Next lIndex
```

In Listing 3-5, we have a comment that adds value to the code. Not only does it describe the intent, rather than the operation of the code, it also explains the entire loop structure. After reading this comment, you know what you're looking at as you delve into the code within the loop.

As with most rules, there are exceptions to the internal comment guidelines specified above. The most important exception concerns comments used to clarify control structures. If...Then statements and Do... Loops can make code difficult to understand as they become wider, because you can no longer see the entire control structure in a single code window. At that point, it becomes difficult to remember what the applicable control expression was. For example, when evaluating a lengthy procedure we have often found ourselves looking at something like the code snippet shown in Listing 3-6.

Listing 3-6 Inscrutable Control Structures

```
        End If

        lNumInputFiles = lNumInputFiles - 1

    Loop

End If
```

In Listing 3-6, what are the logical tests being made by the two If...Then statements, and what expression controls the Do...While loop? After these structures have been filled with a substantial amount of code, you simply cannot tell without scrolling back and forth within the procedure, because the entire block is no longer visible within a single code window. You can alleviate this problem very easily by using the end-of-control-block commenting style shown in Listing 3-7.

Listing 3-7 Understandable Control Structures

```
        End If   ' If bContentsValid Then

        lNumInputFiles = lNumInputFiles - 1

    Loop          ' Do While lNumInputFiles > 0

End If            ' If bInputFilesFound Then
```

The comments in Listing 3-7, although they just restate the code at the top of each control structure, make it completely obvious what you are looking at. These types of comments should be used anywhere you have a control structure within your code that is too large to fit completely into one code window.

Avoiding the Worst Code-Commenting Mistake

It might seem obvious, but the most frequent and damaging mistake related to code commenting is not keeping the comments updated as you modify the code. We have frequently seen projects that appeared at first glance to implement good code-commenting practices, but upon closer examination discovered the comments were created for some ancient version of the project and now bore almost no relationship to the current code.

When attempting to understand a project, bad comments are worse than no comments at all. Bad comments are actively misleading. Always keep your comments current. Old comments can either be deleted or retained as a series of change-tracking records. We recommend removing obsolete in-line comments or they will quickly clutter your code, making it difficult to understand simply due to the number of lines of inapplicable comments that accumulate. Use procedure-level comments as a change-tracking mechanism where necessary.

Code Readability

Code readability is a function of how your code is physically arranged. Good visual layout of code enables you to infer a significant amount of information about the logical structure of the program. This is a key point. Code layout makes not one bit of difference to the computer. Its sole purpose is to assist humans in understanding the code. Like naming conventions, the consistent use of good code layout conventions makes your code self-documenting. The primary tool of code layout is white space. White space includes space characters, tabs and blank lines. The following paragraphs discuss the most important ways to use white space to produce a well-designed code layout.

Group related code elements together and separate unrelated code elements with blank lines. Sections of code separated by blank lines within a procedure can be thought of as serving a similar function to paragraphs within the chapters of a book. They help you determine what things belong together. Listing 3-8 shows an example of how blank lines can improve code readability. Even without the code comments, it would be obvious which lines of code are related.

Listing 3-8 Using Blank Lines to Group Related Sections of Code

```
' Reset Application properties.
Application.ScreenUpdating = True
Application.DisplayAlerts = True
Application.EnableEvents = True
Application.StatusBar = False
Application.Caption = Empty
Application.EnableCancelKey = xlInterrupt
Application.Cursor = xlDefault

' Delete all custom CommandBars
For Each cbrBar In Application.CommandBars
    If Not cbrBar.BuiltIn Then
        cbrBar.Delete
    Else
        cbrBar.Enabled = True
    End If
Next cbrBar

' Reset the Worksheet Menu bar.
With Application.CommandBars(1)
    .Reset
    .Enabled = True
    .Visible = True
End With
```

Within a related section of code, alignment is used to indicate which lines of code belong together. Indentation is used to show the logical structure of the code. Listing 3-9 shows a single section from Listing 3-8 where alignment and indentation have been used to good effect. You can look at this section of code and understand immediately which elements go together as well as deduce the logical flow of the code's execution.

Listing 3-9 Proper Use of Alignment and Indentation

```
' Delete all custom CommandBars
For Each cbrBar In Application.CommandBars
    If Not cbrBar.BuiltIn Then
        cbrBar.Delete
    Else
        cbrBar.Enabled = True
    End If
Next cbrBar
```

Line continuation can be used to make complex expressions and long declarations more readable. Keep in mind that breaking code into continued lines solely for the purpose of making the entire line visible without scrolling is not necessarily a good practice and can often make code more confusing. Listing 3-10 shows examples of judicious use of line continuation.

Listing 3-10 Judicious Use of Line Continuation

```
' Complex expressions are easier to understand
' when properly continued
If (uData.lMaxLocationLevel > 1) Or _
    uData.bHasClientSubsets Or _
    (uData.uDemandType = bcDemandTypeCalculate) Then

End If

' Line continuations make long API declarations easier to read.
Declare Function SHGetSpecialFolderPath Lib "Shell32.dll" _
    (ByVal hwndOwner As Long, _
    ByRef szBuffer As String, _
    ByVal lFolder As Long, _
    ByVal bCreate As Long) As Long
```

VBA Programming Best Practices

General VBA Best Practices

Use of Module Directives

- **Option Explicit**—Always use the Option Explicit statement in every module. The importance of this practice cannot be overstated. Without Option Explicit, any typographical error you make results in VBA automatically creating a new Variant variable. This type of error is very insidious because it may not even cause an immediate runtime error. However, it will certainly cause your application to eventually return incorrect results. This type of bug may very well pass without notice until your application is distributed, and it will be difficult to debug under any circumstances.

    The Option Explicit statement forces you to explicitly declare all the variables you use. Option Explicit causes VBA to throw a compile-time error (initiated by selecting *Debug > Compile* from the VBE menu) whenever an unrecognized identifier name is encountered. This makes it very easy to discover and correct typographical errors. You can ensure that Option Explicit is automatically placed at the top of every module you create by choosing *Tools > Options > Editor* from the VBE menu and checking the *Require Variable Declaration* check box. This setting is strongly recommended.

- **Option Private Module**—The Option Private Module statement makes all procedures within the module where it is used unavailable from the Excel user-interface or from other Excel projects. Use this statement to hide procedures that should not be called from outside your application.

TIP: The Application.Run method can circumvent the Option Private Module statement and run private procedures in modules where this statement has been used.

- **Option Base 1**—The Option Base 1 statement causes all array variables whose lower bound has not been specified to have a lower bound of 1. Do not use the Option Base 1 statement. Instead, always specify both the upper and lower bounds of every array variable you use. A procedure created in a module that uses Option

`Base 1` may malfunction if copied to a module in which this statement isn't used. This behavior inhibits one of the most important procedure design goals, that of reusability.

- **Option Compare Text**—The `Option Compare Text` statement forces all string comparisons within the module where it is used to be text based rather than binary. In a text-based string comparison, upper- and lowercase versions of the same character are treated as identical, whereas in a binary comparison they are different. The `Option Compare Text` statement should be avoided for the same reason `Option Base 1` should be avoided. It makes procedures behave differently when placed in modules with the statement versus modules without it. Text-based comparisons are also much more computationally expensive than binary comparisons, so `Option Compare Text` slows down all string comparison operations in the module where it's located. Most Excel and VBA string comparison functions provide an argument you can use to specify binary or text-based comparison. It's much better to use these arguments to provide text-based comparisons only where you need them.

  There are some rare cases where `Option Compare Text` is required. The most frequent case occurs when you need to do non-case-sensitive string comparisons with the VBA `Like` operator. The only way to get the `Like` operator to perform in a non-case-sensitive manner is to use the `Option Compare Text` statement. In this case, you should isolate the procedures that require this statement in a separate code module so other procedures that don't require this option aren't adversely affected. Be sure to document why you have done this in a module-level comment.

Variables and Constants

Avoid Reusing Variables Each variable declared in your program should serve one purpose only. Using the same variable for multiple purposes saves you only one variable declaration line but introduces massive potential for confusion within your program. If you are trying to determine how a procedure works and you have figured out what a certain variable does in a certain place, you will naturally assume the variable serves the same purpose the next time you see it. If this is not the case, the code logic will become very difficult to understand.

Avoid the Variant Data Type   Avoid the use of the Variant data type whenever possible. Unfortunately, VBA is not a strongly typed programming language. Therefore, you can simply declare variables without specifying their data type and VBA will create these variables as Variants. The main reasons not to use Variants are as follows:

- **Variants are very inefficient**—This is because internally, a Variant is a very complex structure designed to hold any data type in the VBA programming language. Variant values cannot be accessed and modified directly as can fundamental data types such as Long and Double. Instead, VBA must use a series of complex Windows API calls behind the scenes whenever it needs to perform any operation on a Variant.

- **Data stored in a variant can behave unexpectedly**—Because Variants are designed to hold any type of data, the data type that goes into a Variant is not necessarily the data type that will come out of it. When accessing the data in a Variant, VBA will attempt to coerce the data into whatever data type it thinks makes the most sense in the context of the operation. If you must use Variants, always explicitly cast them to the data type you want when using their values.

Beware of Evil Type Coercion   Evil Type Coercion (ETC) is another symptom that results from VBA not being a strongly typed programming language. ETC occurs when VBA automatically converts one data type to another completely unrelated data type. The most frequent examples are Strings that hold numbers being converted to Integers and Booleans being converted to their String equivalents. Don't mix variables of different data types in your code without using the explicit casting functions (CStr, CLng, CDbl and so on) to tell VBA exactly how you want those variables to be treated.

Avoid the As New Declaration Syntax   Never declare object variables using the As New syntax. For example, the following form of an object variable declaration should never be used:

```
Dim rsData As New ADODB.Recordset
```

If VBA encounters a line of code that uses this variable and the variable has not been initialized, VBA will automatically create a new instance of the variable. This is **never** the behavior you want. Good programming practice implies that the programmer should maintain complete control over the creation of all the objects used in the program. If VBA encounters an uninitialized object variable in your code, it is almost certainly the result of a bug, and you want to be notified about it immediately. Therefore, the proper way to declare and initialize the object variable shown above is as follows:

```
Dim rsData As ADODB.Recordset
Set rsData = New ADODB.Recordset
```

Using this style of declaration and initialization, if the object variable is destroyed somewhere in your procedure and you inadvertently reference it again after that point, VBA will immediately throw the runtime error "Object variable or With block variable not set," notifying you of the problem.

Always Fully Qualify Object Names   Always use fully qualified object names in variable declarations and code with their class name prefix. The reason for this is because many object libraries share the same object names. If you just declare a variable with an object name alone and there are multiple object libraries with that object name being referenced by your application, VBA will create a variable from the first library in the *Tools > References* list where it finds the object name you used. This is often not what you want.

UserForm controls present the most common situation where problems result from object variable declarations that aren't fully qualified. For example, if you wanted to declare an object variable to reference a TextBox control on your userform, you might be inclined to do the following:

```
Dim txtBox As TextBox
Set txtBox = Me.TextBox1
```

Unfortunately, as soon as VBA attempts to execute the second line of code, a "Type mismatch" error would be generated. This is because the Excel object library contains a TextBox object and the Excel object library comes before the MSForms object library in the *Tools > References* list. The correct way to write this code is shown here:

```
Dim txtBox As MSForms.TextBox
Set txtBox = Me.TextBox1
```

Never Hard-Code Array Bounds   When you are looping the contents of an array variable, never hard-code the array bounds in loop. Use the `LBound` and `UBound` functions instead, as shown in Listing 3-11.

Listing 3-11 The Correct Way to Loop an Array

```
Dim lIndex As Long
Dim alListItems(1 To 10) As Long

' Load the array here.

For lIndex = LBound(alListItems) To UBound(alListItems)
     ' Do something with each value.
Next lIndex
```

The reason for this is because array bounds frequently change over the course of creating and maintaining an application. If you hard-code the array bounds 1 and 10 in the loop shown above, you will have to remember to update the loop any time the bounds of the `alListItems` array change. Failure to do so is a frequent source of errors. By using `LBound` and `UBound`, you make the loop self-adjusting.

Always Specify the Loop Counter After a `Next` Statement   Listing 3-11 demonstrates another good coding practice. You should always specify the loop counter variable after a `Next` statement. Even though this is not strictly required by VBA, doing so makes your code much easier to understand, especially if the distance between the `For` and `Next` statements is long.

Make Use of Constants   Constants are very useful programming elements. They serve the following purposes in your code, among others:

- Constants eliminate "magic numbers," replacing them with recognizable names. For example, in the following line of code, what does the number 50 mean?

  ```
  If lIndex < 50 Then
  ```

  There is no way of knowing unless you wrote the code and you still remember what 50 represents. If instead you saw the following, you would have a very good idea of what the `If...Then` test was looking for:

```
Const lMAX_NUM_INPUT_FILES As Long = 50

' More code here.

If lIndex < lMAX_NUM_INPUT_FILES Then
```

If you need to know the value of a constant at design time, you can just right-click over the constant name in the VBE and choose *Definition* from the shortcut menu. You will be brought directly to the line where the constant is defined. In break mode at runtime it's even easier. Just hover your mouse over the constant and a tooltip window containing its value will appear.

- Constants improve coding efficiency and avoid errors by eliminating duplicate data. In the preceding example, assume you reference the maximum number of input files in several places throughout your program. At some point you may need to upgrade your program to handle more files. If you have hard-coded the maximum number of input files everywhere you've needed to use it, you will have to locate all of these places and change the number in each one. If you've used a constant, all you need to do is modify the value of the single constant declaration and the new value will automatically be used wherever the constant has been used in your code. This situation is a very frequent source of errors that can be eliminated by simply using constants instead of hard-coded numbers.

Variable Scope

Public variables are dangerous. They can be modified anywhere in your application without warning, making their values unpredictable. They also work against one of the most important programming precepts: encapsulation. Always create variables with the minimum scope possible. Begin by creating all of your variables with local (procedure-level) scope and only widen the scope of a variable when it is absolutely necessary.

As with most of our other rules, there are a few cases where the use of public variables is useful and/or necessary.

- When data must be passed deep into the stack before it is used. For example, if procedure A reads some data, then passes that data to procedure B, which passes it to procedure C, which passes it to procedure D where the data is finally used, a good case can be made that the data should be passed directly from procedure A to procedure D by way of a public variable.

■ Certain inherently public classes, such as an application-level event handling class, require a public object variable so they never go out of scope while your application is running.

Early Binding vs. Late Binding

The distinction between early binding and late binding is widely misunderstood and often confused with how an object is created. The ***only*** thing that affects whether an object is early bound or late bound is how the object variable holding the reference to the object was declared. Variables declared as a specific object data type are always early bound. Variables declared with the Object or Variant data type are always late bound. Listing 3-12 shows an example of a late bound reference, and Listing 3-13 shows an example of an early bound reference.

Listing 3-12 A Late Bound Reference to an ADO Connection Object

```
Dim objConnection As Object

' It doesn't matter how you create the object, it's still
' late bound due to the As Object variable declaration.
Set objConnection = New ADODB.Connection
Set objConnection = CreateObject("ADODB.Connection")
```

Listing 3-13 An Early Bound Reference to an ADO Connection Object

```
Dim cnConnection As ADODB.Connection

' It doesn't matter how you create the object, it's still early
' bound due to the data type used in the variable declaration.
Set cnConnection = New ADODB.Connection
Set cnConnection = CreateObject("ADODB.Connection")
```

Note that to use early binding with objects that are outside the Excel object model you must set a reference to the appropriate object library using the *Tools > References* menu in the Visual Basic Editor. For example, to create early bound variables referencing ADO objects, you must set a reference to the Microsoft ActiveX Data Objects 2.x Library, where *x* is the version of ADO you intend to use.

You should use early bound object variables wherever possible. Early bound object variables provide the following advantages over late bound variables:

- **Improved performance**—When you use an object variable whose data type is known to VBA at compile time, VBA can look up the memory locations of all property and method calls you use with this object and store them with your code. At runtime, when VBA encounters one of these early bound property or method calls, it simply executes the code located at the stored location. (This is a bit of an oversimplification. What VBA actually stores is a numeric offset to the code to be executed from a known starting point in memory, which is the beginning of a structure called the object's VTable.)

  When you use a late bound object variable, VBA has no way of knowing in advance what type of object the variable will contain. Therefore, it cannot optimize any property or method calls at compile time. This means that each time VBA encounters a late bound property or method call at runtime, it must query the variable to determine what kind of object it holds, look up the name of the property or method being executed to determine where in memory it is located and then execute the code located at that memory address. This process is significantly slower than an early bound call.

- **Strict type checking**—In the late bound example in Listing 3-12, if you accidentally set your object variable to reference an ADO Command object instead of a Connection object, VBA would not complain. You would only discover you had a problem downstream in your code when you tried to use a method or property not supported by the Command object. With early binding, VBA will immediately detect that you are trying to assign the wrong type of object reference to your object variable and notify you with a "Type mismatch" error. Incorrect property and method calls can be detected even earlier, before the code is ever run. VBA will attempt to look up the name of the property or method being called from within the appropriate object library at compile time and throw an error if the name cannot be located.

- **IntelliSense availability**—Early bound object variables make for much easier programming as well. Because VBA knows exactly what type of object a variable represents, it can parse the appropriate object library and provide a drop-down list of all available properties and methods for the object as soon as you type a dot operator after the variable's name.

As you might expect, in some cases you need to use late binding rather than early binding. The two most common reasons for using late binding rather than early binding are as follows:

1. When a newer version of an application's object library has broken compatibility with an earlier version.

This is an all too common situation. If you set a reference to the later version of the application's object library in your application and then attempt to run it on a computer that has the earlier version, you will get an immediate compile time error "Can't find project or library," and the reference on the target machine will be prefixed with MISSING. The most insidious thing about this error is that the line of code flagged as being the source of the error will often have nothing to do with the object library actually causing the problem.

If you need to use objects from an application that exhibits this problem and you want to support users with any version of the application, you need to use late binding for all variables referencing objects from the application. If you are creating new objects, you also need to use the CreateObject function with the version-independent ProgID of the object you want to create, rather than the = `New ObjectName` syntax.

2. When you want to use an application that you cannot be sure will exist on the user's computer and that you cannot install yourself.

In this case, you need to use late binding to avoid the compile time error that would immediately result from attempting to run an application that referenced an object library that did not exist on the user's computer. Your application can then check for the existence of the object library in question and exit gracefully if that library is not installed on the user's computer.

TIP: Even if you will eventually use late binding in your code, early binding offers such a great increase in productivity while coding that you should write and test the application using early binding. Convert your code to late binding only for the final round of testing and distribution.

Defensive Coding

Defensive coding refers to various programming practices designed to help you prevent errors rather than having to correct them after they occur.

Write Your Application in the Earliest Version of Excel That You Expect It to Run In

Although the Microsoft Excel team has done a better job than most of maintaining backward compatibility with earlier versions of Excel, there are many subtle differences between the versions. If you are very familiar with a later version of Excel, you can easily write an application that will not run on an earlier version because some feature you used did not exist in that version.

The solution to this problem is to always develop your applications in the earliest version of Excel that you expect them to run in. This may force you to maintain multiple versions of Excel on one computer, or better yet, separate computers for each version of Excel. Either way, this is an essential practice. If you develop an application in Excel 2000, give it to a user in Excel 97 and find out it doesn't run, you will need to debug and remove any code that doesn't work in Excel 97. You will save much time and stress by simply developing the application using Excel 97 to begin with.

Explicitly Use `ByRef` or `ByVal`

If a procedure takes arguments, there are two ways to declare those arguments: ByRef or ByVal.

- **ByRef**—This convention means you are passing the memory address of the variable rather than the value of the variable. If the called procedure modifies a `ByRef` argument, the modification will be visible in the calling procedure.
- **ByVal**—This convention means you are passing a value to the procedure. A procedure can make changes to a `ByVal` argument, but these changes will not be visible to the calling procedure. In fact, a procedure can use `ByVal` arguments exactly as if they were locally declared variables.

Always explicitly declare your procedure arguments as `ByRef` or `ByVal`. If you do not specify this, all arguments are created `ByRef` by default. You should declare procedure arguments `ByVal` unless you have a specific need for the calling procedure to see changes made to the arguments. Declaring arguments `ByVal` will prevent changes made to those arguments from being propagated back to the calling procedure.

The only exceptions are when you are passing large strings (very large strings), which are far more efficiently passed `ByRef`, or when your procedure argument is of a type, such as an array, that cannot be passed `ByVal`. Be aware that declaring procedure arguments `ByVal` does leave you more exposed to Evil Type Coercion. A `ByRef` procedure argument ***must*** be passed the same data type as it is declared to accept; otherwise a compile time error will result. By contrast, VBA will attempt to coerce a value passed to a `ByVal` procedure argument into a compatible data type.

Explicitly Call the Default Property of an Object

With the possible exception of the Item property of a Collection object, it's never a good idea to implicitly invoke the default property of an object just by using the object's name in an expression. Listing 3-14 shows the right way and the wrong way of accessing the default property of an object using an `MSForms.TextBox` control for demonstration purposes (the Text property is the default property of an `MSForms.TextBox` control).

Listing 3-14 Default Properties

```
' The right way.
txtUsername.Text = "My Name"

' The wrong way
txtUsername = "My Name"
```

By avoiding the implicit use of default properties, you make your code much more readable and protect yourself from errors if the default behavior of the object changes in some future version of Excel or VBA.

Validate Arguments Before Using Them in Procedures

If your procedure accepts input arguments that must have certain properties in order to be valid—for example, if they must be within a specific range of values—verify that the values passed to those arguments are valid before attempting to use them in your procedure. The idea is to catch erroneous input as soon as possible so that you can generate a meaningful error message and simplify your debugging.

Wherever possible, create test harnesses to validate the behavior of your procedures. A test harness is a wrapper procedure that can call the procedure being tested multiple times, passing it a wide range of arguments, and test the result to be sure it is correct. *Chapter 16 — VBA Debugging* discusses test harnesses in detail.

Use Guard Counters to Protect Against Infinite Loops

Program your loops to automatically handle infinite loop conditions. One of the most common mistakes made when using `Do...While` or `While...Wend` loops is to create a situation where the loop control condition is never satisfied. This causes the loop to run forever (or until you can force your code to break by pressing Ctrl+Break if you are lucky, or by using the Windows Task Manager to shut down your application if you are not). Always add a counter that automatically bails out when the number of loops executed is known to be more than the highest number that should ever occur in practice. Listing 3-15 shows a `Do...While` loop with an infinite loop guard structure.

Listing 3-15 Guard Against Infinite Loops

```
Dim bContinueLoop As Boolean
Dim lCount As Long

bContinueLoop = True
lCount = 1

Do

    ' The code that goes here should set the
    ' bContinueLoop variable to False once the
    ' loop has achieved its purpose.

    ' This infinite loop guard exits the loop
    ' unconditionally after 10000 iterations.
    lCount = lCount + 1
    If lCount > 10000 Then Exit Do

Loop While bContinueLoop
```

The only purpose of the `lCount` variable within the loop is to force the loop to exit if the code within the loop fails to set the control variable to exit within 10,000 iterations. (The appropriate number would depend on the particular situation.) This type of construct adds very little overhead to your loop; if performance is a significant concern, however, use the infinite loop guard until you are sure all the code within the loop is functioning properly, and then delete it or comment it out.

Use Debug > Compile Early and Often

Never let your code stray more than a few changes away from being able to run a flawless *Debug > Compile*. Failing to adhere to this practice will lead to long, inefficient debugging sessions.

Use CodeNames to Reference Sheet Objects

Always reference worksheets and chart sheets in your application by their CodeName. Depending on sheet tab names to identify sheets is risky because you or your users may change these tab names, breaking any code that uses them.

Validate the Data Types of Selections

If you write a procedure designed to operate on a specific type of object the user has selected, always check the object type of the selection using either the `TypeName` function or the `If TypeOf...Is` construct. For example, if you need to operate on a range selected by the user, ensure that the selection really is a Range object before continuing, as shown in Listing 3-16.

Listing 3-16 Verify That the Selection Is the Correct Object Type

```
' Code designed to operate on a range.
If TypeOf Selection Is Excel.Range Then
    ' OK, it's a Range object.
    ' Continue code execution.
Else
    ' Error, it's not a Range object.
    MsgBox "Please select a range.", vbCritical, "Error!"
End If
```

Change Control

Change control, also known as version control, at the most basic level involves two practices: maintaining a set of prior versions of your application that you can use to recover from various programming or technical errors and documenting changes made to your application over time.

Saving Versions

When most professional programmers talk about version control, they mean the use of dedicated version control software, such as Microsoft Visual Source Safe. However, this type of software is expensive, has a steep learning curve and doesn't integrate well with applications built in Excel. This is because Excel doesn't store its modules natively as separate text files. The version control method we will suggest here is quick, simple, requires no special software and delivers the most crucial benefits of a traditional version control system.

The most important objective of a version control system is to enable you to recover an earlier version of your project if you have encountered some significant problem with the version you are currently working on. If a significant code modification has gone terribly wrong or you suddenly find yourself with a corrupt file, you will be in a very difficult position if you do not have a recent backup to help you recover.

A simple version control system that can save you from these problems would be implemented in a fashion similar to the following. First create a folder named Backup as a subfolder to the folder in which your project is stored. Each time you prepare to make a significant addition or modification to your project, or at minimum once a day, use a file-compression utility such as WinZip to zip all the files in your project folder into a file with the following name format: Backup_YYYYMMDDHH.zip, where Y stands for year, M stands for month, D stands for day and H stands for hour. This naming format will give your backup file a unique name that will sort in correct sequential order when viewed in Windows Explorer. Move this file into your Backup folder and continue working.

If you encounter a problem, you can recover your project from the most recent backup. You will obviously lose some work, but if you save backup versions diligently you can minimize the loss. Each time you are sure you have a fully tested build of your project, you can delete most of the intermediate files from your Backup folder. It is advisable to retain at least weekly backups throughout the life of a project.

Documenting Changes with Comments

When you are maintaining code, if you make a significant change to the logic of a procedure you should also make a note with a brief description of the change, the date it was made and your name in the procedure-level comment block (see Listing 3-3). All nontrivial modifications to your code should be noted with an internal comment that includes the date the change was made and the name of the developer who made the change if there are multiple developers working on the application.

Conclusion

Whether you use the naming convention proposed here or create your own, use a naming convention consistently across all your applications and over time. It will make your code self-documenting and easy to follow. Code the separate logical tiers of your application as independent entities. This will prevent changes in one logical tier from forcing you to rebuild much of your application. Comment your code liberally at all levels. When trying to understand the purpose of a section of code, it's a lot easier if that purpose is explained by a code comment than if you have to figure it out yourself. Following these and all the other best practices presented in this chapter will result in robust, understandable and maintainable applications.

CHAPTER 4

Worksheet Design

There is a tremendous amount of Excel user interface design that can and should be accomplished using the built-in features of Excel alone, with no VBA required. One of the guiding principles of Excel development is "let Excel be Excel." Don't try to reinvent the wheel. Excel provides a wide variety of prepackaged, performance-optimized features you can use to build your application's user interface. This chapter examines how you can produce a fully functional user interface with just the features Excel provides for this purpose.

There are two fundamental sections of an Excel worksheet user interface: those designed to be visible to the user and through which the user operates your application, and those designed to be hidden from the user and used only by your application to perform the tasks required of it. We cover each of these sections in more detail in this chapter.

Principles of Good Worksheet UI Design

The following list provides some design guidelines that apply to all worksheet user interfaces:

1. Use formatting to create visual contrast between cells designed to serve different purposes—input cells versus formula cells, for example—as well as visual separation between different sections of your user interface.
2. Use consistent formatting based on the purpose of each cell. For example, don't format input cells with a white background in one area and a green background in another.
3. Don't use garish colors. Your choice of formatting should not distract from the task at hand.

4. Create a logical, well-structured flow through your user interface. Your user interface should flow from left to right then top to bottom within a worksheet and from left to right among multiple worksheets.

5. Make it obvious to users what they are supposed to do each time they are required to perform some action. Techniques for doing this include the use of cell comments, validation lists, default values, good descriptive field names and so on.

6. Use dynamic input-verification techniques to provide feedback as quickly as possible if the user has done something wrong. Waiting until the user has completed the entire form to point out data-entry errors should be viewed as a last resort, to be used only when there are no good alternatives.

7. Don't create an environment that potentially allows the user to make catastrophic mistakes. Protect all of your user interface worksheets, leaving only cells that require data entry unlocked. This prevents critical formulas from being accidentally overwritten.

8. Don't allow the user to get lost. Restrict the area of the worksheet within which the user can navigate to the working area of your user interface.

Program Rows and Columns: The Fundamental UI Design Technique

When you design a user interface on an Excel worksheet, one of the first things you should do is leave row 1 and column A empty. This section of the worksheet will be hidden from the user and will allow your application to perform many tasks associated with an advanced Excel UI, including error checking, storing validation lists and calculating intermediate values. In very complex worksheet user interfaces, it is not uncommon to have several initial rows and/or columns used as hidden work areas. These are called *program rows* and *program columns*.

An Excel worksheet user interface is typically laid out in a table format, left to right, top to bottom. Implementing design principle 6 described above is most easily accomplished if you have a hidden area you can use to automatically examine each of the user's entries and determine whether they meet all the criteria that are enforceable using worksheet-based constructs. The result of these tests can then be used by conditional formatting and/or VBA-based validation to signal users when they have entered data incorrectly.

In the simple timesheet example shown in Figure 4-1, the user completes the first three columns of the table. The last column of the table is calculated by the worksheet. The first column of the worksheet itself is designed to be a hidden column. It performs a simple validation check on each row of the timesheet table. It counts the number of entries made by the user in each row and returns True if the number of entries is incorrect (which is to say the user has not completed all of the required entries for that row).

A6		▾	=	=IF(COUNTA(C6:E6)=0,FALSE,COUNTA(C6:E6)<>3)		
	A	B	C	D	E	F	G
1							
2							
3	errHasError		Activity	Start Time	Stop Time	Total Hours	
4	FALSE		General Programming	8:00 AM	12:00 PM	4:00	
5	FALSE		Phone Conference	1:00 PM	2:00 PM	1:00	
6	TRUE		Technical Support	2:00 PM			
7	FALSE						
8	FALSE						
9	FALSE						

Figure 4-1 An Example of Hidden Column Data Validation

Here there are only two possible valid conditions. Either a row has not yet been used and therefore has zero entries, or a row has been completely filled out, in which case there will be three entries. Any other condition is an error. Notice that the error-checking formula for row 6 indicates there is a data-entry error in that row. This is because the user has not yet entered a Stop Time. The user may very well eliminate this error by entering a Stop Time after he completes this task. If he doesn't, it is a simple matter for your application to examine the validation range in column A and determine there is an error.

Defined Names

Defined names are an integral part of worksheet user interface design. Defined names are a superset of the more commonly understood named range feature. Defined names include named constants, named ranges and named formulas. Each type of defined name serves an important purpose and all nontrivial Excel worksheet user interfaces use some or all of the defined name types. The naming conventions used for the defined names demonstrated in this chapter are described in *Chapter 3 — Excel and VBA Development Best Practices*.

Named Constants

A defined name can refer to a constant value. For example, the setHiddenCols defined constant shown in Figure 4-2 refers to the value 1.

This name illustrates a typical use of defined constants: storing settings that will be made to a user interface worksheet. In this case it indicates the number of initial columns that will be hidden. Named constants can also serve all of the same purposes on a worksheet that VBA constants serve in a VBA program, as discussed in *Chapter 3 — Excel and VBA Development Best Practices*.

Two particularly important uses of named constants are workbook identification and version identification. Each UI workbook you create should have a unique named constant that identifies it as belonging to your application. The add-in for your application can then use this constant to determine whether the currently active workbook belongs to it. You should also include a version constant so you can pinpoint exactly what version of your application a given workbook belongs to. This becomes very important when you upgrade the application such that prior version user interface workbooks must be updated in some way.

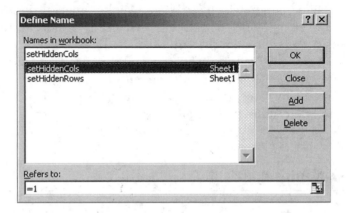

Figure 4-2 A Sample Named Constant

Named Ranges

Named ranges enable you to reference a location on a worksheet with a friendly name that conveys information about that location, rather than using a range address that cannot be interpreted without following it back to the cell or cells it refers to. As the example below shows, named ranges also enable you to accomplish things you cannot accomplish with directly entered cell addresses.

Everyone reading this book should be familiar with fixed named ranges, those referring to a fixed cell or group of cells on a worksheet. This section concentrates on the less well-understood topic of relative named ranges. A *relative* named range is called relative because the location it references is determined relative to the cell in which the name is used. Relative named ranges are defined in such a way that the cell or cells they refer to change depending on where the name is used. There are three types of relative named ranges:

1. **Column relative**—The referenced column changes, but the referenced row remains fixed. These can be identified because the absolute reference symbol ($) appears only before the row number. The address A$1 is an example of a column-relative address.
2. **Row relative**—The referenced row changes, but the referenced column remains fixed. These can be identified because the absolute reference symbol ($) appears only before the column letter. The address $A1 is an example of a row-relative address.
3. **Fully relative**—Both the referenced row and the referenced column change. In fully relative named ranges, neither the row nor the column is prefixed with the absolute reference symbol ($). The address A1 is an example of a fully relative address.

To create a relative named range, you must first select a cell whose position you will define the name relative to. This cell is your *starting point*. This cell is not the only cell where the name can be used; it simply gives you a point from which to define the relative name.

In the next example, we demonstrate how to define and use a fully relative named range that enables you to create formulas that automatically adjust the range they refer to when a row is inserted directly above them. First let's see why this is important.

Figure 4-3 shows a simple table showing the sales for three hypothetical regions. The total sales for all three regions are calculated using the built-in SUM worksheet function, which you can see displayed in the formula bar.

Now assume we need to add a fourth region to our list. We will insert a new row directly above the Total Sales row and add Region D. Figure 4-4 shows the result.

B5	▼	=	=SUM(B2:B4)		
Name Box		**B**	**C**	**D**	
1		Sales			
2	Region A	10			
3	Region B	10			
4	Region C	10			
5	Total Sales	30			
6					
7					
8					

Figure 4-3 Total Sales Using a Standard Formula

B6	▼	=	=SUM(B2:B4)		
	A	**B**	**C**	**D**	
1		Sales			
2	Region A	10			
3	Region B	10			
4	Region C	10			
5	Region D	10			
6	Total Sales	30			
7					
8					

Figure 4-4 Insert an Additional Region to the List

Because the new region was inserted at the bottom of the list, the SUM function range did not adjust and the Total Sales number reported by the function is now wrong. This example was designed to make the problem blindingly obvious. In real-world worksheets, this type of mistake is frequent and rarely so obvious. In fact, it is one of the most common errors we discover when auditing malfunctioning worksheets.

This error is easy to avoid by defining a fully relative named range that always refers to the cell directly above the cell where the name is used. To do this, choose *Insert > Name > Define* to display the Define Name dialog (or better yet, use the Ctrl+F3 keyboard shortcut). As you can see in Figure 4-5, our starting point is cell B6 and we have defined a fully relative, sheet-level named range called ptrCellAbove that refers to cell B5.

Next we modify our SUM function so it references the ptrCellAbove named range rather than a specific ending cell address, as shown in Figure 4-6.

Not only does our SUM function now display the correct answer, you can insert as many rows directly above it as you like and it will always sum the correct area. This feat can only be accomplished through the use of a fully relative named range. We use relative named ranges extensively in our sample application.

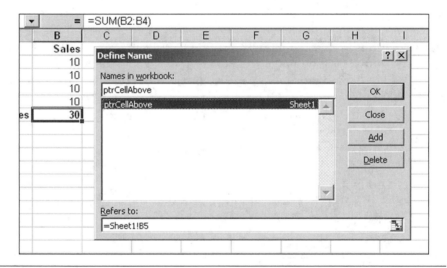

Figure 4-5 Creating a Fully Relative Named Range

	A	B	C	D	E
1		Sales			
2	Region A	10			
3	Region B	10			
4	Region C	10			
5	Region D	10			
6	Total Sales	40			
7					
8					

B6 = =SUM(B2:ptrCellAbove)

Figure 4-6 Using a Fully Relative Named Range in a Worksheet Function

Named Formulas

The least understood and most powerful defined name type is the named formula. Named formulas are built from the same Excel functions as regular worksheet formulas and like worksheet formulas they can return simple values, arrays and range references.

Named formulas enable you to package up complex but frequently used formulas into a single defined name. This makes the formula much easier to use, because all you need to do is enter the defined name you've assigned to it rather than the entire formula. It also makes the formula easier to maintain because you can modify it in one place (the Define Name dialog) and the changes will automatically propagate to every cell where the defined name is used.

In the *Practical Example* section of this chapter, we show an example of how to use a named formula to package a complex worksheet formula into a defined name to make it more maintainable and easier to use.

Named formulas can also be used to create ***dynamic lists***. A dynamic list formula is used to return a reference to a list of entries on a worksheet when the number of entries in the list is variable. Worksheet user interface development makes extensive use of dynamic lists for data-validation purposes, a topic we cover in depth in the *Data Validation* section later in the chapter, but let's revisit the timesheet from Figure 4-1 to show a quick example.

In this type of user interface, we wouldn't want users to enter whatever activity name they want in the Activity column. To make our data consistent from user to user, we would define a data-validation list of acceptable activity names and users would pick the activity that most closely described what they were doing from our predefined data-validation list.

We'll put our activity list on a background worksheet (one not designed to be seen by the user) and create a dynamic list named formula that refers to it. Figure 4-7 shows this named formula.

The valActivitiesList named formula can now be used as the data-validation list for the timesheet Activity column. A dynamic list named formula consists of the following parts:

- **Starting point**—The point at which the list begins. In this case, our starting point is cell wksData!$A$1.
- **Data area**—The full range in which items of our list might be located. This includes not only cells that are currently being used, but also cells that might be used in the future. In this case, our data area is the entire column A, or wksData!$A:$A.

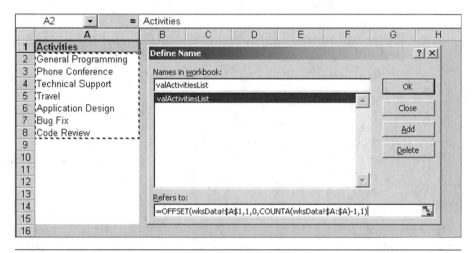

Figure 4-7 A Dynamic Named Formula

- **List formula**—A formula that determines the number of items currently in the list and returns a range reference to just those items. This is a combination of the OFFSET and COUNTA worksheet functions.

Scope of Defined Names

Defined names can have one of two scopes: worksheet level or workbook level. These are roughly analogous to private and public variables. Like variables, defined names should be given the most limited scope possible. Always use worksheet-level defined names unless you must make a name workbook level.

When your workbook contains a large number of defined names, using worksheet-level defined names helps reduce the number of names you have to look through in the Define Name dialog all at once. Worksheet-level defined names can be used from other worksheets in most cases. When they are used from another worksheet, they are just prefixed with the name of the worksheet from which they originated. This makes auditing worksheets that use defined names much simpler because you don't have to look up every defined name you come across in the Define Names dialog in order to determine which worksheet it references.

It is also often useful to have the same defined name on multiple worksheets in your user interface workbook. Two good examples of this are general-purpose, fully relative range names such as the ptrCellAbove range we discussed earlier and names that hold the values of settings you want to make to each worksheet using VBA code. We cover the latter in more detail in *Chapter 5 — Function, General and Application-Specific Add-ins*.

Some circumstances require you to use workbook-level defined names. Figure 4-7 demonstrates the most common case. A defined name that refers to a range located on a different worksheet that you want to use in a data-validation list must be a workbook-level defined name. This is a limitation inherent in Excel's data-validation feature.

In some cases, a workbook-level defined name is simply appropriate, such as when the name truly refers to the entire workbook rather than to any individual worksheet. This would be the case with a named constant used to identify the version number of a workbook. In the practical example section of *Chapter 7 — Using Class Modules to Create Objects*, we demonstrate the use of a workbook-level defined constant to identify workbooks that belong to our application.

Styles

Advantages of Styles

Styles provide a number of advantages that make them an integral part of any worksheet user interface. They provide a simple, flexible way to apply similar formatting to all the cells in your worksheet user interface that serve a similar purpose. The consistent use of styles also gives the user clear visual clues about how your user interface works. Using our timesheet example from Figure 4-1, Figure 4-8 shows how different styles define different areas of the worksheet user interface.

Styles enable you to apply the multiple formatting characteristics required for each user interface range all at once. Formatting characteristics commonly applied through the use of styles include number format, font type, background shading and cell protection. Other style properties, such as text alignment and cell borders, are less commonly used because they tend to be different, even within cells of the same style. Custom styles, which we discuss in the next section, can be configured to ignore the formatting characteristics you don't want to include in them.

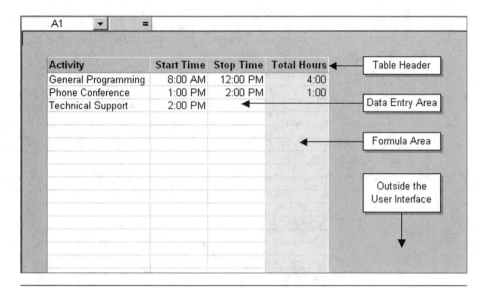

Figure 4-8 Using Styles as Visual Indicators of the Structure of Your User Interface

If you need to change the format of a certain area of your user interface, you can just modify the appropriate style and all of the cells using that style will update automatically. Here's an all-too-common real-world example of where this is very useful.

You've created a complex, multisheet data-entry workbook using white as the background color for data-entry cells. When you show this to your client or boss, they decide they want the data-entry cells to be shaded light yellow instead of white. If you didn't use styles to construct your user interface, you would have to laboriously reformat every data-entry cell in your workbook. If you did use styles, all that's required is to change the pattern color of your data-entry style from white to light yellow and every data-entry cell in your workbook will update automatically. Given the frequency with which people change their minds about how their applications should look, using styles throughout an application can save you a significant amount of time and effort.

Creating and Using Styles

Adding custom styles is not the most intuitive process in Excel, but after you've seen the steps required, you'll be creating styles like an expert in no time. Custom styles are created using the *Format > Style* menu. This opens the Style dialog, shown in Figure 4-9, from which all style confusions originate.

When the Style dialog first opens, it automatically displays the formatting characteristics of the cell that was selected when the dialog was invoked. In Figure 4-9, the Style dialog was invoked while the selected cell was in the Start Time column shown in Figure 4-8. As you can see, this cell was formatted with the Input style, so this is the style displayed by the Style dialog.

To create a new style, enter the name of the style you want to create in the *Style name* combo box, as shown in Figure 4-10.

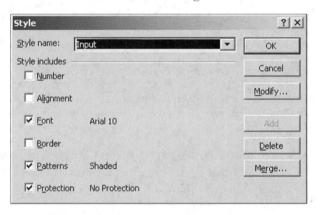

Figure 4-9 The Excel Style Dialog

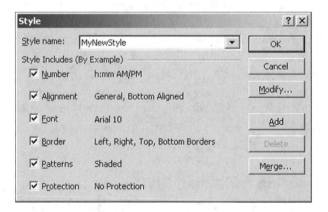

Figure 4-10 A New Style Is Always Based on the Style of the Cell Selected When the Style Dialog Is Displayed

After you do this, you will encounter one of the more confusing aspects of the Style dialog. All the *Style Includes* check boxes will be checked and their values will be set to the format of the cell that was selected when the Style dialog was invoked. This occurs even if those format characteristics are not part of the style currently applied to that cell.

For example, Number, Alignment and Border attributes were excluded from the Input style that was displayed in the Style dialog immediately before we created our new style. All three of those attributes are included in our new style, however, and their specific values are drawn from the format that was applied to the cell that was selected when the Style dialog was first invoked. This is what the *By Example* in parenthesis after the *Style Includes* title means. Don't worry; all of these attributes can easily be changed.

First, remove the checkmark from beside any format option that you don't want to include in your style. When a style is applied to a range, only the format options you checked will be applied. Next, click the Modify button to define the properties of your new style. This will display the Format Cells dialog, shown in Figure 4-11.

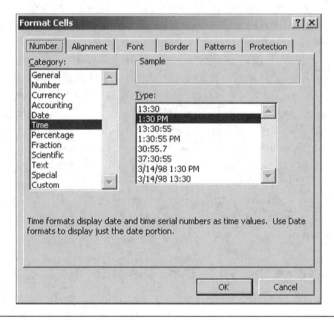

Figure 4-11 The Format Cells Dialog as Invoked from the Style Dialog Modify Button

Notice that the six tabs on the Format Cells dialog correspond exactly to the six *Style Includes* options shown in Figure 4-10. This is no accident. Styles are just a way of grouping multiple cell format characteristics under a single name so that they can be applied and maintained simultaneously through that name.

NOTE: If you remove the checkmark from a *Style Includes* option but then change any of the characteristics of that option in the Format Cells dialog, the option will automatically become checked again in the Style dialog.

Modifying Styles

Modifying an existing style is exactly like creating a new style except that after selecting the *Format > Style* menu, you pick the style you want to modify from the *Style name* combo box rather than entering a new style name. Each time you select a style in the *Style name* combo box, that style will have its settings summarized and displayed for you in the *Style Includes* section of the dialog. Click the Modify button to display the Format Cells dialog and change any of the format options for the currently selected style.

There is one minor caution to keep in mind when creating new styles or modifying existing styles. After you have configured the style using the Format Cells dialog, be sure to click the Add button on the Style dialog to save your changes. If you click the OK button, your changes will be saved, but the style you have created or modified will also be applied to the currently selected cell. This is often not the result you want. Getting into the habit of using the Add button to add and update styles will save you from having to undo changes to a cell you didn't intend to change. After you have used the Add button to create or modify a Style, you can safely use the Cancel button to dismiss the Style dialog without losing your work or formatting the currently selected cell.

Adding the Style Drop-Down to the Toolbar

If you're familiar with Word, you'll notice styles in Word are considered so important that a special style drop-down is automatically present on the Formatting toolbar. This not only enables you to quickly apply a style to a selection, but also displays the style associated with the section of the document where your cursor is located. Excel has the same toolbar control, but for some reason, styles in Excel were not deemed important enough by Microsoft to have this control appear by default. You can add this control to one of your Excel toolbars manually, however, and if you plan on making full use of styles in Excel you should do so. Here's how.

Start by selecting *View > Toolbars > Customize* from the Excel menu. In the Customize dialog, select the *Commands* tab. In the *Commands* tab, select the Format item from the *Categories* list. As shown in Figure 4-12, the Style drop-down will be the fifth item in the *Commands* list box.

Drag this control from the *Commands* list box and drop in onto one of your existing toolbars. You will now have a Style control that provides the same benefits as the Style control in Word. You can select a group of cells and apply a style to all of those cells by simply selecting the style name from the Style drop-down. And when you select a cell, the name of the style applied to that cell will automatically be displayed in the Style drop-down. This feature proves very helpful when creating complex worksheet user interfaces that utilize many different styles.

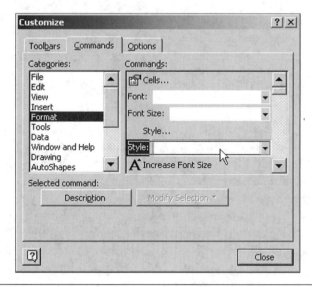

Figure 4-12 Selecting the Style Drop-Down from the List of Format Controls

User Interface Drawing Techniques

Using Borders to Create Special Effects

To keep the user focused on the elements of your worksheet user interface, it is often helpful to modify the normal style so all unused areas of the worksheet have a consistent, light gray background color. This practice has been demonstrated in most of the user interface examples shown so far and will be used in our sample application. On top of this light gray background, you can use cell borders to create some interesting special effects. One of the most commonly used border-based special effects gives a range of cells a 3D appearance, either raised or sunken. Figure 4-13 shows examples of both effects.

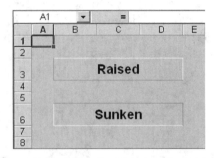

Figure 4-13 Using Borders to Create 3D Visual Effects

To create a raised effect, you just add a white border to the top and right sides of your range and add a 50 percent gray border to the left and bottom sides of your range. To create a sunken effect, you do exactly the opposite. The width of the borders can be used to control the degree of the effect.

When you've applied a background color to a worksheet, as we've done in the example above, Excel's standard gridlines are obscured. In many cases gridlines are a useful visual guide for the user, so you want to put them back. Although there is no way to force Excel's standard gridlines to display over a background color, you can easily simulate gridlines by adding 25 percent gray borders with the lightest width to the area where you want the gridlines to appear. Figure 4-14 shows this effect.

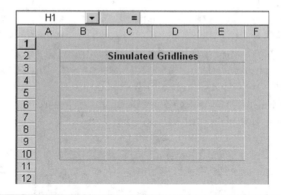

Figure 4-14 Using Borders to Simulate Gridlines

Creating Well-Formatted Tables

Tables used within an Excel worksheet user interface typically have one or more of the following elements:

- Table description
- Row and column descriptions
- Data-entry area
- Formula result area

Each section of your table should be formatted with a unique style that you use consistently throughout your user interface. Figure 4-15 shows a sample table with all four of the elements described above.

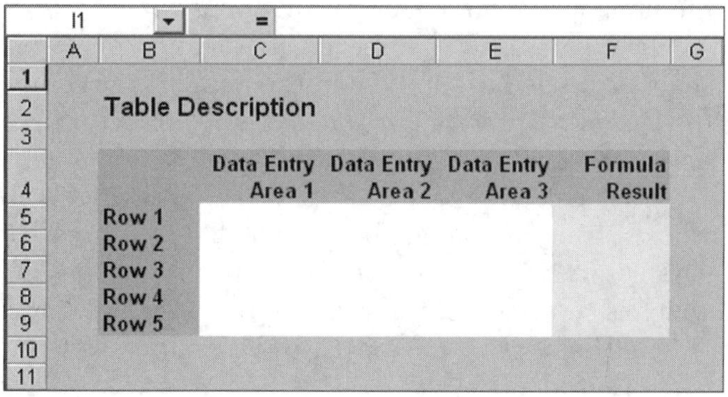

Figure 4-15 A Basic Worksheet User Interface Table Layout

As you can see, in its simplest form the table is not very attractive. You can give your tables a much more professional appearance by using borders to provide a 3D effect and simulated gridlines and by increasing the row heights and column widths to provide more visual separation. Turning off the row and column headers and the formula bar completes the effect. The table now looks like a completely custom user interface. Figure 4-16 shows the table with these added effects.

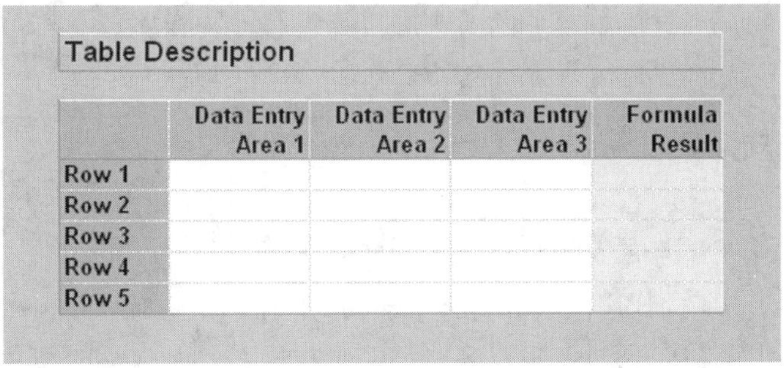

Figure 4-16 A Fully Formatted Worksheet User Interface Table

Cell Comments for Help Text

Cell comments are one of the most important user interface features provided by Excel. Their utility stems from the fact that in many cases they can serve the same purpose as a help file without requiring users to do anything more complicated than hover their mouse cursor over the commented cell. Note that cell comments have several limitations that may make them inappropriate in certain situations:

If you are using the freeze panes feature on a worksheet and the worksheet is scrolled beyond the freeze point, if the comment window overlaps the frozen row and/or column it will be cut off at the point where the window is frozen.

Each cell comment is also associated with a specific status bar message whose structure cannot be modified. The status bar message displayed when users hover their mouse over a comment has the following structure, which is shown graphically in Figure 4-17:

Cell **address** commented by **username at the time the comment was created**

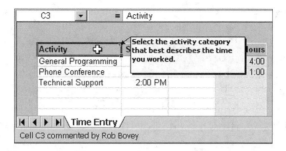

Figure 4-17 The Format of an Excel Comment Status Bar Message

The only part of this message you can modify is the *user name at the time the comment was created* section, which displays the contents of the *User name* entry located under the *Tools > Options > General* tab of the Excel menu. If you are a consultant creating a worksheet user interface for a client, it's unlikely your client will want to see your name in the status bar each time they view a cell comment. In that case, one of the best workarounds is to change the *User name* setting on your machine to your client's company name while you create the comments for their user interface. After the comments have been created, the user name displayed in the status bar is fixed and will not be affected when you change your *User name* setting back to your own name.

Remember that cell comments can be rich-text formatted. This means you can use formatting such as bold and italic fonts within the comment text as well as multiple fonts. Rich-text formatting enables you to create some very sophisticated help messages. Figure 4-18 shows a rich-text-formatted cell comment from a real-world worksheet user interface.

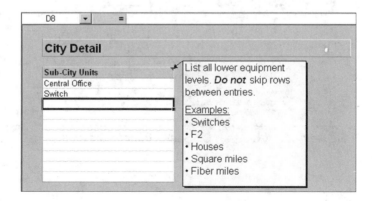

Figure 4-18 A Rich-Text-Formatted Cell Comment

Using Shapes

The ability to use shapes (objects drawn using the various options on the Drawing or Forms toolbars) on an Excel worksheet is a very powerful user interface technique. Shapes are located in a special drawing layer that exists above the cells on a worksheet, so shapes cover (and obscure) worksheet cells. Shapes are also connected to the underlying worksheet through their properties, which allow them to do the following:

- Move and size with the worksheet cells they cover
- Move but don't size with the worksheet cells they cover
- Don't move or size with the worksheet cells they cover

Almost all shapes can contain text. A shape's text can either be manually entered or it can be linked dynamically to a specific cell on a worksheet by selecting the shape and entering the address of that cell as a formula in the formula bar. As you can imagine, the ability to assign formulas to shapes opens up a wide array of options for creating dynamic user interfaces. Shapes can also be given a macro assignment that will cause them to execute the specified macro whenever the user clicks them. Just right-click over the shape and choose *Assign Macro* from the shortcut menu. Figure 4-19 shows an excellent example of how shapes can be used to create a custom toolbar-like area across the top of a worksheet user interface.

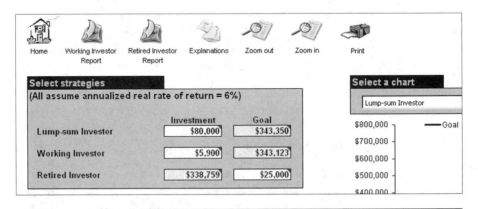

Figure 4-19 A Custom On-Sheet Toolbar Created with Shapes

Data Validation

Data validation is one of the most useful yet underutilized features for worksheet user interface design. It enables you to ensure that most, if not all, of the inputs made in your user interface are correct by disallowing input that does not match the rules you specify. Data validation can be as simple as restricting cell entries to whole numbers or as complex as restricting cell entries to items on a list whose contents are conditionally determined based on an entry made in a previous cell.

We assume you understand the basic use of data validation and instead demonstrate two of the more complex validation scenarios that can be created with this feature. Most complex data validation scenarios involve data validated lists or custom data validation formulas.

Unique Entries

If you need the user to enter only unique item names in a data-entry list, you can use a custom data-validation formula to enforce uniqueness. First select the entire data-entry area you need to validate. Then choose *Data > Validation* from the menu and select the *Custom* option from the *Allow* list. The basic syntax of the formula you need to enter is the following:

```
=COUNTIF(<entire range>,<relative reference to input cell>)=1
```

The first argument to the COUNTIF function is a fixed reference to the entire data-entry area that must contain unique entries. The second argument to the COUNTIF function is a relative reference to the currently selected cell in the data-input range.

If each entry is unique, the COUNTIF function evaluates to 1 and the entire formula evaluates to True, meaning the data is valid. If the COUNTIF function locates more than one instance of an entry in the data-entry area the entire formula will evaluate to False and data validation will prevent that entry from being made. Figure 4-20 shows an example of this validation setup and Figure 4-21 shows it in action.

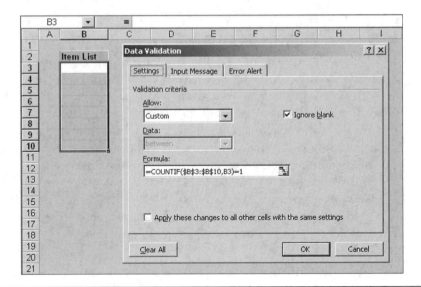

Figure 4-20 Data Validation Configuration to Force Unique Entries in a List

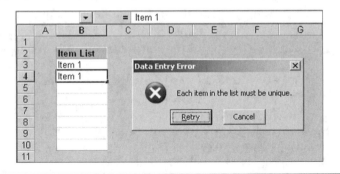

Figure 4-21 Unique Entries Data Validation in Action

Cascading Lists

In this type of validation, the specific data validation list that is displayed for a cell is determined by the entry selected in a previous cell. In Figure 4-22, the data validation list for the Item column is determined by the selection in the Category column. All of the data validation lists are located in the hidden column A. The Categories list is the data validation list for the Category column. The Fruits list is the data validation list for the Item column when the Category selected is Fruits. The Vegetables list is the data validation list for the Item column when the Category selected is Vegetables.

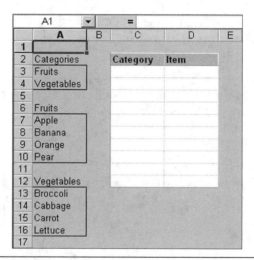

Figure 4-22 Initial Setup for Cascading Data-Validation Lists

The data validation list formula for the Category column is simple: =$A$3:$A$4. The data validation list formula for the Item column is a bit more complicated. It has to check the value of the corresponding Category entry and do one of three things: display no list if the Category entry has not been selected, display the list of fruits if Fruits has been selected or display the list of vegetables if Vegetables has been selected. The formula that does all this is shown below:

```
=IF(C3=$A$3,$A$7:$A$10,IF(C3=$A$4,$A$13:$A$16,$A$1)))
```

Note the trailing reference to cell $A$1 in this formula. The purpose this serves is to create an empty validation list in the Item column if nothing has been selected in the Category column. It wouldn't make sense to allow the user to select an Item prior to selecting a Category. As Figure 4-23 shows, this formula successfully displays two completely different data validation lists depending on the category selection.

This logic can be extended to as many categories as the maximum formula length of 1024 characters will allow. However, for cases with large numbers of categories, a table-driven approach that you'll see used in our sample timesheet application is much easier to set up and maintain.

Note that one drawback of this type of validation is that it doesn't work in both directions. In the scenario described above, there is nothing to stop a user from accidentally changing the category entry in a row where a specific item has already been selected. In the next section we show how to use conditional formatting to provide a visual indication that this kind of error has been made.

NOTE: In Excel 97 there is a bug such that in most circumstances, data-validation lists will not function when the freeze panes feature has been applied to a worksheet.

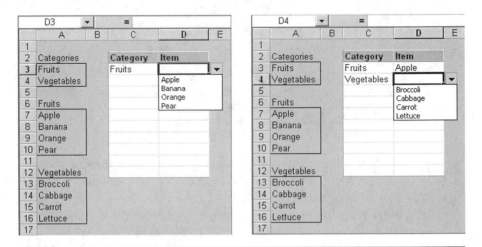

Figure 4-23 Cascading List Validation in Action

Conditional Formatting

Conditional formatting is one of the most powerful features available for Excel user interface construction. It enables you to substitute simple formulas for what would otherwise be reams of VBA code. Conditional formatting works by modifying the appearance of the cells it has been applied to only if one or more conditions that you specify have been met. Conditional formatting overrides any style setting when the condition is triggered. When the condition that triggered the conditional formatting is no longer true, the affected cell regains its original format.

The two most common uses for conditional formatting in Excel user interface development are the creation of dynamic tables and calling out error conditions.

Creating Dynamic Tables

When building nontrivial worksheet-based user interfaces, you will often be faced with the problem of providing a table that in extreme cases will allow the entry of some large number of rows but for the most common scenarios will only require a few. Rather than hard-coding a visible table with the maximum possible number of rows, you can use conditional formatting to create a table that expands dynamically as data is entered into it. We demonstrate how this is done beginning with the sample table shown in Figure 4-24.

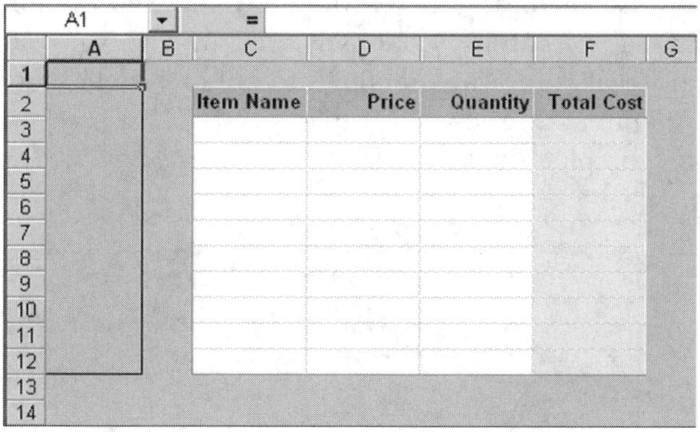

Figure 4-24 Data-Entry Table Prior to the Addition of Dynamic Formatting

Let's assume this table really requires 200 rows for the largest projects but that most users only need a few rows of input. Therefore, you want to hide the unused area of the table. As you can see, the first step in creating a dynamic table is to draw the entire table on the worksheet. You then use conditional formatting to hide the unused area of the table and reveal rows dynamically as needed. The trigger for displaying a data-entry row will be the user entering a new name into the Item Name column. For that reason, we always need to leave an empty Item Name entry cell at the bottom of the table.

When creating a dynamic table, it's a good idea to also create an outline showing the extent of the table in one of your hidden columns. After we've added the conditional formatting, the table will disappear. This makes the table difficult to maintain if you haven't provided yourself with a visual marker indicating its extent. The empty bordered area in column

A serves this purpose in our example. This area doesn't need to be empty. It could include error-checking formulas, for example. As long as it gives you a visual indication of the extent of the hidden area of the table, it serves its purpose.

Our dynamic table requires three different conditionally formatted sections. Referencing Figure 4-25, the first section will encompass range C3:C12, the second section will encompass range D3:F12 and the third range will encompass range G3:G12. We'll add the conditional formats one step at a time so you can see the results as they occur. To make the operation of the conditional formats more obvious we'll add data to the first row of the table. Keep in mind that the purpose of all three conditional formatting sections is the same: to simulate the appearance of a table that is just large enough to hold the data that has been entered into it. Figure 4-25 shows the table with the first section of conditional formatting completed.

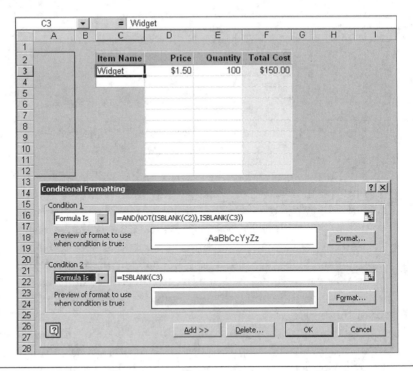

Figure 4-25 Conditional Formatting for the First Column

In addition to the purpose described above, the first conditional format serves to leave a blank cell in front of the first unused table row in order to help prompt the user to enter the next item. The second conditional format is shown in Figure 4-26. It clears all unused rows in columns D through F and draws a bottom border below the first unused row in the table, thereby helping to complete the table outline.

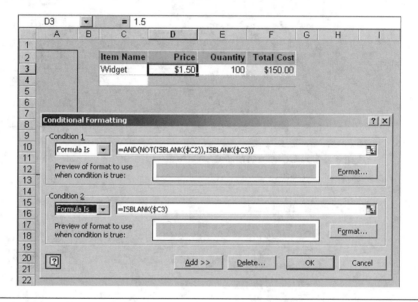

Figure 4-26 Conditional Formatting for the Remaining Columns Within the Table

You can see the white border on the far right side of the table is missing in Figure 4-27. The purpose of the third conditional format is to complete the simulated table by drawing this border. Figure 4-27 shows the third conditional format.

Figure 4-28 shows the fully formatted table with some additional entries. Each time a new entry is made, the conditional format reveals the row in which the entry was placed and adds a new prompt row below it.

The one major caveat when considering the use of conditional formatting to create dynamic tables is that calculation must be set to automatic in order for it to work. If your user interface is so calculation intensive that you need to set calculation to manual, then you cannot create dynamic tables using this method (or use any other type of formula-based conditional formatting for that matter).

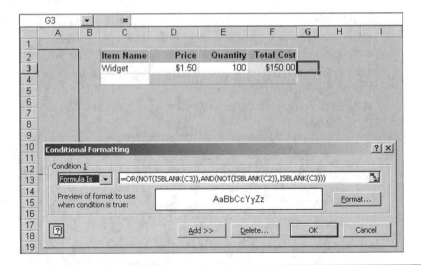

Figure 4-27 Conditional Formatting Outside the Table to Create the Right-Hand Border

	A	B	C	D	E	F	G
1							
2			Item Name	Price	Quantity	Total Cost	
3			Widgets	$1.50	100	$150.00	
4			Pieces	$1.00	50	$50.00	
5			Parts	$2.00	125	$250.00	
6							
7							
8							

Figure 4-28 The Complete Dynamically Formatted Table

Calling Out Error Conditions

Conditional formatting can also work alone or in concert with formulas in hidden rows and columns to highlight invalid entries as soon as they are made. This should not be your method of first choice for pointing out data-entry errors. Always try to use data validation to prevent data-entry errors from being made in the first place.

The most common situation in which errors cannot be prevented by data validation is when you have two data-entry columns such that the entry in the first column determines the allowable entries in the second column. In Figure 4-29 we revisit our cascading data-validation list example from Figure 4-22.

Even though both columns' lists are data validated, an error can creep in if the user initially selects a valid category and item combination but then accidentally changes the category name at some later point in time. This type of mistake cannot be prevented by data validation, so we need to provide some visual indication that there is a mismatch between the category and item selections if this error occurs. This is a task for conditional formatting.

As you can see in Figure 4-29, we've inserted a second hidden column. In this column we've created an error check for each row that verifies the entry selected in the Item column is valid for the selection in the Category column.

	B3	▼	=	=IF(ISBLANK(E3),FALSE,IF(D3=A
	A	B	C	D	E	F
1						
2	Categories	HasError		Category	Item	
3	Fruits	FALSE		Fruits	Apple	
4	Vegetables	FALSE		Vegetables	Broccoli	
5		FALSE				
6	Fruits	FALSE				
7	Apple	FALSE				
8	Banana	FALSE				
9	Orange	FALSE				
10	Pear	FALSE				
11		FALSE				
12	Vegetables	FALSE				
13	Broccoli					
14	Cabbage					
15	Carrot					
16	Lettuce					
17						

Figure 4-29 The Error Check Formula Column for the Conditional Format

The error check formula is a bit complicated, so we break it down in Listing 4-1. Keep in mind that the purpose of the error check formula is to return True if the corresponding row in the table has a data-entry error and False otherwise.

Listing 4-1 The Error Check Formula Outlined

```
=IF(ISBLANK(E3),FALSE,
    IF(D3=$A$3,
        ISERROR(MATCH(E3,$A$7:$A$10,0)),
        ISERROR(MATCH(E3,$A$13:$A$16,0))
    )
)
```

The only type of error that can occur in this situation is the Item column entry not matching the Category column entry. If there is no Item column entry, the row is not complete and we cannot determine the validity of the Category column entry. The outer IF function checks for this condition and returns FALSE if this is the case. When there is an entry in the Item column, the inner IF function determines the correct list from which to try and locate the Category entry. The formula then uses the MATCH function wrapped in the ISERROR function to return TRUE if the Category entry is located in the correct list or FALSE if it isn't.

The next thing we do is add a conditional format to the table that checks the value of the HasError column. If the HasError column indicates there is an error in one of the table rows, our conditional format will give that row a bright red shade. Error condition highlighting is one exception to the rule of not using garish colors in your user interface. We do recommend using red, however, because this is almost universally recognized as a warning color. Figure 4-30 shows the conditional format required to accomplish this.

The result of the conditional format in response to an error condition is shown in Figure 4-31, where we've changed the Category column entry in the second table row from Vegetables to Fruits so it no longer matches the entry in the Item column.

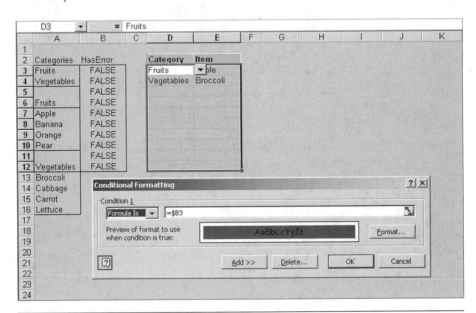

Figure 4-30 Setting Up Conditional Formatting to Flag an Error Condition

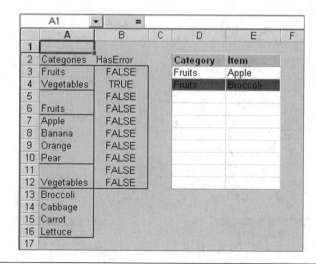

Figure 4-31 Conditional Formatting Flagging a Bad Entry in the Table

Using Controls on Worksheets

Using controls placed directly on worksheets is typically not the best user interface design. For most Excel application development, we recommend you use custom command bars as entry points into your code and substitute data-validation lists for combo box controls. (Command bars are given a full-chapter treatment in *Chapter 8 — Advanced Command Bar Handling*.) In some circumstances, placing controls directly on your worksheet user interface is the best option, so here we cover some of the things you need to watch out for when you do this.

When you do need to use controls on a worksheet, you must choose between ActiveX controls and controls from the Forms toolbar. As a general rule, we recommend you use Forms controls unless you absolutely need ActiveX controls. Forms controls are very lightweight and don't exhibit the many quirks you'll run into when using ActiveX controls on worksheets. Figure 4-32 shows a worksheet in which Forms controls have been used to great effect.

Because everyone reading this chapter should be familiar with how controls work, we just cover the details critical to deciding whether you can use Forms controls in your worksheet user interface or whether you need ActiveX controls.

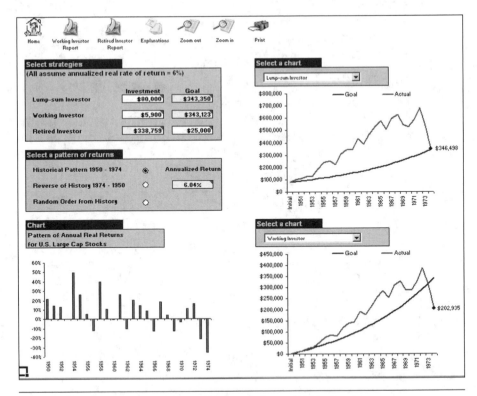

Figure 4-32 Good Use of Forms Controls on a Worksheet

Advantages of Forms Controls

- Forms controls can be used on Chart sheets, ActiveX controls cannot.
- Forms controls are more tightly linked to Excel. You can select a Label or Button control and enter a formula in the formula bar that will dynamically set the captions of those controls. And unlike its ActiveX counterpart, a Forms control Listbox will update its contents in response to changes to a dynamic named range that has been assigned to its Input range property.
- It is a simple matter to assign multiple Forms controls to run the same VBA procedure. Doing the same with ActiveX controls requires a more complicated class-based approach.
- If you use multiple windows or the split-panes feature in your application to show two different views of the same worksheet, ActiveX controls will only work in the original window. Forms controls will work in any window.

Advantages of ActiveX Controls

- You can modify the appearance of ActiveX controls to a much greater degree than Forms controls.
- There are more varieties of ActiveX controls than there are Forms controls.
- ActiveX controls have a wide variety of event procedures that you can respond to, whereas Forms controls can only run a single macro.

NOTE: If you use ActiveX controls on worksheets in Excel 97, you will frequently run into problems with VBA code that will not run in response to a control being selected. This is because the selected control has "stolen" the focus from the worksheet. With the exception of the CommandButton control, which has a TakeFocusOnClick property that can be set to False to eliminate this problem, the first line of code associated with an ActiveX control on a worksheet under Excel 97 should select a cell on the worksheet to return the focus to it.

Practical Example

In this section we begin building a real-world Excel application that illustrates the points made in the chapter text. Our application will be a time-tracking system that will start as a simple, no-frills timesheet and work its way up to being a full-featured Excel application as we progress through the book. Due to space constraints, we do not show every detail involved in creating this application. We demonstrate the major features and allow you to examine the rest by perusing the finished sample of the application that is available on the accompanying CD. This timesheet application will henceforth be referred to by its acronym PETRAS, which stands for Professional Excel Timesheet Reporting and Analysis System.

The first version of PETRAS will be a simple workbook containing a time-entry table on one worksheet and data-validation lists on a second hidden worksheet. The user will be expected to complete the time-entry table each week and manually copy the workbook to a central location for consolidation. You can find this version of PETRAS on the accompanying CD in the \Application\Ch04-Worksheet Design\ folder. It is displayed in Figure 4-33.

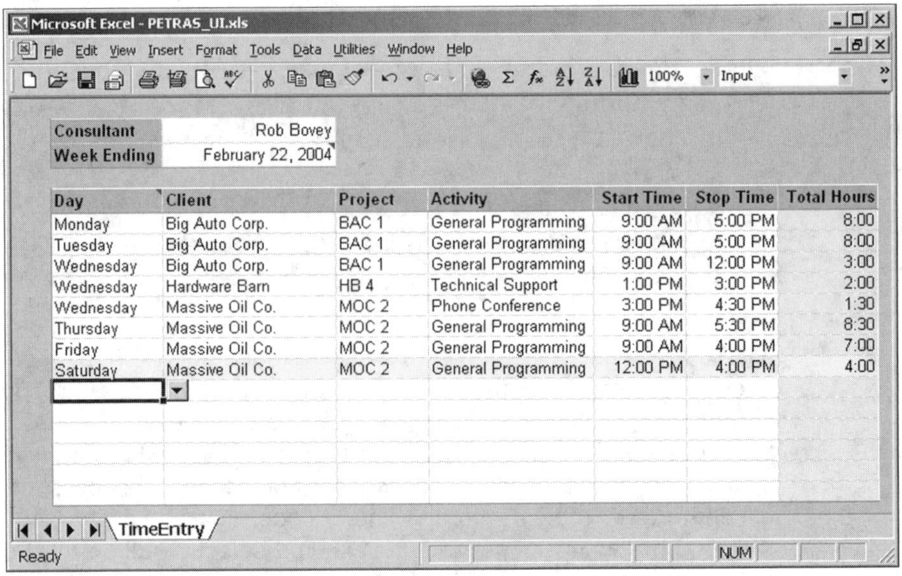

Figure 4-33 The First Version of the PETRAS Application

Most of the user interface design techniques that have been discussed in this chapter have been used in the PETRAS application, including all variations of defined names, styles to differentiate areas by purpose, table formatting techniques, use of comments for help text, data validation and conditional formatting. Let's quickly cover examples of how each of these techniques is used in practice.

Hidden Rows and Columns

We've taken advantage of hidden rows and columns in the PETRAS application for two purposes: error checking and background data processing. Figure 4-34 shows an open version of the PETRAS user interface workbook.

This worksheet has two types of hidden columns. The two initial hidden columns are what we called program columns early in the chapter. We also have two hidden columns in the middle of the user interface. These two columns are used to create a data table that makes the process of automatically consolidating data simpler, while not requiring the user to enter duplicate data for each row. As you'll see in *Chapter 5 — Function, General and Application-Specific Add-ins*, we will have special-purpose code that uses the setHideCols named range, shown in the first row, to ensure these columns are hidden.

	A	B	C	D	E	F	G
1	errHasErrors			setHideCols			
2	FALSE						
3	FALSE					Consultant	Rob Bovey
4	FALSE					Week Ending	February 22, 2004
5							
6	FALSE	FALSE	Consultant	EndDate	Day	Client	Prc
7	FALSE	FALSE	Rob Bovey	02/22/04	Monday	Big Auto Corp.	BA
8	FALSE	FALSE	Rob Bovey	02/22/04	Tuesday	Big Auto Corp.	BA
9	FALSE	FALSE	Rob Bovey	02/22/04	Wednesday	Big Auto Corp.	BA
10	FALSE	FALSE	Rob Bovey	02/22/04	Wednesday	Hardware Barn	HB
11	FALSE	FALSE	Rob Bovey	02/22/04	Wednesday	Massive Oil Co.	MC
12	FALSE	FALSE	Rob Bovey	02/22/04	Thursday	Massive Oil Co.	MC
13	FALSE	FALSE	Rob Bovey	02/22/04	Friday	Massive Oil Co.	MC
14	FALSE	FALSE	Rob Bovey	02/22/04	Saturday	Massive Oil Co.	MC
15	FALSE	FALSE					
16	FALSE	FALSE					
17	FALSE	FALSE					
18	FALSE	FALSE					
19	FALSE	FALSE					
20	FALSE	FALSE					
21							

Figure 4-34 The PETRAS Application with all Rows and Columns Visible

Defined Names

The Total Hours column in Figure 4-33 is calculated using a named formula called `forTimeDiff`. We used a defined formula for this purpose because the logic required is complex and therefore it makes sense to encapsulate it. The `forTimeDiff` named formula makes use of relative defined names to reference each part of the row from which it needs to gather the data required to perform its calculation. Listing 4-2 shows this defined formula.

Listing 4-2 The `forTimeDiff` Named Formula

```
=IF(COUNTA(inpEntryRow)<6,"",
    IF(inpStop>inpStart,
        inpStop-inpStart,
        (1+inpStop)-inpStart
    )
)
```

The input-type defined names (those with the inp prefix) are all row-relative defined names that refer to fixed columns on the TimeEntry worksheet, as follows:

inpEntryRow = TimeEntry!$F3:$K3

inpStart = TimeEntry!$J3

inpStop = TimeEntry!$K3

If there are fewer than six entries in the current row, the formula simply returns an empty string. We cannot allow total hours to be calculated for a row that has not been completed. After all of the entries in a row have been completed, we must compare the start and stop times. These times are entered as Excel date serial time values; therefore they are decimal values less than or equal to 1 that have no indication of the date worked. We set up the timesheet in this manner as a convenience to the user. It allows the user to simply enter a start time and a stop time without also having to enter a specific date for each time.

If the stop time is greater than the start time we know both entries refer to the same day. We can then just subtract the start time from the stop time to calculate the number of hours worked. If the stop time is less than or equal to the start time, we know the user began working prior to midnight on one day and finished working after midnight on the next day. In this case, we add 1 to the stop time, which is equivalent to adding one day in the Excel date serial format, to force it to be greater than the start time. We then subtract the start time from the result. This enables us to account for situations in which users work past midnight.

Styles

Note that PETRAS uses the same styles we introduced in Figure 4-8. We use separate styles to identify row and column headers, input areas, formula results and areas that are outside the user interface. The TimeEntry worksheet in Figure 4-33 is designed to be protected, and once protected, the only cells that can be modified by the user are cells having the Input style (the style with the white background).

User Interface Drawing Techniques

The PETRAS application demonstrates two of our recommended user interface drawing techniques. As shown in Figure 4-33, we've used borders to give the time-entry table a 3D appearance and a simulated grid to help guide the user. We've also provided cell comments to answer the most common questions the user may have about the user interface. Figure 4-35 shows the cell comment describing the Day column.

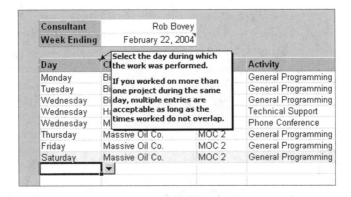

Figure 4-35 A Cell Comment Used as Help Text

Data Validation

Data validation has been used in every input cell in the PETRAS user interface. Most of the data validation derives from dynamic lists stored on the hidden wksProgramData worksheet, part of which is shown in Figure 4-36.

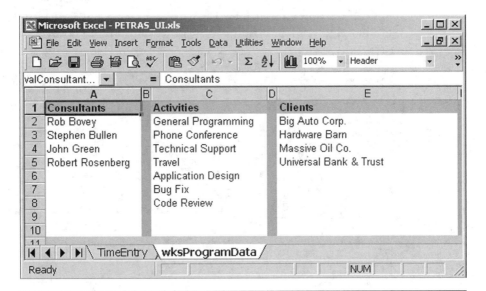

Figure 4-36 The Hidden wksProgramData Worksheet

The Consultants column on the wksProgramData worksheet provides the data-validation list for the Consultant entry on the TimeEntry worksheet. Similarly, the Activities column on the wksProgramData worksheet provides the data-validation list for the Activity column on the TimeEntry worksheet and so on. A complete picture of the various data validation techniques used on the TimeEntry worksheet can be gained by examining the sample application. Note that a more complex example of the cascading lists data-validation technique described earlier in this chapter is used to connect the Client and Project columns on the TimeEntry worksheet.

Conditional Formatting

In Figure 4-33, you can see that conditional formatting has been used to provide a clear visual indication of time entries that were made on a weekend. This is because work done on weekend days typically costs a higher hourly rate than work done on a weekday. Conditional formatting is also used to call out the error condition created when the user changes the first column entry of a cascading validation list pair if the second entry has already been made. In Figure 4-37 below, the user has mistakenly changed a Client entry to a client that does not match the Project entry previously made. Note how conditional formatting makes it instantly recognizable that changing the client entry was the wrong thing to do in this case.

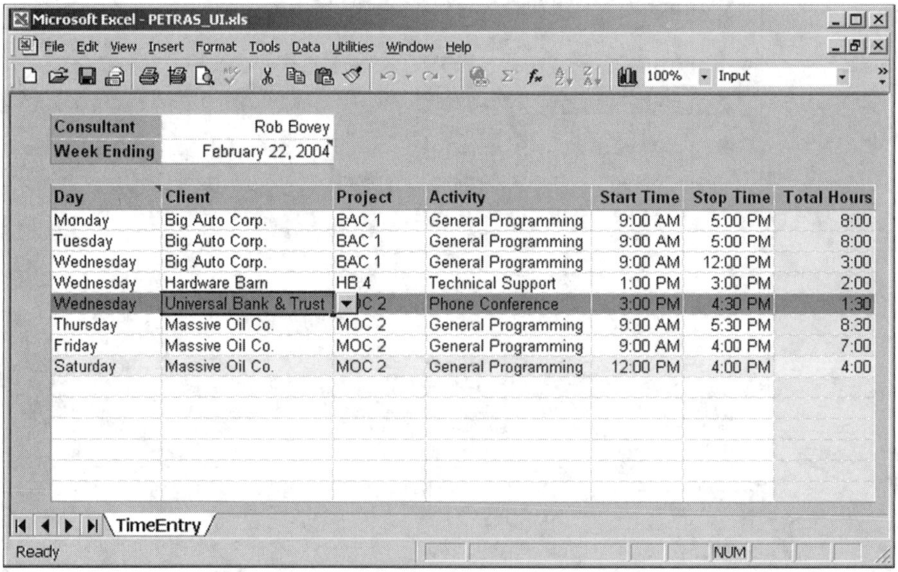

Figure 4-37 Conditional Formatting Notifies the User of a Data-Entry Error

Conclusion

We've discussed many user-interface building techniques in this chapter; all of them implemented using Excel's built-in features. However, don't lose sight of the fact that the most important thing about an Excel user interface is not how many cool techniques you've used. Users don't care about cool techniques. They want an intuitive user interface that makes it easy for them to get their job done. Ideally your user interface should not draw attention to itself at all. It should just be so well designed and constructed that users can dive right in and start working without having to spend any significant time figuring things out. Adhering to the eight principles described at the beginning of this chapter can help you design user interfaces that do their job so well no one notices them. This is the best user interface design of all.

CHAPTER 5

Function, General and Application-Specific Add-ins

Add-ins are the primary constituents of most nontrivial Excel applications. This chapter discusses the most important duties add-ins perform within an Excel application, as well as details about the activities various types of add-in must perform. This chapter does not cover dictator applications, as that is the subject of the next chapter.

The Four Stages of an Application

Every application has four distinct stages, regardless of the type of add-in used to implement it. These stages are development/maintenance, startup, runtime and shutdown. This section briefly discusses all four stages and identifies the activities and services that must be provided by the application during each stage. Some of the topics covered do not apply to all types of applications, but we cover them all to give you a complete high-level overview of what an application must accomplish. We do not go into great detail on the topics covered in this section. Some will be obvious to readers of this book and others are covered extensively either later in this chapter or in later chapters of the book.

Development/Maintenance

During this stage you are either writing the application's code for the first time or updating existing code in the application. Either way, the purpose of this stage is to build or fix the application rather than to run it. You can make your life easier during this stage by using VBA code to help build and maintain the application you are writing. There are two major categories of code that helps to build code:

- **Code templates**—These can be as simple as basic subroutine and function frameworks manually copied from a stored module, or as complex as third-party code-generation tools. The Excel Visual Basic Editor (VBE) provides a very rudimentary tool for creating template subroutines, functions and property procedures through the *Insert > Procedure* menu.
- **Development utilities**—You should strive to automate as many routine development processes as possible. Your application should contain a dedicated code module, or even a separate utility application, for VBA utilities that assist you in creating and maintaining the application. In the *A Table-Driven Approach to UI Worksheet Management* section later in the chapter, we demonstrate a utility for automatically managing the settings on your user interface worksheets.

Startup

When your application is starting up, it must perform a number of tasks depending on what type of application it is and the conditions it finds during the startup process.

- **Check the environment**—Check any environmental conditions that must be satisfied in order for your application to run. This might include verifying that the appropriate version of Windows and Excel are installed as well as verifying the existence of any additional programs and files your application depends on. If the startup check fails, you can exit gracefully with a clear error message to the user rather than allowing your application to continue until it encounters a runtime error.
- **Save all settings that must be restored on exit**—If your application modifies the user's Excel environment, it must save the original settings so they can be restored prior to exiting. This topic is covered extensively in *Chapter 6 — Dictator Applications*.
- **Build any dynamic user interface elements**—These include application-specific command bars, Excel Application-level settings, workbook templates and so forth.

- **Register any user-defined functions**—If your add-in contains user-defined functions (UDFs) you want to expose to the user, you need to add some basic information about them to the Excel Function Wizard. We cover this topic in the *Function Library Add-ins* section later in the chapter.

- **Set the initial user interface configuration**—The specific settings made will depend on the type of add-in and the conditions discovered at startup. For example, if there were an application workbook open that belonged to your application when the add-in was opened, you would enable all of your application's menu bars and toolbars. Otherwise you would probably disable most of them. This type of dynamic command bar modification is covered in the *Practical Example* section of *Chapter 7 — Using Class Modules to Create Objects*.

Runtime

Runtime is the stage during which your application is performing the operations that constitute its primary purpose.

- **Handle requests from the user**—These include calls generated by command bar controls, Forms controls on worksheets, ActiveX controls on userforms and worksheets and any keyboard shortcuts your application has provided for the user.

- **Handle Excel application events**—During runtime your application must also be prepared to respond to (and in some cases suppress) events generated by Excel itself. Excel application event handling is covered extensively in *Chapter 7 — Using Class Modules to Create Objects*.

- **Handle runtime errors**—Although we would like our applications to run flawlessly all the time, every application eventually encounters a runtime error. These errors cannot be allowed to stop your application dead in its tracks. Instead, they must be handled gracefully and in such a way that the user has some idea of what went wrong. Error handling is covered extensively in *Chapter 12 — VBA Error Handling*.

- **Call code located in other add-ins**—If you have set a reference to another add-in using the *Tools > References* menu in the VBE during development, you can call public procedures located in standard modules in the referenced add-in directly by name. Without references, you can accomplish the same thing by using the `Application.Run` function.

- **Provide other services**—Add-ins also provide other services at runtime, the most common being UDFs. We cover UDFs in detail in the *Function Library Add-ins* section later in this chapter.

Shutdown

The shutdown stage is when your application is exiting, either normally at the request of the user or abnormally as the result of an error condition. Either way there are activities that must be performed at this stage.

- **Unregister any user-defined functions**—If your add-in registered any UDFs with the Excel Function Wizard on startup, it should unregister these functions on shutdown.
- **Remove all application-specific user interface components**—This means removing all the application-specific items created during the startup phase (command bars, application-specific workbooks and so forth).
- **Restore the original environment**—If your application made any persistent changes to the Excel environment, it must save the original settings on startup and restore them on shutdown. This process is generically known as saving and restoring the user's workspace. This topic is covered extensively in *Chapter 6 — Dictator Applications*.

Function Library Add-ins

It is quite common to encounter VBA add-ins that serve no other purpose than to provide a library of UDFs. These add-ins are called function library add-ins. Add-ins are the best container for hosting VBA user-defined functions because as long as the user has the add-in containing the functions open, those functions will be available to all currently open workbooks. UDFs located in a specific workbook are only available to worksheets in that workbook.

Function library add-ins are the simplest type of add-in from the perspective of the operational tasks they must accomplish. Although the functions it contains may be quite complex, the function library add-in itself has only two responsibilities: registering its UDFs with the Excel Function Wizard on startup and unregistering them on shutdown. In this section, we first create a sample UDF and then show the options available to the add-in for handling its registration duties.

An Example UDF

A common situation encountered when creating worksheet models is the need to use a combination of the IF and ISERROR worksheet functions to test the result of another function for an error condition. If the function being tested evaluates to an error value, you construct the IF function to return some default value in its place. If the function being tested does not evaluate to an error value, you construct the IF function to execute the function being evaluated a second time and return its result.

When the function being tested is very long and/or complex, the resulting formula is doubly long and/or complex because you must evaluate the function being tested twice. This situation can be generalized by the following pseudo-formula:

```
=IF(ISERROR(<long_function>),<default>,<long_function>)
```

In this section, we write a UDF that performs this operation with just one pass of the function being evaluated. We'll call our UDF IFERROR and its syntax will be the following:

```
=IFERROR(<long_function>,<default>)
```

Listing 5-1 shows the VBA code required to implement our IFERROR function.

Listing 5-1 The IFERROR User-Defined Function

```
Public Function IFERROR(ByRef ToEvaluate As Variant, _
                        ByRef Default As Variant) As Variant
    If IsError(ToEvaluate) Then
        IFERROR = Default
    Else
        IFERROR = ToEvaluate
    End If
End Function
```

The `ToEvaluate` argument is a value, cell reference or directly entered function expression to be evaluated. If `ToEvaluate` contains an error value, the `Default` argument is returned, otherwise `ToEvaluate` is returned. The `Default` argument can also be a value, cell reference or directly entered expression.

Both arguments and the function return value of the IFERROR function are specified as Variant data types in order to provide the maximum flexibility in the types of arguments the function can accept and return. As discussed in *Chapter 3 — Excel and VBA Development Best Practices*, the Variant data type can have a negative impact on performance. If you know, for example, that you will always be passing cell references to both IFERROR arguments, you can significantly improve the performance of the function by changing the data type of its arguments and return value to the Range data type.

UDF Naming Conventions

Custom worksheet functions and their arguments (if any) should be given reasonably short descriptive names. You should do your best to make your UDFs look and feel like built-in Excel worksheet functions. Therefore, you should not apply the naming conventions described in *Chapter 3 — Excel and VBA Development Best Practices* to UDFs.

Making Your UDF Appear Native

You can make your UDFs appear more like native Excel functions by registering them with the Excel Function Wizard. This involves giving them descriptions and assigning them to categories that will assist the user in figuring out how to use them. There are two ways to do this; the first is simple but limited, the second complex but complete.

The first way is to use the `Application.MacroOptions` method. The major advantages of the `Application.MacroOptions` method are the relatively lengthy function description allowed and the fact that it removes your UDF from the default User Defined category when it places it under the category you specify. The disadvantages of this method are that the function description and category are the only options you can specify and you cannot create categories that don't already exist in the Function Wizard. Listing 5-2 shows an Auto_Open procedure that uses the `Application.MacroOptions` method to register our IFERROR function.

Listing 5-2 Registering a UDF with Application.MacroOptions

```
Sub Auto_Open()
    Dim sDescription As String
    sDescription = "Provides a short-cut replacement " & _
        "for the common worksheet function construct:" & _
        vbLf & "=IF(ISERROR(<function>),<default>,<function>)"
    Application.MacroOptions Macro:="IFERROR", _
                             Description:=sDescription, _
                             Category:=9
End Sub
```

Excel's function categories are specified by numeric values that correspond to the position of the category in the Excel Function Wizard category list, where All = 0, Financial = 1 and so on. If you do not specify a category number, your UDF will be assigned to category 14, User Defined, by default. If you specify a category number that does not exist, a runtime error will occur. Table 5-1 shows the full set of available category numbers, along with their corresponding category names. Not all of these categories are commonly used.

Table 5-1 UDF Function Category Numbers and Names

Category Number	Category Name
0	All
1	Financial
2	Date & Time
3	Math & Trig
4	Statistical
5	Lookup & Reference
6	Database
7	Text
8	Logical
9	Information
10	Commands
11	Customizing
12	Macro Control
13	DDE/External
14	User Defined

Listing 5-3 shows an Auto_Close procedure that uses the `Application.MacroOptions` method to unregister our IFERROR function. The only drawback to this method is it leaves your function name listed in the All category with no description.

Listing 5-3 Unregistering a UDF with Application.MacroOptions

```
Private Sub Auto_Close()
    Application.MacroOptions Macro:="IFERROR", _
                             Description:=Empty, _
                             Category:=Empty
End Sub
```

Keep in mind that the `Application.MacroOption` examples shown above register and unregister a single function. If your add-in contains multiple UDFs, you will need to add one call to the `Application.MacroOptions` method for each UDF in both the Auto_Open and the Auto_Close procedure.

The second way to provide descriptions for your UDFs requires you to execute an XLM macro function to both register and unregister them. XLM is the native Excel programming language that predates VBA but is still supported in Excel. More than ten years after it supposedly became obsolete, there are still things that XLM does better than VBA, and this is a good example.

The advantage of this method is it gives you complete control over all aspects of the description and categorization of your function. The disadvantage of this method is the XLM macro string, which must contain all names, descriptions and other information, is limited to 255 characters in length. This means your descriptions must be kept short. Your UDF will also continue to appear in the default User Defined category even though it also appears in any new category that you specify. Credit for originally devising this technique goes to worksheet function expert Laurent Longre.

The code required to demonstrate this method will not fit within the limited confines of a printed page, so you will need to examine the MRegister module in the Function.xls workbook located on the CD in the *Concepts* folder for this chapter to see how it works. The code in this module is commented extensively to help you understand it and is designed so the entire module can be copied into another project and work correctly.

You will just need to modify the function descriptions and add room for additional functions to suit your needs. One procedure call placed in your add-in's Auto_Open procedure will register all of your UDFs and one procedure call placed in your add-in's Auto_Close procedure will unregister all of your UDFs.

NOTE: If you do not do anything to prevent it, any public function in your add-in will automatically be listed in the User Defined category in the Excel Function Wizard. This will occur even if your function isn't designed to be used as a worksheet function at all. The solution to this problem is to add the `Option Private Module` directive to the top of any module that contains public functions. This will not prevent public worksheet functions from being used as such, but it will prevent them from being automatically added to the User Defined functions category.

Creating a Friendly Name and Description for Your Function Library Add-in

Function library add-ins are typically placed in the add-ins list of the Excel Add-ins dialog accessed through the *Tools > Add-ins* menu. This enables the user to easily load and unload them as the need arises. We discuss the various ways of making your add-in appear in the *Tools > Add-ins* dialog in *Chapter 24 — Providing Help, Securing, Packaging and Distributing*. You should provide a friendly name and a short description for any add-in that appears in the Add-ins dialog. These can be made to appear when the add-in's entry is selected by setting two specific file properties of the add-in workbook.

First, set the IsAddin property of the add-in's ThisWorkbook object to False so you can access the add-in workbook from the Excel user interface. Then choose *File > Properties* from the Excel menu. On the *Summary* tab of the resulting Properties dialog, you provide a friendly name for your add-in using the *Title* entry. The description for your add-in is entered in the *Comments* field. Figure 5-1 shows the name and description for our sample function library add-in.

Figure 5-2 shows how the name and description added in the Properties dialog appear in the Add-ins dialog.

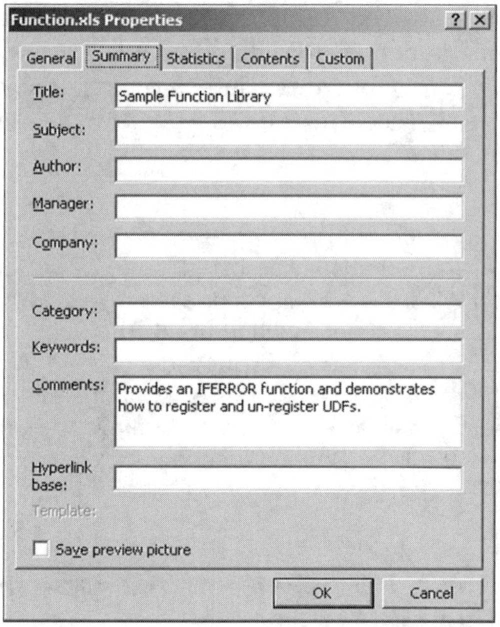

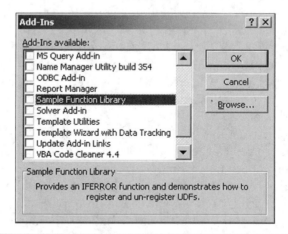

Figure 5-1 Adding a Name and Description to an Add-in

Figure 5-2 The Add-in Name and Description in the Add-ins Dialog

Critical UDF Details

The following are some critical details you need to understand in order to develop VBA user-defined functions.

- One of the most common mistaken beliefs about UDFs is that they can change the value of cells other than the one they've been entered into. This is not the case. Whether a UDF is programmed in a VBA add-in (described in this chapter) a VB6 automation add-in (described in *Chapter 21 — Writing Add-ins with Visual Basic 6*) or a C/C++ XLL (described in *Chapter 19 — XLLs and the C API*), a user-defined function can only modify the value of the cell into which it has been entered.

- A UDF cannot change any properties of the cell it has been entered into other than the value of that cell. Attempting to set the pattern or borders of a cell from within a UDF, for example, will not work, although neither does it cause a VBA or function return value error.

- UDFs must be located in standard code modules. They cannot be placed in class modules, userforms or the code modules behind workbooks or worksheets.

- Do not attempt to change the values of UDF arguments that are declared ByRef. As we discuss in a moment, UDFs can only change the value of the cell into which they have been entered. Attempting to modify the value of a ByRef argument violates this principle and will cause your UDF to return a #VALUE! error if you attempt to modify a ByRef argument that has been declared as a Range object.

- Put all range references used by your function in the function's argument list. If you refer to ranges not in the argument list from within your UDF, changes to those ranges will not cause your UDF to recalculate, possibly leading to incorrect results being displayed. You can use the `Application.Volatile` method to force your UDF to recalculate whenever calculation is triggered anywhere in Excel, but this can cause serious degradation of calculation performance and some types of worksheet event handling and should be used only as a last resort.

VBA UDF Problems

The biggest problem with most VBA UDFs is that using them creates hard-coded links from the workbooks where they are used to the add-in that contains them. If you physically move the source add-in, workbooks that use the functions it contains will not be able to locate it, even if the add-in is opened prior to opening any workbooks that use its functions. If you use the XLM UDF registration method described in the section on *Creating a Friendly Name and Description for Your Function Library Add-in*, you can avoid this problem.

VBA functions also do not automatically capitalize correctly when you enter them into a worksheet cell. Capitalization does not affect the operation of the function, but it gives the function a strange appearance. And after you have entered a UDF in all lowercase characters, you will find it almost impossible to get it to convert to uppercase characters even when it is defined that way in the source code in the add-in.

TIP: When writing any worksheet function for Excel 97, always use an error handler. An unhandled error that occurs inside a UDF in Excel 97 for any reason will cause many different problems depending on how the function calculation was triggered. The worst of these problems will halt your VBA program in its tracks if the calculation was triggered by VBA code.

General Add-ins

General add-ins, also known as utility add-ins, are designed to enhance Excel by extending its feature set or providing connections between it and other programs. All Excel utility add-ins fall into this category, including most of the add-ins you will find in the *Tools* folder of the CD that accompanies this book. Like function library add-ins, general add-ins are designed to work with any arbitrary workbook the user opens. General add-ins are typically contained within a single .xla workbook, although larger examples may be distributed across multiple files. General add-ins are typically placed in the add-ins list of the Excel Add-ins dialog so the user can easily load and unload them as the need arises. They are provided with a friendly name and description in exactly the same way as described for a function library add-in in the previous section.

The most common method for providing the user access to features in a general add-in is through a menu and/or toolbar. Event handling is also frequently used to respond to user actions, while keyboard shortcuts can be provided to run commonly used features.

Because general add-ins must operate correctly no matter what state Excel is currently in, any event handling class you use must respond to changes in the Excel environment that would prevent your add-in from operating correctly. An example would be the user closing the last open workbook. In response to this situation, your event handler should disable access to the features of your add-in that require an open workbook to function correctly. Event handling is covered in more detail in *Chapter 7 — Using Class Modules to Create Objects*.

The individual entry-point procedures of your add-in must also verify that the current state of Excel is valid for them to run. For example, if a procedure is designed to operate on a chart, but there is no chart currently active, your procedure must detect this and provide the user with an explanatory error message rather than falling over with a runtime error caused by an attempt to reference a nonexistent chart.

Application-Specific Add-ins

Application-specific add-ins differ from the previous two add-in types in that they are designed to implement self-contained Excel applications. They may integrate with the standard Excel user interface, as does the add-in shown in the *Practical Example* section later in the chapter, or they may take over the Excel user interface entirely, as demonstrated in *Chapter 6 — Dictator Applications*. In either case, an application-specific add-in is designed to operate only on workbooks that have been specifically designed for it. Still, most of the same operations and requirements apply to application-specific add-ins as apply to function libraries and general add-ins. Application specific add-ins simply add an additional element, the worksheet user interface.

A Table-Driven Approach to UI Worksheet Management

A significant part of the responsibility of an application-specific add-in is to manage the user interface workbook and worksheet settings. It's possible to store, apply and remove these settings on an ad hoc basis, but when dealing with large and/or complex user interfaces it is much better to let VBA do the work for you.

In this section, we demonstrate a table-driven approach to managing worksheet user interface settings. Typically, a number of settings must be made prior to your application being run by the end user. However, these settings will get in your way during development. The solution is to create an automated system for defining, applying and removing these settings. This is just one of many areas in Excel development that lends itself to a table-driven methodology.

Table-Driven Methodology Defined

In a nutshell, table-driven methods use a worksheet table to store data that describes the task you are trying to accomplish. One or more VBA procedures read the data from the table and automatically perform that task. The biggest advantage of a table-driven method for accomplishing a specific task is it tends to be easily reusable from project to project.

Common tasks that lend themselves to table-driven solutions are managing workbook and worksheet user interface setup, building command bars and saving and restoring the user's workspace. We even demonstrate a table-driven method for creating userforms in *Chapter 10 — Userform Design and Best Practices*.

Typical Worksheet User Interface Settings

A number of settings or configuration details tend to be common to all worksheet user interfaces, including the following

- **Hidden rows and columns**—As discussed in *Chapter 4 — Worksheet Design*, having hidden rows and columns at your disposal is a valuable user interface construction technique. However, you don't want these rows and columns to be hidden when you are performing development or maintenance work on the user interface.
- **Protection**—Workbook and worksheet protection are fundamental to good user interface design. Protecting the user interface prevents users from modifying areas of the user interface that should not be modified.
- **Scroll area**—Setting a scroll area for each user interface worksheet prevents users from getting lost by preventing them from scrolling beyond the area used by your application.

- **Enable selection**—This property works with the scroll area property to keep the user focused on your user interface. It prevents the user from even selecting cells that are outside the boundaries of your UI.
- **Row and column headers**—Although there are some exceptions, you typically do not want to display Excel's row and column headers on your user interface worksheets. Row and column headers serve as guidelines for constructing and maintaining a user interface, so they should be visible during that process. In most well-designed user interfaces, however, they will just be a distraction to the user. Therefore, you want them visible during development and hidden at runtime.
- **Sheet visibility**—In most nontrivial workbook-based user interfaces, you will have one or more worksheets that are designed to perform background tasks that should not be seen or modified by the user. Once again, however, you want these sheets to be visible during development and maintenance.

The Settings Table

Let's see how a table-driven methodology can help us create and manipulate the user interface settings described above. The first thing we need is a settings table. This table will list the names of the user interface worksheets in the first column and the names of the settings in the first row. At the intersection of each row and column is the value that will be applied to a specific worksheet for that setting. Figure 5-3 shows an example of a user interface settings table.

	A	B	C	D	E	F	G
1	Worksheets	setProgRows	setProgCols	setScrollArea	setProtect	setRowColHeaders	setVisible
2	wksProgramData	0	0		FALSE	TRUE	FALSE
3	wksLists	0	0		FALSE	TRUE	FALSE
4	wksErrors	0	0		FALSE	TRUE	FALSE
5	wksEntryValidation	0	0		FALSE	TRUE	FALSE
6	wksOutputData	0	0		FALSE	TRUE	FALSE
7	wksOutputCalcs	0	0		FALSE	TRUE	FALSE
8	wksDescription	1	1	$B$2:$K$60	TRUE	FALSE	TRUE
9	wksExecSummary	1	1	$B$2:$N$50	TRUE	FALSE	TRUE
10	wksCF	1	1	$B$2:$N$51	TRUE	FALSE	TRUE
11	wksCFSummary	1	1	$B$2:$AD$36	TRUE	FALSE	TRUE
12	wksIS	1	1	$B$2:$AD$28	TRUE	FALSE	TRUE
13	wksBS	1	1	$B$2:$AD$25	TRUE	FALSE	TRUE
14	wksGeneral	1	1	$B$2:$G$42	TRUE	FALSE	TRUE
15	wksCostAreas	1	1	$B$2:$L$128	TRUE	FALSE	TRUE
16	wksCostAreaMap	1	3	$B$2:$M$128	TRUE	FALSE	TRUE
17	wksCostAreaCounts	1	1	$B$2:$O$140	TRUE	FALSE	TRUE
18	wksProducts	1	1	$B$2:$S$18	TRUE	FALSE	TRUE
19	wksClients	2	2	$B$2:$AG$136	TRUE	FALSE	TRUE

Figure 5-3 A User Interface Settings Table

This table would typically be located on a worksheet in your add-in. The VBA code used to manage these settings would be located in a utility module in the add-in. A utility module is a standard code module that holds code designed to assist the programmer during development and not used by the application itself. In situations where add-in size needs to be minimized, this table and its associated code could be located in a separate utility workbook that is only used during development and maintenance. However, you will still need to have some user interface management code located in the add-in to set the properties of your user interface when your application is run.

There are two things to note about this table. First, you can see that all of the worksheet names in the first column follow our worksheet naming convention. This is because they are the CodeNames of the worksheets, not their sheet tab names. As mentioned in *Chapter 3 — Excel and VBA Development Best Practices*, you should never rely on sheet tab names because they may change frequently or unexpectedly. A worksheet's CodeName provides a permanent, unique name by which you can identify the worksheet.

Second, beginning in column B you can see that the column headers are defined names (remember that the set prefix identifies a defined name that represents a setting). This is because all of these settings will be stored as sheet-level defined names on the worksheets to which they apply. This allows all of the information required to manage a worksheet to be encapsulated within that worksheet.

Also notice that some of the settings in the body of the table are blank. This indicates the setting does not apply to that worksheet and the setting name will not be defined on that worksheet. Later you will see that the VBA code that implements these settings ignores settings whose defined names are missing.

The Utility Code

The VBA code that implements the table-driven settings needs to accomplish two objectives:

1. It needs to read the settings table and add the specified defined names with the specified values to each worksheet listed in the table.
2. It needs to loop each worksheet in the user interface workbook, read the value of each defined name listed in the settings table and record the value of that setting in the appropriate cell of the settings table.

These tasks will be implemented as two separate procedures. If we have code to create the settings defined in the settings table, you may be asking yourself, why do we also need code to read these settings back into the table? Good question.

The answer is that when you are working directly on the user interface workbook you will often find it easier to manually update the value of a defined name for a setting you've just altered. For example, if you need to add additional hidden program columns to several sheets, it's very easy to update their respective setProgCols defined names as you go along. After you've made these adjustments, you can quickly synchronize the settings table and the user interface workbook by reading the values of all the defined names from the workbook back into the settings table.

As you can see in Listing 5-4, the code required to apply the settings in the settings table to the worksheets in the user interface workbook is relatively simple. The defined names that reference the list of worksheets in the first column and the list of settings in the first row are both dynamic. If you add worksheets or settings, these names automatically expand to include them.

Keep in mind that this code does not actually ***apply*** any settings in the user interface workbook. It simply records the settings we want to apply on each worksheet using worksheet-level defined names. A procedure in the application that runs as part of the startup code will read these defined names and apply the settings they specify.

Listing 5-4 Code to Write Settings to the User Interface Worksheets

```
Private Const msFILE_TEMPLATE As String = "PetrasTemplate.xlt"
Private Const msRNG_NAME_LIST As String = "tblRangeNames"
Private Const msRNG_SHEET_LIST As String = "tblSheetNames"

Public Sub WriteSettings()

    Dim rngSheet As Range
    Dim rngSheetList As Range
    Dim rngName As Range
    Dim rngNameList As Range
    Dim rngSetting As Range
    Dim sSheetTab As String
    Dim wkbTemplate As Workbook
    Dim wksSheet As Worksheet
```

```vba
' Turning off screen updating and calculation
' will speed the process significantly.
Application.ScreenUpdating = False
Application.Calculation = xlCalculationManual

' The time entry workbook.
Set wkbTemplate = Application.Workbooks(msFILE_TEMPLATE)
' The list of worksheets in the first column.
Set rngSheetList = wksUISettings.Range(msRNG_SHEET_LIST)
' The list of setting names in the first row.
Set rngNameList = wksUISettings.Range(msRNG_NAME_LIST)

' The outer loop processes all the worksheets in the
' first column of the table.
For Each rngSheet In rngSheetList

    ' We need an object reference to the worksheet so we
    ' can easily add a sheet-level defined name to it.
    ' The sSheetTabName() function converts a CodeName
    ' into its corresponding sheet tab name.
    sSheetTab = sSheetTabName(wkbTemplate, rngSheet.Value)
    Set wksSheet = wkbTemplate.Worksheets(sSheetTab)

    ' The inner loop adds each setting to the current sheet.
    ' If the setting already exists it will be replaced.
    For Each rngName In rngNameList

        ' The value of the setting is contained in the cell
        ' where the worksheet row and range name column
        ' intersect.
        Set rngSetting = Intersect(rngSheet.EntireRow, _
                                rngName.EntireColumn)

        ' We only create defined names for settings that
        ' have been given a non-zero-length value.
        If Len(rngSetting.Value) > 0 Then
            wksSheet.Names.Add rngName.Value, _
                        "=" & rngSetting.Value
        End If

    Next rngName

Next rngSheet
```

```
Application.ScreenUpdating = True
Application.Calculation = xlCalculationAutomatic

End Sub
```

The sample add-in discussed in the *Practical Example* section later in this chapter contains code that automatically applies these settings to the user interface workbook when it is first opened. The MUtility module of the application also contains a procedure that automatically removes all these settings from the user interface workbook to make it easier to maintain.

Using VBA to Dynamically Modify Your Worksheet User Interface

You can leverage the power of VBA to improve your user interface in many ways. Many of them, including techniques such as context-specific command bar enabling and dynamic hiding and unhiding of rows and columns, require the use of Excel event trapping, which we cover in *Chapter 7 — Using Class Modules to Create Objects*.

A simple example that we'll add to our sample application is a feature that clears the data-entry cells on a worksheet. A one-click method for clearing all input cells on the current user interface worksheet is often very helpful to users. To do this, just create a named range that includes all the data-input cells on each data-entry worksheet and give it an obvious name such as rgnClearInputs. This must be a sheet-level defined name created on all data-entry worksheets in your workbook. Listing 5-5 shows the VBA implementation of our clear data-entry area feature.

Listing 5-5 VBA Implementation of a Clear Data-Entry Area Feature

```
Public Sub ClearDataEntryAreas()

    Dim rngToClear As Range

    ' Make sure the active worksheet has the rgnClearInputs
    ' defined name (i.e. it's an input worksheet).
    On Error Resume Next
        Set rngToClear = ActiveSheet.Range("rgnClearInputs")
    On Error GoTo 0
```

```
' If the worksheet is an input worksheet, clear the
' contents of the input area.
If Not rngToClear Is Nothing Then rngToClear.ClearContents

End Sub
```

Practical Example

Features

The add-in for our PETRAS timesheet application will perform the following operations:

- Open and initialize the application
- Build a toolbar that gives the user access to each feature of the application
- Open and initialize the time-entry workbook
- Enable the user to save a copy of the time entry workbook to a predefined consolidation location
- Enable the user to add more data-entry rows to the time-entry worksheet
- Enable the user to clear the data-entry area so the timesheet can easily be reused
- Enable the user to close the PETRAS application
- Add a custom property that will allow the consolidation application to locate all instances of our time-entry workbook

Let's look at how the add-in accomplishes these tasks. We'll assume the WriteSettings utility procedure shown in Listing 5-4 has been run on the time-entry workbook and the settings saved prior to running the add-in.

Open and Initialize the Application

The first operation the add-in performs when it is opened is to initialize the application and then open and initialize the user interface workbook. This is accomplished by the Auto_Open procedure, shown in Listing 5-6.

Listing 5-6 The PETRAS Add-in Auto_Open Procedure

```
Public Sub Auto_Open()

    Dim wkbBook As Workbook

    ' The very first thing your application should do upon
    ' startup is attempt to delete any copies of its
    ' command bars that may have been left hanging around
    ' by an Excel crash or other incomplete exit.
    On Error Resume Next
        Application.CommandBars(gsBAR_TOOLBAR).Delete
    On Error GoTo 0

    ' Initialize global variables.
    InitGlobals

    ' Make sure we can locate our time entry workbook before
    ' we do anything else.
    If Len(Dir$(gsAppDir & gsFILE_TIME_ENTRY)) > 0 Then

        Application.ScreenUpdating = False
        Application.StatusBar = gsSTATUS_LOADING_APP

        ' Build the command bars.
        BuildCommandBars

        ' Determine if the time entry workbook is already
        ' open. If not, open it. If so, activate it.
        On Error Resume Next
        Set wkbBook = Application.Workbooks(gsFILE_TIME_ENTRY)
        On Error GoTo 0

        If wkbBook Is Nothing Then
            Set wkbBook = Application.Workbooks.Open( _
                            gsAppDir & gsFILE_TIME_ENTRY)
        Else
            wkbBook.Activate
        End If

        ' Make the worksheet settings for the time entry
        ' workbook
        MakeWorksheetSettings wkbBook
```

```
    ' Reset critical application properties.
    ResetAppProperties

Else
    MsgBox gsERR_FILE_NOT_FOUND, vbCritical, gsAPP_NAME
    ShutdownApplication
End If

End Sub
```

The first thing the add-in does is blindly attempt to delete any previous instance of its toolbar. This should be considered a best practice. Application toolbars can be left behind due to an incomplete shutdown, which will then cause an error when you try to create them again the next time your application is run. Then the add-in initializes any global variables. In this case we have two: a variable that holds the full path where the add-in is located and a variable that indicates when the add-in is in the process of shutting down.

As mentioned in *Chapter 3 — Excel and VBA Development Best Practices*, you should use as few global variables as possible. When you do use them, you must make sure they are in a known state at the beginning of every procedure where they might be accessed. Encapsulating this logic in an InitGlobals procedure that can be called wherever it's needed is a good way to manage this process.

After the add-in has performed these two basic tasks, it checks to see whether it can locate the user interface workbook. If the user interface workbook is located, execution continues. Otherwise, an error message displays and the application exits. This makes sense because there is nothing the add-in can do without the user interface workbook.

Build a Toolbar That Gives the User Access to Each Feature

Next the add-in builds its toolbar. The techniques used to do this are basic, hard-coded VBA command bar building techniques that should be familiar to all readers of this book. Therefore, we do not go into any detail on this. An entire chapter is devoted to advanced command bar building techniques, *Chapter 8 — Advanced Command Bar Handling*.

The add-in exposes four distinct features for the user through the application toolbar, as shown in Figure 5-4. Each of these features is discussed in the sections that follow.

Figure 5-4 The PETRAS Application Toolbar

Open and Initialize the Time-Entry Workbook

After the command bars have been constructed, the add-in checks to see whether the user interface workbook is already open. If this workbook is not open, the `Auto_Open` procedure opens it. If this workbook is open, the Auto_Open procedure activates it. The next step is to initialize the user interface workbook. During this process, all the settings that were saved to the user interface workbook's worksheets by the WriteSettings procedure in Listing 5-4 are read and applied by the MakeWorksheetSettings procedure. Listing 5-7 shows this procedure.

Listing 5-7 The MakeWorksheetSettings Procedure

```
Public Sub MakeWorksheetSettings(ByRef wkbBook As Workbook)

    Dim rngCell As Range
    Dim rngSettingList As Range
    Dim rngHideCols As Range
    Dim sTabName As String
    Dim vSetting As Variant
    Dim wksSheet As Worksheet

    Set rngSettingList = wksUISettings.Range(gsRNG_NAME_LIST)

    For Each wksSheet In wkbBook.Worksheets

        ' The worksheet must be unprotected and visible in order
        ' to make many of the settings. It will be protected and
        ' hidden again automatically by the settings code if it
        ' needs to be protected and/or hidden.
        wksSheet.Unprotect
        wksSheet.Visible = xlSheetVisible

        ' Hide any non-standard columns that need hiding.
        Set rngHideCols = Nothing
        On Error Resume Next
```

```
Set rngHideCols = wksSheet.Range(gsRNG_SET_HIDE_COLS)
On Error GoTo 0
If Not rngHideCols Is Nothing Then
    rngHideCols.EntireColumn.Hidden = True
End If

For Each rngCell In rngSettingList

    ' Determine if the current worksheet requires the
    ' current setting.
    vSetting = Empty
    On Error Resume Next
    If rngCell.Value = "setScrollArea" Then
        ' The scroll area setting must be treated
        ' differently because it's a range object.
        Set vSetting = Application.Evaluate( _
            "'" & wksSheet.Name & "'!" & rngCell.Value)
    Else
        vSetting = Application.Evaluate( _
            "'" & wksSheet.Name & "'!" & rngCell.Value)
    End If
    On Error GoTo 0

    If Not IsEmpty(vSetting) Then
        If rngCell.Value = "setProgRows" Then
            If vSetting > 0 Then
                wksSheet.Range("A1").Resize(vSetting) _
                    .EntireRow.Hidden = True
            End If
        ElseIf rngCell.Value = "setProgCols" Then
            If vSetting > 0 Then
                wksSheet.Range("A1").Resize(, _
                    vSetting).EntireColumn.Hidden = True
            End If
        ElseIf rngCell.Value = "setScrollArea" Then
            wksSheet.ScrollArea = vSetting.Address
        ElseIf rngCell.Value = "setEnableSelect" Then
            wksSheet.EnableSelection = vSetting
        ElseIf rngCell.Value = "setRowColHeaders" Then
            wksSheet.Activate
            Application.ActiveWindow _
                .DisplayHeadings = vSetting
        ElseIf rngCell.Value = "setVisible" Then
            wksSheet.Visible = vSetting
```

```
          ElseIf rngCell.Value = "setProtect" Then
              If vSetting Then
                  wksSheet.Protect , True, True, True
              End If
          End If
      End If

    Next rngCell

  Next wksSheet

  ' Leave the Time Entry worksheet active.
  sTabName = sSheetTabName(wkbBook, gsSHEET_TIME_ENTRY)
  wkbBook.Worksheets(sTabName).Activate

End Sub
```

The MakeWorksheetSettings procedure loops through all the worksheets in the specified workbook and applies all the settings that we have defined for each worksheet. We have designed this procedure to accept a reference to a specific workbook object as an argument rather than having it assuming it needs to operate on the user interface workbook because this design will allow us to generalize the application to handle multiple user interface workbooks if we need to at some later time. The settings table on which this procedure is based can be seen on the wksUISettings worksheet of the PetrasAddin.xla workbook.

After the user interface workbook has been initialized, the last thing we do is run a procedure that ensures all Excel application properties are set to their default values. This is the ResetAppProperties procedure shown in Listing 5-8.

Listing 5-8 The ResetAppProperties Procedure

```
Public Sub ResetAppProperties()
    Application.StatusBar = False
    Application.ScreenUpdating = True
    Application.DisplayAlerts = True
    Application.EnableEvents = True
    Application.EnableCancelKey = xlInterrupt
    Application.Cursor = xlDefault
End Sub
```

This procedure is useful because we can make whatever application settings we like during the code execution required for a feature, and as long as we call this procedure before we exit we know that all critical application properties will be left in known good states. If we didn't happen to use one of the properties reset by this procedure, it doesn't matter. The values set by the ResetAppProperties procedure are the default values for each property. Therefore we aren't changing them if they weren't used.

Save a Copy of the Time-Entry Workbook to a Predefined Consolidation Location

The first toolbar button will save a copy of the time-entry workbook to a centralized consolidation location. From here, a procedure in the PETRAS reporting application will consolidate the time-entry workbooks from all the consultants into a single report. Listing 5-9 shows the procedure that implements this feature.

Listing 5-9 The PostTimeEntriesToNetwork Procedure

```
Public Sub PostTimeEntriesToNetwork()

    Dim sSheetTab As String
    Dim sWeekEndDate As String
    Dim sEmployee As String
    Dim sSaveName As String
    Dim sSavePath As String
    Dim wksSheet As Worksheet
    Dim wkbBook As Workbook
    Dim vFullName As Variant


    ' Don't do anything unless our time entry workbook is active
    ' wkbBook will return a reference to it if it is.
    If bIsTimeEntryBookActive(wkbBook) Then

        ' Make sure the TimeEntry worksheet does not have any
        ' data entry errors.
        sSheetTab = sSheetTabName(wkbBook, gsSHEET_TIME_ENTRY)
        Set wksSheet = wkbBook.Worksheets(sSheetTab)
        If wksSheet.Range(gsRNG_HAS_ERRORS).Value Then
            MsgBox gsERR_DATA_ENTRY, vbCritical, gsAPP_NAME
            Exit Sub
        End If
```

```
    ' Create a unique name for the time entry workbook.
    sWeekEndDate = Format$( _
            wksSheet.Range(gsRNG_WEEK_END_DATE).Value, _
            "YYYYMMDD")
    sEmployee = wksSheet.Range(gsRNG_EMPLOYEE_NAME).Value
    sSaveName = sWeekEndDate & " - " & sEmployee & ".xls"


    ' Check the registry to determine if we already have a
    ' consolidation path specified. If so, save the time
    ' entry workbook to that location. If not, prompt the
    ' user to identify a consolidation location, save that
    ' location to the registry and save the time entry
    ' workbook to that location.
    sSavePath = GetSetting(gsREG_APP, gsREG_SECTION, _
            gsREG_KEY, "")
    If Len(sSavePath) = 0 Then
        ' No path was stored in the registry. Prompt the
        ' user for one.
        vFullName = Application.GetOpenFilename( _
                Title:=gsCAPTION_SELECT_FOLDER)
        If vFullName <> False Then
            ' NOTE: The InStrRev function was not available
            ' in Excel 97.
            sSavePath = Left$(vFullName, _
                InStrRev(vFullName, "\"))
            SaveSetting gsREG_APP, gsREG_SECTION, _
                gsREG_KEY, sSavePath
        Else
            ' The user cancelled the dialog.
            MsgBox gsMSG_POST_FAIL, vbCritical, gsAPP_NAME
            Exit Sub
        End If
    End If

    wkbBook.SaveCopyAs sSavePath & sSaveName
    MsgBox gsMSG_POST_SUCCESS, vbInformation, gsAPP_NAME

Else
    MsgBox gsMSG_BOOK_NOT_ACTIVE, vbExclamation, gsAPP_NAME
End If

End Sub
```

This procedure shows the safety mechanism we use to prevent runtime errors from occurring if the user clicks one of our toolbar buttons without the user interface workbook being active. Prior to performing any action, we verify that this workbook is active using the bIsTimeEntryBookActive (wkbBook) function call. This function returns an object reference to the time-entry workbook via its ByRef Workbook argument if the time-entry workbook is active. If the time-entry workbook is not active, we display an error message to the user and exit.

After we verify the time-entry workbook is active, we check the error flag in the hidden column on the time-entry worksheet to determine whether the timesheet has any data-entry errors. If the flag indicates errors, we display a message to the user and exit. If there are no data-entry errors, the next task is to create a unique name for the workbook and look for our consolidation path in the registry. If the consolidation path has not yet been saved to the registry, we prompt the user to specify the path that should be used.

Finally, we use the SaveCopyAs method of the Workbook object to post a copy of the workbook to the central consolidation location. We then display a message to the user indicating that the process succeeded.

Allow the User to Add More Data-Entry Rows to the Time-Entry Worksheet

In the version of the time-entry workbook demonstrated in *Chapter 4 — Worksheet Design*, the number of data-entry rows was fixed. In this version, the second toolbar button will enable the user to add additional rows to the time-entry table as needed. Listing 5-10 shows the procedure that implements this feature.

Listing 5-10 The AddMoreRows Procedure

```
Public Sub AddMoreRows()

    Const lOFFSET_COLS As Long = 5
    Const lINPUT_COLS As Long = 6

    Dim rngInsert As Range
    Dim wkbBook As Workbook
    Dim wksSheet As Worksheet
```

```
' Don't do anything unless our time entry workbook is active
If bIsTimeEntryBookActive(wkbBook) Then

    ' Get a reference to the TimeEntry worksheet and the
    ' insert row range on it. All new rows will be inserted
    ' above this range.
    Set wksSheet = wkbBook.Worksheets(sSheetTabName( _
                            wkbBook, gsSHEET_TIME_ENTRY))
    Set rngInsert = wksSheet.Range(gsRNG_INSERT_ROW)

    ' Add a new row to the time entry table.
    wksSheet.Unprotect
    rngInsert.EntireRow.Insert
    rngInsert.Offset(-2, 0).EntireRow.Copy _
        Destination:=rngInsert.Offset(-1, 0)
    rngInsert.Offset(-1, lOFFSET_COLS) _
        .Resize(1, lINPUT_COLS).ClearContents
    wksSheet.Protect , True, True, True

Else
    MsgBox gsMSG_BOOK_NOT_ACTIVE, vbExclamation, gsAPP_NAME
End If

End Sub
```

In the AddMoreRows procedure, we use the same method to determine whether a time-entry workbook is active as we used in the PostTimeEntriesToNetwork procedure. After we've determined we have a valid workbook active, inserting a new row is a three-step process:

1. Insert a new row directly above the last row in the table. The last row in the table is marked by the gsRNG_INSERT_ROW defined name.

2. Copy the row above the newly inserted row and paste it onto the newly inserted row. This ensures all functions, formatting and validation required to make the table operate and appear correctly are transferred to the newly inserted row.

3. The contents of the data-entry area of the newly inserted row is cleared of any data that may have been transferred to the new row by the previous step. The new data-entry row is now clean and ready to be used.

Allow the User to Clear the Data-Entry Area So the Timesheet Can Be Reused

The third toolbar button, Clear Data Entries, simply clears the values from all the data-entry areas on the timesheet. The code to implement this feature was discussed in the *Using VBA to Dynamically Modify Your Worksheet User Interface* section above, so we don't repeat it here.

Allow the User to Close the PETRAS Application

The fourth and last toolbar button simply closes the PETRAS application workbooks and removes its toolbar. The ExitApplication procedure that implements this feature is shown in Listing 5-11.

Listing 5-11 The ExitApplication Procedure

```
Public Sub ExitApplication()
    ShutdownApplication
End Sub
```

This is a one-line stub procedure that just calls the ShutdownApplication procedure, which actually performs the tasks required to shut down the application. We place the shutdown logic in a separate procedure because it must be called from the ExitApplication procedure as well as from the Auto_Close procedure. These two procedures reflect the two ways the user could exit our application: selecting the Exit PETRAS toolbar button or using one of Excel's built-in exit features. Listing 5-12 shows the code for the ShutdownApplication procedure.

Listing 5-12 The ShutdownApplication Procedure

```
Public Sub ShutdownApplication()

    ' Blow past any errors on application shutdown.
    On Error Resume Next

    ' This flag prevents this procedure from being called a
    ' second time by Auto_Close if it has already been called
    ' by the ExitApplication procedure.
    gbShutdownInProgress = True
```

```
' Delete command bar.
Application.CommandBars(gsBAR_TOOLBAR).Delete

' Close the time entry workbook, allowing the user to
' save changes.
Application.Workbooks(gsFILE_TIME_ENTRY).Close

' If there are no workbooks left open, quit Excel
' Otherwise just close this workbook.
If lCountVisibleWorkbooks() = 0 Then
    ThisWorkbook.Saved = True
    Application.Quit
Else
    ThisWorkbook.Close False
End If

End Sub
```

The ShutdownApplication procedure is an example of a procedure where you want to ignore any errors. The application is closing down, so there isn't anything useful that could be done about any errors that did occur. Therefore, we tell VBA to ignore any errors in the procedure by using the On Error Resume Next statement. *Chapter 12 — VBA Error Handling* covers this statement in detail.

The first thing the ShutdownApplication procedure does is set a global flag variable that will prevent it from being called twice if the user initiated shutdown by clicking the Exit PETRAS toolbar button. The process of closing the add-in workbook will cause the Auto_Close procedure to fire. The Auto_Close procedure also calls ShutdownApplication, but it checks the value of the gbShutdownInProgress variable first and simply exits if shutdown is already in progress.

Then the ShutdownApplication procedure deletes the application toolbar. It then closes the user's time-entry workbook. If this workbook has not been saved, we allow Excel to prompt the user to save the workbook. After the time-entry workbook has been closed, we check to see whether any other *visible* workbooks are open. If no visible workbooks are open, we can assume the user started Excel just to run our application and therefore we can close Excel. If there are still visible workbooks open, we assume the user was working with Excel before our application was opened and therefore we just close our add-in and leave Excel open for the user to continue working with.

The *visible* workbooks distinction is an important one because many users have a hidden Personal.xls workbook or other utility workbook always open. We want to ignore these hidden workbooks when trying to determine whether we should close Excel or leave Excel open on exit. Listing 5-13 shows the procedure that counts the number of visible workbooks.

Listing 5-13 The lCountVisibleWorkbooks Procedure

```
Public Function lCountVisibleWorkbooks() As Long
    Dim lCount As Long
    Dim wkbBook As Workbook
    For Each wkbBook In Application.Workbooks
        If wkbBook.Windows(1).Visible Then
            lCount = lCount + 1
        End If
    Next wkbBook
    lCountVisibleWorkbooks = lCount
End Function
```

Add a Custom Property to Allow the Consolidation Application to Locate All Instances of Our Time-Entry Workbook

After all employees have saved their time-entry workbooks to the centralized consolidation location, the consolidation application needs to be able to definitively locate these workbooks. There may be other files located in the consolidation directory that the consolidation application needs to ignore. We solve this problem by adding a custom document property called PetrasTimesheet to our time-entry workbook. This allows the consolidation application to uniquely identify any time-entry workbooks created by our application.

To add a custom document property, activate the PetrasTemplate.xls workbook and choose *File > Properties* from the Excel menu. In the Properties dialog, select the *Custom* tab. Enter PetrasTimesheet in the *Name* box and enter Yes in the *Value* box. Click the *Add* button to add this property to the workbook. Figure 5-5 shows the result.

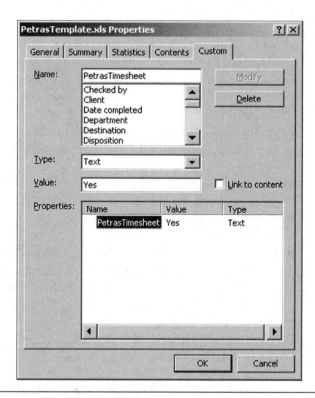

Figure 5-5 Adding the Custom Document Property

Application Organization

We briefly cover the way in which the PETRAS add-in has been organized into code modules. The PetrasAddin.xla workbook is a very simple, entirely procedural based application at this point. It consists of six standard code modules whose names provide a reasonable indication of the type of code they contain. These modules are the following:

- **MEntryPoints**—This module contains the procedures called from the toolbar buttons of our toolbar. These procedures are entry points in the sense that they are the only way for the user to execute code in the application. The ClearDataEntryAreas procedure shown in Listing 5-5, the PostTimeEntriesToNetwork procedure shown in Listing 5-9, the AddMoreRows procedure shown in

Listing 5-10 and the ExitApplication procedure shown in Listing 5-11 are all located in this module.

- **MGlobals**—This module contains the definitions of all public constants and variables used by our application as well as an InitGlobals procedure used to ensure our global variables are always properly initialized.

- **MOpenClose**—This module contains the code required to start up and shut down the application. The Auto_Open procedure shown in Listing 5-6 is located in this module.

- **MStandardCode**—This module contains standard code library procedures that are reused without modification in many different projects. The ResetAppProperties procedure shown in Listing 5-8 is one example.

- **MSystemCode**—This module contains core procedures written specifically for this application. In a larger application, you would have many modules of this type, each of which would have a more detailed descriptive name (for example, MPrinting, MCalculation or MExport).

- **MUtilities**—This module contains procedures designed solely for use by the programmer during construction and maintenance of the application. Procedures in this module will never be run by the end user and in fact are hidden from the user by the `Option Private Module` directive. The WriteSettings procedure shown in Listing 5-4 is located in this module.

Conclusion

This chapter has covered a complete list of stages all Excel applications go through. It has described the various types of add-ins and the types of operations that each is required to perform. It has demonstrated a table-driven method for maintaining and applying critical settings in a user interface workbook and demonstrated a simple example of an application-specific add-in application.

CHAPTER 6

Dictator Applications

Dictator applications take control of the entire Excel session, modifying the user interface to make it appear and behave like a normal Windows program. By doing this, the applications can leverage Excel's rich user interface features and/or make extensive use of Excel's calculation engine and analysis features, while maintaining a high degree of control over the user. This chapter explains how to create a simple dictator application, providing a basic template from which you can build your own. Later chapters in this book add more features to the basic application we present here.

Structure of a Dictator Application

As mentioned in *Chapter 2 — Application Architectures*, most dictator applications have the following logical structure:

- A startup routine to perform version and dependency checks and so forth
- A core set of routines, to:
  - Take a snapshot of the Excel environment settings and to restore those settings
  - Configure and lock down the Excel application
  - Create and remove the dictator application's command bars
  - Handle copying and pasting data within the worksheet templates (if using worksheet-based data-entry forms)
  - Provide a library of common helper routines and classes
- A backdrop worksheet, to display within the Excel window while userforms are being shown, usually with some form of application-specific logo (if we're primarily using forms for the user interface)
- Multiple independent applets, which provide the application's functionality
- Multiple template worksheets used by the applets, such as data-entry forms or preformatted report templates

Each of these points is discussed in more detail below in the order in which they occur within a typical dictator application. In the simplest dictator applications, these elements are all contained within a single workbook, although spreading them over multiple workbooks can make maintenance easier when a team of developers works on a large application.

Startup and Shutdown

Version and Dependency Checks

All versions of Excel from 97 to 2003 share the same file format, so if our application requires a minimum version level (for example, Excel 2000 in our case), we need to check that our user hasn't just opened the application in Excel 97. The easiest way to do this is to check the value of the `Application.Version` property. The original version of Excel 97 was version 8.0, which incremented to 8.0e with the various service packs. Each major release of Excel increments the version number, so Excel 2000 is version 9.0, Excel 2002 is version 10.0 and Excel 2003 is version 11.0. In Listing 6-1, we check that the user is running Excel 2000 or later.

Listing 6-1 Checking the Excel Version

```
'Check that the version is at least Excel 2000
If Val(Application.Version) < 9 Then
  MsgBox "The PETRAS Reporting application " & _
         "requires Excel 2000 or later.", _
         vbOKOnly, gsAPP_TITLE

  ThisWorkbook.Close False
  Exit Sub
End If
```

After we know we're running in an appropriate version of Excel, we have to check that the user has installed any extra components we require, such as the Analysis Toolpak or Solver add-ins, or other applications that we're automating, such as Word or Outlook. For add-ins, we can either check the `Application.Addins` collection, or check that the file exists based on the `Application.LibraryPath`. To check that other applications are installed, we can either look directly in the registry (using API calls) or use `CreateObject` to try to create a new instance of the application and test for failure. This is covered in more detail in *Chapter 18 — Controlling Other Office Applications*.

Storing and Restoring Excel Settings

To take full control of the Excel session, dictator applications typically customize the interface to a high degree, such as hiding the toolbars and formula bar and changing numerous application settings. Unfortunately (and despite repeated requests to Microsoft), Excel assumes these changes are the user's choice of settings and should be preserved for the next session; there's no way to tell Excel these are temporary settings, for this session only. To solve this problem, we have to take a snapshot of the Excel settings when our application starts, store them away somewhere and reset them as part of our application's shutdown processing. The easiest place to store the settings is in a worksheet in the add-in, although our preference is to store them in the registry, so they can be recovered if the application crashes (see below). The biggest issue with using the registry is if the company's security policy is such that registry access is blocked. In that case, Excel won't be able to store any user settings, so it doesn't matter that we won't be able to store/restore them either. Listing 6-2 shows a typical routine to store the Excel settings.

Listing 6-2 Storing Excel Settings in the Registry

```
Public Const gsREG_APP As String = "Company\Application"
Public Const gsREG_XL_ENV As String = "Excel Settings"

Sub StoreExcelSettings()

  Dim cbBar As CommandBar
  Dim sBarNames As String
  Dim objTemp As Object
  Dim wkbTemp As Workbook

  'Skip errors in case we can't use the registry
  On Error Resume Next

  'Check if we've already stored the settings
  '(so don't want to overwrite them)
  If GetSetting(gsREG_APP, gsREG_XL_ENV, "Stored", "No") _
     = "No" Then

    'Some properties require a workbook open, so create one
    If ActiveWorkbook Is Nothing Then
      Set wkbTemp = Workbooks.Add
    End If
```

```vb
'Indicate that the settings have been stored.
'This key will be deleted in RestoreSettings.
SaveSetting gsREG_APP, gsREG_XL_ENV, "Stored", "Yes"

'Store the current Excel settings in the registry
With Application
  SaveSetting gsREG_APP, gsREG_XL_ENV, _
      "DisplayStatusBar", CStr(.DisplayStatusBar)

  SaveSetting gsREG_APP, gsREG_XL_ENV, _
      "DisplayFormulaBar", CStr(.DisplayFormulaBar)

  'etc.

  'Which commandbars are visible
  For Each cbBar In .CommandBars
    If cbBar.Visible Then
      sBarNames = sBarNames & "," & cbBar.Name
    End If
  Next
  SaveSetting gsREG_APP, gsREG_XL_ENV, _
      "VisibleCommandBars", sBarNames

  'Special items for Excel 2000 and up
  If Val(.Version) >= 9 Then
    SaveSetting gsREG_APP, gsREG_XL_ENV, _
        "ShowWindowsInTaskbar", _
        CStr(.ShowWindowsInTaskbar)
  End If

  'Special items for Excel 2002 and up
  If Val(.Version) >= 10 Then
    Set objTemp = .CommandBars
    SaveSetting gsREG_APP, gsREG_XL_ENV, _
        "DisableAskAQuestion", _
        CStr(objTemp.DisableAskAQuestionDropdown)

    SaveSetting gsREG_APP, gsREG_XL_ENV, _
        "AutoRecover", CStr(.AutoRecover.Enabled)
  End If
End With

'Close up the temporary workbook
```

```
    If Not wkbTemp Is Nothing Then wkbTemp.Close False
    End If

End Sub
```

Listing 6-3 shows the corresponding routine to restore the settings, which should be called during the application's shutdown processing.

Listing 6-3 Restoring Excel Settings During Shutdown

```
Sub RestoreExcelSettings()

  Dim vBarName As Variant
  Dim objTemp As Object

  'Restore the original Excel settings from the registry
  With Application

    'Check that we have some settings to restore
    If GetSetting(gsREG_APP, gsREG_XL_ENV, "Stored", "No") _
        = "Yes" Then

      .DisplayStatusBar = CBool(GetSetting(gsREG_APP, _
          gsREG_XL_ENV, "DisplayStatusBar", _
          CStr(.DisplayStatusBar)))

      .DisplayFormulaBar = CBool(GetSetting(gsREG_APP, _
          gsREG_XL_ENV, "DisplayFormulaBar", _
          CStr(.DisplayFormulaBar)))

      'etc.

      'Show the correct toolbars
      On Error Resume Next
      For Each vBarName In Split(GetSetting(gsREG_APP, _
          gsREG_XL_ENV, "VisibleCommandBars"), ",")

        Application.CommandBars(vBarName).Visible = True
      Next
      On Error GoTo 0

      'Specific stuff for Excel 2000 and up
```

```
     If Val(.Version) >= 9 Then
        .ShowWindowsInTaskbar = CBool(GetSetting(gsREG_APP, _
            gsREG_XL_ENV, "ShowWindowsInTaskbar", _
            CStr(.ShowWindowsInTaskbar)))
     End If

     'Specific stuff for Excel 2002 and up
     If Val(.Version) >= 10 Then
        Set objTemp = .CommandBars
        objTemp.DisableAskAQuestionDropdown = _
            CBool(GetSetting(gsREG_APP, gsREG_XL_ENV, _
            "DisableAskAQuestion", _
            CStr(objTemp.DisableAskAQuestionDropdown)))

        .AutoRecover.Enabled = CBool(GetSetting(gsREG_APP, _
            gsREG_XL_ENV, "AutoRecover", _
            CStr(.AutoRecover.Enabled)))
     End If

     'Once restored, delete all the registry entries
     DeleteSetting gsREG_APP, gsREG_XL_ENV
   End If
End With

'Restore the Excel menus
RestoreMenus


End Sub
```

Toolbar customizations are stored in a file with an .xlb extension, where the filename differs with each version of Excel. Each time a permanent change is made to the toolbars, information about the change is added to the file. By their very nature, dictator applications usually make lots of changes to the toolbars, resulting in the XLB file growing quite rapidly (although it can be reduced by creating the toolbars with the `temporary` parameter set to True). This results in slowing Excel's startup processing and eventually causes Excel to crash at startup. To avoid this, the best way to restore the user's toolbar configuration is to find and open the XLB file just before the application closes. By doing so, Excel doesn't see any changes, so the XLB file isn't modified. The RestoreMenus routine to do this is shown in Listing 6-4.

Listing 6-4 Restoring Excel Toolbars During Shutdown

```vba
Public Const gsMENU_BAR As String = "PETRAS Menu Bar"

Sub RestoreMenus()

  Dim cbCommandBar As CommandBar
  Dim sPath As String
  Dim sToolbarFile As String
  Dim vBarName As Variant

  On Error Resume Next

  'Reopen the xlb toolbar customization file
  '(if it exists), to avoid it growing in size
  sPath = Application.StartupPath

  'Work out the name of the correct toolbar file to open,
  'depending on the version of Excel
  If Val(Application.Version) = 9 Then
    sToolbarFile = Left$(sPath, InStrRev(sPath, "\")) & _
        "Excel.xlb"
  Else
    sToolbarFile = Left$(sPath, InStrRev(sPath, "\")) & _
        "Excel" & Val(Application.Version) & ".xlb"
  End If

  'If there is one, reopen the toolbar file
  If Dir(sToolbarFile) <> "" Then
    Workbooks.Open sToolbarFile, ReadOnly:=True
  Else
    'If not, we have to tidy up ourselves

    'Re-enable all the toolbars
    For Each cbCommandBar In Application.CommandBars
      cbCommandBar.Enabled = True
    Next

    'Delete our Application's toolbar
    Application.CommandBars(gsMENU_BAR).Delete
  End If

End Sub
```

Handling Crashes

It is an unfortunate fact of Excel application development that at some point, Excel might crash while our application is being used. If/when that happens, our normal shutdown processing will not have the chance to run, so Excel will restart with our application's settings instead of the user's. If we want, we can handle this by copying the RestoreExcelSettings routine into a new workbook, calling it from the Workbook_Open procedure and saving it as another add-in that we distribute with our application. Our StoreExcelSettings routine can be modified to copy the add-in to the `Application.StartupPath` and our RestoreExcelSettings routine can be modified to delete it. In doing so, the add-in will be left behind if Excel crashes and will be opened and run by Excel when it restarts, resetting the environment to the way the user had it.

Configuring the Excel Environment

After we've taken the snapshot of the user's environment settings, we can configure Excel to suit our application, such as:

- Setting the application caption and icon
- Hiding the formula bar and status bar
- Setting calculation to manual (because recalcs will be under program control)
- Setting `Application.IgnoreRemoteRequests = True`, so double-clicking a workbook in Explorer opens a new instance of Excel instead of reusing our instance
- Switching off Windows in TaskBar, because we're likely to have multiple processing workbooks open that we don't want the user to be able to switch to
- Switching off the Ask a Question drop-down from the command bars
- Preventing the ability to customize the command bars
- Switching off auto-recover (in Excel 2002 and later)

Supporting a Debug Mode

When developing and debugging our dictator application, we will need a mechanism to enable us to access the VBE, hidden sheets and so on and allow quick and easy switching between Excel's interface and our application's, yet prevent our users from doing the same. A simple method is to check for the existence of a specific file in a specific directory at startup and set a global `gbDebugMode` Boolean variable accordingly. We can then configure the Excel environment differently for debug and production modes. In debug mode, we'll keep all Excel's shortcut keys active and set up an extra shortcut to switch back to Excel's menus (by calling the RestoreExcelSettings routine from Listing 6-4). In production mode, we'll disable all Excel's shortcut keys and ensure the VBE window is hidden. Listing 6-5 shows a typical routine to configure the Excel environment for a dictator application. If testing this routine, we recommend you do so with the debug.ini file created.

Listing 6-5 Configuring the Excel Environment for a Dictator Application

```
Public gvaKeysToDisable As Variant
Public gbDebugMode As Boolean

Sub InitGlobals()

  gvaKeysToDisable = Array("^{F6}", "+^{F6}", "^{TAB}", _
    "+^{TAB}", "%{F11}", "%{F8}", "^W", "^{F4}", _
    "{F11}", "%{F1}", "+{F11}", "+%{F1}", "^{F5}", _
    "^{F9}", "^{F10}")

  'Use the existence of a debug file to set whether we're
  'in debug mode
  gbDebugMode = Dir(ThisWorkbook.Path & "\debug.ini") <> ""

End Sub


Sub ConfigureExcelEnvironment()

  Dim objTemp As Object
  Dim vKey As Variant

  With Application
    'Set the Application properties we want
    .Caption = gsAPP_TITLE
    .DisplayStatusBar = True
    .DisplayFormulaBar = False
    .Calculation = xlManual
```

```
      .DisplayAlerts = False
      .IgnoreRemoteRequests = True
      .DisplayAlerts = True

      .Iteration = True
      .MaxIterations = 100

      'Specific items for Excel 2000 and up
      If Val(.Version) >= 9 Then
         .ShowWindowsInTaskbar = False
      End If

      'Specific items for Excel 2002 and up
      If Val(.Version) >= 10 Then
         Set objTemp = .CommandBars
         objTemp.DisableAskAQuestionDropdown = True
         objTemp.DisableCustomize = True
         .AutoRecover.Enabled = False
      End If

      'We'll have slightly different environment states, _
      'depending on whether we're debugging or not
      If gbDebugMode Then
         'Since we have blitzed the environment, we should
         'set a hot key combination to restore it.
         'That key combination is Shift+Ctrl+R
         .OnKey "+^R", "RestoreExcelSettings"
      Else
         'Make sure the VBE isn't visible
         .VBE.MainWindow.Visible = False

         'Disable a whole host of shortcut keys
         For Each vKey In gvaKeysToDisable
            .OnKey vKey, ""
         Next
      End If
   End With

End Sub
```

Note that the initial value of *every* persistent environment property changed in the configuration routine should be stored at startup and restored at shutdown, so any extra properties you need to change must be added to all three routines. We're assuming the dictator application shuts down Excel when it closes, so there's no need to store such things as the application title and so forth.

Customizing the User Interface

Preparing a Backdrop Graphic

At this point, we have a locked-down empty screen, ready for us to add our application's user interface. The first UI element to add will typically be some sort of background graphic to display as our application's "desktop." The simplest version of this is to have a single worksheet contained in our application workbook that is copied to a new, visible workbook. The workbook is then maximized, has the appropriate worksheet display attributes set and the display range is zoomed to fill the Excel window, as shown in Listing 6-6. The workbook windows can then be protected to remove the control box and maximize/minimize buttons:

Listing 6-6 Code to Prepare a Background Graphic Workbook

```
Public gwbkBackDrop As Workbook
Public Const gsBACKDROP_TITLE As String = "BackdropWkbk"

Sub PrepareBackDrop()

  Dim wkbBook As Workbook

  If Not WorkbookAlive(gwbkBackDrop) Then

    'See if there's already a backdrop workbook out there
    Set gwbkBackDrop = Nothing
    For Each wkbBook In Workbooks
      If wkbBook.BuiltinDocumentProperties("Title") = _
          gsBACKDROP_TITLE Then

        Set gwbkBackDrop = wkbBook
        Exit For
      End If
    Next

    If gwbkBackDrop Is Nothing Then
```

```
      'Copy the backdrop sheet out of this workbook
      'into a new one for display
      wksBackdrop.Copy
      Set gwbkBackDrop = ActiveWorkbook
      gwbkBackDrop.BuiltinDocumentProperties("Title") = _
          gsBACKDROP_TITLE
    End If
  End If

With gwbkBackDrop
  .Activate

  'Select the full region that encompasses the backdrop
  'graphic, so we can use Zoom = True to size it to fit
  .Worksheets(1).Range("rgnBackDrop").Select

  'Set the Window View options to hide everything
  With .Windows(1)
    .WindowState = xlMaximized
    .Caption = ""
    .DisplayHorizontalScrollBar = False
    .DisplayVerticalScrollBar = False
    .DisplayHeadings = False
    .DisplayWorkbookTabs = False

    'Zoom the selected area to fit the screen
    .Zoom = True
  End With

  'Prevent selection or editing of any cells
  With .Worksheets(1)
    .Range("ptrCursor").Select
    .ScrollArea = .Range("ptrCursor").Address
    .EnableSelection = xlNoSelection
    .Protect DrawingObjects:=True, _
             UserInterfaceOnly:=True
  End With

  'Protect the backdrop workbook, to remove the
  'control menu
  .Protect Windows:=True
  .Saved = True
End With
```

```
End Sub


'Function to test if a given workbook object variable
'points to a valid workbook
Function WorkbookAlive(wbkTest As Workbook) As Boolean

  On Error Resume Next

  If Not wbkTest Is Nothing Then
    WorkbookAlive = wbkTest.Sheets(1).Name <> ""
  End If

End Function
```

A more complex version will contain multiple potential backdrop sheets, each designed for a specific screen resolution or window size. At runtime, the appropriate sheet is selected, based on the window's height or width.

Sheet-Based vs. Form-Based User Interfaces

There are two primary styles of user interface for dictator applications: those that use worksheets for the main data-entry forms and those that use userforms. Both styles can be combined with a custom menu structure, although it is slightly harder with a form-based user interface.

Worksheet-based user interfaces are very similar to the application-specific add-ins discussed in *Chapter 5 — Function, General and Application-Specific Add-ins* and are designed to make maximum use of Excel's rich cell-editing features, such as auto-complete, data validation and conditional formatting. Although the use of Excel's rich functionality is a compelling choice, care must be taken to ensure the users do not accidentally destroy the data-entry form. If you decide on a worksheet-based user interface, use worksheets for all your major data-entry forms and reports; dialogs should only be used for minor tasks and wizards.

Form-based user interfaces are typically found in applications that use Excel primarily for its calculation and analysis features, rather than the rich editing experience. The data-entry forms tend to be much simpler than those where a worksheet is used, which is often perceived as a benefit for both the user and the developer; the reduced functionality and tighter control that userforms provide can result in less chance for your users to make mistakes and hence a more robust solution. If you decide to use a form-based user interface, worksheets should only be used for reporting. Designing a form-based user interface is covered in detail in *Chapter 10 — Userform Design and Best Practices*.

Trying to mix the two user interface styles rarely works well; it is just too cumbersome to make worksheets behave like dialogs (such as tabbing between controls) and vice versa (such as auto-complete), particularly if the worksheet also includes some forms controls (such as buttons, check boxes and so on). When deciding which style to use, base the decision on where users are likely to spend the majority of their time. Will it be better (for the user) to provide the rich editing features of a worksheet, or the tighter control of a userform?

Handling Cut, Copy and Paste

The biggest issue with sheet-based user interfaces is having to override Excel's default handling of cut, copy, paste and drag/drop. As discussed in *Chapter 4 — Worksheet Design*, most of the editable cells in a data-entry worksheet will be given specific styles, data validation and conditional formats. Unfortunately, Excel's default copy/paste behavior will overwrite the formatting of the cell being pasted to and Excel's default cut behavior is to format the cell being cut with the Normal style (which is usually used for the sheet background). Excel's drag/drop feature is the same as cut and paste and will also destroy the data-entry sheet if used. The only way to avoid this is to switch off drag/drop and code our own cut, copy and paste routines, such as those shown in Listing 6-7.

Listing 6-7 Code to Handle Cut, Copy and Paste for Data-Entry Worksheets

```
Dim mbCut As Boolean
Dim mrngSource As Range

'Initialise cell copy-paste
Public Sub InitCutCopyPaste()

    'Hook all the cut, copy and paste keystrokes
    Application.OnKey "^X", "DoCut"
    Application.OnKey "^x", "DoCut"
    Application.OnKey "+{DEL}", "DoCut"

    Application.OnKey "^C", "DoCopy"
```

```
  Application.OnKey "^c", "DoCopy"
  Application.OnKey "^{INSERT}", "DoCopy"

  Application.OnKey "^V", "DoPaste"
  Application.OnKey "^v", "DoPaste"
  Application.OnKey "+{INSERT}", "DoPaste"

  Application.OnKey "{ENTER}", "DoPaste"
  Application.OnKey "~", "DoPaste"

  'Switch off drag/drop
  Application.CellDragAndDrop = False

End Sub

'Handle Cutting cells
Public Sub DoCut()

  If TypeOf Selection Is Range Then
    mbCut = True
    Set mrngSource = Selection
    Selection.Copy
  Else
    Set mrngSource = Nothing
    Selection.Cut
  End If

End Sub

'Handle Copying cells
Public Sub DoCopy()
  If TypeOf Selection Is Range Then
    mbCut = False
    Set mrngSource = Selection
  Else
    Set mrngSource = Nothing
  End If

  Selection.Copy
End Sub

'Handle pasting cells
```

```
Public Sub DoPaste()
  If Application.CutCopyMode And Not mrngSource Is Nothing Then
    Selection.PasteSpecial xlValues
    If mbCut Then
      mrngSource.ClearContents
    End If

    Application.CutCopyMode = False
  Else
    ActiveSheet.Paste
  End If
End Sub
```

Custom Command Bars

Most dictator applications will include a set of menus and toolbars to provide access to the application's functionality. Dictator applications usually have quite complex menu structures, mixing both Excel's menu items (such as Print and Print Preview) and custom items. The maintenance of these menu items can be greatly eased by using a table-driven approach to building the command bars, as discussed in *Chapter 8 — Advanced Command Bar Handling*.

Processing and Analysis

Many dictator applications use Excel for its data processing, calculation and analysis features, rather than its rich UI. All the processing should be performed using hidden sheets, under program control, with only the results being shown to the users. This enables us to design our processing sheets for maximum calculation efficiency, without having to worry whether they would be readable by our users. This topic is covered in detail in *Chapter 14 — Data Manipulation Techniques*.

Presenting Results

Excel worksheets are extremely good presentation vehicles for detailed reports and charts; indeed, the requirement to use Excel for the application's reporting mechanism is often the main factor for choosing to create the application entirely in Excel. In practice, report styles and layouts are usually dictated by the client (to conform to a house style), but we explain how to get the most out of Excel's charting engine in *Chapter 15 — Advanced Charting Techniques*.

Practical Example

PETRAS Timesheet

The PETRAS timesheet add-in has not been updated for this chapter.

PETRAS Reporting

In *Chapter 5 — Function, General and Application-Specific Add-ins*, we introduced the client side of the PETRAS application, with which our users enter their weekly timekeeping information and save the resulting workbook to a central location on the network. This chapter introduces the central consolidation, analysis and reporting application, written as a simple, single-workbook dictator application.

In this version of the application, we're assuming the consolidation will be done weekly, as soon as all the source timesheets have been received. The data will be extracted from each timesheet workbook and copied to a single table in a results workbook, from which we'll generate a single pivot table to provide a rudimentary analysis capability. The results workbook can then be saved. We also allow previous results workbooks to be opened, so the consolidation can be repeated (for instance, if a timesheet arrives late). Later chapters add many more features to the application.

The application can be found on the CD in the folder \Application\Ch06—Dictator Applications and includes the following files:

- **PetrasTemplate.xls**—The client data-entry template, unchanged from Chapter 5
- **PetrasAddin.xla**—The client data-entry support add-in, unchanged from Chapter 5
- **PetrasReporting.xla**—The main reporting application
- **PetrasConsolidation.xlt**—A template to use for new results workbooks, containing an area for importing timesheet data to and a pre-formatted pivot table, which references the consolidation area
- **Debug.ini**—A dummy file that tells the application to run in debug mode

The main reporting workbook, PetrasReporting.xla, contains the following items:

- **MGlobals**—This module contains the declarations of our global constants and variables.
- **MOpenClose**—This module contains the startup and shutdown code, including code similar to Listing 6-1 to check the Excel version.
- **MWorkspace**—This module contains the code to store, configure and restore the Excel environment, very similar to Listing 6-2, Listing 6-3, Listing 6-5 and Listing 6-6.
- **MCommandbars**—This module contains code to create and destroy our menus, including code like Listing 6-4 to restore them.
- **MEntryPoints**—This module contains the routines called by our menus.
- **MStandardCode**—This module contains the WorkbookAlive function shown in Listing 6-6, a function to check whether a given file has a specific custom document property (see below) and will contain more common utility routines as they're added throughout the book.
- **MSystemCode**—This module contains code specific to this application, including a routine to enable/disable some of our menu items and the main routine to perform the data consolidation.
- **wksBackDrop**—This is the worksheet used for the backdrop graphic.

The example application uses the code shown in Listing 6-8 to set up the menu structure item by item. It is quite a lengthy routine, for only eight menu items. Fortunately, it will be replaced in *Chapter 8 — Advanced Command Bar Handling*, to use a table-driven command bar builder, enabling us to implement a much more comprehensive menu structure without adding new code for every item.

Listing 6-8 Code to Set Up the Menu Structure

```
Sub SetUpMenus()

    Dim cbCommandBar As CommandBar
    Dim oPopup As CommandBarPopup
    Dim oButton As CommandBarButton
```

```
' Hide all the toolbars
On Error Resume Next
For Each cbCommandBar In Application.CommandBars
    cbCommandBar.Visible = False
    cbCommandBar.Enabled = False
Next
Application.CommandBars(gsMENU_BAR).Delete
On Error GoTo 0

'Create our menu bar
Set cbCommandBar = Application.CommandBars.Add( _
                    gsMENU_BAR, , True, True)


'The File menu
Set oPopup = cbCommandBar.Controls.Add(msoControlPopup)
With oPopup
    .Caption = "&File"

    'File > New
    Set oButton = .Controls.Add(msoControlButton)
    With oButton
        .Caption = "&New Consolidation..."
        .BeginGroup = True
        .FaceId = 18
        .ShortcutText = "Ctrl+N"
        .OnAction = "MenuFileNew"
        Application.OnKey "^N", "MenuFileNew"
        Application.OnKey "^n", "MenuFileNew"
    End With

    'File > Open
    Set oButton = .Controls.Add(msoControlButton)
    With oButton
        .Caption = "&Open..."
        .BeginGroup = False
        .FaceId = 23
        .ShortcutText = "Ctrl+O"
        .OnAction = "MenuFileOpen"
        Application.OnKey "^O", "MenuFileOpen"
        Application.OnKey "^o", "MenuFileOpen"
    End With

    'File > Close
```

```
    Set oButton = .Controls.Add(msoControlButton)
    With oButton
        .Caption = "&Close"
        .BeginGroup = False
        .FaceId = 106
        .OnAction = "MenuFileClose"
        .Enabled = False
    End With

    'File > Save
    'Use the standard Save button
    Set oButton = .Controls.Add(msoControlButton, 3)
    With oButton
        .BeginGroup = True
        .Enabled = False
    End With

    'File > Save As
    'Use the standard Save As button
    Set oButton = .Controls.Add(msoControlButton, 748)
    With oButton
        .BeginGroup = False
        .Enabled = False
    End With

    'File > Exit
    Set oButton = .Controls.Add(msoControlButton)
    With oButton
        .Caption = "&Exit"
        .BeginGroup = True
        .OnAction = "MenuFileExit"
    End With
End With

'The Processing menu
Set oPopup = cbCommandBar.Controls.Add(msoControlPopup)
With oPopup
    .Caption = "&Processing"

    'Processing > Consolidate
    Set oButton = .Controls.Add(msoControlButton)
    With oButton
```

```
            .Caption = "&Consolidate Timesheets"
            .BeginGroup = True
            .OnAction = "MenuConsolidate"
            .Enabled = False
        End With
    End With

    'The Help menu
    Set oPopup = cbCommandBar.Controls.Add(msoControlPopup)
    With oPopup
        .Caption = "&Help"

        'Help > About
        Set oButton = .Controls.Add(msoControlButton)
        With oButton
            .Caption = "&About PETRAS Reporting"
            .BeginGroup = True
            .OnAction = "MenuHelpAbout"
        End With
    End With

    cbCommandBar.Visible = True
    'Protect the command bars, to prevent customization
    Application.CommandBars("Toolbar List").Enabled = False

End Sub
```

Identifying Workbooks

Dictator applications often need to identify whether a particular workbook was created from a particular template, or otherwise "belongs" to the application. One way to do this without needing to open the workbook is to add a custom document property to the template file, as shown in Figure 6-1.

The dictator application can then use Excel's FileSearch object to test whether the file has that property, using the function shown in Listing 6-9. In our example application, we've added the PetrasTimesheet property to the data-entry template and the PetrasResults property to the consolidation results template.

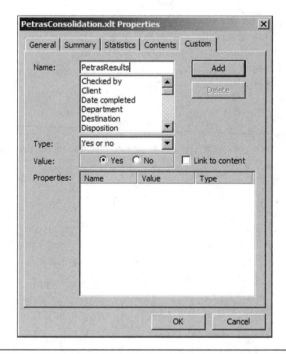

Figure 6-1 Adding an Identifying Custom Document Property to a Template

Listing 6-9 Using the FileSearch Object to Check for a Custom Document Property

```
'Function to test whether a file has the given
'Yes/No property set to Yes
Function FileHasYesProperty(ByVal sFile As String, _
        ByVal sProperty As String) As Boolean

  Dim lSeparator As Long

  'Using the FileSearch object
  With Application.FileSearch

    'Start a new search
    .NewSearch

    'For all file types
    .FileType = msoFileTypeAllFiles
```

```
'For the given file in the given directory
lSeparator = InStrRev(sFile, "\")
.Filename = Mid$(sFile, lSeparator + 1)
.LookIn = Left$(sFile, lSeparator)

'Having the given Yes/No property set to Yes
.PropertyTests.Add sProperty, msoConditionIsYes, _
                Connector:=msoConnectorAnd

'Look for the file
.Execute

'If we found it, that file has that property!
FileHasYesProperty = .FoundFiles.Count > 0
End With

End Function
```

Using the PETRAS Reporting Application

In *Chapter 5 — Function, General and Application-Specific Add-ins*, we explained how to use the PETRAS timesheet add-in and template to create weekly timesheet workbooks and store them in a central location. The following steps can be used to consolidate and analyze your timesheets using the PETRAS reporting dictator application:

1. Start Excel and use *File > Open* to open the PetrasReporting.xla workbook.
2. Select the *File > New Consolidation* menu, as shown in Figure 6-2. This will create a new, empty consolidation workbook and then display a standard file open dialog.
3. Select the timesheet workbooks to include in the consolidation by multiselecting the individual files (or using Ctrl+A to select all the files in a folder) and click OK to begin the consolidation. The application will extract the timesheet data from all the selected files, importing it into the consolidation workbook.
4. Review the consolidated data in the SourceData worksheet and analyze the data in the PivotTable worksheet.

Figure 6-2 The PETRAS Reporting Application Menu Structure

Conclusion

Dictator applications enable us to leverage Excel's rich user interface, calculation engine, analysis and/or presentation features, while simulating the look and behavior of a normal Windows program.

The Excel workspace will usually require a significant amount of configuration and customization for the dictator application. Unfortunately, Excel will remember most of these configurations and try to reuse them for the next (user) session. To work around Excel's behavior, we must store the initial state of the user's settings when our application starts and restore them when we close down.

When using a worksheet-based user interface, extreme care must be taken to prevent accidental corruption of the sheet, often as a result of a cut, copy or paste operation.

The practical example for this chapter is a complete, but simple, dictator application template for you to use as a starting point for your own applications. Later chapters in this book add many more features to the application.

CHAPTER 7

Using Class Modules to Create Objects

Class modules are used to create objects. There are many reasons for you as a developer to create your own objects, including the following:

- To encapsulate VBA and Windows API code to make it transportable and easy to use and reuse, as shown in *Chapter 9 — Understanding and Using Windows API Calls*
- To trap events
- To raise events
- To create your own objects and object models

In this chapter we assume you are already familiar with writing VBA code to manipulate the objects in Excel and are familiar with the Excel object model that defines the relationships among those objects. We also assume you are familiar with object properties, methods and events. If you have written code in the ThisWorkbook module, any of the modules behind worksheets or charts or the module associated with a userform, you have already worked with class modules. One of the key features of these modules, like all class modules, is the ability to trap and respond to events.

The goal of this chapter is to show you how to create your own objects. We begin by explaining how to create a single custom object and then show how you can create a collection containing multiple instances of the object. We continue with a demonstration of how to trap and raise events within your classes.

Creating Objects

Suppose we want to develop code to analyze a single cell in a worksheet and categorize the entry in that cell as one of the following:

- Empty
- Containing a label
- Containing a constant numeric value
- Containing a formula

We can readily accomplish this by creating a new object with the appropriate properties and methods. Our new object will be a Cell object. It will have an Analyze method that determines the cell type and sets the CellType property to a numeric value that can be used in our code. We will also have a DescriptiveCellType property so we can display the cell type as text.

Listing 7-1 shows the CCell class module code. This class module is used to create a custom Cell object representing the specified cell, analyze the contents of the cell and return the type of the cell as a user-friendly text string.

Listing 7-1 The CCell Class Module

```
Option Explicit

Public Enum anlCellType
    anlCellTypeEmpty
    anlCellTypeLabel
    anlCellTypeConstant
    anlCellTypeFormula
End Enum

Private muCellType As anlCellType
Private mrngCell As Excel.Range

Property Set Cell(ByRef rngCell As Excel.Range)
    Set mrngCell = rngCell
End Property

Property Get Cell() As Excel.Range
    Set Cell = mrngCell
End Property

Property Get CellType() As anlCellType
    CellType = muCellType
End Property

Property Get DescriptiveCellType() As String
```

```
    Select Case muCellType
        Case anlCellTypeEmpty
            DescriptiveCellType = "Empty"
        Case anlCellTypeFormula
            DescriptiveCellType = "Formula"
        Case anlCellTypeConstant
            DescriptiveCellType = "Constant"
        Case anlCellTypeLabel
            DescriptiveCellType = "Label"
    End Select
End Property

Public Sub Analyze()
    If IsEmpty(mrngCell) Then
        muCellType = anlCellTypeEmpty
    ElseIf mrngCell.HasFormula Then
        muCellType = anlCellTypeFormula
    ElseIf IsNumeric(mrngCell.Formula) Then
        muCellType = anlCellTypeConstant
    Else
        muCellType = anlCellTypeLabel
    End If
End Sub
```

The CCell class module contains a public enumeration with four members, each of which represents a cell type. By default, the enumeration members will be assigned values from zero to three. The enumeration member names help make our code more readable and easier to maintain. The enumeration member values are translated into user-friendly text by the DescriptiveCellType property.

Listing 7-2 shows the AnalyzeActiveCell procedure. This procedure is contained in the standard module MEntryPoints.

Listing 7-2 The AnalyzeActiveCell Procedure

```
Public Sub AnalyzeActiveCell()

    Dim clsCell As CCell

    ' Create new instance of Cell object
    Set clsCell = New CCell

    ' Determine cell type and display it
```

```
Set clsCell.Cell = Application.ActiveCell
clsCell.Analyze
MsgBox clsCell.DescriptiveCellType

End Sub
```

If you select a cell on a worksheet and run the AnalyzeActiveCell procedure, it creates a new instance of the CCell class that it stores in the clsCell object variable. The procedure then assigns the active cell to the Cell property of this Cell object, executes its Analyze method and displays the result of its DescriptiveCellType property. This code is contained in the Analysis1.xls workbook in the \Concepts\Ch07—Using Class Modules to Create Objects folder on the CD that accompanies this book.

Class Module Structure

A class module contains the blueprint for an object. You can use it to create as many instances of the object as you require. It defines the methods and properties of the object. Any public subroutines or functions in the class module become methods of the object. Any public variables or property procedures become properties of the object.

Property Procedures

Rather than rely on public variables to define properties, it is better practice to use property procedures. These give you more control over how properties are assigned values and how they return values. Property procedures enable you to validate the data that is passed to the object and to perform related actions where appropriate. They also enable you to make properties read only or write only if you want.

The CCell class uses two private module level variables to store its properties internally. muCellType holds the cell type in the form of an anlCellType enumeration member value. mrngCell holds a reference to the single-cell Range that an object created from the CCell class will represent.

Property procedures control the interface between these variables and the outside world. Property procedures come in three forms:

- **Property Let**—Used to assign a value to a property
- **Property Set**—Used to assign an object to a property
- **Property Get**—Used to return the value or the object reference in a property to the outside world

The property name presented to the outside world is the same as the name of the property procedure. The CCell class uses Property Set Cell to enable you to assign a Range reference to the Cell property of the Cell object. The property procedure stores the reference in the mrngCell variable. This procedure could have a validation check to ensure that only single-cell ranges can be specified. There is a corresponding Property Get Cell procedure that allows this property to be read.

The CCell class uses two Property Get procedures to return the cell type as an enumeration member value or as descriptive text. These properties are read-only because they have no corresponding Property Let procedures.

Methods

The CCell class has one method defined by the Analyze subroutine. It determines the type of data in the cell referred to by the mrngCell variable and assigns the corresponding enumeration member to the muCellType variable. Because it is a subroutine, the Analyze method doesn't return a value to the outside world. If a method is created using a function, it can return a value. The Analyze method could be converted to a function that returned the text value associated with the cell type, as shown in Listing 7-3.

Listing 7-3 The Analyze Method of the Cell Object

```
Public Function Analyze() As String

    If IsEmpty(mrngCell) Then
        muCellType = anlCellTypeEmpty
    ElseIf mrngCell.HasFormula Then
        muCellType = anlCellTypeFormula
    ElseIf IsNumeric(mrngCell.Formula) Then
        muCellType = anlCellTypeConstant
    Else
        muCellType = anlCellTypeLabel
    End If

    Analyze = Me.DescriptiveCellType

End Function
```

We could then analyze the cell and display the return value with the following single line of code instead of the original two lines:

```
MsgBox clsCell.Analyze()
```

Creating a Collection

Now that we have a Cell object, we will want to create many instances of the object so we can analyze a worksheet or ranges of cells within a worksheet. The easiest way to manage these new objects is to store them in a collection. VBA provides a Collection object that we can use to store objects and data. The Collection object has four methods:

- Add
- Count
- Item
- Remove

There is no restriction on the type of data that can be stored within a Collection object, and items with different data types can be stored in the same Collection object. In our case, we want to be consistent and store just Cell objects in our collection.

To create a new Collection, the first step is to add a new standard module to contain global variables. This module will be called MGlobals. Next, add the following variable declaration to the MGlobals module to declare a global Collection object variable to hold the collection, as follows:

```
Public gcolCells As Collection
```

Now add the CreateCellsCollection procedure shown in Listing 7-4 to the MEntryPoints module. The modified code is contained in the Analysis2.xls workbook in the \Concepts\Ch07—Using Class Modules to Create Objects folder on the CD that accompanies this book.

Listing 7-4 Creating a Collection of Cell Objects

```
Public Sub CreateCellsCollection()

    Dim clsCell As CCell
```

```
Dim rngCell As Range

' Create new Cells collection
Set gcolCells = New Collection

' Create Cell objects for each cell in Selection
For Each rngCell In Application.Selection
    Set clsCell = New CCell
    Set clsCell.Cell = rngCell
    clsCell.Analyze
    'Add the Cell to the collection
    gcolCells.Add Item:=clsCell, Key:=rngCell.Address
Next rngCell

' Display the number of Cell objects stored
MsgBox "Number of cells stored: " & CStr(gcolCells.Count)

End Sub
```

We declare gcolCells as a public object variable so that it persists while the workbook is open and is visible to all procedures in the VBA project. The CreateCellsCollection procedure creates a new instance of the collection and loops through the currently selected cells, creating a new instance of the Cell object for each cell and adding it to the collection. The address of each cell, in $A$1 reference style, is used as a key to uniquely identify it and to provide a way of accessing the Cell object later.

We can loop through the objects in the collection using a For... Each loop or we can access individual Cell objects by their position in the collection or by using the key value. Because the Item method is the default method for the collection, we can use code like the following to access a specific Cell object:

```
Set rngCell = gcolCells(3)
Set rngCell = gcolCells("$A$3")
```

Creating a Collection Object

The collection we have established is easy to use but it lacks some features we would like to have. As it stands, there is no control over the type of objects that can be added to the collection. We would also like to add a method to the collection that enables us to highlight cells of the same type and another method to remove the highlights.

We will first add two new methods to the CCell class module. The Highlight method adds color to the Cell object according to the CellType. The UnHighlight method removes the color. Listing 7-5 shows the new code.

Note that we are applying the principle of encapsulation. All the code that relates to the Cell object is contained in the CCell class module, not in any other module. Doing this ensures that the code can be easily found and maintained and means that it can be easily transported from one project to another.

Listing 7-5 New Code for the CCell Class Module

```
Public Sub Highlight()
  Cell.Interior.ColorIndex = Choose(muCellType + 1, 5, 6, 7, 8)
End Sub

Public Sub UnHighlight()
  Cell.Interior.ColorIndex = xlNone
End Sub
```

We can now create a new class module named CCells to contain the Cells collection, as shown in Listing 7-6. The complete code is contained in the Analysis3.xls workbook in the \Concepts\Ch07—Using Class Modules to Create Objects folder on the CD that accompanies this book.

Listing 7-6 The CCells ClassModule

```
Option Explicit

Private mcolCells As Collection

Property Get Count() As Long
    Count = mcolCells.Count
End Property

Property Get Item(ByVal vID As Variant) As CCell
    Set Item = mcolCells(vID)
End Property
```

```
Private Sub Class_Initialize()
    Set mcolCells = New Collection
End Sub

Public Sub Add(ByRef rngCell As Range)
    Dim clsCell As CCell
    Set clsCell = New CCell
    Set clsCell.Cell = rngCell
    clsCell.Analyze
    mcolCells.Add Item:=clsCell, Key:=rngCell.Address
End Sub

Public Function NewEnum() As IUnknown
    Set NewEnum = mcolCells.[_NewEnum]
End Function

Public Sub Highlight(ByVal uCellType As anlCellType)
    Dim clsCell As CCell
    For Each clsCell In mcolCells
        If clsCell.CellType = uCellType Then
            clsCell.Highlight
        End If
    Next clsCell
End Sub

Public Sub UnHighlight(ByVal uCellType As anlCellType)
    Dim clsCell As CCell
    For Each clsCell In mcolCells
        If clsCell.CellType = uCellType Then
            clsCell.UnHighlight
        End If
    Next clsCell
End Sub
```

The mcolCells Collection object variable is declared as a private, module-level variable and is instantiated in the Initialize procedure of the class module. Because the Collection object is now hidden from the outside world, we need to write our own Add method for it. We also have created Item and Count property procedures to emulate the corresponding properties of the collection. The input argument for the Item property is declared as a Variant data type because it can be either a numeric index or the string key that identifies the collection member.

The Highlight method loops through each member of the collection. If the CellType property of the Cell object is the same as the type specified by the uCellType argument, we execute the Cell object's Highlight method. The UnHighlight method loops through the collection and executes the UnHighlight method of all Cell objects whose type is the same as the type specified by the uCellType argument.

We've modified the public Collection variable declaration in MGlobals to refer to our new custom collection class, as shown here:

```
Public gclsCells As CCells
```

We've also modified the CreateCellsCollection procedure in the MEntryPoints module to instantiate and populate our custom collection, as shown in Listing 7-7.

Listing 7-7 MEntryPoints Code to Create a Cells Object Collection

```
Public Sub CreateCellsCollection()

    Dim clsCell As CCell
    Dim lIndex As Long
    Dim lCount As Long
    Dim rngCell As Range

    Set gclsCells = New CCells

    For Each rngCell In Application.ActiveSheet.UsedRange
        gclsCells.Add rngCell
    Next rngCell

    ' Count the number of formula cells in the collection.
    For lIndex = 1 To gclsCells.Count
        If gclsCells.Item(lIndex).CellType = anlCellTypeFormula Then
            lCount = lCount + 1
        End If
    Next lIndex

    MsgBox "Number of Formulas = " & CStr(lCount)

End Sub
```

We declare gclsCells as a public object variable to contain our custom Cells collection object. The CreateCellsCollection procedure instantiates gclsCells and uses a `For...Each` loop to add all the cells in the active worksheet's used range to the collection. After loading the collection, the procedure counts the number of cells that contain formulas and displays the result.

The MEntryPoints module contains a ShowFormulas procedure that can be executed to highlight and unhighlight the formula cells in the worksheet. Several additional variations are provided for other cell types.

This code illustrates two shortcomings of our custom collection class. You can't process the members of the collection in a `For...Each` loop. You must use an index and the Item property instead. Also, our collection has no default property, so you can't shortcut the Item property using the standard collection syntax gclsCells(1) to access a member of the collection. You must specify the Item property explicitly in your code. We explain how to solve these problems using Visual Basic or just a text editor in the next section.

Addressing Class Collection Shortcomings

It is possible to make your custom collection class behave like a built-in collection. It requires nothing more than a text editor to make the adjustments, but first we explain how to do it by setting procedure attributes using Visual Basic 6 (VB6) to better illustrate the nature of the changes required.

Using Visual Basic

In VB6, unlike Visual Basic for Applications used in Excel, you can specify a property to be the default property of the class. If you declare the Item property to be the default property, you can omit .Item when referencing a member of the collection and use a shortcut such as gclsCells(1) instead.

If you have VB6 installed you can export the code module CCells to a file and open that file in VB6. Place your cursor anywhere within the Item property procedure and select *Tools > Procedure Attributes* from the menu to display the Procedure Attributes dialog. Then click the *Advanced >>* button and under the Advanced options select (Default) from the *Procedure ID* combo box. This will make the Item property the default property for the class. When you save your changes and import this file back into your Excel VBA project, the attribute will be recognized even though there is no way to set attribute options within the Excel Visual Basic editor.

VB6 also enables you to set up the special procedure in Listing 7-8.

Listing 7-8 Code to Allow the Collection to be Referenced in a `For ... Each` Loop

```
Public Function NewEnum() As IUnknown
    Set NewEnum = mcolCells.[_NewEnum]
End Function
```

This procedure must be given an attribute value of –4, which you enter directly into the *Procedure ID* combo box in the Procedure Attributes dialog. Giving the NewEnum procedure this attribute value enables a `For ... Each` loop to process the members of the collection. After you have made this addition to your class module in VB6 and saved your changes, you can load the module back into your Excel VBA project, and once again the changes will be recognized.

Using a Text Editor

Even without VB6, you can easily create these procedures and their attributes using a text editor such as Notepad. Export the CCells class module to a file and open it using the text editor. Modify your code to look like the example shown in Listing 7-9.

Listing 7-9 Viewing the Code in a Text Editor

```
Property Get Item(ByVal vID As Variant) As CCell
Attribute Item.VB_UserMemId = 0
    Set Item = mcolCells(vID)
End Property

Public Function NewEnum() As IUnknown
Attribute NewEnum.VB_UserMemId = -4
    Set NewEnum = mcolCells.[_NewEnum]
End Function
```

When the modified class module is imported back into your project, the Attribute lines will not be visible, but the procedures will work as expected. You can now refer to a member of the collection as gclsCells(1) and use your custom collection class in a `For ... Each` loop as shown in Listing 7-10.

Listing 7-10 Referencing the Cells Collection in a `For ... Each` Loop

```
For Each clsCell In gclsCells
    If clsCell.CellType = anlCellTypeFormula Then
        lCount = lCount + 1
    End If
Next clsCell
```

Trapping Events

A powerful capability built in to class modules is the ability to respond to events. We want to extend our Analysis application so that when you double-click a cell that has been analyzed, all the cells of the same type will be highlighted. When you right-click the cell, the highlight will be removed. We also want to ensure that cells are reanalyzed when they are changed so that our corresponding Cell objects are kept up to date. The code shown in this section is contained in the Analysis4.xls workbook in the *Concepts\Ch07—Using Class Modules to Create Objects* folder on the CD that accompanies this book.

To trap the events associated with an object you need to do two things:

- Declare a ***WithEvents*** variable of the correct object type in a class module.
- Assign an object reference to the variable.

The events we want to trap are associated with the Worksheet object. Therefore, we need to create a WithEvents object variable in the CCells class module that references the worksheet containing the Cell objects. The appropriate WithEvents variable declaration is made at the module-level within the CCells class and looks like the following:

```
Private WithEvents mwksWorkSheet As Excel.Worksheet
```

As soon as you add this variable declaration to the CCells class module, you can select the WithEvents variable name from the drop-down menu at the top left of the module and use the drop-down menu at the top right of the module to see the events that can be trapped, as shown in Figure 7-1. Event names listed in bold are currently being trapped within the class, as you will see in a moment.

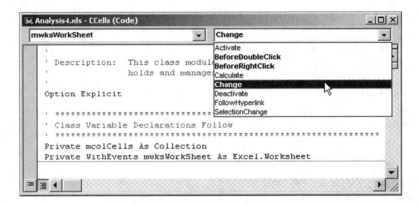

Figure 7-1 The Worksheet Event Procedures Available in CCells

Selecting an event from the drop-down creates a shell for the event procedure in the module. You need to add the procedures shown in Listing 7-11 to the CCells class module. They include a new property named Worksheet that refers to the Worksheet object containing the Cell objects held by the collection, as well as the code for the BeforeDoubleClick, BeforeRightClick and Change events.

Listing 7-11 Additions to the CCells Class Module

```
Property Set Worksheet(wks As Excel.Worksheet)
    Set mwksWorkSheet = wks
End Property


Private Sub mwksWorkSheet_BeforeDoubleClick( _
        ByVal Target As Range, Cancel As Boolean)
    If Not Application.Intersect(Target, _
        mwksWorkSheet.UsedRange) Is Nothing Then
        Highlight mcolCells(Target.Address).CellType
        Cancel = True
    End If
End Sub

Private Sub mwksWorkSheet_BeforeRightClick( _
        ByVal Target As Range, Cancel As Boolean)
    If Not Application.Intersect(Target, _
        mwksWorkSheet.UsedRange) Is Nothing Then
```

```
            UnHighlight mcolCells(Target.Address).CellType
            Cancel = True
        End If
End Sub


Private Sub mwksWorkSheet_Change(ByVal Target As Range)
    Dim rngCell As Range
    If Not Application.Intersect(Target, _
            mwksWorkSheet.UsedRange) Is Nothing Then
        For Each rngCell In Target.Cells
            mcolCells(rngCell.Address).Analyze
        Next rngCell
    End If
End Sub
```

The CreateCellsCollection procedure in the MEntryPoints module needs to be changed as shown in Listing 7-12. The new code assigns a reference to the active worksheet to the Worksheet property of the Cells object so the worksheet's events can be trapped.

Listing 7-12 The Updated CreateCellsCollection Procedure in the MEntryPoints Module

```
Public Sub CreateCellsCollection()

    Dim clsCell As CCell
    Dim rngCell As Range

    Set gclsCells = New CCells
    Set gclsCells.Worksheet = ActiveSheet

    For Each rngCell In ActiveSheet.UsedRange
        gclsCells.Add rngCell
    Next rngCell

End Sub
```

You can now execute the CreateCellsCollection procedure in MEntryPoints to create a new collection with all the links in place to trap the double-click and right-click events for the cells in the worksheet. Double-clicking a cell changes the cell's background of all similar cells to a color that depends on the cell's type. Right-clicking a cell removes the background color.

Raising Events

Another powerful capability of class modules is the ability to raise events. You can define your own events and trigger them in your code. Other class modules can trap those events and respond to them. To illustrate this, we will change the way our Cells collection tells the Cell objects it contains to execute the Highlight and UnHighlight methods. The Cells object will raise an event that will be trapped by the Cell objects. The code shown in this section is contained in the Analysis5.xls workbook in the \Concepts\ Ch07—Using Class Modules to Create Objects folder on the CD that accompanies this book.

To raise an event in a class module you need two things:

■ An ***Event*** declaration at the top of the class module.
■ A line of code that uses ***RaiseEvent*** to cause the event to take place.

The code changes shown in Listing 7-13 should be made in the CCells class module.

Listing 7-13 Changes to the CCells Class Module to Raise an Event

```
Option Explicit

Public Enum anlCellType
    anlCellTypeEmpty
    anlCellTypeLabel
    anlCellTypeConstant
    anlCellTypeFormula
End Enum

Private mcolCells As Collection
Private WithEvents mwksWorkSheet As Excel.Worksheet

Event ChangeColor(uCellType As anlCellType, bColorOn As Boolean)

Public Sub Add(ByRef rngCell As Range)
    Dim clsCell As CCell
    Set clsCell = New CCell
    Set clsCell.Cell = rngCell
    Set clsCell.Parent = Me
    clsCell.Analyze
```

```
        mcolCells.Add Item:=clsCell, Key:=rngCell.Address
End Sub

Private Sub mwksWorkSheet_BeforeDoubleClick( _
            ByVal Target As Range, Cancel As Boolean)
    If Not Application.Intersect(Target, _
            mwksWorkSheet.UsedRange) Is Nothing Then
        RaiseEvent ChangeColor( _
            mcolCells(Target.Address).CellType, True)
        Cancel = True
    End If
End Sub

Private Sub mwksWorkSheet_BeforeRightClick( _
            ByVal Target As Range, Cancel As Boolean)
    If Not Application.Intersect(Target, _
            mwksWorkSheet.UsedRange) Is Nothing Then
        RaiseEvent ChangeColor( _
            mcolCells(Target.Address).CellType, False)
        Cancel = True
    End If
End Sub
```

Note that we moved the anlCellType Enum declaration into the parent collection class module. Now that we have created an explicit parent-child relationship between the CCell and CCells class, any public types used by both classes must reside in the parent class module; otherwise, circular dependencies between the classes that cannot be handled by VBA will be created.

In the declarations section of CCells we declare an event named ChangeColor that has two arguments. The first argument defines the cell type to be changed and the second argument is a Boolean value to indicate whether we are turning color on or off. The BeforeDoubleClick and BeforeRightClick event procedures have been changed to raise the new event and pass the cell type of the target cell and the on or off value. The Add method has been updated to set a new Parent property of the Cell object. This property holds a reference to the Cells object. The name reflects the relationship between the Cells object as the parent object and the Cell object as the child object.

Trapping the event raised by the Cells object in another class module is carried out in exactly the same way we have trapped other events. We create a WithEvents object variable and set it to reference an instance of the class that defines and raises the event. The changes shown in Listing 7-14 should be made to the CCell class module.

Listing 7-14 Changes to the CCell Class Module to Trap the ChangeColor Event

```
Option Explicit

Private muCellType As anlCellType
Private mrngCell As Excel.Range
Private WithEvents mclsParent As CCells

Property Set Parent(ByRef clsCells As CCells)
    Set mclsParent = clsCells
End Property

Private Sub mclsParent_ChangeColor(uCellType As anlCellType, _
                                        bColorOn As Boolean)
    If Me.CellType <> uCellType Then Exit Sub
    If bColorOn Then
        Highlight
    Else
        UnHighlight
    End If
End Sub
```

A new module-level object variable mclsParent is declared WithEvents as an instance of the CCells class. A reference to a Cells object is assigned to mclsParent in the Parent Property Set procedure. When the Cells object raises the ChangeColor event, it will be trapped by all the Cell objects. The Cell objects will take action in response to the event if they are of the correct cell type.

A Family Relationship Problem

Unfortunately, we have introduced a problem in our application. Running the CreateCellsCollection procedure multiple times creates a memory leak. Normally when you overwrite an object in VBA, VBA cleans up the old version of the object and reclaims the memory that was used to hold it. You can also set an object equal to Nothing to reclaim the memory used by it. It is good practice to do this explicitly when you no longer need an object, rather than relying on VBA to do it.

```
Set gclsCells = Nothing
```

When you create two objects that store references to each other, the system will no longer reclaim the memory they used when they are set to new versions or when they are set to Nothing. When analyzing the worksheet in Analysis5.xls with 574 cells in the used range, there is a loss of about 250KB of RAM each time CreateCellsCollection is executed during an Excel session.

> **NOTE:** If you are running Windows NT, 2000 or XP, you can check the amount of RAM currently used by Excel by pressing Ctrl+Shift+Esc to display the Processes window in Task Manager and examining the Mem Usage column for the row where the Image Name column is EXCEL.EXE.

One way to avoid this problem is to make sure you remove the cross-references from the linked objects before the objects are removed. You can do this by adding a method such as the Terminate method shown in Listing 7-15 to the problem classes, in our case the CCell class.

Listing 7-15 The Terminate Method in the CCell Class Module

```
Public Sub Terminate()
    Set mclsParent = Nothing
End Sub
```

The code in Listing 7-16 is added to the CCells class module. It calls the Terminate method of each Cell class contained in the collection to destroy the cross-reference between the classes.

Listing 7-16 The Terminate Method in the CCells Class Module

```
Public Sub Terminate()
    Dim clsCell As CCell
    For Each clsCell In mcolCells
        clsCell.Terminate
        Set clsCell = Nothing
```

```
    Next clsCell
    Set mcolCells = Nothing
End Sub
```

The code in Listing 7-17 is added to the CreateCellsCollection procedure in the MEntryPoints module.

Listing 7-17 The CreateCellsCollection Procedure in the MEntryPoints Module

```
Public Sub CreateCellsCollection()
    Dim clsCell As CCell
    Dim rngCell As Range

    ' Remove any existing instance of the Cells collection
    If Not gclsCells Is Nothing Then
        gclsCells.Terminate
        Set gclsCells = Nothing
    End If

    Set gclsCells = New CCells
    Set gclsCells.Worksheet = ActiveSheet

    For Each rngCell In ActiveSheet.UsedRange
        gclsCells.Add rngCell
    Next rngCell

End Sub
```

If CreateCellsCollection finds an existing instance of gclsCells, it executes the object's Terminate method before setting the object to Nothing.
The gclsCells Terminate method iterates through all the objects in the collection and executes their Terminate methods.

In a more complex object model with more levels, you could have
objects in the middle of the structure that contain both child and parent
references. The Terminate method in these objects would need to run the
Terminate method of each of its children and then set its own Parent property to Nothing.

Creating a Trigger Class

Instead of raising the ChangeColor event in the CCells class module, we can set up a new class module to trigger this event. Creating a trigger class gives us the opportunity to introduce a more efficient way to highlight our Cell objects. We can create four instances of the trigger class, one for each cell type, and assign the appropriate instance to each Cell object. That means each Cell object is only sent a message that is meant for it, rather than hearing all messages sent to all Cell objects.

The trigger class also enables us to eliminate the parent/child relationship between our CCells and CCell classes, thus removing the requirement to manage cross-references. Note that it will not always be possible or desirable to do this. The code shown in this section is contained in the Analysis6.xls workbook in the *\Concepts\Ch07—Using Class Modules to Create Objects* folder on the CD that accompanies this book.

Listing 7-18 shows the code in a new CTypeTrigger class module. The code declares the ChangeColor event, which now only needs one argument to specify whether color is turned on or off. The class has Highlight and UnHighlight methods to raise the event.

Listing 7-18 The CTypeTrigger Class Module

```
Option Explicit

Public Event ChangeColor(bColorOn As Boolean)

Public Sub Highlight()
    RaiseEvent ChangeColor(True)
End Sub

Public Sub UnHighlight()
    RaiseEvent ChangeColor(False)
End Sub
```

Listing 7-19 contains the changes to the CCell class module to trap the ChangeColor event raised in CTypeTrigger. Depending on the value of bColorOn, the event procedure runs the Highlight or UnHighlight methods.

Listing 7-19 Changes to the CCell Class Module to Trap the ChangeColor Event of CTypeTrigger

```
Option Explicit

Private muCellType As anlCellType
Private mrngCell As Excel.Range
Private WithEvents mclsTypeTrigger As CTypeTrigger

Property Set TypeTrigger(clsTrigger As CTypeTrigger)
    Set mclsTypeTrigger = clsTrigger
End Property

Private Sub mclsTypeTrigger_ChangeColor(bColorOn As Boolean)
    If bColorOn Then
        Highlight
    Else
        UnHighlight
    End If
End Sub
```

Listing 7-20 contains the changes to the CCells module. An array variable maclsTriggers is declared to hold the instances of CTypeTrigger. The Initialize event redimensions maclsTriggers to match the number of cell types and the For ... Next loop assigns instances of CTypeTrigger to the array elements. The Add method assigns the correct element of maclsTriggers to each Cell object according to its cell type. The result is that each Cell object only listens for messages that apply to its own cell type.

Listing 7-20 Changes to the CCells Class Module to Assign References to CTypeTrigger to Cell Objects

```
Option Explicit

Public Enum anlCellType
    anlCellTypeEmpty
    anlCellTypeLabel
    anlCellTypeConstant
    anlCellTypeFormula
End Enum
```

```vb
Private mcolCells As Collection
Private WithEvents mwksWorkSheet As Excel.Worksheet
Private maclsTriggers() As CTypeTrigger

Private Sub Class_Initialize()
    Dim uCellType As anlCellType
    Set mcolCells = New Collection
    ' Initialize the array of cell type triggers,
    ' one element for each of our cell types.
    ReDim maclsTriggers(anlCellTypeEmpty To anlCellTypeFormula)
    For uCellType = anlCellTypeEmpty To anlCellTypeFormula
        Set maclsTriggers(uCellType) = New CTypeTrigger
    Next uCellType
End Sub

Public Sub Add(ByRef rngCell As Range)
    Dim clsCell As CCell
    Set clsCell = New CCell
    Set clsCell.Cell = rngCell
    clsCell.Analyze
    Set clsCell.TypeTrigger = maclsTriggers(clsCell.CellType)
    mcolCells.Add Item:=clsCell, Key:=rngCell.Address
End Sub

Public Sub Highlight(ByVal uCellType As anlCellType)
    maclsTriggers(uCellType).Highlight
End Sub

Public Sub UnHighlight(ByVal uCellType As anlCellType)
    maclsTriggers(uCellType).UnHighlight
End Sub

Private Sub mwksWorkSheet_BeforeDoubleClick( _
            ByVal Target As Range, Cancel As Boolean)
    If Not Application.Intersect(Target, _
            mwksWorkSheet.UsedRange) Is Nothing Then
        Highlight mcolCells(Target.Address).CellType
        Cancel = True
    End If
End Sub

Private Sub mwksWorkSheet_BeforeRightClick( _
            ByVal Target As Range, Cancel As Boolean)
```

```
    If Not Application.Intersect(Target, _
            mwksWorkSheet.UsedRange) Is Nothing Then
        UnHighlight mcolCells(Target.Address).CellType
        Cancel = True
    End If
End Sub


Private Sub mwksWorkSheet_Change(ByVal Target As Range)

    Dim rngCell As Range
    Dim clsCell As CCell

    If Not Application.Intersect(Target, _
            mwksWorkSheet.UsedRange) Is Nothing Then
        For Each rngCell In Target.Cells
            Set clsCell = mcolCells(rngCell.Address)
            clsCell.Analyze
            Set clsCell.TypeTrigger = _
                maclsTriggers(clsCell.CellType)
        Next rngCell
    End If

End Sub
```

Practical Example

PETRAS Timesheet

In our practical example for this chapter, we add an application-level event
handling class to our PETRAS timesheet application that will make two
significant changes. First, it will enable us to convert the time-entry workbook into an Excel template. This will simplify creation of new time-entry
workbooks for new purposes as well as allow multiple time entry workbooks to be open at the same time. Second, the event handler will automatically detect whether a time entry workbook is active and enable or disable our toolbar buttons accordingly. Table 7-1 summarizes the changes
made to the PETRAS timesheet application for this chapter.

Table 7-1 Changes to PETRAS Timesheet Application for Chapter 7

Module	Procedure	Change
PetrasTemplate.xlt		Changed the normal workbook into a template workbook
CAppEventHandler		Added an application-level event handling class to the add-in
MEntryPoints	NewTimeSheet	New procedure to create timesheets from the template workbook
MOpenClose	Auto_Open	Removed timesheet initialization logic and delegated it to the event handling class
MSystemCode		Moved all time-entry workbook management code into the event handling class

The Template

A template workbook reacts differently than a normal workbook when opened using the Excel `Workbooks.Open` method. A normal workbook will simply be opened. When a template workbook is opened a new, unsaved copy of the template workbook will be created. To create a template workbook from a normal workbook, choose *File > Save As* from the Excel menu and select the Template entry from the *Save as type* drop-down. As soon as you select the Template option, Excel will unhelpfully modify the directory where you are saving your workbook to the Office Templates directory, so don't forget to change this to the location where you are storing your application files.

After we begin using a template workbook, the user has complete control over the workbook filename. We will determine whether a given workbook belongs to us by checking for the unique named constant setIsTimeSheet that we have added to our template workbook for this purpose.

A template workbook combined with an application-level event handler enables us to support multiple instances of the time entry workbook being open simultaneously. This might be needed, for example, if there is a requirement to have a separate time sheet for each client or project.

Moving to a template user interface workbook also requires that we give the user a way to create new time sheet workbooks, because it is no longer a simple matter of opening and reusing the same fixed timesheet workbook over and over. In Figure 7-2, note the new toolbar button labeled *New Time Sheet*. This button enables the user to create new instances of our template.

Figure 7-2 The PETRAS Toolbar with the New Time Sheet Button

As shown in Listing 7-21, the code run by this new button is very simple.

Listing 7-21 The NewTimeSheet Procedure

```
Public Sub NewTimeSheet()
    Application.ScreenUpdating = False
    InitGlobals
    Application.Workbooks.Add gsAppDir & gsFILE_TIME_ENTRY
    Application.ScreenUpdating = True
End Sub
```

We turn off screen updating and call InitGlobals to ensure that our global variables are properly initialized. We then simply open the template workbook and turn screen updating back on. When you open a template workbook from VBA, it is treated differently than a normal workbook. Rather than opening PetrasTemplate.xlt, a new copy of PetrasTemplate.xlt, called PetrasTemplate1, is created. Each time the user clicks the New Time Sheet button, he gets a completely new, independent copy of PetrasTemplate.xlt.

The act of opening the template triggers the NewWorkbook event in our event handing class. This event performs all the necessary actions required to initialize the template. This event procedure is shown in the next section.

The Application-Level Event Handler

Within our application-level event handling class, we encapsulate many of the tasks that were previously accomplished by procedures in standard modules. For example, the MakeWorksheetSettings procedure and the bIsTimeEntryBookActive function that we encountered in *Chapter 5* —

Function, General and *Application-Specific Add-ins* are now both private procedures of the class. We will describe the layout of the class module in Listing 7-22, then explain what the pieces do, instead of showing all of the code here. You can examine the code yourself in the PetrasAddin.xla workbook of the sample application for this chapter on the CD, and are strongly encouraged to do so.

Listing 7-22 Class Module Layout of the CAppEventHandler Class

Module-Level Variables
```
Private WithEvents mxlApp As Excel.Application
```

Class Event Procedures
```
Class_Initialize
Class_Terminate
mxlApp_NewWorkbook
mxlApp_WorkbookOpen
mxlApp_WindowActivate
mxlApp_WindowDeactivate
```

Class Method Procedures
```
SetInitialStatus
```

Class Private Procedures
```
EnableDisableToolbar
MakeWorksheetSettings
bIsTimeEntryBookActive
bIsTimeEntryWorkbook
```

Because the variable that holds a reference to the instance of the CAppEventHandler class that we use in our application is a public variable, we use the InitGlobals procedure to manage it. The code required to do this is shown below.

In the declarations section of the MGlobals module:

```
Public gclsEventHandler As CAppEventHandler
```

In the InitGlobals procedure:

```
' Instantiate the Application event handler
If gclsEventHandler Is Nothing Then
    Set gclsEventHandler = New CAppEventHandler
End If
```

The InitGlobals code checks to see whether the public gclsEventHandler variable is initialized and initializes it if it isn't. InitGlobals is called at the beginning of every nontrivial entry-point procedure in our application, so if anything causes our class variable to lose state, it will be instantiated again as soon as the next entry-point procedure is called. This is a good safety mechanism.

When the public gclsEventHandler variable is initialized, it causes the Class_Initialize event procedure to execute. Inside this event procedure, we initialize the event handling mechanism by setting the class module-level WithEvents variable to refer to the current instance of the Excel Application, as follows:

```
Set mxlApp = Excel.Application
```

Similarly, when our application is exiting and we destroy our gclsEventHandler variable, it causes the Class_Terminate event procedure to execute. Within this event procedure we destroy the class reference to the Excel Application object by setting the mxlApp variable to Nothing.

All the rest of the class event procedures, which are those belonging to the mxlApp WithEvents variable, serve the same purpose. They "watch" the Excel environment and enable or disable our toolbar buttons as appropriate when conditions change.

Disabling toolbar buttons when they can't be used is a much better user interface technique than displaying an error message when the user clicks one in the wrong circumstances. You don't want to punish the user (that is, display an error message in response to an action) when he can't be expected to know he has done something wrong. Note that we always leave the *New Time Sheet* and *Exit PETRAS* toolbar buttons enabled. The user should always be able to create a new timesheet or exit the application.

In addition to enabling and disabling the toolbar buttons, the mxlApp_NewWorkbook and mxlApp_WorkbookOpen event procedures detect when a time entry workbook is being created or opened for the first time, respectively. At this point they run the private MakeWorksheetSettings procedure to initialize that time entry workbook. All of the mxlApp event procedures are shown in Listing 7-23. As you can see, the individual procedures are very simple, but the cumulative effect is very powerful.

Listing 7-23 The mxlApp Event Procedures

```
Private Sub mxlApp_NewWorkbook(ByVal Wb As Workbook)
    If bIsTimeEntryWorkbook(Wb) Then
        EnableDisableToolbar True
        MakeWorksheetSettings Wb
    Else
        EnableDisableToolbar False
    End If
End Sub


Private Sub mxlApp_WorkbookOpen(ByVal Wb As Excel.Workbook)
    If bIsTimeEntryWorkbook(Wb) Then
        EnableDisableToolbar True
        MakeWorksheetSettings Wb
    Else
        EnableDisableToolbar False
    End If
End Sub


Private Sub mxlApp_WindowActivate(ByVal Wb As Workbook, _
                                  ByVal Wn As Window)
    ' When a window is activated, check to see if it belongs
    ' to one of our workbooks. Enable all our toolbar controls
    ' if it does.
    EnableDisableToolbar bIsTimeEntryBookActive()
End Sub


Private Sub mxlApp_WindowDeactivate(ByVal Wb As Workbook, _
                                    ByVal Wn As Window)
    ' When a window is deactivated, disable our toolbar
    ' controls by default. They will be re-enables by the
    ' WindowActivate event procedure if required.
    EnableDisableToolbar False
End Sub
```

The full power of having an event handling class in your application is difficult to convey on paper. We urge you to experiment with the sample application for this chapter to see for yourself how it works in a live setting. Double-click the PetrasAddin.xla file to open Excel and see how the application toolbar behaves. Create new timesheet workbooks, open non-timesheet workbooks and switch back and forth between them. The state of the toolbar will follow your every action.

It is also educational to see exactly how much preparation the application does when you create a new instance of the timesheet workbook. Without the PetrasAddin.xla running, open the PetrasTemplate.xlt workbook and compare how it looks and behaves in its raw state with the way it looks and behaves as an instance of the timesheet within the running application.

PETRAS Reporting

The PETRAS reporting application has been modified in much the same way, and for the same reasons, as the PETRAS timesheet add-in. By adding a class module to handle application-level events, we can enable the user to have multiple consolidation workbooks open at the same time and switch between them using the new *Window* menu, as shown in Figure 7-3.

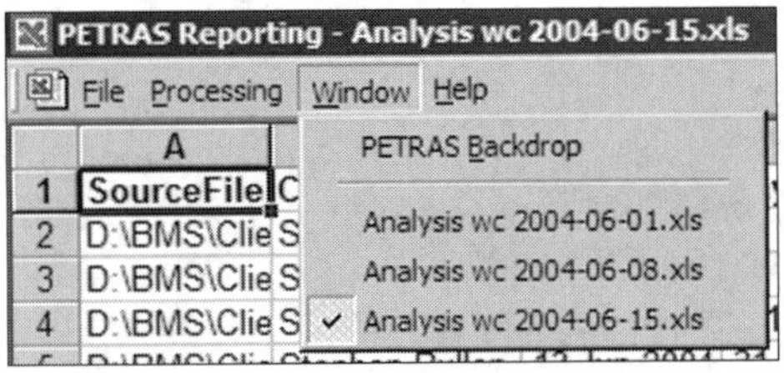

Figure 7-3 The PETRAS Reporting Menu Bar with the New Window Menu

Table 7-2 summarizes the changes made to the PETRAS reporting application for this chapter. Rather than repeat much of the previous few pages, we suggest you review the PetrasReporting.xla workbook to see exactly how the multiple-document interface has been implemented.

Table 7-2 Changes to the PETRAS Reporting Application for Chapter 7

Module	Procedure	Change
CAppEventHandler		Added an application-level event handling class to the application to manage multiple consolidation workbooks.
MCommandBars	SetUpMenus	Added code to create the Window menu.
MSystemCode		Added procedures to add, remove and place a checkmark against an item in the Window menu.
MEntryPoints	MenuWindowSelect	New procedure to handle selecting an item within the Window menu. All Window menu items call this routine.

Conclusion

You use class modules to create objects and their associated methods, properties and events. You can collect child objects in a parent object so that you can create a hierarchy of objects to form an object model. You can use class modules to trap the events raised by other objects including the Excel application. You can raise your own events in a class module.

When you set up cross-references between parent and child objects so that each is aware of the other, you will create a structure that is not simple to remove from memory when it is no longer useful. You need to add extra code to remove these cross-references.

Class modules are a powerful addition to a developer's toolkit. The objects created lead to code that is easier to write, develop, maintain and share than traditional code. Objects are easy to use because they encapsulate complex code in a form that is very accessible. All you need to know to use an object are its methods, properties and events. Objects can be shared because the class modules that define them are encapsulated (self-contained) and therefore very transportable from one project to another. All you need to do is copy the class module to make the object available in another project.

As a developer, you can easily add new methods, properties and events to an object without changing the existing interface. Your objects can evolve without harming older systems that use them. Most developers find class modules very addictive. The more you use them, the more you like them and the more uses you find for them. They will be used extensively throughout the rest of this book.

CHAPTER 8

Advanced Command Bar Handling

This chapter starts off by covering some best practices for command bar design. Then we introduce our table-driven command bar building methodology. This feature, which you can easily add to your own applications, removes most of the difficulties associated with building and maintaining nontrivial custom command bars. We show you how to create and use custom icon/mask file combinations in Excel 2002 and higher (a feature also supported by the command bar builder). We then finish up by explaining how to hook CommandBarControl events in order to intercept clicks from CommandBarControls in ways that are not possible using a simple OnAction macro assignment.

NOTE: Whenever we use the noun *control* in this chapter, we are referring to the generic CommandBarControl object. This noun is used whenever the topic we are currently discussing applies equally to any of the specific control objects that can be represented by a generic CommandBarControl.

Command Bar Design

Before we get into command bar creation, let's cover a few best practices for command bar design. Try to follow all of these practices when designing your custom command bars and controls:

- Emulate Excel's menu bar. Users are already familiar with the Excel menu structure, so if your application emulates it users will have some immediate familiarity with your application. This is especially true for dictator applications, whose menus may include a large number of the same features that would normally appear on Excel's menu bar.

- Don't use more than three menu sublevels. Although the table-driven command bar builder that we will describe in the next section provides a means to create menus deeper than three levels, this is not something you should do unless absolutely necessary. Users tend to get lost when your menu structure exceeds three sublevels.

- If you are adding one or more top-level menus to the built-in menu bar, those menus should be located directly to the left of the Window menu. This is a longstanding user interface convention that most users are familiar with.

- Unless you have a very good reason for not doing so, always dock your custom toolbars at the top of the Excel window. There are a reasonable number of situations where it is appropriate to create floating toolbars, but remember that your users can always undock your toolbar if they want. Even less frequently, but still on occasion, it is useful to dock a toolbar at the bottom of the Excel window. Right and left docking, even though the command bar builder supports them, are never recommended. We have never seen a situation where these positions are appropriate. The vast majority of users have never encountered a toolbar docked on the right or left sides, and the necessity of doing so is almost always an indication of poor user interface design.

- Physically group controls that perform related functions. Your application will be much easier to use if similar controls are located near each other.

- Separate related groups of controls from each other using separator bars, but try not to have more than four our five menus or toolbar buttons in a row without a separator. Separator bars are created using the BeginGroup property, which we cover in the next section.

- Select or create icons whose appearance visually implies the action performed by their control. This seems obvious, but it's very difficult in a custom application with a large number of features. Put as much thought and creativity into the appearance of your icons as possible. Features whose icons bear no visual resemblance to their function will be much harder for users to remember than those whose icons clearly imply their function. Think, for example, how easy it is to determine which toolbar button you need to click to print a document. Do your best to emulate this close association between function and appearance.

Table-Driven Command Bars

For small-scale Excel applications with a few toolbar buttons and/or menu items, it is perfectly acceptable to hard-code the creation of the command bars and controls your application requires using a custom VBA procedure. (We do recommend that you isolate command bar building code in a separate procedure for ease of maintenance.) When you begin building large-scale applications with multiple dedicated toolbars and menus, hard-coded command bars become very time-consuming to create and difficult to maintain.

The solution to this problem is a widely used technique within the Excel development community known as *table-driven* command bar building. As we discussed in *Chapter 4 — Worksheet Design*, table-driven is a generic term referring to any process that performs some operation guided by information stored in a dedicated table on a worksheet.

Table-driven command bar building is one of the more complex table-driven methodologies. Implemented correctly, however, it is easy to use and far superior to anything that can be accomplished using VBA alone. Even when we resort to using Visual Basic ActiveX DLLs, a technique we cover extensively in *Chapter 20 — Combining Excel and Visual Basic 6*, we use an Excel add-in workbook with a three-line stub procedure assigned to each of the command bar controls that calls the ActiveX DLL. This add-in workbook allows us to use worksheets, which would otherwise be unavailable, to implement table-driven command bars and other table-driven methodologies.

In this section we describe the most sophisticated table-driven command bar builder available. As with all other applications described in the book, this command bar builder is included on the CD that accompanies this book and can be integrated into any of your applications.

Introducing the Table-Driven Command Bar Builder

The table-driven command bar builder consists of three parts that form a self-contained unit you can plug directly into any application: a worksheet table that defines the command bars and controls to be built and two code modules that read this table and build the command bars and controls it specifies.

To use the command bar builder in your application, you need to copy the wksCommandBars worksheet and the MCommandBars and

MPastePicture modules into your project. In the *Putting It All Together* section later in the chapter we demonstrate the workbook containing the version of the command bar builder that you should use in your projects.

After you have added definitions of the command bars and controls you want to build to the wksCommandBars worksheet, your application just needs to call one procedure on startup and all of those command bars and controls will be built to your specifications. A second procedure can be called on shutdown to dismantle the command bars and controls specified in the table. We cover this in more detail in the *Practical Example* section at the end of the chapter.

We spend most of this section explaining how to write command bar definitions in the command bar definition table. It's best to think of the code that reads and implements the command bars and controls defined by the table as a black box. This code is too lengthy and complex to cover in any detail in this chapter, but you are strongly encouraged to examine the code if you want to understand how it works. The code is open and heavily commented, so it should be reasonably approachable to the seasoned programmer.

The Command Bar Definition Table

The reason we are spending so much time describing the command bar definition table is because you will spend 99 percent of your command bar building time working with it. The only thing you need to do with the code, after adding it to your project, is call the build command bars procedure on startup and the reset command bars procedure on shutdown.

The command bar definition table is too wide to display entirely in a screen shot on the printed page, but we will give you the flavor for what it looks like with the partial example shown in Figure 8-1.

The custom menu bar created by this command bar definition table entry is shown in Figure 8-2.

Keep in mind this is only a small section from the upper-left corner of the command bar definition table. The actual table contains at least 25 columns of settings and as many rows as required to define all of the command bars and controls required for the application.

One of the features making the command bar definition table so easy for experienced programmers to use is that it contains sheet-level defined constants corresponding to every enumeration member used when building command bars and controls with VBA. Therefore, wherever the table calls for an enumeration member such as `msoBarTop` or

	A	B	C	D	E	F
1	Command Bar Name	Control Caption	Control Caption	Control Caption	Position	IsMenubar
2	Custom Menu Bar				1	TRUE
3		&File				
4			&New			
5			&Open			
6			&Close			
7			&Save			
8			Save &As			
9			Print Pre&view			
10			&Print...			
11			E&xit			
12		&Edit				
13			&Copy			
14			&Paste			
15			Paste &Special...			
16		&Custom				
17			Sample Submenus &1			
18				Sub Item &1		
19				Sub Item &2		
20				Sub Item &3		
21			Sample Submenus &2			
22				Sub Item &1		
23				Sub Item &2		
24				Sub Item &3		
25		&Help				
26			&About...			
27	Stop					

Figure 8-1 A Partial Command Bar Definition Table

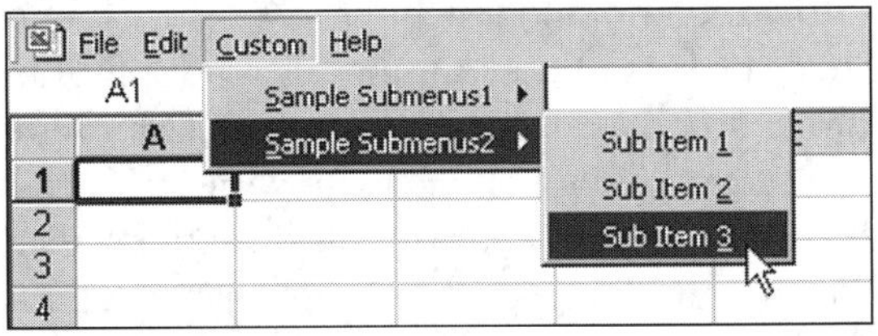

Figure 8-2 A Custom Menu Bar Created by the Command Bar Builder

`msoButtonIconAndCaption`, you can use those names exactly as you would in VBA by just preceding them with an equal sign when you enter them into a cell. Their numeric values will appear in the cell, but if you select the cell and check the formula bar you will see the enumeration member name. Figure 8-3 shows an example of this.

N3	▼	=	=msoControlPopup	
M	**N**	**O**	**P**	**Q**
1 Control ID	Control Type	Control Style	Face ID	Begin Group
2				
3	10			
4 1	1	3	18	
5 1	1	3	23	
6 1	1	3	106	
7 1	1	3	3	TRUE
8 1	1	3	748	
9 1	1	3	109	TRUE
10 1	1	3	4	
11 1	1	3		TRUE

Figure 8-3 Defined Constants in the Command Bar Definition Table

In the sections that follow, we will provide complete descriptions of the purpose and usage of each of the settings in the command bar definition table. In the actual table there are cell comments at the top of each column that give brief but reasonably complete explanations of the purpose of the column. This will enable you to use the table without having to continually refer back to this chapter. The setting names in the column headers of the command bar definition table are identical or very similar to the names of the VBA properties they represent on the command bar or control being defined. This allows you to leverage all of your existing knowledge of how to build command bars and controls in VBA when using the table-driven command bar builder.

Most settings in the command bar definition table are not required. In addition, some settings apply to CommandBar objects, some to CommandBarControl objects and some to both. Table 8-1 contains a summary of the command bar definition table settings, showing which objects each setting applies to, which settings are required and what the default value is for each optional setting, if any.

Beginning with the Position column and continuing through the last column in the table, the column values apply to the command bar or control whose name or caption is specified in the same row in one of the first four columns of the table. If a setting does not apply to the type of object specified in the initial columns, it will be ignored. Similarly, if the entry in the initial columns specifies an existing command bar or control object, most settings in subsequent columns are ignored.

Table 8-1 Command Bar Definition Table Settings Summary

Setting	CommandBar	Command BarControl	Required	Default
Command Bar Name	✓		Yes	None
Control Caption		✓	Yes	None
Position	✓		No	msoBarTop
IsMenubar	✓		No	False
Visible	✓		No	False
Width	✓	✓	No	None
Protection	✓		No	msoBarNoCustomize
IsTemporary	✓	✓	No	True
IsEnabled	✓	✓	No	True
OnAction		✓	No	None
Control ID		✓	No	1 (Custom)
Control Type		✓	No	msoControlButton
Control Style		✓	No	msoButtonAutomatic
Face ID		✓	No	None
Begin Group		✓	No	False
Before		✓	No	System Default
Tooltip		✓	No	System Default
Shortcut Text		✓	No	None
Tag		✓	No	None
Parameter		✓	No	None
State		✓	No	msoButtonUp
ListRange		✓	No	None
Lists		✓	No	None

Command Bar Name

The command bar builder has the flexibility to create new command bars as well as add controls to existing command bars. Regardless of whether you are creating a new command bar or adding controls to an existing command bar, you enter the name of the command bar in this column. The command bar builder checks each command bar name specified in this column to see whether it already exists. If the specified command bar already exists, the command bar builder assumes you are adding controls to that command bar. If no command bar with the specified name exists, the command bar builder creates a new command bar with the specified name using the settings specified in later columns.

There must be two entries in the Command Bar Name column for every command bar you build or modify. The first entry must be the name or index number of the command bar being created or modified. The second entry is simply the word Stop. The Stop entry must be placed in the row directly below the last row of the command bar definition specified by the first entry. These two entries in the first column work together to bracket the command bar definition so the command bar building code knows where the definition starts and ends.

In Figure 8-1, notice how the command bar name Custom Menu Bar is placed at the top of the Command Bar Name column in cell A2 and the word Stop is placed at the bottom in cell A27. As shown in this example, ***there cannot be any entries between the command bar name value and the Stop keyword***. You can stack as many command bar definitions in the table as you like. The only rule is that each subsequent definition must be separated from the previous definition by at least one blank row.

Control Caption

There are three Control Caption columns by default. This is because good user interface design suggests you should not use more than three cascading menu levels. If you really must have additional levels, you can simply insert additional Control Caption columns to the right of the existing three.

Similar to the Command Bar Name column, the Control Caption columns can be used to create new controls or add subcontrols to existing controls. If the command bar builder code detects that the caption in the Control Caption column refers to an existing control on the current command bar, it will assume you want to add subcontrols to it. Otherwise it will create a new control with the specified caption using the settings specified in later columns.

Regardless of whether you are creating a single control or a cascading series of menus, each control must occupy its own row. The position of a control's caption within the series of Control Caption columns determines the level at which the control will be added. Look again at Figure 8-1. Notice that even though all three Control Caption columns have entries, no row has a Control Caption entry in more than one of the three columns. ***This is an absolute requirement***.

You can provide an accelerator key for your control by placing an ampersand directly to the left of the character that you want to use as the accelerator key character. The control can then be activated from the keyboard by pressing the Alt key and the specified character simultaneously. This feature only applies to controls that display their caption and are currently visible.

NOTE: When a control displays a dialog, standard user interface conventions dictate that the caption of the control, if it displays one, should be followed by an ellipsis. See the Excel *File > Print...* menu for an example of this convention.

Position

The Position setting applies only to CommandBar objects. It specifies the position on the screen where the CommandBar will appear when it is displayed. This setting must be one of the following `msoBarPosition` enumeration members:

- `msoBarBottom`—The command bar will be docked at the bottom of the screen.
- `msoBarFloating`—The command bar will not be docked but instead will float over the screen.
- `msoBarLeft`—The command bar will be docked on the left side of the screen.
- `msoBarPopup`—This setting is used to specify command bars that will be displayed when the user right-clicks with the mouse. The command bar will be displayed at the position where the user right-clicked. Command bars with this position setting must be displayed in response to one of the BeforeRightClick event procedures using the syntax:

```
Application.CommandBars("Name").ShowPopup
```

- `msoBarRight`—The command bar will be docked on the right side of the screen.
- `msoBarTop`—The command bar will be docked at the top of the screen. This is the default value if no position is specified.

IsMenubar

The IsMenubar setting applies only to CommandBar objects. If set to True, the specified command bar will be the menu bar when it is visible. You can define multiple command bars as menu bars for different purposes, but only one menu bar can be visible at a time. If the IsMenubar setting is False, the command bar will be a toolbar or popup depending on the Position setting. The IsMenubar property must be False for command bars with the Position property value `msoBarPopup` or a runtime error will occur. Therefore, the command bar builder code will enforce this value for `msoBarPopup` command bars regardless of the value actually entered in the table. The default value for the IsMenubar setting is False.

Visible

The Visible setting applies only to CommandBar objects. If set to True, the specified CommandBar will be visible, subject to the following limitations:

- If more than one command bar has both the IsMenubar and Visible settings set to True, the last such command bar in the table will be the menu bar that is actually displayed. All other menu bars will be hidden.
- The Visible property does not apply to and has no effect on command bars with the Position value `msoBarPopup`.

The default value of the Visible setting is False. This enables you to create a large number of command bars when your application starts up and then display them on demand as needed.

Width

The Width setting applies to CommandBar and CommandBarControl objects. The Width setting must be a positive whole number greater than zero. This setting is not required and there is no default value. If the Width setting is not specified, the width of the command bar or control will be determined automatically by VBA. If the Width setting is not specified for a command bar, VBA will make the command bar wide enough to display all of the controls it contains on a single row. If the Width setting is not specified for a control, VBA will make the control wide enough to display its icon and/or caption.

For CommandBar objects, the Width setting applies only when the Position setting is `msoBarFloating`. The Width setting is ignored for all other command bar Position settings. You cannot make a command bar wider than its automatically calculated width. Setting the width of a floating command bar to a value narrower than its automatically calculated width enables you to stack controls in multiple rows rather than displaying a long, single-row command bar.

For CommandBarControl objects, the Width setting always applies and you can set it to any positive whole number greater than zero. If the specified width is too narrow to display the caption and/or icon of the control, however, it will be ignored. Note that all controls on the same popup menu list will have the width of the widest control in the list regardless of their individual Width settings.

There are no hard-and-fast rules for deciding exactly what the Width setting should be. The best approach is to first build your command bars and controls without specifying the Width setting. Then use the Immediate window to examine the width property that has been automatically assigned by VBA. You can use that as a starting point from which to increase or decrease the width of your command bars and/or controls.

Protection

The Protection setting applies only to CommandBar objects. This setting specifies what type of modifications the user will be allowed to make to the command bar. This setting must be one or more of the following `msoBarProtection` enumeration members. To apply multiple Protection values, just add the values together in the Protection cell for the command bar in question.

- `msoBarNoChangeDock`—The user cannot change the position at which the command bar is docked.
- `msoBarNoChangeVisible`—The user cannot change the visibility status of the command bar. If the command bar is visible, the user cannot hide it; if the command bar is hidden, the user cannot display it.
- `msoBarNoCustomize`—The user cannot add or remove controls on the command bar.
- `msoBarNoHorizontalDock`—The user cannot dock the command bar in any horizontal position, either top or bottom. Without any additional protection values, the command bar can still be

docked vertically. To prevent a command bar from being docked anywhere, just add the `msoBarNoHorizontalDock` and the `msoBarNoVerticalDock` enumeration member values together in the Protection cell.

- `msoBarNoMove`—The command bar cannot be moved. Be careful with this option because it will prevent the user from moving the command bar under any circumstances. For example, if you create a floating command bar whose width causes it to appear partially off-screen, the users will not be able to move the command bar into a position where they can access all of its controls.

- `msoBarNoProtection`—The user can make any changes to the command bar that he wants.

- `msoBarNoResize`—The user cannot modify the width or height of the command bar.

- `msoBarNoVerticalDock`—The user cannot dock the command bar in any vertical position, either left or right.

There are two ways a user can delete your command bar regardless of its Protection setting, even if you have disabled the *View > Toolbars > Customize* menu. Both of these methods provide "back doors" to display the Customize dialog. It is particularly important to disable these options in dictator applications where deleting a custom command bar may leave the user with no way to properly exit the application.

First, if the *Toolbar List* command bar is enabled, the user will be able to delete your custom command bar by right-clicking anywhere over the command bar area and selecting *Customize* from the shortcut menu. To disable the *Toolbar List* command bar, execute the following line of code:

```
Application.CommandBars("Toolbar List").Enabled = False
```

Second, if any empty toolbar docking surface is exposed on screen (typically beyond the right side of a toolbar), the user can double-click anywhere within this area and the Customize dialog will display. There is no way to directly disable this feature, so you must indirectly disable it by ensuring that no uncovered toolbar docking area is left exposed by your application. The easiest way to do this is to add a nonfunctional CommandBarButton control (one with no Caption or OnAction assignment) at the end of each of your toolbars and set it to be wide enough so it will cover the entire toolbar docking area regardless of the user's screen resolution.

IsTemporary

The IsTemporary setting applies to CommandBar and Command-BarControl objects. If set to False, the specified command bar or control will be persisted between Excel sessions. Setting this property to True causes the command bar or control to be discarded when the current session of Excel exits. The default value for this setting is True.

The command bar builder will rebuild all command bars and controls defined in the table each time your application runs, so the occasions when you want your custom command bars or controls to be persisted between Excel sessions are very rare. Leave this setting blank so the default value is used unless you have a very good reason to do otherwise.

IsEnabled

The IsEnabled setting applies to CommandBar and CommandBarControl objects. This setting determines whether the command bar or control is enabled on startup. A value of True causes the command bar or control to be enabled. A value of False causes the command bar or control to be disabled. Disabled command bars will not be visible to the user. The IsEnabled property overrides the Visible property for command bars in this respect. Disabled controls will be visible but will appear grayed out. The default value for this property is True.

OnAction

This setting applies to CommandBarControl objects. It holds the name of the procedure that will be run by the control. This procedure must be a public procedure located in a standard code module. If you want to trap the Click or Change event rather than assigning a procedure to the OnAction property, you can leave this setting blank. We cover control event trapping in the *Hooking Command Bar Control Events* section later in this chapter. If the Control ID setting is anything other than 1, the OnAction setting is ignored. You will understand why this is the case when we describe the Control ID setting next.

Control ID

This setting applies to CommandBarControl objects. Giving this setting a value of 1 means that you are creating a custom control whose properties are specified by the rest of the columns in the table. Any value other than 1 is interpreted as the ID of a built-in Excel control. In that case, the built-in control specified by the Control ID value will be added to your command bar, along with its function and appearance. If you specify a built-in control using the Control ID setting, the following command bar definition table settings will be ignored:

- OnAction
- Control Type
- Control Style
- Shortcut Text
- State
- ListRange
- Lists

You can determine the ID you need to use in order to add a built-in control to your command bar in the following manner. Assume you want to add the *Print* menu item from the *File* menu on the *Worksheet Menu Bar* to your custom command bar. Enter the following into the VBE Immediate window:

```
? CommandBars("File").Controls("Print...").ID
 4
```

The Immediate window is covered in more detail in *Chapter 16 — VBA Debugging*, but for now note that the ? character tells the Immediate window to print the result of the expression that follows it. In this case, the result is the number 4, shown directly below the expression. This is the ID of the *Print* control. To add this control to your custom command bar, you just place 4 in the Control ID column of the appropriate row in the command bar definition table.

NOTE: A quirk in the Office CommandBars object model enables you to access the top-level menus of the Excel menu bar as CommandBar objects in their own right. If you loop the contents of the CommandBars collection, you won't find these menus contained in it, but you can access them using the syntax shown above just the same.

Control Type

This setting applies to CommandBarControl objects. It is used to specify what type of control you want. This setting must be one of the following `msoControlType` enumeration members:

- `msoControlButton`—This is a menu or toolbar button that simply executes the specified OnAction procedure when it is clicked. The majority of CommandBarControls that you see on Excel's menus and toolbars are this type of control.
- `msoControlComboBox`—This is a combo box control that enables users to either select an entry from a predefined list or enter a new value of their choosing. An example of this type of control is the Zoom combo box on the Standard toolbar. You can select from a predefined list of zoom values or supply your own.
- `msoControlDropdown`—This control looks exactly like the `msoControlComboBox` control but the only option allowed is to select an item from the predefined list.
- `msoControlEdit`—This is an edit box control that allows the user to enter an arbitrary text value.
- `msoControlPopup`—This type of control is used to create a submenu containing a list of one or more menu items. All of the top-level menus on the Excel menu bar are of type `msoControlPopup`. Rather than doing anything directly, they just display their associated submenu. This is the *only* control type that can display a submenu.

For custom controls, the default value for this setting is `msoControlButton`. We examine how you use each of these control types in more detail in the *Putting It All Together* section later in this chapter.

NOTE: If you look in the VBE Object Browser, you will discover that there are anywhere from 21 to 27 different `msoControlType` enumeration members depending on the version of Excel you are using. Unfortunately, you are limited to one of the five members listed above when building custom CommandBarControls.

Controls with some of the other enumeration member types can be added to a custom command bar by adding a built-in control of those types (by adding the Borders button from the Formatting toolbar, for example, whose type is `msoControlSplitButtonPopup`). Some of the `msoControlType` enumeration members simply haven't been implemented. `msoControlOCXDropdown` is one example.

Control Style

This setting applies to CommandBarControl objects. It specifies the visual layout of the control. This setting does not apply to the Control Types `msoControlEdit` or `msoControlPopup`. It applies to the other control types in the following manner:

- `msoControlButton`—Must be one of the following `msoButtonStyle` enumeration members:
  - `msoButtonAutomatic`—This is the default value for controls of type `msoControlButton`. For a menu item, this is equivalent to `msoButtonIconAndCaption`. For a toolbar button, this is equivalent to `msoButtonIcon`.
  - `msoButtonCaption`—This style displays only the caption assigned to the control. Any icon assigned to the control is ignored.
  - `msoButtonIcon`—This style is a bit confusing. It displays only the *icon* for toolbar buttons and only the *caption* for menu items. If no icon is specified for a toolbar button with this style, a blank button will be created.
  - `msoButtonIconAndCaption`—This style displays the icon and places the caption to the right of the icon for both menu items and toolbar buttons.
  - `msoButtonIconAndCaptionBelow`—This style has exactly the same effect as `msoButtonIconAndCaption` for menu items. For toolbar buttons it displays the caption centered below the icon.
  - `msoButtonIconAndWrapCaption`—This style is similar to the `msoButtonIconAndCaption` style, but it wraps long captions to the right of the icon instead of displaying them on a single line. This style gives very poor visual results when used with menu items, so we recommend against using it for that type of control.
  - `msoButtonIconAndWrapCaptionBelow`—For toolbar buttons this style is similar to the `msoButtonIconAndCaptionBelow` style except that long captions are wrapped beneath the button icon. For menu items this style gives exactly the same poor results as the `msoButtonIconAndWrapCaption` style, so we recommend against using it for that type of control.

- `msoButtonWrapCaption`—This style is similar to the `msoButtonCaption` style in that it ignores any icon assigned to the control. The difference is that it wraps long captions rather than displaying them on a single line.
- `msoControlComboBox` and `msoControlDropdown`—Must be one of the following `msoComboStyle` enumeration members:
  - `msoComboNormal`—This is the default value for controls of type `msoControlComboBox` and `msoControlDropdown`. It simply displays the control with no caption.
  - `msoComboLabel`—This style displays the caption directly to the left of the combo box or drop-down control.

Because the Control Style setting does not apply to controls of type `msoControlPopup`, you cannot modify the default appearance of this type of control. There is no workaround for this limitation. Because the Control Style setting does not apply to controls of type `msoControlEdit`, you cannot provide a caption for these controls. If your edit box control is located on a toolbar, you can work around this limitation by adding a nonfunctional `msoControlButton` with the `msoButtonCaption` style that displays the caption you desire directly to the left of the edit box control. We demonstrate this workaround in the *Putting It All Together* section later in this chapter.

Face ID

This setting applies to CommandBarControl objects. It specifies the icon that will be associated with the control. The Face ID setting can be specified in one of three ways:

1. You can use the icon from a built-in control by specifying its ID as the value for the Face ID setting.
2. You can use a custom icon by specifying its name. This icon must be a 16×16 pixel graphic that has been placed on the wksCommandBars worksheet. We will demonstrate this in the *Putting It All Together* section later in the chapter.
3. When operating under Excel 2002 or higher, you have the option of specifying an icon and a mask. This method provides significantly superior visual results for these versions of Excel. Both the icon and the mask must be 16×16 pixel graphics that are located on the wksCommandBars worksheet. The icon and mask picture

names must be entered together into the Face ID cell separated by a forward slash (/) character. We discuss this method in more detail in the *Loading Custom Icons from Files* and *Hooking Command Bar Control Events* sections later in the chapter.

Note that the icon picture from the icon/mask pair will automatically be used in versions of Excel earlier than Excel 2002, making method three equivalent to method two when running on down-level versions of Excel.

The most important characteristic of a custom icon is that its background appear transparent when applied to a control. To use custom icons under Excel 97/2000, you must use the *Set Transparent Color* control from the Picture toolbar to specify a transparent background color for the single picture that will become the custom icon for your control. This method is illustrated by the before and after pictures shown in Figure 8-4 and Figure 8-5.

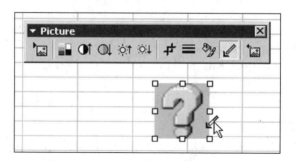

Figure 8-4 An Icon Picture Before Setting the Transparent Background

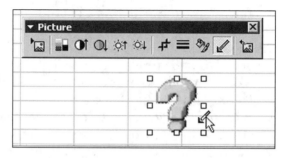

Figure 8-5 An Icon Picture After Setting the Transparent Background

Just place the *Set Transparent Color* control cursor over the color in your picture that you want to become transparent and click. That color will disappear and the background will show through it.

We have demonstrated this example with a picture that has been enlarged enough so that you can see what is happening. This is typically the way you would perform this operation in the real world as well. A 16×16 picture is too small to accurately point at the desired background color when you are dealing with a complex icon. Just stretch the picture out to a size large enough so that you can see what you are doing, set the transparent background color, then revert the picture to its original size in the following manner:

1. Right-click over the picture and choose *Format Picture* from the shortcut menu.
2. In the Format Picture dialog, select the *Size* tab.
3. Click the *Reset* button in the lower-right corner of the *Size* tab.

Excel 97/2000, Excel 2002 and Excel 2003 all use different UI drawing techniques, so picture backgrounds set to be transparent in one version of Excel will not appear transparent in other versions. As you will see in the section on *Loading Custom Icons from Files* later in the chapter, two new methods were added to the CommandBarButton object in Excel 2002 that enable you to load pictures directly into the control in a manner that is independent of their appearance on the worksheet.

For this reason we recommend that you use the icon/mask method described in point 3 above for creating custom icons in Excel 2002 and higher, while setting the transparent background color of the icon picture using Excel 97/2000. This gives the command bar builder an appropriately formatted icon for use in Excel 97/2000. It will automatically use method two under these versions of Excel. You do not have to do anything special to the mask picture, because the mask is not used under Excel 97/2000.

Begin Group

This setting applies to CommandBarControl objects. It is a True/False setting that specifies whether a separator bar will be placed above or to the left of the specified control depending on context. A value of True adds a separator bar. False is the default value for this setting; so if False is specified or this setting is left blank, no separator bar will be created.

Before

This setting applies to CommandBarControl objects. It is used to position a new control before an existing control. If the controls are arranged horizontally, the Before setting will place your control to the left of the control specified. If the controls are arranged vertically, the Before setting will place your control above the control specified.

The existing control can be specified either by its name or ID number. This setting is not required and there is no default value. If this setting is left blank or if the control specified by this setting cannot be located, this setting will be ignored. In this case, the control will be added at the system default position, which is at the end of the current set of controls on the same level. The Before setting is typically used to position controls that are being added to built-in Excel command bars.

Tooltip

This setting applies to CommandBarControl objects. It specifies the text that will be contained in the yellow tooltip message that displays when the user hovers the mouse pointer over the control. This setting does not apply to controls of type `msoControlPopup` or to any child control of an `msoControlPopup` control. If the Tooltip setting is not specified, the system default value displayed in the tooltip is the caption of the control.

Shortcut Text

This setting applies to CommandBarControl objects. It displays the keyboard shortcut that will be assigned to the control directly to the right of the caption for the control. This setting applies only to controls of type `msoControlButton` that are child controls of an `msoControlPopup` control (that is, menu items on a submenu). Specifying this setting does not actually assign the specified keyboard shortcut to the macro assigned to the OnAction setting of the control. You must do this separately in your own code. The Shortcut Text setting is not required and there is no default value.

Tag

This setting applies to CommandBarControl objects. It enables you to store String data for your own use. The Tag setting does not modify the appearance or function of the control in any way. One common use of this setting is to differentiate among controls that have been assigned the same OnAction procedure.

Assume you have assigned the OnAction settings of three controls to the same procedure. You then assign the values 1, 2 and 3 to the Tag settings of the first, second and third controls, respectively. When the specified OnAction procedure is called by one of these controls, you can identify the control that called it in the manner shown in Listing 8-1 and conditionally redirect program execution based on the result.

Listing 8-1 Distinguishing Controls Using the Tag Setting

```
Public Sub MyProcedure()

    Dim lControl As Long

    ' Retrieve the Tag value of the control that
    ' called this procedure.
    lControl = CLng(CommandBars.ActionControl.Tag)

    Select Case lControl
        Case 1
            ' Perform the action for control 1.
        Case 2
            ' Perform the action for control 2.
        Case 3
            ' Perform the action for control 3.
    End Select

End Sub
```

As you will see in the *Hooking Command Bar Control Events* section later in the chapter, the Tag setting is also used to specify the custom controls whose events you want to hook as a group.

Parameter

This setting applies to CommandBarControl objects. It is functionally identical to the Tag setting. It is a place for the programmer to store String data that will not have any effect on the appearance or function of the control.

State

This setting applies to CommandBarControl objects. It enables you to create checked menu items or depressed toolbar buttons. The value for this setting must be one of the following `msoButtonState` enumeration members:

- `msoButtonDown`—For toolbar buttons this creates the visual effect of the button being depressed. For menu items, the effect depends on whether there is an icon displayed with the menu item. For menu items with icons, the icon will appear depressed in a fashion very similar to the effect on toolbar buttons. For menu items without an icon, a depressed check mark will be added to the left of the menu caption.
- `msoButtonMixed`—For all current versions of Excel, this value is indistinguishable from `msoButtonDown`. It is included in the command bar builder in case it becomes supported for some different purpose in a future version of Excel.
- `msoButtonUp`—This is the default value for this setting. A State value of `msoButtonUp` has no effect on the appearance of newly created controls. This value only comes into play as a way to remove the effect of the `msoButtonDown` or `msoButtonMixed` values.

The State setting applies only to custom controls of type `msoControlButton`. Keep in mind that the State property is a dynamic property of the control. The command bar builder will create the control with whatever initial State value you specify, but after the control has been created you will need to write custom code to modify the State property appropriately in response to user actions. We demonstrate this in the *Putting It All Together* section later in the chapter.

ListRange and Lists

These settings apply to CommandBarControl objects of type `msoControlComboBox` or `msoControlDropdown`. We discuss these settings together because they are, in effect, a single setting that specifies the list to be loaded into a combo box or drop-down control. The purpose of these settings is as follows:

- **ListRange**—This value specifies the address of the range on the wksCommandBars worksheet that holds the list to be loaded into the control. The specified range must be located in the Lists column. Like all other settings described so far, the ListRange setting must be located on the same row as the control to which it applies.

- **Lists**—This setting is a list of values that will be loaded into the control. This is the only setting that does not have to be located on the same row as the control it applies to, and as we discuss below, it should not be located in rows that are part of any command bar or control definition.

You should always place your lists below the last command bar definition in the table. By doing this, if you need to insert or delete rows in a command bar definition, you will not inadvertently alter one of your lists. For similar reasons, use a dynamic formula to create the list address value for the ListRange setting. If you hard-code the list address and then insert or delete rows in the command bar definition table, the list address will no longer be valid. Use of a dynamically adjusting formula to specify the list location solves this problem. An example of a dynamically adjusting List address formula is shown here:

```
=ADDRESS(ROW(Y48),COLUMN(Y48))&":"&ADDRESS(ROW(Y53),COLUMN(Y53))
```

This formula indicates that the Lists setting is located in column Y of the command bar definition worksheet. The list currently starts in row 48 of that column and ends in row 53 of that column. Notice, however, that this formula uses relative addresses. If you insert or delete rows above the list, the addresses specified in the formula will automatically adjust to the new location of the list. The result of this formula, as displayed in the ListRange cell and as read by the command bar builder code, is shown here:

```
$Y$48:$Y$53
```

The command bar builder will use the range specified by this address as the list to be loaded into the control defined in the row in which the ListRange setting is located. Note that the last command bar definition in this example ends at row 47. Therefore, placing the list below row 47 ensures that any subsequent insertions or deletions within the command bar definition table will not have any effect on the contents of the list. We demonstrate this technique in the *Putting It All Together* section later in the chapter.

Post Mortem

Although it seems as if every command bar and control property under the sun has been covered here, we're not even close. Only the most frequently used properties have been included in the command bar builder. Other properties that you may find an occasional need for can always be manually coded into your application.

Examples of properties that are not included in the command bar builder are the Height and RowIndex properties of the CommandBar object, because in our experience these properties are rarely used when building command bars. Properties of the CommandBarControl object that are not supported include the DescriptionText property, because it simply duplicates the purpose of the Tag and/or Parameter properties and the HyperLinkType property, because it is so rarely used.

There are also dynamic properties such as IsEnabled and State whose initial values are set by the command bar builder, but whose subsequent values must be managed by custom code in your application as the need to change them arises.

Putting It All Together

In this section we create several common variations of command bars that are not associated with any application. We use these examples to demonstrate many of the settings described in the previous section.

In this example we use the version of the command bar builder code that has been integrated with the error handling system to be described in *Chapter 12 — VBA Error Handling*. Because the primary focus of this section is creating a valid command bar definition table, this should not cause any problems. All of the error handling techniques you'll see in the code for this example are fully explained in *Chapter 12 — VBA Error Handling*.

The error handled command bar builder is the one we strongly recommend you use in your own projects, so bear with us if you're looking at the code and it isn't clear what all of it does. If you do use this version of the command bar builder, you will need to import one additional module besides the three listed at the beginning of the chapter. This is the MErrorHandler module containing all the error handling code referenced by the command bar builder.

The code for this example is located in the CommandBarDemo.xls workbook that can be found on the CD in the *Concepts\Ch08—Advanced Command Bar Handling* folder. We strongly recommend that you open this workbook and follow along while you read this section. The command bar definition table is physically too large to enable us to use screen shots to display all of the important information we'll be discussing.

The command bars in the CommandBarDemo.xls workbook will be built automatically whenever the workbook is opened. Three types of custom command bar are demonstrated:

1. A custom menu containing submenus added to the existing worksheet menu bar
2. A custom toolbar
3. A custom right-click command bar

Figure 8-6 shows the complete set of custom command bars created by the CommandBarDemo.xls workbook. To remove the custom command bars and close the workbook, select *Custom > Exit* from the Excel menu.

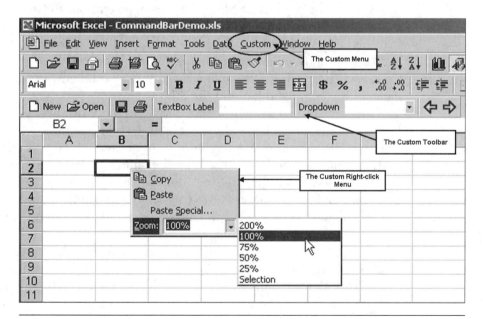

Figure 8-6 The Custom Command Bars Example

Adding a Custom Menu with Submenus to the Worksheet Menu Bar

Figure 8-7 shows the command bar definition table layout required to add a new top-level menu to the Worksheet Menu Bar.

	A	B	C	D	E
1	**Command Bar Name**	**Control Caption**	**Control Caption**	**Control Caption**	**Position**
2	Worksheet Menu Bar				
3		&Custom			
4			Sub Menu &1		
5			Sub Menu &2		
6				Sub Menu Item &1	
7				Sub Menu Item &2	
8				Sub Menu Item &3	
9			&Exit		
10	Stop				

Figure 8-7 Adding a Custom Menu to the Worksheet Menu Bar

Notice that Worksheet Menu Bar has been entered for the Command Bar Name setting value. The command bar building code will recognize that this command bar already exists and will add all subsequently defined controls to the existing command bar. As explained in the section on the Command Bar Name setting above, there can be no entries between the name of the command bar and the Stop keyword.

The new top-level menu we are adding to the Worksheet Menu Bar is located in the first of the three Control Caption columns. Its name is Custom. The ampersand character in front of the first letter of the control caption indicates the letter C will be the shortcut key for this menu. We have also used the Before setting (not shown here) in the command bar definition table to specify that the Custom menu will be added directly to the left of the Window menu. This is the standard position for custom menus added to the Worksheet Menu Bar.

All subsequent controls will be constructed as child menus at some level below the Custom menu. You can verify this is the case because the Control Caption column entries visually display the menu hierarchy. In this case, no Control Caption entries exist below the Custom entry, so all subsequent controls must be children of this menu. The full Custom menu is shown in Figure 8-8.

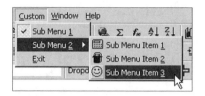

Figure 8-8 The Custom Menu

Unless specified otherwise, all the custom controls in this example have their OnAction settings assigned to the GeneralDemo procedure shown in Listing 8-2. When a menu or toolbar button with this OnAction assignment is clicked, a message box containing the caption of the control that called the procedure will display. This is a very simple example of how you can use a single procedure to handle multiple controls.

Listing 8-2 The GeneralDemo Procedure

```
Public Sub GeneralDemo()
    Dim sCaller As String
    sCaller = CommandBars.ActionControl.Caption
    MsgBox sCaller & " was clicked.", vbInformation, gsAPP_TITLE
End Sub
```

The Custom menu has three submenus:

1. Submenu 1—We use this control to demonstrate the use of the State setting. This control is initially created with its State set to msoButtonDown, as demonstrated by the depressed checkmark displayed to the left of the control in Figure 8-8. Submenu 1 is assigned to a special procedure called StateDemo that toggles the State of the control between msoButtonDown and msoButtonUp each time it is clicked. The StateDemo procedure is shown in Listing 8-3.

Listing 8-3 The StateDemo Procedure

```
Public Sub StateDemo()
    Dim ctlCaller As CommandBarButton
    Dim sMsg As String
```

```
    Set ctlCaller = CommandBars.ActionControl
    If ctlCaller.State = msoButtonDown Then
        ' Switch to msoButtonUp.
        ctlCaller.State = msoButtonUp
        sMsg = "The state has been switched to up."
    Else
        ' Switch to msoButtonDown.
        ctlCaller.State = msoButtonDown
        sMsg = "The state has been switched to down."
    End If
    MsgBox sMsg, vbInformation, gsAPP_TITLE
End Sub
```

2. **Submenu 2**—We use this control to demonstrate third-level submenus (often referred to as submenu items). Submenu 2 is a control of type `msoControlPopup`. As shown in Figure 8-7, it contains three submenu items. Each of these submenu items has had its FaceID setting assigned to the ID number of a built-in control. As explained in the section on the FaceID setting above, assigning the ID number of a built-in control to the FaceID setting of a custom control enables you to give your control the appearance of the built-in control without taking on any of its other characteristics.

3. **Exit**—This is just a plain vanilla submenu control that is used to exit the demo application. Its OnAction setting is assigned to the AppExit procedure, which initiates shutdown of the application.

Adding a Custom Toolbar

Figure 8-9 shows the command bar definition table layout required to create our custom toolbar. Because the toolbar requires only a single level of Control Caption settings, we've used the freeze panes feature to scroll the table over to show some of the additional settings used to create the controls on the toolbar.

If you're following along with the actual workbook example, you'll see that the row in the command bar definition table used to specify the toolbar required only a single setting: Visible = TRUE. This lack of a requirement for explicit settings in most of the command bar definition table columns is pervasive and it represents one of the primary strengths of this system.

	O13	▼	=	=msoButtonIconAndCaption		

	A	B	L	M	N	O
1	Command Bar Name	Control Caption	OnAction	Control ID	Control Type	Control Style
12	Custom Toolbar					
13		New	GeneralDemo			3
14		Open	GeneralDemo			3
15		Save		3		
16		Print		4		
17		TextBox Label				2
18		Textbox	HandleTextBox		2	
19		Dropdown	HandleDropDown		3	1
20		Previous	GeneralDemo			
21		Next	GeneralDemo			
22	Stop					

Figure 8-9 Adding a Custom Toolbar

The default values for all settings are designed to be the values you will use most frequently when building command bars and controls. Therefore, the command bar definition table requires very few entries for the majority of command bars and controls you will build with it. Just be sure you understand what the default entries are. If you're ever unsure, read the cell comment at the top of the column. Any defaults will be listed there as well as any other critical information required to use the setting controlled by that column correctly.

The toolbar built by the command bar definition in Figure 8-9 is shown in Figure 8-10.

Figure 8-10 The Custom Toolbar

The controls on the Custom Toolbar are used to demonstrate a number a features of the command bar builder:

- **New and Open**—As you can see in Figure 8-9, there is no Control ID value specified for the New or Open buttons. This means they will be created as custom controls. Both OnAction settings use the GeneralDemo procedure shown in Listing 8-2 and their FaceID settings (not shown) are the ID numbers of the built-in New and Open controls, respectively.

What makes these controls different from your average toolbar buttons are their Control Style settings. As shown in Figure 8-9, these controls have a Control Style of `msoButton IconAndCaption`. Rather than simply displaying an icon alone, this style displays the controls with their captions to the right of their icons. This is a somewhat unusual but often very useful display technique when you have room on your toolbar to use it. The meanings of toolbar buttons often tend to be obscure based on the icon alone. Adding a caption to a toolbar button can make its purpose much more obvious.

- **Save and Print**—As you can see in Figure 8-9, these buttons have Control ID values other than 1. In this case the Control ID values are the ID values for the built-in Save and Print controls, respectively. This means the built-in Save and Print controls have been added to our custom toolbar with all of their appearance and function intact. These controls have no OnAction setting because they would ignore it. Clicking either one of these controls causes them to perform the same action they would perform as built-in controls.
- **TextBox Label and TextBox**—This set of controls is used to demonstrate how you can add a text box control to your toolbar and fake a caption for it by placing a nonfunctional CommandBarButton control with the desired caption to the left of the text box control. In Figure 8-9 you can see that the OnAction settings of the text box control is assigned to a special-purpose procedure called HandleTextBox, shown in Listing 8-4.

Listing 8-4 The HandleTextBox Procedure

```
Public Sub HandleTextBox()
    Dim ctlCaller As CommandBarControl
    Set ctlCaller = CommandBars.ActionControl
    MsgBox "You entered: '" & ctlCaller.Text & "'."
End Sub
```

This procedure performs exactly the same function as the GeneralDemo procedure except it displays the value entered in the text box control.

- **Dropdown**—This control demonstrates how to add a control of type `msoControlComboBox` or `msoControlDropdown` to your toolbar. This specific example demonstrates an `msoControlDropdown` control, but the two types of controls are almost identical. Everything you see in this example can be applied to a control of type `msoControlComboBox`.

In Figure 8-9, note that the Control Style setting for the drop-down control has a value of 1. This is the value of the `msoComboLabel` style. It causes the caption of the drop-down to display to the left of the control itself. The OnAction setting of the drop-down control is assigned to the custom HandleDropDown procedure shown in Listing 8-5.

Listing 8-5 The HandleDropDown Procedure

```
Public Sub HandleDropDown()
    Dim ctlCaller As CommandBarComboBox
    Set ctlCaller = CommandBars.ActionControl
    MsgBox "You selected: '" & ctlCaller.Text & "'."
End Sub
```

After you select an entry from the drop-down list, this procedure displays the list item you selected.

- **Previous and Next**—These controls demonstrate how to apply custom icons to your controls. In Figure 8-11, you can see the Previous and Next Control Caption settings, their Face ID settings that specify named pictures and the two pictures named by the Face ID settings, which happen to be located in the Begin Group column. (They can be located anywhere on the wksCommandBars worksheet.)

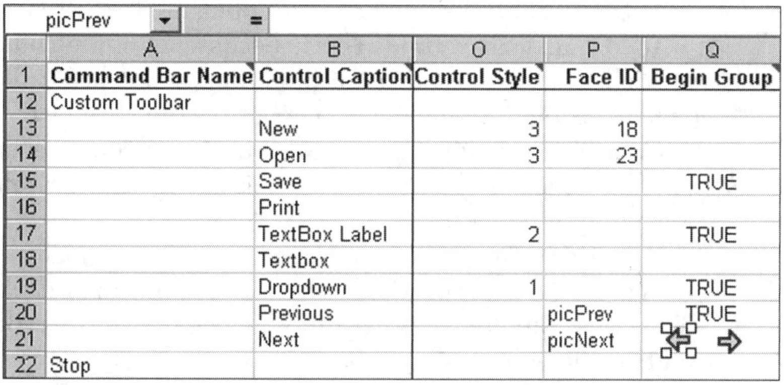

	A	B	O	P	Q
picPrev					=
1	**Command Bar Name**	**Control Caption**	**Control Style**	**Face ID**	**Begin Group**
12	Custom Toolbar				
13		New	3	18	
14		Open	3	23	
15		Save			TRUE
16		Print			
17		TextBox Label	2		TRUE
18		Textbox			
19		Dropdown	1		TRUE
20		Previous		picPrev	TRUE
21		Next		picNext	
22	Stop				

Figure 8-11 Custom Icons on the Toolbar

In Figure 8-11 the picture for the Previous button is selected and you can see that its name, as shown in the name box directly to the left of the formula bar, is exactly the same as the name specified for the Previous control in its Face ID setting (cell P20).

For simplicity's sake we have not demonstrated the icon/mask combination in this Face ID example. The Face ID settings shown above will work in any version of Excel, although not necessarily with optimal appearance. We cover the more complex icon/mask method of setting the Face ID property in the sections that follow.

Adding a Custom Right-Click Command Bar

Figure 8-12 shows the command bar definition table layout required to create our custom right-click command bar. If you examine the Position setting for this command bar, you will see that its value has been set to msoBarPopup.

	A	B	L	M	N
1	Command Bar Name	Control Caption	OnAction	Control ID	Control Type
24	Custom Popup				
25		Copy		19	
26		Paste		22	
27		Paste Special		755	
28		Zoom		1733	
29	Stop				

Figure 8-12 Adding a Custom Right-Click Command Bar

The only control setting on this command bar with values assigned to it is the Control ID setting. This is because all of the controls on our custom right-click menu are built-in controls. Not just built-in controls by appearance, but the actual built-in controls specified by the ID numbers in the Control ID column, including all of their features and attributes. The right-click command bar built by this command bar table definition is shown in Figure 8-13.

We have replaced the built-in command bar normally invoked by right-clicking over a worksheet cell with our custom right-click command bar. This was accomplished using the workbook-level SheetBeforeRightClick event, as shown in Listing 8-6.

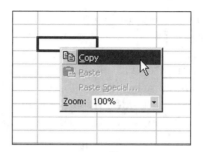

Figure 8-13 The Custom Right-Click Command Bar

Listing 8-6 The Workbook_SheetBeforeRightClick Event Handler

```
Private Sub Workbook_SheetBeforeRightClick(ByVal Sh As Object, _
                  ByVal Target As Range, Cancel As Boolean)

    Dim cbrBar As CommandBar

    ' Only attempt to display the custom right-click
    ' command bar if it exists.
    On Error Resume Next
        Set cbrBar = Nothing
        Set cbrBar = Application.CommandBars("Custom Popup")
    On Error GoTo 0

    If Not cbrBar Is Nothing Then
        ' Show our custom right-click command bar.
        cbrBar.ShowPopup
        ' Cancel the default action of the right-click.
        Cancel = True
    End If

End Sub
```

As Figure 8-13 shows, the controls on our custom right-click menu are behaving exactly like their corresponding Excel controls. Because we have not yet copied anything, both the Paste and Paste Special menus are disabled. The Copy menu is enabled, allowing us to copy a range. The Zoom control is enabled because we can modify the zoom at any time.

We do not need to take any action to make these controls behave in this manner because we are using the built-in controls themselves. Excel ensures they behave appropriately. In the *Hooking Command Bar Control Events* section, you will see how we can have the best of both worlds. By hooking command bar control events, we can utilize the appearance of built-in controls provided by Excel while also having them run the custom code of our choice rather than perform their normal actions.

Loading Custom Icons from Files

As explained in the section on the FaceID setting above, each version of Excel from 2000 onward uses a slightly different UI drawing technique. This means custom icons stored as pictures on a worksheet will only appear correctly in the version of Excel in which they were optimized.

For applications running under Excel 2002 or higher, there is a second way to apply custom icons to command bar controls that eliminates the problems associated with the different drawing techniques used by different versions of Excel. The command bar builder supports this method automatically, but in this section we will explain how to use it manually so you can take advantage of it in an application that does not use the command bar builder.

Beginning with Office XP, two new properties were added to the CommandBarButton object. These two properties enable you to load icons directly into the control. The Picture property specifies the bitmap to be used as the foreground of the icon and the Mask property specifies the bitmap that indicates which areas of the icon should be rendered as transparent background. In the next section, we show you how to create these bitmaps.

Because this method requires two bitmap files for each icon, if you have a large number of custom icons it can become unwieldy due to the number of files you must distribute. In *Chapter 20 — Combining Excel and Visual Basic 6* we show how you can package up all of your custom icons into a single DLL resource file. Alternatively, if you are using the command bar builder, you can host both the icon and mask picture files on the wksCommandBars worksheet.

Creating Bitmap Files for Icons and Masks

If you plan to create custom icons on a regular basis, it probably makes sense to purchase a special-purpose icon creation program. For the occasional custom icon, however, every version of Windows comes with a perfectly serviceable icon creation tool: Microsoft Paint.

The type of file you will need to create for use as a CommandBarButton icon is a 16×16 pixel 16-color bitmap. The icon file will contain the artistic foreground picture you think of as your icon. The mask file is an overlay for the icon file in which everything foreground is colored black and everything you want to be transparent background is colored white.

To create a custom icon, open Microsoft Paint. Paint will open with a blank default image canvas. Select *Image > Attributes* from the Paint menu. In the Attributes dialog, set *Width* and *Height* to 16, *Units* to Pixels and *Colors* to Color. These settings are shown in Figure 8-14.

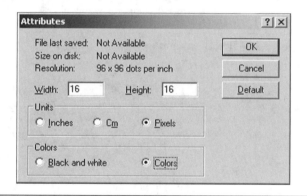

Figure 8-14 The Icon Attributes Settings

Click the OK button on the Attributes dialog and select *View > Zoom > Custom* from the Paint menu. Select 800% as your *Zoom to* setting. The resulting image canvas is shown in Figure 8-15.

You are now ready to draw your icon. Drawing icons well requires much practice. The appearance of a 16×16 pixel image at 800 percent magnification is often nothing like its appearance at normal size. We've provided a simple custom icon image you can use for testing purposes. This icon is called Arrows.bmp and is located on the CD in the *\Concepts\Ch08—Advanced Command Bar Handling* folder. This icon is shown loaded into Paint in Figure 8-16.

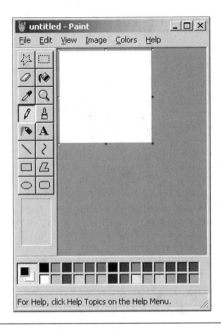

Figure 8-15 The Blank Icon Canvas in Paint

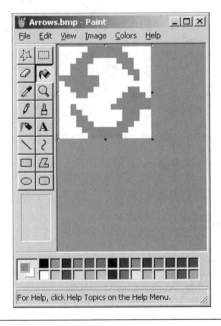

Figure 8-16 The Arrows Icon

The mask file for the arrows icon is called ArrowsMask.bmp and is located in the same CD folder as the Arrows.bmp file. As you can see in Figure 8-17, this file simply replaces the blue foreground color of the original icon with black. When loaded into the CommandBarButton, the areas of the icon corresponding to the black areas of the mask will display, while the areas of the icon corresponding to the white areas of the mask will be transparent.

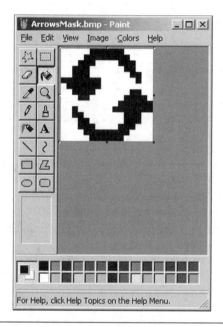

Figure 8-17 The Mask File for the Arrows Icon

Using Bitmap Files as CommandBarButton Icons

Now that we have our icon and mask bitmaps, it's a simple matter to apply them to a CommandBarButton. The procedures shown in Listing 8-7 build a command bar with a single button that uses our custom arrow icon and mask. You can find this code in the LoadPictureAndMask.xls workbook located on the CD in the \Concepts\Ch08—Advanced Command Bar Handling folder. Note that this example only works in Excel 2002 or later.

Listing 8-7 Adding a Custom Icon to a CommandBarButton

```
Public Sub CreateBar()

    Dim cbrBar As CommandBar
    Dim ctlControl As CommandBarButton
    Dim sPath As String

    ' Make sure any previously created version of our demo
    ' command bar is deleted.
    RemoveBar

    ' We're assuming that the bitmap files used to create the
    ' custom icon are located in the same path as this workbook.
    sPath = ThisWorkbook.Path
    If Right$(sPath, 1) <> "\" Then sPath = sPath & "\"

    ' Create a toolbar-type command bar.
    Set cbrBar = CommandBars.Add("Demo", msoBarTop, False, True)
    cbrBar.Visible = True

    ' Add the command bar button control.
    Set ctlControl = cbrBar.Controls.Add(msoControlButton)
    ' Load the foreground bitmap file.
    ctlControl.Picture = LoadPicture(sPath & "Arrows.bmp")
    ' Load the mask bitmap file.
    ctlControl.Mask = LoadPicture(sPath & "ArrowsMask.bmp")

End Sub

Public Sub RemoveBar()
    On Error Resume Next
    CommandBars("Demo").Delete
End Sub
```

To create the command bar button with the custom icon, run the CreateBar procedure. To remove the demo command bar and its button, run the RemoveBar procedure. The resulting custom icon appears as shown in Figure 8-18.

Figure 8-18 The Arrows Custom Icon

Hooking Command Bar Control Events

In Office 2000, Microsoft added the Click event to the Command-BarButton object and the Change event to the CommandBarComboBox object to provide an event-based mechanism for working with command bar controls in addition to the OnAction property. The primary reason for this was to allow controls to be used by non-VBA code, such as COM Add-ins, which were introduced at the same time. There are, however, subtle differences in the behavior of a control when using an event hook compared to using the OnAction property. We can exploit this behavior to our advantage in VBA.

Why Use an Event Hook

Setting the OnAction property is usually the easiest option for custom command bar controls; when the control is clicked, the procedure specified by the OnAction property is called. Using an event hook enables us to interact with controls in three additional ways that cannot be accomplished using the OnAction property:

1. Hook the Click events of the built-in controls, giving us a Before_xxx event for any control that we hook.

2. Hook the Click events of both built-in and custom controls in other Office applications, including the VBE. For example, if we're using Excel to automate Word, our Excel code can respond to the user clicking a control in Word—either a built-in Word control or one we have created.

3. Hook the Click events of both built-in and custom controls from outside VBA, such as when automating Excel from Visual Basic (*Chapter 20 — Combining Excel and Visual Basic 6*), within COM Add-ins (*Chapter 21 — Writing Add-ins with Visual Basic 6*) or in VSTO solutions (*Chapter 22 — Using VB.NET and the Visual Studio Tools for Office*).

What Can an Event Hook Do

When hooking custom controls, event hooks behave exactly like OnAction procedures. They run when the control is clicked. When hooking built-in controls, however, the event hook is called *before the built-in process*, effectively giving us a Before_xxx event in which to run any code we want and/or cancel the built-in processing.

For example, in *Chapter 6 — Dictator Applications* we used an OnKey assignment to ensure that the Ctrl+V keyboard shortcut pasted only values into our data-entry forms. If we also hook the *Edit > Paste* menu, we could check to see whether the cell being pasted into was within our data-entry form. If so, we would replace it with a *Paste Special > Values* and cancel Excel's default paste behavior using the CancelDefault argument supplied by the Click event procedure. Otherwise we would let Excel perform a normal paste operation.

Within the Click event procedure we could also use the `Application.OnTime` method to run a routine immediately after Excel has done its normal process, effectively giving us an After_xxx event. This method will only work within an Excel-based add-in.

We can also use event hooks to implement custom controls that are enabled and disabled automatically as the environment changes. For example, the built-in *Paste Values* control is only enabled when there is something on the clipboard to paste and a cell selected to paste into. We can use event hooks to create our own custom buttons that are enabled and disabled in the same way. All we need to do is create a copy of the *Paste Values* control, give it a different icon, add our own code to the click event and cancel the default behavior. Because our custom controls are based on a built-in control, Excel handles their enable/disable behavior for us. We will demonstrate this in *The Paste Special Command Bar* example below.

The Importance of the Tag Property

When you use a WithEvents object declaration to hook a CommandBarButton or CommandBarComboBox, you're not actually hooking that specific instance of the control, but rather that control ID for built-in controls or that ID/Tag property combination for custom controls. This means when you hook one of the built-in controls, your event will be fired whenever *any* instance of that control is clicked, a big advantage over having to search for every instance of the control and hook each one (including having to determine whether the user has dragged a new one on to their toolbar at some point during your application's operation).

Custom controls with an ID of 1 and no Tag assignment are treated as unique, individual controls for the purposes of a WithEvents assignment. This is a safety mechanism built in to the event hooking system. If hooking any custom control with an ID/Tag combination of 1/<blank> meant hooking all custom controls with that ID/Tag combination you might be hooking a very large number of controls indeed, including many that didn't even belong to your application.

To take advantage of multiple simultaneous event hooks for our custom controls, we need to assign the same Tag value to all of the custom controls we want to hook together. We can then use the Parameter value of the Ctrl argument passed to the event to identify which control was clicked and decide what to do with it.

We can also have a custom control emulate the enabled/disabled behavior of a built-in control automatically. We do this by assigning the ID value of the built-in control whose behavior we want to emulate to the Control ID value of our custom control. We then give that control a unique Tag value and set up the event hook. Excel will manage the enabled/disabled behavior of our custom control but the control will run the code we assign to it in the event handler.

This is actually just a special case of hooking a built-in control. And because we are hooking the ID of a built-in control, that built-in control will also activate our event handler. We can use the Tag value of the Ctrl argument passed to the event procedure to determine whether the event was fired by our custom control or the built-in control whose behavior our custom control emulates. If there is no Tag, we know the built-in control called the event. In this case we simply do nothing and allow Excel to perform its default process for the control. If the Tag property is set, we know our custom control called the event. In this case we cancel Excel's default action and run our own code in its place.

If we want to have multiple custom controls, all with the same enabled/disabled behavior but each with different actions, we can give these controls the same Control ID and Tag values so they all fire the same event hook, then use the Parameter value to uniquely identify each control in order to conditionally execute the correct code for it in the event handler. This is all very confusing, but it will become clear once you see the example in the next section.

The Paste Special Command Bar

After you have copied a range, Excel provides a number of very useful paste special options that are buried under the *Edit > Paste Special* menu. Built-in toolbar buttons are provided for two commonly used paste special options: *Paste Values* and *Paste Formatting*. What we want, however, is a toolbar that exposes **all** of the most commonly used paste special options.

All of the buttons on this toolbar should have the same enabled/disabled behavior exhibited by the built-in *Paste Values* button, but they should run the operation-specific code that we assign to them. In this section we take advantage of command bar control event hooking to create this toolbar. The workbook that implements this example is called PasteSpecialBar.xls and is located on the CD in the \Concepts\Ch08—Advanced Command Bar Handling folder. We strongly recommend that you open this workbook and examine it while you read this section.

The Paste Special Toolbar Definition

The first step in creating our Paste Special toolbar is to write the correct definition for it in the command bar definition table. The complete command bar definition table for this toolbar is too wide to fit within a single screen shot, so we show a series of screen shots that utilize the Excel freeze panes feature to display several of the most important sections of the definition table. Showing the entire command bar definition table for our Paste Special toolbar would require more screen shots than we have room for, so please follow along with the example workbook provided on the CD.

In Figure 8-19 we show the basic structure and definition of the Paste Special toolbar and its controls.

	A	B	L	M	N
1	Command Bar Name	Control Caption	OnAction	Control ID	Control Type
2	Paste Special				
3		All		370	
4		Formulas		370	
5		Values		370	
6		Formatting		370	
7		Comments		370	
8		Validation		370	
9		Column Widths		370	
10	Stop				

Figure 8-19 The Basic Paste Special Toolbar Definition

Our Paste Special toolbar will be constructed as an msoBarFloating CommandBar with seven controls of type msoControlButton. Note that all of the controls on the toolbar have been assigned the same built-in Control ID value 370. This number is the ID of the built-in *Paste Values* CommandBarButton. What we are doing is creating seven identical copies of the built-in *Paste Values* control that we will later modify to perform different actions. We do this because even after our modifications, Excel will treat these controls as if they were copies of the *Paste Values* control for the purpose of enabling and disabling them. This is exactly what we want.

In Figure 8-20 we demonstrate how we are setting the appearance of our seven controls.

Let's start with the Values button. Because all of the controls on our toolbar are copies of the built-in *Paste Values* control, and this control is actually included on our toolbar, we don't have to specify anything for its Face ID setting. It will take on the appearance of the *Paste Values* control by default. Next, look at the Face ID setting for the Formatting control. Because Excel provides a built-in *Paste Formatting* control, we can just use its Face ID rather than having to create a custom icon for our Formatting control.

	A	B	O	P
1	**Command Bar Name**	**Control Caption**	**Control Style**	**Face ID**
2	Paste Special			
3		All	☐ ☐	picAll/picAllMask
4		Formulas	☐ ☐	picFormulas/picFormulasMask
5		Values		
6		Formatting		369
7		Comments	☐ ☐	picComments/picCommentsMask
8		Validation	☐ ☐	picValidation/picValidationMask
9		Column Widths	☐ ☐	picWidths/picWidthsMask
10	Stop			

Figure 8-20 The Paste Special Toolbar Face ID Assignments

For all the other controls on our toolbar, we have provided custom icons and masks. The purpose and usage of icons and masks has been covered extensively in the *Face ID* topic and the *Loading Custom Icons From Files* section above, so we do not repeat that information here. What we do is describe how this feature has been implemented on the command bar definition table shown in Figure 8-20.

The pictures for the icons and masks have been placed in the unused Control Style column. This column is unused because the default value `msoButtonIcon` is exactly what we want for our controls. These pictures could theoretically be located anywhere on the wksCommandBars worksheet, but for ease of maintenance we recommend you place your icon and mask pictures on the same row as the control to which they apply and as close as possible to the Face ID column in which they are named. Although it is somewhat difficult to differentiate when looking at a black-and-white screen shot, in all cases the icon is the picture on the left and the mask is the picture on the right.

If you examine the value of the Face ID setting for each of the controls utilizing an icon and mask you will see that it consists of the icon picture name and the mask picture name separated by a forward slash (/) character. For Excel versions 2002 and higher, both of these pictures will be used to create the icon for the control. For Excel versions 2000 and lower, only the icon picture will be used and its appearance on the control will be exactly the same as its appearance on the worksheet. Therefore, if your application will be run on Excel 97 or Excel 2000, you should set the transparent background color of the icon picture in Excel 2000 and save the workbook in that version of Excel, as we have done here.

Figure 8-21 shows the Tag and Parameter settings for our controls.

	A	B	U	V
1	**Command Bar Name**	**Control Caption**	**Tag**	**Parameter**
2	Paste Special			
3		All	pxlPasteSpecial	All
4		Formulas	pxlPasteSpecial	Formulas
5		Values		
6		Formatting	pxlPasteSpecial	Formatting
7		Comments	pxlPasteSpecial	Comments
8		Validation	pxlPasteSpecial	Validation
9		Column Widths	pxlPasteSpecial	ColWidths
10	Stop			

Figure 8-21 The Paste Special Toolbar Tag and Parameter Assignments

Except for the Values control, all the controls have been assigned the same Tag setting value. This is what allows all of these controls' events to be trapped by the same event handler. The Tag value is not required for the Values control because it is a built-in copy of the Excel *Paste Values* control. Because all of our controls are copies of this control, our event handler will trap its event automatically. In the event code that we show in a moment, event calls from the built-in *Paste Values* control are ignored and Excel is allowed to handle them as if they had not been trapped at all.

When the Paste Special toolbar is first created, there is nothing on the clipboard and therefore all of the controls are in the disabled state, as shown in Figure 8-22.

Figure 8-22 The Paste Special Toolbar with All Controls Disabled

Achieving this effect requires absolutely no work on our part. By using the *Paste Values* control as the basis for all the custom controls on the Paste Special toolbar, Excel manages enabling and disabling the controls appropriately for us. After a range has been copied, Excel automatically enables all of our controls, as shown in Figure 8-23.

Figure 8-23 The Paste Special Toolbar with All Controls Enabled

Now let's look at the code required to manage these controls. A WithEvents class module called CControlEvents is used to trap the events for our controls. A reference to this class must be created in and held by a global variable so that event trapping continues throughout the life of our application. Therefore, we must add the following object variable declaration to the MGlobals module of our example workbook:

```
Public gclsControlEvents As CControlEvents
```

It seems obvious, but bears mentioning, that the global class variable cannot be instantiated until after we have built the command bars specified in the command bar definition table. Otherwise, there would be no controls to hook. Both of these tasks are accomplished in the Auto_Open procedure, a fragment of which is shown in Listing 8-8. As in our *Putting It All Together* example, the version of the command bar builder code used here has been integrated with the error handling system to be described in *Chapter 12 — VBA Error Handling*.

Listing 8-8 Instantiating the Event Handler in the Auto_Open Procedure

```
' Initialize global variables.
InitGlobals

' Build the custom command bars specified in the
' wksCommandBars table.
If Not bBuildCommandBars() Then Err.Raise glHANDLED_ERROR

' Instantiate the control event handler class variable.
Set gclsControlEvents = New CControlEvents
```

The complete code from the CControlEvents class module that actually traps and handles the control events is shown in Listing 8-9.

Listing 8-9 The CControlEvents Class Module

```
Private WithEvents mctlPasteSpecial As Office.CommandBarButton

Private Sub Class_Initialize()
    ' Find and hook one of our custom buttons.
    ' The Click event will fire when *any* of the controls with
    ' the same ID and Tag are clicked, as well as when the
    ' built-in control whose ID we're using is clicked.
    ' We've given all our controls the same ID and Tag, so
    ' we're handling the click events for all our controls
    ' using a single hook and event handler.
    Set mctlPasteSpecial = _
                CommandBars.FindControl(Tag:=gsMENU_TAG)
End Sub

Private Sub Class_Terminate()
    Set mctlPasteSpecial = Nothing
End Sub

Private Sub mctlPasteSpecial_Click( _
                ByVal Ctrl As Office.CommandBarButton, _
                CancelDefault As Boolean)

    Dim uPasteType As XlPasteType

    ' This is called for all instances of the built-in
    ' Paste Special > Values button as well as our custom
    ' Paste Special buttons, so check if it's one of ours.
    ' If the button is not one of ours, we'll do nothing
    ' and Excel will perform its normal action for that
    ' button.
    If Ctrl.Tag = gsMENU_TAG Then

        ' It is one of ours, so set the appropriate paste type.
        Select Case Ctrl.Parameter
            Case gsMENU_PS_ALL
                uPasteType = xlPasteAll
            Case gsMENU_PS_FORMULAS
```

```
            uPasteType = xlPasteFormulas
        Case gsMENU_PS_VALUES
            uPasteType = xlPasteValues
        Case gsMENU_PS_FORMATS
            uPasteType = xlPasteFormats
        Case gsMENU_PS_COMMENTS
            uPasteType = xlPasteComments
        Case gsMENU_PS_VALIDATION
            uPasteType = 6   ' xlPasteValidation in 2002+
        Case gsMENU_PS_COLWIDTHS
            uPasteType = 8   ' xlPasteColumnWidths in 2002+
    End Select

    ' If the paste special doesn't succeed, fail silently.
    On Error Resume Next
        Selection.PasteSpecial uPasteType
    On Error GoTo 0

    ' We handled the event, so cancel its default behavior.
    CancelDefault = True

    End If

End Sub
```

When the global gclsControlEvents class variable is instantiated by the Auto_Open procedure, the first thing that happens is the Class_Initialize event fires. This event locates a single instance of a control on our Paste Special toolbar and assigns it to the internal WithEvents class variable. As we have explained previously, this is enough to cause *all* the controls on our toolbar to be hooked by our event handler (as well as any built-in *Paste Values* controls on which our custom controls are based).

Because Excel is managing whether our controls are enabled or disabled, when our mctlPasteSpecial_Click event does fire, we know the user has clicked one of our controls *and* there is something on the clipboard that can potentially be pasted. The first item of business is then to determine whether the control that fired the click event is one of our custom controls. We do this by comparing the Tag property exposed by the Ctrl argument to the Tag value that we have assigned to each of our custom controls. If the Tag property of the Ctrl argument doesn't match the Tag value we have assigned to our custom controls, we know that a built-in

Excel control fired the event procedure. In this case we just exit the procedure without doing anything. This allows Excel to perform the default action for that built-in control, which is the behavior we want.

If the Tag property of the control that fired the event matches the Tag value we assigned to our custom controls, we know we're dealing with one of our custom controls. In this case we continue processing. The action we take depends on the value of the Parameter property of the control that fired the event. The Parameter property is used to distinguish among our custom controls because the Control ID and Tag properties are identical for all of them. This is what allows them all to fire the same event procedure.

In this case, the Parameter value is used to specify the type of paste special operation that should be performed. Within the event procedure we convert the Parameter value into one of the `xlPasteType` enumeration values. After we have the correct paste special enumeration value, we attempt to perform the specified operation. This paste special operation is wrapped in `On Error Resume Next/On Error GoTo 0` so no error will be generated if the paste special operation being attempted is not valid for the current version of Excel or the contents of the clipboard. We explain the use of the various permutations of the `On Error` statement in more detail in *Chapter 12 — VBA Error Handling*.

Practical Example

Because we have not yet introduced the topic of error handling, the command bar builder that we integrate into the sample application at this point does not make use of any error handling techniques. This is not the preferred method, but we are using it to avoid confusing the addition of an automated command bar builder, discussed in this chapter, with the addition of error handling, covered in *Chapter 12 — VBA Error Handling*.

The toolbar for our PETRAS add-in is a very simple one compared to the examples that we've seen already. We show it again in Figure 8-24 to refresh your memory.

Figure 8-24 The PETRAS Add-in Toolbar

PETRAS Timesheet

As Figure 8-24 shows, all five buttons on the toolbar are custom buttons and all of them use built-in Excel command bar control Face ID values, so there is no need to attach external pictures to them. A partial view of the command bar definition table is shown in Figure 8-25. We've frozen panes at column B and scrolled the right pane to column O to show some of the more interesting control settings. To see the entire table, just set the IsAddin property of the PetrasAddin.xla workbook to False so the wksCommandBars worksheet is visible in the Excel user interface.

	O3	▼	=	=msoButtonIconAndCaption		
	A		B	O	P	Q
1	**Command Bar Name**		**Control Caption**	**Control Style**	**Face ID**	**Begin Group**
2	PETRAS Toolbar					
3			New Time Sheet	3	2520	
4			Post to Network	3	107	TRUE
5			Add More Rows	3	296	TRUE
6			Clear Data Entries	3	47	TRUE
7			Exit PETRAS	2		TRUE
8	Stop					

Figure 8-25 The PETRAS Add-in Command Bar Definition Table

The code within the add-in looks exactly like it did when we last saw it except for the addition of two code modules: MCommandBars and MPastePicture. These hold the code that reads the command bar definition table and builds the command bars it specifies. The procedure call used to create the command bar in the Auto_Open procedure is exactly the same as before. The difference is now it calls the BuildCommandBars procedure in the MCommandBars module instead of our previous, hard-coded command bar building procedure of the same name that was located in the MSystemCode module.

There has been one simple change in the Auto_Close procedure. Rather than removing our custom toolbar with the line:

```
Application.CommandBars(gsBAR_TOOLBAR).Delete
```

we are now calling the MCommandBars procedure designed to work backward through the command bars table and remove the command bars and controls it specifies:

```
ResetCommandBars
```

We've done this for illustration purposes only. In the simple case of a single, fully custom toolbar, the first line of code is the more efficient method for removal. When you begin building complex applications that use a combination of modified built-in and fully customized command bars, however, you will find it much easier to let the command bar builder remove your application's command bars based on the command bar definition table that defined them in the first place.

A summary of the changes made to the PETRAS timesheet application to implement the table-driven command bar builder is shown in Table 8-2.

Table 8-2 Changes to the PETRAS Timesheet Application for Chapter 8

Module	Procedure	Change
MCommandBars (new module)		New module containing the command bar building code.
MPastePicture (new module)		New module to support the command bar builder. Used to add a picture to and retrieve a picture from the clipboard.
MOpenClose	Auto_Open	The BuildCommandbars procedure is now called from the new MCommandBars module instead of MSystemCode.
MSystemCode	BuildCommandBars	This procedure was removed because the task of building the command bars is now handled by the table-driven command bar builder.

PETRAS Reporting

Previous versions of the PETRAS reporting application have had a very simple menu structure, little more than the usual *File > New, Open, Close, Save* and *Exit* menus and a *Window* menu to switch between results workbooks. When we're displaying a results workbook, however, we would really like to provide most (but not all) of Excel's built-in menus, to enable our users to work directly with the workbook. Adding the command bar builder to the application makes this a trivial task of including the appropriate built-in menu IDs. In the definition table shown in Figure 8-26, for example, we've been able to include Excel's entire Edit menu (and all its submenus) just by specifying its control ID of 30003.

Command Bar Name	Control Caption	Control Caption	OnAction	Control ID	Control Type	Face ID	Begin Group	Shortcut Text	Parameter
PETRAS Menu Bar									
	&File				10				
		&New Consolidation...	MenuFileNew			18	TRUE	Ctrl+N	Backdrop,Results
		&Open...	MenuFileOpen			23		Ctrl+O	Backdrop,Results
		&Close	MenuFileClose			106			Results
		&Save					TRUE	Ctrl+S	Results
		Save &As...		748					Results
		Page Set&up...		247					Results
		Prin&t Area		30255					Results
		Print Pre&view		109					Results
		Print...		4				Ctrl+P	Results
		&Exit	MenuFileExit				TRUE		Backdrop,Results
	&Edit			30003	10				Results
	&View			30004	10				Results
	&Insert			30005	10				Results
	F&ormat			30006	10				Results
	&Data			30011	10				Results
		&Consolidate Timesheets	MenuConsolidate				TRUE		Results
	&Window				10				
		&Arrange...		298					Results
		Split		302			TRUE		Results
		&Freeze Panes		443					Results
		PETRAS &Backdrop	MenuWindowSelect				TRUE		Backdrop,Results
	&Help				10				
		Microsoft Excel &Help		984				F1	Results
		&About PETRAS Reporting	MenuHelpAbout				TRUE		Backdrop,Results
Stop									

Figure 8-26 The PETRAS Reporting Command Bar Definition Table

If you look at the *OnAction* and *Control ID* columns of the table, you'll see that we have been able to add lots of very rich functionality to our application just by borrowing Excel's standard menus. In fact, all of these features have been added without us having to write **any** code to implement them!

Application Contexts

As dictator applications become more and more complex, we need an easier way to handle the enabling and disabling of the menu items than coding them individually. One approach is to introduce the concept of an application context, which is an identifier to specify what part of the application is being displayed. Typical contexts in Excel dictator applications include the following:

- **Backdrop**—The static backdrop sheet is being displayed, so almost all menus not related to beginning work or exiting the application are disabled.
- **DataEntry**—We're in a data-entry worksheet, so a limited set of editing menus are enabled
- **Results**—We're in a results workbook, so all the editing and formatting menus are enabled.

We can specify the contexts in which each menu item (or an entire popup toolbar) should be enabled by listing the applicable contexts in the Parameter column of the definition table. In the PETRAS reporting application, we're only using the Backdrop and Results contexts.

Because the context is usually determined by the worksheet currently being displayed, we can use the application WindowActivate event to trigger the enabling/disabling by using code like that shown in Listing 8-10.

Listing 8-10 The Code to Implement Application Contexts

```
Private Sub mxlApp_WindowActivate(ByVal Wb As Workbook, _
                                  ByVal Wn As Window)

    'Set the correct context, depending if we have a results
    'workbook or not.
    If IsResultsWorkbook(Wb) Then
        EnableDisableMenus gsCONTEXT_RESULTS
    Else
        EnableDisableMenus gsCONTEXT_BACKDROP
    End If
End Sub


'Enable/disable menu items, depending on the
'application context.
Sub EnableDisableMenus(ByVal sContext As String)

    Dim cbCommandbar As CommandBar

    On Error Resume Next

    'Enable/disable key menu items, by calling the
    'EnableDisableMenuBar procedure, which recursively operates
    'on all Menu items in the structure
    EnableDisableMenuBar Application.CommandBars(gsMENU_BAR), _
        sContext, ""

    'Enable/disable all the toolbars
    For Each cbCommandbar In Application.CommandBars
        If cbCommandbar.Type <> msoBarTypeMenuBar Then
            cbCommandbar.Enabled = (sContext = gsCONTEXT_RESULTS)
        End If
    Next
```

```
    'Enable/disable the associated shortcut keys
    If sContext = gsCONTEXT_RESULTS Then
        Application.OnKey "^s"
        Application.OnKey "^S"
    Else
        Application.OnKey "^s", ""
        Application.OnKey "^S", ""
    End If

End Sub

'Recursive routine to process the menu bar hierarchy,
'enabling/disabling items based on their context.
Private Sub EnableDisableMenuBar(cbBar As CommandBar, _
            sContext As String, sBarContext As String)

  Dim ctlControl As CommandBarControl

  On Error Resume Next

  'Loop through all the controls on this bar
  For Each ctlControl In cbBar.Controls

    If TypeOf ctlControl Is CommandBarPopup Then
      'If it's a popup, recurse down to process its menus
      EnableDisableMenuBar ctlControl.CommandBar, _
                        sContext, ctlControl.Parameter

    ElseIf ctlControl.Parameter = "" Then
      'If the control doesn't have a parameter, use the
      'commandbar's parameter. This allows us to add entire
      'Excel built-in commandbars to our app, without
      'specifying every menu item on them
      ctlControl.Enabled = InStr(1, sBarContext, _
                                sContext) > 0
    Else
      'Otherwise enable/disable the bar
      ctlControl.Enabled = InStr(1, ctlControl.Parameter, _
                                sContext) > 0
    End If
  Next

End Sub
```

Adding the table-driven command bar builder required a number of relatively minor changes throughout the PETRAS reporting application, detailed in Table 8-3.

Table 8-3 Changes to the PETRAS Reporting Application for Chapter 8

Module	Procedure	Change
MOpenClose	Auto_Open	Set initial application context at end of routine.
MCommandBars		Replaced the entire module with the table-driven command bar builder.
MPastePicture (new module)		New module to support the command bar builder. Used to add a picture to and retrieve a picture from the clipboard.
MGlobals		Added constants for application contexts.
MEntryPoints	MenuWindowSelect	We were using the Parameter to test for the PETRAS Backdrop menu item. Changed to use the caption instead, as the Parameter is now used for the application context.
CAppEventHandler	mxlApp_WindowActivate	Identify the application context and pass it to EnableDisableMenus, as shown in Listing 8-10.
MSystemCode	EnableDisableMenus	Implemented Listing 8-10, to enable/disable the menus based on application context instead of hard-coding each menu item.
MSystemCode	AddToWindowMenu	Set the Parameter value to Backdrop,Results when adding the workbook window menu items.
MWorkspace	RestoreExcelSettings	Moved the code to re-enable the toolbars to here, from the old RestoreMenus routine (which has been replaced by the command bar builder).
wksCommandBars (new worksheet)		New worksheet to hold the command bar definition table.

Conclusion

The purpose of this chapter is to simplify command bar building in your applications to save time and allow you to focus more effort on good design. To assist in that effort, we've covered a number of best practice design principles that you should follow. Command bars are the user's entry point into your application. Make them easy to discover, use and remember.

We've introduced you to a table-driven command bar building methodology that will remove most of the work associated with building and maintaining command bars for your application. We've shown you how to create custom icon and mask pictures that enable you to avoid the problems associated with divergent appearance of custom command bar button icons among various current versions of Excel. We've also explained how to hook the events generated when the user clicks command bar controls so that you can control the behavior of those controls in a more granular fashion.

CHAPTER 9

Understanding and Using Windows API Calls

In the *Programming with the Windows API* chapter of our *Excel 2002 VBA Programmers Reference*, we approached the subject of using Windows API calls by explaining how to locate the definitions for various functions on the MSDN Web site and translate those functions for use in VBA. The idea was to enable readers to browse through the API documentation and use anything of interest they found.

In reality, extremely few people use Windows API calls in that manner; indeed, trying to include previously unexplored API calls in our Excel applications is very likely to result in a maintenance problem, because it's doubtful that another developer will understand what we were trying to do. Instead, most of us go to Google and search the Web or the newsgroups for the answer to a problem and find that the solution requires the use of API calls. (Searching Google for "Excel Windows API" results in more than 200,000 Web pages and 19,000 newsgroup posts.) We copy the solution into our application and hope it works, usually without really understanding what it does. This chapter shines a light on many of those solutions, explaining how they work, what they use the API calls for, and how they can be modified to better fit our applications. Along the way, we fill in some of the conceptual framework of common Windows API techniques and terminology.

By the end of the chapter, you will be comfortable about including API calls in your applications, understand how they work, accept their use in the example applications we develop in this book and be able to modify them to suit your needs.

Overview

When developing Excel-based applications, we can get most things done by using the Excel object model. Occasionally, though, we need some information or feature that Excel doesn't provide. In those cases, we can usually go directly to the files that comprise the Windows operating system to find what we're looking for. The first step in doing that is to tell VBA the function exists, where to find it, what arguments it takes and what data type it returns. This is done using the Declare statement, such as that for GetSystemMetrics:

```
Declare Function GetSystemMetrics Lib "user32" _
                (ByVal nIndex As Long) As Long
```

This statement tells the VBA interpreter that there is a function called GetSystemMetrics located in the file user32.exe (or user32.dll, it'll check both) that takes one argument of a Long value and returns a Long value. Once defined, we can call GetSystemMetrics in exactly the same way as if it is the VBA function:

```
Function GetSystemMetrics(ByVal nIndex As Long) As Long
End Function
```

The Declare statements can be used in any type of code module, can be Public or Private (just like standard procedures), but must always be placed in the Declarations section at the top of the module.

Finding Documentation

All of the functions in the Windows API are fully documented in the *Windows Development/Platform SDK* section of the MSDN library on the Microsoft Web site, at `http://msdn.microsoft.com/library`, although the terminology used and the code samples tend to be targeted at the C++ developer. A Google search will usually locate documentation more appropriate for the Visual Basic and VBA developer, but is unlikely to be as complete as MSDN. If you're using API calls found on a Web site, the Web page will hopefully explain what they do, but it is a good idea to always check the official documentation for the functions to see whether any limitations or other remarks may affect your usage.

Unfortunately, the MSDN library's search engine is significantly worse than using Google to search the MSDN site. We find that Google always gives us more relevant pages than MSDN's search engine. To use Google to search MSDN, browse to `http://www.google.com` and click the Advanced Search link. Type in the search criteria and then in the Domain edit box type msdn.microsoft.com to restrict the search to MSDN.

Finding Declarations

It is not uncommon to encounter code snippets on the Internet that include incorrect declarations for API functions—such as declaring an argument's data type as Integer or Boolean when it should be Long. Although using the declaration included in the snippet will probably work (hopefully the author tested it), it might not work for the full range of possible arguments that the function accepts and in rare cases may cause memory corruption and data loss. The official VBA-friendly declarations for many of the more commonly used API functions can be found in the win32api.txt file, which is included with a viewer in the Developer Editions of Office 97–2002, Visual Basic 6 and is available for download from `http://support.microsoft.com/?kbid=178020`. You'll notice from the download page that the file hasn't been updated for some time. It therefore doesn't include the declarations and constants added in recent versions of Windows. If you're using one of those newer declarations, you'll have to trust the Web page author, examine a number of Web pages to check that they all use the same declaration or create your own VBA-friendly declaration by following the steps we described in the *Excel 2002 VBA Programmers Reference*.

Finding the Values of Constants

Most API functions are passed constants to modify their behavior or specify the type of value to return. For example, the GetSystemMetrics function shown previously accepts a parameter to specify which metric we want, such as SM_CXSCREEN to get the width of the screen in pixels or SM_CYSCREEN to get the height. All of the appropriate constants are shown on the MSDN page for that declaration. For example, the GetSystemMetrics function is documented at `http://msdn.microsoft.com/library/en-us/sysinfo/base/getsystemmetrics.asp` and shows more than 70 valid constants.

Although many of the constants are included in the win32api.txt file mentioned earlier, it does not include constants added for recent versions of Windows. The best way to find these values is by downloading and installing the core Platform SDK from `http://www.microsoft.com/msdownload/platformsdk/sdkupdate/`. This includes all the C++ header files that were used to build the DLLs, in a subdirectory called *include*. The files in this directory can be searched using normal Windows file searching to find the file that contains the constant we're interested in. For example, searching for SM_CXSCREEN gives the file winuser.h. Opening that file and searching within it gives the following lines:

```
#define SM_CXSCREEN              0
#define SM_CYSCREEN              1
```

These constants can then be included in your VBA module by declaring them as Long variables with the values shown:

```
Const SM_CXSCREEN As Long = 0
Const SM_CYSCREEN As Long = 1
```

Sometimes, the values will be shown in hexadecimal form, such as 0x8000, which can be converted to VBA by replacing the *0x* with *&h* and adding a further *&* on the end, such that

```
#define KF_UP               0x8000
```

becomes

```
Const KF_UP As Long = &h8000&
```

Understanding Handles

Within VBA, we're used to setting a variable to reference an object using code like

```
Set wkbBackDrop = Workbooks("Backdrop.xls")
```

and releasing that reference by setting the variable to Nothing (or letting VBA do that for us when it goes out of scope at the end of the procedure). Under the covers, the thing that we see as the Backdrop.xls workbook is just an area of memory containing data structured in a specific way that only Excel understands. When we set the variable equal to that object, it is just given the memory location of that data structure. The Windows operating system works in a very similar way, but at a much more granular level; almost everything within Windows is maintained as a small data structure somewhere. If we want to work with the item that is represented by that structure (such as a window), we need to get a reference to it and pass that reference to the appropriate API function. These references are known as *handles* and are just ID numbers that Windows uses to identify the data structure. Variables used to store handles are usually given the prefix h and are declared As Long.

When we ask for the handle to an item, some functions—such as FindWindow—give us the handle to a shared data structure; there is only one data structure for each window, so every call to FindWindow with the same parameters will return the same handle. In these cases, we can just discard the handle when we're finished with it. In most situations, however, Windows allocates an area of memory, creates a new data structure for us to use and returns the handle to that structure. In these cases, we *must* tidy up after ourselves, by explicitly telling Windows that we've finished using the handle (and by implication, the memory used to store the data structure that the handle points to). If we fail to tidy up correctly, each call to our routine will use another bit of memory until Windows crashes—this is known as a *memory leak*. The most common cause of memory leaks is forgetting to include tidy-up code within a routine's error handler. The MSDN documentation will tell you whether you need to release the handle and which function to call to do it.

Encapsulating API Calls

GetSystemMetrics is one of the few API calls that can easily be used in isolation—it has a meaningful name, takes a single parameter, returns a simple result and doesn't require any preparation or cleanup. So long as you can remember what SM_CXSCREEN is asking for, it's extremely easy to call this function; `GetSystemMetrics(SM_CXSCREEN)` gives us the width of the screen in pixels.

In general practice, however, it is a very good idea to wrap your API calls inside their own VBA functions and to place those functions in modules dedicated to specific areas of the Windows API, for the following reasons:

- The VBA routine can include some validity checks before trying to call the API function. Passing invalid data to API functions will often result in a crash.
- Most of the textual API functions require string variables to be defined and passed in, which are then populated by the API function. Using a VBA routine hides that complexity.

- Many API functions accept parameters that we don't need to use. A VBA routine can expose only the parameters that are applicable to our application.
- Few API functions can be used in isolation; most require extra preparatory and clean up calls. Using a VBA routine hides that complexity.
- The API declarations themselves can be declared Private to the module in which they're contained, so they can be hidden from use by other developers who may not understand how to use them; their functionality can then be exposed through more friendly VBA routines.
- Some API functions, such as the encryption or Internet functions, require an initial set of preparatory calls to open resources, a number of routines that use those resources and a final set of routines to close the resources and tidy up. Such routines are ideally encapsulated in a class module, with the Class_Initialize and Class_Terminate procedures used to ensure the resources are opened and closed correctly.
- By using dedicated modules for specific areas of the Windows API, we can easily copy the routines between applications, in the knowledge that they are self-contained.

When you start to include lots of API calls in your application, it quickly becomes difficult to keep track of which constants belong to which functions. We can make the constants much easier to manage if we encapsulate them in an enumeration and use that enumeration for our VBA function's parameter, as shown in Listing 9-1. By doing this, the applicable constants are shown in the Intellisense list when the VBA function is used, as shown in Figure 9-1. The ability to define enumerations was added in Excel 2000.

Listing 9-1 Encapsulating the GetSystemMetrics API Function and Related Constants

```
'Declare all the API-specific items Private to the module
Private Declare Function GetSystemMetrics Lib "user32" _
        (ByVal nIndex As Long) As Long
Private Const SM_CXSCREEN As Long = 0
Private Const SM_CYSCREEN As Long = 1

'Wrap the API constants in a public enumeration,
```

```
'so they appear in the Intellisense dropdown
Public Enum SystemMetricsConstants
  smScreenWidth = SM_CXSCREEN
  smScreenHeight = SM_CYSCREEN
End Enum

'Wrapper for the GetSystemMetrics API function,
'using the SystemMetricsConstants enumeration
Public Function SystemMetrics( _
      ByVal uIndex As SystemMetricsConstants) As Long

  SystemMetrics = GetSystemMetrics(uIndex)
End Function
```

Figure 9-1 By Using the Enumeration, the Relevant Constants Appear in the Intellisense Drop-Down

Working with the Screen

The procedures included in this section all relate to the Windows screen and can be found in the MScreen module of the API Examples.xls workbook.

Reading the Screen Resolution

The GetSystemMetrics API function has been used to illustrate the general concepts above. It can be used to discover many of the simpler aspects of the operating system, from whether a mouse or network is present to the height of the standard window title bar. By far its most common use in Excel is to find the screen resolution, to check that it is at least a minimum size (for example, 800×600) or to work out which userform to display if you have different layouts optimized for different resolutions. The code in Listing 9-2 wraps the GetSystemMetrics API function, exposing it as separate ScreenWidth and ScreenHeight functions.

Listing 9-2 Reading the Screen Resolution

```
'Declare all the API-specific items Private to the module
Private Declare Function GetSystemMetrics Lib "user32" _
        (ByVal nIndex As Long) As Long
Private Const SM_CXSCREEN = 0      'Screen width
Private Const SM_CYSCREEN = 1      'Screen height

'The width of the screen, in pixels
Public Function ScreenWidth() As Long
  ScreenWidth = GetSystemMetrics(SM_CXSCREEN)
End Function

'The height of the screen, in pixels
Public Function ScreenHeight() As Long
  ScreenHeight = GetSystemMetrics(SM_CYSCREEN)
End Function
```

Finding the Size of a Pixel

In general, Excel measures distances in points, whereas most API functions use pixels and many ActiveX controls (such as the Microsoft Flexgrid) use twips. A point is defined as being 1/72 (logical) inches, and a twip is defined as 1/20th of a point. To convert between pixels and points, we need to know how many pixels Windows is displaying for each logical inch. This is the DPI (dots per inch) set by the user in *Control Panel > Display > Settings > Advanced > General > Display*, which is usually set at either Normal size (96 DPI) or Large size (120 DPI). In versions of Windows prior to XP, this was known as Small Fonts and Large Fonts. The value of this setting can be found using the GetDeviceCaps API function, which is used to examine the detailed capabilities of a specific graphical device, such as a screen or printer.

Device Contexts

One of the fundamental features of Windows is that applications can interact with all graphical devices (screens, printers, or even individual picture files) in a standard way. This is achieved by operating through a layer of indirection called a device context, which represents a drawing layer. An application obtains a reference (handle) to the drawing layer for a specific device (for example, the screen), examines its capabilities (such as the size of a dot, whether it can draw curves and how many colors it supports), draws onto the drawing layer and then releases the reference. Windows takes care of exactly how the drawing layer is represented on the graphical device. In this example, we're only examining the screen's capabilities.

The code to retrieve the size of a pixel is shown in Listing 9-3. Remember that when adding this code to an existing module, the declarations must always be placed at the top of the module.

Listing 9-3 Finding the Size of a Pixel

```
Private Declare Function GetDC Lib "user32" _
        (ByVal hwnd As Long) As Long

Private Declare Function GetDeviceCaps Lib "gdi32" _
        (ByVal hDC As Long, ByVal nIndex As Long) As Long

Private Declare Function ReleaseDC Lib "user32" _
        (ByVal hwnd As Long, ByVal hDC As Long) As Long

Private Const LOGPIXELSX = 88      'Pixels/inch in X

'A point is defined as 1/72 inches
Private Const POINTS_PER_INCH As Long = 72

'The size of a pixel, in points
Public Function PointsPerPixel() As Double

  Dim hDC As Long
  Dim lDotsPerInch As Long

  hDC = GetDC(0)
  lDotsPerInch = GetDeviceCaps(hDC, LOGPIXELSX)
  PointsPerPixel = POINTS_PER_INCH / lDotsPerInch
  ReleaseDC 0, hDC

End Function
```

The first thing to notice about this routine is that we cannot just call GetDeviceCaps directly; we need to give it a handle to the screen's device context. This handle is obtained by calling the GetDC function, where the zero parameter conveniently gives us the device context for the screen. We then call GetDeviceCaps, passing the constant LOGPIXELSX, which asks for the number of pixels per logical inch horizontally. (For screens, the horizontal and vertical DPI is the same, but it might not be for printers, which is why circles on screen often print out as ovals.) With Normal size chosen, we get 96 dots per inch. We divide the 72 points per inch by the 96 DPI, telling us that a dot (that is, pixel) is 0.75 points; so if we want to move something in Excel by one pixel, we need to change its Top or Left by 0.75. With Large Size selected, a pixel is 0.6 points.

Every time we use GetDC to obtain a handle to a device context, we use up a small amount of Window's graphical resources. If we didn't release the handle after using it, we would eventually use up all of Window's graphical resources and crash. To avoid that, we have to be sure to release any resources we obtain, in this case by calling ReleaseDC.

Working with Windows

Everything that we see on the screen is either a window or is contained within a window, from the Windows desktop to the smallest popup tooltip. Consequently, if we want to modify something on the screen, we always start by locating its window. The windows are organized into a hierarchy, with the desktop at the root. The next level down includes the main windows for all open applications and numerous system-related windows. Each application then owns and maintains its own hierarchy of windows. Every window is identified by its window handle, commonly referred to as **hWnd**. By far the best tool for locating and examining windows is the Spy++ utility that is included with Visual Studio. Figure 9-2 shows the Spy++ display for the window hierarchy of a typical Excel session.

Window Classes

As well as showing the hierarchy, the Spy++ display shows three key attributes for each window: the handle (in hexadecimal), the caption and the class. Just like class modules, a window class defines a type of window. Some classes, such as the ComboBox class, are provided by the Windows operating system, but most are defined as part of an application. Each window class is usually associated with a specific part of an application, such as *XLMAIN* being Excel's main application window. Table 9-1 lists the window classes shown in the Spy++ hierarchy and their uses, plus some other window classes commonly encountered during Excel application development.

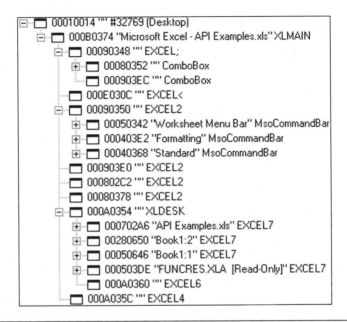

Figure 9-2 The Spy++ Display of the Excel Window Hierarchy

Table 9-1 Excel Window Classes and Their Uses

Window Class	Usage
XLMAIN	The main Excel application window.
EXCEL;	The left half of the formula bar, including the Name drop-down.
ComboBox	A standard Windows combo box (in this case, it's the Name drop-down).
EXCEL<	The edit box section of the formula bar.
EXCEL2	The four command bar docking areas (top, left, right and bottom).
MsoCommandBar	A command bar.
XLDESK	The Excel desktop.
EXCEL7	A workbook window. In this example, Book1 has two windows open.
EXCELE	A window used to provide in-sheet editing of embedded charts.
EXCEL4	The status bar.

Finding Windows

The procedures shown in the sections that follow can be found in the MWindows module of the API Examples.xls workbook.

To work with a window, we first need to find its handle. In Excel 2002, the hWnd property was added to the Application object, giving us the handle of the main Excel application window. In previous versions and for all other top-level windows (that is, windows that are direct children of the desktop), we can use the FindWindow API call, which is defined as follows:

```
Declare Function FindWindow Lib "user32" Alias "FindWindowA" _
        (ByVal lpClassName As String, _
         ByVal lpWindowName As String) As Long
```

To use the FindWindow function, we need to supply a class name and/or a window caption. We can use the special constant vbNullString for either, which tells the function to match on any class or caption. The function searches through all the immediate children of the desktop window (known as *top-level windows*), looking for any that have the given class and/or caption that we specified. To find the main Excel window in versions prior to Excel 2002, we might use the following:

```
hWndExcel = FindWindow("XLMAIN", Application.Caption)
```

ANSI vs. Unicode and the Alias Clause

You might have noticed that the declaration for FindWindow contains an extra clause that we haven't used before—the *Alias* clause. All Windows API functions that have textual parameters come in two flavors: Those that operate on ANSI strings have an A suffix, whereas those that operate on Unicode strings have a W suffix. So while all the documentation and searches on MSDN talk about FindWindow, the Windows DLLs do not actually contain a function of that name—they contain two functions called FindWindowA and FindWindowW. We use the Alias statement to provide the actual name (case sensitive) for the function contained in the DLL. In fact, as long as we provide the correct name in the Alias clause, we can give it any name we like:

```
Declare Function Foo Lib "user32" Alias "FindWindowA" _
        (ByVal lpClassName As String, _
```

```
      ByVal lpWindowName As String) As Long

ApphWnd = Foo("XLMAIN", Application.Caption)
```

Although VBA stores strings internally as Unicode, it always converts them to ANSI when passing them to API functions. This is usually sufficient, and it is quite rare to find examples of VB or VBA calling the Unicode versions. In some cases, however, we need to support the full Unicode character set and can work around VBA's conversion behavior by calling the W version of the API function and using StrConv to do an extra ANSI-to-Unicode conversion within our API function calls:

```
Declare Function FindWindow Lib "user32" Alias "FindWindowW" _
        (ByVal lpClassName As String, _
        ByVal lpWindowName As String) As Long

ApphWnd = FindWindow(StrConv("XLMAIN", vbUnicode), _
            StrConv(Application.Caption, vbUnicode))
```

Finding Related Windows

The problem with the (very common) usage of FindWindow to get the main Excel window handle is that if we have multiple instances of Excel open that have the same caption, there is no easy way to tell which one we get, so we might end up modifying the wrong instance! It is a common problem if the user typically doesn't have his workbook windows maximized, because all instances of Excel will then have the same caption of "Microsoft Excel."

A more robust and foolproof method is to use the FindWindowEx function to scan through all children of the desktop window, stopping when we find one that belongs to the same process as our current instance of Excel. FindWindowEx works in exactly the same way as FindWindow, but we provide the parent window handle and the handle of a child window to start searching after (or zero to start with the first). Listing 9-4 shows a specific ApphWnd function, which calls a generic FindOurWindow function, which uses the following API functions:

- GetCurrentProcessID to retrieve the ID of the instance of Excel running the code

- GetDesktopWindow to get the handle of the desktop window, that we pass to FindWindowEx to look through its children (because all application windows are children of the desktop)
- FindWindowEx to find the next window that matches the given class and caption
- GetWindowThreadProcessID to retrieve the ID of the instance of Excel that owns the window that FindWindowEx found

Listing 9-4 Foolproof Way to Find the Excel Main Window Handle

```
'Get the handle of the desktop window
Declare Function GetDesktopWindow Lib "user32" () As Long

'Find a child window with a given class name and caption
Declare Function FindWindowEx Lib "user32" _
        Alias "FindWindowExA" _
        (ByVal hWnd1 As Long, ByVal hWnd2 As Long, _
        ByVal lpsz1 As String, ByVal lpsz2 As String) _
        As Long

'Get the process ID of this instance of Excel
Declare Function GetCurrentProcessId Lib "kernel32" () _
        As Long

'Get the ID of the process that a window belongs to
Declare Function GetWindowThreadProcessId Lib "user32" _
        (ByVal hWnd As Long, ByRef lpdwProcessId As Long) _
        As Long

'Foolproof way to find the main Excel window handle
Function ApphWnd() As Long

  'Excel 2002 and above have a property for the hWnd
  If Val(Application.Version) >= 10 Then
    ApphWnd = Application.hWnd
  Else
    ApphWnd = FindOurWindow("XLMAIN", Application.Caption)
  End If

End Function
```

```
'Finds a top-level window of the given class and caption
'that belongs to this instance of Excel, by matching the
'process IDs
Function FindOurWindow( _
          Optional sClass As String = vbNullString, _
          Optional sCaption As String = vbNullString)

    Dim hWndDesktop As Long
    Dim hWnd As Long
    Dim hProcThis As Long
    Dim hProcWindow As Long

    'Get the ID of this instance of Excel, to match to
    hProcThis = GetCurrentProcessId

    'All top-level windows are children of the desktop,
    'so get that handle first
    hWndDesktop = GetDesktopWindow

    Do
        'Find the next child window of the desktop that
        'matches the given window class and/or caption.
        'The first time in, hWnd will be zero, so we'll get
        'the first matching window. Each call will pass the
        'handle of the window we found the last time,
        'thereby getting the next one (if any)
        hWnd = FindWindowEx(hWndDesktop, hWnd, sClass, _
                            sCaption)

        'Get the ID of the process that owns the window
        GetWindowThreadProcessId hWnd, hProcWindow

        'Loop until the window's process matches this process,
        'or we didn't find a window
    Loop Until hProcWindow = hProcThis Or hWnd = 0

    'Return the handle we found
    FindOurWindow = hWnd

End Function
```

The FindOurWindow function can also be used to safely find any of the top-level windows that Excel creates, such as userforms.

After we've found Excel's main window handle, we can use the FindWindowEx function to navigate through Excel's window hierarchy. Listing 9-5 shows a function to return the handle of a given Excel workbook's window. To get the window handle, we start at Excel's main window, find the desktop (class XLDESK) and then find the window (class EXCEL7) with the appropriate caption.

Listing 9-5 Function to Find a Workbook's Window Handle

```
Private Declare Function FindWindowEx Lib "user32" _
      Alias "FindWindowExA" _
      (ByVal hWnd1 As Long, ByVal hWnd2 As Long, _
      ByVal lpsz1 As String, ByVal lpsz2 As String) _
      As Long

'Function to find the handle of a given workbook window
Function WorkbookWindowhWnd(wndWindow As Window) As Long

   Dim hWndExcel As Long
   Dim hWndDesk As Long

   'Get the main Excel window
   hWndExcel = ApphWnd

   'Find the desktop
   hWndDesk = FindWindowEx(hWndExcel, 0, _
                        "XLDESK", vbNullString)

   'Find the workbook window
   WorkbookWindowhWnd = FindWindowEx(hWndDesk, 0, _
                        "EXCEL7", wndWindow.Caption)

End Function
```

Windows Messages

At the lowest level, windows communicate with each other and with the operating system by sending simple messages. Every window has a main message-handling procedure (commonly called its wndproc) to which messages are sent. Every message consists of four elements: the handle of the window to which the message is being sent, a message ID and two numbers that provide extra information about the message (if required). Within each wndproc, there is a huge case statement that works out what to do for each message ID. For example, the system will send the WM_PAINT message to a window when it requires the window to redraw its contents.

It will probably come as no surprise that we can also send messages directly to individual windows, using the SendMessage function. The easiest way to find which messages can be sent to which window class is to search the MSDN library using a known constant and then look in the See Also list for a link to a list of related messages. Look down the list for a message that looks interesting, then go to its details page to see the parameters it requires. For example, if we look again at Figure 9-1, we can see that the EXCEL; window contains a combo box. This combo box is actually the Name drop-down to the left of the formula bar. Searching the MSDN library (using Google) with the search term "combo box messages" gives us a number of relevant hits. One of them takes us to msdn.microsoft.com/library/en-us/shellcc/platform/ commctls/comboboxes/comboboxes.asp. Looking down the list of messages we find the CB_SETDROPPEDWIDTH message that we can use to change the width of the drop-down portion of the Name box. In Listing 9-6, we use the SendMessage function to make the Name drop-down 200 pixels wide, enabling us to see the full text of lengthy defined names.

Listing 9-6 Changing the Width of the Name Drop-Down List

```
Private Declare Function FindWindowEx Lib "user32" _
       Alias "FindWindowExA" _
       (ByVal hWnd1 As Long, ByVal hWnd2 As Long, _
       ByVal lpsz1 As String, ByVal lpsz2 As String) _
       As Long

Private Declare Function SendMessage Lib "user32" _
       Alias "SendMessageA" _
       (ByVal hwnd As Long, ByVal wMsg As Long, _
       ByVal wParam As Long, Byval lParam As Long) _
       As Long

'Not included in win32api.txt, but found in winuser.h
```

```
Private Const CB_SETDROPPEDWIDTH As Long = &H160&

'Make the Name dropdown list 200 pixels wide
Sub SetNameDropdownWidth()

   Dim hWndExcel As Long
   Dim hWndFormulaBar As Long
   Dim hWndNameCombo As Long

   'Get the main Excel window
   hWndExcel = ApphWnd

   'Get the handle for the formula bar window
   hWndFormulaBar = FindWindowEx(hWndExcel, 0, _
                    "EXCEL;", vbNullString)

   'Get the handle for the Name combobox
   hWndNameCombo = FindWindowEx(hWndFormulaBar, 0, _
                    "combobox", vbNullString)

   'Set the dropdown list to be 200 pixels wide
   SendMessage hWndNameCombo, CB_SETDROPPEDWIDTH, 200, 0

End Sub
```

Changing the Window Icon

When creating a dictator application, the intent is usually to make it look as though it is a normal Windows application and not necessarily running within Excel. Two of the giveaways are the application and worksheet icons. These can be changed to our own icons using API functions. We first use the ExtractIcon function to get a handle to an icon from a file, then send that icon handle to the window in a WM_SETICON message, as shown in Listing 9-7. The SetIcon routine is given a window handle and the path to an icon file, so it can be used to set either the application's icon or a workbook window's icon. For best use, the icon file should contain both 32×32 and 16×16 pixel versions of the icon image. Note that when setting the workbook window's icon, Excel doesn't refresh the image to the left of the menu bar until a window is maximized or minimized/restored, so you may need to toggle the WindowState to force the update.

Listing 9-7 Setting a Window's Icon

```
Private Declare Function ExtractIcon Lib "shell32.dll" _
        Alias "ExtractIconA" _
        (ByVal hInst As Long, _
        ByVal lpszExeFileName As String, _
        ByVal nIconIndex As Long) As Long

Private Declare Function SendMessage Lib "user32" _
        Alias "SendMessageA" _
        (ByVal hwnd As Long, ByVal wMsg As Long, _
        ByVal wParam As Long, Byval lParam As Long) _
        As Long

Private Const WM_SETICON As Long = &H80

'Set a window's icon
Sub SetIcon(ByVal hWnd As Long, ByVal sIcon As String)

  Dim hIcon As Long

  'Get the icon handle
  hIcon = ExtractIcon(0, sIcon, 0)

  'Set the big (32x32) and small (16x16) icons
  SendMessage hWnd, WM_SETICON, 1, hIcon
  SendMessage hWnd, WM_SETICON, 0, hIcon

End Sub
```

Changing Windows Styles

If you look at all the windows on your screen, you might notice that they all look a little different. Some have a title bar, some have minimize and maximize buttons, some have an [x] to close them, some have a 3D look, some are resizable, some are a fixed size and so on. All of these things are individual attributes of the window and are stored as part of the window's data structure. They're all on/off flags stored as bits in two Long numbers. We can use the GetWindowLong function to retrieve a window's style settings, switch individual bits on or off and write them back using SetWindowLong. Modifying windows styles in this way is most often done for userforms and is covered in *Chapter 10 — Userform Design and Best Practices*.

Working with the Keyboard

The behavior of many of Excel's toolbar buttons and some of the dialog buttons changes if the Shift key is held down when the button is clicked. For example, the Increase decimal toolbar button normally increases the number of decimal places shown in a cell, but decreases the number of decimal places if it is clicked with the Shift key held down. Similarly, when closing Excel, if you hold down the Shift key when clicking the No button on the Save Changes? dialog, it acts like a "No to All" button. We can do exactly the same in our applications by using API functions to examine the state of the keyboard. The procedures included in this section can be found in the MKeyboard module of the API Examples.xls workbook.

Checking for Shift, Ctrl, Alt, Caps Lock, Num Lock and Scroll Lock

The GetKeyState API function tells us whether a given key on the keyboard is currently held down or "on" (in the case of Caps Lock, Num Lock and Scroll Lock). The function is used by passing a code representing the key we're interested in and returns whether the key is being held down or is "on." Listing 9-8 shows a function to determine whether one of the six "special" keys is currently pressed. Note that we have again encapsulated the key code constants inside a more meaningful enumeration.

Listing 9-8 Checking Whether a Key Is Held Down

```
Private Declare Function GetKeyState Lib "user32" _
        (ByVal vKey As Long) As Integer

Private Const VK_SHIFT As Long = &H10
Private Const VK_CONTROL As Long = &H11
Private Const VK_MENU As Long = &H12
Private Const VK_CAPITAL = &H14
Private Const VK_NUMLOCK = &H90
Private Const VK_SCROLL = &H91

Public Enum GetKeyStateKeyboardCodes
  gksKeyboardShift = VK_SHIFT
  gksKeyboardCtrl = VK_CONTROL
  gksKeyboardAlt = VK_MENU
```

```
    gksKeyboardCapsLock = VK_CAPITAL
    gksKeyboardNumLock = VK_NUMLOCK
    gksKeyboardScrollLock = VK_SCROLL
End Enum

Public Function IsKeyPressed _
        (ByVal lKey As GetKeyStateKeyboardCodes) As Boolean

    Dim iResult As Integer

    iResult = GetKeyState(lKey)

    Select Case lKey
    Case gksKeyboardCapsLock, gksKeyboardNumLock, _
        gksKeyboardScrollLock

      'For the three 'toggle' keys, the 1st bit says if it's
      'on or off, so clear any other bits that might be set,
      'using a binary AND
      iResult = iResult And 1

    Case Else
      'For the other keys, the 16th bit says if it's down or
      'up, so clear any other bits that might be set, using a
      'binary AND
      iResult = iResult And &H8000
    End Select

    IsKeyPressed = (iResult <> 0)

End Function
```

Bit Masks

The value obtained from the call to GetKeyState should not be interpreted as a simple number, but as its binary representation where each individual bit represents whether a particular attribute is on or off. This is one of the few functions that return a 16-bit Integer value, rather than the more common 32-bit Long. The MSDN documentation for GetKeyState says that "If the high-order bit is 1, the key is down, otherwise the key is up. If the low-order bit is 1, the key is on, otherwise the key is off." The first sentence is applicable for all keys (down/up), whereas the second is only applicable to the Caps Lock, Num Lock and Scroll Lock keys. It is possible for both bits to be set, if the Caps Lock key is held down and "on." The low-order bit is the rightmost bit, and the high-order bit is the leftmost (16th) bit. To examine whether a specific bit has been set, we have to apply a ***bit mask***, to zero-out the bits we're not interested in, by performing a binary AND between the return value and a binary value that has a single 1 in the position we're interested in. In the first case, we're checking for a 1 in the first bit, which is the number 1. In the second case, we're checking for a 1 in the 16th bit, i.e. the binary number 1000 0000 0000 0000, which is easiest to represent in code as the hexadecimal number &h8000. After we've isolated that bit, a zero value means off/up and a nonzero value means on/down.

Testing for a Key Press

As mentioned previously, at the lowest level, windows communicate through messages sent to their wndproc procedure. When an application is busy (such as Excel running some code), the wndproc only processes critical messages (such as the system shutting down). All other messages get placed in a queue and are processed when the application next has some spare time. This is why using SendKeys is so unreliable; it's not until the code stops running (or issues a DoEvents statement) that Excel checks its message queue to see whether there are any key presses to process.

We can use Excel's message queuing to allow the user to interrupt our code by pressing a key. Normally, if we want to allow the user to stop a lengthy looping process, we can either show a modeless dialog with a Cancel button (as explained in *Chapter 10 — Userform Design and Best Practices*), or allow the user to press the Cancel key to jump into the routine's error handler (as explained in *Chapter 12 — VBA Error Handling*). An easier way is to check Excel's message queue during each iteration of the loop to see whether the user has pressed a key. This is achieved using the PeekMessage API function:

```
Declare Function PeekMessage Lib "user32" _
        Alias "PeekMessageA" _
       (ByRef lpMsg As MSG, _
        ByVal hWnd As Long, _
        ByVal wMsgFilterMin As Long, _
        ByVal wMsgFilterMax As Long, _
        ByVal wRemoveMsg As Long) As Long
```

Structures

If you look at the first parameter of the PeekMessage function, you'll see it is declared As MSG and is passed ByRef. MSG is a windows *structure* and is implemented in VBA as a user-defined type. To use it in this case, we declare a variable of that type and pass it in to the function. The function sets the value of each element of the UDT, which we then read. Many API functions use structures as a convenient way of passing large amounts of information into the function, instead of having a long list of parameters. Many messages that we send using the SendMessage function require a structure to be passed as the final parameter (as opposed to a single Long value). In those cases, we use a different form of the SendMessage declaration, where the final parameter is declared As Any and is passed ByRef:

```
Declare Function SendMessageAny Lib "user32" _
        Alias "SendMessageA" _
        (ByVal hwnd As Long, ByVal wMsg As Long, _
        ByVal wParam As Long, _
        ByRef lParam As Any) As Long
```

When we use this declaration, we're actually sending a pointer to the memory where our UDT is stored. If we have an error in the definition of our UDT, or if we use this version of the declaration to send a message that is not expecting a memory pointer, the call will at best fail and possibly crash Excel.

Listing 9-9 shows the full code to check for a key press.

Listing 9-9 Testing for a Key Press

```
'Type to hold the coordinates of the mouse pointer
Private Type POINTAPI
  x As Long
  y As Long
End Type

'Type to hold the Windows message information
Private Type MSG
  hWnd As Long        'the window handle of the app
  message As Long     'the type of message (e.g. keydown)
  wParam As Long      'the key code
  lParam As Long      'not used
  time As Long        'time when message posted
```

```
    pt As POINTAPI      'coordinate of mouse pointer
End Type

'Look in the message buffer for a message
Private Declare Function PeekMessage Lib "user32" _
        Alias "PeekMessageA" _
        (ByRef lpMsg As MSG, ByVal hWnd As Long, _
        ByVal wMsgFilterMin As Long, _
        ByVal wMsgFilterMax As Long, _
        ByVal wRemoveMsg As Long) As Long

'Translate the message from a key code to a ASCII code
Private Declare Function TranslateMessage Lib "user32" _
        (ByRef lpMsg As MSG) As Long

'Windows API constants
Private Const WM_CHAR As Long = &H102
Private Const WM_KEYDOWN As Long = &H100
Private Const PM_REMOVE As Long = &H1
Private Const PM_NOYIELD As Long = &H2

'Check for a key press
Public Function CheckKeyboardBuffer() As String

    'Dimension variables
    Dim msgMessage As MSG
    Dim hWnd As Long
    Dim lResult As Long

    'Get the window handle of this application
    hWnd = ApphWnd

    'See if there are any "Key down" messages
    lResult = PeekMessage(msgMessage, hWnd, WM_KEYDOWN, _
            WM_KEYDOWN, PM_REMOVE + PM_NOYIELD)

    'If so ...
    If lResult <> 0 Then

        '... translate the key-down code to a character code,
        'which gets put back in the message queue as a WM_CHAR
        'message ...
        lResult = TranslateMessage(msgMessage)
```

```
'... and retrieve that WM_CHAR message
lResult = PeekMessage(msgMessage, hWnd, WM_CHAR, _
            WM_CHAR, PM_REMOVE + PM_NOYIELD)

'Return the character of the key pressed,
'ignoring shift and control characters
CheckKeyboardBuffer = Chr$(msgMessage.wParam)
End If

End Function
```

When we press a key on the keyboard, the active window is sent a WM_KEYDOWN message, with a low-level code to identify the physical key pressed. The first thing we need to do, then, is to use PeekMessage to look in the message queue to see whether there are any pending WM_KEYDOWN messages, removing it from the queue if we find one. If we found one, we have to translate it into a character code using TranslateMessage, which sends the translated message back to Excel's message queue as a WM_CHAR message. We then look in the message queue for this WM_CHAR message and return the character pressed.

Working with the File System and Network

The procedures included in this section can be found in the MFileSys module of the API Examples.xls workbook.

Finding the User ID

Excel has its own user name property, but does not tell us the user's network logon ID. This ID is often required in Excel applications for security validation, auditing, logging change history and so on. It can be retrieved using the API call shown in Listing 9-10.

Listing 9-10 Reading the User's Login ID

```
Private Declare Function GetUserName Lib "advapi32.dll" _
        Alias "GetUserNameA" _
        (ByVal lpBuffer As String, _
        ByRef nSize As Long) As Long
```

```
'Get the user's login ID
Function UserName() As String

  'A buffer that the API function fills with the login name
  Dim sBuffer As String * 255

  'Variable to hold the length of the buffer
  Dim lStringLength As Long

  'Initialize to the length of the string buffer
  lStringLength = Len(sBuffer)

  'Call the API function, which fills the buffer
  'and updates lStringLength with the length of the login ID,
  'including a terminating null - vbNullChar - character
  GetUserName sBuffer, lStringLength

  If lStringLength > 0 Then
     'Return the login id, stripping off the final vbNullChar
     UserName = Left$(sBuffer, lStringLength - 1)
  End If

End Function
```

Buffers

Every API function that returns textual information, such as the user name, does so by using a buffer that we provide. A buffer comprises a String variable initialized to a fixed size and a Long variable to tell the function how big the buffer is. When the function is called, it writes the text to the buffer (including a final Null character) and (usually) updates the length variable with the number of characters written. (Some functions return the text length as the function's result instead of updating the variable.) We can then look in the buffer for the required text. Note that VBA stores strings in a very different way than the API functions expect, so whenever we pass strings to API functions, VBA does some conversion for us behind the scenes. For this to work properly, we *always* pass strings by value (ByVal) to API functions, even when the function updates the string. Some people prefer to ignore the buffer length information, looking instead for the first vbNullChar character in the buffer and assuming that's the end of the retrieved string, so you may encounter usage like that shown in Listing 9-11.

Listing 9-11 Using a Buffer, Ignoring the Buffer Length Variable

```
'Get the user's login ID, without using the buffer length
Function UserName2() As String
  Dim sBuffer As String * 255
  GetUserName sBuffer, 255
  UserName2 = Left$(sBuffer, InStr(sBuffer, vbNullChar) - 1)
End Function
```

Changing to a UNC Path

VBA's intrinsic ChDrive and ChDir statements can be used to change the active path prior to using `Application.GetOpenFilename`, such that the dialog opens with the correct path preselected. Unfortunately, that can only be used to change the active path to local folders or network folders that have been mapped to a drive letter. Note that once set, the VBA CurDir function will return a UNC path. We need to use API functions to change the folder to a network path of the form \\server\share\path, as shown in Listing 9-12. In practice, the SetCurDir API function is one of the few that can be called directly from your code.

Listing 9-12 Changing to a UNC Path

```
Private Declare Function SetCurDir Lib "kernel32" _
        Alias "SetCurrentDirectoryA" _
        (ByVal lpPathName As String) As Long

'Change to a UNC Directory
Sub ChDirUNC(ByVal sPath As String)

  Dim lReturn As Long

  'Call the API function to set the current directory
  lReturn = SetCurDir(sPath)

  'A zero return value means an error
  If lReturn = 0 Then
    Err.Raise vbObjectError + 1, "Error setting path."
  End If

End Sub
```

Locating Special Folders

Windows maintains a large number of special folders that relate to either the current user or the system configuration. When a user is logged in to Windows with relatively low privileges, such as the basic User account, it is highly likely that the user will only have full access to his personal folders, such as his *My Documents* folder. These folders can usually be found under *C:\Documents and Settings\UserName*, but could be located anywhere. We can use an API function to give us the correct paths to these special folders, using the code shown in Listing 9-13. Note that this listing contains a subset of all the possible folder constants. The full list can be found by searching MSDN for "CSIDL Values." The notable exception from this list is the user's Temp folder, which can be found by using the GetTempPath function. Listing 9-13 includes a special case for this folder, so that it can be obtained through the same function.

Listing 9-13 Locating a Windows Special Folder

```
Private Declare Function SHGetFolderPath Lib "shell32" _
       Alias "SHGetFolderPathA" _
       (ByVal hwndOwner As Long, ByVal nFolder As Long, _
       ByVal hToken As Long, ByVal dwFlags As Long, _
       ByVal pszPath As String) As Long

Private Declare Function GetTempPath Lib "kernel32" _
       Alias "GetTempPathA" _
       (ByVal nBufferLength As Long, _
       ByVal lpBuffer As String) As Long

'More Commonly used CSIDL values.
'For the full list, search MSDN for "CSIDL Values"
Private Const CSIDL_PROGRAMS As Long = &H2
Private Const CSIDL_PERSONAL As Long = &H5
Private Const CSIDL_FAVORITES As Long = &H6
Private Const CSIDL_STARTMENU As Long = &HB
Private Const CSIDL_MYDOCUMENTS As Long = &HC
Private Const CSIDL_MYMUSIC As Long = &HD
Private Const CSIDL_MYVIDEO As Long = &HE
Private Const CSIDL_DESKTOPDIRECTORY As Long = &H10
Private Const CSIDL_APPDATA As Long = &H1A
Private Const CSIDL_LOCAL_APPDATA As Long = &H1C
Private Const CSIDL_INTERNET_CACHE As Long = &H20
```

```
Private Const CSIDL_WINDOWS As Long = &H24
Private Const CSIDL_SYSTEM As Long = &H25
Private Const CSIDL_PROGRAM_FILES As Long = &H26
Private Const CSIDL_MYPICTURES As Long = &H27

'Constants used in the SHGetFolderPath call
Private Const CSIDL_FLAG_CREATE As Long = &H8000&
Private Const SHGFP_TYPE_CURRENT = 0
Private Const SHGFP_TYPE_DEFAULT = 1
Private Const MAX_PATH = 260

'Public enumeration to give friendly names for the CSIDL values
Public Enum SpecialFolderIDs
   sfAppDataRoaming = CSIDL_APPDATA
   sfAppDataNonRoaming = CSIDL_LOCAL_APPDATA
   sfStartMenu = CSIDL_STARTMENU
   sfStartMenuPrograms = CSIDL_PROGRAMS
   sfMyDocuments = CSIDL_PERSONAL
   sfMyMusic = CSIDL_MYMUSIC
   sfMyPictures = CSIDL_MYPICTURES
   sfMyVideo = CSIDL_MYVIDEO
   sfFavorites = CSIDL_FAVORITES
   sfDesktopDir = CSIDL_DESKTOPDIRECTORY
   sfInternetCache = CSIDL_INTERNET_CACHE
   sfWindows = CSIDL_WINDOWS
   sfWindowsSystem = CSIDL_SYSTEM
   sfProgramFiles = CSIDL_PROGRAM_FILES

   'There is no CSIDL for the temp path,
   'so we need to give it a dummy value
   'and treat it differently in the function
   sfTemporary = &HFF
End Enum

'Get the path for a Windows special folder
Public Function SpecialFolderPath( _
        ByVal uFolderID As SpecialFolderIDs) As String

   'Create a buffer of the correct size
   Dim sBuffer As String * MAX_PATH
   Dim lResult As Long

   If uFolderID = sfTemporary Then
```

```
  'Use GetTempPath for the temporary path
  lResult = GetTempPath(MAX_PATH, sBuffer)

  'The GetTempPath call returns the length and a
  'trailing \ which we remove for consistency
  SpecialFolderPath = Left$(sBuffer, lResult - 1)
Else
  'Call the function, passing the buffer
  lResult = SHGetFolderPath(0, _
          uFolderID + CSIDL_FLAG_CREATE, 0, _
          SHGFP_TYPE_CURRENT, sBuffer)

  'The SHGetFolderPath function doesn't give us a
  'length, so look for the first vbNullChar
  SpecialFolderPath = Left$(sBuffer, _
                      InStr(sBuffer, vbNullChar) - 1)
End If

End Function
```

The observant among you might have noticed that we've now come across all three ways in which buffers are filled by API functions:

- GetUserName returns the length of the text by modifying the input parameter.
- GetTempPath returns the length of the text as the function's return value.
- SHGetFolderPath doesn't return the length at all, so we search for the first vbNullChar.

Deleting a File to the Recycle Bin

The VBA Kill statement is used to delete a file, but does not send it to the recycle bin for potential recovery by the user. To send a file to the recycle bin, we need to use the SHFileOperation function, as shown in Listing 9-14:

Listing 9-14 Deleting a File to the Recycle Bin

```
'Structure to tell the SHFileOperation function what to do
Private Type SHFILEOPSTRUCT
  hwnd As Long
```

```
    wFunc As Long
    pFrom As String
    pTo As String
    fFlags As Integer
    fAnyOperationsAborted As Boolean
    hNameMappings As Long
    lpszProgressTitle As String
End Type

Private Declare Function SHFileOperation Lib "shell32.dll" _
        Alias "SHFileOperationA" _
        (ByRef lpFileOp As SHFILEOPSTRUCT) As Long

Private Const FO_DELETE = &H3
Private Const FOF_SILENT = &H4
Private Const FOF_NOCONFIRMATION = &H10
Private Const FOF_ALLOWUNDO = &H40

'Delete a file, sending it to the recycle bin
Sub DeleteToRecycleBin(ByVal sFile As String)

    Dim uFileOperation As SHFILEOPSTRUCT
    Dim lReturn As Long

    'Fill the UDT with information about what to do
    With FileOperation
        .wFunc = FO_DELETE
        .pFrom = sFile
        .pTo = vbNullChar
        .fFlags = FOF_SILENT + FOF_NOCONFIRMATION + _
                  FOF_ALLOWUNDO
    End With

    'Pass the UDT to the function
    lReturn = SHFileOperation(FileOperation)

    If lReturn <> 0 Then
      Err.Raise vbObjectError + 1, "Error deleting file."
    End If

End Sub
```

There are two things to note about this function. First, the function uses a user-defined type to tell it what to do, instead of the more common method of having multiple input parameters. Second, the function returns a value of zero to indicate success. If you recall the SetCurDir function in Listing 9-12, it returns a value of zero to indicate failure! The only way to know which to expect is to check the Return Values section of the function's information page on MSDN.

Browsing for a Folder

All versions of Excel have included the GetOpenFilename and GetSaveAsFilename functions to allow the user to select a filename to open or save. Excel 2002 introduced the common Office FileDialog object, which can be used to browse for a folder, using the code shown in Listing 9-15, which results in the dialog shown in Figure 9-3.

Listing 9-15 Using Excel 2002's FileDialog to Browse for a Folder

```
'Browse for a folder, using the Excel 2002 FileDialog
Sub BrowseForFolder()

  Dim fdBrowser As FileDialog

  'Get the File Dialog object
  Set fdBrowser = Application.FileDialog(msoFileDialogFolderPicker)

  With fdBrowser

    'Initialize it
    .Title = "Select Folder"
    .InitialFileName = "c:\"

    'Display the dialog
    If .Show Then
      MsgBox "You selected " & .SelectedItems(1)
    End If
  End With

End Sub
```

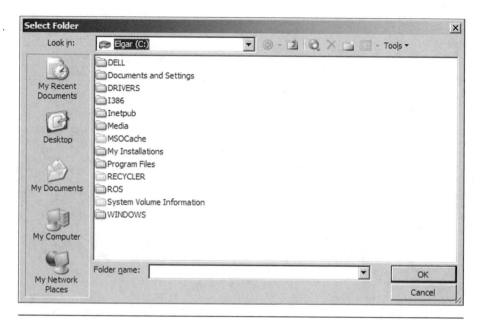

Figure 9-3 The Standard Office 2002 Folder Picker Dialog

We consider this layout far too complicated, when all we need is a simple tree view of the folders on the computer. We can use API functions to show the standard Windows Browse for folder dialog shown in Figure 9-4, which our users tend to find much easier to use. The Windows dialog also gives us the option to display some descriptive text to tell our users what they should be selecting.

Callbacks

So far, every function we've encountered just does its thing and returns its result. However, a range of API functions (including the SHBrowseForFolder function that we're about to use) interact with the calling program while they're working. This mechanism is known as a *callback*. Excel 2000 added a VBA function called AddressOf, which provides the address in memory where a given procedure can be found. This address is passed to the API function, which calls back to the procedure found at that address as required. For example, the EnumWindows function iterates through all the top-level windows, calling back to the procedure with the details of each window it finds. Obviously, the procedure being called must be defined exactly as Windows expects it to be so the API function can pass it the correct number and type of parameters.

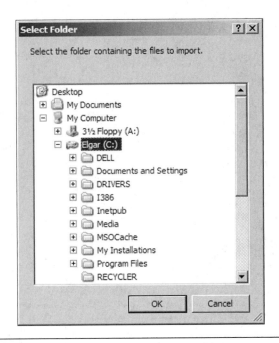

Figure 9-4 The Standard Windows Folder Picker Dialog

The SHBrowseForFolder function uses a callback to tell us when the dialog is initially shown, enabling us to set its caption and initial selection, and each time the user selects a folder, enabling us to check the selection and enable/disable the OK button. The full text for the function is contained in the MBrowseForFolder module of the API Examples.xls workbook and a slightly simplified version is shown in Listing 9-16.

Listing 9-16 Using Callbacks to Interact with the Windows File Picker Dialog

```
'UDT to pass information to the SHBrowseForFolder function
Private Type BROWSEINFO
  hOwner As Long
  pidlRoot As Long
  pszDisplayName As String
  lpszTitle As String
  ulFlags As Long
  lpfn As Long
  lParam As Long
  iImage As Long
End Type
```

```
'Commonly used ulFlags constants

'Only return file system directories.
'If the user selects folders that are not
'part of the file system (such as 'My Computer'),
'the OK button is grayed.
Private Const BIF_RETURNONLYFSDIRS As Long = &H1

'Use a newer dialog style, which gives a richer experience
Private Const BIF_NEWDIALOGSTYLE As Long = &H40

'Hide the default 'Make New Folder' button
Private Const BIF_NONEWFOLDERBUTTON As Long = &H200


'Messages sent from dialog to callback function

Private Const BFFM_INITIALIZED = 1
Private Const BFFM_SELCHANGED = 2


'Messages sent to browser from callback function
Private Const WM_USER = &H400

'Set the selected path
Private Const BFFM_SETSELECTIONA = WM_USER + 102

'Enable/disable the OK button
Private Const BFFM_ENABLEOK = WM_USER + 101


'The maximum allowed path
Private Const MAX_PATH = 260

'Main Browse for directory function
Declare Function SHBrowseForFolder Lib "shell32.dll" _
        Alias "SHBrowseForFolderA" _
        (ByRef lpBrowseInfo As BROWSEINFO) As Long

'Gets a path from a pidl
Declare Function SHGetPathFromIDList Lib "shell32.dll" _
        Alias "SHGetPathFromIDListA" _
        (ByVal pidl As Long, _
         ByVal pszPath As String) As Long
```

```
'Used to set the browse dialog's title
Declare Function SetWindowText Lib "user32" _
        Alias "SetWindowTextA" _
        (ByVal hwnd As Long, _
        ByVal lpString As String) As Long

'A versions of SendMessage, to send strings to the browser
Private Declare Function SendMessageString Lib "user32" _
        Alias "SendMessageA" (ByVal hwnd As Long, _
        ByVal wMsg As Long, ByVal wParam As Long, _
        ByVal lParam As String) As Long

'Variables to hold the initial options,
'set in the callback function
Dim msInitialPath As String
Dim msTitleBarText As String

'The main function to initialize and show the dialog
Function GetDirectory(Optional ByVal sInitDir As String, _
        Optional ByVal sTitle As String, _
        Optional ByVal sMessage As String, _
        Optional ByVal hwndOwner As Long, _
        Optional ByVal bAllowCreateFolder As Boolean) _
        As String

    'A variable to hold the UDT
    Dim uInfo As BROWSEINFO

    Dim sPath As String
    Dim lResult As Long

    'Check that the initial directory exists
    On Error Resume Next
    sPath = Dir(sInitDir & "\*.*", vbNormal + vbDirectory)
    If Len(sPath) = 0 Or Err.Number <> 0 Then sInitDir = ""
    On Error GoTo 0

    'Store the initials setting in module-level variables,
    'for use in the callback function
    msInitialPath = sInitDir
    msTitleBarText = sTitle

    'If no owner window given, use the Excel window
```

```
'N.B. Uses the ApphWnd function in MWindows
If hwndOwner = 0 Then hwndOwner = ApphWnd

'Initialise the structure to pass to the API function
With uInfo
    .hOwner = hwndOwner
    .pszDisplayName = String$(MAX_PATH, vbNullChar)
    .lpszTitle = sMessage
    .ulFlags = BIF_RETURNONLYFSDIRS + BIF_NEWDIALOGSTYLE _
        + IIf(bAllowCreateFolder, 0, BIF_NONEWFOLDERBUTTON)

    'Pass the address of the callback function in the UDT
    .lpfn = LongToLong(AddressOf BrowseCallBack)
End With

'Display the dialog, returning the ID of the selection
lResult = SHBrowseForFolder(uInfo)

'Get the path string from the ID
GetDirectory = GetPathFromID(lResult)

End Function



'Windows calls this function when the dialog events occur
Private Function BrowseCallBack (ByVal hwnd As Long, _
        ByVal Msg As Long, ByVal lParam As Long, _
        ByVal pData As Long) As Long

Dim sPath As String

'This is called by Windows, so don't allow any errors!
On Error Resume Next

Select Case Msg
Case BFFM_INITIALIZED
    'Dialog is being initialized,
    'so set the initial parameters

    'The dialog caption
    If msTitleBarText <> "" Then
        SetWindowText hwnd, msTitleBarText
    End If
```

```
    'The initial path to display
    If msInitialPath <> "" Then
      SendMessageString hwnd, BFFM_SETSELECTIONA, 1, _
                        msInitialPath
    End If

  Case BFFM_SELCHANGED
    'User selected a folder
    'lParam contains the pidl of the folder, which can be
    'converted to the path using GetPathFromID
    'sPath = GetPathFromID(lParam)

    'We could put extra checks in here,
    'e.g. to check if the folder contains any workbooks,
    'and send the BFFM_ENABLEOK message to enable/disable
    'the OK button:
    'SendMessage hwnd, BFFM_ENABLEOK, 0, True/False
  End Select

End Function



'Converts a PIDL to a path string
Private Function GetPathFromID(ByVal lID As Long) As String

  Dim lResult As Long
  Dim sPath As String * MAX_PATH

  lResult = SHGetPathFromIDList(lID, sPath)

  If lResult <> 0 Then
    GetPathFromID = Left$(sPath, InStr(sPath, Chr$(0)) - 1)
  End If

End Function

'VBA doesn't let us assign the result of AddressOf
'to a variable, but does allow us to pass it to a function.
'This 'do nothing' function works around that problem
Private Function LongToLong(ByVal lAddr As Long) As Long
  LongToLong = lAddr
End Function
```

Let's take a closer look at how this all works. First, most of the shell functions use things called PIDLs to uniquely identify folders and files. For simplicity's sake, you can think of a PIDL as a handle to a file or folder, and there are API functions to convert between the PIDL and the normal file or folder name.

The GetDirectory function is the main function in the module and is the function that should be called to display the dialog. It starts by validating the (optional) input parameters, then populates the BROWSEINFO user-defined type that is used to pass all the required information to the SHBrowseForFolder function. The **hOwner** element of the UDT is used to provide the parent window for the dialog, which should be the handle of the main Excel window, or the handle of the userform window if showing this dialog from a userform. The **ulFlags** element is used to specify detailed behavior for the dialog, such as whether to show a Make Folder button. The full list of possible flags and their purpose can be found on MSDN by searching for the SHBrowseForFolder function. The **lpfn** element is where we pass the address of the callback function, BrowseCallBack. We have to wrap the AddressOf value in a simple LongToLong function, because VB doesn't let us assign the value directly to an element of a UDT.

After the UDT has been initialized, we pass it to the SHBrowseForFolder API function. That function displays the dialog and Windows calls back to our BrowseCallBack function, passing the BFFM_INITIALIZED message. We respond to that message by setting the dialog's caption (using the SetWindowText API function) and the initial folder selection (by sending the BFFM_SETSELECTIONA message back to the dialog with the path string).

Every time the user clicks a folder, it triggers a Windows callback to our BrowseCallBack function, passing the BFFM_SELCHANGED message and the ID of the selected folder. All the code to respond to that message is commented out in this example, but we could add code to check whether the folder is a valid selection for our application (such as whether it contains any workbooks) and enable/disable the OK button appropriately (by sending the BFFM_ENABLEOK message back to the dialog).

When the user clicks the OK or Cancel button, the function returns the ID of the selected folder and execution continues back in the GetDirectory function. We get the textual path from the returned ID and return it to the calling code.

Practical Examples

All the routines included in this chapter have been taken out of actual Excel applications, so are themselves practical examples of API calls.

The PETRAS application files for this chapter can be found on the CD in the folder \Application\Ch09—*Understanding and Using Windows API Calls* and now includes the following files:

- **PetrasTemplate.xlt**—The timesheet template
- **PetrasAddin.xla**—The timesheet data-entry support add-in
- **PetrasReporting.xla**—The main reporting application
- **PetrasConsolidation.xlt**—A template to use for new results workbooks
- **Debug.ini**—A dummy file that tells the application to run in debug mode
- **PetrasIcon.ico**—A new icon file, to use for Excel's main window

PETRAS Timesheet

Until this chapter, the location used by the Post to Network routine has used Application.GetOpenFilename to allow the user to select the directory to save the timesheet workbook to. The problem with that call is that the directory must already contain at least one file. In this chapter, we add the BrowseForFolder dialog and use that instead of GetOpenFilename, which allows empty folders to be selected.

We've also added a new feature to the timesheet add-in. In previous versions you were prompted to specify the consolidation location the first time you posted a timesheet workbook to the network. When you selected a location, that location was stored in the registry and from there on out the application simply read the location from the registry whenever you posted a new timesheet.

What this didn't take into account is the possibility that the consolidation location might change. If it did, you would have no way, short of editing the application's registry entries directly, of switching to the new location. Our new Specify Consolidation Folder feature enables you to click a button on the toolbar and use the Windows browse for folders dialog to modify the consolidation folder. The SpecifyConsolidationFolder procedure is shown in Listing 9-17 and the updated toolbar is shown in Figure 9-5.

Listing 9-17 The New SpecifyConsolidationFolder Procedure

```
Public Sub SpecifyConsolidationFolder()

    Dim sSavePath As String

    InitGlobals

    ' Get the current consolidation path.
    sSavePath = GetSetting(gsREG_APP, gsREG_SECTION, _
            gsREG_KEY, "")

    ' Display the browse for folders dialog with the initial
    ' path display set to the current consolidation folder.
    sSavePath = GetDirectory(sSavePath, _
            gsCAPTION_SELECT_FOLDER, gsMSG_SELECT_FOLDER)

    If Len(sSavePath) > 0 Then
        ' Save the selected path to the registry.
        If Right$(sSavePath, 1) <> "\" Then _
            sSavePath = sSavePath & "\"
        SaveSetting gsREG_APP, gsREG_SECTION, _
            gsREG_KEY, sSavePath
    End If

End Sub
```

Table 9-2 summarizes the changes that have been made to the timesheet add-in for this chapter.

Figure 9-5 The Updated PETRAS Timesheet Toolbar

Table 9-2 Changes to the PETRAS Timesheet Add-in to Use the BrowseForFolder Routine

Module	Procedure	Change
MBrowseForFolder (new module)		Included the entire MBrowseForFolder module shown in Listing 9-16
MEntryPoints	PostTimeEntriesToNetwork	Added call to the GetDirectory function in MBrowseForFolder
	SpecifyConsolidationFolder	New feature to update the consolidation folder location

PETRAS Reporting

The changes made to the central reporting application for this chapter are to display a custom icon for the application and to enable the user to close all the results workbooks simultaneously, by holding down the Shift key while clicking the *File > Close* menu. The detailed changes are shown in Table 9-3, and Listing 9-18 shows the new MenuFileClose routine that includes the check for the Shift key.

Table 9-3 Changes to the PETRAS Reporting Application for Chapter 9

Module	Procedure	Change
MAPIWrappers (new module)	ApphWnd	Included Listing 9-4 to obtain the handle of Excel's main window
MAPIWrappers (new module)	SetIcon	Included Listing 9-7 to display a custom icon, read from the new PetrasIcon.ico file.
MAPIWrappers	IsKeyPressed	Included Listing 9-8 to check for the Shift key held down when clicking *File > Close*
MGlobals		Added a constant for the icon filename
MWorkspace	ConfigureExcelEnvironment	Added a call to SetIcon
MEntryPoints	MenuFileClose	Added check for Shift key being held down, shown in Listing 9-17, doing a Close All if so

Listing 9-18 The New MenuFileClose Routine, Checking for a Shift+Close

```
'Handle the File > Close menu
Sub MenuFileClose()

  Dim wkbWorkbook As Workbook

  'Ch09+
  'Check for a Shift+Close
  If IsKeyPressed(gksKeyboardShift) Then

    'Close all results workbooks
    For Each wkbWorkbook In Workbooks
      If IsResultsWorkbook(wkbWorkbook) Then
        CloseWorkbook wkbWorkbook
      End If
    Next
  Else
    'Ch09-

    'Close only the active workbook
    If IsResultsWorkbook(ActiveWorkbook) Then
      CloseWorkbook ActiveWorkbook
    End If
  End If

End Sub
```

Later chapters, particularly *Chapter 10 — Userform Design and Best Practices*, use more of the routines and concepts introduced in this chapter.

Conclusion

The Excel object model provides an extremely rich set of tools for us to use when creating our applications. By including calls to Windows API functions, we can enhance our applications to give them a truly professional look and feel.

This chapter has explained most of the uses of API functions that are commonly encountered in Excel application development. All the fundamental concepts have been explained and you should now be able to interpret and understand new uses of API functions as you encounter them.

All of the example routines included in this chapter have been taken from actual Excel applications and are ready for you to use in your own workbooks.

CHAPTER 10

Userform Design and Best Practices

Userforms are a fundamental part of most applications' user interfaces, ranging from custom message and input boxes to very complex data-entry forms. This chapter explains how to get the most out of Excel's userforms.

Principles

When we design and code userforms, we strive to adhere to a small set of basic principles whenever possible, explained below. We have found that following these principles has resulted in userforms that are easy to use, easy to code and easy to maintain. Although some of these principles may seem a little artificial at first, experience has shown that sticking to them gives long-term rewards.

Keep It Simple

A userform should not need a help file to explain how to fill it in. When presented with a userform, our users should intuitively be able to use it. In practice, this means having a relatively small number of controls on a userform that are well positioned, clearly labeled and in appropriate groupings and orders to match the task for which the userform will be used. When designing a userform to help with a complex task, a wizard style should be used, breaking the userform down into multiple steps, each of which adheres to the Keep It Simple, Stupid (KISS) principle. There are, of course, situations that require complex userforms. In these cases, extra effort should be invested to make the userform as simple to use as possible. Making a complex userform as easy as possible for the user usually requires the most effort on the part of the programmer and often results in quite complex code!

Display Canvas, Not Business Rules

A userform is a user interface element, not a place to implement business logic. The user interaction should always be separated from the business response to that interaction, at least logically if not physically. In practice, this means that the only code that should be included in controls' event procedures is either (a) changing another control's properties, or (b) calling functions in the business logic layer. Conversely, the code in the business logic layer should never refer directly to controls on the userform and ideally should not assume that a specific display mechanism is being used (such as a set of option buttons vs. a list box).

So what is business logic in this context? Figure 10-1 shows a simple userform with a combo box to select a region and a two-column list to show sales by product.

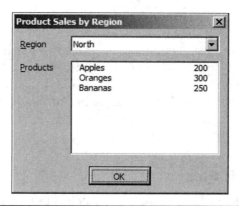

Figure 10-1 A Simple Userform

If the code in the combobox_change event procedure identifies the region, retrieves the products for the region, retrieves the total sales for each product and adds them to the list box, it's implementing business logic and is doing too much.

When the user selects a new region, there are two things we need to specify: (1) the appropriate response, and (2) the data required to satisfy that response. In our example, the appropriate response is to populate the list of products and the data required to satisfy the response is the list of products and the total sales for each.

At a minimum, the data required to satisfy the response should be obtained from the business logic layer. In this case, we would have a function in the business logic layer that takes a region as a parameter and returns an array of products and total sales. It does this by retrieving the underlying data from the data access layer and populating the array. Code in the combobox_change event would read the selected region from the combo box, call the business logic layer function to get the array of products and sales and write that array to the list box. Listing 10-1 shows an example of this mechanism.

Listing 10-1 The User Interface Layer Determines the Response

```
'***********************************
'* User Interface Layer, FSimpleForm
'***********************************

'Handle selecting a different region
Private Sub cboRegion_Change()

  Dim vaProductSales As Variant

  'Get the Product/Sales array for the selected region
  'from the business logic layer
  vaProductSales = GetProductSalesForRegion(cboRegion.Value)

  'Populate the list box
  lstProducts.List = vaProductSales

End Sub
```

At the extreme, we introduce a new user interface support (UIS) layer that contains the code to determine the appropriate response for each user action. The event procedure would then contain a single line that calls a procedure in the UIS layer, passing the selected region. The UIS layer calls the function in the business logic layer to retrieve the array of products and total sales, then tells the userform to populate the list with the array. This mechanism treats the userform as nothing more than a drawing and inter-action layer and is an extremely useful way to handle complex forms. An example of this technique can be found in the UISLayer.xls workbook on the CD. In Listing 10-2, the UIS layer is physically located in a separate class module that tells the userform what to do by raising custom events. For more details about class modules and custom events, see *Chapter 7— Using Class Modules to Create Objects*.

Listing 10-2 The User Interface Support Layer Determines the Response

```
'**************************************
'* User Interface Layer in
'* userform FComplexForm
'**************************************

'UIS Event handler
Dim WithEvents mclsUISComplexForm As CUISComplexForm


'Initialize our UIS class
Private Sub UserForm_Initialize()
   Set mclsUISComplexForm = New CUISComplexForm
End Sub

'

' Control events, to handle the user telling us
' to do something. In most cases, we just pass it
' on to the UIS class.
'

'Handle selecting a different region
Private Sub cboRegion_Change()

   'Tell the UIS layer that the user
   'just selected a different region
   mclsUISComplexForm.RegionSelected cboRegion.Value

End Sub



'

' UIS class events, to handle the UIS layer
' telling us to do something
'


'Populate the Product Sales List
Private Sub mclsUISComplex_PopulateProductList( _
      vaProductSales As Variant)

   lstProducts.List = vaProductSales
End Sub
```

```
'***************************************************
'* User Interface Support Layer
'* in class CUISComplexForm
'***************************************************

'Events to tell the userform what to do
Public Event PopulateProductList(vaProductSales As Variant)


'The user selected a different region.
Public Sub RegionSelected(ByVal sRegion As String)

    Dim vaProductSales As Variant

    'Get the Product/Sales array from the business logic layer
    vaProductSales = GetProductSalesForRegion(sRegion)

    'Tell the userform to populate the products list
    RaiseEvent PopulateProductList(vaProductSales)

End Sub
```

There is obviously more overhead in using an intermediate UIS layer, but it reduces most of the userform event procedures to one-line calls into the UIS layer, enabling us to concentrate on the detail of the user experience within the userform module. This makes the userform itself much easier to maintain. Notice also that the UIS class has no knowledge of how the information is obtained or displayed—all it knows is that when it's given a region, it should tell the userform that there's a new list of products. The UIS class could be used by multiple versions of the same userform—perhaps with each one optimized for different screen resolutions.

Use Classes, Not the Default Instance

Whenever we add a userform to a project, we automatically get a default instance of the userform created for us. This is effectively a global variable that has the same name as the userform's class name, declared As New. This means that as soon as we refer to the userform, Excel creates the default instance for us (this is known as *auto-instantiation*). When we unload the userform, the default instance is destroyed and when we refer to it again, the default instance is re-created. Consider a userform,

FMyForm, containing a single text box, txtName. The code in Listing 10-3 shows the userform and displays the name.

Listing 10-3 Using the Userform's Default Instance

```
Sub TestDefaultInstance()

  'Show the userform
  FMyForm.Show

  'Show the contents of the text box
  MsgBox "The name is: " & FMyForm.txtName.Text

End Sub
```

Run the procedure, type a name into the text box and close the userform using the [x] in the top-right corner. The procedure runs without any errors, but the message box doesn't show us the name we typed in! This is because when the [x] was clicked, the userform was unloaded and anything entered into it was lost. Within the MsgBox line, the reference to FMyForm caused Excel to create a new instance of the userform, in which the name is blank.

Do not use default instances. Userforms are just a special type of class module and they should be treated like class modules. By doing so, we gain control over when the userform is created and destroyed, preventing the type of bug demonstrated in Listing 10-3. Listing 10-4 shows the same routine, treating the userform as a class. This time, the name is displayed correctly.

Listing 10-4 Using the Userform Like a Class

```
Sub TestClassInstance()

  'Define our object variable
  Dim frmMyForm As FMyForm

  'Set our object variable to be a new instance of the userform
  Set frmMyForm = New FMyForm

  'Show the userform
  frmMyForm.Show
```

```
'Show the contents of the text box
MsgBox "The name is: " & frmMyForm.txtName.Text

'If showing the userform modeless, we have to unload it
Unload frmMyForm

End Sub
```

Unfortunately, using a userform like this gives us a minor problem that we need to be aware of and workaround: If the userform is unloaded while our object variable is referring to it, we will often get an automation error. This is easily avoided by ensuring our userform is only ever hidden instead of being unloaded. The code in Listing 10-5 can be added to any userforms that have the standard OK and Cancel buttons.

Listing 10-5 Hiding Instead of Unloading a Form

```
'Store whether the user OK'd or Cancel'd
Dim mbOK As Boolean

'Handle the OK button
Private Sub cmdOK_Click()
    mbOK = True
    Me.Hide
End Sub

'Handle the Cancel button
Private Sub cmdCancel_Click()
    mbOK = False
    Me.Hide
End Sub

'Make the [x] behave the same as Cancel
Private Sub UserForm_QueryClose(Cancel As Integer, _
                                CloseMode As Integer)

    If CloseMode = vbFormControlMenu Then
        cmdCancel_Click
        Cancel = True
    End If
```

```
End Sub

'Return whether the OK or Cancel button was clicked
Public Property Get OK() As Boolean
    OK = mbOK
End Property
```

Expose Properties and Methods, Not Controls

Following the philosophy of treating a userform like a class, we should only interact with the userform via properties and methods that we add to the userform's class module; we should never refer to individual controls from outside the userform's module, nor should we set any properties of the userform itself. Proper encapsulation dictates that everything to do with a userform should be contained within the userform. By adding properties and methods to isolate a userform's controls from external code, we gain the ability to rename or change the style of any of the controls, knowing that we won't be breaking any code that uses the userform.

Imagine a userform with a set of three option buttons to select a level of detail for a report. If we were to allow external code to directly access the controls, we might be tempted to write code like Listing 10-6 (where we've assumed the form includes the code from Listing 10-5).

Listing 10-6 Using a Userform's Controls Directly

```
Sub UseTheControls()

  Dim frmOptions As FOptions
  Set frmOptions = New FOptions

  'Show the userform
  frmOptions.Show

  If frmOptions.OK Then
    'Which option was selected?
    If frmOptions.optDetailed.Value Then
      RunDetailedReport

    ElseIf frmOptions.optNormal.Value Then
      RunNormalReport
```

```
   ElseIf frmOptions.optSummary.Value Then
      RunSummaryReport
   End If
 End If

End Sub
```

The result of doing this is that the calling code is very tightly bound to the physical layout of the userform, so if we want to change the userform's layout—such as to use a combo box instead of the three option buttons—we have to check wherever the userform is used and change that code as well as the code within the userform's module.

Instead, we should expose everything using property procedures, so the calling code does not need to know how the property is physically represented on the userform. Listing 10-7 adds a DetailLevel property to the userform, returning the level of detail as an enumeration, which the calling code uses to decide which report to run.

Listing 10-7 Using Property Procedures

```
'
'Within the userform FOptions
'
'Enum for the levels of detail
Public Enum odlOptionDetailLevel
   odlDetailLevelDetailed
   odlDetailLevelNormal
   odlDetailLevelSummary
End Enum

'Property to return the level of detail
Public Property Get DetailLevel() As odlOptionDetailLevel

   'Which option was selected?
   If optDetailed.Value Then
      DetailLevel = odlDetailLevelDetailed

   ElseIf optNormal.Value Then
      DetailLevel = odlDetailLevelNormal

   ElseIf optSummary.Value Then
```

```vba
        DetailLevel = odlDetailLevelSummary
    End If

End Property

'
'The calling code
'
Sub UseAProperty()

  Dim frmOptions As FOptions
  Set frmOptions = New FOptions

  'Show the userform
  frmOptions.Show

  If frmOptions.OK Then
    'Which option was selected?
    If frmOptions.DetailLevel = odlDetailLevelDetailed Then
      RunDetailedReport

    ElseIf frmOptions.DetailLevel = odlDetailLevelNormal Then
      RunNormalReport

    ElseIf frmOptions.DetailLevel = odlDetailLevelSummary Then
      RunSummaryReport
    End If
  End if

End Sub
```

Now if we want to change the option buttons to a combo box, all of the changes are contained within the userform and its code module, making maintenance much easier and much less prone to introducing new bugs. Unfortunately, all the controls on a userform and all the userform's properties are always exposed to external code, so any properties and methods we add get lost in the IntelliSense list. In *Chapter 11 — Interfaces*, we explain how to define and use our own interfaces, which allow us to expose only the properties and methods that we want to be called.

Control Fundamentals

There are a few fundamental details that we simply have to get right when working with controls on userforms.

Naming

As we discussed in *Chapter 3 — Excel and VBA Development Best Practices*, all our controls should be given meaningful names and include a two- or three-character prefix to identify the control type. This enables us to easily identify the control in code and when setting the tab order. For example, we have no idea which button CommandButton1 is, but we can easily identify cmdOK and so on.

Layering

If we include the background, userforms have three drawing layers. When we add a control to a userform, it gets added to one of the top two layers, depending on the type of control. The three layers are identified as follows:

1. The userform background and its scrollbar
2. The Label, CheckBox, ComboBox, CommandButton, Image, OptionButton, RefEdit, ScrollBar, SpinButton, TabStrip, ToggleButton and TextBox controls
3. The Frame, ListBox, MultiPage and other ActiveX controls

Controls in layer 2 can overlap each other, but will always be drawn behind controls in layer 3, whereas all the controls in layer 3 can overlap each other. Fortunately, layer 3 includes the Frame control, so if we want to draw any of the other controls on top of a layer 3 control, we can put it inside a frame. Within a layer, we can arrange our controls' z-order using the *Format > Order* menu items.

Positioning

All controls on a userform should be aligned both horizontally and vertically with a consistent amount of space between them. When people read forms, they read the text of each control, so it is the text that we should align and not the edges of the controls. If we have Snap to Grid switched on and add a text box and a label to a userform, the label will need to be moved down (usually by four pixels) to ensure the text of the label aligns with the text entered into the text box. This can be done by editing the label's Top property, to add four pixels, but how big is a pixel? In *Chapter 9 — Understanding and Using Windows API Calls*, we explained that the pixel size depends on the user's choice of dots per inch, but is usually 0.75 points for the Normal setting of 96 DPI and 0.6 points for the Large setting of 120 DPI. So to move a control by one pixel, we have to add 0.75 or 0.6. Moving and sizing controls pixel by pixel is made much easier by using the *VBE Tools Control Nudger* toolbar, shown in Figure 10-2. This toolbar is part of the VBE Tools add-in, included on the CD in the *Tools*\\ folder.

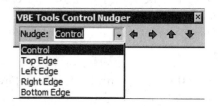

Figure 10-2 The VBE Tools Control Nudger Toolbar

Tab Orders and Accelerator Keys

As designers of userforms, we tend to be "mousers" and often forget that many people prefer to use the keyboard to navigate around userforms. We must remember to facilitate keyboard usage by ensuring we give our controls the correct tab order and/or accelerator keys. The tab order should match the natural reading order—left to right and top to bottom—and should include labels as well as controls. If the userform includes some container controls, such as the Frame and MultiPage controls, we must remember to set the tab order for the controls they contain as well as for those directly on the userform. We do this by ensuring the container control is selected before clicking *View > Tab Order*.

Accelerator keys enable us to use the Alt+key combination to jump directly to the control. The accelerator key for a control is identified by an underscore under the appropriate letter of the control's caption. If we set the accelerator key for a label and use that accelerator key, the focus will jump to the next control in the userform's tab order. This behavior allows us to provide keyboard access to controls that do not have a caption, such as list boxes, edit boxes and so forth.

Data Binding

Many userform controls have properties that allow them to be bound to worksheet cells to specify their contents and/or return their value/text. Don't use them. They are there for beginners to create simple, quick-and-dirty forms, but they very quickly become more trouble than they're worth. Using VBA to set the controls' contents and handle the data entry gives us much more flexibility and enables us to validate the data before updating cells.

Event Handling

The MSForms controls used on userforms have a fairly rich event model. Deciding which event to use for a given purpose can be quite daunting. Our recommendation is to follow the principle of keeping it simple and use the basic Change or Click events for most situations.

In particular, don't try to intercept the KeyDown or KeyPress events in an attempt to force numeric entry into a control. If your code prevents letters, it also prevents the valid use of exponential notation, such as 1E3 for 1000. If you try to prevent multiple decimal separators, you have to make sure you're allowing the decimal separator set in the Regional Settings applet; and if the user put the decimal in the wrong place, you're forcing them to delete the wrong one before typing the new one. It is much better (and easier for us) to allow the user to type in whatever he chooses, then validate the entry using VBA's IsNumeric() function.

Control events are fired both by user action and when the control is changed in code. We can use Application.EnableEvents to turn events on and off for Excel's objects, but that has no effect on the MSForms object model. We can get the same level of control over when events are handled by using a module-level variable that is checked at the start of all our event procedures, as shown in Listing 10-8.

Listing 10-8 Handling Controls' Events

```
'Module-level variable to control events firing
Dim mbStopEvents As Boolean


'Handle clicking a 'Get Data' button
Private Sub btnGetNames_Click()
```

```
Dim vaNames As Variant

'Get a list of names from somewhere
vaNames = Array("Rob", "Stephen", "John", "Robert")

'Turn off events while populating the controls
mbStopEvents = True

'Populate controls.
'The Clear method triggers the Change event.
lstNames.Clear
lstNames.List = vaNames

'Turn events on again
mbStopEvents = False

'Select the first name, allowing the Change event to fire
If lstNames.ListCount > 0 Then
  lstNames.ListIndex = 0
End If

End Sub


'Handle selecting a name
Private Sub lstNames_Change()

  'Don't do anything if we've stopped events
  If mbStopEvents Then Exit Sub

  'Process selecting a name from the list
  MsgBox "You selected " & lstNames.Text

End Sub
```

Validation

Most userforms have controls for data entry and a pair of OK and Cancel buttons. When the OK button is clicked, the data is written to the sheet/database/object model. When the Cancel button is clicked, the data is ignored. At some point between the user entering data and that data being stored, it must be validated. Many people are tempted to use the BeforeUpdate event for their validation code, because it has a Cancel property that can be used to force the user to enter valid data. Don't use it. Our userforms should never get in the way of users, or interrupt their work, yet should also provide feedback as soon as possible, to give them the opportunity (but not force them) to correct their mistakes. Our recommendation is to use an unobtrusive form of validation in each control's AfterUpdate event and an intrusive form of validation in the OK button's Click event. By intrusive, we mean something that stops the user from continuing, such as displaying a message box. By unobtrusive, we mean something that alerts the user to an error situation, but allows them to continue, such as turning the background red and setting the tooltip to show the error message. Listing 10-9 shows the code to validate a simple userform that contains two sales figures, and Figure 10-3 shows the userform with an error in the first edit box.

Listing 10-9 Validating Controls

```
Option Explicit

'When exiting the controls, we perform some
'nonintrusve validation, by calling the
'CheckNumeric function
Private Sub txtSalesNorth_AfterUpdate()
  CheckNumeric txtSalesNorth
End Sub

Private Sub txtSalesSouth_AfterUpdate()
  CheckNumeric txtSalesSouth
End Sub


'In the OK button, we use the same CheckNumeric
'function to show some intrusive validation
'messages.
Private Sub btnOK_Click()

  Dim dNorth As Double
  Dim dSouth As Double
  Dim sError As String
  Dim sAllErrors As String
  Dim bFocusSet As Boolean
```

```
'Validate the North Sales text box,
'returning the value or some error text
If Not CheckNumeric(txtSalesNorth, dNorth, sError) Then

   'Set the focus to the first control with an error
   If Not bFocusSet Then
     txtSalesNorth.SetFocus
     bFocusSet = True
   End If

   'Build an error string, so we display all errors on the
   'userform in one error message
   sAllErrors = sAllErrors & "North Sales:" & sError & vbLf
End If

'Validate the South Sales text box,
'returning the value or some error text
If Not CheckNumeric(txtSalesSouth, dSouth, sError) Then

   'Set the focus to the first control with an error
   If Not bFocusSet Then
     txtSalesSouth.SetFocus
     bFocusSet = True
   End If

   'Build an error string, so we display all errors on the
   'userform in one error message
   sAllErrors = sAllErrors & "South Sales:" & sError & vbLf
End If

'Display any errors we got
If Len(sAllErrors) > 0 Then
   MsgBox "Please correct the following error(s):" & _
          vbLf & sAllErrors, vbOKOnly
Else
   'No errors, so store the result
   ActiveSheet.Range("rngNorthSales").Value = dNorth
   ActiveSheet.Range("rngSouthSales").Value = dSouth

   'And unload the userform
   Unload Me
End If

End Sub
```

```vb
'The Cancel button just unloads the userform.
'This assumes the form is self-contained, so the
'calling routine doesn't need to know if the user
'OK'd or Cancelled the form.
Private Sub btnCancel_Click()
   Unload Me
End Sub


'Function to check a control (textbox or combobox) for
'numeric entry
'
'Parameters:  txtData [in]  The textbox or combobox
'             dResult [out] The numeric value from the box
'             sError  [out] The text of the error message
'
Function CheckNumeric(ByRef txtData As MSForms.Control, _
    Optional ByRef dResult As Double, _
    Optional ByRef sError As String) As Boolean

   Const sERR As String = ". Error: "
   Dim lErrPos As Long

   'Remove any existing tooltip error text
   lErrPos = InStr(1, txtData.ControlTipText, sERR)
   If lErrPos > 0 Then
     txtData.ControlTipText = Left$(txtData.ControlTipText, _
         lErrPos - 1)
   End If

   'Check for valid entry
   If txtData.Text = "" Then
     'Allow empty
     dResult = 0
     sError = ""
     CheckNumeric = True

     'And give the text box its usual background
     txtData.BackColor = vbWindowBackground

   ElseIf IsNumeric(txtData.Text) Then
     'Numeric, so set the return values
     dResult = CDbl(txtData.Text)
     sError = ""
```

```
      CheckNumeric = True

      'And give the text box its usual background
      txtData.BackColor = vbWindowBackground
  Else
      'Not numeric, so set the return values
      dResult = 0
      sError = "Entry is not a number."
      CheckNumeric = False

      'Give the text box a red background
      txtData.BackColor = vbRed

      'And add the error message to the tooltip
      txtData.ControlTipText = txtData.ControlTipText & _
          sERR & sError
  End If

End Function
```

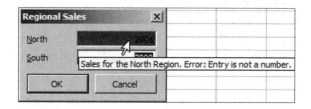

Figure 10-3 An Unobtrusive Error Indicator

Visual Effects

Userform Window Styles

We mentioned briefly in *Chapter 9 — Understanding and Using Windows API Calls* that we can use a few API functions to modify the appearance of a window's border and/or title bar. Listing 10-10 shows the SetUserformAppearance procedure to do just that for userforms, enabling us to independently set the following attributes:

- Whether the userform has a title bar
- Whether the title bar is the normal size or the small size used for floating toolbars

- Whether the userform is resizable
- Whether the userform has a maximize button
- Whether the userform has a minimize button
- Whether the userform has a close button
- Whether the userform has an icon and the icon to use

To set the appearance for a userform we call the SetUserform Appearance procedure from the Userform_Initialize event, passing in the required set of values from the UserformWindowStyles enumeration, added together. This code is included on the CD in the MFormStyles module in the UserformStyles.xls workbook and uses the FindOurWindow and SetIcon procedures shown in *Chapter 9 — Understanding and Using Windows API Calls*.

Listing 10-10 Modifying a Userform's Window Styles

```
'Windows API calls to do all the dirty work
Private Declare Function GetWindowLong Lib "user32" Alias _
    "GetWindowLongA" (ByVal hWnd As Long, _
    ByVal nIndex As Long) As Long

Private Declare Function SetWindowLong Lib "user32" Alias _
    "SetWindowLongA" (ByVal hWnd As Long, _
    ByVal nIndex As Long, ByVal dwNewLong As Long) As Long

Private Declare Function GetSystemMenu Lib "user32" _
    (ByVal hWnd As Long, ByVal bRevert As Long) As Long

Private Declare Function DeleteMenu Lib "user32" _
    (ByVal hMenu As Long, ByVal nPosition As Long, _
    ByVal wFlags As Long) As Long

Private Declare Function DrawMenuBar Lib "user32" _
    (ByVal hWnd As Long) As Long

'Window API constants
Private Const GWL_STYLE As Long = (-16)
Private Const GWL_EXSTYLE As Long = (-20)
Private Const WS_CAPTION As Long = &HC00000
Private Const WS_SYSMENU As Long = &H80000
Private Const WS_THICKFRAME As Long = &H40000
Private Const WS_MINIMIZEBOX As Long = &H20000
Private Const WS_MAXIMIZEBOX As Long = &H10000
```

```
Private Const WS_EX_DLGMODALFRAME As Long = &H1
Private Const WS_EX_TOOLWINDOW As Long = &H80
Private Const SC_CLOSE As Long = &HF060

'Public enum of our userform styles
Public Enum UserformWindowStyles
  uwsNoTitleBar = 0
  uwsHasTitleBar = 1
  uwsHasSmallTitleBar = 2
  uwsHasMaxButton = 4
  uwsHasMinButton = 8
  uwsHasCloseButton = 16
  uwsHasIcon = 32
  uwsCanResize = 64
  uwsDefault = uwsHasTitleBar Or uwsHasCloseButton
End Enum


'Routine to set a userform's window style,
'called from Userform_Initialize event
Sub SetUserformAppearance(ByRef frmForm As Object, _
        ByVal lStyles As UserformWindowStyles, _
        Optional ByVal sIconPath As String)

  Dim sCaption As String
  Dim hWnd As Long
  Dim lStyle As Long
  Dim hMenu As Long

  'Find the window handle of the form
  sCaption = frmForm.Caption
  frmForm.Caption = "FindThis" & Rnd
  hWnd = FindOurWindow("ThunderDFrame", frmForm.Caption)
  frmForm.Caption = sCaption

  'If we want a small title bar, we can't have an icon,
  'max or min buttons as well
  If lStyles And uwsHasSmallTitleBar Then
    lStyles = lStyles And Not (uwsHasMaxButton Or _
        uwsHasMinButton Or uwsHasIcon)
  End If

  'Get the normal windows style bits
```

```
lStyle = GetWindowLong(hWnd, GWL_STYLE)

'Update the normal style bits appropriately

'If we want and icon or Max, Min or Close buttons,
'we have to have a system menu
ModifyStyles lStyle, lStyles, uwsHasIcon Or _
        uwsHasMaxButton Or uwsHasMinButton Or _
        uwsHasCloseButton, WS_SYSMENU

'Most things need a title bar!
ModifyStyles lStyle, lStyles, uwsHasIcon Or _
        uwsHasMaxButton Or uwsHasMinButton Or _
        uwsHasCloseButton Or uwsHasTitleBar Or _
        uwsHasSmallTitleBar, WS_CAPTION

ModifyStyles lStyle, lStyles, uwsHasMaxButton, WS_MAXIMIZEBOX
ModifyStyles lStyle, lStyles, uwsHasMinButton, WS_MINIMIZEBOX
ModifyStyles lStyle, lStyles, uwsCanResize, WS_THICKFRAME

'Update the window with the normal style bits
SetWindowLong hWnd, GWL_STYLE, lStyle

'Get the extended style bits
lStyle = GetWindowLong(hWnd, GWL_EXSTYLE)

'Modify them appropriately
ModifyStyles lStyle, lStyles, uwsHasSmallTitleBar, _
        WS_EX_TOOLWINDOW

'The icon is different to the rest--
'we set a bit to turn it off, not on!
If lStyles And uwsHasIcon Then
  lStyle = lStyle And Not WS_EX_DLGMODALFRAME

  'Set the icon, if given
  If Len(sIconPath) > 0 Then
    SetIcon hWnd, sIconPath
  End If
Else
  lStyle = lStyle Or WS_EX_DLGMODALFRAME
End If
```

```
'Update the window with the extended style bits
SetWindowLong hWnd, GWL_EXSTYLE, lStyle

'The Close button is handled by removing it from the
'control menu, not through a window style bit
If lStyles And uwsHasCloseButton Then
   'We want it, so reset the control menu
   hMenu = GetSystemMenu(hWnd, 1)
Else
   'We don't want it, so delete it from the control menu
   hMenu = GetSystemMenu(hWnd, 0)
   DeleteMenu hMenu, SC_CLOSE, 0&
End If

'Refresh the window with the changes
DrawMenuBar hWnd

End Sub


'Helper routine to check if one of our style bits is set
'and set/clear the corresponding Windows style bit
Private Sub ModifyStyles(ByRef lFormStyle As Long, _
      ByVal lStyleSet As Long, _
      ByVal lChoice As UserformWindowStyles, _
      ByVal lWS_Style As Long)

   If lStyleSet And lChoice Then
      lFormStyle = lFormStyle Or lWS_Style
   Else
      lFormStyle = lFormStyle And Not lWS_Style
   End If

End Sub
```

Disabling the Close Button

Even though the procedure shown in Listing 10-10 can be used to remove the close menu from a userform, the standard Windows keystroke of Alt+F4 to close a window can still be used to close the form. We handle this by hooking the UserForm_QueryClose event, as shown in Listing

10-11. The QueryClose event can be used without removing the Close button, but that gives conflicting messages to the user; you're showing an enabled Close button, but it doesn't do anything.

Listing 10-11 Preventing the User Closing the Userform

```
'Set the form to have a (small) title bar, but no Close button
Private Sub UserForm_Initialize()

  SetUserformAppearance Me, uwsHasSmallTitleBar

End Sub

'Prevent the form being closed using Alt+F4
Private Sub UserForm_QueryClose(Cancel As Integer, _
    CloseMode As Integer)

  Cancel = (CloseMode = vbFormControlMenu)

End Sub
```

Displaying Graphics, Charts, WordArt and So Forth on Userforms

Userforms have very limited graphics capabilities; although we can set the colors and fonts of the controls and use empty labels to draw rectangles, we can't draw diagonal lines, arrows, ovals and so on. Neither can we embed other objects on to the userform to display charts, WordArt and so forth. We can, however, draw our graphics on a worksheet, copy them to the clipboard and paste them as pictures to use for the background of many of the MSForms controls. To set the picture, select the control (or the userform itself), click in the Picture property box in the Properties window and either click the ellipsis to select an image file or just press Ctrl+V to paste a picture from the clipboard. Most of the controls stretch the picture to fill the control, but with the Image, Frame and Page controls and the userform background, we can control the picture sizing (zoom, stretch or crop), alignment (within the control) and whether the picture is tiled to fill the control.

At runtime, we can use Excel's CopyPicture method to copy a range, chart or other drawing object to the clipboard and our PastePicture function to retrieve the image from the clipboard as a standard Picture object that can be assigned to the Picture property of the MSForms controls. The function uses lots of complex Windows API calls to extract the picture from the clipboard, so it's best to treat it as a "black box" by just copying the entire MPastePicture module into your project. We did this in *Chapter 8 — Advanced Command Bar Handling* to set a command bar button's Picture and Mask properties. The MPastePicture module can be found in the PastePicture.xls example workbook, which demonstrates how to display a chart on a userform, shown in Figure 10-4. The relevant part of the code to update the chart is shown in Listing 10-12.

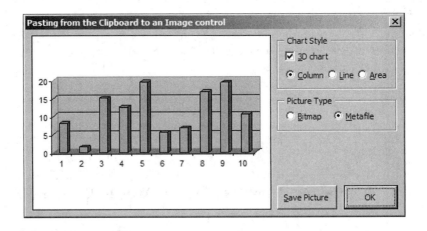

Figure 10-4 Displaying a Chart on a Userform

Listing 10-12 Displaying a Chart on a Userform

```
'Update the chart image on the form
Private Sub UpdateChart()

  Dim chtChart As Chart
  Dim lPicType As Long

  'Find the chart object on the sheet
  Set chtChart = Sheet1.ChartObjects(1).Chart

  'Do we want a metafile or a bitmap?
  'If scaling the image, xlPicture will give better results
```

```
'If not scaling, xlBitmap will give a 'truer' rendition.
'obMetafile is the 'Metafile' option button on the form
lPicType = IIf(obMetafile, xlPicture, xlBitmap)

'Copy the chart to the clipboard, as seen on screen
chtChart.CopyPicture xlScreen, lPicType, xlScreen

'Paste the picture from the clipboard into our image control
Set imgChtPic.Picture = PastePicture(lPicType)

End Sub
```

Locking vs. Disabling Controls

When text boxes and combo boxes are disabled, Excel displays the text in gray, but keeps the white background. If there is no text in the box, there is no way for the user to tell whether it is disabled or not. An alternative is to keep the control enabled, but locked and with a gray background. Locking a text box or combo box allows the user to select any text in it, but not change the text. This can be very useful when displaying information to the user that they may want to copy to the clipboard, such as an error message. Figure 10-5 shows a section of a userform containing three text boxes—one disabled, one locked with a gray background and the third used as a label. In our opinion, the middle text box gives the best visual indicator that it is disabled, while keeping the text readable. Listing 10-13 shows the standard routine that we use to "disable" our controls by locking them. Unfortunately, we cannot use the same technique for a list box, because it doesn't redraw the selection indicator when the background color is changed!

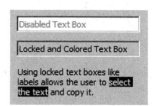

Figure 10-5 Three Text Boxes

Listing 10-13 Standard Procedure to "Disable" a Control by Locking It

```
'Enable/Disable a control by locking it and
'changing the background color
Public Sub EnableControl(ByRef ctlControl As MSForms.Control, _
                    ByVal bEnable As Boolean)

  ctlControl.Locked = Not bEnable
  ctlControl.BackColor = IIf(bEnable, vbWindowBackground, _
                                vbButtonFace)

End Sub
```

Popup Menus

When designing complex userforms, we have a continual trade-off between adding features to make the userform easier to use versus confusing the user by making the userform too cluttered. For example, if we have a list box with a long list of names, we could make it easier to find a name by adding options to sort by forename or surname, in ascending or descending order. We could add these controls as sets of option buttons or combo boxes, but those take up valuable space on the form and make it appear too cluttered. An alternative mechanism is to put those options in a command bar created with the msoBarPopup style, then show that popup when the user right-clicks the list box. Figure 10-6 shows a list box with the popup, and Listing 10-14 shows the code to handle the right-click and show the popup. This code assumes the command bar has already been created and other routines handle the menu item selections.

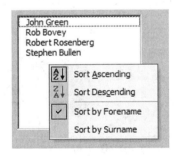

Figure 10-6 A List Box with Popup Sort Menu

Listing 10-14 Showing a Popup for a List Box

```
'Show a Sort Method popup when the list box is right-clicked
Private Sub lstNames_MouseDown(ByVal Button As Integer, _
    ByVal Shift As Integer, ByVal X As Single, _
    ByVal Y As Single)

  '2=Right Button
  If Button = 2 Then
    Application.CommandBars("NameSortPopup").ShowPopup
  End If

End Sub
```

Userform Positioning and Sizing

Positioning Next to a Cell

If we're displaying a userform in response to the user selecting a menu item from the cell's popup menu, it is a nice touch to display the userform directly alongside the cell (assuming there's space for it on the screen). Trying to work out the exact position of a cell on the screen using the Range's position is extremely difficult, because we would have to account for the zoom factor, scroll settings, which toolbars were displayed and whether the Excel application window is maximized. Fortunately there is an easier workaround, which is to make use of the window that Excel uses for editing embedded charts. If we create a chart object over the cell and activate it, Excel moves a window with the class name EXCELE to that position. We can immediately delete the chart object, use API functions to read the position of the EXCELE window and display our userform in the same place. Listing 10-15 shows a procedure to move a userform over a cell and an example of it being used to display a userform alongside of the active cell. You can find this routine on the CD in the MFormPos module of UserformPositioning.xls. Note that the routine uses functions in the MScreen and MWindows modules from the API Examples.xls workbook documented in *Chapter 9 — Understanding and Using Windows API Calls.*

Listing 10-15 Showing a Userform Next to the Active Cell

```
'API Functions to find a window and read its position
Private Declare Function FindWindowEx Lib "user32" _
    Alias "FindWindowExA" (ByVal hWnd1 As Long, _
    ByVal hWnd2 As Long, ByVal lpsz1 As String, _
    ByVal lpsz2 As String) As Long

Private Declare Function GetWindowRect Lib "user32" _
    (ByVal hWnd As Long, lpRect As RECT) As Long

Private Type RECT
   Left As Long
   Top As Long
   Right As Long
   Bottom As Long
End Type


'Routine to move a form to a given cell
Public Sub MoveFormToCell(frmForm As Object, _
    rngCell As Range)

   Dim hWndDesk As Long
   Dim hWndChart As Long
   Dim uChartPos As RECT

   'Create a chart object at the cell, activate it and
   'immediately delete it. That puts the EXCELE chart
   'editing window in the correct place
   With rngCell.Parent.ChartObjects.Add(rngCell.Left, _
         rngCell.Top, 1, 1)

      .Activate
      .Delete
   End With

   'Find the EXCELE window
   hWndDesk = FindWindowEx(ApphWnd, 0, "XLDESK", vbNullString)
   hWndChart = FindWindowEx(hWndDesk, 0, "EXCELE", vbNullString)

   'Read its position
   GetWindowRect hWndChart, uChartPos
```

```
'Move the form to the same position,
'converting pixels to points
frmForm.Left = uChartPos.Left * PointsPerPixel
frmForm.Top = uChartPos.Top * PointsPerPixel

End Sub


'Test procedure to show a form next to the active cell
Sub ShowMyForm()

  Dim frmForm As FMyForm

  Set frmForm = New FMyForm

  'Set the form to show in a custom position
  frmForm.StartUpPosition = 0

  'Move the form over the cell
  MoveFormToCell frmForm, ActiveCell.Offset(0, 1)

  'Show the form
  frmForm.Show

End Sub
```

Responding to Different Resolutions

We regularly see questions in the Microsoft support newsgroups from people who have designed a userform to fill their screen, only to find that it's too big for their users' lower resolutions. The question usually ends "How do I change the user's resolution to display my userform?" The answer is always "You don't." Instead, we have to design our userforms so they are usable on the lowest resolution our users have. Typically, that means a resolution of 800×600 pixels, although people with poor sight or very small screens may use 640×480 pixels. Designing our userforms to fit on a 640×480 display gives us two main issues to solve:

1. We can't fit many controls on a 640×480 userform.
2. Userforms that fit on a 640×480 screen often make very poor use of the space available with larger resolutions.

In practice, most of the userforms we create are quite simple and can usually fit within the bounds of a 640×480 screen. For complex forms, we usually use popup menus, drop-down panes (see later) and/or a wizard style to make the most of the available space and may design multiple versions of the same form, for use with different screen resolutions. The forms for lower resolutions will use more compact controls, such as combo boxes instead of sets of option buttons or list boxes and have less blank space around each control, whereas the forms for higher resolutions will have more controls directly visible, with each control using more space. If we correctly split our code between the form layer and business logic layer, both forms can use the same class for their business logic.

Resizable Userforms

Part of the KISS principle is avoiding overwhelming the user. Experience has shown us that if a userform won't fit on an 800×600 resolution screen, it almost certainly contains too many controls. For that reason, we design our forms to fit on an 800×600 screen, but make them resizable so the user can choose to make better use of the space available if they have a higher-resolution screen. For example, if our userform includes a list box, we allow the list box to change size with the form, thereby allowing the user to see more items in the list. The FormResizer.xls example workbook contains a class module, CFormResizer, which can be included in a project to handle the resizing of any form. The class changes the form's window styles to make it resizable and handles the resizing and repositioning of all the controls on the form.

We define the resize behavior of each control by setting its Tag property to indicate by how much each of its top, left, height and/or width should change in proportion to the change in size of the form. To make one of the properties change as the form is sized, we include the letter T, L, H, or W followed by a number giving the percentage change (or omitted for 100 percent). For example, if we have an OK button in the middle bottom of the form, we would want it to move up/down the same amount as the change in the form's height and move left/right by half the change in the form's width; its Tag would be TL0.5. If we have a form with a pair of list boxes side by side, we would want the left list box to keep its top and left constant, but grow by the full change in the form's height and half the change in the form's width; its Tag would be HW0.5. The right-hand list box would resize the same way, but should also move across by half the change in form's width (so its right edge stays constant relative to the right edge of the form); its Tag would be L0.5HW0.5.

To start including resizable userforms in your applications, copy the CFormResizer class into the project, hook it up to a form using the code shown in Listing 10-16 and set the controls' Tag properties appropriately. It will probably take some trial and error to get the tags correct at first, but will become much easier with practice. For best results, list boxes should have their IntegralHeight property set to False, and due to an Excel bug, they may need an extra blank item added to the bottom of the list for all the items to display correctly.

Listing 10-16 Making a Userform Resizable Using the CFormResizer Class

```
'Declare an object of our CFormResizer class to handle
'resizing for this form
Dim mclsResizer As CFormResizer

'The Resizer class is set up in UserForm_Initialize
Private Sub UserForm_Initialize()

  'Create the instance of the class
  Set mclsResizer = New CFormResizer

  'Tell it which form it's handling
  Set mclsResizer.Form = Me

End Sub


'When the form is resized, the UserForm_Resize event is
'raised, which we just pass on to the Resizer class
Private Sub UserForm_Resize()
    mclsResizer.FormResize
End Sub


'The QueryClose event is called whenever the form is closed.
'We call the FormResize method one last time, to store the
'form's final size and position in the registry
Private Sub UserForm_QueryClose(Cancel As Integer, _
    CloseMode As Integer)

  mclsResizer.FormResize
End Sub
```

Splitter Bars

If our resizable userforms contain two or more list boxes, it may not be always desirable to let them both grow or shrink at the same rate. We can allow our users to decide how much space to give each form by adding a splitter bar between them. We don't actually have a splitter bar control, but we can fake one using a normal Label. The userform shown in Figure 10-7 has two list boxes that are both configured for their width to change at half the rate of the form's change in width, keeping the gap between them central to the form. We've also added a label to fill the gap between the list boxes. For clarity, it is shown here with its name, but would normally be transparent and blank. The label's MousePointer property has been changed to fmMousePointerSizeWE, so we get the standard left/right sizing arrows when the mouse moves over the label. The code in Listing 10-17 uses the label's mouse events to simulate a splitter bar.

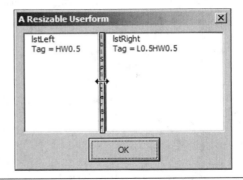

Figure 10-7 A Splitter Bar Between Two List Boxes

Listing 10-17 The Code to Turn a Label into a Splitter Bar

```
'Module variables to handle the splitter bar
Dim mbSplitterMoving As Boolean
Dim mdSplitterOrigin As Double

'When pressing down the left mouse button,
'initiate the dragging and remember where we started
Private Sub lblSplitterBar_MouseDown( _
     ByVal Button As Integer, ByVal Shift As Integer, _
     ByVal X As Single, ByVal Y As Single)

  If Button = 1 Then
    mbSplitterMoving = True
    mdSplitterOrigin = X
```

```
      End If
End Sub

'When releasing the left mouse button,
'stop the dragging
Private Sub lblSplitterBar_MouseUp( _
      ByVal Button As Integer, ByVal Shift As Integer, _
      ByVal X As Single, ByVal Y As Single)

   If Button = 1 Then mbSplitterMoving = False
End Sub

'When moving the mouse over the label
'and we're in 'drag' mode (i.e. dragging the splitter),
'move all the controls appropriately
Private Sub lblSplitterBar_MouseMove( _
      ByVal Button As Integer, ByVal Shift As Integer, _
      ByVal X As Single, ByVal Y As Single)

   Dim dChange As Double

   'Are we doing a drag?
   If mbSplitterMoving Then

      'Find where we moved to
      dChange = (X - mdSplitterOrigin) / PointsPerPixel

      'Adjust the control sizes and positions
      If (lstLeft.Width + dChange > 0) And _
         (lstRight.Width - dChange > 0) Then

         'The left list changes size
         lstLeft.Width = lstLeft.Width + dChange

         'The splitter bar in the middle moves
         lblSplitterBar.Left = lblSplitterBar.Left + dChange

         'The right list moves and changes size
         lstRight.Left = lstRight.Left + dChange
         lstRight.Width = lstRight.Width - dChange
      End If
   End If

End Sub
```

Wizards

Wizard dialogs are normally used when we need to collect a reasonably large amount of data from the user. The only absolute requirement this data must fulfill in order to be a candidate for a wizard dialog is that the bits of data being collected must be logically related to each other in some way. Wizard dialogs are particularly useful where the data being collected has the following characteristics in addition to being logically related:

- The information is complex and varied.
- The information must be supplied in a defined order because earlier selections alter the allowable parameters of later selections.
- The user does not need to understand the relationship between earlier and later choices. The wizard dialog can then abstract this decision-making process away from the user.

The primary purpose of a wizard dialog is to reduce the number of choices the user must make at any one time to a manageable level. An important secondary purpose of a wizard dialog is to allow us to alter the parts of the user interface that depend on the selections the user is currently making without having to do so in a way that is visible to the user and thereby potentially distract them from the task at hand (see *Dynamic Userforms* later for an example).

Design Rules for Wizard Dialogs

1. The first page of a wizard dialog should explain the purpose of the wizard and the steps involved, but always have a "Don't show me this again" check box to automatically skip the first page if the user wants.
2. The last page of a wizard dialog should confirm everything the user has entered and all the choices made, and no actions are performed until the user clicks the Finish button.
3. Always display the step number within the wizard that the user is currently working on as well as the total number of steps left to complete. This information is typically displayed in the title bar, although we've seen perfectly acceptable designs that display it elsewhere.
4. Navigation through the wizard is typically controlled by a series of four buttons: Cancel, Back, Next and Finish. The enabled state of these buttons should be used to provide visual clues to the user

about how they're doing. Track the user's progress through the wizard and watch their input during each step of the wizard. Based on where the user is and what data he has entered, enable only the navigation buttons that makes sense, such as the following:

- First step with no data entered—The Cancel button should be the only button enabled. (Cancel is always enabled.)
- The Next button is only enabled when the page passes all validation checks, as long as the user can determine which are the invalid entries and why (see *Validation* earlier).
- Last step with all data entered and validated—Cancel enabled, Back enabled, Next disabled and Finish enabled.
- The user has completed all wizard steps correctly but then used the Back button to revisit an earlier step—All buttons enabled until the user makes an entry that invalidates the ability of the wizard to finish or move forward.
- In, say, a five-step wizard, if steps four and five allow the user to enter optional information, the Finish button can be enabled after step three. Excel's Chart Wizard is a good example of this.

5. The user can move back and forth through wizards to his heart's content. Therefore, you must always keep track of the status of all steps in the wizard in order to properly set the status of the navigation buttons. It is perfectly appropriate for the user to click Finish from step two of a five-step wizard as long as he has completed all five steps and has just moved back to step two in order to make a minor change.

6. In some wizard designs, selections made on a step affect other selections on that same step. If a selection on a step makes another selection on that same step unnecessary, do not **hide** the controls for the unnecessary selection. Just disable them. Controls that pop in and out of existence in front of the user's face tend to be a confusing distraction.

Creating a Wizard Dialog

The easiest way to create a wizard dialog is to use a MultiPage control, with each page of the control being used for a separate step of the wizard and a common set of buttons at the bottom. Figure 10-8 shows the wizard userform template included on the CD in the WizardDemo.xls workbook, with the MultiPage tabs showing on the right side. Prior to distributing the wizard, the MultiPage should be formatted to not have any tabs showing by setting its Style property to fmTabStyleNone, and reducing both the MultiPage's and userform's width accordingly.

Unfortunately, the MultiPage control is not without its problems, particularly when using non-MSForms controls within a page. If you intend to use the RefEdit control or any of the Windows Common Controls (such as the TreeView and ListView control), you should use a separate Frame control for each step of the wizard instead of a MultiPage control. If using a Frame control, it's easiest to develop the wizard with all the frames visible at the same time, on a userform much larger than the final version. When the wizard is complete, change the frames' left and top so they all overlap and reduce the userform to its correct size.

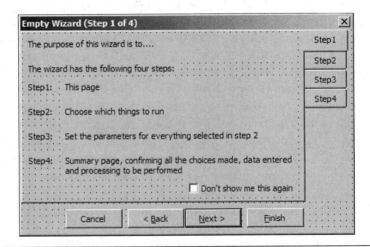

Figure 10-8 An Empty Wizard Userform Using a MultiPage Control for the Steps

Listing 10-18 shows the code for the four navigation buttons, which each call further procedures to initialize and validate the controls in each step. The content of the InitializeStep and bValidateStep procedures will obviously depend on the contents of the step, so have not been shown here. As well as initializing the controls on each page, the InitializeStep procedure should update the userform's caption to show the step number and enable/disable the navigation buttons.

Listing 10-18 The Navigation Code for a Wizard Dialog

```
Private Sub cmdCancel_Click()
  mbUserCancel = True
  Me.Hide
End Sub


Private Sub cmdBack_Click()
  ' Can't go back from step 1.
  If mlStep > 1 Then
    ' No validation is required when moving back.
    mlStep = mlStep - 1
    mpgWizard.Value = mlStep - 1
    InitializeStep mlStep
  End If
End Sub


Private Sub cmdNext_Click()
  ' Can't go forward from the last step.
  If mlStep <= mlNumSteps Then
    ' We validate the controls on the current step
    ' before allowing the user to move forward.
    If bValidateStep(mlStep) Then    ' Validation succeeded.
      mlStep = mlStep + 1
      mpgWizard.Value = mlStep - 1
      InitializeStep mlStep
    Else                ' Validation failed.
      MsgBox gsErrMsg, vbCritical, gsAPP_TITLE
      gsErrMsg = gsEMPTY_STRING
    End If
  End If
End Sub


Private Sub cmdFinish_Click()
  ' The last step must be validated before the user
  ' is allowed to complete the wizard.
  If bValidateStep(mlStep) Then    ' Validation succeeded.
    mbUserCancel = False
    Me.Hide
  Else                ' Validation failed.
    MsgBox gsErrMsg, vbCritical, gsAPP_TITLE
    gsErrMsg = gsEMPTY_STRING
  End If
End Sub
```

Dynamic Userforms

Most userforms that we create are static, which is to say they have a fixed number of controls that are always visible (although may be disabled at certain times). Dynamic userforms display different controls each time the form is shown.

Subset Userforms

The easiest way to create a dynamic userform is to start with a form that has more controls of all types than we'll ever need. When the form is shown, we set the position, caption and so on of all the controls we need, hide the extra controls that we don't use and set the userform's size to encompass only the controls we use. This method is ideal to use when the upper limit on the number of controls is known and when each control is a known type. An example would be a survey, where each question might have between two and five responses for the user to pick between. We create the form with five option buttons, set their captions with the applicable responses for each question and hide the unused buttons.

Code-Created and Table-Driven Userforms

If we cannot predict a reasonable upper limit on the number of controls, or if there could be lots of different types of control that could be shown, having a pre-prepared set of controls on the form becomes increasingly harder to maintain. Instead, we can add controls to the userform at run-time. It's quite rare to find a situation that requires a userform to be created through code; we can usually either design the form directly or use the "subset" technique to hide the controls we don't need to use.

The one situation where code-created userforms make our development life extremely easy is in the use of table-driven dynamic wizards. Imagine a wizard used to generate a batch of reports, with each report using check boxes to set its options. In Step 2 of the wizard, we could display a multiselect list box of the available reports, where the list of reports is read from a table in a worksheet. When the user clicks the Next > button, we populate Step 3 of the wizard with the check boxes appropriate for the selected report(s), where again the check boxes are read from a worksheet table. By implementing a table-driven report wizard, we can add new reports to the wizard just by adding rows to the report and report options lists. An example of this technique can be found on the CD in the ReportWizard.xls workbook and is explained below.

Figure 10-9 shows an extract of the wksReportOptions worksheet, containing the lists of the available reports and their options, and Figure 10-10 shows Step 3 of the Report Wizard dialog, where the Client Detail report has been selected to run.

Report List	Report Options			
	Report	Name	Caption	Default
Client Detail	Client Detail	CDIncProjects	Include Project Details	Y
Client Summary	Client Detail	CDIncTasks	Include Task Details	Y
Staff Detail	Staff Detail	SDIncHolidays	Include Holidays	N
Staff Summary	Staff Detail	SDGroupByClient	Group Results by Client	Y

Figure 10-9 A List of Reports and Their Options

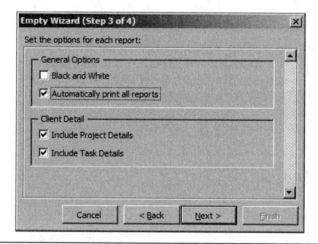

Figure 10-10 The Table-Driven Step 3 of the Report Wizard

In this step, the General Options pane is a permanent part of the wizard and contains options common to all the reports. The report-specific panes, such as the Client Detail pane, are created each time this step is initialized. A separate pane is created for each selected report that has some options (note that the two summary reports have no options), using the code in Listing 10-19.

Listing 10-19 Code to Create the Report Options Panels

```
'Procedure to create the Report Option panels in Step 3
Private Sub CreateReportOptions()
```

```
Dim vaOptions As Variant
Dim lReport As Long
Dim lOption As Long
Dim sReport As String
Dim fraFrame As MSForms.Frame
Dim chkControl As MSForms.CheckBox
Dim ctlControl As MSForms.Control
Dim dFraTop As Double
Dim dCtlTop As Double

'Constants for each column in the Report Options table
Const clREPORT = 1
Const clPARAM = 2
Const clCAPTION = 3
Const clDEFAULT = 4

'Read the report options table into an array
vaOptions = wksReportLists.Range("rngReportOptions").Value

'Clear out existing group boxes
For Each ctlControl In fraReportOptions.Controls
   If TypeOf ctlControl Is MSForms.Frame And _
      ctlControl.Name <> "fraGeneral" Then

      fraReportOptions.Controls.Remove ctlControl.Name
   End If
Next

'Get the position of the top of the first frame
dFraTop = fraGeneral.Top + fraGeneral.Height + 6

'Loop through the reports
For lReport = 0 To lstReports.ListCount - 1

   'Was this one selected to run?
   If lstReports.Selected(lReport) Then

      'Get its name from the list box
      sReport = lstReports.List(lReport)

      'A new report, so clear the frame
      Set fraFrame = Nothing
```

```vba
'Loop through the options array
For lOption = 1 To UBound(vaOptions)


    'Is the option for the selected report?
    If vaOptions(lOption, clREPORT) = sReport Then

        'If we don't have a frame for this report,
        'create one
        If fraFrame Is Nothing Then

            'Add a new frame to the dialog
            Set fraFrame = fraReportOptions.Controls.Add( _
                    "Forms.Frame.1", "fraRpt" & lReport, True)

            'Set the frame's size and position
            With fraFrame
                .Caption = sReport
                .SpecialEffect = fmSpecialEffectSunken
                .Top = dFraTop
                .Left = fraGeneral.Left
                .Width = fraGeneral.Width
            End With

            'Where to put the first control in the frame
            dCtlTop = chkBlackWhite.Top
        End If

        'Add a check box to the report's frame
        Set chkControl = fraFrame.Controls.Add( _
                "Forms.CheckBox.1", _
                vaOptions(lOption, clPARAM), True)

        'Set its size and position, caption and value
        With chkControl
            .Top = dCtlTop
            .Left = chkBlackWhite.Left
            .Width = chkBlackWhite.Width
            .Height = chkBlackWhite.Height

            .Caption = vaOptions(lOption, clCAPTION)
            .Value = GetSetting(gsREG_APP, gsREG_SECTION, _
                    vaOptions(lOption, clPARAM), _
```

```
                         vaOptions(lOption, clDEFAULT)) = "Y"
             End With

             'Move to the next control position
             dCtlTop = dCtlTop + chkAutoPrint.Top - _
                     chkBlackWhite.Top
          End If
       Next

       If Not fraFrame Is Nothing Then
          'If we have a frame for this report, work out how
          'high it needs to be
          fraFrame.Height = fraGeneral.Height - _
               chkAutoPrint.Top + dCtlTop - _
               (chkAutoPrint.Top - chkBlackWhite.Top)

          'Calculate the position for the next report's frame
          dFraTop = fraFrame.Top + fraFrame.Height + 6
       End If
     End If
  Next

  'Set the scroll area of the Report Options frame,
  'in case our report options don't fit
  fraReportOptions.ScrollHeight = dFraTop

End Sub
```

To keep this example simple, we have only used check boxes for the report's options and forced each check box to be shown on a different row. A real-world version of this technique would have many more columns for the report options, allowing all control types to be used and having more control over their position and style.

Scroll Regions

The observant reader will have noticed that the last line of the procedure shown in Listing 10-19 sets the ScrollHeight of the fraReportOptions frame. This is the frame that contains all the report option panes and was formatted to show a vertical scrollbar in Figure 10-10. Setting the frame's ScrollHeight enables us to add more controls to the frame than can be seen at one time; when the ScrollHeight is bigger than the frame's height, the user can use the scrollbars to see the additional controls. Although this should be considered a last resort in most userform design situations, it can prove very useful when creating dynamic forms that might extend beyond the visible area.

Dynamic Control Event Handling and Control Arrays

The biggest downside of adding controls at runtime is that we cannot add procedures to the userform's code module to handle their events. In theory, we could use the VBA Extensibility library to create a userform in a new workbook, add both controls and event procedures to it and then show the form, but we've yet to encounter a situation that requires such a cumbersome solution. We can, however, use a separate pre-prepared class module to handle (most of) the events of the controls we add to the form. The class module shown in Listing 10-20 uses a variable declared WithEvents to handle the events of any TextBox it's hooked up to. The Change event is used to perform nonintrusive validation of the control, checking that it is a number using the CheckNumeric function from earlier. Ideally, we would prefer to use either the BeforeUpdate or AfterUpdate events to perform the validation, so it's done when the user leaves the control instead of every time it's changed. Unfortunately, those events belong to the generic MSForms.Control object and are not exposed to us when we declare a WithEvents object in this way.

Listing 10-20 Class to Handle a Text Box's Events

```
'Class CTextBoxEvents

'WithEvents variable to hook the events for a text box
Private WithEvents mtxtBox As MSForms.TextBox

'Allow the calling code to set the control to hook
Public Property Set Control(txtNew As MSForms.TextBox)
  Set mtxtBox = txtNew
End Property

'Validate the text box with each change.
'Ideally, we'd using the AfterUpdate event, but
'we don't get it through the WithEvents variable
Private Sub mtxtBox_Change()
  CheckNumeric mtxtBox
End Sub
```

Every time we add a text box to the form, we create a new instance of the class to handle its events and store all the class instances in a module-level collection, as shown in Listing 10-21.

Listing 10-21 Assigning Event Handler Classes to Controls Created at Runtime

```
'Module-level collection to store instances of our
'event handler class
Dim mcolEvents As Collection

'Build the userform in the initialize routine
Private Sub UserForm_Initialize()

  Dim sBoxes As String
  Dim lBoxes As Long
  Dim lBox As Long
  Dim lblLabel As MSForms.Label
  Dim txtBox As MSForms.TextBox
  Dim clsEvents As CTextBoxEvents

  'Ask the user how many boxes to show
  sBoxes = InputBox("How many boxes (1-5)?", , "3")

  'Validate the entry
  If sBoxes = "" Then Exit Sub
  If Not IsNumeric(sBoxes) Then Exit Sub

  lBoxes = CLng(sBoxes)
  If lBoxes < 1 Then lBoxes = 1
  If lBoxes > 5 Then lBoxes = 5

  'Initialize the collection of event handler classes
  Set mcolEvents = New Collection

  'Create the required number of boxes
  For lBox = 1 To lBoxes

    'Add a label to the form
    Set lblLabel = Me.Controls.Add("Forms.Label.1", _
            "lbl" & lBox)
```

```
With lblLabel
   .Top = (lBox - 1) * 21.75 + 9
   .Left = 6
   .Width = 50
   .Height = 9.75
   .WordWrap = False
   .Caption = "Text Box " & lBox
End With

'Add the text box to the form
Set txtBox = Me.Controls.Add("Forms.TextBox.1", _
         "txt" & lBox)

With txtBox
   .Top = (lBox - 1) * 21.75 + 6
   .Left = 56
   .Width = 50
   .Height = 15.75
End With

'Create a new instance of the event handler class
Set clsEvents = New CTextBoxEvents

'Tell it to handle the events for the text box
Set clsEvents.Control = txtBox

'Add the event handler instance to our collection,
'so it stays alive during the life of the form
mcolEvents.Add clsEvents
   Next

End Sub
```

We can use the same technique to handle the events of controls in non-dynamic userforms as well. Imagine a form with 50 text boxes, all requiring numeric validation. We could include all 50 Change event procedures in our code and accept the maintenance overhead that brings, or we could use the class module from Listing 10-20 to handle the validation for all our text boxes. The code in Listing 10-22 iterates through all the controls on the form, hooking up new instances of the event handler class for every text box it finds.

Listing 10-22 Class to Handle a Text Box's Events

```
'Collection to store instances of our event handler class
Dim mcolEvents As Collection

'Hook the events for all the Text Boxes
Private Sub UserForm_Initialize()

  Dim ctlControl As MSForms.Control
  Dim clsEvents As CTextBoxEvents

  'Initialize the collection of event handler classes
  Set mcolEvents = New Collection

  'Loop through all the controls
  For Each ctlControl In Me.Controls

    'Check if it's a text box
    If TypeOf ctlControl Is MSForms.TextBox Then

      'Create a new instance of the event handler class
      Set clsEvents = New CTextBoxEvents

      'Tell it to handle the events for the text box
      Set clsEvents.Control = ctlControl

      'Add the event handler instance to our collection,
      'so it stays alive during the life of the form
      mcolEvents.Add clsEvents
    End If
  Next

End Sub
```

Modeless Userforms

Most of the dialogs that we normally come into contact with are modal, which is to say that neither the application nor the user can do anything until the form is dismissed. When the Show statement is processed, by default the application window is disabled (so none of the menus are available), the form is displayed and the code stops. Snippets of code can run in response to control events, but it's not until the user closes the form that execution continues on the line after the Show statement.

When a userform is shown modeless, however, code execution continues immediately after the Userform_Initialize and Userform_Activate event procedures have finished, with the userform remaining displayed. If the code comes to an end while a modeless userform is displayed, the form remains open and both the userform and the application window can be used.

NOTE: Excel 97 does not support modeless userforms.

Splash Screens

The simplest use for a modeless userform is as an introductory splash screen. The userform is shown modeless at the start of the Auto_Open or Workbook_Open procedure and unloaded at the end of the procedure. Listing 10-23 shows a simple example, where the form uses the SetUserformAppearance procedure from earlier to remove the title bar.

Listing 10-23 Showing a Splash Screen at Startup

```
Sub Auto_Open()

  Dim frmSplash As FSplashScreen

  'Show the form modelessly
  Set frmSplash = New FSplashScreen
  frmSplash.Show vbModeless

  'Process the startup code
  Application.Wait Now + TimeValue("00:00:5")

  'Unload the splash screen
  Unload frmSplash
  Set frmSplash = Nothing

End Sub
```

```
'The FSplashScreen Userform's Code Module
Option Explicit

'Set the form to have no title bar
Private Sub UserForm_Initialize()

  'Adjust the height for the missing caption
  Me.Height = Me.InsideHeight

  SetUserformAppearance Me, uwsNoTitleBar

End Sub

'Prevent the form being closed using Alt+F4
Private Sub UserForm_QueryClose(Cancel As Integer, CloseMode As Integer)

  Cancel = (CloseMode = vbFormControlMenu)

End Sub
```

Progress Bars

A rather more interesting use of modeless forms is to display progress information to the user during lengthy looping operations. Figure 10-11 shows a simple progress bar userform, where the progress indicator is made up of two overlapping Frame controls, each containing a label. The back frame has a white background and a label with blue text, and the front frame has a blue background and a label with white text. As the progress is updated, the width of the front frame is adjusted, allowing us to see more of the blue background. This makes the bar appear to fill up as the progress increases.

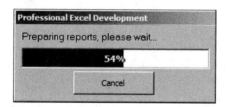

Figure 10-11 A Modeless Progress Bar

The code for the progress bar form is too lengthy to show here, but is included on the CD in the ModelessForms.xls example workbook. The FProgressBar form can be copied from the example workbook into your project and controlled using code such as that shown in Listing 10-24.

Listing 10-24 Using the Progress Bar Userform

```
Sub ShowProgress()

  Dim lLoop As Long
  Dim lIterations As Long
  Dim frmProgress As FProgressBar

  lIterations = 2000

  'Initialize the progress bar
  Set frmProgress = New FProgressBar
  frmProgress.Title = "Professional Excel Development"
  frmProgress.Text = "Preparing reports, please wait..."
  frmProgress.Min = 1
  frmProgress.Max = lIterations

  'Show the progress bar
  frmProgress.ShowForm

  For lLoop = 1 To lIterations
    'Check if the user cancelled
    If frmProgress.Cancelled Then Exit For

    'Update the progress
    frmProgress.Progress = lLoop

    'Do Stuff
  Next lLoop

  'Unload the progress bar form
  Unload frmProgress

End Sub
```

Combining with Menu Items

If we display a modeless userform and then allow our code to finish, the form is left active on the screen, and both the form and the application can be used. This behavior can be used to very good effect in form-based dictator applications. In this design, the worksheet is only ever used for a backdrop graphic display; all the interaction with the user is done through userforms. Most form-based applications have a central "switchboard" form, with a set of buttons to show subforms for each functional area. Those forms have their own buttons to show other forms and so on. It is usually very difficult to navigate around the application. If we use modeless userforms, however, the menus are available, so we can implement a menu structure that enables the user to quickly switch between parts of the application.

To implement this design, we need to be able to communicate with all the forms, so they can be notified when the user clicks a menu item to jump to another form, or when the application is about to exit, or if the Save menu item is clicked. All the forms will have to include the same set of standard functions, shown in Listing 10-25, that can be called from a central "form-handler" routine.

Listing 10-25 Standard Routines to Be Included in All Modeless Forms

```
' Called prior to navigating to another form.
' Allows the form to validate and store its data, then unload
' If validation fails, the navigation can be cancelled
Public Sub BeforeNavigate(ByRef Cancel As Boolean)
End Sub


' Called prior to saving the data workbook
' Allows the form to validate and store its data
' If validation fails, the navigation can be cancelled
Public Sub BeforeSave(ByRef Cancel As Boolean)
End Sub


' Called after saving the data workbook
' Allows the form to update its display
' (e.g. if showing the file name)
Public Sub AfterSave()
End Sub


' Called when the application is about to be closed
```

```
' The form should unload itself, but could cancel the close
Public Sub AppExit(ByRef Cancel As Boolean)
End Sub
```

With all the userforms having the same set of standard routines, we can write a simple centralized routine to manage them all, shown in Listing 10-26.

Listing 10-26 The Central Control Routine to Handle Navigation Between Forms

```
' Global variable to hold the form currently being displayed
Dim gfrmActiveForm As Object

' A single OnAction procedure for most menu items, where the
' form name is obtained from the menu item's Parameter
Sub FormMenuClick()
    ShowForm Application.CommandBars.ActionControl.Parameter
End Sub

'Common routine to switch between forms
Sub ShowForm(ByVal sForm As String)

    Dim bCancel As Boolean

    'If there's an active form, tell it to save and unload
    If Not gfrmActiveForm Is Nothing Then
        gfrmActiveForm.BeforeNavigate bCancel
    End If

    'If the save/close wasn't cancelled,
    If Not bCancel Then
        'Show the next form, assuming it is in the same workbook
        Set gfrmActiveForm = VBA.Userforms.Add(sForm)
        gfrmActiveForm.Show vbModeless
    End If
End Sub

'The OnAction routine for the File > Save menu item
Sub MenuFileSave()

    Dim bCancel As Boolean
```

```
'If there's an active form, tell it to save its data
If Not gfrmActiveForm Is Nothing Then
  gfrmActiveForm.BeforeSave bCancel
End If

If Not bCancel Then
  'Save the data workbook if not cancelled
  gwkbDataWorkbook.Save

  'If there's an active form, tell it to do its post-save
  'processing (if any)
  If Not gfrmActiveForm Is Nothing Then
    gfrmActiveForm.AfterSave
  End If
End If

End Sub
```

Using this mechanism, we can add more userforms to the application without having to add any extra code to control their display; as long as they include the standard set of procedures shown in Listing 10-25, they will plug in to the central control procedure. All we need to do is add the form module to the workbook and add some extra lines to the table used by the command bar builder, to include the new form in our application's menu structure.

Control Specifics

Most of the controls that we use in our forms are well documented and well understood, so documenting them here would be of little benefit to the reader. Instead, this section of the chapter explains how to use some of the lesser-known controls, or how to use them in innovative ways.

ComboBox

The ComboBox is the unsung hero of the MSForms toolbox. By changing the style of the drop-down button, we can use a combo box as a normal drop-down list, as a text box, as a filename entry box or as a totally customized drop-down control. Figure 10-12 shows four combo boxes, with the bottom one shown in its dropped state, revealing a custom drop-down pane for specifying a filter.

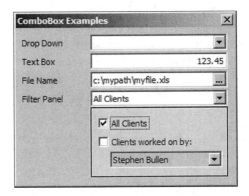

Figure 10-12 Combo Box Styles

Drop-Down List/Combo

The default behavior for a combo box is to allow the user to select an item from a list or type in entries that do not exist in the supplied list; when the arrow is clicked, the list is shown below the combo box. When the user clicks on an item from the list, the selected item is shown in the control and the list is hidden.

Text Box

If we set the ShowDropButtonWhen property to fmShowDrop-ButtonNever and the Style property to fmStyleDropDownCombo, the result is a control that looks and behaves exactly like a text box. This allows us to have a single control that can be used to select an item from a list, or allow direct entry. For example, in the userform in Figure 10-12, the top drop-down may be a list of attributes about a person, such as age, sex and so on, whereas the second drop-down would be used to fill in the value for the selected attribute. When Age is selected from the drop-down, we would want to be able to type a number directly into the control, but when Sex is selected, we would want to show a drop-down to choose between Male and Female.

Filename Box

By changing the DropButtonStyle to fmDropButtonStyleEllipsis, we create a control that looks like a filename box. The user would expect a File Open dialog to appear when he clicks the button. We can do exactly that by hooking the DropButtonClick event, as shown in Listing 10-27.

Listing 10-27 Handle the Ellipsis in the Filename Combo

```
'Handle clicking the ellipsis in the Filename combo
Private Sub cboFileName_DropButtonClick()

  Dim vFile As Variant

  'Get the filename
  vFile = Application.GetOpenFilename()

  'Write it to the control
  If TypeName(vFile) = "String" Then
    cboFileName.Text = vFile
  End If

  'Toggle the Enabled property to move the focus
  'to the next control
  cboFileName.Enabled = False
  cboFileName.Enabled = True

End Sub
```

One annoying aspect of hooking the DropButtonClick event is that we can't cancel it, so the control shows an empty list after we've obtained the filename. One workaround for this is to toggle the Enabled property of the control, which forces the focus to move to the next control in the tab order.

Drop-Down Panes

The fourth combo box shown in Figure 10-12 is used to implement a totally customized drop-down pane, to display a simple filter selection. This would typically be used above a list box, to filter the items in the list. The code to handle the filter pane is shown in Listing 10-28.

Listing 10-28 Code to Manage a Custom Drop-Down Pane

```
'Boolean to identify if the filter has changed
Dim mbFilterChanged As Boolean

'Set up the form
Private Sub UserForm_Initialize()
  cboFilter.AddItem "All Clients"
```

```vba
    cboFilter.ListIndex = 0

    cboConsultant.List = Array("Stephen Bullen", "Rob Bovey", _
                            "John Green")
    cboConsultant.ListIndex = 0
End Sub

'When clicking the drop-down, show the filter frame
Private Sub cboFilter_DropButtonClick()

  mbFilterChanged = False
  fraFilter.Visible = True
  fraFilter.SetFocus

End Sub

'Changing any of the filter options
'sets the 'Filter Changed' Boolean
Private Sub optAllClients_Click()
  mbFilterChanged = True
  cboConsultant.Enabled = optClientsForConsultant.Value
End Sub

Private Sub optClientsForConsultant_Click()
  mbFilterChanged = True
  cboConsultant.Enabled = optClientsForConsultant.Value
End Sub

Private Sub cboConsultant_Change()
  mbFilterChanged = True
End Sub

'When exiting the frame, check for updates to the filter
Private Sub fraFilter_Exit(ByVal Cancel As _
    MSForms.ReturnBoolean)

  CheckFilterFrame
End Sub

'When clicking outside the frame,
'check and close the filter panel
Private Sub UserForm_MouseDown(ByVal Button As Integer, _
    ByVal Shift As Integer, ByVal X As Single, _
```

```
    ByVal Y As Single)

  CheckFilterFrame
End Sub

'Handle clicking outside the frame,
'to check for updates and close the panel
Private Sub CheckFilterFrame()

   'If it's visible, update the list
   If fraFilter.Visible Then
     If mbFilterChanged Then ApplyFilter
   End If

   fraFilter.Visible = False
End Sub

'Apply the changed filter options
Private Sub ApplyFilter()
   'Update the text of the filter dropdown
   If optAllClients Then
     cboFilter.List(0) = "All Clients"
   Else
     cboFilter.List(0) = "Clients for " & cboConsultant.Text
   End If
   'Update the contents of the list box

End Sub
```

The custom drop-down pane is a standard Frame control, initially set to be invisible and with a slightly lighter background color, containing the controls used for our filter. When the user clicks the combo box's drop-down button, we use the DropButtonClick event to initialize a Boolean variable mbFilterChanged (used to identify whether changes are made within the frame), then make the frame visible and give it the focus; this makes the frame appear to "drop down" from the combo box. We include code in the change event for all the controls in the frame to set the Boolean variable to True, indicating that the frame's content has changed. The user can exit the frame by tabbing to or clicking another control (causing the Exit event to fire), or by clicking somewhere else on the userform (which we detect with the Userform_MouseDown event). In both cases, we call the CheckFilterFrame procedure to hide the frame, check whether any of the controls were changed and apply the new filter. In this case, we're just updating the text shown in the combo box to show the filter settings. The combo box style is set to fmStyleDropDownList, so that clicking anywhere in the combo box will cause the DropButtonClick event to fire. We have a single item in the combo box's list, with the ListIndex to zero to show it in the control. To update the text shown in the combo box, we change the text of that item.

Windows Common Controls

There is an OCX file available on most computers called mscomctl.ocx, usually found in the *C:\windows\system32* folder that contains a set of controls collectively known as the Microsoft Windows Common Controls 6.0. Although it theoretically might not exist, we have yet to see a computer with Office installed that doesn't have this file—it is so widely used that anything other than a plain vanilla Windows installation will include the file. It contains the following controls that can be used in our userforms. To access these controls, right-click the control toolbox, select the Additional Controls, menu and put a tick mark beside each of the controls you intend to use:

- Microsoft ImageComboBox Control 6.0
- Microsoft ImageList Control 6.0
- Microsoft ListView Control 6.0
- Microsoft ProgressBar Control 6.0
- Microsoft Slider Control 6.0
- Microsoft StatusBar Control 6.0
- Microsoft TabStrip Control 6.0
- Microsoft ToolBar Control 6.0
- Microsoft TreeView Control 6.0
- Microsoft UpDown Control 6.0

Some of these controls, such as the TabStrip and UpDown controls, are very similar to the standard MSForms controls, but the others can be used to improve the usability of our forms. For example, the ListView is similar to the File pane of Windows Explorer, and enables us to display a list of items with icons, giving us many formatting possibilities for each item in the list. The ListView's "report" style is very similar in appearance to the normal List control, but enables us to display each item using a different font, color and so forth. The TreeView control is an excellent way to display hierarchical data, and the ImageList and ImageCombo controls can be used where displaying thumbnails may be more appropriate than text.

To fully document each of the Windows Common Controls is beyond the scope of this book, but the CommonControls.xls example workbook contains the userform shown in Figure 10-13, with fully commented code to explain its operation.

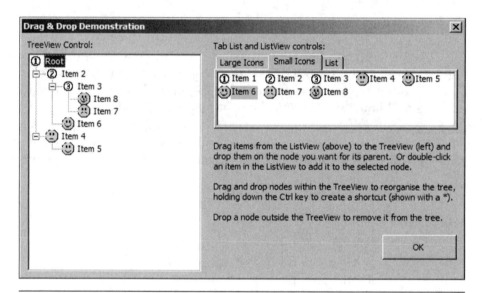

Figure 10-13 Using the Windows Common Controls

The official documentation for the Windows Common Controls can be found in the MSDN library within the Visual Basic 6.0 section. For example, the documentation for the TreeView starts at `http://msdn.microsoft.com/library/en-us/cmctl198/html/vbobjTreeView.asp`. The only issue to be aware of when using the Windows Common Controls on userforms is that they do not like to be placed inside the MultiPage control. Trying to modify a control that is not on the active page usually fails.

Drag and Drop

The normal MSForms controls do not support drag-and-drop operations between controls. If we want to implement drag and drop between controls on our forms (such as being able to drag an item from one list box and drop it on another), we have to either use the Windows Common Controls or use a Visual Basic form. The CommonControls.xls workbook contains fully commented code that implements drag and drop between the ListView and TreeView controls as well as within the TreeView control to change its structure.

Practical Examples

PETRAS Timesheet

The PETRAS timesheet add-in has not been changed for this chapter.

PETRAS Reporting

At this stage of the PETRAS reporting application, it would be artificial to add a suite of userforms just to demonstrate the techniques discussed in this chapter. Therefore, the only change made to the reporting application for this chapter is to display a progress bar while consolidating all the timesheet workbooks. When we modify the application to use a database back end in *Chapter 13 — Programming with Databases*, we will add a set of userforms to the reporting application for the user to maintain the static lists of consultants, clients, projects and so on. The code changes required to add the progress bar are detailed in Table 10-1.

Table 10-1 Changes to the PETRAS Reporting Application for Chapter 10

Module	Procedure	Change
FProgressBar (new form)		Added the FProgressBar form shown in Figure 10-11
MSystemCode	ConsolidateWorkbooks	Modified to use the FProgressBar form instead of writing the progress to the status bar

Conclusion

As programmers, we tend to think that our code is the most important part of an application and dismiss the userforms as mere eye candy. Our users, on the other hand, don't see the code, only the interface that we provide them. The userforms are the most important part of our application to the users, and they will like or dislike our applications based primarily on how well the userforms are designed. For this reason and more, userform design should be as much a priority as any other part of our application development. Taking the time to design userforms that are easy to use, easy to maintain and that adapt to the user's environment can give our workbook the polished appearance expected of a professionally developed application.

CHAPTER 11

Interfaces

The previous few chapters have explained class modules in some depth and the various parts they can play in our applications—handling events, encapsulating functionality and creating our own object models. We've seen that userforms and the workbook and worksheet code modules are just special types of class module. This chapter takes a step further into object-oriented design by explaining how one class can appear to be many different types of object and how many different classes can appear to be the same type of object. We show that by using the techniques explained in this chapter, we can improve the robustness of our solution, simplify the development experience and reduce the amount of code we need to write. As an example, we convert our central consolidation and reporting application to use a plug-in architecture for its userforms, enabling us to extend the application without having to add any more code to the core routines.

What Is an Interface?

An interface is a list of public properties, methods, events, user-defined-types, constants and/or enumerations that we can use to interact with an object. When we dimension a variable to be a certain object type, we're actually specifying the **interface** that the variable will use to talk to an object. When we later make the variable refer to an object, we're specifying which **object** we want to talk to, through that interface. When the code is run, the compiler checks to see whether the object has the interface we specified, and throws a Type Mismatch error if it doesn't, as shown in Listing 11-1.

Listing 11-1 A Type Mismatch Error

```
'Declare a variable that will talk to objects through the
'Worksheet interface
Dim wksInput As Worksheet

'Sheet1 in our workbook has the Worksheet interface,
'so we can talk to it
Set wksInput = Sheet1

'The ThisWorkbook object doesn't have the Worksheet interface,
'so we get a Type Mismatch error.
Set wksInput = ThisWorkbook
```

Whenever we create a class module, the VBA compiler also creates a default interface for that class. The default interface is given the same name as the class and contains a list of all the public properties, methods etc. that we add to the class. When we dimension a variable using `Dim clsTheClass As CClassName`, we're saying that the variable will use the *interface* CClassName. When we use code like `Set clsTheClass = New CClassName`, we're creating an object that is a new instance of the *class* CClassName, then setting the variable to refer to the object, as in Listing 11-2.

Listing 11-2 Variables, Interfaces and Classes

```
'Declare a variable to use the CClassName interface
Dim clsTheClass As CClassName

'Create a new instance of the CClassName class
'and set our variable to refer to it
Set clsTheClass = New CClassName
```

The code in the class defines how the object behaves, whereas the interface defines how we access the code. By hiding this implementation detail from us, VBA makes it much easier for us to work with class modules—we don't need to care whether we're dealing with a class or an interface. Unfortunately, it also hides the useful fact that we can define our own custom interfaces and mix and match classes and interfaces if we want to! The rest of this chapter examines a few ways that we can improve our applications by doing just that.

Code Reuse

One of the basic tenets of good programming is to write routines that can be reused as much as possible. For example, a generic sorting routine, such as the simple bubble sort shown in Listing 11-3, can be used to sort an array of any simple data type.

Listing 11-3 A Generic Bubble Sort

```
'A simple, generic, slow bubble sort, to sort a 1D array
Sub Generic1DBubbleSort(ByRef vaArray As Variant)

    Dim bDoAgain As Boolean
    Dim vTemp As Variant
    Dim iIndex As Integer

    Do
        'Assume we're done
        bDoAgain = False

        'Loop through the array, comparing the names
        For iIndex = LBound(vaArray) To UBound(vaArray) - 1

            'If we found some in the wrong order, ...
            If vaArray(iIndex) > vaArray(iIndex + 1) Then

                '... swap them ...
                vTemp = vaArray(iIndex)
                vaArray(iIndex) = vaArray(iIndex + 1)
                vaArray(iIndex + 1) = vTemp

                '... and remember to loop again.
                bDoAgain = True
            End If
        Next
    Loop While bDoAgain

End Sub
```

Unfortunately, we can't use this routine to sort objects, because there is nothing in the code to say which property to sort on; every type of object would need a specific version of the routine. Let's assume that we're writing an application for a publishing company to manage the production of a book, we're using an object-oriented design and we have a CAuthor class and a CReviewer class (among others). The CAuthor class might look something like Listing 11-4 (but with more properties than just the name!).

Listing 11-4 A CAuthor Class

```
'Name:          CAuthor
'Description:    Class to represent a book's author

Option Explicit

Dim msAuthName As String

Public Property Let AuthorName(sNew As String)
   msAuthName = sNew
End Property

Public Property Get AuthorName() As String
   AuthorName = msAuthName
End Property
```

At some point in the application, we have the requirement to produce a list of Authors, sorted by the author's name. Because this is a collection of objects we're sorting, we cannot just pass them to a generic routine; we have to use a specific routine for each object type such as that shown in Listing 11-5 to sort a collection of Authors using the AuthorName property.

Listing 11-5 A Bubble Sort for the CAuthor Class

```
'A simple bubble sort, to sort a collection of CAuthor objects
Sub BubbleSortAuthors(ByRef colAuthors As Collection)

   Dim bDoAgain As Boolean
   Dim iIndex As Integer
   Dim clsAuthorLow As CAuthor
   Dim clsAuthorHigh As CAuthor

   Do
      'Assume we're done
      bDoAgain = False
```

```
'Loop through the collection, comparing the names
For iIndex = 1 To colAuthors.Count - 1

    'Get the Author objects from the collection at this point
    Set clsAuthorLow = colAuthors(iIndex)
    Set clsAuthorHigh = colAuthors(iIndex + 1)

    'If we found some in the wrong order, ...
    If clsAuthorLow.AuthorName > clsAuthorHigh.AuthorName Then

        '... swap them ...
        colAuthors.Remove iIndex + 1
        colAuthors.Add clsAuthorHigh, , iIndex

        '... and remember to loop again.
        bDoAgain = True
    End If
Next
Loop While bDoAgain

End Sub
```

Similarly, we might need specific routines to sort collections of CReviewer, CEditor, CDistributor and so forth objects. Wouldn't it be much better if we could have a single routine that could sort collections of any of those objects? If we use a custom interface, we can!

Defining a Custom Interface

If we want to create a generic sort routine that will work with any of our classes, we need to be able to talk to each class in the same way—that is, through the same interface—by saying to each one "I don't care what class you are, just give me something to sort you by." To achieve that, we need to give each of our classes a custom interface, through which we can ask for the item to sort with. Our custom interface will be called ISortableObject (by convention, interfaces start with a capital *I*) and will have a single property called SortKey. The generic object sorting routine can then use that interface to ask each object for its key, without caring what type of class it is.

As mentioned previously, whenever we create a class module, the VBA compiler also creates an interface of the same name, containing all the public properties, methods and events that we add to the class. All we need to do to define a custom interface, then, is to create a new class module that contains the properties and methods we want to use, but doesn't have any code in the routines. VBA will create the interface for us behind the scenes, which we can then add to our other classes. So we can define our ISortableObject interface by adding a new class module, giving it the name ISortableObject and a public SortKey property, as shown in Listing 11-6.

Listing 11-6 A ISortableObject Interface Class

```
'Name:          ISortableObject
'Description:   Class to define the ISortableObject interface
'Author:        Stephen Bullen

'Get the key to use in the generic sorting routine
Public Property Get SortKey() As Variant
End Property
```

That's all there is to it. Note that we've defined the SortKey property to return a Variant data type, so we can use the same generic routine for other objects that it may be more appropriate to sort by a number or date.

Implementing a Custom Interface

After we've defined our interface, we have to add it to all the classes that we want to use it with. We do this by adding the Implements keyword at the top of the class module:

```
Implements IsortableObject
```

Figure 11-1 shows that as soon as we add that line to the class, the interface name appears in the object dropdown at the top-left of the code pane, just like an object on a userform.

When the interface name is selected in that drop-down, the right-hand drop-down lists the methods and properties defined for that interface, as shown in Figure 11-2.

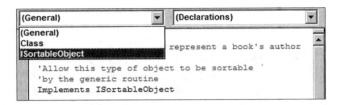

Figure 11-1 The Interface Appears in the Object Drop-Down

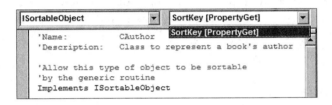

Figure 11-2 With the Interface Selected, the Properties and Methods Appear in the Right-Hand Drop-Down

Clicking one of the methods adds an outline procedure to the code module, just as it does for a userform object's event. We just need to add code to that routine to return the value to use when sorting this type of object. The complete, sortable CAuthor class is shown in Listing 11-7, where the code to implement the ISortableObject interface has been highlighted.

Listing 11-7 The Sortable CAuthor Class

```
'Name:          CAuthor
'Description:   Class to represent a book's author

'Allow this type of object to be sortable
'by the generic routine
Implements ISortableObject

Dim msAuthName As String

Public Property Let AuthorName(sNew As String)
  msAuthName = sNew
End Property

Public Property Get AuthorName() As String
```

```
    AuthorName = msAuthName
End Property
```

```
'Return the value to be used when sorting this object
Private Property Get ISortableObject_SortKey() As Variant
  ISortableObject_SortKey = AuthorName
End Property
```

Note that the name of the ISortableObject_SortKey routine is the concatenation of the interface name and the property name and that it is a Private property of the CAuthor class, so won't appear on the CAuthor interface.

Using a Custom Interface

With the custom ISortableObject interface defined and implemented in our CAuthor class, we can modify our BubbleSortAuthors routine to be able to sort collections of any class that implements our ISortableObject interface, shown in Listing 11-8. All we need to do is to define our data types As ISortableObject instead of As CAuthor, use the SortKey property instead of AuthorName and change the variable names to be more generic.

Listing 11-8 A Bubble Sort for Classes That Implement ISortableObject

```
'A simple bubble sort, to sort a collection of objects
'that implement ISortableObject
Sub BubbleSortSortableObjects(ByRef colSortable As Collection)

  Dim bDoAgain As Boolean
  Dim iIndex As Integer
  Dim clsSortable1 As ISortableObject
  Dim clsSortable2 As ISortableObject

  Do
    'Assume we're done
    bDoAgain = False

    'Loop through the collection, comparing the names
```

```
     For iIndex = 1 To colSortable.Count - 1

        'Get the objects from the collection at this point
        Set clsSortable1 = colSortable(iIndex)
        Set clsSortable2 = colSortable(iIndex + 1)

        'If we found some in the wrong order, ...
        If clsSortable1.SortKey > clsSortable2.SortKey Then

           '... swap them ...
           colSortable.Remove iIndex + 1
           colSortable.Add clsSortable2, , iIndex

           '... and remember to loop again.
           bDoAgain = True
        End If
     Next
  Loop While bDoAgain

End Sub
```

We can then use this routine with any type of object that implements the ISortableObject interface, as shown in Listing 11-9. This technique assumes that the values provided by each object's ISortableObject_SortKey property can be used within a "greater than" comparison.

Listing 11-9 Using the Generic Sorting Routine for a Collection of CAuthors

```
Sub AuthorSortExample()

  Dim vItem As Variant
  Dim colAuthors As Collection
  Dim clsAuthor As CAuthor

  Set colAuthors = New Collection

  'Populate the Authors collection
  For Each vItem In Array("Stephen Bullen", "Rob Bovey", _
      "John Green")

     Set clsAuthor = New CAuthor
```

```
      clsAuthor.AuthorName = CStr(vItem)
      colAuthors.Add clsAuthor
   Next

   'Sort the Authors using the generic routine
   BubbleSortSortableObjects colAuthors

   'Show the sorted list
   For Each clsAuthor In colAuthors
      Debug.Print clsAuthor.AuthorName
   Next

End Sub
```

That was a very quick introduction to custom interfaces, so let's recap what we've achieved and why we're doing it. When we create nontrivial object models, we often end up with multiple object types (that is, classes) that have a lot of properties in common, but some significant differences. We also often need to process many of those object types in similar ways (such as sorting them). We could do this using a variable declared As Object and hope that all our classes use the same names for their common properties, but that is neither robust nor efficient. Instead, we can define a custom interface which contains the properties and methods that are common to our objects and add code to each class to implement the interface. Our processes can then communicate with any of those object types through the custom interface, making our code much more robust, efficient, maintainable and reusable.

Polymorphic Classes

The ability of a class to appear to be many different types of object is called *polymorphism* and is something that many of the classes in Excel's object model use. For example, we can access the different aspects of the various menu item types using their detailed interfaces—CommandBarPopUp, CommandBarButton, CommandBarComboBox and so on—or iterate through them all using the more generic set of properties that they expose through the CommandBarControl interface. We can make our own classes polymorphic by simply defining and implementing multiple custom interfaces, in the same way that we added the ISortableObject interface.

For example, another requirement for our fictional book-publishing application might be to generate a letter for everyone involved in the book's production. Ideally we would like to be able to put all the CAuthor, CReviewer, CEditor and CDistributor objects into a single collection, sort the collection and then loop through it to generate the letters. Adding all the objects into one collection is not a problem—the Collection object can handle mixed object types. Assuming all those classes have implemented our ISortableObject interface, sorting the collection is not an issue either— our generic sorting routine doesn't care what type of object it's looking at, so long as it implements the interface. The problem comes when we want to generate the letters—how do we iterate through the collection of mixed object types to get the contact details? The answer, of course, is to add another custom interface to those classes, through which we can access the contact details and other properties that are common to all the objects (assuming we've extended the earlier CAuthor class to include those details). We might choose to call it the IContactDetails interface, shown in Listing 11-10, and include the name, postal address and so forth.

Listing 11-10 The IContactDetails Interface Class

```
'Name:          IContactDetails
'Description:    Class to define the IContactDetails interface
'Author:         Stephen Bullen

'Get/set the name
Public Property Get Name() As String
End Property

Public Property Let Name(sNew As String)
End Property

'Get/set the postal address
Public Property Get Address() As String
End Property

Public Property Let Address(sNew As String)
End Property
```

The extended CAuthor, CReviewer, CEditor and CDistributor classes can implement that interface, resulting in the CAuthor class looking like Listing 11-11, where the extra code to implement the IContactDetails interface has been highlighted.

Listing 11-11 The CAuthor Class Implementing the IContactDetails Interface

```
'Name:          CAuthor
'Description:    Class to represent a book's author

'Allow this type of object to be sortable
'by the generic routine
Implements ISortableObject

'Provide access through the IContactDetails interface
Implements IContactDetails

Dim msAuthName As String
Dim msAddress As String

'Set/get the Author name
Public Property Let AuthorName(sNew As String)
  msAuthName = sNew
End Property

Public Property Get AuthorName() As String
  AuthorName = msAuthName
End Property

'Set/Get the address
Public Property Let Address(sNew As String)
  msAddress = sNew
End Property

Public Property Get Address() As String
  Address = msAddress
End Property

'Implement the ISortableObject class
Private Property Get ISortableObject_SortKey() As Variant
  ISortableObject_SortKey = AuthorName
End Property

'Implement the IContactDetails interface,
'by calling through to the default interface's properties
Private Property Let IContactDetails_Name(RHS As String)
```

```
   Me.AuthorName = RHS
End Property

Private Property Get IContactDetails_Name() As String
   IContactDetails_Name = Me.AuthorName
End Property

Private Property Let IContactDetails_Address(RHS As String)
   Me.Address = RHS
End Property

Private Property Get IContactDetails_Address() As String
   IContactDetails_Address = Me.Address
End Property
```

When using the interface and procedure name drop-downs to add the Property Let procedures, the VB editor always uses RHS as the variable name for the new property value (because that represents the "right-hand side" of the property assignment expression). If the code will be doing anything other than just passing the value on to another procedure, it is a very good idea to give the variable a more meaningful name, in line with the best practices on naming conventions explained in *Chapter 3 — Excel and VBA Development Best Practices*.

After we've added the interface to all our classes, we can add the classes to a single collection, sort the collection using the ISortableObject interface and iterate through it using the IContactDetails interface, shown in Listing 11-12. The ShowDetails procedure processes the contact details for each object in the collection, again using the IContactDetails interface, and is explained later.

Listing 11-12 Sorting and Listing Mixed Classes That Implement ISortableObject and IContactDetails

```
Sub CombinedIterateExample()

   Dim vItem As Variant
   Dim colMailList As Collection
   Dim clsAuthor As CAuthor
   Dim clsReviewer As CReviewer
```

```
Dim clsDetails As IContactDetails

Set colMailList = New Collection

'Add the Authors to the collection
For Each vItem In Array("Stephen Bullen", "Rob Bovey", _
    "John Green")

  Set clsAuthor = New CAuthor
  clsAuthor.AuthorName = CStr(vItem)
  colMailList.Add clsAuthor
Next

'Add some Reviewers to the collection
For Each vItem In Array("Dick Kusleika", _
    "Beth Melton", "Shauna Kelly", "Jon Peltier")

  Set clsReviewer = New CReviewer
  clsReviewer.ReviewerName = CStr(vItem)
  colMailList.Add clsReviewer
Next

'Sort the Mailing list using the generic routine
BubbleSortSortableObjects colMailList

'Although colMailList is a collection of mixed object types,
'they all implement the IContactDetails interface, so we can
'process them all by using an object variable declared
'As IContactDetails
For Each clsDetails In colMailList
  ShowDetails clsDetails
Next

End Sub
```

We can use the TypeOf function to test whether a class implements a certain interface and switch between interfaces by declaring a variable as the type of interface we want to look through, then setting it to refer to the object, as shown in Listing 11-13. Regardless of which interface we're looking through, the VB TypeName() function will always return the object's class name.

Listing 11-13 Checking an Object's Interfaces

```
'Show the details of any given object
Sub ShowDetails(objUnknown As Object)

    'Two variables that we can use to look at the object
    'through two different interfaces
    Dim clsAuthor As CAuthor
    Dim clsDetails As IContactDetails

    'Check if this object has the full CAuthor interface
    If TypeOf objUnknown Is CAuthor Then

        'Yes, so look at the object through the CAuthor interface
        Set clsAuthor = objUnknown

        'Write a special message for the authors
        Debug.Print clsAuthor.AuthorName & " wrote the book"

        'Does the object implement the IContactDetails interface?
    ElseIf TypeOf objUnknown Is IContactDetails Then

        'Yes, so look at it through that interface
        Set clsDetails = objUnknown

        'And write a message for everyone that helped
        Debug.Print clsDetails.Name & " helped with the book"
    Else
        'An object we can't use, so write the class name
        Debug.Print "Unknown Object: " & TypeName(objUnknown)
    End If

End Sub
```

Improving Robustness

The ability to iterate through a collection of different object types could be achieved without using a custom interface, by declaring the variable As Object and ensuring that all the classes we want to access have the same properties and methods. However, that makes the object late bound, so it's slower, doesn't show any IntelliSense, coding errors aren't caught until runtime and it relies on all the classes using the same names for their properties. Had we tried to implement the preceding functionality using a generic Object type, we would have had a few issues to resolve:

- Having started with CAuthor.AuthorName and CReviewer.ReviewerName, we would have had to add a common .Name property to both, resulting in two properties that do the same thing. Alternatively, we could have checked the rest of the application and changed AuthorName and ReviewerName to Name wherever it was used.
- We would have to expose *all* the properties of the class on its (single) default interface, including those such as the SortKey property that are only used for specific "internal" functionality.
- If we design our application to use the generic Object type instead of custom interfaces to iterate through mixed object types, we rely on an *implicit* agreement that our objects will have the correct property names and any errors due to missing, renamed or simply mistyped properties won't be found until run time.

Taking the extra step to define and use a custom interface gives us all the benefits of early binding (speed, IntelliSense and compile-time type checking) as well as *explicitly* stating how the classes and their consumers interact, which can only help to improve the robustness of our applications.

Simplifying Development

One of the most used time-saving tools in the Visual Basic Editor is the IntelliSense popup that appears after typing a period (.) after an object. This popup lists all the methods and properties that are defined in the interface for that type of object. Unfortunately, when we try to set properties or call methods in a worksheet or userform class, the IntelliSense list contains so many items that it's hard to find the properties and methods that we need to use. If we follow the recommendations for encapsulating our code, for example, we shouldn't be setting any of a userform's properties from outside the form; we should instead be exposing the form's functionality through our own properties and methods. When viewing the IntelliSense popup for a userform, it shows our properties and methods mixed in with those of the form. Defining and using our own interface for the form enables us to restrict the list of properties and methods to only those that we choose to expose.

A Progress Bar

Many applications include some form of progress indication to show the status of lengthy routines. It's likely that such an indication will be used in multiple places in our application and it makes sense to implement it as a common function that can be called from all our routines. If we have an object-oriented design, we would ideally like to treat it just like any other object, using something like the code in Listing 11-14.

Listing 11-14 Using a ProgressBar Class

```
Sub LongRoutine()

  Dim pbProgBar As ProgressBar
  Dim iCounter As Integer

  Set pbProgBar = New ProgressBar

  pbProgBar.Title = "Professional Excel Development"
  pbProgBar.Text = "Preparing report, please wait..."
  pbProgBar.Min = 0
  pbProgBar.Max = 1000
  pbProgBar.Progress = 0
  pbProgBar.Show

  For iCounter = 0 To 1000
    pbProgBar.Progress = iCounter
  Next

  pbProgBar.Hide

End Sub
```

There is nothing in this code to suggest that the progress indication is a userform. The code is only saying that we want to display some type of progress indication to the user; the way in which it's presented is entirely encapsulated within the ProgressBar class and could just as easily be a userform, a message in the status bar or an audible prompt.

To help other developers that might use the ProgressBar class, it would be ideal if the IntelliSense list only showed the seven properties and methods (Title, Text, Min, Max, Progress, Show and Hide) that we should be using to control the progress bar. Unfortunately, if the ProgressBar was a userform class, the IntelliSense list would show our 7 items lost among the other 57 properties and methods of userforms.

As well as making it harder to pick out the correct properties and methods to use, exposing the normal userform properties makes it tempting for the consumer of the progress bar class to set some of the other properties of the form. At worst, that could break the way in which the progress bar works, or make the progress bar appear differently in different parts of the application. At best, it would make it much harder for us to modify the implementation of the progress bar itself; our new implementation may break the nonstandard way in which the progress bar class has been used, so we would have to check (and test) everywhere that it's referred to.

By using a custom interface, we can **guarantee** that all users of the progress bar class are only able to use the properties and methods that we define in that interface. Doing so removes the temptation to use the normal userform properties and makes it impossible for consumers of the class to use the progress bar form in non-standard ways. This enables us to totally separate the **implementation** of the progress indication from the **use** of the progress indication; as long as we keep the same interface, we can implement it as a userform or as a simple class module that just updates the status bar.

The IProgressBar Interface

As before, we define the interface to use for our progress bar form by creating a new class module, giving it the name IProgressBar and adding empty routines for each of the elements on the interface, as shown in Listing 11-15.

Listing 11-15 The IProgressBar Interface Class

```
'Set and get the title
Public Property Let Title(sNew As String)
End Property

Public Property Get Title() As String
End Property
```

```
'Set and get the descriptive text
Public Property Let Text(sNew As String)
End Property

Public Property Get Text() As String
End Property

'Set and get the minimum value for the bar
Public Property Let Min(dNew As Double)
End Property

Public Property Get Min() As Double
End Property

'Set and get the maximum value for the bar
Public Property Let Max(dNew As Double)
End Property

Public Property Get Max() As Double
End Property

'Set and get the progress point
Public Property Let Progress(dNew As Double)
End Property

Public Property Get Progress() As Double
End Property

'Show the progress bar
Public Sub Show()
End Sub

'Hide the progress bar
Public Sub Hide()
End Sub
```

The FProgressBar Form

The FProgressBar form implements the IProgressBar interface by displaying the progress indication on a userform. The progress bar is made up of two superimposed frames, each containing a label. The back frame and label is blue-on-white, and the front frame and label is white-on-blue. The progress measure controls the width of the front frame, to give the appearance of the progress bar shown in Figure 11-3.

The complete FProgressBar form can be found on the CD, in the workbook *Concepts\Ch11—Interfaces\Progress Bars.xls*, but is reproduced in a simple form in Listing 11-16.

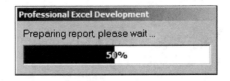

Figure 11-3 A Simple Progress Bar Form

Listing 11-16 The FProgressBar Form Module Implementing the IProgressBar Interface

```
'
' Name:          FProgressBar
' Description:    Displays a modeless progress bar on the screen
' Author:        Stephen Bullen

Option Explicit

' Implement the IProgressBar interface
Implements IProgressBar

' Store the Min, Max and Progress values in module variables
Dim mdMin As Double
Dim mdMax As Double
Dim mdProgress As Double
Dim mdLastPerc As Double

' Initialize the form to show blank text
Private Sub UserForm_Initialize()
  lblMessage.Caption = ""
  Me.Caption = ""
End Sub

'Ignore clicking the [x] on the dialog
Private Sub UserForm_QueryClose(Cancel As Integer, _
                        CloseMode As Integer)
```

```
    If CloseMode = vbFormControlMenu Then Cancel = True
End Sub

' Let the calling routine set/get the caption of the form
Private Property Let IProgressBar_Title(RHS As String)
   Me.Caption = RHS
End Property

Private Property Get IProgressBar_Title() As String
   IProgressBar_Title = Me.Caption
End Property

' Let the calling routine set/get the descriptive text
Private Property Let IProgressBar_Text(RHS As String)

   If RHS <> lblMessage.Caption Then
     lblMessage.Caption = RHS
   End If

End Property

Private Property Get IProgressBar_Text() As String
   IProgressBar_Text = lblMessage.Caption
End Property

' Let the calling routine set/get the Minimum scale
Private Property Let IProgressBar_Min(RHS As Double)
   mdMin = RHS
End Property

Private Property Get IProgressBar_Min() As Double
   IProgressBar_Min = mdMin
End Property

' Let the calling routine set the Maximum scale
Private Property Let IProgressBar_Max(RHS As Double)
   mdMax = RHS
End Property

Private Property Get IProgressBar_Max() As Double
   IProgressBar_Max = mdMax
End Property
```

```
' Let the calling routine set the progress amount.
' Update the form to show the progress.
Private Property Let IProgressBar_Progress(RHS As Double)

   Dim dPerc As Double

   mdProgress = RHS

   'Calculate the progress percentage
   If mdMax = mdMin Then
     dPerc = 0
   Else
     dPerc = Abs((RHS - mdMin) / (mdMax - mdMin))
   End If

   'Only update the form every 0.5% change
   If Abs(dPerc - mdLastPerc) > 0.005 Then
     mdLastPerc = dPerc

     'Set the width of the inside frame,
     'rounding to the pixel
     fraInside.Width = Int(lblBack.Width * dPerc / _
                       0.75 + 1) * 0.75

     'Set the captions for the blue-on-white and
     'white-on-blue text
     lblBack.Caption = Format(dPerc, "0%")
     lblFront.Caption = Format(dPerc, "0%")

     'Refresh the form if it's being shown
     If Me.Visible Then
       Me.Repaint
     End If
   End If

End Property

Private Property Get IProgressBar_Progress() As Double
   IProgressBar_Progress = mdProgress
End Property


'Show the form modelessly
Private Sub IProgressBar_Show()
```

```
  Me.Show vbModeless
End Sub

'Hide the form
Private Sub IProgressBar_Hide()
  Me.Hide
End Sub
```

The only differences between this code and the "plain" Progress Bar form we saw in *Chapter 10 — Userform Design and Best Practices* are that the Title, Text, Min, Max and Progress properties have been exposed via the IProgressBar interface and we've added our own Show and Hide methods to show and hide the form using that interface. The difference between the IntelliSense displays when using our custom IProgressBar interface instead of the form's default interface can be seen in Figure 11-4 and Figure 11-5. By implementing the interface, the consumer of our progress bar form has a much clearer display of the properties and methods that should be used to control the progress bar. Figure 11-4 shows the IntelliSense popup we get if we add the progress bar properties directly to the form, and Figure 11-5 shows the much simpler IntelliSense list we get when using the custom interface.

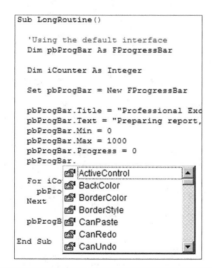

Figure 11-4 Using the Form's Default Interface Shows All the Userform's Properties in the IntelliSense List, Obscuring the Ones for the Progress Bar Itself

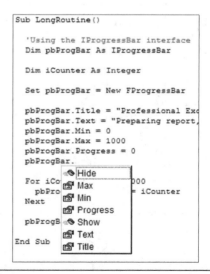

Figure 11-5 Using the Custom IProgressBar Interface Limits the IntelliSense List to Only the Items We Want to Expose, Simplifying the Use of the Form

The CProgressBar Class

After we know that the consumer of our progress bar is accessing it through our custom interface, we are free to modify the implementation of the progress indication in any way we like. As long as we keep the interface the same, we *know* the code that uses the class will continue to work. The opposite is also true; as consumers of the class, we *know* as long as the interface is kept the same, the creator of the class cannot change the name of any of the properties or methods and in doing so break our code. By way of example, the code in Listing 11-17 implements the interface using a class module instead of a userform and displays the progress on Excel's status bar.

Listing 11-17 The CProgressBar Class Implementing the IProgressBar Interface

```
' Class to show a progress indication in the status bar.
' Implements to IProgressBar interface to allow easy switching
' between showing the progress on the status bar (this class)
' or on a userform (the FProgressBar form).

Option Explicit

'Implement the IProgressBar interface
Implements IProgressBar

'Module-level variables to store the property values
Dim msTitle As String
Dim msText As String
Dim mdMin As Double
Dim mdMax As Double
Dim mdProgress As Double
Dim mbShowing As Boolean
Dim msLastCaption As String


'Assume an initial progress of 0-100
Private Sub Class_Initialize()
  mdMin = 0
  mdMax = 100
End Sub
```

```
'Set and get the title
Private Property Let IProgressBar_Title(RHS As String)
   msTitle = RHS
   If mbShowing Then UpdateStatusBar
End Property

Private Property Get IProgressBar_Title() As String
   IProgressBar_Title = msTitle
End Property


'Set and get the descriptive text
Private Property Let IProgressBar_Text(RHS As String)
   msText = RHS
   If mbShowing Then UpdateStatusBar
End Property

Private Property Get IProgressBar_Text() As String
   IProgressBar_Text = msText
End Property


'Set and get the minimum value for the bar
Private Property Let IProgressBar_Min(RHS As Double)
   mdMin = RHS
   If mbShowing Then UpdateStatusBar
End Property

Private Property Get IProgressBar_Min() As Double
   IProgressBar_Min = mdMin
End Property


'Set and get the maximum value for the bar
Private Property Let IProgressBar_Max(RHS As Double)
   mdMax = RHS
   If mbShowing Then UpdateStatusBar
End Property

Private Property Get IProgressBar_Max() As Double
   IProgressBar_Max = mdMax
End Property
```

```
'Set and get the progress point
Private Property Let IProgressBar_Progress(RHS As Double)
  mdProgress = RHS
  If mbShowing Then UpdateStatusBar
End Property

Private Property Get IProgressBar_Progress() As Double
  IProgressBar_Progress = msprogress
End Property


'Show the progress bar
Private Sub IProgressBar_Show()
  mbShowing = True
  mdLastProgress = 0
  UpdateStatusBar
End Sub


'Hide the progress bar
Private Sub IProgressBar_Hide()
  Application.StatusBar = False
  mbShowing = False
End Sub


'Private routine to show the progress indication
'on the status bar
Private Sub UpdateStatusBar()

  Dim dPerc As Double
  Dim sCaption As String

  'Calculate the progress percentage
  If mdMax = mdMin Then
    dPerc = 0
  Else
    dPerc = Abs((mdProgress - mdMin) / (mdMax - mdMin))
  End If

  'Create the caption
  If Len(msTitle) > 0 Then sCaption = msTitle
```

```
If Len(msTitle) > 0 And Len(msText) > 0 Then
  sCaption = sCaption & ": "
End If

If Len(msText) > 0 Then sCaption = sCaption & msText

'Calculate and add the formatted percentage
sCaption = sCaption & " (" & Format$(dPerc, "0%") & ")"

'Update the status bar if it's changed
If sCaption <> msLastCaption Then
  msLastCaption = sCaption
  Application.StatusBar = sCaption
End If

End Sub
```

The calling code can very easily switch between using either the form or the status bar for the progress display (perhaps according to a user's preference), as shown in Listing 11-18.

Listing 11-18 Using the IProgressBar Interface Allows the Choice Between the Form and the Class

```
Sub LongRoutine(bProgressInForm As Boolean)

  'Always use the IProgressBar interface
  Dim pbProgBar As IProgressBar

  Dim iCounter As Integer

  If bProgressInForm Then
    'Use the progress bar form
    Set pbProgBar = New FProgressBar
  Else
    'Use the status bar class
    Set pbProgBar = New CProgressBar
  End If

  'The rest of the code is unchanged
  pbProgBar.Title = "Professional Excel Development"
```

```
pbProgBar.Text = "Preparing report, please wait..."
pbProgBar.Min = 0
pbProgBar.Max = 1000
pbProgBar.Progress = 0
pbProgBar.Show

For iCounter = 0 To 1000
   pbProgBar.Progress = iCounter
Next

pbProgBar.Hide

End Sub
```

A Plug-in Architecture

You saw in *Chapter 10 — Userform Design and Best Practices* how it was possible to create a user interface consisting of modeless userforms, in which the interaction with the user occurs within userforms (as opposed to worksheets), yet with the command bars still usable. To allow the forms to respond to menu bar clicks (such as saving, moving to another form or closing the application), we had to ensure that all our forms had the same basic set of routines, that could be called by our common menu handler. Those routines were called BeforeNavigate, BeforeSave, AfterSave and AppExit. We had in fact created our own implicit interface, without knowing it. By making that interface explicit, we can improve robustness and reliability and simplify the development of the application. We'll call this interface IPlugInForm and define it as shown in Listing 11-19, where we've also added a Show method, to be able to show the form through this interface.

Listing 11-19 The IPlugInForm Interface Class

```
'Name:           IPlugInForm
'Description:     Interface to be implemented by each form
'Author:         Stephen Bullen
```

```vb
'The form's name
Public Property Get Name() As String
End Property

'Show the form
Public Sub Show(Optional ByVal Style As _
                FormShowConstants = vbModal)
End Sub

'The user clicked a menu item to navigate to a different form
'Save any changes on the form and unload
Public Sub BeforeNavigate(ByRef bCancel As Boolean)
End Sub

'The user clicked the Save button
'Save any changes on the form and unload
Public Sub BeforeSave(ByVal bSaveAs As Boolean, _
                ByRef bCancel As Boolean)
End Sub

'After the save completed
'Update the form with any new information
Public Sub AfterSave(ByVal bSaveAs As Boolean)
End Sub

'The user clicked the Close button to exit the application
'Tidy up and unload the form
Public Sub AppExit()
End Sub
```

If all of our forms implement this interface, the central control routine shown in Listing 10-26 in *Chapter 10 — Userform Design and Best Practices* can declare the gfrmActiveForm variable As IPlugInForm instead of As Object and call the same methods as before. Using the interface enables us to be explicit about what the code is doing, prevents typing errors, ensures none of our common routines are "accidentally" deleted from the forms and helps enforce a common structure throughout the application.

Practical Example

The PETRAS application files for this chapter can be found on the CD in the folder \Application\Ch11—Interfaces and include the following files:

- **PetrasTemplate.xlt**—The timesheet template
- **PetrasAddin.xla**—The timesheet data-entry support add-in
- **PetrasReporting.xla**—The main reporting application
- **PetrasConsolidation.xlt**—A template to use for new results workbooks
- **Debug.ini**—A dummy file that tells the application to run in debug mode
- **PetrasIcon.ico**—An icon file, to use for Excel's main window

PETRAS Timesheet

The PETRAS timesheet add-in has not been updated for this chapter.

PETRAS Reporting

At this stage in the development of the application, it would be artificial to add a suite of userforms, just so we could demonstrate the implementation of a plug-in architecture. However, such a suite of forms will be added to the application in *Chapter 13 — Programming with Databases* for maintenance of the static lists of Consultants, Clients, Projects and so forth.

For this chapter, we will modify the progress bar handling to display the consolidation progress unobtrusively in the status bar if we're consolidating fewer than ten timesheet workbooks, but pop up a cancelable progress bar userform if consolidating ten or more timesheets. As such, we'll be including the IProgressBar interface from Listing 11-15, the FProgressBar form from Listing 11-16 and the CProgressBar class from Listing 11-17. In this example, the form has an extra Cancel button and the interface has been enhanced to add a Cancelled property, set to True when the Cancel button is clicked. The code changes required for this enhancement are detailed in Table 11-1.

Table 11-1 Changes to the PETRAS Reporting Application for Chapter 11

Module	Procedure	Change
IProgressBar (new class)		Added class to define the IProgressBar interface, copied from Listing 11-15, adding Cancelable property.
CProgressBar (new class)		Added class to show the progress in the status bar, copied from Listing 11-17.
FProgressBar		Moved various methods to be exposed through the IProgressBar interface instead of the default interface. The resulting code is similar to Listing 11-16.
MSystemCode	ConsolidateWorkbooks	Modified to use the IProgressBar interface and test whether to use the CProgressBar class or FProgressBar form.

Conclusion

Whenever we create a class module in VBA, the compiler creates both the class and a default interface for it. The code in the class defines how the object behaves, and the interface defines how we access the code. With a small amount of effort, we can define our own custom interfaces and implement them in our classes, enabling us to treat different classes as if they were the same type of object.

When developing userforms, we can use a custom interface to expose only the properties and methods that apply to the functionality we're providing, without cluttering the IntelliSense list with all the basic userform's properties. By doing this, we can make our code more generic, more robust, more reliable, easier to write and easier to maintain.

By implementing a standard custom interface in all our forms, reports and processes, we can design an application architecture that is totally extensible, without requiring any changes to the core application. If working in a multideveloper team, this interface can be extended across workbooks, allowing each developer to work independently on the application's functions, safe in the knowledge that his work will not directly impede any of the other developers.

CHAPTER 12

VBA Error Handling

Error handling is one of the most commonly omitted features in Excel applications. This is not an acceptable state of affairs. The last thing you want your users to see is an unvarnished Excel or VBA runtime error. They will most surely not understand what they are seeing and they will often panic, lose faith in your application, or both. A good error handling system will not prevent errors from occurring, but it will make the process much less distressing for your users and much easier for you to diagnose and correct.

All the errors discussed in this chapter are runtime errors. These are errors that occur while your code is executing. The other type of error, the compile-time error, should not be a factor at this point. A good developer will have ensured his project cleanly passes a *Debug > Compile* in the VBE before attempting to execute it.

Error-Handling Concepts

Unhandled vs. Handled Errors

Runtime errors fall into two broad categories: **unhandled errors** and **handled errors**. Simply put, an unhandled error is one that is not caught by an error handling mechanism in the procedure where it occurs, whereas a handled error is caught by such an error handler. This is not to imply that all unhandled errors are bad. In some situations, you can reasonably choose not to handle errors in a certain procedure, instead deferring them to an error handler further up the call stack. The error is converted from an unhandled error into a handled error at the point where it reaches an error handling mechanism. What is unacceptable is an error that remains unhandled all the way until it reaches the user. Figure 12-1 shows the result of an unhandled error.

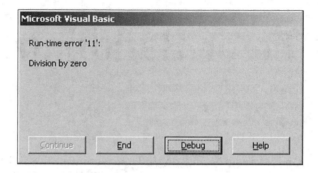

Figure 12-1 An Unhandled Error Message

The Err Object

When any kind of runtime error occurs, the affected code is said to be in error mode. An intrinsic, global VBA object called the Err object is populated with information about the error. Almost every error handling mechanism makes use of the Err object, so it is helpful to understand its most commonly used properties and methods.

- `Err.Clear`—This method clears all the properties of the Err object, canceling the current error.
- `Err.Description`—This property contains a short string that describes the error.
- `Err.HelpFile`—This property contains the full path and filename of the help file containing a description of the error.
- `Err.HelpContext`—This property contains the help context ID within the help file of the topic that describes the error.
- `Err.LastDLLError`—Theoretically, this property returns any error code generated by calls to a DLL, such as a Windows API call. In practice, this value is very unreliable because Windows may execute DLL functions automatically that overwrite the information in this property before your code gets a chance to look at it. It's best never to rely on the `LastDLLError` property.
- `Err.Number`—This property returns the number associated with the most recent runtime error. When your error handler needs to take different actions based on the type of error that occurred, you should use this property to distinguish among different types of errors.

- `Err.Raise`—This method enables you to intentionally raise errors within your application. We discuss this topic in detail later in the chapter.
- `Err.Source`—This property identifies the source of the error. It is not very useful for providing information about VBA runtime errors because it simply returns the name of the project in which the error occurred. However, as we discuss later in this chapter, you can populate this property yourself with more detailed information when raising custom errors.

NOTE: All contents of the Err object are cleared automatically when code execution encounters a Resume statement, an On Error statement, Exit Sub, Exit Function, Exit Property, End Sub, End Function, or End Property.

What Is an Error Handler

An error handler is a labeled section of a procedure that you designate as the place where code will resume executing whenever a runtime error occurs. An `On Error GoTo <Line>` statement, discussed in the next section, is used to make this designation. The error handler must be a separate block of code within the procedure, with the only way into it being an error and the only way out being a Resume, Exit Sub, or Exit Function. Listing 12-1 shows an example of a procedure with a very simple error handler.

Listing 12-1 A Procedure with a Simple Error Handler

```
Public Sub MyProcedure()

    On Error GoTo ErrorHandler

    ' Lots of code here.

    Exit Sub

ErrorHandler:
    MsgBox Err.Description, vbCritical, "Error!"
End Sub
```

In this procedure, the section of code identified by the `ErrorHandler` label has been designated as the error handler for the procedure by the `On Error GoTo ErrorHandler` statement. Note the `Exit Sub` statement prior to the ErrorHandler section. This prevents the procedure from executing the code in the ErrorHandler section if no error has occurred.

Designating a section of code as an error handler *enables* it. When a runtime error occurs and code execution branches to the error handler, it is said to be *active*. This difference is not academic. If an error handler is active (currently in the process of handling an error) and another error occurs as a result of something the code in that error handler does, the new error cannot be handled by the same error handler. If this occurs, control will be passed to the error handler of the next highest procedure in the call stack.

Why is this important? There are some circumstances in which you need to perform an operation that may generate another error inside an error handler. If this is the case, put this code into a separate procedure with its own error handler and call that procedure from the active error handler. Multiple error handlers can be active at the same time, so an error that occurs in and is handled by this separate procedure will not affect the error handler that called it.

NOTE: There is only a single global Err object. Its properties are set by the error that occurred most recently. If you think you will run into an error within an error situation, as described above, save any information about the original error in your own variables so you don't lose it.

Error Handler Scope

The scope of an error handler, which is the body of code that will activate it if a runtime error occurs, includes the procedure that the error handler is defined in as well as any called procedures that do not have their own error handlers. If a calling procedure has a designated error handler but the procedures it calls do not, the error handler of the calling procedure will be activated by any errors that occur. The simple code example in Listing 12-2 will illustrate this more clearly.

Listing 12-2 The Scope of an Error Handler

```
Public Sub EntryPointProcedure()

    On Error GoTo ErrorHandler

    SubProcedure1

    Exit Sub

ErrorHandler:
    MsgBox Err.Description, vbCritical, "Error!"
End Sub

Private Sub SubProcedure1()
    SubProcedure2
End Sub

Private Sub SubProcedure2()
    Dim lTest As Long
    ' This error will activate the error handler
    ' in the entry point procedure.
    lTest = 1 / 0
End Sub
```

In this example, only EntryPointProcedure has defined an error handler. EntryPointProcedure calls SubProcedure1 and SubProcedure1 calls SubProcedure2. If a runtime error occurs in **any** of these three procedures, code execution will immediately branch to the error handler defined in EntryPointProcedure.

There are some cases where this is a valid and reasonable error handling technique, but usually it's not the best choice. First, you lose any information about where the error actually occurred. Second, if any of the called procedures need to perform cleanup prior to exiting (destroy object, close connections, reset public variables and so on), this cleanup code will be skipped. Code execution branches unconditionally to the top-level procedure's error handler and it cannot be made to return to the procedure where the error occurred (even with the use of the Resume statement, which we will discuss later in the chapter). For these reasons, it is usually best if each procedure in your application handles its own errors.

The On Error Statement

The three variants of the On Error statement provide the foundation of VBA's error handling capability.

On Error GoTo <Label>

This statement is used to specify an error handler for a procedure. Literally, what it tells VBA to do is branch code execution to the line in the procedure identified by <Label> when a runtime error occurs. The code below this line is considered the error handler for the procedure.

On Error Resume Next

This statement is both very dangerous and very useful at the same time. It tells VBA to ignore any errors that occur and continue with the next line of code until you tell it to do otherwise. First let's make it very clear what you should not do with this statement. All too often I receive code from a client where the first line in several very large procedures is On Error Resume Next. Don't do this! On Error Resume Next is not a substitute for writing code correctly in the first place. If you have a large procedure that will not run unless you place On Error Resume Next at the top of it, then that procedure is almost certainly poorly written.

With that out of the way, let's talk about the circumstances in which On Error Resume Next is useful and necessary. You will sometimes encounter situations where you expect an error to occur during normal program execution at least some of the time. In cases such as this you do not want the error to activate your error handler. Instead you want code execution to continue in some conditional fashion based on whether or not an error occurred.

For example, assume a procedure needs to use an existing workbook that may or may not be open when the procedure is executed. In this case, you would use On Error Resume Next to temporarily bypass error handling while you test to determine whether the workbook is open. The moment you finish this test you would re-enable the error handler using the On Error Goto <Label> statement. Listing 12-3 shows an example of this.

Listing 12-3 When to Use On Error Resume Next

```
Public Sub OnErrorResumeNextDemo()

    Dim wkbCalcs As Workbook

    On Error GoTo ErrorHandler

    ' Lots of code here.

    ' Test if the Calcs.xls workbook is open.
    Set wkbCalcs = Nothing
    On Error Resume Next
        Set wkbCalcs = Application.Workbooks("Calcs.xls")
    On Error GoTo ErrorHandler

    ' If the workbook wasn't open we need to open it.
    If wkbCalcs Is Nothing Then
        Set wkbCalcs = Application.Workbooks.Open( _
                        ThisWorkbook.Path & "\Calcs.xls")
    End If

    ' Lots more code here.

    Exit Sub

ErrorHandler:
    MsgBox Err.Description, vbCritical, "Error!"
End Sub
```

Notice that On Error Resume Next is used to disable error handling for just the single line of code that determines if the Calcs.xls workbook is already open. This should be the norm. Always keep the number of lines of code affected by On Error Resume Next to an absolute minimum. If you do not turn it off immediately when you no longer need it, you will very likely suppress errors you did not intend to suppress.

As with almost all rules, there are a few exceptions to the ban on entire procedures being "wrapped" in On Error Resume Next. The first situation concerns a special type of procedure in which an error is an integral part of the logic of the procedure. In the code in Listing 12-3, for example, we could substitute the in-place test for the Calcs.xls workbook being open with a general-purpose function that could be used anywhere this type of test was required. The result would look like the function in Listing 12-4, which is wrapped entirely in `On Error Resume Next` by design.

Listing 12-4 An Entire Function Wrapped in On Error Resume Next

```
Private Function bIsBookOpen(ByVal sBookName As String, _
                ByRef wkbBook As Workbook) As Boolean

  ' Checks to see if the specified workbook is open. If it is,

  ' a reference to it is returned in the wkbBook argument.

  On Error Resume Next

  Set wkbBook = Application.Workbooks(sBookName)

  bIsBookOpen = (Len(wkbBook.Name) > 0)

End Function
```

The second situation that requires wrapping an entire procedure in `On Error Resume Next` involves application shutdown code. When your application is closing, you typically attempt to perform some cleanup. If an error occurs during this process, there really isn't anything useful an error handler can accomplish. It's typically better to use `On Error Resume Next` to bypass any errors and continue performing whatever cleanup the application can accomplish before it closes. You can see an example of this in the shutdown code for our sample add-in.

The third situation that requires wrapping an entire procedure in `On Error Resume Next` involves application shutdown code and class Terminate events. When your application or class is going away, there's not much point in activating an error handler. The best choice for when an error occurs in these types of procedure is usually to skip the line that caused the error and continue to execute as much of the code as possible. We cover these cases later in the chapter.

On Error GoTo 0

This statement disables any previously enabled error handler in the current procedure. It has no effect in procedures that do not contain error handling, even if they have been called by a higher-level procedure that does contain error handling. In Listing 12-2, for example, placing On Error GoTo 0 in SubProcedure1 would not prevent errors that occurred in that procedure from being handled by the still enabled error handler in EntryPointProcedure.

The Resume Statement

The Resume statement is used to deactivate an error handler and cause code execution to resume at a specific location that depends on which variation of the statement is used. The Resume statement can only be used inside an active error handler. Using it under any other circumstances will cause a runtime error to occur.

No variety of the Resume statement can cause code execution to resume in any procedure other than the one where the current error handler is located. This means if the current error handler has trapped an error from a lower-level procedure, Resume cannot cause code execution to return to that procedure.

You must be very careful with the Resume statement because you can very easily create an infinite loop in your code with it. There are three variations of the Resume statement.

Resume

This is the most dangerous Resume statement of them all. It causes code execution to return to the line of code that caused the error (or the call to a subprocedure where the error originated if the error did not originate in the current procedure). The implicit assumption is that your error handler has done something to correct the error condition. If this is not the case, the error will just occur again, triggering the error handler, which resumes execution on the line of code that caused the error and so on. This is the dreaded infinite loop condition and in many situations the only way to stop it is to use Ctrl+Alt+Del to shut down Excel.

With this warning very clear, though, the Resume statement can be quite useful. If you are attempting to make a connection to a remote database over a slow or congested network, for example, it is not uncommon to fail one or more times. When a connection failure occurs, an error is thrown and your error handler is activated. You can increment a counter in your error handler and use Resume to try connecting again. If you are unable to connect successfully after a certain number of attempts, you can have your error handler bail out with an error message to the user. We demonstrate this use of resume in *Chapter 13 — Programming with Databases*.

The `Resume` statement is also very useful within the context of built-in debugging aides. When your code has a special flag set that indicates it is in debug mode, your error handler can direct code execution to a branch that automatically places the code into break mode and allows you to resume code execution on the line of code that generated the error in order to debug the problem. You will see the error handling constructs that assist debug mode in this chapter, but we do not cover debugging in detail until *Chapter 16 — VBA Debugging*.

Resume Next

The `Resume Next` statement causes code execution to continue on the first executable line of code after the one that generated the error. The `Resume Next` statement will not return to a lower-level procedure if that's where the error was generated. Instead, it will resume execution in the procedure that handled the error on the line of code immediately following the call to the procedure branch where the error was generated.

Resume <Label>

The `Resume <Label>` statement causes code execution to continue on the line of code following the specified label. The label must be located in the same procedure as the error handler. Like the `Resume` statement, the `Resume <Label>` statement can cause an infinite loop in your code if the error is located below the specified label.

Raising Custom Errors

Although it may seem counterintuitive, deliberately generating runtime errors in your code can be a very useful technique and it is fully supported by VBA. The reasons for using these custom errors are better dealt with in the context of procedure error handling as a whole, so we defer a detailed discussion of this topic until later in the chapter. In this section we cover the mechanics of raising custom errors.

Custom errors are raised using the `Raise` method of the `Err` object. The syntax of this method is as follows:

```
Err.Raise Number, Source, Description, HelpFile, HelpContextID
```

The arguments to the `Err.Raise` method correspond to the properties of the Err object, which we described above. When you raise a custom error, you can set these arguments however you like. All of them except the Number argument are optional.

One caveat is you cannot use an error number for a custom error that is already used by an Excel or VBA error. (You can raise predefined errors using their error numbers.) The numbers 513 through 65535 are reserved for custom errors. VBA also provides the special constant vbObjectError for creating custom error numbers that are typically used with classes. Any number added to the vbObjectError constant is guaranteed to be an error number that is not used by any Windows process. An example of a custom error number created using the vbObjectError constant is shown here:

```
Err.Raise vbObjectError + 1024
```

The Source argument of the error should be set to the name of the procedure in which the error was raised. The Description of a custom error should be a reasonably brief but clear description of the reason the error was raised. The HelpFile and HelpContextID arguments enable you to provide the user with additional information about the error if your project uses a help file. Otherwise, these arguments can be ignored. Help files are covered in more detail in *Chapter 24 — Providing Help, Securing, Packaging and Distributing*.

The Single Exit Point Principle

One of the fundamental good architectural practices in any procedure is to have a single exit point. This means that after your error handler has finished handling an error, it should redirect code execution back into the body of the procedure so the procedure will be exited at the same point under all circumstances. The practical reason for this is that it's very common for some type of cleanup to be required before a procedure exits. Even if a procedure currently requires no cleanup, this may very well change as a result of some future code modification. If your error handlers are already structured to use a single exit point, you have one less modification to make.

The mechanism for implementing a single exit point is the Resume <Label> statement discussed previously. In this case <Label> identifies the point in each procedure at which code execution resumes after an error has occurred and been handled. We will give this label the name ErrorExit. The ErrorExit label has no effect on code execution when the procedure completes without error. Normal code execution just passes this label and continues on to the end of the procedure. When an error occurs, however, this label identifies the point at which the error handler should resume code execution once an error has been handled in order to guarantee that code execution completes at the same point in the procedure with or without an error. You will see examples of single exit point procedures in the sections that follow.

Simple Error Handling

In the simplest form of error handling, error handlers are placed only in *entry point procedures*. Entry point procedures are those procedures from which code execution can be initiated. They are typically the procedures assigned to menu items, toolbar buttons, or controls placed on worksheets, but most event procedures are also entry points, because they initiate execution based on some action made by the user.

If the error handler in an entry point procedure is the only error handler in its call stack, this error handler will trap all errors that occur in all lower-level procedures. A simple error handler will display an error message to the user and exit the procedure. An example of this is shown in Listing 12-5.

Listing 12-5 An Example of a Simple Error Handler

```
Public Sub MyEntryPoint()

    On Error GoTo ErrorHandler

    ' Your code here.

ErrorExit:

    Exit Sub

ErrorHandler:
    MsgBox Err.Description, vbCritical, "Application Name"
    Resume ErrorExit
End Sub
```

Simple error handlers are appropriate only for the most trivial applications. An example might be a utility add-in that provides a number of simple features that require a small amount of code and do not require any significant cleanup. The primary purpose of a simple error handler is to shield users from raw runtime errors such as the one shown in Figure 12-1.

Complex Project Error Handler Organization

There are two or three complex error handling system designs commonly used in Excel VBA applications and several minor variations on each of those. If designed correctly, all of them will accomplish the same purpose; gracefully handling runtime errors encountered by your application. The complex error handling system we introduce in this section has the following characteristics:

- All nontrivial procedures contain error handlers.
- All procedure error handlers call a central error handling function. This function tracks and logs each error, decides whether or not to display an error message to the user and tells the calling procedure how to proceed by way of its return value.
- All entry point procedures are subroutines. An entry point procedure is any procedure in which code execution begins. This includes subroutines in standard modules called by toolbar buttons and event procedures executed in response to some user action.
- All nontrivial lower-level procedures (all procedures that are called by entry point procedures) are Boolean functions whose return value indicates whether the function succeeded or failed.

We cover all of these points in detail as this section progresses, but we wanted to give you a high-level overview of how our error handling system works.

An important point to keep in mind as you read this section is that entry point procedures must only be triggered directly by some user action. One entry point procedure must never call another entry point procedure or the error handling system described here will break down. If two entry point procedures need to run the same code, the common code should be factored out into a lower-level function that can be called by both entry point procedures.

Procedure Error Handlers

Listing 12-6 shows two error handler procedure skeletons. The first is an example of an entry point subroutine, the second an example of a lower-level, Boolean function. We have placed a call from the entry point subroutine to the lower-level function to demonstrate how the error handling system would work. We explain the purpose of the various constants shown in Listing 12-6 as well as the function call inside the error handlers in *The Central Error Handler* section later in the chapter.

Listing 12-6 Subroutine and Function Error Handlers

```
Private Const msMODULE As String = "MMyModule"

Public Sub MyEntryPointSubroutine()

    Const sSOURCE As String = "MyEntryPointSubroutine()"

    On Error GoTo ErrorHandler

    ' Call the lower level function.
    If Not bMyLowerLevelFunction() Then
        Err.Raise glHANDLED_ERROR
    End If

ErrorExit:

    ' Cleanup code here.

    Exit Sub

ErrorHandler:
    If bCentralErrorHandler(msMODULE, sSOURCE, , True) Then
        Stop
        Resume
    Else
        Resume ErrorExit
    End If
End Sub

Private Function bMyLowerLevelFunction() As Boolean
```

```
    Const sSOURCE As String = "bMyLowerLevelFunction()"

    Dim bReturn As Boolean   ' The function return value

    On Error GoTo ErrorHandler

    ' Assume success until an error is encountered.
    bReturn = True

    ' Operational code here.

ErrorExit:

    ' Cleanup code here.

    bMyLowerLevelFunction = bReturn
    Exit Function

ErrorHandler:
    bReturn = False
    If bCentralErrorHandler(msMODULE, sSOURCE) Then
        Stop
        Resume
    Else
        Resume ErrorExit
    End If
End Function
```

The general layout of the error handlers is very similar in both cases. The only significant difference is the function must return a value indicating success or failure without violating the single exit point principle, so we have added the structure required to accomplish that to the function's error handler.

Listing 12-6 shows examples of very simple error handlers. They don't try to respond to errors other than by invoking the central error handler and exiting. In many situations, you will be aware of errors that might occur but can be corrected in the error handler and allow code execution to continue. A more complex error handler, such as the one shown in Listing 12-7, enables you to accomplish this.

Listing 12-7 A More Complex Error Handler

```
ErrorHandler:

    Select Case Err.Number

    Case 58
        ' File already exists. Resolve the problem and resume.
        Resume
    Case 71
        ' Disk not ready. Resolve the problem and resume.
        Resume
    Case Else
        ' The error can't be resolved here. Invoke the central
        ' error handling procedure.
        If bCentralErrorHandler(msMODULE, sSOURCE, , True) Then
            ' If the program is in debug mode, execution
            ' continues here.
            Stop
            Resume
        Else
            Resume ErrorExit
        End If
    End Select

End Function
```

A Select Case statement is used to identify error numbers that can be handled within the error handler. If the number of the error trapped is not one of those handled by a specific Case clause, it falls through to the Case Else clause, which invokes the central error handler.

NOTE: In the context of error handling, the word *trap* refers to an error handler being activated by an error. It is synonymous with the word *catch*, which is commonly used in its place.

A typical error handling scenario based on the examples shown in Listing 12-6 and Listing 12-7 would play out something like this. MyEntryPointSubroutine calls bMyLowerLevelFunction to perform some operation. An error occurs in bMyLowerLevelFunction that cannot be handled by its error handler. The error handler in bMyLower LevelFunction calls the central error handler. The central error handler logs the error and passes a value back to bMyLowerLevelFunction that tells it to exit. bMyLowerLevelFunction exits and returns False to the MyEntryPointSubroutine calling procedure. In MyEntryPointSubroutine, a custom error is raised (because bMyLowerLevelFunction returned False), which then calls the central error handler again. Because an entry point subroutine called the central error handler, an error message is displayed to the user. After the central error handler has completed its duties, code execution resumes in MyEntryPointSubroutine, which then exits.

In *The Central Error Handler* section below, we describe how the central error handler determines when an error message should be displayed and how it influences program execution after the error is handled.

Trivial Procedures

At the beginning of this section we stated that all **nontrivial** procedures contain error handlers. That begs the question of what is a trivial procedure that wouldn't require an error handler. A trivial procedure is either so simple that an error cannot occur within it or is structured such that any errors that do occur are ignored. Listing 12-8 shows examples of both types.

Listing 12-8 Trivial Procedures Don't Require Error Handlers

```
' This subroutine is so simple that no errors
' will ever be generated within it.
Public Sub ResetAppProperties()
    Application.StatusBar = False
    Application.ScreenUpdating = True
    Application.DisplayAlerts = True
    Application.EnableEvents = True
    Application.EnableCancelKey = xlInterrupt
    Application.Cursor = xlDefault
End Sub


' Any errors that occur in this function are ignored.
Private Function bIsBookOpen(ByVal sBookName As String, _
                   ByRef wkbBook As Workbook) As Boolean
    On Error Resume Next
    Set wkbBook = Application.Workbooks(sBookName)
    bIsBookOpen = (Len(wkbBook.Name) > 0)
End Function
```

The Central Error Handler

The central error handler is the heart of any complex error handling system. It consists of a procedure designed to log errors to an error log file or other persistent location and display error messages to the user, as well as provide facilities that allow the programmer to debug errors during development. (We cover debugging in detail in *Chapter 16 — VBA Debugging*.) The module containing the central error handler also contains all error handling-related constants, making the error handling system fully encapsulated. Listing 12-9 shows an example of a complete central error handler.

Listing 12-9 A Central Error Handler

```
Public Const gbDEBUG_MODE As Boolean = False
Public Const glHANDLED_ERROR As Long = 9999
Public Const glUSER_CANCEL As Long = 18

Private Const msSILENT_ERROR As String = "UserCancel"
Private Const msFILE_ERROR_LOG As String = "Error.log"

Public Function bCentralErrorHandler( _
          ByVal sModule As String, _
          ByVal sProc As String, _
          Optional ByVal sFile As String, _
          Optional ByVal bEntryPoint As Boolean) As Boolean

     Static sErrMsg As String

     Dim iFile As Integer
     Dim lErrNum As Long
     Dim sFullSource As String
     Dim sPath As String
     Dim sLogText As String

     ' Grab the error info before it's cleared by
     ' On Error Resume Next below.
     lErrNum = Err.Number
     ' If this is a user cancel, set the silent error flag
     ' message. This will cause the error to be ignored.
     If lErrNum = glUSER_CANCEL Then sErrMsg = msSILENT_ERROR
     ' If this is the originating error, the static error
     ' message variable will be empty. In that case, store
```

```
' the originating error message in the static variable.
If Len(sErrMsg) = 0 Then sErrMsg = Err.Description

' We cannot allow errors in the central error handler.
On Error Resume Next

' Load the default filename if required.
If Len(sFile) = 0 Then sFile = ThisWorkbook.Name

' Get the application directory.
sPath = ThisWorkbook.Path
If Right$(sPath, 1) <> "\" Then sPath = sPath & "\"

' Construct the fully-qualified error source name.
sFullSource = "[" & sFile & "]" & sModule & "." & sProc

' Create the error text to be logged.
sLogText = "   " & sFullSource & ", Error " & _
                    CStr(lErrNum) & ": " & sErrMsg

' Open the log file, write out the error information and
' close the log file.
iFile = FreeFile()
Open sPath & msFILE_ERROR_LOG For Append As #iFile
Print #iFile, Format$(Now(), "mm/dd/yy hh:mm:ss"); sLogText
If bEntryPoint Then Print #iFile,
Close #iFile

' Do not display silent errors.
If sErrMsg <> msSILENT_ERROR Then

    ' Show the error message when we reach the entry point
    ' procedure or immediately if we are in debug mode.
    If bEntryPoint Or gbDEBUG_MODE Then
        Application.ScreenUpdating = True
        MsgBox sErrMsg, vbCritical, gsAPP_TITLE
        ' Clear the static error message variable once
        ' we've reached the entry point so that we're ready
        ' to handle the next error.
        sErrMsg = vbNullString
    End If

    ' The return value is the debug mode status.
```

```
            bCentralErrorHandler = gbDEBUG_MODE

    Else
        ' If this is a silent error, clear the static error
        ' message variable when we reach the entry point.
        If bEntryPoint Then sErrMsg = vbNullString
        bCentralErrorHandler = False
    End If

End Function
```

This is a lot to digest, so let's dissect it piece by piece. First the constant declarations:

- gbDEBUG_MODE—This public Boolean constant is used by the developer to set the debug mode status of the application. When you are testing your application or attempting to locate errors in your code, you want your error handlers to behave differently than they do when your application is deployed to end users. Setting the gbDEBUG_MODE constant to True causes the central error handler function to display an error message immediately after an error occurs and then return True.

    As shown in Listing 12-6 and Listing 12-7, when the central error handler function returns True, the procedure error handler drops into a VBA Stop statement followed by a Resume statement. The Stop statement puts the project into Break mode and the Resume statement enables you to single step back to the line of code in the procedure where the error occurred. You can then debug the error. Again, we discuss debugging in detail in *Chapter 16 — VBA Debugging*.

- glHANDLED_ERROR—This public Long constant is an error number you can use to raise custom errors. As we discussed in the section on raising custom errors, when you raise a custom error you must supply an error number not already used by Excel or VBA. The glHANDLED_ERROR constant has a value of 9999, which is not within the range of error number values used by VBA. It also has the advantage of being easily recognizable as a custom error number for debugging purposes. In all but the most complex error handling scenarios, a single custom error number can be used for all of your custom errors.

- glUSER_CANCEL—This public Long constant is set to the VBA error value 18. This error value occurs when the user cancels program execution by pressing the Esc or Ctrl+Break keys. Unless it is absolutely critical that your program not be interrupted, such as during startup and shutdown, you should always allow the user to halt program execution. The best way to do this is to add the following statement at the beginning of each entry point procedure:

```
Application.EnableCancelKey = xlErrorHandler
```

This will cause VBA to treat a user cancel as a runtime error with an `Err.Number = 18` that is routed through your error handler. When the central error handler sees this error number, it converts it into a special error message string, which we cover next, that causes the error to be ignored.

- msSILENT_ERROR—This private String constant is assigned to the static error message variable in the central error handling function whenever a user cancel error (`Err.Number = glUSER_CANCEL`) is detected. Because this error message variable is static, it holds its value between calls to the central error handler. This means no matter how deep in the call stack the program was when the user cancelled execution, the error handler will pass the error up the stack and out the entry point procedure without displaying an error message to the user. Silent errors also will not trigger the procedure debugging mechanism, even if the application is in debug mode.

- msFILE_ERROR_LOG—This private String constant specifies the name of the text file to which all error messages will be written. The error log file will always be located in the same directory as the workbook containing the central error handler. The information stored in the error log file is designed to help you debug errors that have occurred on a user's computer that you may not necessarily have access to. The error log file will show you the exact error message, the procedure where the error originated and the call stack that led to the error. Combined with a brief verbal report from the user about exactly what they were doing when the error occurred, this information is usually sufficient to enable you to debug the problem.

Now we examine the code in the central error handler function line by line to see how an error is treated under various conditions. First let's look at the arguments to the function. The first three arguments to the bCentralErrorHandler function identify the code module, procedure and filename from which the function was called. This information is written to the error log file for use in debugging runtime errors. The fourth argument to the bCentralErrorHandler function indicates whether or not it was called from an entry point procedure. If the application is not in debug mode, an error message is displayed to the user only when the error reaches the originating entry point procedure. If the application is in debug mode, the fourth argument is ignored, an error message is displayed immediately and the central error handler returns False so that you can begin debugging the error.

Notice that within the bCentralErrorHandler function we have declared a static String variable. This variable is used to store the original error message so we can display it to the user when we reach the entry point, regardless of how many procedures deep in the stack we are when the error occurs. This static variable will hold its value until we explicitly change it.

As soon as code execution has entered the bCentralErrorHandler function, we must read and store any information we need from the VBA Err object. The reason for this will become apparent very shortly.

```
lErrNum = Err.Number
' If this is a user cancel, set the silent error flag
' message. This will cause the error to be ignored.
If lErrNum = glUSER_CANCEL Then sErrMsg = msSILENT_ERROR
' If this is the originating error, the static error
' message variable will be empty. In that case, store
' the originating error message in the static variable.
If Len(sErrMsg) = 0 Then sErrMsg = Err.Description
```

First we read and store the error number. Then, if the error number indicates that the user has cancelled program execution, we store the msSILENT_ERROR flag message in our static error message variable. If the error number does not indicate a user cancel and the static error message variable does not already contain a value, we store the error description in the static error message variable. In this way, we store only the original error message and persist it through any additional calls to the central error handler function. The static variable is cleared only after the entry point procedure has been reached and the error message displayed to the user.

The reason we must persist any necessary Err object values immediately upon entering the central error handler function is because we cannot allow any errors to occur in this function. Therefore the entire function is wrapped in `On Error Resume Next`:

```
' We cannot allow errors in the central error handler.
On Error Resume Next
```

As soon as code execution passes the `On Error Resume Next` statement, all properties of the Err object are automatically cleared. If you have not stored the original values from the Err object's properties at this point, they are lost forever. In the next section of code we construct several String values that the error handler requires.

```
' Load the default filename if required.
If Len(sFile) = 0 Then sFile = ThisWorkbook.Name

' Get the application directory.
sPath = ThisWorkbook.Path
If Right$(sPath, 1) <> "\" Then sPath = sPath & "\"

' Construct the fully-qualified error source name.
sFullSource = "[" & sFile & "]" & sModule & "." & sProc

' Create the error text to be logged.
sLogText = "   " & sFullSource & ", Error " & _
                    CStr(lErrNum) & ": " & sErrMsg
```

You will notice from Listing 12-9 that the sFile argument is optional. If no value for this argument is passed, the central error handler assumes it is being called from within the current workbook and it loads this argument's value with `ThisWorkbook.Name`. The next task is to get the path to the current workbook. This is where the error log file will be created (or updated if it has already been created). In the next line of code we construct a fully qualified location that identifies where the call to the bCentralErrorHandler function originated. This location identifier has the following format:

```
[FileName]CodeModuleName.ProcedureName
```

The last string we construct in this section is the complete error log file entry. This consists of the fully qualified location string created above, prefixed with the date and time the error occurred and suffixed with the error number and the error message. We will see examples of error log file entries later in this chapter.

Our next task is to write the entry in the application error log file. As shown below, we use standard VBA file I/O techniques to create or append to the error log file:

```
' Open the log file, write out the error information and
' close the log file.
iFile = FreeFile()
Open sPath & msFILE_ERROR_LOG For Append As #iFile
Print #iFile, Format$(Now(), "mm/dd/yy hh:mm:ss"); sLogText
If bEntryPoint Then Print #iFile,
Close #iFile
```

We first acquire an available file number and use it to create or open the error log file specified by the msFILE_ERROR_LOG constant and located in the path created in the previous section. We then write the log file entry string created above to the log file. If the bCentralErrorHandler function has been called by an entry point procedure, we write an additional blank line to the error log file to provide visual separation between this and subsequent errors. After that we close the error log file.

The last section of the central error handler determines whether and when an error message is displayed and whether the central error handler triggers debug mode behavior in the procedure that called it.

```
' Do not display or debug silent errors.
If sErrMsg <> msSILENT_ERROR Then

    ' Show the error message when we reach the entry point
    ' procedure or immediately if we are in debug mode.
    If bEntryPoint Or gbDEBUG_MODE Then
        Application.ScreenUpdating = True
        MsgBox sErrMsg, vbCritical, gsAPP_TITLE
        ' Clear the static error message variable once
        ' we've reached the entry point so that we're ready
        ' to handle the next error.
        sErrMsg = vbNullString
    End If

    ' The return vale is the debug mode status.
```

```
        bCentralErrorHandler = gbDEBUG_MODE

Else
        ' If this is a silent error, clear the static error
        ' message variable when we reach the entry point.
        If bEntryPoint Then sErrMsg = vbNullString
        bCentralErrorHandler = False
End If
```

The primary deciding factor on when to display an error message and when to ignore it is the value of the static sErrMsg variable. Remember that this variable holds the value of the original error message that triggered the central error handler. If the value of this variable indicates that the original error was the result of the user canceling program execution, then no error message is displayed, the static error message variable is cleared to prepare the central error handler for the next error, and the return value of the central error handler is False, so as not to trigger any debug actions.

If the static error message variable indicates any error other than a user cancel error, then an error message is displayed. If the application is in debug mode (gbDEBUG_MODE = True), an error message displays as soon as the error occurs and the central error handler returns True so the calling procedure can begin executing debug code. If the application is not in debug mode, an error message displays only when the error handling code reaches the entry point procedure. In this case, the central error handler function returns False throughout so as not to trigger any procedure-level debug code.

Error Handling in Classes and Userforms

Classes and userforms present some unique error handling challenges that we cover in this section. As explained previously, event procedures in classes and userforms should almost always be considered entry point procedures. The Initialize, Activate and Terminate events are exceptions to this rule. The user does not directly trigger these events. Instead, they are fired as a side effect of a class being created or destroyed or a userform being created, shown or destroyed. Error handling for these events is a little tricky, so we discuss them in detail.

Initialize and Activate Events

Errors that occur in Initialize or Activate events are typically catastrophic errors that render the class or userform in which they occur unusable. Therefore, they normally cannot be handled in any way that would mitigate them. If you are going to place code in either of these event procedures, the best option is not to give them an error handler at all. This will delegate the handling of any errors that occur inside these event procedures to the error handler of the procedure that attempted to create the object.

An option that gives you much more control over the initialization process, and any errors that arise as a result of it, is to create your own custom Initialize method. This Boolean function would replace the Initialize and Activate event procedures, so those events would no longer need to be trapped in your code. In the *Putting It All Together* section below, we show an example of a custom Initialize method in a userform.

Terminate Events

Errors that occur in Terminate events are unusual in that, assuming proper programming techniques have been used, neither are they catastrophic nor can they be mitigated. When the Terminate event is fired, the class or userform has performed its function and is being destroyed. If you need to place code in the Terminate event of a class or userform, it is best to simply ignore any errors that occur by using the `On Error Resume Next` statement at the beginning of the procedure.

Putting It All Together

Although we've described all the pieces of an error handling system, it may not be clear how all those pieces fit together. In this section we show a small but complete program that demonstrates the basic error handling techniques. This program is admittedly contrived, but the idea behind it is to have a complete program with as little distraction from non-error-handling-related code as possible. The complete program can be found in the *Concepts* folder of the CD in the workbook named ErrorHandlingDemo.xls.

The error handling demo program consists of a single entry point procedure that displays a userform and then calls a function that intentionally generates an error depending on whether the user clicks the OK or Cancel button on the userform. Figure 12-2 shows the userform for our error handling demo and Listing 12-10 shows the code behind this userform.

Figure 12-2 The Error Handling Demo Userform

Listing 12-10 The Code Behind the Error Handling Demo Userform

```
Private Const msMODULE As String = "FDemo"

Private bUserCancel As Boolean

Public Property Get UserCancel() As Boolean
    UserCancel = bUserCancel
End Property

Private Sub cmdOK_Click()
    bUserCancel = False
    Me.Hide
End Sub

Private Sub cmdCancel_Click()
    bUserCancel = True
    Me.Hide
End Sub

Private Sub UserForm_QueryClose(Cancel As Integer, _
                                CloseMode As Integer)
```

```
    ' Route any X-close button calls through
    ' the cmdCancel_Click procedure.
    If CloseMode = vbFormControlMenu Then
        Cancel = True
        cmdCancel_Click
    End If
End Sub

Public Function Initialize() As Boolean

    Const sSOURCE As String = "Initialize()"

    Dim bReturn As Boolean  ' The function return value

    On Error GoTo ErrorHandler

    ' Assume success until an error is encountered.
    bReturn = True

    ' Set the UserForm caption.
    Me.Caption = gsAPP_TITLE

ErrorExit:

    Initialize = bReturn
    Exit Function

ErrorHandler:
    bReturn = False
    If bCentralErrorHandler(msMODULE, sSOURCE) Then
        Stop
        Resume
    Else
        Resume ErrorExit
    End If
End Function
```

The first thing to notice is the userform has a read-only UserCancel property. The value of this property is determined by which button the user clicks. If the OK button is clicked, the UserCancel property will return False (meaning the user did not cancel the userform). If the Cancel button is clicked, the UserCancel property will return True. In the code for the calling procedure we will demonstrate how to raise a custom user cancel error in response to the UserCancel method returning True that will cause the error handler to exit silently rather than displaying an error.

The second thing to notice is we are trapping clicks to the X-close button on the userform with the UserForm_QueryClose event procedure and rerouting them to the cmdCancel_Click event procedure. This makes a click on the X-close button behave exactly like a click on the Cancel button.

The last thing to notice is the userform contains a custom Initialize method. This method is a Boolean function that returns True if initialization succeeds and False if an error occurred during initialization. This method is called prior to showing the userform. The calling function then examines the return value of the method and does not attempt to show the userform if initialization failed.

Listing 12-11 shows the function that will purposely cause an error.

Listing 12-11 The bCauseAnError Function

```
Public Function bCauseAnError() As Boolean

    Const sSOURCE As String = "bCauseAnError()"

    Dim bReturn As Boolean    ' The function return value
    Dim lTest As Long

    On Error GoTo ErrorHandler

    ' Assume success until an error is encountered.
    bReturn = True

    ' Cause a divide by zero error.
    lTest = 1 / 0

ErrorExit:

    bCauseAnError = bReturn
    Exit Function

ErrorHandler:
    bReturn = False
    If bCentralErrorHandler(msMODULE, sSOURCE) Then
        Stop
        Resume
```

```
    Else
        Resume ErrorExit
    End If
End Function
```

This function is exactly the same as the one we showed in Listing 12-6 with some code added that causes it to throw a divide by zero error. Now we can tie things together with the entry point procedure that runs the application. The code for this procedure is shown in Listing 12-12.

Listing 12-12 The EntryPoint Subroutine

```
Public Sub EntryPoint()

    Const sSOURCE As String = "EntryPoint"

    Dim bUserCancel As Boolean
    Dim frmDemo As FDemo

    On Error GoTo ErrorHandler

    Set frmDemo = New FDemo
    Load frmDemo
    ' If UserForm initialization failed, raise a custom error.
    If Not frmDemo.Initialize() Then Err.Raise glHANDLED_ERROR
    frmDemo.Show
    ' If the user pressed the Cancel button, raise a custom
    ' user cancel error. This will cause the central error
    ' handler to exit the program without displaying an
    ' error message.
    If frmDemo.UserCancel Then Err.Raise glUSER_CANCEL

    ' If the user pressed the OK button, run the function that
    ' is designed to cause an error.
    If Not bCauseAnError() Then Err.Raise glHANDLED_ERROR

ErrorExit:

    ' Clean up the UserForm
    Unload frmDemo
    Set frmDemo = Nothing

    Exit Sub
```

```
ErrorHandler:
    If bCentralErrorHandler(msMODULE, sSOURCE, , True) Then
        Stop
        Resume
    Else
        Resume ErrorExit
    End If
End Sub
```

The EntryPoint subroutine is run from a button located on Sheet1 of the ErrorHandlingDemo.xls workbook. This application has only two possible execution paths. Clicking the OK button on the userform triggers the first and clicking the Cancel button on the userform triggers the second. Let's examine what happens in each case and see the resulting error log entries.

The EntryPoint subroutine first creates a new instance of the FDemo UserForm, loads it and calls the userform's custom Initialize method. In this sample application the userform will never fail to initialize. We have provided this custom Initialize method to demonstrate how you would initialize a userform in a way that is linked into the error handling system.

Next, the EntryPoint subroutine shows the FDemo userform. As you can see in Figure 12-2, the only actions available to the user are clicking the OK or Cancel buttons. Clicking the OK button sets the FDemo userform's UserCancel property to False, meaning the user did not cancel. Clicking the Cancel button sets the UserCancel property to True, meaning the user did cancel. Clicking either button also hides the userform, allowing the EntryPoint subroutine to continue executing.

Because the FDemo userform is hidden rather than unloaded, when code execution returns to the EntryPoint subroutine the userform is still in memory. This allows the EntryPoint subroutine to check the value of the FDemo UserCancel property to determine what the user has asked it to do.

If the UserCancel property is True, the EntryPoint subroutine needs to exit without displaying an error message but still running its cleanup code. It accomplishes this by raising a custom user cancel error. If you recall from the discussion of the central error handler, VBA uses the error number 18 to indicate the user has cancelled program execution, we have defined a public constant that holds this value, and when the central error handler sees a user cancel error it exits silently. Therefore, to exit as a result of the user clicking Cancel in the FDemo userform, the EntryPoint subroutine raises a custom error with the error number glUSER_ CANCEL. The line of code used to accomplish this is shown here:

```
If frmDemo.UserCancel Then Err.Raise glUSER_CANCEL
```

This notifies the central error handler of the error. The central error handler logs the error and returns control to the EntryPoint procedure so it can complete its cleanup activities prior to exiting.

The central error handler records all errors, including user cancel errors, in the error log. The error.log file will be located in the same directory as the ErrorHandlingDemo.xls workbook. The entry made in response to the user clicking the FDemo Cancel button will be similar to the entry shown below except it will be written to a single line in the error log file:

```
03/30/04 20:23:37  [ErrorHandlingDemo.xls]
MEntryPoints.EntryPoint, Error 18: UserCancel
```

If the user did not cancel program execution, the EntryPoint subroutine continues with the next line of code. This line is a call to the function that is designed to intentionally throw a divide by zero error. As you can see in Listing 12-11, this function's error handler will first call the central error handler to notify it of the error, then cause the function to return False in order to notify the calling procedure that an error has occurred. In this case, the error is catastrophic, so the calling procedure must terminate the program. It does this by raising a custom handled error, as shown below:

```
If Not bCauseAnError() Then Err.Raise glHANDLED_ERROR
```

Because this error was raised from an entry point procedure, the original error message stored by the central error handler will be displayed to the user, as shown in Figure 12-3.

Figure 12-3 The Error Message Displayed to the User

In this case the central error handler will log two entries: one from the function where the error originated and one from the entry point procedure.

```
03/30/04 20:44:20  [ErrorHandlingDemo.xls]
MSystemCode.bCauseAnError(), Error 11: Division by zero
03/30/04 20:44:20  [ErrorHandlingDemo.xls]
MEntryPoints.EntryPoint, Error 9999: Division by zero
```

Note that the first error number recorded is the original VBA error number, while the second error number (and any subsequent error numbers) is the value of our predefined glHANDLED_ERROR constant. If there are multiple procedures in the call stack when an error occurs, the central error handler will create a log entry for each one. This provides helpful information when debugging an error because it provides a record of the call stack at the time the error occurred.

After the error has been logged and the error message displayed, the central error handler returns control to the EntryPoint subroutine so it can complete its cleanup prior to exiting.

Practical Example

PETRAS Timesheet

In the *Practical Example* section of this chapter, we retrofit our time-entry add-in with a complete centralized error handling system. This is the best example to examine if you want to see how a real-world error handling system is constructed.

The process of retrofitting our add-in with error handling is tedious but uncomplicated. All entry point procedures are outfitted with the entry point version of the error handling code and all subprocedures are converted into Boolean functions and outfitted with the function version of the error handling code.

The only code example from the new version of the PETRAS add-in that we show here is the Auto_Open procedure, in Listing 12-13. This is the entry point procedure that makes the most calls to lower-level procedures. It also has the unique requirement to shut down the application if an error occurs. This makes it the most interesting example of error handling in the add-in. You are encouraged to examine the complete revised code for the PETRAS add-in, located on the CD in the *Application* folder for this chapter, for a complete view of the error handling system.

Listing 12-13 The PETRAS Add-in Auto_Open Procedure with Error Handling

```
Public Sub Auto_Open()

    Const sSOURCE As String = "Auto_Open"

    Dim bErrorOut As Boolean
    Dim wkbBook As Workbook

    ' The very first thing your application should do upon
    ' startup is attempt to delete any copies of its
    ' command bars that may have been left hanging around
    ' by an Excel crash or other incomplete exit.
    On Error Resume Next
        Application.CommandBars(gsBAR_TOOLBAR).Delete
    On Error GoTo ErrorHandler

    ' Initialize global variables.
    If Not bInitGlobals() Then Err.Raise glHANDLED_ERROR

    ' Assume False until an error is encountered.
    bErrorOut = False

    ' Make sure we can locate our time entry workbook before we
    ' do anything else.
    If Len(Dir$(gsAppDir & gsFILE_TIME_ENTRY)) = 0 Then _
        Err.Raise glHANDLED_ERROR, sSOURCE, gsERR_FILE_NOT_FOUND

    Application.ScreenUpdating = False
    Application.EnableEvents = False
    Application.StatusBar = gsSTATUS_LOADING_APP

    ' Build the command bars.
    If Not bBuildCommandBars() Then Err.Raise glHANDLED_ERROR

    ' Set the initial state of the application.
    If Not gclsEventHandler.SetInitialStatus() Then _
                                    Err.Raise glHANDLED_ERROR
```

```
ErrorExit:

    ' Reset critical application properties.
    ResetAppProperties

    ' If an error occurred during the Auto_Open procedure,
    ' the only option is to exit the application.
    If bErrorOut Then ShutdownApplication

    Exit Sub

ErrorHandler:
    ' This variable informs the clean up section when an error
    ' has occurred.
    bErrorOut = True
    If bCentralErrorHandler(msMODULE, sSOURCE, , True) Then
        Stop
        Resume
    Else
        Resume ErrorExit
    End If
End Sub
```

This version of the Auto_Open procedure is very different from the version we last saw in *Chapter 8 — Advanced Command Bar Handling*. You will notice that with the exception of the ResetAppProperties procedure and the ShutdownApplication procedure, every procedure called by Auto_Open is now a Boolean function whose return value indicates success or failure.

The ResetAppProperties procedure is an exception because it is the rare case of a procedure in which nothing can go wrong. This type of procedure was described in the *Trivial Procedures* section above and the ResetAppProperties procedure itself was shown in Listing 12-8. The ShutdownApplication procedure is an exception because it is the last procedure run before the application closes. Similar to the bCentralErrorHandler function we examined in Listing 12-9, it doesn't make any sense to try and handle errors that occur in this procedure, so the entire ShutdownApplication procedure is wrapped in On Error Resume Next.

We've also added a new bErrorOut flag variable. This is because the cleanup section for the Auto_Open procedure (the section of code between the `ErrorExit` label and the `Exit Sub` statement) needs to know whether an error has occurred when it is executed. The error handler for the Auto_Open procedure sets the bErrorOut variable to True when an error occurs. It then calls the central error handler and, after the central error handler returns, it redirects code execution to the cleanup section, starting directly below the `ErrorExit` label. If the bErrorOut variable indicates to the cleanup section that an error has occurred, the cleanup section initiates application shutdown by calling the ShutdownApplication procedure.

PETRAS Reporting

As mentioned in the section *Complex Project Error Handler Organization* earlier in this chapter, there are two or three complex error handling system designs commonly used in Excel VBA applications and several minor variations on each of those. Throughout this chapter, we've demonstrated the concepts of error handling using a system known as the ***function return value*** method. In this system, every subprocedure is written as a Boolean function whose return value indicates success or failure. If an error occurs, it is trapped in the function's error handler, which logs the error and then sets the function's return value to False. The calling procedure tests the return value and (usually) raises another error to trigger its own error handler, and so the error bubbles up the call stack. Listing 12-14 shows the order in which lines are executed in a nested set of procedures.

Listing 12-14 The Order of Execution When Using the Function Return Value System

```
Sub EntryPoint()

    Const sSOURCE As String = "EntryPoint"

1   On Error GoTo ErrorHandler

2   If Not bSubProc1() Then
20      Err.Raise glHANDLED_ERROR
    End If

ErrorExit:
    'Run some cleanup code
23  Exit Sub
```

```
ErrorHandler:
21  If bCentralErrorHandler(msMODULE, sSOURCE, , True) Then
        Stop
        Resume
    Else
22      Resume ErrorExit
    End If
End Sub

Function bSubProc1() As Boolean

    Const sSOURCE As String = "bSubProc1"
    Dim bReturn As Boolean

3   On Error GoTo ErrorHandler
4   bReturn = True

5   If Not bSubProc2() Then
14      Err.Raise glHANDLED_ERROR
    End If

ErrorExit:
    'Run some cleanup code
18  bSubProc1 = bReturn
19  Exit Function

ErrorHandler:
15  bReturn = False
16  If bCentralErrorHandler(msMODULE, sSOURCE) Then
        Stop
        Resume
    Else
17      Resume ErrorExit
    End If
End Function

Function bSubProc2() As Boolean

    Const sSOURCE As String = "bSubProc2"
    Dim bReturn As Boolean

6   On Error GoTo ErrorHandler
```

```
7    bReturn = True

     'Cause an error
8    Debug.Print 1 / 0

ErrorExit:
     'Run some cleanup code
12   bSubProc2 = bReturn
13   Exit Function

ErrorHandler:
9    bReturn = False
10   If bCentralErrorHandler(msMODULE, sSOURCE) Then
         Stop
         Resume
     Else
11       Resume ErrorExit
     End If
End Function
```

You'll notice that in the vast majority of cases, the calling procedure handles a False return value just by raising another error to trigger its own error handler.

Error handling in VBA is designed such that any unhandled errors and any errors raised within an error handler automatically fire the error handler of the calling procedure. So if we raise an error within the subprocedure's error handler, it will automatically trigger the calling procedure's error handler, without the calling procedure having to test for a False return value and trigger the error handler itself. The same will happen if we raise an error at the end of the central error handler. This is known as the *re-throw* system of error handling and has been implemented in the PETRAS reporting application. The main advantages of the re-throw system are that we can use it within Sub, Property and Function procedures, and our functions' return values can be used for their results instead of success/failure indicators. The main disadvantage is that it becomes slightly harder for us to include complex cleanup code if an error occurs.

Listing 12-15 is taken from the MErrorHandler module of the PETRASReporting.xla workbook and shows a modified central error handler that implements the re-throw system by default, but enables us to override the re-throw behavior in the exceptional cases when we need to run complex post-error cleanup code. This is very similar to Listing 12-9, with the extra code to implement the re-throw method highlighted.

Listing 12-15 A Central Error Handler Implementing the Re-Throw System

```
Public Function bCentralErrorHandler( _
        ByVal sModule As String, _
        ByVal sProc As String, _
        Optional ByVal sFile As String, _
        Optional ByVal bEntryPoint As Boolean = False, _
        Optional ByVal bReThrow As Boolean = True) As Boolean

    Static sErrMsg As String

    Dim iFile As Integer
    Dim lErrNum As Long
    Dim sFullSource As String
    Dim sPath As String
    Dim sLogText As String

    ' Grab the error info before it's cleared by
    ' On Error Resume Next below.
    lErrNum = Err.Number

    ' If this is a user cancel, set the silent error flag
    ' message. This will cause the error to be ignored.
    If lErrNum = glUSER_CANCEL Then sErrMsg = msSILENT_ERROR

    ' If this is the originating error, the static error
    ' message variable will be empty. In that case, store
    ' the originating error message in the static variable.
    If Len(sErrMsg) = 0 Then sErrMsg = Err.Description

    ' We cannot allow errors in the central error handler.
    On Error Resume Next

    ' Load the default filename if required.
    If Len(sFile) = 0 Then sFile = ThisWorkbook.Name

    ' Get the application directory.
    sPath = ThisWorkbook.Path
    If Right$(sPath, 1) <> "\" Then sPath = sPath & "\"

    ' Construct the fully qualified error source name.
    sFullSource = "[" & sFile & "]" & sModule & "." & sProc

    ' Create the error text to be logged.
```

```
sLogText = "   " & sFullSource & ", Error " & _
            CStr(lErrNum) & ": " & sErrMsg

' Open the log file, write out the error information and
' close the log file.
iFile = FreeFile()
Open sPath & msFILE_ERROR_LOG For Append As #iFile
Print #iFile, Format$(Now(), "dd mmm yy hh:mm:ss"); sLogText
If bEntryPoint Or Not bReThrow Then Print #iFile,
Close #iFile

' Do not display or debug silent errors.
If sErrMsg <> msSILENT_ERROR Then

    ' Show the error message when we reach the entry point
    ' procedure or immediately if we are in debug mode.
    If bEntryPoint Or gbDEBUG_MODE Then
        Application.ScreenUpdating = True
        MsgBox sErrMsg, vbCritical, gsAPP_TITLE
        ' Clear the static error message variable once
        ' we've reached the entry point so that we're ready
        ' to handle the next error.
        sErrMsg = vbNullString
    End If

    ' The return vale is the debug mode status.
    bCentralErrorHandler = gbDEBUG_MODE

Else
    ' If this is a silent error, clear the static error
    ' message variable when we reach the entry point.
    If bEntryPoint Then sErrMsg = vbNullString
    bCentralErrorHandler = False
End If

'If we're using re-throw error handling,
'this is not the entry point and we're not debugging,
're-raise the error, to be caught in the next procedure
'up the call stack.
'Procedures that handle their own errors can call the
'central error handler with bReThrow:=False to log the
'error, but not re-raise it.
If bReThrow Then
```

```
        If Not bEntryPoint And Not gbDEBUG_MODE Then
            On Error GoTo 0
            Err.Raise lErrNum, sFullSource, sErrMsg
        End If
    Else
        'Error is being logged and handled,
        'so clear the static error message variable
        sErrMsg = vbNullString
    End If

End Function
```

Listing 12-16 shows the order in which lines are executed in a nested set of procedures when the re-throw system is implemented.

Listing 12-16 The Order of Execution When Using the Re-Throw System

```
Sub EntryPoint()

    Const sSOURCE As String = "EntryPoint"

1   On Error GoTo ErrorHandler

2   SubProc1

ErrorExit:
11  Exit Sub

ErrorHandler:
    'Run simple cleanup code here

9   If bCentralErrorHandler(msMODULE, sSOURCE, , True) Then
        Stop
        Resume
    Else
10      Resume ErrorExit
    End If
End Sub

Sub SubProc1()

    Const sSOURCE As String = "SubProc1"
```

```
3    On Error GoTo ErrorHandler

4    SubProc2

     Exit Sub

ErrorHandler:
     'Run simple cleanup code here

8    If bCentralErrorHandler(msMODULE, sSOURCE) Then
         Stop
         Resume
     End If
End Sub

Sub SubProc2()

     Const sSOURCE As String = "bSubProc2"

5    On Error GoTo ErrorHandler

     'Cause an error
6    Debug.Print 1 / 0

     Exit Sub

ErrorHandler:
     'Run simple cleanup code here

7    If bCentralErrorHandler(msMODULE, sSOURCE) Then
         Stop
         Resume
     End If
End Sub
```

Using the re-throw method, we can only include cleanup code at the start of our error handlers (before the call to the central error handler), so we have to be extremely careful to ensure that the cleanup code does not cause any more errors to occur and does not reset the Err object. In practice, this means the re-throw method is best used when there is no cleanup required, or when the cleanup is trivial and could not cause an error.

In Listing 12-15, we added an optional parameter to the central error handler that enables us to stop the error being re-raised. This results in exactly the same behavior as the function return value system, thereby allowing us to use that method in the exceptional cases that require complex cleanup code. This parameter is used in the ConsolidateWorkbooks procedure to handle errors that occur while extracting the data from a timesheet workbook. In that case, we call the central error handler to log the error, then close the problem timesheet workbook and continue with the next one.

Whether to use the function return value or re-throw system of error handling is largely a philosophical decision. Both have their advantages and disadvantages and will be more or less appropriate for different situations. Either system is better than having no error handling at all.

Conclusion

In this chapter we've covered a lot of ground that may be unfamiliar to many readers. Look closely at the sample applications for this chapter and read the chapter again if error handling concepts continue to be unclear. One of the best ways to discover how an error handler works is to use debugging techniques to single step through an application as it handles an error. We cover debugging techniques in detail in *Chapter 16 — VBA Debugging*. After reading that chapter, you might want to revisit this chapter and examine the sample applications in more detail using VBA debugging techniques.

CHAPTER 13

Programming with Databases

A large percentage of nontrivial Excel applications require some sort of data store that is separate from the rest of the application, usually in the form of a database. In this chapter we cover the basics of database design and data access using SQL and ADO. We do not go into great detail on any of these topics. All of them are book-length subjects in their own right. After some brief introductory material, we demonstrate these technologies by showing how to use them for their most common purposes. At the end of the chapter, we suggest additional books that you can use for in-depth study of the topics we introduce here.

An Introduction to Databases

The biggest problem for Excel-centric developers making the jump to applications based on a back-end database is understanding the fundamental differences between how data is treated in Excel and how data is treated in a database. A database requires a significant amount of rigor from the data when compared to an Excel worksheet. You can enter almost anything you want on a worksheet, but database tables are much more picky. Even some of the things you *can* enter in database tables you shouldn't.

Database tables have a concept of being formally related to each other, a concept that doesn't exist at all in Excel. Modifications made to databases take effect immediately. There's no need to "save" the data. Unfortunately, there's also no way to undo a change made to data in a database once that change has been committed.

As you can see, working with databases is significantly different from working with Excel worksheet tables. This section covers the most important things you need to know about how databases work and why you would want to use one.

NOTE: Those of you who are very familiar with databases and the terminology surrounding them will notice that we use some nonstandard terms to describe database concepts in this section. This is intentional and is designed to explain these concepts in terms that Excel programmers with limited database experience will find easier to understand.

Why Use a Database

For many purposes Excel is a perfectly adequate data container. However, certain common circumstances will force you to confront a database. These circumstances include the following:

- **An existing database**—The data your Excel application requires may already be stored in a database. In that case, you'll need to use the existing database, if for no other purpose than to extract the data your application requires.
- **Capacity constraints**—An Excel worksheet can hold only a limited amount of data, 65,536 rows to be exact. It is not uncommon for a large application to be required to deal with *millions* of rows of data. You cannot hope to store this much data in Excel, so you are forced to use a database, which can easily manage this volume of data.
- **Operational requirements**—Excel is not a multiuser application. It does have some very unreliable sharing capabilities, but as a general rule, if one person is using an Excel workbook that contains data, anyone else who wants to use it must wait for that person to finish. Databases, by contrast, are inherently multiuser applications. They are designed from the ground up to allow many people to access the same data at the same time. If your application requires multiple users to access the same data at the same time, then you probably need a database.

Relational Databases

A relational database is a set of tables containing data organized into specific categories. Each table contains data categories in columns. Each row contains a unique instance of data for the categories defined by the columns. A relational database is structured such that data can be accessed in many different ways without having to reorganize the tables. A relational database also has the important advantage of being easy to extend. After the original database has been created, new tables can be added without requiring all existing applications that use the database to be modified. The standard method used to access relational data is Structured Query Language (SQL), which we describe in the *Data Access Techniques* section later in the chapter.

File-Based Databases vs. Client-Server Databases

There are two broad categories of relational databases: file-based databases and client-server databases. The fundamental difference between them has to do with where the data access logic is executed.

In a file-based database, the database consists of one or more files that simply contain the data. When an application accesses a file-based database, all of the data access logic is executed on the client computer where the application resides. The advantages of file-based databases are that they are inexpensive, relatively simple and require little ongoing maintenance. The disadvantages of file-based databases are that they can create significant network traffic, they are limited in the amount of data they can store and limited in the number of simultaneous users who can access them. Microsoft Access and Microsoft Visual FoxPro are two examples of file-based databases.

In a client-server database, databases are contained within a larger server application. This database server is responsible for executing the data access requests from client applications. The advantages and disadvantages of client server databases are more or less the mirror image of those for file-based databases. Client server databases reduce network traffic by handling the data access logic on the server. They can store very large amounts of data and handle very large numbers of simultaneous users. However, client-server databases are expensive, complex and require routine maintenance to keep them operating efficiently. Microsoft SQL Server and Oracle are two examples of client-server databases.

Normalization

Normalization is the process of optimizing the data in your database tables. Its goal is to eliminate redundant data and ensure that only related data is stored in each table. Normalization can be taken to extreme lengths. But for most developers most of the time, understanding the first three rules of normalization and ensuring that your database is in third normal form is all you'll ever need to do. (We cover the first three normal forms in detail in the sections that follow.)

NOTE: Prior to normalizing your data, you must be sure all of the rows in every table are unique. A database table should not contain duplicate rows of data and normalization will not correct this problem.

Before we can talk about normalization, we need to cover the concept of a *primary key*. A primary key consists of one or more columns in a data table whose value(s) uniquely identify each row in the table. Let's take a look at a simple example. Figure 13-1 shows a database table containing a list of author information.

FirstName	LastName	City	Country
Robert	Bovey	Seattle	United States
Stephen	Bullen	Carlow	Ireland
John	Green	Sydney	Australia
Robert	Rosenberg	Los Angeles	United States

Figure 13-1 The Authors Table

Notice that there are two instances of the name Robert in the FirstName column. These names refer to two different people, but if you were trying to use only this column to identify rows there would be no way to distinguish these from duplicate entries. To uniquely identify rows in this table, we must designate the FirstName *and* LastName columns as the primary key. If you combine the values of these two columns there is no longer any duplication, so all rows are uniquely identified. In the text that follows, primary key columns are often referred to simply as *key columns*, whereas any columns that do not belong to the primary key are referred to as *nonkey columns*.

For our discussion of normalization, we use the BillableHours table shown in Figure 13-2. This table contains data that might have been extracted from one of our PETRAS time-entry workbooks. As it stands, this data is very denormalized and not suitable for use in a relational database. The primary key for this table consists of the combination of the Consultant, Date, Project and Activity columns.

Figure 13-2 The Initial BillableHours Table

First Normal Form

There are two requirements a data table must meet to satisfy the first normal form:

1. All column values are *atomic*. This means there are no values that can be split into smaller meaningful parts.

   We have one column that obviously violates this requirement. The Consultant column consists of both the first name and the last name of each consultant. This data must be separated into two distinct columns, FirstName and LastName, to satisfy the first normal form.

2. Repeating groups of data should be eliminated by moving them into new tables.

   The Consultant column, even after separating it into first name and last name, violates this requirement. The solution is to create a separate Consultants table to hold this data. Each consultant will be assigned a unique consultant ID number that will be used in the BillableHours table to identify the consultant.

The result of transforming our BillableHours table into first normal form is two tables—the modified BillableHours table shown in Figure

13-3 and the new Consultants table shown in Figure 13-4. The first column in the BillableHours table, which previously held each consultant's name, has been replaced with a unique ConsultantID number created in the new Consultants table.

ConsultantID	Date	Client	Project	Activity	Hours	Rate	Charge
1	4/3/2004	Big Auto Corp.	BAC 1	General Programming	8	$150	$1,200
1	4/3/2004	Big Auto Corp.	BAC 1	Application Design	6	$200	$1,200
3	4/3/2004	Big Auto Corp.	BAC 1	Bug Fix	4	$100	$400
3	4/3/2004	Big Auto Corp.	BAC 1	Phone Conference	1	$75	$75
3	4/3/2004	Big Auto Corp.	BAC 1	Travel	4	$100	$400
4	4/3/2004	Hardware Barn	HB 2	Bug Fix	3	$100	$300
2	4/3/2004	Hardware Barn	HB 2	Travel	5	$100	$500
4	4/3/2004	Hardware Barn	HB 2	Phone Conference	2	$75	$150
4	4/3/2004	Hardware Barn	HB 2	Travel	3	$100	$300
2	4/3/2004	Hardware Barn	HB 2	Bug Fix	2	$100	$200
2	4/3/2004	Massive Oil Co.	MOC 3	Phone Conference	2	$75	$150
4	4/3/2004	Massive Oil Co.	MOC 3	Phone Conference	1	$75	$75
3	4/3/2004	Massive Oil Co.	MOC 3	Code Review	2	$150	$300
1	4/3/2004	Massive Oil Co.	MOC 3	General Programming	5	$150	$750
3	4/3/2004	Massive Oil Co.	MOC 3	Travel	6	$100	$600
3	4/3/2004	Universal Bank & Trust	UBT 4	Application Design	4	$200	$800
1	4/3/2004	Universal Bank & Trust	UBT 4	General Programming	6	$150	$900

Record: 18 of 18

Figure 13-3 The BillableHours Table in First Normal Form

ConsultantID	FirstName	LastName
1	Rob	Bovey
2	Stephen	Bullen
3	John	Green
4	Robert	Rosenberg

Record: 4 of 4

Figure 13-4 The New Consultants Table

This not only allows us to satisfy first normal form, but also allows us to handle the situation in which two consultants have the same first and last names. In the original table there would have been no way to distinguish between two consultants with the same name.

Before we go any further we must explain the concept of a **_foreign key_**. A foreign key is a column in one table that uniquely identifies records in some other table. In the case above, the ConsultantID column in the

BillableHours table is a foreign key column, each of whose values identify a single, unique consultant in the new Consultants table. The use of foreign keys is ubiquitous in relational databases. As we will see in the upcoming section on *Relationships and Referential Integrity*, foreign keys are used to create connections between related tables in a database.

Second Normal Form

There are two requirements a data table must meet to satisfy the second normal form:

1. The table must be in first normal form.

Each successive normal form builds upon the previous normal form. Because our BillableHours table is already in first normal form, this requirement has been satisfied.

2. Each column in the table must depend on the whole primary key. This means if any column in the primary key were removed, you could no longer uniquely identify the rows in any nonkey column in the table.

The primary key in our BillableHours table consists of a combination of the ConsultantID, Date, Project and Activity columns. Do we have any columns that are not dependent on all four of these key columns? Yes. The Client column depends only on the Project column, because a project name uniquely identifies the client for whom the project is completed.

To solve this problem we will remove the client column from the BillableHours table and create a new Clients table. We will also create a new Projects table that provides each project with a unique ID number, and use this project ID rather than the project name in the BillableHours table. This will serve two purposes. The new Projects table will provide a link from the BillableHours table to the Clients table (which we discuss in more detail later in the chapter). It will also enable us to handle the situation in which two clients have the same project name.

The result of transforming our BillableHours table into second normal form is three tables. The modified BillableHours table, shown in Figure 13-5, the new Clients table, shown in Figure 13-6, and the new Projects table, shown in Figure 13-7 (this is in addition to the Consultants table we created in the previous section).

NOTE: The sharp-eyed among you may have noticed that the Rate column in the BillableHours table also violates second normal form. This is absolutely correct, so give yourself a gold star if you caught this. However, this column is part of such a good example for demonstrating third normal form that we've decided to postpone it for that topic.

ConsultantID	Date	ProjectID	Activity	Hours	Rate	Charge
1	4/3/2004	1	General Programming	8	$150	$1,200
1	4/3/2004	1	Application Design	6	$200	$1,200
3	4/3/2004	1	Bug Fix	4	$100	$400
3	4/3/2004	1	Phone Conference	1	$75	$75
3	4/3/2004	1	Travel	4	$100	$400
4	4/3/2004	5	Bug Fix	3	$100	$300
2	4/3/2004	5	Travel	5	$100	$500
4	4/3/2004	5	Phone Conference	2	$75	$150
4	4/3/2004	5	Travel	3	$100	$300
2	4/3/2004	5	Bug Fix	2	$100	$200
2	4/3/2004	11	Phone Conference	2	$75	$150
4	4/3/2004	11	Phone Conference	1	$75	$75
3	4/3/2004	11	Code Review	2	$150	$300
1	4/3/2004	11	General Programming	5	$150	$750
3	4/3/2004	11	Travel	6	$100	$600
3	4/3/2004	16	Application Design	4	$200	$800
1	4/3/2004	16	General Programming	6	$150	$900

Record: 18 of 18

Figure 13-5 The BillableHours Table in Second Normal Form

ClientID	ClientName
1	Big Auto Corp.
2	Hardware Barn
3	Massive Oil Co.
4	Universal Bank & Trust
(AutoNumber)	

Record: 4 of 4

Figure 13-6 The New Clients Table

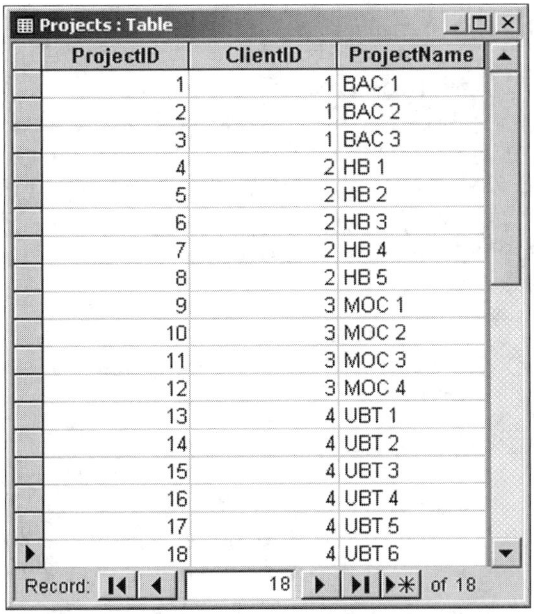

Projects : Table

ProjectID	ClientID	ProjectName
1	1	BAC 1
2	1	BAC 2
3	1	BAC 3
4	2	HB 1
5	2	HB 2
6	2	HB 3
7	2	HB 4
8	2	HB 5
9	3	MOC 1
10	3	MOC 2
11	3	MOC 3
12	3	MOC 4
13	4	UBT 1
14	4	UBT 2
15	4	UBT 3
16	4	UBT 4
17	4	UBT 5
18	4	UBT 6

Record: 18 of 18

Figure 13-7 The New Projects Table

Third Normal Form

There are three requirements a data table must meet to satisfy third normal form:

1. The table must be in second normal form.

   This requirement has been met by the modifications we made in the previous section.
2. Nonkey columns cannot describe other nonkey columns.

   This requirement can be memorably expressed as "Nonkey columns must represent the key, the whole key and nothing but the key." In our BillableHours table, the Rate column depends only on the Activity key column. All the other key columns could be removed from the table and the values in the Rate column could still be uniquely associated with the remaining Activity column.

   We can solve this problem by creating a new table to hold the list of Activities and their associated rates. The BillableHours table will retain only an activity ID number in place of the previous Activity and Rate columns.

3. The table cannot contain **derived data**.

Derived data refers to a column in a data table whose values have been created by applying a formula or transformation to the values in one or more other columns in the table. In our BillableHours table, the Charge column is a derived column that is the result of multiplying the Rate column by the Hours column. Columns containing derived data should simply be removed from the table and calculated "on the fly" whenever their values are required.

The result of transforming our BillableHours table into third normal form is two tables: the modified BillableHours table, shown in Figure 13-8 and the new Activities table shown in Figure 13-9.

Note that our third normal form BillableHours table consists of a set of primary key columns, the ConsultantID, Date, ProjectID and ActivityID columns, and a nonkey Hours column that depends on the entire primary key and nothing but the primary key. If any primary key column were removed from the table, it would no longer be possible to uniquely identify any of the entries in the Hours column. Because there are no other nonkey columns in the table, the Hours column cannot possibly depend on any nonkey columns. Our data is now ready to be used in a relational database.

ConsultantID	Date	ProjectID	ActivityID	Hours
1	4/3/2004	1	1	8
1	4/3/2004	1	5	6
3	4/3/2004	1	6	4
3	4/3/2004	1	2	1
3	4/3/2004	1	4	4
4	4/3/2004	5	6	3
2	4/3/2004	5	4	5
4	4/3/2004	5	2	2
4	4/3/2004	5	4	3
2	4/3/2004	5	6	2
2	4/3/2004	11	2	2
4	4/3/2004	11	2	1
3	4/3/2004	11	7	2
1	4/3/2004	11	1	5
3	4/3/2004	11	4	6
3	4/3/2004	16	5	4
1	4/3/2004	16	1	6

Record: 18 of 18

Figure 13-8 The BillableHours Table in Third Normal Form

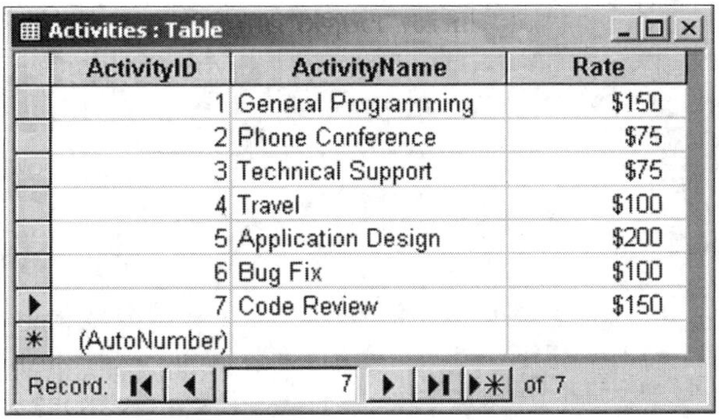
Activities : Table

ActivityID	ActivityName	Rate
1	General Programming	$150
2	Phone Conference	$75
3	Technical Support	$75
4	Travel	$100
5	Application Design	$200
6	Bug Fix	$100
7	Code Review	$150
(AutoNumber)		

Record: 7 of 7

Figure 13-9 The New Activities Table

When Not to Normalize

In the vast majority of cases, you will always want to follow the normalization rules outlined above when preparing your data for storage in a relational database. As with almost every other rule, however, there are exceptions.

The most common exception has to do with derived columns. When we transformed our BillableHours table into third normal form we eliminated the derived column that showed the total charge for each line item. This is generally a good practice because if you have derived columns you must also create logic to ensure those columns are updated correctly if the values of any of the columns they depend on change. This creates overhead that is best deferred until you actually need to query the derived value.

In some cases, however, it makes sense to store derived data. This is usually the case when the data is derived from columns that are very unlikely to change. If the columns that the derived data depends on are unlikely to change, the derived data is also unlikely to change. In this case you can improve the performance of queries that access the derived data by calculating it in advance and storing the result so the query can simply retrieve its value rather than having to calculate it on the fly.

Relationships and Referential Integrity

The ability to take advantage of ***relationships*** and ***referential integrity*** are two of the primary advantages that relational databases provide over Excel for data storage. The ability to create formal relationships between tables enables you to avoid massive repetition of data and its associated frequency of data-entry errors that lead to bad or "dirty" data. Referential integrity enables you to ensure that data entered in one table is consistent with data entered in other related tables. Neither one of these capabilities is available to data stored in Excel.

Foreign Keys

Before we can discuss relationships and referential integrity, we need to have a firm understanding of foreign keys. A foreign key is a column in one table (the **referencing** table) containing data that uniquely identifies records from another table (the **referenced** table). The foreign key serves to connect the two tables and ensures that only valid data from the referenced table can be entered in the referencing table. The ActivityID column in the BillableHours table shown in Figure 13-8 is a foreign key that refers to the ActivityID column in the Activities table in Figure 13-9.

For a column to serve as a foreign key, it must either be the primary key of the referenced table or a column on which a unique index has been defined. We cover unique indexes later in the chapter. A foreign key can also consist of multiple columns, as long as the constraints above are followed. Foreign keys provide the basis of creating relationships between tables.

In this section we will be using the Microsoft Access Relationships window to visually display the effect of relationships and referential integrity. Figure 13-10 shows the relationship described above between the BillableHours table and the Activities table. Each table's primary key columns are shown in bold.

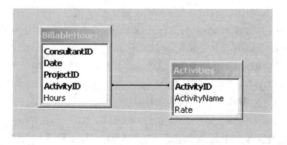

Figure 13-10 The Relationship Between the BillableHours and Activities Tables

Types of Relationships

The vast majority of relationships between database tables fall into one of three categories: one to one, one to many, and many to many.

One to One

In this type of relationship, each row in one table is associated with a single row in another table. One-to-one relationships are not frequently encountered. The most common reason for creating a one-to-one relationship is to divide a single table into its most frequently accessed sections and least frequently accessed sections. This can improve performance by making the most frequently accessed table smaller. All things being equal, the rows in a small table can be accessed more quickly than the rows in a large table. A smaller table is also more likely to remain in memory or require less bandwidth to transfer to the client depending on the type of database being used. Consider the hypothetical Parts table shown in Figure 13-11.

Figure 13-11 The Parts Table

Assume this table has a very large number of rows, and the only columns you want to access in most cases are the PartNumber, PartName, UnitPrice and Weight columns. You can improve the performance of queries against your Parts table by dividing it into two tables, with the most frequently accessed columns in one table and the rest in a second table. Each row in these two new tables will be related to exactly one row in the other table and the two tables will share a primary key. The result of this partitioning is shown in Figure 13-12.

The Access Relationship window indicates a one-to-one relationship by placing the number 1 on each side of the relationship line connecting the two tables.

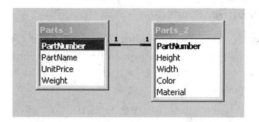

Figure 13-12 The Parts Table Divided into Two Tables with a One-to-One Relationship

One to Many

This is by far the most common type of relationship. In a one-to-many relationship, a single row in one table can be related to zero, one or many rows in another table. As Figure 13-13 shows, every relationship created in the process of normalizing our BillableHours table is a one-to-many relationship.

The Access Relationship window indicates a one-to-many relationship by placing the number 1 on the one side of the relationship line and the infinity symbol on the many side of the relationship line. Each row in the Consultants, Projects and Activities table can be related to zero, one or many rows in the BillableHours table. The one or many part of the relationship should be obvious; the zero part may require some additional explanation.

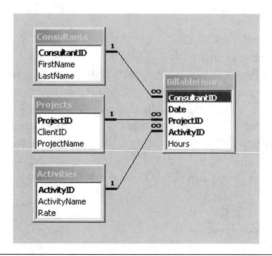

Figure 13-13 One-to-Many Relationships

If a new consultant has joined the company but not yet logged any billable hours, that consultant would be represented by a row in the Consultants table. However, the row representing the new consultant would not be associated with any rows in the BillableHours table. The Consultants table would have a one-to-many relationship with the BillableHours table, and the row representing the new consultant in the Consultants table would be associated with zero rows in the BillableHours table.

NOTE: Some of you may be thinking that Excel's data-validation list feature provides the same benefit as a one-to-many database relationship. Unfortunately, this is not true. Although it's a very useful feature, a data-validation list only enforces a one-time relationship check, at the time an entry is selected from the list. Unlike a database relationship, after an entry has been selected from a data-validation list it does not maintain any connection to the list from which it was selected.

Many to Many

In this type of relationship, each row in one table can be related to multiple rows in the other table. This concept can be a bit difficult to visualize. We demonstrate it by extending the example we used in the *Normalization* section to include the role each consultant plays on each project. Our list of roles might look like the Roles table shown in Figure 13-14.

Figure 13-14 The Roles Table

Each project will require multiple roles in order to complete it, and consultants will serve in different roles on different projects. A consultant might be a programmer on one project and a tester on another. On a small project, in fact, one consultant could very well serve multiple roles. This means that role information cannot be attached to either the Projects table or the Consultants table because there are many-to-many relationships between projects and roles as well as consultants and roles. Each project requires multiple roles and each role applies to multiple projects. Likewise, each consultant can serve multiple roles and each role can be served by multiple consultants.

Most relational databases cannot directly represent a many-to-many relationship. When this type of relationship is encountered, however, it can always be broken up into multiple one-to-many relationships linked by an intermediate table. In our Projects, Consultants and Roles example, the many-to-many relationships would be represented in the database as shown in Figure 13-15.

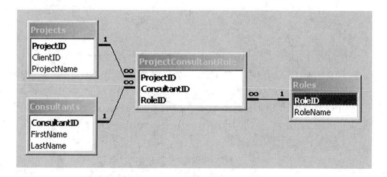

Figure 13-15 Many-to-Many Relationships Resolved into One-to-Many Relationships

The ProjectConsultantRole table serves as the intermediate table that enables us to convert the many-to-many relationships between the Projects and Roles tables and the Consultants and Roles tables into one-to-many relationships with the ProjectConsultantRole table in the middle. The Projects, Consultants and Roles tables now have one-to-many relationships with the ProjectConsultantRole table, allowing the many-to-many relationships between the Projects and Roles tables and the Consultants and Roles tables to be implemented.

Referential Integrity

After your database has been fully normalized and you have established relationships among your tables, referential integrity ensures that the data in those tables remains valid when data is added, modified or deleted. In Figure 13-13, for example, referential integrity ensures that invalid rows cannot be added to the BillableHours table by enforcing the fact that the ConsultantID, ProjectID and ActivityID foreign key columns all refer to valid rows in their respective source tables. (The validity of the Date and Hours columns is ensured by domain constraints that can be added to those columns. The topic of domain constraints is beyond the scope of this chapter.)

NOTE: All modern relational databases support the concept of referential integrity, but the steps required to implement it are completely different from one database to the next. Consult the documentation for your database to determine how to implement referential integrity.

Natural vs. Artificial Primary Keys

There is an ongoing debate within the database community over whether the primary key for a table should be natural, which is to say it should consist of one or more columns that naturally occur in the table, or whether it should be artificial. An artificial key is a unique but otherwise meaningless number that is automatically added to each row in a table. Most modern relational databases provide a special column type that will automatically generate a unique number for every row added to a table.

To oversimplify the debate, natural keys tend to be advocated by people who primarily design databases, whereas artificial keys tend to be advocated by people who must live and work with databases. The argument really comes down to two points: providing easily usable foreign keys and ensuring the true uniqueness of records in a table.

The formal task of a primary key can be divided into two very similar but subtly different tasks: uniquely identifying each row in a table and ensuring every row in a table is unique. The first task provides a foreign key that can be used by other tables to uniquely identify a specific row in a table while the second task enforces data integrity by ensuring that you cannot create duplicate records in a table.

When you have a table with a primary key that is performing both tasks simultaneously, problems begin to arise when you need to reference that table from another table through the use of a foreign key. Take, for example, our BillableHours table. This table requires the use of four columns to construct a natural primary key. If you need to reference the BillableHours table from another table in your database, you will need to add a foreign key to that table consisting of all four of these columns. This is because all four columns are required to uniquely identify a record in the BillableHours table. As you can imagine, this can become very unwieldy. Assume we have an Invoices table that needs to reference the BillableHours table. An example of how this would be accomplished using a natural key is shown in Figure 13-16.

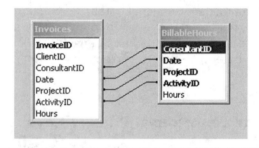

Figure 13-16 Using a Natural Key for the Billable Hours Table

The alternative is to separate the two tasks of the primary key between two different constructs. The task of uniquely identifying a row in the table can be accomplished with a single column that provides a unique number for each row. This column becomes the primary key for the table. When you need to reference this table from another table, the only column you will need to import as the foreign key is the single numeric primary key column. In Figure 13-17 we have added an artificial primary key to the BillableHours table. This is just a number that uniquely identifies each row in the table. See how much simpler this makes the task of referencing a record in the BillableHours table from the Invoices table.

If all we did was create an artificial primary key consisting of an automatically generated unique value that had no real meaning, you could easily enter two completely identical rows in the BillableHours table and the database would make them artificially unique by creating a unique value in the artificial primary key column. The task of ensuring data uniqueness can be accomplished with a unique index.

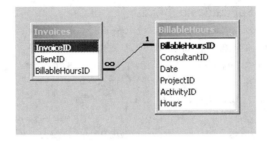

Figure 13-17 Using an Artificial Key for the BillableHours Table

A unique index is a special construct you can create that includes one or more columns in a table. The values in the column(s) on which the unique index is defined must be unique. The index will not allow duplicate values to be entered. In the case of our BillableHours table, a unique index would include the ConsultantID, Date, ProjectID and ActivityID columns. Note that these columns are the columns that originally formed the natural primary key.

At the risk of antagonizing those on the opposite side of this debate, we recommend the use of artificial primary keys. Artificial primary keys make database construction and use much simpler in practice, and you can easily enforce true uniqueness in every table by creating a unique index on the columns that would otherwise form the natural primary key.

NOTE: All modern relational databases support the creation of unique indexes, but the method used to create them is completely different from one database to the next. Consult the documentation for your database to determine how to create unique indexes on a table.

Designing the Data Access Tier

As you saw in *Chapter 3 — Excel and VBA Development Best Practices*, the data access code in an application forms a unique logical tier that should be separated from the other application tiers. The main reason for this is over the lifetime of a nontrivial Excel application, the data-storage mechanism is very likely to change. For example, when data-storage requirements are simple, data can be stored in an Excel workbook. As the amount of data and the number of users who need to access it grows, a file-based database may be required. Some applications will grow so large and attract so many users that their data access needs can only be met by a client-server database.

Your application should be designed so changes in the data access tier have a minimal impact on the rest of the application when moving from one data storage mechanism to another. Application tiers other than the data access tier should have no knowledge or implicit reliance on any particular data storage mechanism. It is the job of the data access tier to abstract away the particular data storage mechanism used and present all data to the business logic tier in the same format, regardless of whether the data comes from a local Excel workbook or a remote SQL Server database.

In an ideal design, the public methods of the data access tier will be driven by the needs of the business logic tier. The business logic tier should be able to call the data access tier to retrieve, input, update or delete data in a manner that reflects the application logic. The application logic will be translated into the specific actions required to accomplish the physical task on whatever data storage mechanism is in use. If possible, all data should be transferred between the business logic tier and the data access tier by way of user-defined types. Use ADO recordsets if absolutely necessary, but be aware that the use of recordsets introduces some undesired linkages between business logic and data access tiers, in the form of the physical ordering of the data in the recordset, for example. ADO will be described in more detail in the next section.

Data Access with SQL and ADO

An Introduction to ActiveX Data Objects (ADO)

ADO is the data access technology designed by Microsoft to make data access as simple and transparent as possible, regardless of how or where the data is stored. Previous data access technologies, most notably DAO and ODBC, are still in use. However, these technologies have been officially deprecated, meaning that Microsoft will no longer enhance them and may drop support for them at any time. For several years, as of this writing, ADO has been the sole designated data access technology for now and the future.

Data Access Technology Defined

A data access technology such as ADO can be thought of as a connector between your application and the data-storage mechanism it uses. ADO allows your application to "talk" to databases in the VBA programming language. You do still need to understand the use of SQL, which will be discussed throughout the rest of this chapter, but you do not need to understand the low-level APIs required to translate SQL-based requests between VBA and the target data-storage application. ADO abstracts these low-level requirements into a set of common objects, properties and methods that are used in the same way no matter what data-storage application you're working with.

NOTE: For simple applications where the data is stored entirely within open Excel workbooks, you will rarely need to use a separate data access technology such as ADO. VBA will do the job quite nicely. However, your data access code should still be separated into its own logical tier in order to minimize the number of problems you'll encounter if you need to move to a data storage mechanism that does require the use of ADO.

How does ADO accomplish this? It operates through a lower-level technology called OLE DB. You can think of OLE DB as ADO for C++ programmers. OLE DB cannot be used directly from VBA, but ADO translates the OLE DB data access mechanisms into a form VBA understands.

The root of OLE DB's ability to make all data storage applications look the same is a component called a ***provider***. There is an OLE DB provider for each data-storage application. This provider translates the unique, low-level APIs of that application into a common OLE DB interface. (The concept of interfaces is covered extensively in *Chapter 11 — Interfaces*.) Providers for the most commonly used databases are packaged with ADO.

If you need to use ADO to access a database for which a provider has not been supplied, there are two potential options. You can obtain a native OLE DB provider for that database from a third-party vendor if one is available. If no third-party provider is available you can fall back on the OLE DB provider for ODBC. ODBC was an early industry standard low-level data access technology pioneered by Microsoft. Any database application that supports ODBC can be accessed by ADO using the OLE DB provider for ODBC. We discuss the topic of providers from an ADO point of view in more detail later in this section.

ADO Objects

ADO is built on a very simple yet extremely flexible object model. For the vast majority of purposes you will require only three top-level objects: Connection, Command and Recordset, and three collections that belong to these top-level objects: Errors, Parameters and Fields. The top-level objects are not organized hierarchically. Rather they can each be created and used along with or independently of the others. As shown in Figure 13-18, the core ADO object model can be visualized as a triangle among the three top-level objects with the collections attached to the top-level object they belong to.

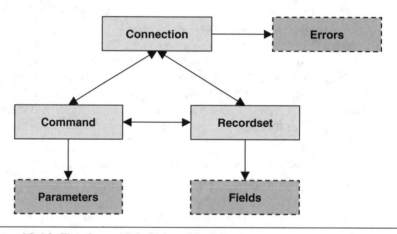

Figure 13-18 The Core ADO Object Model

A brief description of the general purpose of each object and collection is provided below. We show specific code examples that use each of these objects and collections later in the chapter.

Top-Level Objects

- **Connection**—The primary purpose of the Connection object is exactly what its name implies: connecting to a database. In keeping with the flexibility of ADO, however, a Connection object can be used to execute SQL statements or stored procedures directly.
- **Command**—The Command object is typically used to execute SQL statements or stored procedures that do not return data and/or require parameters.
- **Recordset**—The Recordset object is used to execute SQL statements or stored procedures that will return data to your application.

Collections

- **Errors**—The Errors collection is used by ADO to return any errors generated by the provider used to connect to the data source. These errors are not ADO errors. ADO objects generate runtime errors.
- **Parameters**—The Parameters collection is used to store the variable arguments that will be passed to a SQL statement or stored procedure. This allows you to construct a reusable Command object containing all the static information to which you simply pass different parameters for each call.
- **Fields**—The Fields collection is used to access the data contained in a Recordset object. A recordset can be thought of as containing a table in which only one row is active at a time. The Fields collection exposes the values in the columns corresponding to the active row.

Connecting to Data Sources

Before you can do anything with the data in a data source you must establish a connection to the data source. As with most tasks involving ADO, there is more than one way to do this. A connection can be specified by setting individual properties of an ADO Connection object or by grouping all the required properties into a *connection string*. We will demonstrate how to establish connections using connection strings.

A connection string tells ADO what provider to use, what data source to connect to and any other details required to establish the connection (a user name and password, for example). A connection string consists of a series of property-value pairs, each followed by a semicolon. The first property specified in your connection string should be the *Provider* property. This tells ADO what provider you want to use. The provider determines the structure of the rest of the connection string. Each provider has a unique set of additional properties, some of which are required and some of which are optional.

If no provider is specified, the default provider is the OLE DB provider for ODBC. This is for backward compatibility with old-style ODBC connection strings. This is rarely the provider you want to use, so always specify the provider in your connection strings. Sample connection strings for several common data sources are shown below.

Access

The OLE DB Provider for Microsoft Jet is used to connect to Access databases. The syntax for a typical connection string to an Access database is shown in Listing 13-1.

Listing 13-1 An Access Database Connection String

```
Dim sConnect As String

sConnect = "Provider=Microsoft.Jet.OLEDB.4.0;" & _
           "Data Source=C:\Files\MyDatabase.mdb;" & _
           "User ID=UserName;" & _
           "Password=Password;"
```

As you can see, the first argument specifies the provider you want to use. After you have specified the OLE DB Provider for Microsoft Jet, the only other property that is always required is the Data Source property. This tells OLE DB where the Access database you want to connect to is located. If your Access database is password-protected, you can pass it the user name and password required to open it using the User ID and Password properties.

NOTE: Microsoft has deprecated the OLE DB Provider for Microsoft Jet. This means that it still works but is no longer actively distributed and that support for it will end at some point in the future. ADO version 2.5 was the last version of ADO with which this provider was distributed. If you or your users do not have this version of ADO installed, you can download it from the Microsoft Web site at `http://msdn.microsoft.com/downloads/`.

SQL Server

The OLE DB Provider for SQL Server is used to connect to SQL Server databases. The base connection string syntax for this provider is shown in Listing 13-2.

Listing 13-2 Base Connection String Syntax for SQL Server

```
Dim sConnect As String

sConnect = "Provider=SQLOLEDB;" & _
           "Data Source=Server\Instance;" & _
           "Initial Catalog=DatabaseName;"
```

The ***Data Source*** property specifies the server and instance you want to connect to. SQL Server 2000 and later can have multiple server instances, each containing multiple databases. In prior versions of SQL Server, you would just specify the server name. In either case, the server name is typically the same as the name of the computer on which SQL Server is installed. The ***Initial Catalog*** property is used to specify the database you want to connect to.

There are two common syntax variations used when connecting to a SQL Server database. The variation you need to use depends on how the login security has been configured on the SQL Server you are connecting to. Unlike Access, SQL Server always requires some sort of login credentials. The two types of SQL Server security are ***standard security*** and ***Windows integrated security***. Standard security means that you log in to SQL Server with a user name and password specific to SQL Server. Integrated security means your Windows network login credentials are used to validate your connection to SQL Server. The connection string used for standard security is shown in Listing 13-3. The connection string used for integrated security is shown in Listing 13-4.

Listing 13-3 Connection String for SQL Server with Standard Security

```
Dim sConnect As String

sConnect = "Provider=SQLOLEDB;" & _
           "Data Source=ServerName\InstanceName;" & _
           "Initial Catalog=DatabaseName;" & _
           "User ID=UserName;" & _
           "Password=Password;"
```

Listing 13-4 Connection String for SQL Server with Integrated Security

```
Dim sConnect As String

sConnect = "Provider=SQLOLEDB;" & _
           "Data Source=ServerName\InstanceName;" & _
           "Initial Catalog=DatabaseName;" & _
           "Integrated Security=SSPI"
```

Excel

You can connect to an Excel workbook using either the OLE DB Provider for ODBC or the OLE DB Provider for Microsoft Jet. We demonstrate the use of the latter. The syntax for this is shown in Listing 13-5.

Listing 13-5 Connection String for an Excel Workbook

```
Dim sConnect As String

sConnect = "Provider=Microsoft.Jet.OLEDB.4.0;" & _
           "Data Source=C:\Files\MyWorkbook.xls;" & _
           "Extended Properties=""Excel 8.0;HDR=YES"";"
```

Note the ***Extended Properties*** property. This property consists of two values. The first tells the Jet provider you are connecting to an Excel workbook. The second tells the provider how to interpret the data in the sheet or range you specify in your SQL statements. A value of HDR=YES indicates the first row of data contains the column names. If this value is omitted or if it is specified as HDR=NO, the provider will assume all values in the table are data and there are no column names.

Using the Connection String

After you have built your connection string, you can assign it to the ConnectionString property of the ADO Connection object or pass it directly to various properties and methods of other top-level ADO objects. Listing 13-6 demonstrates how to open a connection to an Access database using the Connection object.

NOTE: To use ADO from your Excel VBA project, you must set a reference to the Microsoft ActiveX Data Objects 2.x library, where x represents the highest numbered library available on your system.

Listing 13-6 Opening a Connection to an Access Database

```
Public gcnAccess As ADODB.Connection

Sub OpenAccessConnection()
```

```
Dim sConnect As String

sConnect = "Provider=Microsoft.Jet.OLEDB.4.0;" & _
           "Data Source=E:\MyDatabase.mdb;"

Set gcnAccess = New ADODB.Connection
gcnAccess.ConnectionString = sConnect
gcnAccess.Open

' Code to use the connection goes here.

gcnAccess.Close

End Sub
```

Connecting to other data sources works exactly the same way. We show other ways that the connection string can be used in later sections.

Note that our ADO Connection object was declared as a global variable. This is required to enable a very important ADO feature called *connection pooling*. Creating and tearing down a connection to a database is a resource-intensive process. If your application will be performing a large number of database operations, you do not want ADO to have to create and destroy a connection for each one of them. To enable connection pooling, you must do the following:

- Declare your ADO Connection object as a global or module-level variable.
- Create your ADO connection on application startup and then close it.
- Each time a procedure needs to use the connection it should open the connection, use it and then close it.
- Do not set the Connection object to Nothing until your application is shutting down.

By following these procedures you will allow ADO (or more accurately, the underlying OLE DB provider) to hold the database connection open behind the scenes and provide your procedures with an existing connection on request rather than forcing it to create a new connection each time one is needed.

Error Handling Connections

When talking theoretically about making database connections, the connection attempts always succeed and you continue along your merry way. In the real world, this is not always the case. When you are attempting to access a database that is not located on the same computer as your code, any number of things can cause the connection attempt to fail.

The solution to this problem is to use your error handler to look for the error that is generated when a connection attempt fails and then handle it appropriately. Because congested network conditions or very busy databases can both cause transient connection problems, the best strategy is to retry the connection attempt a few times before giving up and informing the user that a connection to the database could not be established.

The code required to accomplish this for an attempted connection to a SQL Server database is shown in Listing 13-7. For general details on the error handling technique used here, refer back to *Chapter 12 — VBA Error Handling*.

Listing 13-7 Error Handling a Connection Attempt

```
Public gcnConnect As ADODB.Connection

Public Sub ConnectToDatabase()

    Const sSOURCE As String = "ConnectToDatabase"

    Dim lAttempt As Long
    Dim sConnect As String

    On Error GoTo ErrorHandler

    ' Create the connection string.
    sConnect = "Provider=SQLOLEDB;" & _
               "Data Source=ServerName\InstanceName;" & _
               "Initial Catalog=DatabaseName;" & _
               "Integrated Security=SSPI"

    ' Attempt to open the connection.
    Application.StatusBar = "Attempting to connect..."
    Set gcnConnect = New ADODB.Connection
    gcnConnect.ConnectionString = sConnect
    gcnConnect.Open
```

```
    ' Close connection to enable connection pooling.
    gcnConnect.Close

ErrorExit:

    Application.StatusBar = False
    Exit Sub

ErrorHandler:

    ' We will try to make the connection three times before
    ' bailing out.
    If lAttempt < 3 And gcnConnect.Errors.Count > 0 Then
        If gcnConnect.Errors(0).NativeError = 17 Then
            Application.StatusBar = "Retrying connection..."
            lAttempt = lAttempt + 1
            Resume
        End If
    End If

    If bCentralErrorHandler(msMODULE, sSOURCE, , True) Then
        Stop
        Resume
    Else
        Resume ErrorExit
    End If

End Sub
```

The error indicating a connection failure is a provider error, so we must examine the Connection object's Errors collection in order to determine whether a connection attempt failed. The Errors collection may contain multiple errors, but the first item in the collection is almost always the one that describes the root cause of the error. Unlike most collections that you'll encounter in VBA, the Connection object Errors collection is indexed beginning with zero.

The process of retrying connection attempts can be lengthy. Therefore we've added status bar messages to keep our users updated. Otherwise they may think the application is frozen and attempt to end it with Ctrl+Alt+Del.

Data Access Techniques

There are four fundamental *data manipulation* operations you can perform on the data in a data source. You can retrieve existing data, you can add new data, you can modify existing data and you can delete existing data. In this section we demonstrate how to perform these operations using SQL and ADO.

Any data-manipulation operation can be performed on any data source by passing plain-text SQL statements directly to the data source using ADO. Relational databases also allow you to store prefabricated SQL statements, known as stored queries or stored procedures. When working with client-server databases especially, if you have the option you should always prefer stored procedures. They are far more efficient than plain-text SQL statements and you can create far more complex data access logic within them.

For the plain-text SQL statements we demonstrate below we will show only the most common syntax elements. Actual SQL statements can be much more complex and will have database-specific extensions available that are only valid when you are working with that database. To keep this section focused, all the examples shown use Access as the data source. The nice thing about ADO is that its usage is almost identical regardless of the data source you are working with. However, please see our previous book, the *Excel 2002 VBA Programmer's Reference*, for detailed examples of data access using SQL Server, Excel and even text files.

Retrieving Data

In this section we demonstrate how to retrieve data using SQL and ADO. Excel also provides a number of automated features for retrieving and analyzing data. These will be covered in *Chapter 14 — Data Manipulation Techniques*. The SQL SELECT statement is used to accomplish data retrieval. The basic syntax of the SELECT statement is shown in Listing 13-8.

Listing 13-8 The SQL SELECT Statement

```
SELECT     <column list>
FROM       <table list>
WHERE      <criteria>
ORDER BY <column list>
```

We've placed each clause of the SELECT statement on a separate line for readability purposes. In reality, white space has no effect on a SQL statement and you can arrange it on a single line or multiple lines as you see fit. Just make sure that at least one space separates each element in the statement from the next and the clauses appear in the order shown above. The meaning of each clause is the following:

- **SELECT**—This clause is a comma-delimited list of columns you want to retrieve.
- **FROM**—This clause contains the names of one or more tables that contain the data you want to retrieve. If multiple tables are specified, you will need to perform a *join*. There are various types of joins available in SQL and a discussion of them all is beyond the scope of this chapter. However, the most common join type is the INNER JOIN, which uses the following syntax:

```
FROM table1 INNER JOIN table2 ON table1.IDCol = table2.IDCol
```

We demonstrate an INNER JOIN in the example below.
- **WHERE**—This clause contains any criteria that restrict what data should be returned. It is typically expressed as a Boolean condition in the form of `column_name = value`. The WHERE clause is optional and can be omitted if you just want to retrieve all the data in a table.
- **ORDER BY**—This clause indicates which columns you want the data sorted by. The ORDER BY clause is optional if you are not concerned about the order in which the data is returned to you.

For our SELECT example, we will use our normalized BillableHours table shown in Figure 13-8 and the related Consultants table shown in Figure 13-4. We will assume the database is located in the same directory as the workbook that is calling it. Listing 13-9 shows a plain-text SQL query that retrieves all of the billable hours records for consultant Rob Bovey.

Listing 13-9 Retrieving Data from Access

```
Public Sub SelectFromAccess()

    Dim rsData As ADODB.Recordset
    Dim sPath As String
```

```
Dim sConnect As String
Dim sSQL As String

' Clear the destination worksheet.
Sheet1.UsedRange.Clear

' Get the database path (same as this workbook).
sPath = ThisWorkbook.Path
If Right$(sPath, 1) <> "\" Then sPath = sPath & "\"

' Create the connection string.
sConnect = "Provider=Microsoft.Jet.OLEDB.4.0;" & _
            "Data Source=" & sPath & "Figures3.mdb;"

' Build the SQL query.
sSQL = "SELECT FirstName + ' ' + LastName, Date, Hours " & _
        "FROM BillableHours AS b " & _
        "INNER JOIN Consultants AS c " & _
        "ON b.ConsultantID = c.ConsultantID " & _
        "WHERE FirstName = 'Rob' AND LastName = 'Bovey';"

' Retrieve the data using ADO.
Set rsData = New ADODB.Recordset
rsData.Open sSQL, sConnect, _
            adOpenForwardOnly, adLockReadOnly, adCmdText
If Not rsData.EOF Then
    Sheet1.Range("A1").CopyFromRecordset rsData
Else
    MsgBox "No data located.", vbCritical, "Error!"
End If

rsData.Close
Set rsData = Nothing

End Sub
```

There are several interesting techniques to point out in Listing 13-9. First examine the SQL used to specify the data we want to retrieve. This shows a little bit of the flexibility available in the SQL SELECT statement. In the SELECT clause, we show how you can concatenate the values of multiple database columns into a single result column.

We have also joined two tables in the FROM clause. We need to do this because even though the data we want is located in the BillableHours table, the consultant's name that we want to restrict our data to is located in the Consultants table. In the FROM clause, we link the two tables on their common column, the ConsultantID column. Recall from our previous discussion on relationships that the ConsultantID column is the primary key of the Consultants table and a foreign key in the BillableHours table.

Next, notice we have used multiple restriction conditions in the WHERE clause. We need to specify both the value of the FirstName and LastName columns to uniquely identify the consultant whose data we want to retrieve. To do this, we just link the two Boolean conditions with the SQL AND operator.

Last, notice how we make use of the connection string in this example. Rather than creating an ADO Connection object, we simply pass the connection string directly to the ADO Recordset object's Open method. This is a very useful technique when you will only be performing a single query and you don't need advanced features of the ADO Connection object such as connection pooling.

After we've opened the recordset, we check to see whether we got any data. This is accomplished by examining the recordset's EOF property. EOF stands for *end of file*. If no data was returned, the recordset's row pointer will be pointing to the end of the recordset and the EOF property will be True, otherwise the row pointer will be pointing to the first record in the recordset and the value of EOF will be False.

If we successfully retrieved the data we asked for, we dump it onto Sheet1 using the CopyFromRecordset method of the Excel Range object. The CopyFromRecordset method provides an extremely fast method for extracting the data from a recordset onto a worksheet. The CopyFromRecordset method returns only the data, not the column names. An alternative method that adds the column names and then adds the data by looping the recordset one row at a time is shown in the code fragment in Listing 13-10.

Listing 13-10 Looping a Recordset by Rows

```
If Not rsData.EOF Then
    ' Add the column headers.
    For lColumn = 0 To rsData.Fields.Count - 1
        With Sheet1.Range("A1")
            .Offset(0, lColumn).Value = _
                        rsData.Fields(lColumn).Name
        End With
```

```
    Next lColumn

    ' Add the data.
    lRow = 1
    Do While Not rsData.EOF
        For lColumn = 0 To rsData.Fields.Count - 1
            With Sheet1.Range("A1")
                .Offset(lRow, lColumn).Value = _
                        rsData.Fields(lColumn).Value
            End With
        Next lColumn
        lRow = lRow + 1
        rsData.MoveNext
    Loop
Else
    MsgBox "No data located.", vbCritical, "Error!"
End If
```

Inserting Data

Inserting new data into a database is accomplished using the SQL INSERT statement. The basic syntax of the INSERT statement is shown in Listing 13-11. An explanation of each clause of the statement follows.

Listing 13-11 The SQL INSERT Statement

```
INSERT INTO <table name> (<column list>)
VALUES (<value list>)
```

- **INSERT INTO**—This clause includes the name of the table into which you are inserting the data and a comma-delimited list of columns that will be receiving data enclosed in parenthesis. You are not required to list the columns if you will be supplying data in the VALUES clause for every required column in the table in the same order in which they appear in the table. Certain types of columns cannot be included in the INSERT clause. These include any AutoNumber column in an Access database table.

■ **VALUES**—This clause includes a comma-delimited list of values to be inserted into the table enclosed in parenthesis. When a list of columns is provided in the INSERT INTO clause, there must be a corresponding value for each of these columns in the VALUES clause.

To illustrate the INSERT statement, we'll add a new consultant to our Consultants table. The code to accomplish this is shown in Listing 13-12.

Listing 13-12 Inserting Data into Access

```
Public Sub InsertIntoAccess()

    Dim cnAccess As ADODB.Connection
    Dim sPath As String
    Dim sConnect As String
    Dim sSQL As String

    ' Get the database path (same as this workbook).
    sPath = ThisWorkbook.Path
    If Right$(sPath, 1) <> "\" Then sPath = sPath & "\"

    ' Create the connection string.
    sConnect = "Provider=Microsoft.Jet.OLEDB.4.0;" & _
                "Data Source=" & sPath & "Figures3.mdb;"

    ' Build the SQL query.
    sSQL = "INSERT INTO Consultants (FirstName, LastName)" & _
            "VALUES ('John', 'Smith');"

    ' Use the Connection object to execute the SQL statement.
    Set cnAccess = New ADODB.Connection
    cnAccess.ConnectionString = sConnect
    cnAccess.Open
    cnAccess.Execute sSQL, , adCmdText + adExecuteNoRecords
    cnAccess.Close
    Set cnAccess = Nothing

End Sub
```

In this example we've demonstrated how you can execute SQL statements using the ADO Connection object alone. The Connection object has an Execute method that we've used to insert our new record into the Consultants table. The first argument to the Execute method is the SQL statement we want to execute. The second argument is a return value that tells us the number of records affected after the method has completed. We don't need this because we know our INSERT statement only inserts a single record. If the insert fails for some reason a runtime error will be generated by ADO.

The last argument tells the Execute method what we are giving it in the first argument as well as how to process the call. adCmdText is an enumeration member that tells the Execute method we are passing it a SQL text string. This is the same value we passed to the last argument of the Recordset.Open method in Listing 13-9 above. If this value is not specified, ADO will determine for itself what is being passed in the first argument, but telling it to begin with saves time. adExecuteNoRecords is an enumeration member that tells the Execute method how to process the call. In this case, it means the Execute method should not return a recordset. The Execute method will always return a recordset unless told to do otherwise, even if a recordset it not logically required and is therefore empty. Telling the Execute method we don't need a recordset returned saves the time and resources required to create and return the unnecessary empty recordset.

Updating Data

Updating data in a database is accomplished using the SQL UPDATE statement. The basic syntax of the UPDATE statement is shown in Listing 13-13. An explanation of each clause of the statement follows.

Listing 13-13 The SQL UPDATE Statement

```
UPDATE    <table name>
SET       <column name> = <value>
WHERE     <criteria>
```

- **UPDATE**—This clause contains the name of the table that holds the data to be updated.
- **SET**—This clause provides the column name to be updated and the value it will be updated with.

■ **WHERE**—This clause contains the criterion that identifies the row to be updated. It is expressed as a Boolean condition in the form of `column_name = value`. The WHERE clause is technically optional, but beware. If you do not supply a WHERE clause in the UPDATE statement then every row in the table will be updated with the specified value. This is rarely what you want to do and it is impossible to reverse.

To illustrate the UPDATE statement, we'll use an Access stored parameter query to modify the name of one of the clients in our Clients table from Figure 13-6. The Access stored query is called qryUpdateClient and its contents are shown in Listing 13-14.

Listing 13-14 The qryUpdateClient Parameter Query

```
UPDATE   Clients
SET      ClientName = [CName]
WHERE    ClientID = [ID];
```

As you can see, this query takes two parameters. The CName parameter is used to modify the client name and the ID parameter is used to uniquely identify the client whose name we want to update. The code to execute this query is shown in Listing 13-15.

Listing 13-15 Updating Access Data

```
Public Sub UpdateAccess()

    Dim cmAccess As ADODB.Command
    Dim objParams As ADODB.Parameters
    Dim lAffected As Long
    Dim sPath As String
    Dim sConnect As String

    ' Get the database path (same as this workbook).
    sPath = ThisWorkbook.Path
    If Right$(sPath, 1) <> "\" Then sPath = sPath & "\"

    ' Create the connection string.
    sConnect = "Provider=Microsoft.Jet.OLEDB.4.0;" & _
               "Data Source=" & sPath & "Figures3.mdb;"
```

```
' Create the Command object.
Set cmAccess = New ADODB.Command
cmAccess.ActiveConnection = sConnect
cmAccess.CommandText = "qryUpdateClient"
cmAccess.CommandType = adCmdStoredProc

' Create and append the parameters.
Set objParams = cmAccess.Parameters
objParams.Append cmAccess.CreateParameter("CName", _
                        adVarChar, adParamInput, 50)
objParams.Append cmAccess.CreateParameter("ID", _
                        adInteger, adParamInput, 0)
Set objParams = Nothing

' Load the parameters and execute the query.
cmAccess.Parameters("CName").Value = "Hardware House"
cmAccess.Parameters("ID").Value = 2
cmAccess.Execute lAffected, , adExecuteNoRecords

' Verify the correct number of records updated.
If lAffected <> 1 Then
    MsgBox "Error updating record.", vbCritical, "Error!"
End If

Set cmAccess = Nothing

End Sub
```

We are again bypassing the ADO Connection object, this time assigning the connection string directly to the Command object's ActiveConnection property. Also notice that instead of a plain-text SQL statement we are now using the name of the Access stored query. Where the type of the plain-text queries we used previously was adCmdText, the type of a stored query is adCmdStoredProc.

This example illustrates the use of the ADO Command object's Parameters collection. For each parameter in the Access parameter query, we must create a Parameter object and add it to the Parameters collection. These parameters must be created and added to the collection in exactly the same order as they appear in the SQL of the Access parameter query. We create and store the parameters in a single line of code by passing the result of the Command object's CreateParameter method to the Parameters collection Append method. We use four arguments of the CreateParameter method:

- **Name**—This is the name of the parameter. It must be the same name that appears in the Access parameter query for the parameter.
- **Type**—This is an enumeration member specifying the data type of the parameter. adVarChar means a Text parameter and adInteger means a Long Integer parameter.
- **Direction**—This is an enumeration member indicating which direction the parameter is used to pass data. adParamInput indicates the parameter will be used to pass data from our code to the database.
- **Size**—This value indicates the size of the parameter. It is only required for Text data types. In the case of our CName parameter, the column being updated has a maximum width of 50 characters. For numeric data types like the ID parameter, you can simply pass zero to this argument.

After we have created the parameters and added them to our Command object's Parameters collection, we load them with the values we want to send to the database and then execute the stored query. The first argument to the Command object's Execute method is a return value indicating the number of records affected. We are using the lAffected variable to retrieve this value and checking it to ensure that exactly one record was updated. As in our insert example, we do not require a recordset to be returned, so we're using the third argument of the Command object to prevent this from happening.

Deleting Data

Deleting data in a database is accomplished using the SQL DELETE statement. The basic syntax of the DELETE statement is shown in Listing 13-16. An explanation of each clause of the statement follows.

Listing 13-16 The SQL DELETE Statement

```
DELETE FROM <table name>
WHERE <criteria>
```

- **DELETE FROM**—This clause contains the name of the table that holds the data to be deleted.
- **WHERE**—This clause contains the criterion that identifies the row to be deleted. It is expressed as a Boolean condition in the form of `column_name = value`. The WHERE clause is technically optional, but beware. If you do not supply a WHERE clause in the DELETE statement, then every row in the table will be deleted. This is rarely what you want to do and it is impossible to reverse.

To illustrate the DELETE statement, we'll remove the consultant we added to the Consultants table with our insert example in Listing 13-12. The code to accomplish this is shown in Listing 13-17.

Listing 13-17 Deleting Access Data

```
Public Sub DeleteFromAccess()

    Dim cmAccess As ADODB.Command
    Dim lAffected As Long
    Dim sPath As String
    Dim sConnect As String
    Dim sSQL As String

    ' Get the database path (same as this workbook).
    sPath = ThisWorkbook.Path
    If Right$(sPath, 1) <> "\" Then sPath = sPath & "\"

    ' Create the connection string.
    sConnect = "Provider=Microsoft.Jet.OLEDB.4.0;" & _
               "Data Source=" & sPath & "Figures3.mdb;"

    ' Build the SQL query.
    sSQL = "DELETE FROM Consultants " & _
           "WHERE FirstName = 'John' AND LastName = 'Smith';"

    ' Create and execute the Command object.
    Set cmAccess = New ADODB.Command
    cmAccess.ActiveConnection = sConnect
    cmAccess.CommandText = sSQL
    cmAccess.CommandType = adCmdText
    cmAccess.Execute lAffected, , adExecuteNoRecords
```

```
' Verify the correct number of records deleted.
If lAffected <> 1 Then
    MsgBox "Error deleting record.", vbCritical, "Error!"
End If

Set cmAccess = Nothing

End Sub
```

All of the techniques used here should be familiar from previous examples so we will not cover them in any detail.

Further Reading

As we stated at the beginning of the chapter, the subjects covered here are all book-length topics in their own right. Therefore, we would be remiss if we didn't recommend some good books you could use to pursue the full breadth of these topics. The books recommended below have been found very useful by the authors of this book. We have no financial stake in any of them. These recommendations are based purely on quality.

Professional SQL Server 2000 Database Design

Authored by Louis Davidson
ISBN 1861004761 - Wrox

Although the title contains "SQL Server 2000," the first half of this book provides very detailed coverage of data normalization and relational database design in a software-agnostic manner. If the first section of this chapter was unclear or left you wanting more information, this is the book for you. Sadly, this book is now out of print, but used copies can be readily obtained through Amazon.com.

ADO 2.6 Programmer's Reference

Authored by David Sussman
ISBN 186100463X - Wrox

Professional ADO 2.5 Programming

Authored by David Sussman et al.
ISBN 1861002750 - Wrox

Unfortunately, there were not very many excellent books on "classic ADO" to begin with. Now that Microsoft has moved on to ADO.NET (a completely different technology regardless of the similar acronym) what few good books there were are going out of print very quickly. That applies to both of these titles, although again, you can readily find used copies through Amazon.com.

The *ADO 2.6 Programmer's Reference* is exactly what its title would suggest: a very comprehensive reference to the ADO object model. It is essentially a high-quality ADO dictionary. *Professional ADO 2.5 Programming* assumes that you understand all the basic concepts of ADO and goes on to show you how to apply them in a series of advanced application scenarios.

Professional SQL Server 2000 Programming

Authored by Robert Vieira
ISBN 0764543792 - Wrox

If you want to learn about SQL Server, there is no better place to start than here. The best way to describe the scope of this book is that it starts where ADO ends. It is tightly focused on pure SQL Server topics. It provides excellent SQL Server-specific coverage of SQL, stored procedures, views, indexes, transactions, and the tools used to manage and program SQL Server, among many other topics.

Access 2002 Developer's Handbook Set

Authored by Paul Litwin, Ken Getz and Mike Gunderloy
ISBN 0782140114 - Sybex

This is the latest update of an ongoing series of first-class Access development books that began with Access 95. This book touches on all aspects of Access development, from running Access SQL directly against an Access database to developing reports in the Access user interface. If you want a comprehensive reference to Access development, this should be your first choice.

Practical Example

In this section we will move our data into an Access database. We've provided a ready-made Access database for this project. Creating an Access database is easy and after you've created the database you no longer need Access to use it.

PETRAS Timesheet

All of the data access logic in our application has been isolated in a single module called MDataAccess. This will make it easy for us to change our back-end data store, to SQL Server for example, as our data access needs become more significant. We are also using the connection pooling feature of ADO to improve performance. Listing 13-18 shows the function that is called from the Auto_Open procedure to initialize our Connection object.

Listing 13-18 Initializing the Connection Object

```
Private mcnConnection As ADODB.Connection

Public Function bCreateDBConnection() As Boolean

    Const sSOURCE As String = "bCreateDBConnection()"

    Dim bReturn As Boolean
    Dim sPath As String
    Dim sConnect As String

    On Error GoTo ErrorHandler

    ' Assume success until an error is encountered.
    bReturn = True

    ' First look for the database path in the registry.
    sPath = GetSetting(gsREG_APP, gsREG_SECTION, gsREG_KEY, "")

    ' If we didn't find a database location entry in the
    ' registry, assume it is located in the same folder
    ' as this workbook.
    If Len(sPath) = 0 Then
        sPath = ThisWorkbook.Path
        If Right$(sPath, 1) <> "\" Then sPath = sPath & "\"
```

```
    End If

    ' Make sure we can locate the database file.
    If Len(Dir$(sPath & msFILE_DATABASE)) = 0 Then _
        Err.Raise glHANDLED_ERROR, sSOURCE, gsERR_NO_DATABASE

    ' Create the connection string.
    sConnect = "Provider=Microsoft.Jet.OLEDB.4.0;" & _
               "Data Source=" & sPath & msFILE_DATABASE & ";"

    Set mcnConnection = New ADODB.Connection
    mcnConnection.ConnectionString = sConnect
    mcnConnection.Open
    mcnConnection.Close

ErrorExit:

    bCreateDBConnection = bReturn
    Exit Function


ErrorHandler:
    bReturn = False
    If bCentralErrorHandler(msMODULE, sSOURCE) Then
        Stop
        Resume
    Else
        Resume ErrorExit
    End If
End Function
```

This function first ensures we can locate our database file. It then instantiates the module-level Connection object, then opens and closes the connection to our database. This enables the ADO connection pooling feature. The Connection object remains active as long as the application is running, being opened and closed as it is used. When the application shuts down we destroy the connection object by calling the procedure shown in Listing 13-19.

Listing 13-19 Destroying the Connection Object

```
Public Sub DestroyConnection()
    Set mcnConnection = Nothing
End Sub
```

Modifying the Application to Load Data-Validation Lists from the Database

In previous versions of our time-entry workbook template, the data-validation lists in the wksProgramData worksheet were hard-coded. If these lists changed, you would need to distribute a new copy of the template to all of your users. In this section we will modify the application so it automatically loads the latest versions of these lists from our new database whenever a time-entry workbook is opened.

The procedure that accomplishes this task is located in our MDataAccess module and called by our application event handler whenever a time-entry workbook is created, opened or detected on application startup. The entire procedure is long and very repetitive, so we will only show a representative sample of it in Listing 13-20.

Listing 13-20 Loading the Application Data

```
Public Function bLoadInitialData( _
             ByRef wkbTemplate As Workbook) As Boolean

    Const sSOURCE As String = "bLoadInitialData()"

    Dim rsData As ADODB.Recordset
    Dim bReturn As Boolean
    Dim lColOffset As Long
    Dim rngCell As Range
    Dim rngClients As Range
    Dim rngProjects As Range
    Dim sSQL As String
    Dim sSQLBase As String
    Dim wksProgData As Worksheet

    On Error GoTo ErrorHandler

    ' Assume success until an error is encountered.
    bReturn = True

    Application.StatusBar = gsSTATUS_LOADING_DATA

    ' Clear any existing data from the wksProgramData worksheet.
    Set wksProgData = wkbTemplate.Worksheets(gsSHEET_PROG_DATA)
    wksProgData.UsedRange.Offset(1, 0).ClearContents
```

```
    ' Create the Recordset object we'll use for all the queries.
    Set rsData = New ADODB.Recordset

    ' Get a connection from the pool.
    mcnConnection.Open

    ' Load each of the program data lists.
    ' Consultants
    sSQL = "SELECT FirstName + ' ' + LastName, ConsultantID" & _
            " FROM Consultants;"
    rsData.Open sSQL, mcnConnection, adOpenForwardOnly, _
            adLockReadOnly, adCmdText
    If Not rsData.EOF Then
        wksProgData.Range(gsRNG_CONSULT_TOP).Offset(1, 0) _
            .CopyFromRecordset rsData
    Else
        Err.Raise glHANDLED_ERROR, sSOURCE, _
            "Error retrieving consultant data."
    End If
    rsData.Close

    ' Load the rest of the lists here...

ErrorExit:

    Set rsData = Nothing
    ' Close the connection to return it to the pool.
    mcnConnection.Close

    Application.StatusBar = False
    bLoadInitialData = bReturn
    Exit Function

ErrorHandler:
    bReturn = False
    If bCentralErrorHandler(msMODULE, sSOURCE) Then
        Stop
        Resume
    Else
        Resume ErrorExit
    End If
End Function
```

The select operation using the recordset should look very familiar. It is essentially identical to the operation we demonstrated in the *Retrieving Data* section above. Notice how we open our module-level Connection object at the beginning of the procedure and close it at the end. This is the proper way to make use of a pooled connection.

Modifying the Application to Save Time Entries to the Database

In previous versions of our application, the entire completed time-entry workbook was saved to a central consolidation location. In this section we modify the application to save just the billable hours data to our new database. We've added a new hidden section to our time-entry worksheet that converts the data entered by the user into a format that can be loaded into the database.

The data from the visible UI is rearranged into a format that is identical to the BillableHours table in the database. All text column selections are converted to their ID numbers by looking them up in the appropriate wksProgramData worksheet table, and the total hours number is converted from Excel's date serial format into numeric format by multiplying by 24. The conversion section of the time-entry worksheet is shown in Figure 13-19.

	J	K	L	M	N	O	P	Q
1					setHideCols			
2								
3			ptrNumEntries	ConsultantID				
4			5	1				
5				tblBillableHours				
6	**Total Hours**		EntryComplete	ConsultantID	DateWorked	ProjectID	ActivityID	Hours
7	8:00		TRUE	1	04/19/04	6	1	8
8	8:00		TRUE	1	04/20/04	6	1	8
9	8:00		TRUE	1	04/21/04	9	5	8
10	8:00		TRUE	1	04/22/04	9	5	8
11	8:00		TRUE	1	04/23/04	9	1	8
12			FALSE					
13			FALSE					
14			FALSE					
15			FALSE					
16			FALSE					
17			FALSE					
18			FALSE					
19			FALSE					
20			FALSE					
21								

Figure 13-19 Time-Entry Data-Conversion Section

For performing the insert operation on the time-entry data, we've created a user-defined type structure that is used to pass data between the business logic tier and the data access tier. The definition of this type structure is shown in Listing 13-21.

Listing 13-21 The BILLABLE_HOUR Type Structure

```
Public Type BILLABLE_HOUR
    lConsultantID As Long
    dteDateWorked As Date
    lProjectID As Long
    lActivityID As Long
    dHours As Double
End Type
```

The data access tier procedure that consumes this type structure and inserts its data into the database is shown in Listing 13-22.

Listing 13-22 The bInsertTimeEntry Function

```
Public Function bInsertTimeEntry( _
                     ByRef uData As BILLABLE_HOUR) As Boolean

    Const sSOURCE As String = "bInsertTimeEntry()"

    Dim cmInsert As ADODB.Command
    Dim bReturn As Boolean
    Dim sSQL As String

    On Error GoTo ErrorHandler

    ' Assume success until an error is encountered.
    bReturn = True

    ' Create the SQL statement to insert the data.
    sSQL = "INSERT INTO BillableHours (ConsultantID, " & _
           "DateWorked, ProjectID, ActivityID, Hours) " & _
           "VALUES (" & CStr(uData.lConsultantID) & ", " & _
           "#" & uData.dteDateWorked & "#, " & _
           CStr(uData.lProjectID) & ", " & _
           CStr(uData.lActivityID) & ", " & _
           CStr(uData.dHours) & ");"
```

```
    ' Open the connection so we can use it.
    mcnConnection.Open

    Set cmInsert = New ADODB.Command
    Set cmInsert.ActiveConnection = mcnConnection
    mcnConnection.Execute sSQL, , adCmdText + adExecuteNoRecords

ErrorExit:

    Set cmInsert = Nothing
    ' Close the connection to return it to the pool.
    mcnConnection.Close

    bInsertTimeEntry = bReturn
    Exit Function

ErrorHandler:
    bReturn = False
    If bCentralErrorHandler(msMODULE, sSOURCE) Then
        Stop
        Resume
    Else
        Resume ErrorExit
    End If
End Function
```

Our new PostTimeEntriesToDatabase procedure, shown in Listing 13-23, simply loops the processed entries in the hidden section of the time entry worksheet, loads each of them into the BILLABLE_HOUR type structure one at a time and passes them to the bInsertTimeEntry function to be inserted into the database.

Listing 13-23 The PostTimeEntriesToDatabase Procedure

```
Public Sub PostTimeEntriesToDatabase()

    Const sSOURCE As String = "PostTimeEntriesToDatabase"

    Dim uData As BILLABLE_HOUR
    Dim rngCell As Range
    Dim rngTable As Range
    Dim sSheetTab As String
```

```
Dim wksSheet As Worksheet
Dim wkbBook As Workbook

On Error GoTo ErrorHandler

If Not bInitGlobals() Then Err.Raise glHANDLED_ERROR

' We know the active workbook is a time-entry workbook
' because our application event handling class would have
' disabled the menu that runs this procedure if it wasn't.
Set wkbBook = Application.ActiveWorkbook

' Make sure the TimeEntry worksheet does not have any
' data entry errors.
sSheetTab = sSheetTabName(wkbBook, gsSHEET_TIME_ENTRY)
Set wksSheet = wkbBook.Worksheets(sSheetTab)
If wksSheet.Range(gsRNG_HAS_ERRORS).Value Then
    Err.Raise glHANDLED_ERROR, sSOURCE, gsERR_DATA_ENTRY
End If

' Warn the user that this action cannot be reversed
' and give them a chance to bail out.
If MsgBox(gsMSG_WARN_POST, vbExclamation + vbYesNo, _
                            gsAPP_TITLE) = vbYes Then

    ' Loop each entry in the time sheet and save it to
    ' the database.
    Set rngTable = wksSheet.Range(gsRNG_BILLABLE_HOURS)
    For Each rngCell In rngTable

        uData.lConsultantID = rngCell.Value
        uData.dteDateWorked = rngCell.Offset(0, 1).Value
        uData.lProjectID = rngCell.Offset(0, 2).Value
        uData.lActivityID = rngCell.Offset(0, 3).Value
        uData.dHours = rngCell.Offset(0, 4).Value

        If Not bInsertTimeEntry(uData) Then
            Err.Raise glHANDLED_ERROR
        End If

    Next rngCell
```

```
    ' Clear the time entry worksheet and display a success
    ' message to the user.
    wksSheet.Range(gsRNG_CLEAR_INPUTS).ClearContents
    MsgBox gsMSG_POST_SUCCESS, vbInformation, gsAPP_TITLE

  End If

ErrorExit:

  Exit Sub

ErrorHandler:
  If bCentralErrorHandler(msMODULE, sSOURCE, , True) Then
      Stop
      Resume
  Else
      Resume ErrorExit
  End If
End Sub
```

Table 13-1 shows a summary of the changes made to the PETRAS timesheet application for this chapter.

Table 13-1 Changes to the PETRAS Timesheet Application for Chapter 13

Module	Procedure	Change
CAppEventHandler	bInitializeWorkbook	Centralized workbook initialization code here
	bLoadInitialData	Call this procedure to load initial timesheet data
MDataAccess		New module to handle all the database connectivity
MEntryPoints	PostTimeEntriesToNetwork	Converted to PostTimeEntriesToDatabase
	SpecifyConsolidationFolder	Converted to SpecifyDatabaseLocation
Auto_Open	bCreateDBConnection	Call this procedure to create pooled Connection object
	ShutdownApplication	Destroy pooled Connection object on close

PETRAS Reporting

The PETRAS reporting application has had a number of changes and additions, partly to demonstrate the database handling concepts introduced in this chapter, but also to demonstrate some of the more interesting concepts introduced in *Chapter 10 — Userform Design and Best Practices* and *Chapter 11 — Interfaces*.

The immediate result of using a database instead of workbooks to store our timesheet data is that we no longer need a (potentially time-consuming) procedure to consolidate the data. Instead of selecting the files to consolidate, the user now provides a start and end date, which the application uses to extract the required records from the database. The data extraction is done using code very similar to Listing 13-20.

Using a central database also makes it much easier for us to maintain the static lists of consultants, activities, clients and projects. The PETRAS timesheet add-in has been modified to read these lists from the database whenever a new timesheet is created, instead of us being required to distribute new timesheet templates after each update. A set of forms to maintain the lists has been added to the PETRAS reporting application, demonstrating many of the concepts from *Chapters 10 — Userform Design and Best Practices* and *11 — Interfaces*, including the following:

- All the forms follow the KISS principle of being simple for the user.
- All the forms have their code separated between a user interface layer (the form's module) and a separate user interface support (UIS) layer, implemented as a class module specific to each form.
- All the forms are resizable, implemented using the CFormResizer class from Chapter 10.
- The maintenance of the client and project lists has been implemented using a TreeView control to show the client/project hierarchy.
- All the forms have been implemented using the plug-in architecture from Chapter 11, enabling us to add new forms without changing any existing code.

Within this chapter, we've barely been able to scratch the surface of database programming in general and ADO in particular. To show some real-world examples of these technologies, we have used some of the more advanced techniques covered in the *Further Reading* texts. Specifically, we have used ***disconnected recordsets*** to handle the underlying data for our userforms. With these recordsets, we create a connection to the database, populate the recordset, then set the recordset's ActiveConnection property to Nothing. That disconnects the recordset from the physical database file, allowing us to change the data contained in the recordset *without the database being updated*. So when our user adds, deletes or renames the data, we can apply those changes directly to the recordset. If they subsequently cancel the form, we can just discard the recordset and none of their changes will have reached the database. If they click the OK button, we set the recordset's ActiveConnection to a valid database connection and tell the recordset to apply its changes to the database. This makes it extremely easy for us to modify simple lists of data, while allowing the user to cancel their changes.

The code changes required for all these enhancements are detailed in Table 13-2.

Table 13-2 Changes to the PETRAS Reporting Application for Chapter 13

Module	Procedure	Change
General changes for database handling		
MDataAccess		New module to handle all the database connectivity.
MEntryPoints	MenuSpecifyDatabaseLocation	New procedure for the user to select the location of the central PETRAS database file.
MBrowseForFolder		New module to show the standard Browse for Folder dialog.
Extracting data instead of consolidating workbooks		
MSystemCode	ImportData	Renamed from ConsolidateWorkbooks. Extracts data from the database instead of looping through workbooks.
FImportData		New userform to provide a range of dates for extracting timesheet records.
MDataAccess	GetTimesheetData	Retrieve the timesheet records for the given date range, writing the records to the results workbook.
		(continued)

Table 13-2 Changes to the PETRAS Reporting Application for Chapter 13 (*cont.*)

Module	Procedure	Change
FProgressBar, CProgressBar, IProgressBar		The three progress bar modules have been removed, because they are no longer required to show the progress of the consolidation process.
Userforms to maintain the static lists wksCommandBars		New menu structure created for the database interaction.
MEntryPoints		Added procedures called by the new menu items, one for each new form.
FActivities		New form to maintain the list of Activities. The code in the form concentrates on handling the user interaction.
CUISActivities		New class to support the FActivities form. The code in the class concentrates on managing the disconnected recordset, in response to the user actions.
FConsultants		New form to maintain the list of Consultants.
CUISConsultants		New class to support the FConsultants form.
FClients		New form to maintain the lists of Clients and Projects.
CUISClients		New class to support the FClients form.
MDataAccess		New procedures to create the disconnected recordsets for the Activities, Consultants and Clients/Projects forms and to update the database with the changes to the recordsets.
CFormResizer		New class to handle the resizing of the new forms.

Table 13-2 Changes to the PETRAS Reporting Application for Chapter 13 (*cont.*)

Module	Procedure	Change
Implementing the plug-in userform architecture		
IPlugInForm		New class to define the IPlugInForm interface.
FActivities, FConsultants, FClients		The three new data-maintenance forms implement the IPlugInForm interface.
MSystemCode	ShowForm	A generic procedure to show any of the plug-in forms.

Conclusion

We've covered a lot of ground in a very short space in this chapter. We've explained what databases are and under what circumstances you should use them. We've explained how to structure your data properly for storage in a relational database. We've provided a brief introduction to SQL and ADO and demonstrated how you can use them to retrieve and manipulate data in a relational database from your Excel VBA application. Because we cannot possibly do justice to any of these topics in a single chapter, we've also provided you with pointers to some excellent resources for additional information.

The ability to work with databases may have been an optional skill for the professional Excel developer five or six years ago. Today it is an absolute requirement. As different types of applications converge, there are fewer and fewer nontrivial Excel applications that do not require interaction with a back-end database of some kind. If you need to be a true professional Excel developer, you will need to understand how to work with databases.

Data Manipulation Techniques

In this chapter, we turn away slightly from VBA to examine how we can make the most of Excel's advanced data-manipulation features. Although the user interface is usually the only part of our applications that our users will know (or care) about, it is the quality and efficiency of our data processing that provides the solid foundation on which a great user interface can be built.

Excel provides some extremely powerful data-manipulation features, if used in the correct way. The most difficult aspect of organizing our data processing is often deciding which features to use in each situation, and how they can be efficiently combined.

Excel's Data Structures

Excel's data-handling features fall into two distinct groups. Most worksheet functions are designed to operate on individual items of data (usually stored in single cells), whereas features such as pivot tables, filtering and so on operate on large sets of data, usually arranged in tables. There are comparatively few worksheet functions, such as VLOOKUP, MATCH and the Dxxx functions that fill the gap between the two paradigms, operating on tables of data but returning single-value results. The way in which we arrange our data on the sheet can have a significant impact on the ease with which Excel's features can be used.

Most workbooks that we see are organized in what can only be described as a haphazard nature. They often try to combine data entry, analysis and reporting within the same area of the worksheet and are therefore a compromise between format and function. To design the best user interfaces, we have to organize the sheet to appeal to the user (such as including blank rows and/or columns around the data), ignoring the arrangement required by Excel's features (such as having to be in a single table). Conversely, to make the most efficient use of many of Excel's features, we have to organize our data in specific ways, which will probably not be the nicest to look at (such as having to leave lots of white space around pivot tables to allow for their changing shape, or include artificial column and row labels).

Unstructured Ranges

Unstructured ranges are usually encountered in the parts of the workbook designed for data entry. The spatial arrangement of the data will probably have some meaning to the user, with labels and formatting used to identify the data to be typed into each cell. When data is arranged in this unstructured manner, we can only use worksheet functions for our analysis. We cannot directly create pivot tables or charts from this data, nor consolidate, filter or sort the items. In practice, we probably wouldn't want to operate on this data as a whole anyway. They're likely to be single, unrelated items of data, where the lack of a structure is not a problem. Ideally, each data-entry cell should be given an unambiguous name, so we can tell at a glance where it's used by other functions.

The main problem with an unstructured arrangement of data is that every cell has to be treated individually—both by the user and through code—making it hard to copy and paste or import and export the data. The inability to import/export unstructured ranges can be overcome in Excel 2003 Professional by using XML to apply some structure to the cells, as we demonstrate in *Chapter 23 — Excel, XML and Web Services*.

Structured Ranges

Most of the features in Excel that are designed to operate on or with large sets of data require the data to be organized in a tabular arrangement, usually with a header row containing unique labels which Excel can use to identify each column. The most notable exceptions to this are the LOOKUP() function and array formulas (see later), which both work better without including a header row. The *Data > Consolidate* feature works best with an even stricter structure, where the contents of the first column in the data range can be used to identify each row, as you'll see later.

The easiest way for us to set up our data to be most useful to Excel, then, is to put it in a worksheet as a single table, with a header row and consistent data in each column, such as the list of customers shown in Figure 14-1. This data is from the sample NorthWind Access database supplied with Office, usually found at *C:\Program Files\Microsoft Office\Office\ Samples\Northwind.mdb*.

	A	B	C	D	E
1	CompanyName	Country	City	ContactName	Phone
2	Alfreds Futterkiste	Germany	Berlin	Maria Anders	030-0074321
3	Ana Trujillo Emparedados y helados	Mexico	México D.F.	Ana Trujillo	(5) 555-4729
4	Antonio Moreno Taquería	Mexico	México D.F.	Antonio Moreno	(5) 555-3932
5	Around the Horn	UK	London	Thomas Hardy	(171) 555-7788
6	Berglunds snabbköp	Sweden	Luleå	Christina Berglund	0921-12 34 65
7	Blauer See Delikatessen	Germany	Mannheim	Hanna Moos	0621-08460
8	Blondel père et fils	France	Strasbourg	Frédérique Citeaux	88.60.15.31
9	Bólido Comidas preparadas	Spain	Madrid	Martín Sommer	(91) 555 22 82
10	Bon app'	France	Marseille	Laurence Lebihan	91.24.45.40
11	Bottom-Dollar Markets	Canada	Tsawassen	Elizabeth Lincoln	(604) 555-4729
12	B's Beverages	UK	London	Victoria Ashworth	(171) 555-1212
13	Cactus Comidas para llevar	Argentina	Buenos Aires	Patricio Simpson	(1) 135-5555
14	Centro comercial Moctezuma	Mexico	México D.F.	Francisco Chang	(5) 555-3392
15	Chop-suey Chinese	Switzerland	Bern	Yang Wang	0452-076545

Figure 14-1 A Structured Range of Data

Using the techniques shown in *Chapter 13 — Programming with Databases* to retrieve data from a database, we can easily create a structured range by populating the sheet from an ADO recordset. Typical code to do that is shown in Listing 14-1, where rsData is an object variable which refers to an ADO recordset.

Listing 14-1 Creating a Structured Range from an ADO Recordset

```
If Not rsData.EOF Then
    ' Clear the destination worksheet.
    Sheet1.UsedRange.Clear

    ' Add the column headers.
    For lField = 0 To rsData.Fields.Count - 1
        Sheet1.Cells(1, lField + 1).Value = _
                        rsData.Fields(lField).Name
    Next lField

    ' Make the column headers bold, for clarity
    Sheet1.Rows(1).Font.Bold = True

    ' Copy the data from the recordset
    Sheet1.Range("A2").CopyFromRecordset rsData

    ' Give the retrieved data range a name for later use
    Sheet1.Range("A1").CurrentRegion.Name = "Sheet1!MyData"
Else
    MsgBox "No data located.", vbCritical, "Error!"
End If
```

Excel 2003's Lists

Working with a list of data is such a common use of Excel that Microsoft added the ***List*** feature in Excel 2003 to ease many of the tasks associated with them, such as sorting, filtering and adding and removing rows. A range can be converted to a List using the *Data > List > Create List* menu item. Figure 14-2 shows the same table of customers converted to a List (with rows 8 to 90 hidden to save space). Notice the thick (blue) border, the automatic appearance of the autofilter drop downs in the top row and the New Data row in row 93. The List can also be set to automatically show a total row, using the same totaling options that are provided by the SUBTOTAL() function. Showing the total row only makes sense if the list contains numeric data, as the only option for textual data is to count the rows. It would have been more helpful to have a "count distinct" option, but perhaps that will be added in a future version of Excel.

	A	B	C	D	E
1	CompanyName	Country	City	ContactName	Phone
2	Alfreds Futterkiste	Germa	Sort Ascending	Maria Anders	030-0074321
3	Ana Trujillo Emparedados y helados	Mexico	Sort Descending	Ana Trujillo	(5) 555-4729
4	Antonio Moreno Taqueria	Mexico	(All)	Antonio Moreno	(5) 555-3932
5	Around the Horn	UK	(Top 10...) (Custom...)	Thomas Hardy	(171) 555-7788
6	Berglunds snabbköp	Swede	Berlin	Christina Berglund	0921-12 34 65
7	Blauer See Delikatessen	Germa	Helsinki	Hanna Moos	0621-08460
91	Wilman Kala	Finland	London Luleå	Matti Karttunen	90-224 8858
92	Wolski Zajazd	Poland	Mannheim	Zbyszek Piestrzeniewicz	(26) 642-7012
93	*		México D.F.		
94			Warszawa		

Figure 14-2 An Excel 2003 List Range

The biggest benefit of using Lists is that any references to an entire column of the list are automatically updated as data is added or deleted, so we no longer need to worry about whether functions, charts or defined names are referring to the full set of data.

The List object also provides some rudimentary consistency checking, such as ensuring the data in a row stays in sync, but is mainly used by Excel under the covers to handle interaction with SharePoint and to enable the import and export of XML. Unfortunately, SharePoint interaction is beyond the scope of this book, but using Lists for XML import/export is covered in *Chapter 23 — Excel, XML and Web Services*.

Query Tables

Whenever we use one of the *Data > Import External Data* menu items to import a text file, a table from a Web page or a database query, the result is a *query table*. This is just a defined area of the worksheet that encompasses the retrieved data and (optionally) stores the connection information used to obtain the data. If the connection information is stored, the query table can be configured to refresh the data when the file is opened or at regular intervals. We can also tell the query table how to handle different amounts of data, and whether to copy/delete any formulas in adjacent columns.

For anything other than the most basic of database queries, Excel uses the MSQuery application to provide an interface for creating the SQL SELECT statement. If you've used a UI for creating SQL statements before (such as MS Access), the MSQuery interface is easy to understand. Figure 14-3 shows the MSQuery screen, with a query that retrieves some example data from the NorthWind OrderDetails and associated tables.

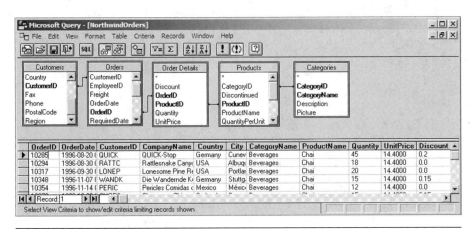

Figure 14-3 The MSQuery UI for Creating SQL Select Statements

The biggest problem with creating query tables is that the SQL produced by MSQuery is such poor quality and includes the full path to the database file being queried. This makes it almost impossible to create a worksheet using a query table to retrieve data from an Access database and expect it to work when installed at a client site. To create a robust solution, we always have to include some VBA code to set the query table's Connection and SQL properties. For example, we would rarely be able to use the built-in ability to refresh the query when the file was opened, because it would fail if the database was moved. Instead, we can use code similar to that shown in Listing 14-2, which sets the database location to the same directory as the workbook and updates the query table's properties before doing the refresh. Note that for this example to work correctly, you will need to copy the NorthWind database to the folder containing your workbook. In practice, we would prompt the user to select the database location the first time the workbook was opened and store that choice in the registry for subsequent use.

Listing 14-2 Refreshing a Query Table When Opening a Workbook

```
Private Sub Workbook_Open()

    Dim sDatabase As String
    Dim sConnect As String
    Dim sSQL As String

    'Where is the database to connect to?
    'This is the usual location of the Northwind database.
    'In practice, this should be a user-configurable option,
    'probably read from the registry.
    sDatabase = Application.Path & "\Samples\Northwind.mdb"

    If Len(Dir(sDatabase)) > 0 Then

        'Create the connection string using ADO
        sConnect = "OLEDB;Provider=Microsoft.Jet.OLEDB.4.0;" & _
                   "Data Source=" & sDatabase & ";"

        'Create a tidy SQL statement, without the file paths
        sSQL = "SELECT O.OrderID, O.OrderDate, CUS.CustomerID, " & _
               "       CUS.CompanyName, CUS.Country, CUS.City, " & _
               "       CAT.CategoryName, P.ProductName, " & _
               "       OD.Quantity, OD.UnitPrice, OD.Discount " & _
               "  FROM Categories CAT, Customers CUS, " & _
               "       `Order Details` OD, Orders O, Products P " & _
               " WHERE CUS.CustomerID = O.CustomerID And " & _
               "       OD.OrderID = O.OrderID And " & _
               "       P.ProductID = OD.ProductID And " & _
               "       CAT.CategoryID = P.CategoryID"

        'Update and refresh the query table
        With wksData.QueryTables(1)
            .Connection = sConnect
            .CommandText = sSQL
            .Refresh
        End With
```

```
      End If

End Sub
```

As well as removing the hard-coded paths to the database file, handling the refresh through VBA also provides the ability to include parameters in the query, such as only retrieving the data for a specific country where the country name could be obtained from worksheet cells.

When creating a query table using Excel's UI, the result is a table that uses ODBC to connect to the database, rather than the ADO connections that we covered in *Chapter 13 — Programming with Databases*. We can easily switch to using an ADO connection if we prefer, by adding the `OLEDB;` prefix to the ADO connection string.

Even though we end up with very similar code to connect to the database and run the query, using query tables is preferable to populating the worksheet from an ADO recordset, as the query table automatically handles whether to insert new rows for extra data and whether to copy any formulas from adjacent columns.

Query tables are very useful features, but are limited in the amount of data they can efficiently handle. As the end result of a query table is a worksheet containing the data, we are limited by Excel's ability to display the data in a worksheet (that is, a maximum of 65,535 rows) and have to devote a significant amount of resources (both display resource and drawing time) to show the data on the worksheet.

Data Processing Features

After we've arranged our data and/or calculations in a tabular form, we can use Excel's data processing features to manipulate it. Obviously, the actual manipulation that needs to be done will depend totally on the problem being solved, so this section describes some of the techniques available and how they can be linked together. It is up to the reader to decide which techniques are most appropriate for their situation!

It Doesn't Have to Be Data

Even though we've only considered data so far, Excel is not a database; it's designed to manipulate numbers. We are not forced to only include raw data in our structured ranges. Some of the most powerful number crunching comes from organizing our *formulas* in a structured, tabular form, then using Excel's data processing features on the results of those calculations. The only caveat with using formulas in our data tables is that the data processing (consolidation, pivot table, filter and so on) will not be updated or refreshed when the source formulas are recalculated. We can easily work around this by including some VBA code to trigger the processing from within the Worksheet_Calculate event (which conveniently occurs after the sheet has been calculated).

Pivot Caches

When Microsoft introduced pivot tables in Excel 95, they realized that it would be much more efficient to store the source data for the pivot tables in a hidden form within the workbook file than within worksheet cells. The hidden data stores are called *pivot caches* and are just like query tables, but without the visual representation and can only be used by pivot tables. They suffer from the same problem of including hard-coded paths to the database within their connection and SQL query information, and the same solution of using VBA to define the connection string and query text applies.

Pivot Tables

Pivot tables are Excel's premier data processing feature. Using either a table in a worksheet as the data source or a pivot cache for direct connection to a database, pivot tables enable us to filter, group, sort, total, count and drill down into our data. Most books about using Excel include a section explaining how to set up and manipulate pivot tables, so we're assuming you already know the basics. With pivot tables, there is only one level of difficulty, so once the basics are understood, the skill is in knowing how to most efficiently use pivot tables to analyze our data and integrate them with the rest of our data processing.

The best way to use pivot tables for data processing in most applications is to create all the pivot tables beforehand, on individual worksheets. If the pivot tables are set up to connect directly to a database, it is usually more efficient to have a single, large pivot cache that feeds multiple pivot tables, than having separate queries for each pivot table. The easiest way to do this is to create the first pivot table normally, then base subsequent pivot tables on the first (in step one of the Pivot Table Wizard). By using the same pivot cache, Excel will only need to store one copy of the data within the workbook and all the pivot tables will be updated when the cache is refreshed. Although it is possible to use the Excel object model to create and modify pivot tables, this should be kept to a minimum, because Excel refreshes and redraws the table with every modification. With anything other than a trivial amount of data, this quickly becomes extremely slow.

In the NWindOrders.xls example workbook, found on the CD in the \Concepts\Ch14—Data Manipulation Techniques folder, the OrderData worksheet contains a query table which retrieves information about each order from the NorthWind sample Access database, shown in Figure 14-4.

	A	B	C	D	E	F	G	H	I	J	K
1	OrderID	OrderDate	CustomerID	CompanyName	Country	City	CategoryName	ProductName	Quantity	UnitPrice	Discount
2	10285	20/08/1996	QUICK	QUICK-Stop	Germany	Cunewalde	Beverages	Chai	45	14.40	0.200
3	10294	30/08/1996	RATTC	Rattlesnake Canyon Grocery	USA	Albuquerque	Beverages	Chai	18	14.40	0.000
4	10317	30/09/1996	LONEP	Lonesome Pine Restaurant	USA	Portland	Beverages	Chai	20	14.40	0.000
5	10348	07/11/1996	WANDK	Die Wandernde Kuh	Germany	Stuttgart	Beverages	Chai	15	14.40	0.150
6	10354	14/11/1996	PERIC	Pericles Comidas clásicas	Mexico	México D.F.	Beverages	Chai	12	14.40	0.000
7	10370	03/12/1996	CHOPS	Chop-suey Chinese	Switzerland	Bern	Beverages	Chai	15	14.40	0.150
8	10406	07/01/1997	QUEEN	Queen Cozinha	Brazil	São Paulo	Beverages	Chai	10	14.40	0.000
9	10413	14/01/1997	LAMAI	La maison d'Asie	France	Toulouse	Beverages	Chai	24	14.40	0.000
10	10477	17/03/1997	PRINI	Princesa Isabel Vinhos	Portugal	Lisboa	Beverages	Chai	15	14.40	0.000
11	10522	30/04/1997	LEHMS	Lehmanns Marktstand	Germany	Frankfurt a.M.	Beverages	Chai	40	18.00	0.200
12	10526	05/05/1997	WARTH	Wartian Herkku	Finland	Oulu	Beverages	Chai	8	18.00	0.150
13	10576	23/06/1997	TORTU	Tortuga Restaurante	Mexico	México D.F.	Beverages	Chai	10	18.00	0.000
14	10590	07/07/1997	MEREP	Mère Paillarde	Canada	Montréal	Beverages	Chai	20	18.00	0.000
15	10609	24/07/1997	DUMON	Du monde entier	France	Nantes	Beverages	Chai	3	18.00	0.000
16	10611	25/07/1997	WOLZA	Wolski Zajazd	Poland	Warszawa	Beverages	Chai	6	18.00	0.000
17	10628	12/08/1997	BLONP	Blondel père et fils	France	Strasbourg	Beverages	Chai	25	18.00	0.000

Figure 14-4 The Query Table for NorthWind Order Details

As well as retrieving the specific data for the order information, we've included extra information such as the company name, country and product category. Adding this extra information will usually have negligible impact on the query execution time or extra data storage requirements, but enables us to perform more diverse analysis using the same raw data. For example, Figure 14-5 shows the PivotTable worksheet from the example workbook, which includes both a breakdown of order quantities by country and product category and a list of our UK customers.

Unfortunately, this technique is limited by the lack of a "distinct count" function to total the data. The "count" function gives the number of records, which in our case is the total number of order detail line items. If we had a "distinct count" function, we would be able to identify the number of orders placed by each customer (by counting the number of distinct order IDs) or the number of customers in each country (by counting the number of distinct customer IDs).

	A	B	C	D	E	F	G
1	Order Quantity Breakdown by Country and Product Category						
2	Sum of Quantity	CategoryName					
3	Country	Beverages	Condiments	Confections	Dairy Products	Grains/Cereals	Meat/Po
4	Argentina	82	45	57	54	20	
5	Austria	982	720	575	1027	580	
22	UK	502	210	318	679	322	
23	USA	1587	821	1617	1559	760	
24	Venezuela	533	166	504	555	244	
25	Grand Total	9532	5298	7906	9149	4562	
26							
27							
28	List of Customers for a Specific Country						
29	Country	UK					
30							
31	Sum of Quantity						
32	CustomerID	CompanyName	Total				
33	AROUT	Around the Horn	650				
34	BSBEV	B's Beverages	293				
35	CONSH	Consolidated Holdings	87				
36	EASTC	Eastern Connection	569				
37	ISLAT	Island Trading	295				
38	NORTS	North/South	30				
39	SEVES	Seven Seas Imports	818				
40	Grand Total		2742				
41							

Figure 14-5 Two Diverse PivotTables, Derived from the Same Pivot Cache

Calculated Pivot Fields

Excel enables us to add extra fields and data to our pivot caches, in the form of **calculated fields** and **calculated items**. A calculated field is an extra column, derived from one or more other fields, such as defining a calculated Profit field as Revenue – Cost, where Revenue and Cost are fields in the data set. These are of very limited use, because Excel always does the Sum of the individual fields before performing the calculation, so we get the following:

Sum of Profit = Sum of Revenue – Sum of Cost

This is okay and marginally useful for the simple cases, but is useless and dangerous if a more complex formula is required. Looking at the NorthWind data in Figure 14-4, we have fields for the Quantity, UnitPrice and Discount, so we might be tempted to add a calculated Revenue field as Quantity × (UnitPrice – Discount). Unfortunately, as Excel sums the individual fields before doing the calculation, we end up multiplying the total quantity sold by the sum of all the prices minus the sum of all the discounts! Unless that is what you really require, it is far better and much safer to add the additional fields at the raw data level, either by including calculated fields in the SQL query, or by adding extra columns alongside the query table, as shown in Figure 14-6.

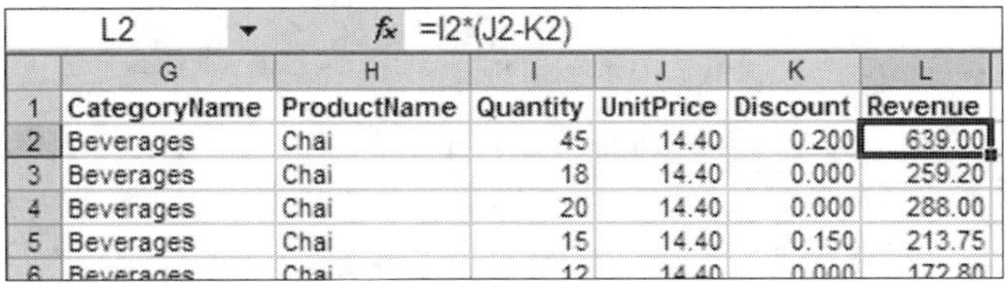

L2 =I2*(J2-K2)

	G	H	I	J	K	L
1	CategoryName	ProductName	Quantity	UnitPrice	Discount	Revenue
2	Beverages	Chai	45	14.40	0.200	639.00
3	Beverages	Chai	18	14.40	0.000	259.20
4	Beverages	Chai	20	14.40	0.000	288.00
5	Beverages	Chai	15	14.40	0.150	213.75
6	Beverages	Chai	12	14.40	0.000	172.80

Figure 14-6 Adding a Calculated Field Alongside a Query Table

When using columns alongside the query table, be sure to tick the *Fill down formulas in columns adjacent to data* check box in the query table Properties dialog to make sure the formulas are copied to new rows. We should also use a defined name to link the pivot table to the query table, which can be adjusted to ensure the pivot tables always refer to the correct data range, including the additional formulas. We create the name to refer to the full range of data and formulas and use that name instead of a direct range reference in Step 2 of the Pivot Table Wizard. The defined name can be updated using the QueryTable_AfterRefresh event shown in Listing 14-3, which also refreshes any pivot caches that use it.

Listing 14-3 Updating Defined Names and Refreshing Pivot Caches When a Query Table Is Refreshed

```
'Code contained within the OrderData worksheet code module

'Variable to hook the Query Table events
Private WithEvents mqtData As QueryTable

'Called from the start of Workbook_Open()
Public Sub Initialise()

    'Set up the event hook for the query table
    Set mqtData = Me.QueryTables(1)

End Sub

'Update dependent data when the QueryTable is refreshed
```

```
Private Sub mqtData_AfterRefresh(ByVal Success As Boolean)

    Dim sRangeName As String
    Dim pcCache As PivotCache

    If Success Then
        'Update the defined name
        sRangeName = Me.Name & "!pdPivotDataRange"
        mqtData.ResultRange.CurrentRegion.Name = sRangeName

        'Refresh any dependent pivot caches
        For Each pcCache In ThisWorkbook.PivotCaches
            If pcCache.SourceData = sRangeName Then
                pcCache.Refresh
            End If
        Next
    End If

End Sub
```

Data Consolidation

Probably the most little-known of Excel's data processing features is its ability to consolidate numeric data from multiple ranges into a single table, matching the data using the labels in both the first row and first column of each range. If a single cell is selected, Excel first creates a unique list of all the column headers and a unique list of all the row headers (that is, the labels in the first column) to create the result table. If a range is already selected, Excel uses the row and column headers that are already there. It then adds (or counts, averages, max, min and so on) all the items of data that share the same row and column header.

This proves extremely useful when consolidating data and calculations that occur over a time series. For example, imagine a project to analyze whether to build and run a new theme park. You might have a workbook for the construction planning, another for the ongoing operations, another for concessions and retail planning and so forth. Each workbook contains a summary table showing the costs, revenue and cash flow for each year. A greatly simplified version is shown in Figure 14-7, but imagine the Construction Planning and Operations tables actually exist in different workbooks and each has been given a defined name.

To consolidate these ranges into a single table, select the top-left cell in the target consolidation area, A15 in this example, and click the *Data > Consolidate* menu to access the Consolidate dialog shown in Figure 14-8.

	A	B	C	D	E	F	G
1	**Construction Planning:**						
2	YEAR	2004	2005	2006	2007	2008	2009
3	Costs	50	100	200	200	40	0
4	CashFlow	-50	-100	-200	-200	-40	0
5							
6							
7	**Operations:**						
8	YEAR	2008	2009	2010	2011	2012	2013
9	Costs	50	10	10	10	10	10
10	Revenue	5	50	90	150	250	500
11	CashFlow	-45	40	80	140	240	490
12							
13							
14	**Consolidated Results:**						
15							
16							

Figure 14-7 Simplified Project Planning

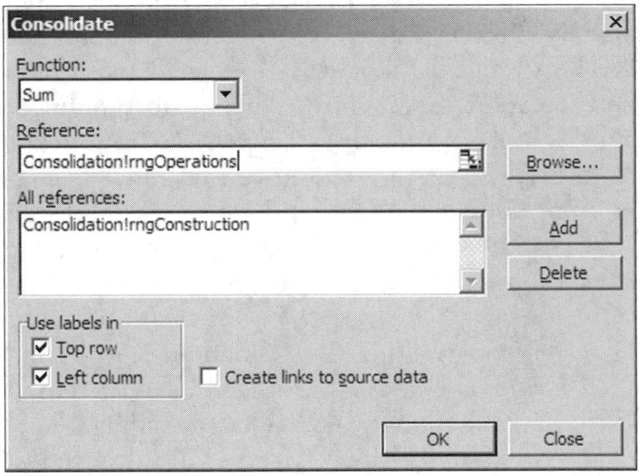

Figure 14-8 The Data Consolidation Dialog

The All references list shows all the source data ranges that will be consolidated. The ranges can be from the same worksheet, a different worksheet, different workbook or even a closed workbook! Yes, this is one of the few Excel features that works as well with closed workbooks as with open ones. To add a source data range, type the reference in the *Reference:* refedit and click the *Add* button. Make sure the two *Use labels in* check boxes are both ticked, to ensure Excel matches both row and column headers. If they're not ticked, Excel matches by position, which is rarely what is required.

When we click the OK button, Excel matches all the labels, adds up all the similar data and gives us the table shown in Figure 14-9.

14	**Consolidated Results:**										
15		2004	2005	2006	2007	2008	2009	2010	2011	2012	2013
16	Costs	50	100	200	200	90	10	10	10	10	10
17	Revenue					5	50	90	150	250	500
18	CashFlow	-50	-100	-200	-200	-85	40	80	140	240	490
19											

Figure 14-9 The Consolidated Results

Advanced Filtering

The ability to extract specific records from a large data set is often the key to successful and efficient data processing. Pivot tables provide some rudimentary filtering capability, but only by hiding individual items of data. Excel's Advanced Filter feature enables us to filter the data using much more complex expressions, either just by hiding records in the original table, or more commonly by copying the resulting records to a new location for further processing. The Advanced Filter dialog is accessed by clicking the *Data > Filter > Advanced Filter* menu and is shown in Figure 14-10.

As can be seen from Figure 14-10, when copying the filtered data to a new location, an advanced filter requires three ranges:

- List range is the range containing the original data to be filtered.
- Criteria range is a worksheet range used to define the criteria to use when filtering the data. Understanding how to get the most from the criteria range is the key to using advanced filtering and is the focus of the rest of this section.
- Copy to is the destination range for the filtered data to be copied to.

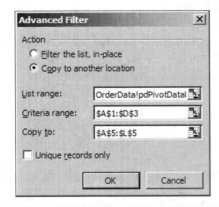

Figure 14-10 The Advanced Filter Dialog

When the OK button is clicked, Excel scans through the source data range, checks each record against the criteria specified in the criteria range and copies the matching records to the next row in the Copy to range. The result is a subset of the original data, arranged as a simple structured data area—that is, not as a list or query table.

Unfortunately, every time the Advanced Filter dialog is shown, the List range is either blanked out or guessed and the Action defaults to Filter in place. It would be much more helpful if Excel remembered the source range and action, which would be possible if only Excel created the filter as a query table. If that were the case, we would also have a one-click Refresh option and be able to tell Excel to automatically copy down adjacent formulas. The best we can do in current versions is to give our ranges some specific names. If the workbook contains the defined names Database, Criteria and/or Extract, Excel will populate the dialog using the ranges pointed to by those names.

To save you some frustration if you're working through these examples, we've included the routine shown in Listing 14-14 in the example workbook to refresh the filter without showing the Advanced Filter dialog. Note that in VBA, we use the AdvancedFilter method on the *source* data range and specify the range to copy the filtered data to.

Listing 14-4 Advanced Filtering with VBA

```
Private Sub cmdRefresh_Click()

    Static rngCriteria As Range
```

```
    Dim rngNewCriteria As Range

    'Provide a default initial selection
    If rngCriteria Is Nothing Then
        Set rngCriteria = Me.Range("A1")
    End If

    'Use error trapping to handle a cancel
    On Error GoTo ErrNoRangeSelected

    'Allow the user to select the criteria range to use
    'Type:=8 allows for selection of ranges.
    Set rngNewCriteria = Application.InputBox( _
        "Select the criteria range to use and click OK.", _
        "Refresh Advanced Filter Extract", _
        rngCriteria.Address, Type:=8)

    'Remember the criteria range for next time
    Set rngCriteria = rngNewCriteria

    'Perform the autofilter
    wksData.Range("pdPivotDataRange").AdvancedFilter _
        xlFilterCopy, rngCriteria, _
        Me.Range("rngAFExtract"), False

ErrNoRangeSelected:
    Exit Sub

End Sub
```

Criteria Ranges

The criteria range is used to specify the equivalent of a SQL WHERE clause, telling Excel which records to return. Figure 14-11 shows an example of a criteria range, in A1:B3.

	A	B
1	Country	CategoryName
2	UK	
3	USA	Beverages
4		

Figure 14-11 An Advanced Filter Criteria Range

The first row of the criteria range contains field names that must match the field names used in the source data table, but can be in any order. Subsequent rows contain the data to match for each field. All the items in a row are joined with an AND operation, while separate rows are joined with an OR operation. Blank cells in the criteria range match to anything. The criteria range shown in Figure 14-11 should be read as "(Country="UK") OR (Country="USA" AND CategoryName="Beverages")," so that will return all orders from the UK and all orders from the USA for Beverages. If we only want the Beverage orders from the UK or USA, we have to include the Beverages filter in both lines, as shown in Figure 14-12, which reads as "(Country="UK" AND CategoryName="Beverages") OR (Country="USA" AND CategoryName="Beverages")."

	A	B
1	Country	CategoryName
2	UK	Beverages
3	USA	Beverages

Figure 14-12 Beverages from the UK or USA

By combining the AND and OR logic in this way, Excel enables us to create extremely complex criteria.

We're not limited to filtering using "equals" relationships. In fact, the default filter for text items is "starts with" so the criteria range shown in Figure 14-12 will also return Beverages orders from the Ukraine! To specify an exact (case insensitive) match, we use an = sign, as shown in Figure 14-13. When typing these in, it's a good idea to start with a quote mark, '=UK, to tell Excel this is text and not a formula, or to format the criteria cells as text before typing the values.

	A	B
1	Country	CategoryName
2	=UK	=Beverages
3	=USA	=Beverages

Figure 14-13 Beverages from Only the UK or USA, and Not Ukraine

As well as using the = sign to specify an exact match, we can include the ? and × wildcard characters to match any one character or any range of characters respectively and use the > and < symbols to match ranges. To specify both a lower and upper limit, we can include the field name multiple times in the criteria range, such as the criteria shown in Figure 14-14 to select the orders from UK customers whose names start with G to N.

	A	B	C
1	Country	CompanyName	CompanyName
2	=UK	>=G	<O

Figure 14-14 Specifying a Range of Matches by Repeating the Field Name

We can also, of course, filter on numeric and date fields in exactly the same way, although we have to be careful if our workbooks will be used in multiple countries with different date orders. For example, if you're American, you might expect the criteria range in Figure 14-15 to return all the records for 2004.

	A	B
1	OrderDate	OrderDate
2	>=1/1/2004	<=12/31/2004

Figure 14-15 Filtering Between to Dates in the USA

When the filter is applied in the UK, it doesn't return any records, as 12/31/2004 is not recognized as a date—it should be 31/12/2004 instead. To avoid these issues, it is a very good idea to use formulas to construct the date criteria. In this example we should replace the hard-coded date in B2 with the formula `="<="&DATE(2004,12,31)`, which displays as the less-readable date number <=38352, but works in all locations. Similarly when filtering for a range of numbers, it is safest to create the criteria entry as a formula such as `=">="&1.23`, thereby allowing Excel to use the correct decimal separators for the location.

As well as specifying that individual fields must have certain values, we can also filter on relationships between the data in multiple fields. To do this, we use a dummy field name that doesn't exist in the source data, such as Calc1, Calc2 and so forth and create a formula using the cells from the first data row of the table (that is, not the header row). The formula must evaluate to TRUE or FALSE and must use relative referencing when referring to the data in the table. As Excel scans through the source table, it increments all the relative row references in the formula, evaluates the formula for that row and matches on a TRUE result. For example, the formula shown in Figure 14-16 will return any orders where the discount is more than 5 percent of the unit price. Note that this is entered as an Excel formula, not as a text string, so you should see the result of the formula (TRUE or FALSE) displayed in the cell.

	A
1	Calc1
2	=OrderData!K2/OrderData!J2>=0.05

Figure 14-16 Filtering Using a Formula

Instead of using cell references, which can be hard to read when the referenced range is on a separate sheet (as in this case), Excel enables us to use the field names in the formula, such as =Discount/UnitPrice>=0.05 in this case. Doing so usually results in the cell displaying a #NAME! error, but that can be safely ignored.

Advanced Functions

The Database Functions

We often see advanced filtering used to select a subset of data, with the result of the filter being used by a few simple worksheet functions, such as SUM, AVERAGE and so on. Depending on the complexity and number of the worksheet functions that refer to the filtered data, it can often be quicker and easier to use Excel's **database functions**. These are equivalent to the normal SUM, AVERAGE, MIN, MAX, COUNT, COUNTA and so forth, but instead of providing a simple range to operate over, we provide a source database, a criteria range to filter the database by and the field in the database to operate on. For example, while AVERAGE(K2:K2156) would give us the overall average discount in our sample workbook, we could use the DAVERAGE() function to calculate the average discount of our UK and USA Beverage sales, ignoring those with zero discount. The criteria range for the database functions follows exactly the same structure and rules as for advanced filtering, so we could use the range shown in Figure 14-17 in this case.

	A	B	C
1	Country	CategoryName	Discount
2	=UK	=Beverages	>0
3	=USA	=Beverages	>0

Figure 14-17 Criteria Range for Discounted UK and USA Beverage Sales

The average nonzero discount for our UK and USA Beverage sales could then be calculated using the worksheet formula:

```
=DAVERAGE(OrderData!pdPivotDataRange,"Discount",$A$1:$C$3)
```

If we use these functions within the advanced filter criteria range, we can perform some extremely powerful filtering. For example, the criteria range shown in formula view in Figure 14-18 will extract all the UK or USA Beverages sales that have a discount greater than the average discount for UK or USA Beverage sales, ignoring those sales where no discount was applied.

	A	B	C	D
1	Country	CategoryName	Discount	Discount
2	=UK	=Beverages	>0	=">"&DAVERAGE(OrderData!pdPivotDataRange,"Discount",$A$1:$C$3)
3	=USA	=Beverages	>0	=D2

Figure 14-18 Using a Database Function Within an Advanced Filter Criteria Range

Here, the first three columns of the criteria range are being used by the DAVERAGE() function to calculate the average discount. The average discount figure is then used to populate the fourth column in the criteria range, which is used by the Advanced Filter.

Array Formulas

The standard worksheet functions that we use every day typically accept one or more parameters and return a result. A few, such as SUM() and AVERAGE(), accept ranges or arrays in their parameters and will return the sum, average and so on of all the data they're given. Most worksheet functions and mathematical operators, however, are given a single number for each of their parameters and return a single number as the result.

Even though a function normally accepts single-figure parameters, we can usually give it a multicell range reference and enter the function using Ctrl+Shift+Enter instead of just pressing the Enter key. Doing this tells Excel to calculate the function as an ***array formula***, whereby the function performs its calculation multiple times, iterating over each cell in the range. The result is an array of numbers, with each element in the array corresponding to one of the cells in the original reference. These results can in turn be fed into the parameters of other functions and so on until they are eventually aggregated (usually summed) to give a final answer. All of the array calculation is done inside Excel and does not usually appear on the worksheet.

The most common use of array formulas is to count and sum lists, using multiple criteria. Excel provides the COUNTIF() and SUMIF() functions that accept a single filter criteria, so we could sum our UK orders using the following function:

```
=SUMIF($E$1:$E$2156,"=UK",$I$1:$I$2156)
```

where column E contains the country names and column I contains the order quantities. If we want the total of our UK Beverages sales, we can no longer use SUMIF, because we need two criteria. We could create a pivot table for it, or use DSUM with a criteria range, but both of those can be overkill if we only have a relatively small list and simple criteria, and cannot be used if we don't have column headers.

Array formulas occupy the middle ground between the simplicity of a worksheet function and the complexity of criteria ranges. If we only have a series of conditions AND'ed together, we can use an array formula of the form:

```
=SUM(ValueRange*(Criteria1)*(Criteria2)*(Criteria...))
```

To get the total orders of UK Beverages from our example data, we could use the following formula:

```
=SUM($I$2:$I$2156*N($E$2:$E$2156="UK")
*N($G$2:$G$2156="Beverages"))
```

Remember to enter it using Ctrl+Shift+Enter. Let's look at the sample data shown in Figure 14-19 (on the following page) to see how it works.

To explain how the array formula works, we need to break it up and explain each part of the formula, starting from the middle and working outward:

- `$E$2:$E$2156="UK"`—Excel scans through each of the cells in the range E2:E2156 in turn, checking whether each one is equal to UK. The result is an array of True or False values. In our case, it is the array {F, F, T, T, T, T, T, T, F, F}.
- `N($E$2:$E$2156="UK")`—The N() function converts its parameter to a number. When given an array of True and False values, it converts each True to 1 and each False to 0. In our case, this is the array {0, 0, 1, 1, 1, 1, 1, 1, 0, 0}. You might see a double-minus

	E	F	G	H	I
	Country	City	CategoryName	ProductName	Quantity
	Germany	Berlin	Beverages	Chartreuse verte	21
	Germany	Berlin	Produce	Rössle Sauerkraut	15
	UK	London	Beverages	Guaraná Fantástica	25
	UK	London	Grains/Cereals	Ravioli Angelo	25
	UK	London	Confections	Valkoinen suklaa	15
	UK	London	Grains/Cereals	Gnocchi di nonna Alice	20
	UK	London	Seafood	Konbu	20
	UK	London	Beverages	Outback Lager	25
	Germany	Berlin	Seafood	Spegesild	2
	Germany	Berlin	Condiments	Vegie-spread	20

Figure 14-19 Sample Data for an Array Formula

being used instead of the N() function, such as `--($E$2:$E$2156="UK")`, which has the same effect and is preferred by some people. You might also see the N() function omitted from complex array formulas, as Excel will often (but not always) do the conversion without being told.

- `$G$2:$G$2156="Beverages"`—Like the test for UK, Excel scans each cell in the range G2:G2156, checking whether each one is equal to Beverages. In our case, the result is the array {T, F, T, F, F, F, F, T, F, F}.

- `N($G$2:$G$2156="Beverages")`—Converts the Beverages True/False array to 1s and 0s, giving the array {1, 0, 1, 0, 0, 0, 0, 1, 0, 0}.

- `$I$2:$I$2156`—A standard range reference, which is directly translated into the array {21, 15, 25, 25, 15, 20, 20, 25, 2, 20}.

- `SUM($I$2:$I$2156*N($E$2:$E$2156="UK")*N($G$2:$G$2156="Beverages"))`—Multiplies the matching elements from each of the intermediate arrays and totals the result, as shown in Figure 14-20.

$I$2:$I$2156	N($E$2:$E$2156="UK")	N($G$2:$G$2156="Beverages")	Result
21	0	1	0
15	0	0	0
25	1	1	25
25	1	0	0
15	* 1	* 0	= 0
20	1	0	0
20	1	0	0
25	1	1	25
2	0	0	0
20	0	0	0
SUM($I$2:$I$2156*N($E$2:$E$2156="UK")*N($G$2:$G$2156="Beverages"))=			50

Figure 14-20 The Inner Workings of an Array Formula

For these situations, the decision to use an array formula instead of a pivot table, advanced filter or database function is largely dependent on the size of the data set and the number of such formulas required. For one or two totals, array formulas are often the most efficient, but as the number of totals increases, it becomes more efficient to perform the filtering before calculating them.

After you've grasped the concept of array formulas, you will probably identify more and more situations where they can be used. A common requirement for many array formulas is to be able to generate a number sequence such as the array {1, 2, 3, 4, 5}. This can be achieved using the awkward-looking formula =ROW(INDIRECT("A1:A5")). The INDIRECT("A1:A5") part returns the range reference A1:A5, and is insensitive to rows being moved, added or deleted. The ROW() part returns an array of the row number of each row in the range, being the array of rows 1 to 5, {1, 2, 3, 4, 5}.

The classic use of such a sequence is in the "sum of digits" calculation often used in credit card checksum formulas. Given an arbitrary number, 672435, what is the sum of each of the digits in the number. In this case it's 6+7+2+4+3+5=27. To calculate it using a formula, we start off with a sequence from 1 to the number of digits, use the sequence in the MID() function to extract each digit in turn (as text), convert it to a number and then sum the resultant array. The complete function is as follows:

```
=SUM(VALUE(MID(B7,ROW(INDIRECT("A1:A"&LEN(B7))),1)))
```

Where B7 contains the number for which we want to calculate the sum of the digits. To understand how it works, let's break it down again:

- LEN(B7) gives the length of the number (that is, the count of its digits; 6 in our case).
- INDIRECT("A1:A"&LEN(B7)) returns the range A1:A6 in our case.
- ROW(INDIRECT("A1:A"&LEN(B7))) returns the row of each cell in the range, giving the array {1, 2, 3, 4, 5, 6}.
- MID(B7,ROW(INDIRECT("A1:A"&LEN(B7))),1) applies the sequence to the startnum parameter of the MID() function, which returns the nth digit from the number as text. In this case, it's the array {"6", "7", "2", "4", "3", "5"}.
- VALUE(MID(B7,ROW(INDIRECT("A1:A"&LEN(B7))),1)) converts the array of text items to numbers, giving the array {6, 7, 2, 4, 3, 5}.
- SUM(VALUE(MID(B7,ROW(INDIRECT("A1:A"&LEN(B7))),1))) sums the numbers in the array, giving 6+7+2+4+3+5=27.

Despite their definite power, array formulas have three main problems: They're relatively slow to calculate, particularly when operating on large data sets; they're relatively difficult to understand, when compared to normal worksheet functions; and they're difficult to test, debug and maintain. If you're using Excel 2002 or later, the *Tools > Auditing > Evaluate Formula* feature can be very useful for analyzing and debugging array formulas.

Our advice is to use array formulas when absolutely necessary, but don't use them just to save a few cells. It is often quicker to create and much easier to understand if intermediate cells are used for extra calculations, instead of trying to perform everything in a single array formula.

Circular References

Excel's online help file and most books mention circular references in terms of "circular reference errors," where you've accidentally created a circular reference by mistyping a range reference. This is, indeed, one of many potential symptoms of spreadsheet errors, which can be quite difficult to track down. If you find yourself in that situation, the findcirc.xla add-in, available for download from www.oaltd.co.uk/Excel, might come in useful. This add-in scans a workbook, trying to locate a circular reference chain and provides the full list of cells involved in the circle. With any luck, you should be able to identify the erroneous references and break the chain.

Much more interesting, though, is the ***intentional*** use of circular references to tidily solve business problems. A great many problems in the world of finance are circular in nature. A typical example is to determine the repayments of a long-term loan. A company may have decided to devote 40 percent of their after-tax profits to repay a loan. The problem is that both the loan repayment and the interest charge can usually be offset against the tax liability, thereby increasing the after-tax profits and allowing the company to repay more of the loan. The problem can be expressed using the following equation:

$$R = (P - R - (B - R) \times I) \times (1 - T) \times 0.4$$

where R is the amount of the loan to repay, P is the profit before financing and tax, B is the balance of the loan, I is the interest rate and T is the tax rate. In this extremely simple example, it is possible to solve for R algebraically, giving the following:

$$R = (P - I \times B) / (1 - I + 1 / 0.4 / (1 - T))$$

In most real-life examples, however, the interest rate may be stepped depending on the outstanding balance, and the tax calculation is unlikely to be as simple as just multiplying by the tax rate. In these situations, we can intentionally use circular references to iterate to a solution. Figure 14-21 shows a worksheet to solve this simple problem using circular references.

	A	B	C
1	**Loan Repayment Calculation**		
2	Using Intentional Circular References		
3			
4			
5	Profit before finance and tax, P:	1,000,000	
6	Initial loan balance, B:	900,000	
7	Loan interest rate, I:	6%	
8	Tax rate, T:	42%	
9	Repayment rate (% of net profit):	40%	
10			
11			
12	Repayment (circ)	180,179	=B17
13	Loan Interest	43,189	=(B6-B12)*B7
14	Profit after financing	776,632	=B5-B12-B13
15	Tax	326,185	=B14*B8
16	Profit after tax	450,447	=B14-B15
17	Repayment (circ)	180,179	=B16*B9
18			

Figure 14-21 Using Circular References to Calculate Loan Repayments

When we created the sheet, we initially put a guessed value in cell B12. After entering the remaining formulas, we added the forward reference in B12, to refer to B17.

By default, Excel disables the calculation of circular references. To enable them, put a tick in the *Tools > Options > Calculation > Iteration* box. The Max Iterations and Max Change settings can be left as their defaults; they have little impact on most circular-reference problems. They come into play if the calculations are particularly slow at converging to a result. The Max Change determines when Excel considers a circular reference to have converged correctly (the new result must be within the given value of the previous iteration), whereas the Max Iterations provides a cut-off point to tell Excel to stop trying. In slowly converging calculations, the Max Iterations may need to be increased to allow the iterations to run until completion. Such situations should be examined to see whether the calculations can be reworked to give a solution that converges within fewer iterations.

The worksheet shown in Figure 14-21 adopts a number of best practices when designing worksheets in general, and specifically when using circular references:

- The title of the worksheet makes it clear that intentional circular references exist on the sheet.
- The input ranges are clearly identified, with a light-colored background.
- Each formula is clearly identified with a label stating what is being calculated.
- All the formulas except the circular reference refer to cells above them; the cell containing the circular reference is the only one with a reference to a cell below it.
- The circular reference is clearly identified by including (circ) in the cell label.
- Both ends of the circular reference have the same label.
- The circular reference in cell B12 refers to the single cell holding the value to be fed back into the circular calculation, and only that cell.

After you've used circular references for a while, you'll notice two common issues. First, if any of the functions within the circle results in an error value, it will propagate to every function in the circle. Second, the ability of the formulas to iterate to a solution can be quite sensitive to the initial guess for the feedback value. Both of these issues can be resolved by including a ***kill switch*** to control whether the circular reference is calculated and an extra cell to provide a seed value for the initial guess. When the kill switch is FALSE, the feedback cell(s) take on the seed value, which should also clear out any residual error values. When the kill switch is TRUE, the feedback cell(s) complete the circle. Figure 14-22 shows the same loan repayment problem with the addition of a kill switch in cell B4 and all other changes highlighted in bold.

Unfortunately, including circular references in our worksheets prevents us from using some of Excel's features. Specifically, the Goal Seek, Data Table and Solver features will only calculate a single iteration of the sheet for each step in their processing, so will never return correct results.

	A	B	C
1	**Loan Repayment Calculation**		
2	Using Intentional Circular References		
3			
4	Iterate?	TRUE	
5	Profit before finance and tax, P:	1,000,000	
6	Initial loan balance, B:	900,000	
7	Loan interest rate, I:	6%	
8	Tax rate, T:	42%	
9	Repayment rate (% of net profit):	40%	
10	**Initial repayment guess**	**100,000**	
11			
12	Repayment (circ)	180,179	=IF(B4,B17,B10)
13	Loan Interest	43,189	=(B6-B12)*B7
14	Profit after financing	776,632	=B5-B12-B13
15	Tax	326,185	=B14*B8
16	Profit after tax	450,447	=B14-B15
17	Repayment (circ)	180,179	=B16*B9
18			

Figure 14-22 Using a Kill Switch to Control the Circular Reference Feedback

Conclusion

In this chapter, we have explained how to organize both our data and calculations such that Excel can readily use them and how to use query tables to access data in external databases, and efficiently link them to pivot tables. We've also explained how to identify and perform calculations on subsets of our data, using advanced filters, database functions and array formulas. We have also lifted the lid on the intentional use of circular references in our applications and explained how to remain in control when doing that.

Armed with these techniques, we can include efficient, robust and scalable data processing in our Excel applications and can easily cope with the most complex data-handling requirements.

Advanced Charting Techniques

Only a few minutes are required to learn the basics of Excel's charting module, but many frustrating hours are required to get a chart looking "just right." Most people create charts using one of the built-in chart types, but are unable to modify them to meet their exact requirements. This chapter introduces and explains the fundamental techniques we can use to impose our will on Excel's charting engine to produce charts that look exactly how we want them to.

The chapter focuses solely on the technical aspects of working with the chart engine. We do not investigate which chart type should be used in any given situation, nor the pros and cons of whether 3D charts can be used to present data accurately, nor whether you should use as few or as many of the colorful formatting options that Excel supports.

Fundamental Techniques

Combining Chart Types

When most people create charts, they start the Chart Wizard and browse through all the standard and custom chart types shown in Step 1, trying to find one that most closely resembles the look they're trying to achieve. More often than not, there isn't a close enough match and they end up thinking that Excel doesn't support the chart they're trying to create. In fact, we can include any number of column, bar, line, XY and/or area series within the same chart. All of the choices on the Custom Types tab of Step 1 of the Chart Wizard are no more than preformatted combinations of these basic styles, with a bit of formatting thrown in. Instead of relying on these custom types, we can usually get better results (and a greater understanding of the chart engine) by creating these combination charts ourselves. Unfortunately, we can't combine the different 3D styles, pie charts or bubble charts with other types.

Let's start by creating a simple column/line combination chart for the data shown in Figure 15-1, where we want the 2004 sales to be shown as columns, with the forecast shown as lines.

The easiest way to start is by selecting the data region, A3:C8 and create a simple column chart from it, as shown in Figure 15-2. We usually find it easiest to start with a column chart, but perhaps that's because it's the default selection in the Chart Wizard, so we can create the chart by selecting the source data, clicking the Chart Wizard toolbar button and then the Finish button on the Chart Wizard.

	A	B	C
1			
2		2004 Fruit Sales	
3		Sales	Forecast
4	Apples	1000	900
5	Oranges	1200	1400
6	Peaches	600	800
7	Pears	700	1100
8	Bananas	1100	1000

Figure 15-1 The Sample Data to Plot as a Combination Column/Line Chart

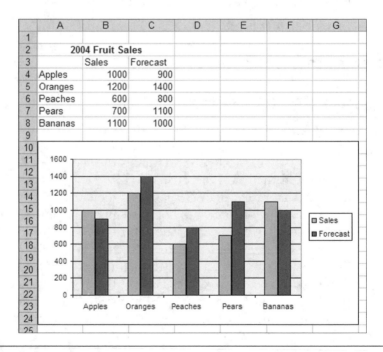

Figure 15-2 The Chart Wizard Created a Standard Column Chart

To change the Forecast values from a column to a line, select the series, click the *Chart > Chart Type* menu item and select one of the 2D Line chart types, choosing to apply the chart type to the selected series, as shown in Figure 15-3.

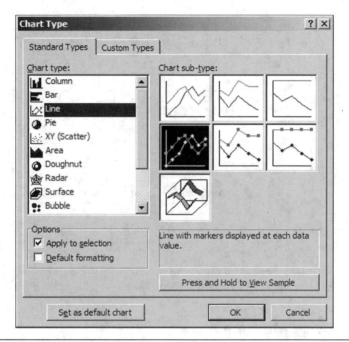

Figure 15-3 Selecting the New Type for the Selected Series

When you click OK, the Forecast series will display as a line, while the Sales series remains as the original column, as shown in Figure 15-4. (We've also modified the format of the Forecast line to make it stand out in the book.)

That's just about all there is to it. Start with a simple column chart with multiple series, select each series in turn, use the *Chart > Chart Type* menu to change its type and then apply the required formatting. The possible combinations are limited only by our imagination and the legibility of the final chart!

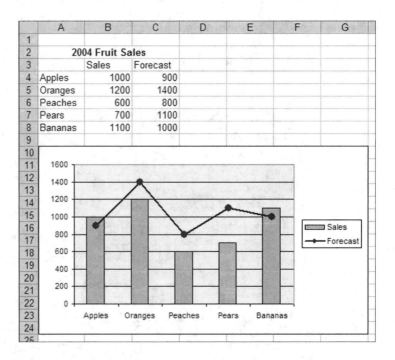

Figure 15-4 The Resulting Combination Column/Line Chart

Using Multiple Axes

When we create one of the standard 2D charts, the plot area can have two sets of axes. The primary axes are usually displayed on the bottom and left, whereas the secondary axes are usually displayed on the top and right. If we have more than one series on the chart, we can choose which set of axes to use for each series by double-clicking the series and making our choice on the Axis tab of the Format Data Series dialog. When instructed to place a series on the secondary axis, Excel usually only displays a secondary Y axis on the chart. This can be changed using the *Chart > Chart Options* menu command, clicking the Axes tab and choosing whatever combination of primary and secondary axes are desired. When two series are plotted on different axes, the axes are scaled independently. Care must be taken to ensure that it is obvious to the viewer which series is plotted on which axis, by adding relevant axis labels and matching them to the series labels, as shown in Figure 15-5.

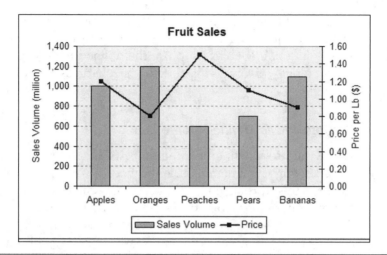

Figure 15-5 Using Labels and Axis Titles to Clearly Identify Which Series Applies to Which Axis

Using Defined Names to Link Charts to Data

A key point to understand is that our charts do not have to refer directly to the cells containing their data. The source data for a chart series is provided by the =SERIES() function, which can be seen in the formula bar when a series is selected. The SERIES() function has the following format:

```
=SERIES(Name, XValues, YValues, PlotOrder)
```

Each of the four parameters can be a constant or array of constants, a direct range reference or a reference to a defined name. All the lines in Listing 15-1 are examples of valid functions.

Listing 15-1 Examples of Valid SERIES() Functions

```
=SERIES(Sheet1!$B$1,Sheet1$A$2:$A$20,Sheet1!$B2:$B20,1)
=SERIES("Sales",Sheet1$A$2:$A$20,Sheet1!$B2:$B20,1)
=SERIES("Horizontal Line",{0,1},{123,123},1)
=SERIES("Book Names",Book1.xls!chtXName,Book1.xls!chtYName,1)
=SERIES("Sheet Names",Sheet1!chtXName,Sheet1!chtYName,1)
```

The last two versions of the SERIES() formula use workbook-level and sheet-level defined names respectively instead of direct cell references. This indirection enables us to use the defined names' definitions to modify the ranges or arrays passed to the chart, as shown in the following examples.

Setting Up the Defined Name Links

When you use a defined name in a SERIES formula, for best results you should begin with a name that references a worksheet range directly. After you have this working correctly, you can modify the name to perform more complex operations. Sometimes, if the formula for the defined name is particularly complex, or if we make an error in its definition, the charting module will refuse to accept the name in the SERIES() function. By starting with a very simple definition for the names, we are able to add them to the SERIES() function without problem.

Figure 15-6 shows a simple line chart, with the series selected and the SERIES() function displayed in the formula bar.

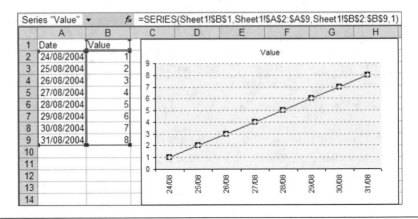

Figure 15-6 A Simple Line Chart

To change the chart to use defined names, we first create two defined names, for the Date and Value ranges. Select *Insert > Name > Define* from the menu and create the following two names:

```
Name:      Sheet1!chtDates
Refers to: =Sheet1!$A$2:$A$9
```

Name: `Sheet1!chtValues`
Refers to: `=Sheet1!$B$2:$B$9`

Now select the chart series and edit the SERIES() formula to read as follows:

`=SERIES("Value",Sheet1!chtDates,Sheet1!chtValues,1)`

That's it! The chart series is now linked to the defined names and the defined names refer to the source data ranges. Obviously, if we had more series in our chart, we would have to create extra names for the values for each additional series. Now that we've set up the linkage, we can modify the Refers To: formulas for the names (their *definitions*) to create some interesting and time-saving effects.

Auto-Expanding Charts

One of the most frequently asked questions in the microsoft.public. excel.charting newsgroup is how to get a chart to automatically include new data as it's typed in. In Excel 2003, if we create a List from the data range and set either the chart or the defined names to refer to an entire column of the List, the reference will automatically be adjusted to include any new data. In previous versions, or if we prefer not to convert the range to a List in Excel 2003, we can use defined names to do the automatic updating.

The trick is to use a combination of the OFFSET() and COUNTA() functions in the definition of the name used for the X values, then define the name used for the Y values as an offset from the X values range. Select a cell in the worksheet, then choose *Insert > Name > Define*. Change the definition of the chtDates range to be the following by selecting the existing chtDates entry, typing the new definition and clicking the Add button:

Name: `Sheet1!chtDates`
Refers to: `=OFFSET(Sheet1!$A$2,0,0,COUNTA`
          `(Sheet1!$A:$A)-1,1)`

The OFFSET() function has the following parameters:

`=OFFSET(SourceRange, RowsToMoveDown, ColumnsToMoveAcross,`
`            NumberOfRowsToInclude, NumberOfColumnsToInclude)`

The COUNTA() function returns the number of non-blank cells in the range, which in our case includes the header row. We therefore subtract one to get the number of data items. Putting the two together gives us a reference that starts in A2, moves down zero rows and across zero columns (so remains in A2), has a number of rows equal to the count of our data items and is one column wide. While in the Define Name dialog with the chtDates name selected, if we tab into the Refers to: box, Excel will highlight the resulting range with its "dancing ants," as shown in Figure 15-7.

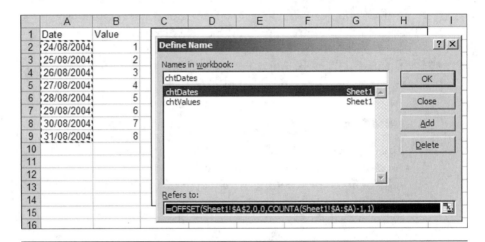

Figure 15-7 Excel's Dancing Ants Showing the Range Referred to by the Defined Name

While we're in the Define Name dialog, we need to modify the definition of the chtValues name. The easiest way to do that is to again use the OFFSET() function, but this time to start at the range referred to by the chtDates name and move one column across, keeping the same height and width:

Name: Sheet1!chtValues
Refers to: =OFFSET(Sheet1!chtDates,0,1)

After clicking OK to apply those changes and return to the worksheet, the chart should be showing exactly the same as before—the new definitions resolve to the same ranges we started off with. The difference now is that if we type a new data point in row 10, it will automatically appear on the chart (assuming calculation is set to Automatic)!

To recap, it works because the COUNTA() function contained within the definition of the chtDates range returns the number of items in column A, which now includes the new entry. That feeds into the OFFSET() function, making it include the new entry in its resulting reference (now A2:A10). The chtValues range is updated to refer to one column across from the expanded chtDates range, so becomes B2:B10 and both those names feed into the chart series =SERIES() function, making the chart redraw to include the new data. The functions used in the defined name assume that the source data is contiguous, starting in cell A2. Blank cells will result in an incorrectly calculated range. More precise formulas are outside the scope of this book, but can easily be found by searching the Google newsgroup archives.

It is fundamental to the rest of this section that you fully understand the mechanism we're using. If anything is unclear, take some time to go through the example, perhaps trying to create an auto-expanding chart with two or three data series.

Scrolling and Zooming a Time Series

In the auto-expanding chart, we were only updating one of the OFFSET() function's parameters. If we modify both the row offset and number of rows, we can provide a simple, codeless mechanism for our users to scroll and zoom through a time series. In the worksheet shown in Figure 15-8, we've added two scrollbars from the Forms toolbar below the chart, set their Min and Max values to correspond to the number of data points and linked their values to the cells in column D, using two defined names ZoomVal and ScrollVal to refer to cells D24 and D25 respectively.

In the definition for the chtDates name for this example, the ScrollVal figure is used for the row offset and the ZoomVal figure provides the number of data points to include in the range:

```
Name:      Sheet1!chtDates
Refers to: =OFFSET(Sheet1!$A$1,Sheet1!ScrollVal,0,
           Sheet1!ZoomVal,1)
```

The chtValues definition is the same as before, =OFFSET(chtDates, 0,1).

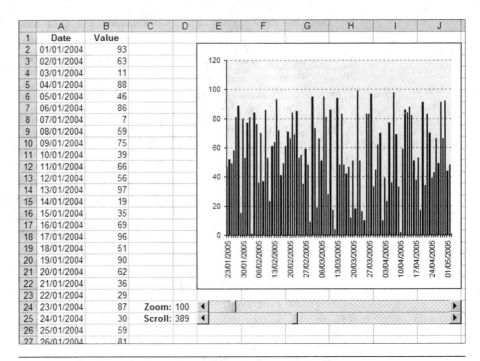

Figure 15-8 Allowing the User to Zoom and Scroll Through Time-Series Data

Transforming Coordinate Systems

In the previous two examples, we've used the OFFSET() function in the defined name to change the range of values drawn on the chart, but keeping the actual data intact. We can also use defined names to modify the data itself prior to plotting it, such as transforming between polar and x, y coordinate systems. In polar coordinates, a point's location is defined by its angle and distance from the origin, rather than the distance-along and distance-up of the standard XY chart. Excel does not have a built-in chart type that will plot data in polar coordinates, but we can use defined names to convert the (angle, length) polar coordinate to (x, y), which can then be drawn on a standard XY chart. We're going to show you how to create the chart shown in Figure 15-9 from the data shown beside it by using defined names. In this example, the length figures are calculated from the angle using the formula `a*sin(a)`.

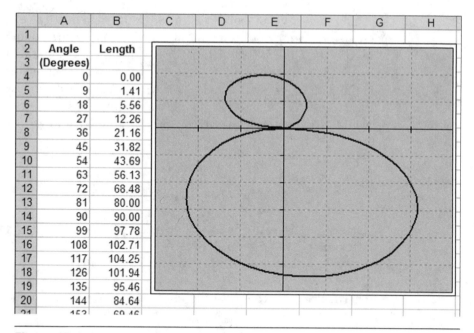

	A	B	C	D	E	F	G	H
1								
2	Angle	Length						
3	(Degrees)							
4	0	0.00						
5	9	1.41						
6	18	5.56						
7	27	12.26						
8	36	21.16						
9	45	31.82						
10	54	43.69						
11	63	56.13						
12	72	68.48						
13	81	80.00						
14	90	90.00						
15	99	97.78						
16	108	102.71						
17	117	104.25						
18	126	101.94						
19	135	95.46						
20	144	84.64						
21	153	69.46						

Figure 15-9 Plotting Polar Coordinates on an XY Scatter Chart

To demonstrate how the various uses of defined names can be combined, we'll implement two levels of indirection. The first level will use the technique from the *Auto-Expanding Charts* section above to automatically handle changing data sets, while a second level will perform the coordinate transformation.

The names to handle the automatic updates are defined as follows:

```
Name:      Sheet1!datAngle
Refers to: =OFFSET(Sheet1!$A$3,1,0,
           COUNTA(Sheet1!$A$3:$A$5000)-1,1)
```

```
Name:      Sheet1!datLength
Refers to: =OFFSET(Sheet1!datAngle,0,1)
```

The observant reader might have noticed that we're using a slight different version of the OFFSET() function in the definition for the datAngle name. The version shown here is slightly more robust, as it counts within a specific range of 5,000 cells, starting with the data header cell. You may have seen a variation on this technique in which the entire column address was used in the COUNTA function. By limiting the range in the way we do here, it doesn't matter whether the user changes the contents of the cells above the data range, such as adding extra titles to the sheet.

With the datAngle and datLength names referring to our source data, we can define two more names to convert from the polar to x, y coordinates:

```
Name:     Sheet1!chtX
Refers to: =Sheet1!datLength*
          COS(Sheet1!datAngle*PI()/180)
```

```
Name:     Sheet1!chtY
Refers to: =Sheet1!datLength*
          SIN(Sheet1!datAngle*PI()/180)
```

The chart series can then use the chtX and chtY names for the X and Y data:

```
=SERIES("Polar Plot",Sheet1!chtX,Sheet1!chtY,1)
```

Charting a Function

So we've used defined names to change the range of cells to plot and to manipulate the data in that range before we plot it. In *Chapter 14 — Data Manipulation Techniques*, we introduced array formulas and explained how they can be used to perform calculations on arrays of data. We also showed a specific array formula that is often used to generate a number sequence for use in other array formulas. What we didn't mention was that we can also use array formulas in our defined names and refer to them from charts! Figure 15-10 shows a worksheet that uses array formulas in defined names to plot a mathematical function over a range of x values, without needing to read any data from the worksheet.

This worksheet combines a number of Excel tricks to generate the x axis values and use them to calculate the y axis results. We create a defined named to generate the values for the x axis and give it the name x, for reasons explained below:

```
Name:     Sheet1!x
Refers to: =$C$6+(ROW(OFFSET($A$1,0,0,$C$8,1))-
          1)*($C$7-$C$6)/($C$8-1)
```

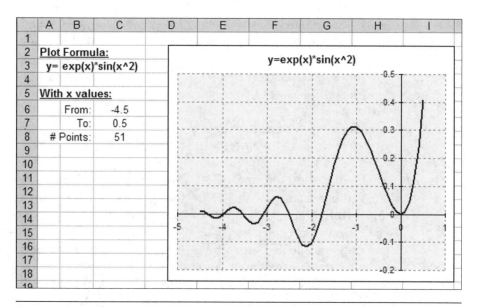

Figure 15-10 Using Array Formulas in Defined Names to Generate and Plot Data

Working through the parts of this array formula:

- `OFFSET($A$1,0,0, $C$8,1)` gives the range A1:A51.
- `ROW(OFFSET($A$1,0,0, $C$8,1))` converts the range to the array {1, 2, 3, ..., 50, 51}.
- `(ROW(OFFSET($A$1,0,0, $C$8,1))-1)` subtracts 1 from each item in the array, giving {0, 1, 2, ..., 49, 50}.
- `($C$7-$C$6)/($C$8-1)` calculates the x axis increment for each point, giving 0.1 in our example.
- `(ROW(OFFSET($A$1,0,0,$C$8,1))-1)*($C$7-$C$6)/($C$8-1)` multiplies each item in the array by the x axis increment, giving the array {0, 0.1, 0.2, ..., 4.9, 5.0}.
- `$C$6+(ROW(OFFSET($A$1,0,0,$C$8,1))-1)*($C$7-$C$6)/($C$8-1)` adds the array to the required x value start point, resulting in the range of x values to use in the chart {–4.5, –4.4, –4.3, ... 0.49, 0.50}.

Unfortunately, if we try to include Sheet1!x in the chart SERIES() function, we get an error about an incorrect range reference. To create the chart, we use the workaround described at the start of this section, by creating two names chtX and chtY that point to worksheet cells, use them to create the chart and then change them to their real definitions:

Name: `Sheet1!chtX`
Refers to: `=Sheet1!x`

Name: `Sheet1!chtY`
Refers to: `=EVALUATE(Sheet1!$B$3&"+x*0")`

The definition for chtX is just a workaround for Excel not allowing us to use the x name in the chart itself. The definition for chtY needs some explaining! Cell `B3` contains the equation to be plotted, `exp(x)*sin(x^2)`, as text. The EVALUATE function is an XLM macro function, equivalent to the VBA Application.Evaluate method, but which can be called from within a defined name. XLM functions were the programming language for Excel 4, replaced by VBA in Excel 5, but still supported in Excel 2003. The documentation for the XLM functions can be downloaded from the Microsoft Web site, by searching for "macrofun.exe" or "xlmacro.exe." At the time of writing, one version of the file is available from `http://support.microsoft.com/?kbid=128175`.

EVALUATE() evaluates the expression it's given, returning a numeric result. In our case, when the expression is evaluated, Excel replaces the x's in the formula with the array of values produced by our Sheet1!x defined name (which is exactly why we called it x) and returns an array containing the result of the function for each of our x axis values. These arrays are plotted on the chart, to give the line for the equation. The `&"+x*0"` part of the chtY definition works around an error in Excel that sometimes causes trig functions to not evaluate as array formulas, by forcing the entire formula to be evaluated as an array.

Faking It

A chart is a visual artifact, designed to impart information to the viewer in a graphical manner. As such, we should mainly be interested in whether the final chart looks correct and performs its purpose of providing clear information. We should not be too bothered about whether the chart has been constructed according to a notional set of generally approved guidelines. In other words, we often need to cheat by using some of the chart engine's features in "creative and imaginative" ways. This section explains a few ways in which we can get creative with Excel's chart engine, by using some of its features in ways they were probably not designed to be used.

Error Bars

When is a line not a line? When it's an error bar! From a purely visual perspective, an error bar is a horizontal or vertical line emanating from a data point, so if we ever have the need to draw horizontal or vertical lines around our data points, we might consider using error bars for those lines. A great example is the step chart shown in Figure 15-11, where the vertical lines show the change in an item's price during a day and the horizontal lines connect the end price from one day to the start price for the next day.

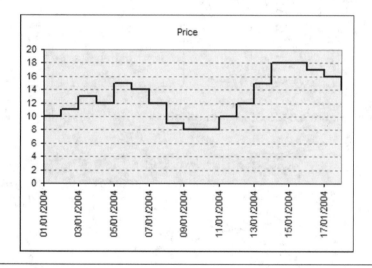

Figure 15-11 A Step Chart

Because Excel doesn't include a built-in Step Chart type, many people believe that Excel can't create them. There are quite a few ways in which it can be done, but the easiest is probably to use an XY chart with both vertical and horizontal error bars. The basic data for the chart consists of a list of dates and end-of-day prices, with a calculated field for the change in price from the end of the previous day. From this basic data, we start with a normal XY chart to plot the price against the date, as shown in Figure 15-12.

Below each data point, we want to display a vertical line equal to the change in price for that day, which we do by specifying a custom minus error value in the Y Error Bars tab of the Format Data Series Dialog, as shown in Figure 15-13.

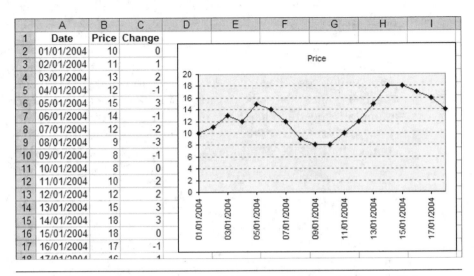

Figure 15-12 Start with a Normal XY (Scatter) Chart of Price vs. Date

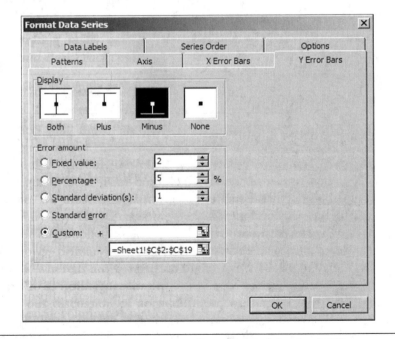

Figure 15-13 Add a Custom Minus Y Error Bar for the Day's Change in Price

The horizontal lines need to join each data point to the bottom of the subsequent point's error bar. That sounds difficult, but because these are daily prices all you need to do is add Plus markers to the X error bars with a fixed value setting of 1. With the error bars configured, you should be seeing a chart something like that shown in Figure 15-14.

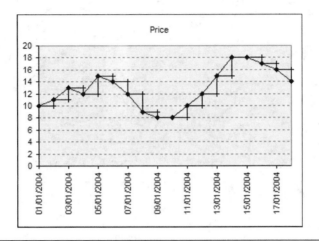

Figure 15-14 The Chart with the Additional Error Bars

All that remains is to double-click the error bar lines and use the Patterns tab to change their color, thickness and marker style, and then double-click the original XY line and format that to have no line and no marker. The result appears to be the step chart from Figure 15-11, even though it's actually only error bars being drawn.

Dummy XY Series

When is an axis not an axis? When it's an XY series with data labels! Excel's value axes are either boringly linear or logarithmic. They do not support breaks in the axis, nor scales that vary along the axis nor many other complex-axis effects. Figure 15-15 shows a chart with a variable Y axis, where the bottom half of the chart plots values from 0 to 100 in steps of 20, but the top half plots 100 to 1,000 in steps of 200:

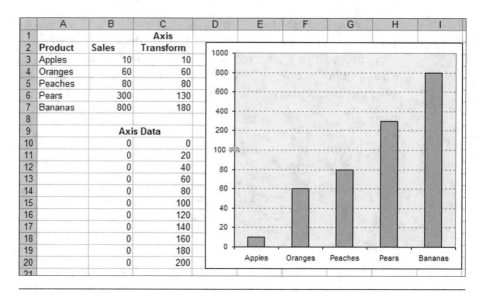

	A	B	C	D	E	F	G	H	I
1			Axis						
2	Product	Sales	Transform						
3	Apples	10	10						
4	Oranges	60	60						
5	Peaches	80	80						
6	Pears	300	130						
7	Bananas	800	180						
8									
9			Axis Data						
10		0	0						
11		0	20						
12		0	40						
13		0	60						
14		0	80						
15		0	100						
16		0	120						
17		0	140						
18		0	160						
19		0	180						
20		0	200						

Figure 15-15 Chart with a Complex Axis Scale

In this chart, the real Y axis goes from zero to 200, but we've added a dummy XY series using the data from `B10:C20`, added data labels to the XY series, set them to display to the left of the point and customized their text to that shown in the figure. The result appears to be a complex axis scale that varies up the chart. The final step is to transform the real sales data in `B3:B7` into the correct values for Excel to plot on its linear 0 to 200 scale, which is done using a simple mapping formula in `C3:C7` of `=IF(B3<=100,B3,100+B3/10)`, which is the data that Excel plots.

We can use this technique to implement any axis scale of our choosing, such as including breaks in our axes, plotting using logarithmic, hyperbolic or probability scales or even including multiple dummy XY series to make the chart appear to have many axes (as long as the user can determine which series is plotted against which axis). This effect can be misleading, if it is not clearly shown that a break in the axis scale exists. The chart in Figure 15-15 looks linear along its entire range, but if plotted on a true linear scale, it would resemble a boomerang with a large angle in the middle. An easy way to indicate a break in the axis is to set an individual point's data marker using a custom image, as we have done. Draw the image using Paint or other graphics program, copy it to the clipboard, select the data point and paste the image.

VBA Techniques

So far, we've concentrated on the techniques we can use to get the most out of Excel's charting engine through the user interface. In this section, we examine how we can use VBA to manipulate charts.

Converting Between Chart Coordinate Systems

When using VBA to work with charts, there are (at least) four different coordinate systems that we often need to convert between:

- The chart series data displayed inside the plot area is in the axis coordinates if it's an XY Scatter chart.
- The mouse pointer coordinates given in the MouseMove etc. events are measured in pixels, with the origin in the top-left corner of the ChartObject window.
- The coordinates of any drawing objects added to the chart are in points, with the origin being the top left of the chart area, slightly inside the ChartObject window.
- The coordinates used by the GET.CHART.ITEM XLM function to locate the vertices of chart objects are in points, but with the origin in the bottom-left corner of the chart area. See the *Locating Chart Items* section later for an example of its use.

Furthermore, if the chart is embedded on a worksheet, the worksheet zoom factor affects the mouse pointer coordinates, but not the data nor location of any drawing objects on the chart.

Listing 15-2 shows a MouseMove event for a chart, within which we convert the X, Y mouse coordinates given to the event into both data coordinates (displayed in the status bar) and drawing object coordinates (which we use to move an oval to follow the mouse pointer). Note that this code uses the PointsPerPixel function defined in *Chapter 9 — Understanding and Using Windows API Calls*:

Listing 15-2 Converting from Mouse Coordinates to Data and Drawing Object Coordinates

```
Private Sub mchtChart_MouseMove(ByVal Button As Long, _
    ByVal Shift As Long, ByVal X As Long, ByVal Y As Long)
```

```
Dim dZoom As Double
Dim dXVal As Double
Dim dYVal As Double
Dim dPixelSize As Double

On Error Resume Next

'The active window zoom factor
dZoom = ActiveWindow.Zoom / 100

'The pixel size, in points
dPixelSize = PointsPerPixel

'Mouse coordinates to (XY) Data coordinates
With mchtChart
   dXVal = .Axes(xlCategory).MinimumScale + _
      (.Axes(xlCategory).MaximumScale - _
       .Axes(xlCategory).MinimumScale) * _
      (X * dPixelSize / dZoom - _
       (.PlotArea.InsideLeft + .ChartArea.Left)) / _
      .PlotArea.InsideWidth

   dYVal = .Axes(xlValue).MinimumScale + _
      (.Axes(xlValue).MaximumScale - _
       .Axes(xlValue).MinimumScale) * _
      (1 - (Y * dPixelSize / dZoom - _
            (.PlotArea.InsideTop + .ChartArea.Top)) / _
      .PlotArea.InsideHeight)
End With

Application.StatusBar = "(" & Application.Round(dXVal, 2) _
     & ", " & Application.Round(dYVal, 2) & ")"

'Mouse coordinates to Drawing Object Points

'We'll only move the oval if the Shift key is pressed
If Shift = 1 Then
  With mchtChart
     dXVal = (X * dPixelSize / dZoom - .ChartArea.Left)
     dYVal = (Y * dPixelSize / dZoom - .ChartArea.Top)

     With .Shapes("ovlPointer")
        .Left = dXVal - .Width / 2
        .Top = dYVal - .Height / 2
```

```
        End With
      End With
    End If

End Sub
```

Locating Chart Items

Sometimes, however hard we try, the only way to get a chart looking exactly how we want it is to add drawing objects to it, such as rectangles, lines, arrows and so on. As soon as we do that, we hit the problem of trying to identify where in the drawing object coordinate space an item on the chart is located, such as the top middle of a specific column in a column chart.

That level of positional information cannot be obtained through the Excel object model, but can be obtained by calling on the long-disused XLM function GET.CHART.ITEM. This function has the following parameters:

```
GET.CHART.ITEM(x_y_index, point_index, item_text)
```

Where:

- `x_y_index` is 1 to return the x position and 2 to return the y position.
- `point_index` depends on the item we're looking at, but is a number from 1 to 8 to identify a specific vertex within the item. For example, 2 is the upper middle of any rectangular item, such as a column in a column chart.
- `item_text` identifies the item we're interested in, such as "Plot" for the plot area, or "S2P4" for the fourth data point in the second series in the chart.

The full list of available parameters can be found in the XLM Macros help file available for download from the Microsoft Web site at `http://support.microsoft.com/?kbid=128175`. The only caveat with using GET.CHART.ITEM is that the chart must be active for it to work. The code in Listing 15-3 moves an arrow on a chart to be from the top-left corner of the inside of the plot area (using normal VBA positioning) to the top middle of the third column of a column chart, resulting in the chart shown in Figure 15-16.

Listing 15-3 Using GET.CHART.ITEM to Locate a Chart Item's Vertices

```
Private Sub cmdMoveArrow_Click()

  Dim rngActive As Range
  Dim dXVal As Double
  Dim dYVal As Double
  Dim chtChart As Chart

  Set rngActive = ActiveCell

  'We have to activate the chart to use GET.CHART.ITEM
  Me.ChartObjects(1).Activate

  'Find the XY position of the middle top of the third column
  'in the data series,
  'returned in XLM coordinates
  dXVal = ExecuteExcel4Macro("GET.CHART.ITEM(1,2,""S1P3"")")
  dYVal = ExecuteExcel4Macro("GET.CHART.ITEM(2,2,""S1P3"")")

  'Get the Chart
  Set chtChart = Me.ChartObjects(1).Chart
  With chtChart

    'Convert the XLM coordinates to Drawing Object coordinates
    'The x values are the same, but the Y values need to be
    'flipped
    dYVal = .ChartArea.Height - dYVal

    'Move and size the Arrow
    .Shapes("linArrow").Left = .PlotArea.InsideLeft
    .Shapes("linArrow").Top = .PlotArea.InsideTop
    .Shapes("linArrow").Width = dXVal - .Shapes("linArrow").Left
    .Shapes("linArrow").Height = dYVal - .Shapes("linArrow").Top
  End With

  rngActive.Activate

End Sub
```

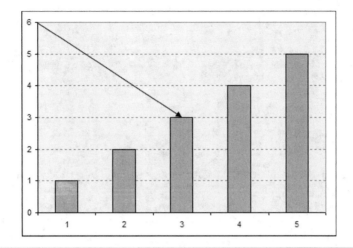

Figure 15-16 Moving an Arrow to Point to the Top Middle of a Column

Calculating Reasonable Axis Scales

Often when we're controlling charts through VBA, we need to set our own values for the axis scales. The code in Listing 15-4 calculates tidy Minimum, Maximum and MajorUnit values. It is a different algorithm than the one Excel uses to determine chart axis scales, but is one that we have found to give pleasant-looking results.

Listing 15-4 Function to Calculate Reasonable Chart Axes Scales

```
Public Type CHART_SCALE
  dMin As Double
  dMax As Double
  dScale As Double
End Type

Public Function ChartScale(ByVal dMin As Double, _
      ByVal dMax As Double) As CHART_SCALE

    Dim dPower As Double, dScale As Double

    'Check if the max and min are the same
    If dMax = dMin Then
        dScale = dMax
        dMax = dMax * 1.01
```

```
        dMin = dMin * 0.99
End If

'Check if dMax is bigger than dMin - swap them if not
If dMax < dMin Then
    dScale = dMax
    dMax = dMin
    dMin = dScale
End If

'Make dMax a little bigger and dMin a little smaller
If dMax > 0 Then
    dMax = dMax + (dMax - dMin) * 0.01
Else
    dMax = dMax - (dMax - dMin) * 0.01
End If
If dMin > 0 Then
    dMin = dMin - (dMax - dMin) * 0.01
Else
    dMin = dMin + (dMax - dMin) * 0.01
End If

'What if they are both 0?
If (dMax = 0) And (dMin = 0) Then dMax = 1

'This bit rounds the maximum and minimum values to
'reasonable values to chart.
'Find the range of values covered
dPower = Log(dMax - dMin) / Log(10)
dScale = 10 ^ (dPower - Int(dPower))

'Find the scaling factor
Select Case dScale
Case 0 To 2.5
    dScale = 0.2
Case 2.5 To 5
    dScale = 0.5
Case 5 To 7.5
    dScale = 1
Case Else
    dScale = 2
End Select
```

```
'Calculate the scaling factor (major unit)
dScale = dScale * 10 ^ Int(dPower)

'Round the axis values to the nearest scaling factor
ChartScale.dMin = dScale * Int(dMin / dScale)
ChartScale.dMax = dScale * (Int(dMax / dScale) + 1)
ChartScale.dScale = dScale
```

```
End Function
```

Conclusion

Although Excel's charting engine has a relatively poor reputation among users, most of that is due to a lack of knowledge about how to exploit the engine, rather than a lack of features. Yes, we would like to see significant improvements in the quality of the graphics, proper support for true 3D contour and XYZ scatter plots and a general overhaul of the user interface to make the advanced techniques shown in this chapter much more discoverable for the average user.

However, after we've spent the time to explore the charting engine and fully understand the techniques introduced here, we realize that the limits of Excel's charting capabilities are to be found in our imagination and creativity, rather than with Excel.

VBA Debugging

Debugging is the most important and probably the least understood aspect of programming. No one writes perfect code on the first try. Being able to efficiently locate and correct the mistakes you've made is a significant part of what separates a great programmer from a skilled amateur. In this chapter we demonstrate how to use the built-in debugging features of the Visual Basic Editor (VBE) to locate and correct bugs in your code as well as provide tips and techniques that will help you become a better debugger.

Basic VBA Debugging Techniques

Run Mode vs. Break Mode

A running application can exist in one of two states. Run mode is exactly what its name would suggest. The application is running normally. In break mode an application is still technically running, but execution has been interrupted. Break mode can be triggered by an unhandled runtime error, a Stop statement, or a break point placed within the code.

In the first group of topics in this section we discuss how the global VBE Error Trapping setting affects how an application will enter break mode. The global error trapping settings are located under the VBE *Tools > Options > General > Error Trapping* menu.

Break on All Errors

This setting is reasonably self-explanatory. When you have selected the Break on All Errors setting, all error handlers will be ignored. The moment any runtime error occurs, an error message will display and you will have the option to end the program or enter break mode on the line of code that caused the error.

Break in Class Module

If an error occurs within a class module procedure that contains an error handler, this setting is equivalent to the *Break on Unhandled Errors* setting that we cover next. This is to say it will not cause code execution to halt in response to the error. If an error occurs within a class module procedure that *does not* contain an error handler, code execution will be interrupted on the line of code in the class module procedure that generated the error. If you've ever experienced a runtime error on a line of code such as Userform1.Show, using this setting will bring you to the line of code within the UserForm class module that actually caused the error.

Break on Unhandled Errors

This setting causes code to break on errors only where there are no error handlers anywhere in the call stack above the procedure in which the error occurred. This is an important distinction. Even if an error occurs in a procedure without an error handler, if that procedure was called by another procedure that does contain an error handler the calling procedure's error handler will handle the error. Code execution will only break when there are no error handlers anywhere in the call stack above the procedure where the error occurred. We cover the call stack in more detail in *The Call Stack* section later in this chapter.

Keep in mind that the error trapping setting is an application-level setting that is persistent in all versions of Excel higher than Excel 97. There is no way to detect or change this setting within your VBA code. Therefore, when you are having strange problems with the error handling behavior on a specific user's computer, the first thing you should do is determine what error trapping setting is currently specified for that instance of Excel.

Debug Mode

Debug mode refers to the state in an application in which error handling has been intentionally bypassed in some fashion. Debug mode is usually built in to the error handling system used by the application. We covered debug mode as a design feature of an error handling system in *Chapter 12 — VBA Error Handling*.

Placing an application into debug mode can also be as simple as changing the VBE Error Trapping setting to *Break on All Errors*. This is not a robust solution for implementing debug mode, however, because many nontrivial applications deliberately generate runtime errors that are designed to be ignored as a normal part of program execution. The *Break on All Errors* setting doesn't distinguish between errors that are a normal part of code execution and those that represent bugs, it just breaks on any of them. If you need to get past a "normal" error to reach an error caused by a bug, you will need a more sophisticated debug mode implementation, such as the one described next.

User-Defined Debug Mode

A user-defined debug mode typically involves a public constant that can be used to disable or modify the behavior of error handling on an application-wide basis. In the error handling system we demonstrated in *Chapter 12 — VBA Error Handling*, debug mode was implemented with the following public constant defined in the MErrorHandler module:

```
Public Const gbDEBUG_MODE As Boolean = False
```

When set to False, the gbDEBUG_MODE constant has no effect and application error handling proceeds normally. When set to True, the gbDEBUG_MODE constant causes the error handler within the procedure where the error occurred to drop into a Stop statement. As we will see in the next section, this initiates break mode and enables us to debug the error.

The gbDEBUG_MODE constant is also used to disable error handling in other contexts. For example, some procedures may not have formal error handling. Procedures that are wrapped entirely in On Error Resume Next are the most common example. When a procedure is constructed in this manner, it implies that any errors that might occur within it are expected and should be ignored. This is not always a valid assumption, so we need some way of conditionally disabling On Error Resume Next. The standard way to accomplish this is shown in Listing 16-1.

Listing 16-1 Conditionally Disabling On Error Resume Next

```
If Not gbDEBUG_MODE Then
    On Error Resume Next
End If
```

The code shown in Listing 16-1 would appear at the top of the procedure in question. If our gbDEBUG_MODE constant has been set to True, all error bypassing is disabled. When the gbDEBUG_MODE constant is set to False, the procedure functions normally, ignoring any errors that occur in the course of its execution.

The Stop Statement

When VBA encounters a Stop statement in your program, code execution is halted at the statement and break mode is initiated. You can then use any of the standard debugging techniques that will be discussed throughout this chapter to step over the Stop statement and debug your program. The Stop statement can be used as part of a larger debug mode infrastructure, as described in *Chapter 12 — VBA Error Handling*, or it can be added to your code on an ad hoc basis when you are attempting to debug errors in very specific locations.

Just remember to remove any ad hoc Stop statements from your code and disable debug mode prior to shipping your application. Failing to do this is one of the most common debugging mistakes we have seen. If VBA encounters a Stop statement in an unprotected VBA application, the user will be unceremoniously dumped into break mode. The vast majority of users will have no idea what has happened or what they should do about it.

Project protection disables the effect of Stop statements, but this can cause even worse problems if debug mode has not been disabled. If a program uses an error handling system similar to the one we presented in *Chapter 12 — VBA Error Handling*, its project is protected and it has been left in debug mode, the program will enter an infinite loop any time a runtime error occurs.

As shown in Listing 16-2, this is because the Stop statement is skipped. Rather than halting at the Stop statement, the Resume statement that immediately follows the Stop statement is executed. This causes VBA to re-execute the line of code that generated the error. This triggers the error handler again and causes the Resume statement to be executed again, ad infinitum.

Listing 16-2 The Perils of Leaving Debug Mode Active

```
ErrorHandler:
    bReturn = False
    If bCentralErrorHandler(msMODULE, sSOURCE) Then
        Stop      ' This will be ignored in a protected project.
        Resume
    Else
```

```
        Resume ErrorExit
    End If
End Function
```

If you are very lucky, the user will understand how to press Ctrl+Break to halt the loop. In most cases, however, the only option they will understand is Ctrl+Alt+Del or worse, the Off button. **Always** remember to disable debug mode prior to shipping your code.

Conditional Compilation Constants

We mention conditional compilation constants very briefly in this section for the sake of completeness. Conditional compilation constants are designed to enable you to compile different versions of your code for different platforms that it will run on. Because VBA is an interpreted rather than a compiled programming language, however, the usefulness of conditional compilation constants is limited.

A conditional compilation constant could be substituted for the normal constant used to control debug mode, but there are no significant benefits to doing so. The single situation in which conditional compilation constants are truly useful in Excel VBA is when you need to write an application that can be run on both the PC and Mac platforms using the same code base. This situation is beyond the scope of this book.

Conditional compilation constants are defined in the VBE using the *Tools > VBAProject Properties* menu (where VBAProject is the actual name of your project). In Figure 16-1 we have created a conditional compilation constant named DEBUG_MODE that could act as a substitute for our gbDEBUG_MODE VBA constant.

The control where conditional compilation constants are defined is located at the bottom of the *General* tab of the Project Properties dialog. Conditional compilation constants defined in the Project Properties dialog have public scope. These constants can only be assigned integer values. They can function as Boolean values using the rule that zero = False and nonzero = True. You can define multiple conditional compilation constants by separating each constant definition in the Project Properties dialog with a colon character.

Conditional compilation constants cannot be treated like standard VBA constants. They have their own special set of statements with which they must be used. The DEBUG_MODE conditional compilation constant would be used in a procedure as shown in Listing 16-3.

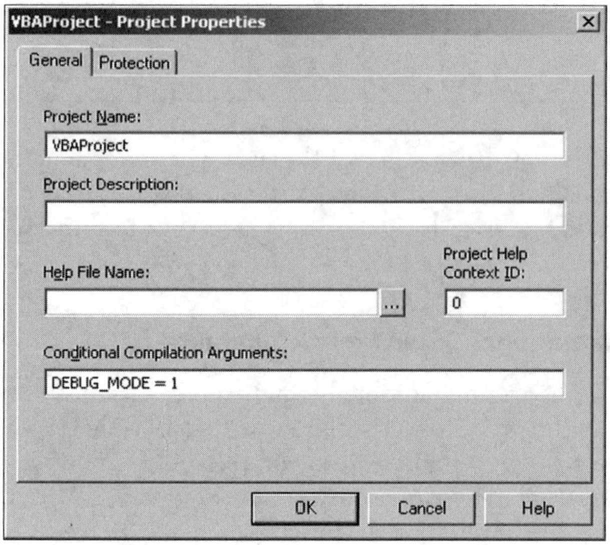

Figure 16-1 Creating Conditional Compilation Constants

Listing 16-3 Using Conditional Compilation Constants

```
#If DEBUG_MODE Then
    On Error GoTo 0
#Else
    On Error Resume Next
#End If
```

The # character before the programming statements used with the conditional compilation constant is required. There are only a few such VBA programming language constructs designed to work with conditional compilation constants.

As you can see, for debugging purposes, conditional compilation constants are no different than normal VBA constants. For this reason we suggest that you use conditional compilation constants only for situations where you truly need conditional compilation. Debugging in VBA is not one of them.

Using Break Points (F9)

Break points are selected positions within your code at which program execution will automatically stop and enter break mode. Break points are conceptually very similar to the Stop statement. The difference is that break points can be added and removed with the click of a mouse or a keyboard shortcut, and they are not saved with your code. If you set break points in your code and then save your project, you will find that they disappear if you close and re-open the project. Stop statements will remain.

As implied above, break points can be set in one of two ways: using your mouse, or using keyboard shortcuts. Figure 16-2 shows a break point being set using the mouse.

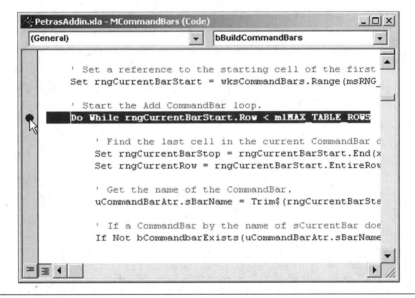

Figure 16-2 Setting a Break Point with Your Mouse

Each code module has a gray bar running down the left side. This is called the ***margin indicator bar***. Clicking the margin indicator bar adds a break point to your code at the point where you clicked. Clicking an existing break point in the margin indicator bar removes that break point.

Setting break points using keyboard shortcuts is just as easy. To set a break point, place the cursor anywhere on the line of code where you want the break point to be located and press the F9 key. A break point will be added to that line of code. Pressing F9 while the cursor is located on an existing break point will remove that break point. Break points can only be set on executable lines of code. Code comments, blank lines and variable declarations are examples of places where you cannot set a break point.

After you have set a break point, run your application as you would normally. When code execution reaches the break point, it will stop and enter break mode. You can then use the debugging techniques discussed in the following sections to step over the break point and debug the problem you are having with your code.

Stepping Through Code

The fundamental skill you must master to become proficient at debugging is stepping through your code. The term "stepping through your code" implies a one-way, deterministic process. This is not the case. Stepping through code can involve moving backward or forward through your code as well as skipping sections of code or allowing sections of code to run but then halting when they have completed.

We discuss the various techniques used to step through code in detail in this section. Keep in mind that the whole point of stepping through code is to see what the code is doing. When you step through code you are duplicating exactly what your program does when it is running normally, but you are doing it one line of code at a time. In later sections we explain in detail how you determine what your code is doing once you are stepping through it.

Every code stepping feature in VBA has both a keyboard shortcut and a toolbar button equivalent. To become truly efficient at code debugging you **must** learn the keyboard shortcuts. For this reason we cover only the keyboard shortcuts required to initiate each technique. It is a simple matter to examine the VBE Debug toolbar and discover the equivalent toolbar buttons for each keyboard shortcut we discuss. You can display the VBE Debug toolbar by choosing *View > Toolbars > Debug* from the VBE menu. We provide a comprehensive list of debugging-related keyboard shortcuts at the end of the chapter.

Step Into (F8)

Stepping into code can be initiated in one of two ways. If you need to examine code execution from the beginning of an entry point procedure, you can place your cursor anywhere inside that procedure and press F8 to begin stepping through its code.

Alternatively, if you want to start your debugging session deeper in the procedure, or even deeper in the call stack, you can place a break point on the first line of code you want to debug and press F5. VBA will run your code until it reaches the break point. You can then use F8 to begin executing your code one line at a time from that point.

As you are stepping through your code, you will notice a yellow line that moves each time you execute one of the step commands. This line is called the ***execution point***. To make it easier to follow, the execution point displays an arrow in the margin indicator bar of the code module, as shown in Figure 16-3.

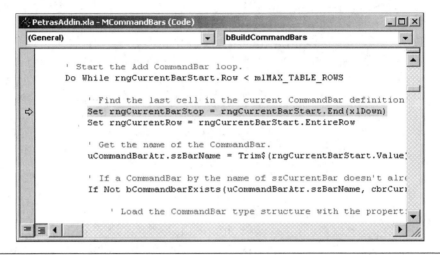

Figure 16-3 The Execution Point Indicator

The execution point indicator can be a bit confusing until you get used to it. It does not represent the line of code you have just executed; rather it shows the line of code that will be executed next. The line of code you just executed is the first executable line of code above the execution point indicator.

The reason VBA debugging works this way will become apparent as you gain experience debugging. Having a clear marker on the line of code that will be executed next tends to be much more valuable than having a marker on the line of code you just executed. The latter is easily determined from the former, but not necessarily vice versa.

With each press of the F8 key the line of code currently highlighted by the execution point indicator will be executed and the execution point indicator will move to the line of code that logically follows based on the results of executing the previous line. This may or may not be the next physical line of code depending on how your program is structured.

Step Over (Shift+F8)

While single stepping through code you will often reach calls to subprocedure that you are sure do not contain any errors. If you continue to press F8, code execution will step into the subprocedure and begin executing its code. What you would rather do in this case is have VBA execute all code associated with the subprocedure call and break again on the line of code that immediately follows it. This is accomplished using the Step Over command, whose keyboard shortcut is Shift+F8.

The Step Over command will execute all code required to pass over the line currently highlighted by the execution point indicator and then break on the next executable line of code that logically follows the result of that execution. If the line of code currently highlighted by the execution point indicator is not a call to an outside procedure, the Step Over command is logically equivalent to the Step Into command.

Step Out (Ctrl+Shift+F8)

If you step into a subprocedure call by accident or if you step into it on purpose and then realize you don't need to continue stepping through it, the Step Out command is your savior. Rather than having to tediously step through the rest of the subprocedure code or physically locate the calling procedure and use the Step To Cursor command described in the next section, you can just press Ctrl+Shift+F8. VBA will run the rest of the subprocedure automatically and break again on the next executable line of code in the calling procedure that logically follows the result of the subprocedure call.

Step to Cursor (Ctrl+F8)

This option would be more accurately called "run to cursor." Whether you are already in break mode or you are just initiating a debugging session, you can simply place your cursor on the line of code where you want execution to break and press the Ctrl+F8 keyboard shortcut. VBA will run your code from the beginning until it reaches the location of your cursor, at which point it will enter break mode. This option works almost exactly like placing a break point on the line. The only difference is that Step to Cursor is transient. As soon as you move the cursor, the step to cursor point changes.

This option is most useful when you are single stepping through your code and you encounter a section of code you are sure does not contain any errors. Just use the arrow keys to move the cursor down to the first exe-cutable line of code beyond this section and press Ctrl+F8. VBA will run all the code between the current execution point and the line marked by the cursor, entering break mode again at the line marked by the cursor. This enables you to avoid tediously single stepping through sections of code where it is not necessary.

Changing the Execution Point, or Set Next Statement (Ctrl+F9)

There are times when you want to either skip lines of code that are about to be executed or retrace the execution steps that got you to where you are. One of the most amazing things about the VBA debugger is that it enables you to do both of these things. You can move the execution point backward and forward as you please using the Set Next Statement command. The execution point can also be dragged to different positions using your mouse. After you have repositioned the execution point you can resume stepping through your code from that point using the commands covered in the previous section.

The difference between changing the execution point using the Set Next Statement command and the step commands that we have previous-ly covered is the following:

- If you reposition the execution point such that it skips lines of code that have not yet been executed, the lines you skipped *will not be executed*.
- If you reposition the execution point such that it resumes execution above the point where it is currently positioned, all of the lines of code between the new position of the execution point and the line of code directly above the previous position of the execution point will be executed *a second time*.

As you can imagine, you must have a very firm understanding of what your code does and where it makes sense to change the execution point to avoid spurious errors or garbage results. For example, if you skip a line of code that sets an object variable and then attempt to execute a line of code that uses the object variable, you will obviously get an "Object variable or with block variable not set" error. Similarly, if you move the execution point backward such that you rerun a block of code that increments a variable, the value of that variable will be incremented beyond the value it would normally reach, resulting in potentially garbage data.

The ability to change the execution point is a very valuable tool. It enables you to safely skip a section of code that you know would otherwise cause an error, or rerun a section of code that you would like to examine a second time without having to restart debugging. Just be sure you are fully aware of what you are doing before you use it.

The Immediate Window (Ctrl+G)

The Immediate window is an interactive debugging tool that is always available for you to use. To display the Immediate window in the VBE, press the Ctrl+G shortcut key, or choose *View > Immediate Window* from the VBE menu. You can do almost anything in the Immediate window that you can do in your VBA project, either at design time or while in break mode, including the following:

- Calling procedures
- Checking or changing the value of variables
- Instantiating and testing classes
- Running single-line loops

The Immediate window is the more powerful cousin of the most basic debugging technique of all; message box debugging. Message box debugging is typically the first debugging method you learn as a VBA programmer. It involves placing message boxes at various locations within your code, each of which display the values of one or more variables and/or location information. The Immediate window enables you to do everything you can do with message box debugging and much more, without the intrusive message boxes.

Debug.Print

The `Debug.Print` statement is the Immediate window's direct equivalent of message box debugging. The `Debug.Print` statement prints the value of the expression that follows it to the Immediate window. Two sample `Debug.Print` statements are shown in Listing 16-4.

Listing 16-4 Sample Debug.Print Statements

```
Dim sSheetTab As String
Dim wkbBook As Workbook

Set wkbBook = Application.ActiveWorkbook
sSheetTab = sSheetTabName(wkbBook, gsSHEET_TIME_ENTRY)

Debug.Print wkbBook.Name
Debug.Print sSheetTab
```

The results of these Debug.Print statements are shown in Figure 16-4.

Figure 16-4 Output From the Debug.Print Statements

As you can see, the output from each Debug.Print statement begins on a new line in the Immediate window. If you are familiar with VBA text I/O functions, note that the Debug.Print statement supports most of the same formatting features supported by the text I/O Print# statement.

It is uncommon to use extensively formatted output from the Debug.Print statement in the Immediate window, so we do not cover these features in any detail other than to say that you can include multiple expressions in a Debug.Print statement separated by commas and they will all be printed on the same line in the Immediate window separated by tabs.

Making the Best Use of the Immediate Window

There are two primary ways in which the Immediate window is used. It can be used as a simple collection point for the output of Debug.Print statements that post results as your code is running normally, or it can be used as an interactive tool while you are stepping through your code. There are two ways to use the immediate window interactively:

■ **To evaluate a variable or expression**—This is accomplished by entering a question mark character (?) followed by the variable or expression that you want to evaluate. The Immediate window is typically used for one-time evaluations. If you want to evaluate the variable or expression multiple times you should add a watch instead. We'll explain how to do this in *The Watch Window* section later in the chapter. Figure 16-5 shows the Immediate window being used to evaluate the value in a worksheet cell that is used in the next line of code to be executed in the module below it.

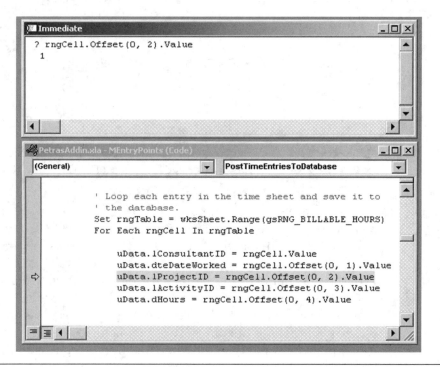

Figure 16-5 Using the Immediate Window to Evaluate an Expression

■ **To execute code**—This can include changing the value of variables that are currently being used in your application, modifying application settings, calling procedures in your code and almost anything else you could normally do in VBA. The only difference between evaluating expressions and executing code using the Immediate window is that you leave out the question mark when executing code. Placing your cursor anywhere within the line of code and pressing enter causes the line of code to be executed.

One common task involving code execution in the immediate window is modifying the value of the `Application.Cursor` property. During long-running VBA procedures, the Excel cursor will often flicker back and forth between an hourglass and the default pointer. This can be confusing to the user, so you force the cursor to display an hourglass at the beginning of the entry point procedure and reset it to its default at the end of the entry point procedure. The problem arises when you want to debug something within this procedure. Even in break mode the cursor setting you make is persistent, and it applies to the VBE as well as the Excel interface. The solution is to use the Immediate window to change the `Application.Cursor` property back to its default value, as shown in Figure 16-6.

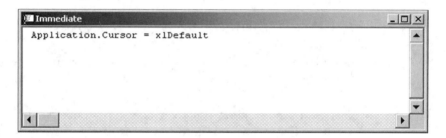

Figure 16-6 Executing a Line of Code in the Immediate Window

Another excellent example of the ability to execute code in the Immediate window is running loops that print out information. Anything you can fit on a single line can be run in the Immediate window and you can string multiple lines of VBA code together by separating them with the colon character (:). Figure 16-7 shows an example of running a loop that prints out the names of all open workbooks in the Immediate window.

Keep in mind that the Immediate window is fully functional even during design time. It's the perfect environment for testing specific lines of code you are unsure about. The Immediate window should become the most commonly used debugging tool in your arsenal.

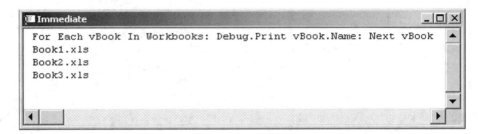

Figure 16-7 Executing a Loop in the Immediate Window

The Call Stack (Ctrl+L)

The call stack refers to the list of procedures that were executed to get you to the procedure you're currently executing in break mode. The call stack is important for two reasons:

1. It shows you the execution path that got you to where you are now. This is especially important when debugging procedures that are called from multiple places within your code. It also enables you to "walk" back up the procedure stack by simply selecting the specific procedure you are interested in.

2. If you want to know exactly which statements in each procedure in the call stack got you into the mess that you are currently debugging, press Ctrl+L to display the Call Stack window. Double-click the procedure name located directly below the name of the procedure you are currently in. The Call Stack window will bring you to the line of code in the procedure you double-clicked that called the procedure in which the error occurred. This process will enable you to continue walking back up the call stack until you reach the line of code in the entry point procedure where the problem call originated.

The Call Stack window is only available while executing code in break mode. A typical example of a Call Stack window you would encounter during break mode is shown in Figure 16-8.

Notice the procedure deepest in the stack is the first procedure listed and the entry point procedure is at the bottom of the list. When debugging procedures that display userforms you will see something a bit strange in the Call Stack window. An example is shown in Figure 16-9.

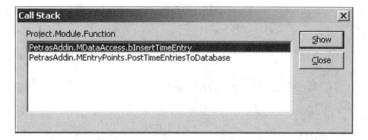

Figure 16-8 The Call Stack Window

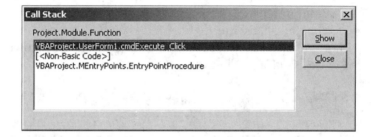

Figure 16-9 Non-Basic Code Entry in the Call Stack Window

The second entry, `[<Non-Basic Code>]`, is an indication that VBA had to perform an operation "under the covers," in this case showing the userform. You can step back and forth to procedures above and below this entry, but you cannot step into this entry because it represents a procedure that is not running within VBA.

The Watch Window

The Watch window is another amazingly multifunctional debugging tool provided by the VBE. Inexplicably, there is no direct keyboard shortcut available to display the Watch window. You can, however, use the standard Windows menu hotkey sequence Alt+V followed by an h character.

The Watch window is typically used to display the value of variables or expressions that you have specified while you are stepping through your code in break mode. But the Watch window contains two features that make it invaluable as a run-time debugging tool as well: *Break When Value*

Is True and *Break When Value Changes*. Both of these features are discussed at length later in this section. Unlike the Immediate window, the Watch window does not operate at design time.

Setting a Basic Watch

The most fundamental feature of the Watch window is its capability to show you the value of a variable or expression that you specify in real time while you are stepping through your code. Adding a watch is very easy, but inexplicably, it is another fundamentally important operation involving the Watch window that has no keyboard shortcut. Therefore, the easiest way to add a watch is to highlight the variable or expression that you want to watch, right-click the highlighted area and choose Add Watch from the shortcut menu. The process of adding a watch is shown in Figure 16-10, Figure 16-11 and Figure 16-12.

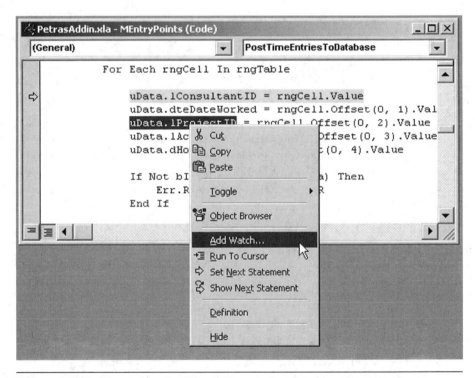

Figure 16-10 Specifying the Watch Expression

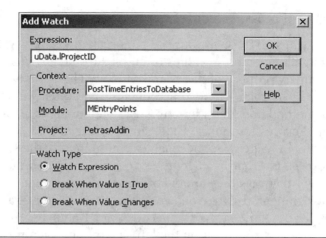

Figure 16-11 Configuring the Watch Expression

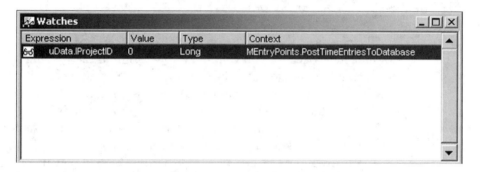

Figure 16-12 The Completed Watch Expression

The watch expression added is shown in Figure 16-12. This sequence assumes that you simply accepted all the default values in the Add Watch dialog shown in Figure 16-11. We discuss why and when you might want to change these defaults later in this section.

As you can see, the Watch window displays the expression being watched, the value of the expression, the data type of the expression and the code module and procedure name within which the watch was defined. You can add as many simultaneous watches as you like. Each watch will be shown on a separate line in the Watch window.

Using a Basic Watch

As you step through your code in break mode, the Watch window will continually update the values of all of the watches you've added. This is the primary purpose of the Watch window. There are typically a large number of things going on in your code and the Watch window provides you with a method to monitor exactly what's happening to all of the critical variables and expressions in the code you're debugging.

The Watch window enables you to modify the value of any variable or expression that is an ***lvalue***. An lvalue is just a fancy computer science term that says the variable or expression can appear on the left side of an assignment. In the following line of code, for example, the expression `Sheet1.Range("A1").Value` is an lvalue because it is valid for this expression to appear on the left side of the assignment operation, which in this case assigns it the value of 25:

```
Sheet1.Range("A1").Value = 25
```

By contrast, the expression `ThisWorkbook.Worksheets.Count` is not an lvalue because you cannot simply assign it a new value. It can only be changed by physically adding or removing worksheets in the workbook.

To modify the value of an lvalue expression in the Watch window, just click the Watch window Value column in the row containing the value you want to modify. The Value column entry will turn into an editable field and you can type in a new value. The new value must be a data type that is valid for the expression you are altering. Figure 16-13 shows us changing the value of the expression `Sheet1.Range("A1").Value` to 99.

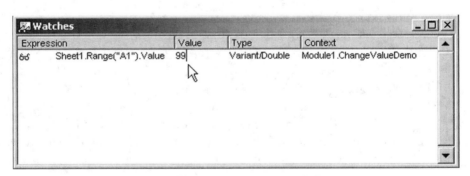

Figure 16-13 Modifying the Value of a Watch Expression

You can also edit the Expression column of the watch. In the case of Figure 16-13, for example, you could change the watch to point at `Range("B1")` instead of `Range("A1")`. Don't be too concerned about trying to determine what you're allowed to change. If you make a mistake, the VBE will display an error message and the Watch window will revert to its previous state. No harm done.

Watch Types

When you create a watch expression, you don't have to accept the default values of all the options in the Watch window. By modifying these defaults you can create watches that are much more powerful than those that simply use the default values.

There are two option categories that you can modify when you add a watch: *Watch Context* and *Watch Type*. We cover them both in following sections. Don't worry if you don't get the values of these options correct when you first add the watch. You can edit any existing watch, which allows you to modify these options. The steps required to edit a watch are shown in Figure 16-14 and Figure 16-15.

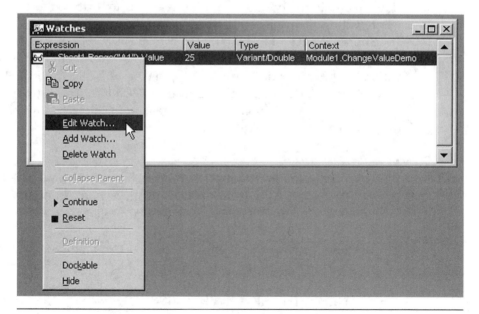

Figure 16-14 Right-Click over a Watch Expression to Edit It

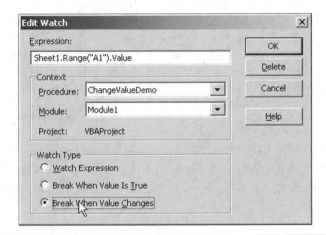

Figure 16-15 Change the Watch Type to Break When Value Changes

Watch Context

The Watch Context options control the scope of the watch expression. Watches can be confined to code executing within a single procedure in a single module (the typical default) or they can apply to code executing any-where within the project.

Suppose, for example, you want to place a watch on a global variable or expression. If you simply add a watch on that variable or expression from within the first procedure where you come across it, the watch will only be valid when code is executing within the procedure where the watch was added. To change this, you change the selections in the two *Watch Context* drop-downs.

Module

We are going to discuss the *Watch Context* options in reverse order of their appearance on the Watch dialog because the *Module* setting drives the *Procedure* setting. You have two options when selecting a *Module* setting:

1. **Select a Specific Module**—All standard modules, class modules, userform modules and document object modules in the current project are available to be selected. When you select a specific module, the values available in the *Procedure* setting will be nar-rowed down to only the procedures that exist within the module you selected. The scope of the watch will then be determined by the value you select in the *Procedure* drop-down.

2. **Select the (All Modules) Value**—This is the first value in the *Module* drop-down. When you select this value, the value of the *Procedure* drop-down will automatically change to the corresponding (All Procedures) value. When you make this selection, the scope of the watch will be global. The Watch window will attempt to evaluate it no matter where code is currently executing within the project.

Procedure

The *Procedure* setting determines what procedure the watch expression will be valid for within the module specified by the *Module* setting. As described above, if the *Module* setting value is (All Modules), then you have no choice over the *Procedure* setting. In this case, its only possible value will be (All Procedures). If a specific code module has been selected in the *Module* setting, there are two options for the *Procedure* setting:

1. **Select the Name of a Specific Procedure**—In this case, the watch expression will only be evaluated when code is executing within the specified procedure or one of the subprocedures called from that procedure. If code is executing in some unrelated procedure, even if it is contained within the same module, the value displayed by the Watch window for the watch expression will be "<Out of context>".

2. **Select the (All Procedures) Value**—Selecting this value means the scope of the watch will be all procedures within the module specified by the *Module* setting. Whenever code is executing within that module, the Watch window will attempt to evaluate the watch. When code is executing within a different module the watch value will display "<Out of context>". The only exception is if code execution reached a different module as the result of a call to a subprocedure originating in the module where the watch was created. In that case the watch will continue to evaluate normally.

Watch Type

The *Watch Type* setting will determine how the Watch window handles the watch. The first option is passive, used only while stepping through code in break mode. The second two options are active and are used to initiate break mode.

Watch Expression

This is the default value for the *Watch Type* setting. It just adds the specified variable or expression as a watch and displays its value while you are stepping through your code in break mode.

Break When Value Is True

This *Watch Type* setting has much in common with the Excel conditional formatting expressions we discussed in *Chapter 3 — Excel and VBA Development Best Practices*. When you specify this watch type, your watch is treated as a Boolean expression and code execution will stop and enter break mode whenever the value of the expression changes from False to True or <out of context> to True.

This type of watch can be constructed as either a Boolean expression or a simple watch expression whose only possible values are True or False. Regardless of the way in which you construct the watch, code execution will stop and enter break mode whenever the value of the watch evaluates to True.

One very common use for this *Watch Type* setting is somewhat counterintuitive but very valuable in practice. The `Application.EnableEvents` property is persistent from the time it is set to False until it is explicitly set to True or Excel is closed, which ever comes first. While this property is False, all Excel events are disabled. One of the most frequent Excel programming bugs is to set `Application.EnableEvents` to False and then forget to set it back to True when you no longer need to disable events. This will obviously cause havoc in any application that depends on trapping Excel events for its operation.

We can very easily debug this problem by telling the Watch window to break code execution whenever the `Application.EnableEvents` property ***does not*** equal True. If the `Application.EnableEvents` property does not equal True, by definition it has been set to False. After you have set this watch, each time code execution breaks you know you have turned off Excel events. You can then examine the code that follows and ensure that `Application.EnableEvents` has been properly reset. We demonstrate setting this watch expression in Figure 16-16.

Note that the watch expression we have defined is `Application.EnableEvents <> True`. When this expression evaluates to True, it means that `Application.EnableEvents` has been set to False. (If `Application.EnableEvents` does not equal True, it must be False.) Also note that we have set the *Context* of this watch to (All Procedures) and (All Modules). This is because the `Application.EnableEvents` property is global to the current instance of Excel, regardless of where it has been set.

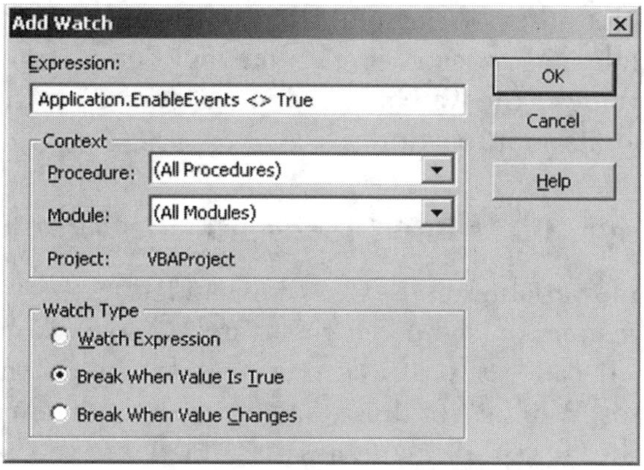

Figure 16-16 Setting a Break When Value Is True Watch

Break When Value Changes

Another common situation you want to watch for is when the value of an expression or variable in your code changes. In this case you are typically not concerned about the specific value to which your variable or expression changed, rather you want code execution to break whenever that value changes to anything other than its current value.

This type of watch can be constructed as either a Boolean expression or a simple watch expression. Regardless of how you construct the watch, code execution will stop and enter break mode whenever the value of the expression changes. In Figure 16-17 we set a watch that will cause code execution to stop and enter break mode whenever the value of the expression `Sheet1.Range("A1").Value` changes.

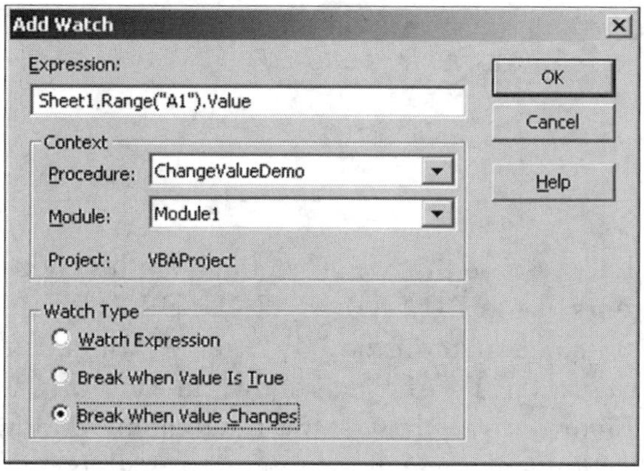

Figure 16-17 Setting a Break When Value Changes Expression

Note that we have set the *Context* settings for this watch to a specific module and procedure. This means code execution will only break when the value of the watch expression is changed by the specified procedure or one of its subprocedures.

Arrays, UDTs and Classes in the Watch Window

Simple variables and expressions added to the Watch window are easy to understand on sight. But the Watch window is much more powerful than this. It can easily handle complex data types such as arrays, UDTs and classes. Watches for these data types are added in exactly the same way that watches for simple variables are added, but the results are quite different.

Recall that in *Chapter 13 — Programming with Databases* we created a BILLABLE_HOURS UDT to hold information about a billable hour entry from our timesheet application. Listing 16-5 shows a section of code from the PostTimeEntriesToDatabase procedure that uses this UDT.

Listing 16-5 Code That Uses the BILLABLE_HOURS UDT

```
Dim uData As BILLABLE_HOUR

For Each rngCell In rngTable

    uData.lConsultantID = rngCell.Value
    uData.dteDateWorked = rngCell.Offset(0, 1).Value
    uData.lProjectID = rngCell.Offset(0, 2).Value
    uData.lActivityID = rngCell.Offset(0, 3).Value
    uData.dHours = rngCell.Offset(0, 4).Value

    If Not bInsertTimeEntry(uData) Then
        Err.Raise glHANDLED_ERROR
    End If

Next rngCell
```

Let's assume that we are debugging this code and we want to watch the contents of the BILLABLE_HOURS UDT. There's no need to add each individual element of the UDT to the Watch window. Just add a watch on the uData UDT variable as shown in Figure 16-18.

Figure 16-19 shows how the Watch window displays a UDT watch expression when you are stepping through code.

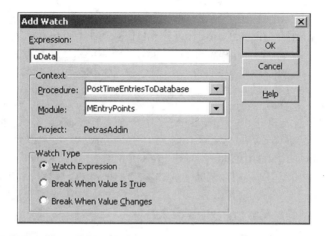

Figure 16-18 Adding a Watch on a UDT Variable

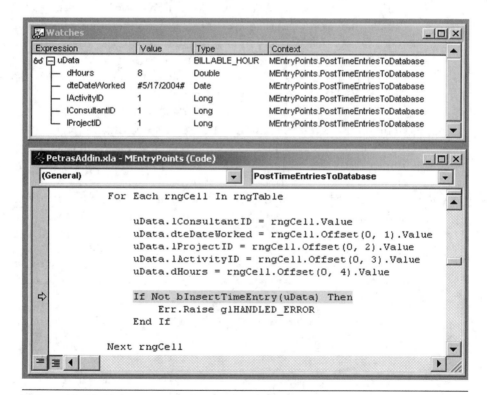

Figure 16-19 Using a Watch on a UDT Variable

Even though we only added a watch to the uData variable, the Watch window understands this is a UDT and it displays the member variables of the UDT in a hierarchical list below the variable the watch was defined on.

Array variables and objects variables are treated the same way. The Watch window recognizes their data types and displays the current values of all their members in a hierarchical list similar to that shown in Figure 16-19. This is a great way to learn the object model of the application you're working with. Set a watch on an object variable, trigger break mode once that variable has been set and then use the Watch window to drill down through that object's properties and child collections.

Quick Watch (Shift+F9)

The Quick Watch window is the little brother of the Watch window. By highlighting a variable or expression while in break mode and pressing Shift+F9, the Quick Watch window allows you to examine all the same details that would be displayed by the Watch window except for the data type. The Quick Watch window also allows you to quickly add the selected variable or expression to the Watch window by invoking the Add button (Alt+A). Figure 16-20 shows an example of the Quick Watch window being used to display the contents of a string variable.

The Quick Watch window is designed for hands-on-the-keyboard debugging. If you're using the mouse, in most cases the Quick Watch window will be unnecessary. This is because the VBE will dynamically display the value of most expressions in a tooltip when you hover your mouse cursor over them. This behavior is shown in Figure 16-21.

Even if you do make use of the tooltip expression evaluation feature, remember how to use the Quick Watch window. You will come across many expressions that just won't be evaluated by the tooltip feature. To see the value of these expressions, you'll need to use the Quick Watch window.

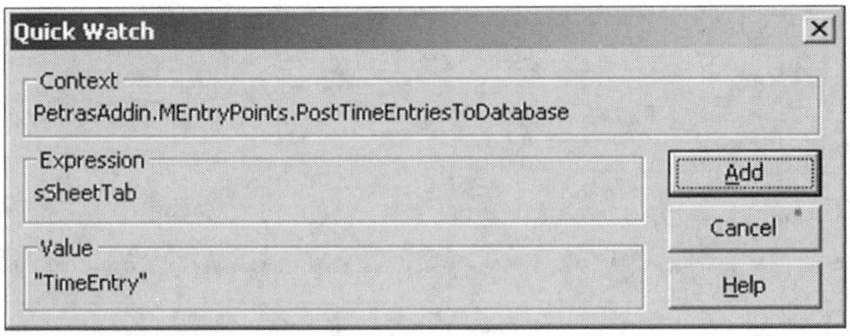

Figure 16-20 The Quick Watch Window

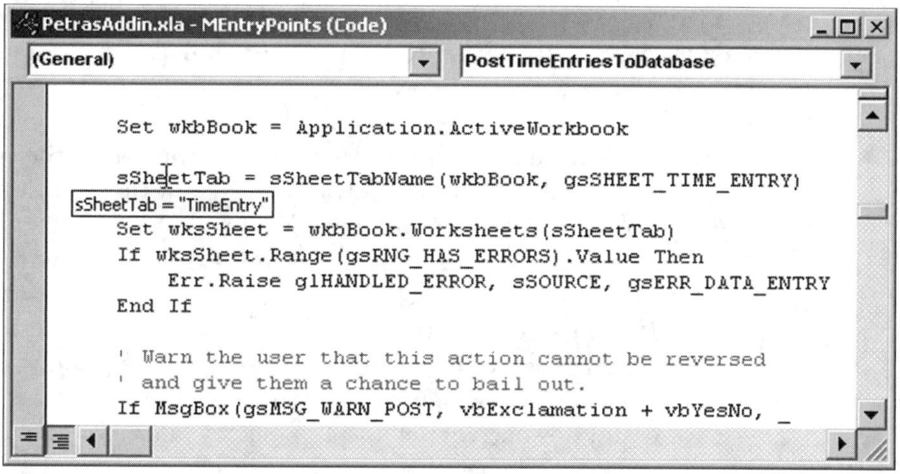

Figure 16-21 Tooltip Expression Evaluation

The Locals Window

The Locals window is another valuable debugging tool closely related to the Watch window that also inexplicably has no built-in keyboard shortcut that can be used to display it. In place of that you can use the standard menu hotkey sequence Alt+V followed by an s character.

The Locals window can be thought of as a specialized version of the Watch window that automatically displays the names, values and data types of all variables and constants that are local to the procedure currently being executed. The Locals window for our debugging session in the PostTimeEntriesToDatabase procedure is shown in Figure 16-22.

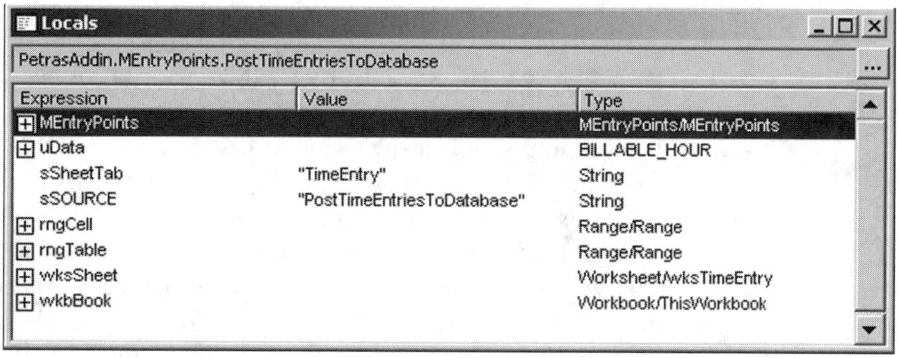

Figure 16-22 The Locals Window in Action

Like the Watch window, you can use the Locals window to change the value of any variable in the watch list. There are also two unique features provided by the Locals window:

1. **Quick access to the call stack**—The button in the upper-right corner of the Locals window directly below the X-close button will display the call stack window and allow you to change the scope of the variables being displayed in the Locals window to any other procedure in the call stack.
2. **The Module Variables entry**—If you look closely at the first line in the Locals window, you'll see that it has the same name as the module within which the current procedure is executing. If you expand this entry it will display a list of values for all module-level variables and constants.

The Object Browser (F2)

Probably the most overlooked and underused tool in the VBA programmer's arsenal is the Object Browser. This is unfortunate, because it is also one of the most important. The Object Browser is your window into the contents of the object libraries you're working with. For every object library marked under the VBE *Tools > References* menu, the Object Browser displays all of the objects, methods, properties, constants and enumerations supported by that object library.

In addition to simply displaying these items, the Object Browser displays a brief description of the syntax required to use each item with hyperlinks to other items where applicable. For constants and enumerations, the Object Browser displays the actual numeric value of the constant or enumeration.

The VBA help system is also directly linked to the object browser. If you need further explanation of some object, property or method you're looking at, you can just select the name of the item in the Object Browser and press F1 to bring up its help topic. (Specific constants and enumerations are rarely associated with help topics.)

The Object Browser is packed with so many useful features that it could almost warrant a chapter in its own right. We cover the most commonly used features of the Object Browser in this section. An example of the Object Browser being used to display information about the ADO object library is shown in Figure 16-23.

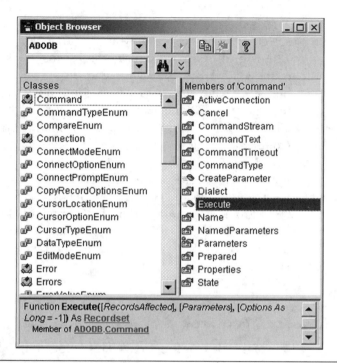

Figure 16-23 The VBE Object Browser

Basic Features

The most commonly used features of the Object Browser window itself are the following:

- **The Object Library Box**—This is the drop-down in the upper-left corner of the Object Library window. It determines which object library will be displayed in the Object Browser. The Object Library Box contains one entry for every referenced object library in the currently active project, one entry for the currently active project itself and a default <All Libraries> entry that causes the Object Browser to display all of the contents of all of the referenced libraries as well as the current project in one big heap. We recommend trying to narrow down the object library you want to examine by selecting it in this drop-down. Having everything displayed all at once makes any one thing difficult to locate.
- **The Classes List**—This is the list that runs down the left side of the Object Browser window. Its name is a bit of a misnomer because it displays modules, constants and enumerations in addition to classes.

This is the second level of detail you will look through after you've selected the object library you want to look in.

- **The Members List**—This is the list that runs down the right side of the Object Browser window. It displays a complete list of members for whatever item is selected in the Classes List. For example, in Figure 16-23 the Command object has been selected in the Classes List, so the Members List displays all the members of the Command object.

- **The Details Window**—This is the window that occupies the bottom of the Object Browser. It provides a description of the item that is currently selected in the Members List. For example, in Figure 16-23 the Execute method of the Command object has been selected in the Members List. The Details window provides a brief description of the syntax of this method with hyperlinks to related items in the object library.

Advanced Features

- **The Search Combo Box**—This is the combo box located directly below the Object Library drop-down. Using the Search combo box you can look for all occurrences of a given term within the object library or libraries currently selected in the Object Library Box. Just type the term you want to search for in the search combo box and click the Search button (the toolbar button that looks like a pair of binoculars). In Figure 16-24, for example, we've searched for all occurrences of the term ActiveConnection within the ADO object library.

- **Show Hidden Members**—It may come as a surprise, but many elements of every object library are hidden from the default Object Browser view. There can be several reasons for this: the hidden features might not be usable from VBA, the hidden features might not be implemented at all, or the hidden features might be older features that Microsoft would like to discourage you from using. This last reason is why we can thank the Microsoft development team for providing us a way to make these hidden features visible. Sometimes these older features are useful, even necessary, for top-quality Excel development. Just don't expect to find any help topics linked to these hidden features. Figure 16-25 shows an excellent example of the value of the Show Hidden Members feature.

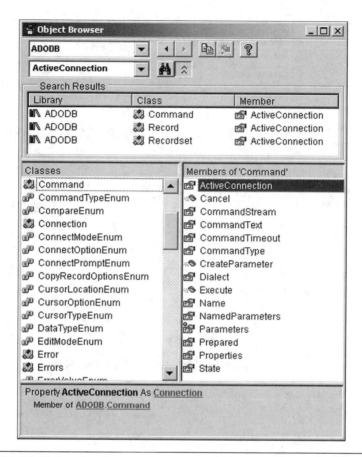

Figure 16-24 Using the Search Feature of the Object Browser

Notice that some of the items in the list are colored in very light gray. These are the hidden members that are revealed when you select the Show Hidden Members option. As discussed in *Chapter 4 — Worksheet Design*, the controls from the Forms toolbar are often the best choice for use of controls on worksheets. Unfortunately, these controls date back prior to the Excel 97 era and even though they are fully supported by VBA it is not obvious how to find information on them unless you have a copy of Excel 5 or 95 running on a spare computer. As shown in Figure 16-25, by using the Object Browser's shortcut menu you can display these hidden objects to learn more about them.

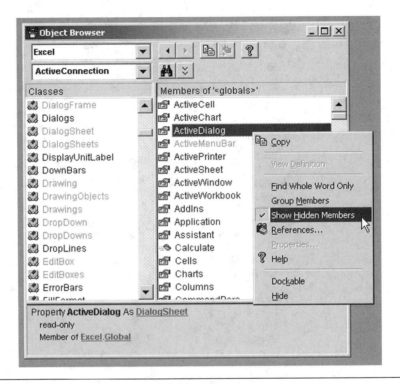

Figure 16-25 Turning On Show Hidden Members

Creating and Running a Test Harness

As discussed in the *Functional Decomposition* section of *Chapter 3 — Excel and VBA Development Best Practices*, you should strive to break your application into as many single-purpose, reusable procedures as possible. After you've done this, however, you need to verify that these procedures work under all circumstances. Testing them manually within your application is tedious, time-consuming and not very thorough.

The proper way to test a procedure is to write a wrapper procedure that calls the procedure to be tested in a loop, passing it all possible combinations of arguments and verifying the results to ensure that they are correct. This wrapper procedure is called a ***test harness*** and we show you how to build one in this section. The workbook containing the procedures we're about to demonstrate is called TestHarnessDemo.xls and is located on the CD in the *\Concepts\Ch16—VBA Debugging* folder.

One frequently useful single-purpose procedure takes a full path and filename string and breaks it into its path and filename components, optionally returning one or both to the calling procedure. The ReturnPathAndFilename procedure shown in Listing 16-6 does this.

NOTE: Because of its use of the VBA InStrRev function, which was first introduced in Excel 2000, the ReturnPathAndFilename procedure will not work in Excel 97.

Listing 16-6 The ReturnPathAndFilename Procedure

```
Public Sub ReturnPathAndFilename(ByRef sFullName As String, _
                        Optional ByRef sPath As String, _
                        Optional ByRef sFile As String)
    Dim lPosition As Long
    lPosition = InStrRev(sFullName, "\")
    sPath = Left$(sFullName, lPosition)
    sFile = Mid$(sFullName, lPosition + 1)
End Sub
```

To verify that this procedure works as expected we need to create a test harness that feeds it large numbers of full path and filename strings and then concatenates the returned split path and filename values and verifies that the specified file exists. If the split is performed incorrectly on any test string, we know there is a bug in the procedure that needs to be fixed. The test harness that performs this operation is shown in Listing 16-7.

Listing 16-7 The Test Harness for the ReturnPathAndFilename Procedure

```
Public Sub TestHarness()

    Dim bSuccess As Boolean
    Dim objSearch As FileSearch
    Dim lCount As Long
    Dim sFullName As String
    Dim sPath As String
    Dim sFilename As String

    ' Use the FileSearch object to get a large number of full
```

```
' path and filename strings to use as test data.
Application.StatusBar = "Retrieving test data..."
Set objSearch = Application.FileSearch
objSearch.NewSearch
objSearch.LookIn = "E:\"
objSearch.SearchSubFolders = True
objSearch.FileType = msoFileTypeExcelWorkbooks

If objSearch.Execute() > 0 Then

    ' Assume the test succeeded until something goes wrong.
    bSuccess = True

    ' Run each path and filename returned by the FileSearch
    ' object through our ReturnPathAndFilename.
    ' Then concatenate the results and verify that they
    ' refer to a valid file.
    For lCount = 1 To objSearch.FoundFiles.Count
        sFullName = objSearch.FoundFiles(lCount)
        Application.StatusBar = "Checking: " & sFullName
        ReturnPathAndFilename sFullName, sPath, sFilename
        If Len(Dir$(sPath & sFilename)) = 0 Then
            ' Combining the path and filename returned by
            ' the ReturnPathAndFilename procedure resulted
            ' in an invalid file specification.
            Debug.Print "Bad split: ", sPath, sFilename
            bSuccess = False
        End If
    Next lCount

    Application.StatusBar = False

    If bSuccess Then
        MsgBox "All tests succeeded."
    Else
        MsgBox "Failures encountered. " & _
            "See list in the Immediate window."
    End If

Else
    MsgBox "No matching files found."
End If

End Sub
```

In the TestHarness procedure we use the FileSearch object to create a large array of full path and filename strings. We loop this array and feed each of these strings to the ReturnPathAndFilename procedure. We then concatenate the path and filename returned by the procedure and verify that it refers to a valid file. If any full path and filename strings are split incorrectly, we print the results to the Immediate window and display an error message upon completion. Otherwise we display a success message.

Using this technique, you can run thousands of full path and filename strings through the function and verify that it handles them correctly in a very short period of time. Verifying as many procedures as possible using the test harness approach should be considered a best programming practice.

Using Assertions

Assertions are a way to guarantee that one or more specific conditions hold true. They can be used to test the validity of variables or expressions at specific points within your program. In VBA programming, assertions are implemented with the Debug.Assert method. The Debug.Assert method takes a Boolean expression as its single argument. If the value of the expression is False, Debug.Assert causes code execution to halt and enter break mode on the line of code where the assertion failed.

Assertions created using Debug.Assert ignore the global error trapping setting defined under the VBE *Tools > Options > General > Error Trapping* menu. A Debug.Assert statement will cause code execution to enter break mode regardless of the global error trapping setting. Listing 16-8 shows an example of Debug.Assert in use.

Listing 16-8 Debug.Assert Example

```
Sub DebugAssertExample()

    Dim lRow As Long
    Dim lColumn As Long

    ' Some code here that sets lRow and lColumn.

    Debug.Assert (lRow > 0) And (lColumn > 0)

    Sheet1.Cells(lRow, lColumn).Value = True

End Sub
```

In this example, we are using two variables to store the row and column number that specifies the Range we access using the Cells method in the last line of code. Because both the row and column number must be greater than zero, we use the `Debug.Assert` statement to halt program execution if either one of them fails this test.

Note that we are able to string two related Boolean tests into a single `Debug.Assert` expression. You can link as many related tests into the same assertion as you want. We recommend, however, that unrelated assertions get separate lines of code. This simplifies the logic of debugging, especially in cases where you may be experiencing multiple errors.

Assertions are especially valuable when debugging intermittent errors or errors that are difficult to reproduce. If you can narrow down the section of code where the error is occurring, you can simply place assertions on all of the important variables and expressions used in that section of code. You then run the program normally, trying various combinations of things until one of your assertions fails and halts your program.

Keep in mind that `Debug.Assert` is purely a debugging tool. It should not be used to test conditions that require validation each time your program runs. For example, if your application needs a specific file to function correctly, you should code a check for that file in your Auto_Open procedure. This is called a ***permanent assertion***, because it is always performed. A permanent assertion is different from the kind created using the `Debug.Assert` statement because it throws a runtime error that can be handled by your project error handling system. An example of this is shown in the excerpt from our PetrasAddin.xla workbook's Auto_Open procedure in Listing 16-9.

Listing 16-9 A Permanent Assertion

```
' Make sure we can locate our time entry workbook before we
' do anything else.
If Len(Dir$(gsAppDir & gsFILE_TIME_ENTRY)) = 0 Then _
    Err.Raise glHANDLED_ERROR, sSOURCE, gsERR_FILE_NOT_FOUND
```

This permanent assertion verifies that we can locate our time entry template workbook and throws a custom error if we can't. Our program can never run properly without its accompanying time-entry template, so this check should be performed whenever the application is run.

Debugging Shortcut Keys that Every Developer Should Know

As with most programming tasks, the fewer times you take your hands off the keyboard during debugging the faster and more productive you will be in the long term. With that in mind, what follows is a list of the most useful debugging-related keyboard shortcuts.

General

F5—Run: Runs the procedure within which the cursor is currently located. If the cursor is not currently located within a procedure that can be run directly, or if the cursor is not located within any procedure, the VBE will prompt you with the Macros dialog, which displays a list of procedures that can be run. If you are already in break mode, F5 will run your code to the next break point or to completion, whichever comes first.

F9—Toggle break point: Toggles between setting and removing a break point on the line of code occupied by the cursor. See the section on *Using Break Points* above for more details on how to effectively use break points.

Ctrl+Shift+F9—Clear all break points: If you have set a number of break points in your code and then corrected the error you were looking for, you may simply want to remove all break points from your code so that you can run it normally and verify your fix. You can quickly remove all break points from your code by pressing Ctrl+Shift+F9.

Ctrl+G—Display the Immediate window: What would be really helpful would be to have a shortcut key, or any simple method for that matter, for clearing the contents of the Immediate window. Unfortunately, no such feature is provided in VBA. In the *Tools* folder of the accompanying CD we provide a link to a freeware add-in called MZTools that offers this feature along with a host of other useful VBE utilities.

Debug Mode Code Execution

F8—Step into: When in break mode, this key enables you to step through your code one line at a time. If you are not in break mode but your cursor is within a valid entry point procedure, code execution will begin and break mode will start on the first line of that procedure.

Shift+F8—Step over: When in break mode, this will step completely over the next line of code to be executed. Whether that line is a simple statement or a complex nested function call, Shift+F8 will execute all the code required to step over the line and resume break mode at the next breakable position.

Ctrl+Shift+F8—Step out of: If you have stepped into a called procedure and determined that what you are looking for is not there, you don't have to continue single stepping through the rest of the procedure to get back out of it. Ctrl+Shift+F8 will tell VBA to finish executing the procedure you are in and will resume break mode on the first breakable line immediately following the call that brought you into the procedure.

Ctrl+F8—Step to cursor: During debugging, you will often encounter a group of statements that you do not need to examine carefully. Rather than single stepping through them, you can place your cursor at the beginning of the next line of code you would like to step through and press Ctrl+F8. VBA will run all the lines of code between your current position and the point where you placed the cursor, then stop and resume break mode at the line where you placed the cursor.

Ctrl+F9—Set next statement: When you are single-step debugging your code, you may see a section that you would like to skip altogether. To do so, just move the cursor down to the next line you want executed and press Ctrl+F9. VBA will skip all the lines of code between the current execution point and resume break mode on the line specified by your cursor position.

Navigation

Shift+F2—Procedure definition: When you place your cursor within the name of a procedure and press this shortcut, you will be taken to the definition of that procedure.

Ctrl+Shift+F2—Last position: This shortcut is the reverse of Shift+F2. It brings you back to the position within your code where you were when you pressed Shift+F2.

Information

Ctrl+L—Call Stack: This shortcut displays the Call Stack window so you can see how you got to the procedure where you're currently located in a deeply nested section of code.

Shift+F9—Quick Watch: This displays the Quick Watch dialog, which displays the context (scope) of the expression you selected, the expression itself and the value of the expression.

F2—Object Browser: This displays the Object Browser.

Conclusion

Excellent debugging skills are one of the primary attributes that separate the professional programmer from the skilled amateur. In this chapter we have covered the vast array of debugging tools and techniques that you have at your disposal in the VBA environment. If ever there were an aspect of programming to which the old adage "practice makes perfect" applies, it is surely debugging. All the dedicated debugging tools described here notwithstanding, the practice of debugging is just as much art as science.

Learning these tools is a starting point, but you must debug a significant amount of real-world code, ideally not all of it your own, before you become truly proficient. Many people have remarked to us, and we believe it to be true, that you learn more from debugging mistakes than you do from getting it right the first time. So go forth and debug!

Optimizing VBA Performance

A common complaint about VBA in general, and particularly routines that automate Excel, is poor performance. Although there is some truth in that, say when compared to C++, it is very often due to poorly structured or poorly written code. This is probably because VBA makes it very easy to write code that works, but quite difficult to write code that works fast. As a general rule, the speed of a well-optimized routine can often be an order of magnitude faster than the original code, and improvements of two orders of magnitude are not uncommon. This chapter explains how to achieve those savings.

Measuring Performance

The end users of your application are the final arbiters of performance, and they rarely use stopwatches to time how long something takes. Instead, they form an impression based on their expectations, past experiences, visual cues and the activity they're performing. As a general guideline, we aim to keep within the times shown in Table 17-1.

Table 17-1 Target Response Times

Action	Response Time
Displaying a simple form	< 2 seconds
Displaying a complex form	< 20 seconds
Selecting items within a form	< 1 second
Typing within a form	Unnoticeable
Preparing a simple report	< 10 seconds
Preparing a complex report	< 30 seconds

All these targets relate to the user experience, so must be checked using a PC similar to the average users' specification. Note also the difference between a "simple" form or report and a "complex" one is purely the users' perception and need not have any relationship to the technical complexity.

Hopefully, you'll find most of the routines you write perform well within these targets, even with the largest data sets they're likely to encounter, so there is little point trying to optimize them. Undoubtedly, though, there will be some that take much, much longer, and they're the ones that will give your application a poor reputation. Radically improving the slowest routines will often give the impression the application is more responsive overall. The rest of this chapter explains the steps that can be taken to achieve massive improvements in the performance of your slowest routines.

After you've optimized the application as much as you can, there are a few tricks you can use to make it seem to perform better—even though it might not be doing so:

- If a routine takes more than about a second, change the cursor to an hourglass at the start of it and back to normal at the end. This tricks users into expecting a delay and they're pleasantly surprised when it finishes quickly.
- If a routine is triggered by the user typing into a text box, never show an hourglass. Showing an hourglass tells the user you expect the routine to be lengthy and no routines triggered by text box Change events should have a noticeable delay.
- If a routine takes more than about five seconds, display a progress bar (such as the ones shown in *Chapter 10 — Userform Design and Best Practices* and *Chapter 11 — Interfaces*) prominently on the screen. A progress bar which quickly reaches 100 percent gives the impression of speed, while a progress bar for a lengthy routine lets users know the routine is advancing, lets them estimate how long there is left and gives them something to concentrate on, and so makes the time seem to go quicker than just staring at an hourglass.

The PerfMon Utility

The PerfMon utility is a set of three DLLs that enable us to monitor and record the performance of a VBA application as it is executing. It achieves this by adding a line of code to the top and bottom of every procedure to notify the monitoring DLL when the procedure starts and finishes. The DLL records the number of times each procedure is called and the maximum, total and average time spent in each. The result is a complete list of all the procedures called and the detailed timings for each, either copied to the clipboard or saved to a text file. Once imported into an Excel worksheet and sorted by total time, the result looks something like Figure 17-1.

	A	B	C	D	E	F	G
1	Tot Dur	11.24252					
2							
3	Project	Module	Proc	Count	Total	Avg	Max
4	prjChapter17	MPerfMon	AlengthyRoutine2	1	11.12998	11.12998	11.12998
5	prjChapter17	MPerfMon	AlengthyRoutine1	1	0.11243	0.11243	0.11243
6	prjChapter17	MPerfMon	AlengthyRoutine	1	0.00009	0.00009	0.00009
7							

Figure 17-1 An Example of the PerfMon Results

We can immediately see the first procedure accounts for nearly the entire processing time and is therefore where we should focus our optimization efforts.

The setup program for the PerfMon utility can be found in the *Tools*\ *Performance Monitor* directory on the CD and installs the following DLLs:

- **PerfMonitor.dll**—An ActiveX DLL that uses the Windows high-performance counter to track the performance of each routine. It is listed in the *Project > References* dialog as *PerfMon: VB/VBA Performance Monitor*.
- **PerfMonOffice.dll**—An add-in for the Office VBE to add and remove the calls to the PerfMonitor DLL.
- **PerfMonVB6.dll**—An add-in for the VB6 IDE to add and remove the calls to the PerfMonitor DLL.

The setup program also installs the *CPerfMon.cls* file, which is a class module that can be included in a VB6 project to enable cross-process performance monitoring for use during development of combined Excel/VB6 solutions (see *Chapter 20 — Combining Excel and Visual Basic 6*).

To start using the utility, click on *Addins > PerfMon > Add PerfMon Calls* and select which procedures to add the calls to, as shown in Figure 17-2.

When you click OK, the utility will add a reference to the PerfMonitor DLL and add calling code to the top and bottom of the selected routine(s), as shown in Listing 17-1.

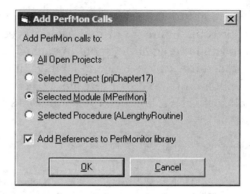

Figure 17-2 The Add PerfMon Calls Dialog

Listing 17-1 A Procedure with the Automatic PerfMon Calls Added

```
Sub ALengthyRoutine()
  PerfMonProcStart "PrjChapter17.MPerfMon.AlengthyRoutine"

  'Do something lengthy

  PerfMonProcEnd "PrjChapter17.MPerfMon.AlengthyRoutine"
End Sub
```

Note that every procedure is given a unique ID, being the concatenation of the project name, module name, procedure name and property type (if it is a property procedure). If you have a particularly long procedure that would be better monitored in separate blocks, extra PerfMon calls can be added manually, taking care to match the ProcStart and ProcEnd calls, as shown in Listing 17-2.

Listing 17-2 A Procedure with Manual PerfMon Calls Added

```
Sub ALengthyRoutine()
  PerfMonProcStart "PrjChapter17.MPerfMon.AlengthyRoutine"

  PerfMonProcStart "PrjChapter17.MPerfMon.AlengthyRoutine1"
  'Do something lengthy
  PerfMonProcEnd "PrjChapter17.MPerfMon.AlengthyRoutine1"

  PerfMonProcStart "PrjChapter17.MPerfMon.AlengthyRoutine2"
  'Do something else lengthy
```

```
PerfMonProcEnd "PrjChapter17.MPerfMon.AlengthyRoutine2"

  PerfMonProcEnd "PrjChapter17.MPerfMon.AlengthyRoutine"
End Sub
```

The last thing to do is to add a line to tell the utility when to start and stop monitoring, as shown in Listing 17-3.

Listing 17-3 Include the Calls to Start and Stop the Monitoring

```
Sub ALengthyRoutine()

  'Start monitoring all procedures from here
  PerfMonStartMonitoring

  PerfMonProcStart "PrjChapter17.MPerfMon.AlengthyRoutine"

  PerfMonProcStart "PrjChapter17.MPerfMon.AlengthyRoutine1"
  'Do something lengthy
  PerfMonProcEnd "PrjChapter17.MPerfMon.AlengthyRoutine1"

  PerfMonProcStart "PrjChapter17.MPerfMon.AlengthyRoutine2"
  'Do something else lengthy
  PerfMonProcEnd "PrjChapter17.MPerfMon.AlengthyRoutine2"

  PerfMonProcEnd "PrjChapter17.MPerfMon.AlengthyRoutine"

  'Stop monitoring and write the results to a file
  'If no file name given, the results will be put on the clipboard
  PerfMonStopMonitoring "c:\MyRoutineTiming.txt"

End Sub
```

The easiest way to analyze the results is to start a new Excel session, click *Data > Get External Data > Import Text File* (Excel 2000) or *Data > Import External Data > Import Data* (Excel XP/2003), select the text file that you gave in the PerfMonStopMonitoring call and click through the Text Import Wizard. It is better to import the data instead of just opening the file, because the latter locks the file and the PerfMon monitor will not then be able to overwrite it with new results for each subsequent run. We can also set the import to use the same filename each time, allowing us to re-import the new results by clicking the Refresh button, shown in Figure 17-3.

	A	B	C	D	E	F	G
1	Tot Dur	11.24252					
2							
3	Project	Module	Proc	Count	Total	Avg	Max
4	prjChapter17	MPerfMon	AlengthyRoutine2	1	11.12998	11.12998	11.12998
5	prjChapter17	MPerfMon	AlengthyRoutine1	1	0.11243	0.11243	0.11243
6	prjChapter17	MPerfMon	AlengthyRoutine	1	0.00009	0.00009	0.00009
7							
8				External Data			
9							
10					Refresh Data		
11							

Figure 17-3 Importing the File Allows Us to Quickly Refresh the Data to Get the New Results

All the timings shown in the results table are in seconds, with an accuracy of at least the millisecond. Note, though, the monitoring calls themselves take a small amount of time, so the results shown will typically be slightly slower than the unmonitored code. Sort the table by the Total Time column to quickly identify the slowest procedures. In this example, we can clearly see the second half of our routine is taking nearly all the time. For best results, the tests should be run without any other applications open, and certainly without switching to them, so Windows can dedicate all its resources to your application.

As these timings will probably be done on a developer-spec machine, we need to calculate a target duration for us to work towards, by comparing the total duration shown in the top-left corner to that experienced by the user and pro-rating it to the users' target time. Obviously, this can only be done when you are timing "end-to-end" processes—that is, from the time the user clicked a button to when the form or report is displayed.

All we then need to do is to think of ways in which the speed of the routines can be improved.

Creative Thinking

The key to improving your application's performance is to remove the bottlenecks by trying to find a different (faster) way to do the same task. Either by rethinking the entire approach—so the task that took so long is no longer needed—or by thinking how to do the task quicker. The trick is to tap in to the creative side of your brain, so instead of "analyzing" the problem and "identifying" a solution, use your imagination to conjure up sentences that start with "I wonder what would happen if I ...." Although this may seem like an alien concept to those of us who are normally analytical instead of artistic, there are a few exercises that can help.

Do a Jigsaw

On the rare occasions that we teach a class on performance optimization, we split the class into pairs and give each pair a child's six-piece jigsaw to build and time how long they take to complete it. The rules of the game are as follows:

- All the pieces must start face down, arranged randomly on the table.
- The jigsaw must be completed and finish face up.
- You are not allowed to be touching any piece when the timer starts.

The first attempt usually takes about 30 seconds. Applying the rule that an optimized routine should be an order of magnitude faster than the first attempt gives us a target of three seconds to do the six-piece jigsaw.

Identify the Steps

The bigger the task, the harder it is to invent a completely new way of performing the task so it will still work. So break it down into smaller steps and try to think how each step could be (a) avoided entirely or (b) speeded up. In VBA terms, the temptation is to focus on each existing procedure, but doing so just locks in the existing design. Instead, look at the process as a whole and identify the transformations, checks and processing that occur. Looking at our jigsaw example, the processing could be broken down into the following steps for each piece:

Pick it up → Turn it over → Identify it → Put it down → Join it up

With six pieces and five things to do for each piece, 30 seconds is a reasonable time, but can any of those steps be removed?

Think Outside the Box

"Think outside the box" is probably the most-used consultant-speak phrase of all time, urging us to come up with some new ideas. But what does it really mean? The origin we most like comes from being asked to join up nine dots, drawing as few connected straight lines as possible—analogous to making a procedure run as fast as possible:

Using five lines is easy (as is our first attempt at coding the VBA routine):

But can you connect all the dots using four straight lines? Visually, the nine dots appear to our brains as a box, which is a visual metaphor for the many rules, regulations and norms that we work (and code) within, usually as a result of our upbringing and education. Connecting the dots using four lines requires us to break through the boundaries of the box and start to consider the area outside it—literally thinking outside the box (but only a little bit!):

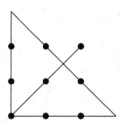

Now you're thinking outside the box, can you do it using three straight lines? You'll have to think further outside the box and also smash through a constraint that was never stated, but has been assumed—you don't have to go through the centre of each dot:

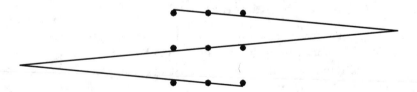

So what other unstated assumptions can we break in order to join the dots using even fewer lines? Just one line, perhaps? If we take the three-line solution to its extreme, we could have one line that spirals around the globe. (It doesn't have to be physically practical.) Or we could break another assumption and use a thicker pen—a paintbrush could cover all the dots in one line!

But our thinking is *still* boxed in—literally. To truly think outside the box requires us to remove the box itself! Was it ever stated we can't cut the paper? Doing so makes a one-line solution trivial:

The final optimization is to realize we can complete the task of joining the dots without drawing any lines at all! If we cut the paper carefully, we can have all the dots touching to begin with. Even better is to break a last assumption and think in terms of a 3D, not 2D, space and stack the dots on top of each other. We've optimized the task of joining the dots to doing nothing!

The next time you're asked to "Think outside the box," step out of your cubicle and ask "What box?"

Break the Rules!

A large part of creative thinking, then, is to break the (often unstated) rules that normally govern our behavior. These rules (usually) exist for some very good reasons, but performance is rarely one of them. For example, passing a variable to a procedure by value (ByVal) is the method recommended in *Chapter 3 — Excel and VBA Development Best Practices*. This is mainly due to defensive programming—knowing the routine being called can't change the value of the variable passed in—but is often (slightly) slower than passing the variable by reference (ByRef), particularly when passing large strings or Variant arrays. The one thing we *must* do when breaking rules it to fully document the rules we're breaking and why we're breaking them (by commenting the code). It's not uncommon for a maintenance developer to think "We're not allowed to do that" and unwittingly undo your optimizations.

Returning to our jigsaw puzzle, what rules can we break in order to speed up the task? The five steps to completing a piece of the puzzle are as follows:

Pick it up → Turn it over → Identify it → Put it down → Join it up

One thing we can do is draw on the table! By tracing around the completed jigsaw pieces (on some flipchart paper), we can tell exactly where each piece goes, enabling us to put it down in its final position. We've combined the "Put it down" and "Join it up" tasks and reduced the time accordingly. In VBA terms, a routine that processes a set of data often has a final step which organizes the results for the next process (such as removing duplicates/blanks, sorting and so on). Try to combine that organization into the processing of the data, so the natural output of the data processing can be passed directly to the next routine.

We can also deface the jigsaw pieces! By numbering the back of each piece and its final position on the flipchart paper, we know before we've even touched a piece exactly where it has to go, and we no longer need the "Identify it" step. The VBA equivalent is to ensure the incoming data is in a structured, known and predictable format before we have to process it. If the incoming data can't be obtained in such a format (by modifying the previous routine), it is often quicker to get it that way at the start of a routine than to have to deal with the lack of structure during the processing. For example, if the routine does a lot of searching through lists, it is much quicker to sort the list first and use a binary search inside the loop than it is to search through an unsorted list each time.

By ensuring we have structured our incoming data (by numbering the jigsaw pieces) and combined the final reorganization into the main processing (by drawing and numbering an outline of each piece of the completed jigsaw), we no longer need to turn the piece over to identify it and so have reduced the processing required for each piece to a simple "Move it." One task for each of our six pieces gives us a processing time of roughly six seconds, which is well on the way to our target of three.

So far we've concentrated on optimizing a routine by changing the way in which things are done, to reduce the amount of processing required. By doing these macro-scale optimizations we've achieved 80 percent of our target 90 percent saving, which is typical for many situations. The last 10 percent comes from making the remaining minimum processing as fast as it can be.

Know the Data

When doing a jigsaw puzzle, with everything else being equal, the second and third attempts are likely to be somewhat quicker than the first. This is simply because the people building the jigsaw will start to recognize which piece is which and where it goes, without needing to check the numbers written on each, shaving another few seconds off the processing time. The last second can be shaved by choosing to do the pieces in a specific order—each person does one of the middle two pieces first, then the two pieces at opposite ends.

The equivalent VBA is in knowing the amount, format, type and so on of the incoming data and hence the most efficient way to process most of it. Often, routines are required to handle slightly different types of data in slightly different ways, but where the differences are rarely sufficient to justify dedicated procedures. It is almost impossible for a routine to be equally efficient at handling all the expected data types. In many cases, the routines we write are fastest when operating within certain limits, such as the typical sizes of lists. The most efficient code to handle lists with up to ten items is unlikely to be the most efficient at handling lists with thousands of items. If we know the data we'll be given and can identify which are the most common situations, we can optimize our routines to handle those situations as efficiently as possible, to maximize overall performance. If this results in particularly poor performance for the rarer cases, we may be forced to include alternative procedures optimized for those. In that case, there would be a trade-off between performance and maintainability.

Ask Questions

What if it was an elephant? What if it was a mouse? The corollary to knowing the data is to consider how you would approach the problem if you had to process incredibly more or incredibly less data. By forcing yourself to consider solutions to out-of-bounds situations, you may think of new ways to streamline the processing that you had previously discounted (maybe subconsciously).

What if I stood on my head? Instead of looking at the code from top to bottom and accepting that B follows A, look at it from bottom to top and keep asking "Does B *have to* follow A? What can I change in B to break that dependency? If I do that, can I get rid of A entirely? Is that any quicker?"

Know the Tool

After we've reduced the processing steps to a minimum and organized the rest to be most efficient when handling the most common situations, the last few percentage points can be saved by ensuring we write the most efficient code. Both in pure VBA and when automating Excel, there are usually a number of alternative ways of doing the same thing, some faster than others. These micro-level optimizations require a very good understanding of the tool being used (that is, VBA and/or Excel), are often counterintuitive and are often different for different data types (Longs vs. Strings vs. Variants). Many of these alternatives are explained in the *Micro-Optimization* section later in this chapter.

Macro-Optimization

The vast majority of the performance improvement will come from restructuring the code to use a more efficient algorithm. This part of the chapter highlights some of the things to look for and provides alternative suggestions for doing the same thing. Whether the suggestions shown here are better or worse than your existing code will depend very much on the situation, particularly on the amount and type of data being processed.

The slowest parts of a procedure will invariably involve either external data retrieval or repeatedly looping through sets of data. Large loops are an opportunity for optimization; any improvement (however minor) that can be made inside a loop is a gain many times over. The performance of external data retrieval is usually dependant on the server and network performance and is something we have little control over. One thing we **can** do to minimize the effect of poor database performance is to load data (such as static lookup lists and so forth) when the application starts instead of when it is required. Users often find it more acceptable to have a longer startup time than sluggish performance after the application is loaded.

Preprocess

Before reading the rest of this paragraph, start Excel and write the fastest possible VBA routine you can to calculate how many 1s there are in the binary representation of the numbers 0 to 255. How did you do it? Did you use the Dec2Bin function from the Analysis Toolpak? Did you use a recursive routine? Did you repeatedly divide by 2 and check whether the result was odd or even? Or did you work out the numbers yourself, hard-code the results in a VBA array and just read them at runtime, as shown in Listing 17-4?

Listing 17-4 How Many 1s Are There in a Binary Number?

```
Function CountTheOnes(ByVal iValue As Integer) As Integer

    Static vaOneCount As Variant

    'Initialize the array
    If IsEmpty(vaOneCount) Then
        vaOneCount = Array(0, 1, 1, 2, 1, ... , 7, 8)
    End If

    'Read the result
    CountTheOnes = vaOneCount(iValue)

End Function
```

By doing as much processing as possible when developing the application, our applications don't need to do the processing at runtime.

Check the Order

The best routines are those whose performance doesn't vary significantly with the volume of data being processed. For example, a routine that copied a set of data from a Variant array into a worksheet range, calculated the worksheet and returned a result would take approximately the same time whether there were ten or a thousand elements in the array. Such routines are said to have an order of 1 and are very hard to achieve in practice.

The next best are those that vary linearly with the volume of data, such as one or more sequential For...Next loops through the data. These routines have an order of n, so if we have ten times as much data, the routine is likely to take approximately ten times as long. With a little thought and work, most routines can be reduced to order n.

Nested loops result in routines that are very sensitive to the volume of data being processed. A routine with two nested loops has an order n^2 and each extra level of nesting adds an extra order to the routine. If these routines are given ten times as much data to process, they're likely to take 100 or 1,000 times as long. If such a routine normally takes 1 second to complete, it might take 15 minutes to process 10 times as much data. In most cases, nested loops are just a quick and easy way to code an algorithm that could be redesigned as multiple sequential loops through the data. Note that nested loops will often be spread over many different procedures, for example where ProcedureA loops through an array and calls ProcedureB for each element, which itself loops through another array to process the element.

As an example, consider the routine in Listing 17-5, which compares two arrays and processes any items that are in both.

Listing 17-5 Compare Two Arrays

```
Sub ProcessLists(asArray1() As String, asArray2() As String)

  Dim lIndex1 As Long
  Dim lIndex2 As Long

  'Loop through the first array
  For lIndex1 = LBound(asArray1) To UBound(asArray1)

    'Loop through the second array
    For lIndex2 = LBound(asArray2) To UBound(asArray2)

      'Do they match?
      If asArray1(lIndex1) = asArray2(lIndex2) Then
        'Yes, so process it
      End If
    Next
  Next

End Sub
```

Without thinking too hard about how to improve this routine, we might be tempted to just add an `Exit For` to jump out of the inner loop after we've found a match, but that still leaves the routine essentially of order n^2. If the two arrays are sorted, we can reduce this to order n by looping through both arrays within the same loop, as shown in Listing 17-6.

Listing 17-6 Process Both Arrays Within One Loop

```
Sub ProcessLists(asArray1() As String, asArray2() As String)

  Dim lIndex1 As Long
  Dim lIndex2 As Long
  Dim iComp As Integer

  lIndex1 = LBound(asArray1)
  lIndex2 = LBound(asArray2)

  'Loop through both arrays together
  Do
     'Compare the elements from both arrays
     iComp = StrComp(asArray1(lIndex1), asArray2(lIndex2))

     If iComp = 0 Then
       'A match, so process it
       Debug.Print asArray1(lIndex1)

       'And advance in both arrays
       lIndex1 = lIndex1 + 1
       lIndex2 = lIndex2 + 1

     ElseIf iComp = -1 Then
        'Item in array1 is before item in array2,
        'so move down array1 and check again
        lIndex1 = lIndex1 + 1

     ElseIf iComp = 1 Then
        'Item in array1 is after item in array2,
        'so move down array2 and check again
        lIndex2 = lIndex2 + 1
     End If

     'Stop when we reach the end of one of the arrays
  Loop Until lIndex1 > UBound(asArray1) Or _
             lIndex2 > UBound(asArray2)

End Sub
```

If the arrays are not sorted, it will probably be quicker to sort them both beforehand, then use the above routine. If the output has to be in a specific order (preventing us from sorting both arrays), we could sort asArray2 and use a binary search routine to see whether the string exists, or use a Dictionary object (see later for an example of each).

Tighten the Loop

Having replaced the nested loops with more efficient algorithms, the next task is to make the code within the remaining loop as tight as possible. As well as implementing all the micro-optimizations shown later in this chapter, the primary goal is to ensure that in each iteration, we only execute the minimum amount of code possible. Returning to the question above "Does B have to follow A?" it is common to see loops that contain code to calculate intermediate results, followed by some tests to check whether the intermediate result should be used (because this reflects the order in which we originally thought about the routine). If we turn the routine on its head, we can do the tests first and only calculate the intermediate results for those elements we know we'll be using.

Fast VBA Algorithms

QuickSort

The QuickSort routine is one of the fastest sorting algorithms and should be used whenever you want to sort an array. It works by doing the following:

1. Select one element from the array, typically taken from the middle
2. Scan through the array moving everything that should come before the selected element to the bottom of the array and everything that should come after the selected element to the top of the array
3. Call itself to sort the bottom half
4. Call itself to sort the top half

For best performance, you should have a number of QuickSort routines for specific data types, such as that shown in Listing 17-7 for one-dimensional string arrays.

Listing 17-7 A QuickSort Routine for One-Dimensional String Arrays

```
'*************************************************************
'*
'* FUNCTION NAME:    QUICKSORT STRING ARRAY - 1D
'*
'* DESCRIPTION:    Sorts the passed array into required order.
'*                 The array must be a 1D string array.
'*
'* PARAMETERS:
'*         asArray          A 1D string array of values to sort
'*         bSortAscending   True = ascending order.
'*         iLow1            The first item to sort between
'*         iHigh1           The last item to sort between
'*
'*************************************************************

Sub QuickSortString1D(asArray() As String, _
          Optional bSortAscending As Boolean = True, _
          Optional iLow1, Optional iHigh1)

   'Dimension variables
   Dim iLow2 As Long, iHigh2 As Long
   Dim sKey As String
   Dim sSwap As String

   On Error GoTo PtrExit

   'If not provided, sort the entire array
   If IsMissing(iLow1) Then iLow1 = LBound(asArray)
   If IsMissing(iHigh1) Then iHigh1 = UBound(asArray)

   'Set new extremes to old extremes
   iLow2 = iLow1
   iHigh2 = iHigh1

   'Get value of array item in middle of new extremes
   sKey = asArray((iLow1 + iHigh1) \ 2)

   'Loop for all the items in the array between the extremes
   Do While iLow2 < iHigh2
```

```vba
    If bSortAscending Then
      'Find the first item that is greater than the mid-point
      Do While asArray(iLow2) < sKey And iLow2 < iHigh1
        iLow2 = iLow2 + 1
      Loop

      'Find the last item that is less than the mid-point
      Do While asArray(iHigh2) > sKey And iHigh2 > iLow1
        iHigh2 = iHigh2 - 1
      Loop
    Else
      'Find the first item that is less than the mid-point
      Do While asArray(iLow2) > sKey And iLow2 < iHigh1
        iLow2 = iLow2 + 1
      Loop

      'Find the last item that is greater than the mid-point
      Do While asArray(iHigh2) < sKey And iHigh2 > iLow1
        iHigh2 = iHigh2 - 1
      Loop
    End If

    'If the two items are in the wrong order, swap them
    If iLow2 < iHigh2 Then
      sSwap = asArray(iLow2)
      asArray(iLow2) = asArray(iHigh2)
      asArray(iHigh2) = sSwap
    End If

    'If the pointers are not together, do the next item
    If iLow2 <= iHigh2 Then
      iLow2 = iLow2 + 1
      iHigh2 = iHigh2 - 1
    End If
  Loop

  'Recurse to sort the lower half of the extremes
  If iHigh2 > iLow1 Then
    QuickSortString1D asArray, bSortAscending, iLow1, iHigh2
  End If

  'Recurse to sort the upper half of the extremes
  If iLow2 < iHigh1 Then
    QuickSortString1D asArray, bSortAscending, iLow2, iHigh1
```

```
    End If

PtrExit:

End Sub
```

Binary Search

A binary search is a very quick way to locate an item within a sorted array. It works by doing the following:

1. Compare the item to look for with the element in the middle of the array.
2. If they match, we found it.
3. If the item to look for is lower than the middle of the array, throw away the top half.
4. If the item to look for is higher than the middle of the array, throw away the bottom half.
5. Repeat 1–5, cutting the array in half each time until we find the item or run out of array.

A binary search routine, such as that shown in Listing 17-8, is practically insensitive to the size of the array passed in, as doubling the size of the array results in only one extra iteration of the routine.

Listing 17-8 A Binary Search Algorithm

```
'***************************************************************
'* Function Name:     BinarySearchString
'*
'* Inputs:
'*   sLookFor   - The string to search for in the array
'*   asArray    - An array of strings, sorted in ascending order
'*   lCompareMethod - either vbBinaryCompare or vbTextCompare
'*              Defaults to vbTextCompare
'*   lNotFound - The value to return if the text isn't found
'*              Defaults to -1
'*
'* Outputs: The position in the array, or -1 if not found
'*
```

```vba
'* Purpose: Uses a binary search algorithm to quickly locate a
'*          string within a sorted array of strings
'*
'*****************************************************************

Function BinarySearchString(ByRef sLookFor As String, _
   ByRef asArray() As String, _
   Optional ByVal lMethod As VbCompareMethod = vbTextCompare, _
   Optional ByVal lNotFound As Long = -1) As Long

   Dim lLow As Long, lMid As Long, lHigh As Long
   Dim iComp As Integer

   On Error GoTo PTR_Exit

   'Assume we didn't find it
   BinarySearchString = lNotFound

   'Get the starting positions
   lLow = LBound(asArray)
   lHigh = UBound(asArray)

   Do
      'Find the midpoint of the array
      lMid = (lLow + lHigh) \ 2

      'Compare the mid-point element to the string
      'being searched for
      iComp = StrComp(asArray(lMid), sLookFor, lMethod)

      If iComp = 0 Then
         'We found it, so return the location and quit
         BinarySearchString = lMid
         Exit Do

      ElseIf iComp = 1 Then
         'The midpoint item is bigger than us--
         'throw away the top half
         lHigh = lMid - 1
      Else
         'The midpoint item is smaller than us--
         'throw away the bottom half
         lLow = lMid + 1
```

```
        End If

    'Continue until our pointers cross
    Loop Until lLow > lHigh

PTR_Exit:

End Function
```

Sort and Scan

The combination of a QuickSort and BinarySearch gives us a very efficient way of comparing two arrays, to process the elements in common, as shown in Listing 17-9.

Listing 17-9 Combining a Sort and Binary Search

```
Sub ProcessLists(asArray1() As String, asArray2() As String)

    Dim lIndex As Long

    'Sort the second array
    QuickSortString1D asArray2

    'Loop through the first array
    For lIndex = LBound(asArray1) To UBound(asArray1)

        'Use the binary search routine to
        'check if the element is in the second array
        If BinarySearchString(asArray1(lIndex), asArray2) <> -1 Then

            'A match, so process it
            Debug.Print asArray1(lIndex)
        End If
    Next

End Sub
```

This is not quite as efficient as the example shown previously that relied on both lists being sorted, but is a very efficient and easy to understand alternative for use when the initial array must be left in its original order.

The SORTSEARCH_INDEX udt

When dealing with large 2D arrays, arrays of objects or multiple keys, it is usually more efficient to create a new indexing array and sort and search that than to try to sort and search the original array. An index array is an array of the SORTSEARCH_INDEX udt, which is defined as follows:

```
Public Type SORTSEARCH_INDEX
   Key As String
   Index As Long
End Type
```

The key is the string used for sorting and searching, which is typically the value from the first column in a large 2D array, the name of an object or a concatenation of the values to sort an array by multiple columns. The index is the row number in the original array. When the udt array is sorted, we can loop through the elements in the sorted order, using the Index property to identify the appropriate row from the original array, as in Listing 17-10.

Listing 17-10 Using the SORTSEARCH_INDEX udt

```
Sub UseIndexSort()

  Dim vaArray As Variant
  Dim lRow As Long
  Dim auIndex() As SORTSEARCH_INDEX

  'Assume vaArray is a multicolumn, multirow Variant array
  'e.g. as read from the worksheet
  vaArray = Selection.Value

  'Create an index array of the same size
  ReDim auIndex(LBound(vaArray) To UBound(vaArray))

  'Populate the index array with the original row number
  'and sort key
  For lRow = LBound(vaArray) To UBound(vaArray)
    auIndex(lRow).Index = lRow
    auIndex(lRow).Key = vaArray(lRow, 1)
  Next
```

```
'Sort the index array
QuickSortIndex auIndex

'Loop through the sorted array
For lRow = LBound(auIndex) To UBound(auIndex)

    'The .Index element of the sorted udt is the row
    'in the original array
    Debug.Print vaArray(auIndex(lRow).Index, 2)
Next

End Sub
```

QuickSortIndex is a version of the QuickSort algorithm for arrays of the SORTSEARCH_INDEX user defined type and can be found on the CD in the workbook \Concepts\Ch17—Optimizing VBA Performance\ *Algorithms.xls*. The workbook also contains a version of the binary search algorithm, BinarySearchIndex, which searches for a string in the index array and returns the row number in the original array.

Micro-Optimization

Both VBA and Excel often provide many ways to do the same thing, some of which are always faster than the others, but some of which are sometimes faster and sometimes slower depending on the data being processed. This section identifies many of the common alternatives. Before blindly using the recommended alternative, you should always confirm the behavior using your own data. This can usually be done in a quick-and-dirty manner, using the code shown in Listing 17-11.

Listing 17-11 A Simple Routine to Compare Two Alternatives

```
Sub CompareThem()

 Dim dStart As Double
 Dim lCounter As Long

 'We often need lots of loops to get a measurable result
 Const 1LOOP_COUNT As Long = 10000
```

```
dStart = Timer

For lCounter = 1 To 1LOOP_COUNT
   'The code for one alternative
Next

Debug.Print "Version 1 took " & (Timer - dStart) & " seconds"

dStart = Timer

For lCounter = 1 To 1LOOP_COUNT
   'the code for the second alternative
Next

Debug.Print "Version 2 took " & (Timer - dStart) & " seconds"

End Sub
```

VBA's built-in Timer call is fairly slow and not very accurate, so we usually have to do each version many, many times to get a measurable result, proving these micro-optimizations will only have a noticeable effect if they're executed many times over.

VBA

Use Matching Data Types

VBA is very forgiving when we mix data types—such as passing a Double to a procedure that expects a String or vice versa. However, there is some overhead associated with the conversion and it can introduce subtle bugs, so it should be avoided. Whenever passing a variable to a procedure, or setting one variable equal to another, always ensure the variables have the same data type.

Perform Explicit Conversions Instead of Implicit Ones

When you are unable to match data types, always tell VBA which conversion to perform, such as CStr(), CDbl() and so on. By being explicit about the conversion you want to perform, you allow wasting the time required by VBA to make the decision itself.

Use Len(string)=0 Instead of string=""

VBA stores strings in memory by storing the length of the string, followed by the characters it contains. As the length of the string is readily available, it is much quicker to check whether it is zero than to ask VBA to perform string comparisons (with all the memory allocations that involves).

Use Left$, Right$, Mid$ and So Forth Instead of Left, Right and Mid

Most of VBA's string-handling functions have both a variant (for example, Left, Right, Mid) and a string (Left$, Right$, Mid$) version. If you use the variant versions with string variables, VBA has to convert the inside string to a variant, pass it to the function, get the result (as a variant) and convert the result back to a string. By using the string version, VBA doesn't need to do the two variant-to-string conversions, which can be relatively slow, particularly with large strings.

Pass Strings and Variant Arrays ByRef Instead of ByVal

Whenever strings and arrays are passed to a procedure by value (ByVal), VBA has to take a copy of the entire string or array and pass the copy to the procedure. If the string or array is passed by reference (ByRef), VBA only has to pass a pointer to the procedure, which is much quicker.

Don't Use Option Compare Text

Adding Option Compare Text to the top of a module forces VBA to perform all string comparisons in a case-insensitive way. In the majority of cases, this will not be required and only wastes time. Instead, every module should have Option Compare Binary set and you should use the CompareMethod parameter of StrComp, Instr and so on to specify when case-insensitive comparisons are required. If you need to use a function that doesn't have a CompareMethod (such as Like), you should either force both strings to upper- or lowercase and do a normal binary compare, or have a specific routine to do the comparison and place it in its own module with Option Compare Text set.

Use Early Binding Wherever Possible

Whenever you declare a variable As Object, VBA doesn't know anything about it until runtime. Every time you call a property or method of the object, VBA has to check whether the method exists, check its parameters and confirm your code can call it. All of that takes time and should be avoided by giving all your variables specific types. If you are using As Object to be able to call the same property (for example, Name) on a number of your own classes, you should implement a custom interface in those classes instead (see *Chapter 11 — Interfaces*).

Use Integer Arithmetic Where Possible

VBA can perform integer arithmetic—particularly division—much faster than floating-point arithmetic. You can tell VBA to use integer arithmetic by declaring your variables As Long, or by using the integer division operator, \:

```
'Slower-uses floating-point operations
dMid = (dLow + dHigh) / 2

'Faster-uses integer operations
lMid = (lLow + lHigh) \ 2
```

Use For Each to Iterate Collections (Not by Index)

VBA's Collection object is designed to be iterated most efficiently using the For Each construct, instead of For Next.

Use For ... Next to Iterate Arrays (Not For Each)

VBA's arrays, however, are faster to iterate by index instead of using For Each.

Use Dictionaries Instead of Collections (If Order Isn't Important)

The *Microsoft Scripting Runtime* library, scrrun.dll, contains a very fast and lightweight Dictionary object, which can be used just like a VBA Collection. As well as being faster, it exposes both the items and the keys used to store them and supports the Exists property to check whether a key exists in the collection. Its biggest drawback is it does not allow items be inserted into the middle of the list, so can't be used when re-ordering is required.

Don't Use If bVariable = True *Then, Just Use* If bVariable Then

If you have a Boolean variable, adding the extra step of comparing it to True in an If statement is just wasting processing cycles. The redundant comparison to True should be removed.

Don't Use IIf()

VBA's IIf() function is a very convenient way to choose between two alternatives. However, it is also extremely slow, compared to the longer multi-line If statement and always evaluates both the True and False expressions.

Use Multiple If...ElseIf...End If Instead of Select Case

Similarly, Select Case is a convenient, clear and easy-to-read construct for choosing between multiple alternatives, but is also slower than the equivalent If...ElseIf construct.

Use With blocks and Object Variables to Reduce the Dots

VBA enables us to navigate through object model hierarchies using the dot (.) operator to access an object's properties or methods. Think of every dot as a small pause in your application and reduce them by using With blocks or an object variable.

Excel

Turn Off ScreenUpdating and Automatic Calculation

The biggest gains when automating Excel are to set `Application.ScreenUpdating = False` and `Application.Calculation = xlManual`. That will stop Excel continually refreshing its display or recalculating everything when data is written to the sheet.

Don't Select Things

The macro recorder produces extremely inefficient code, peppered with code such as this:

```
Range("A1").Select
Selection.Font.Bold = True
```

It is extremely rare to ever need to select anything when controlling Excel from VBA. In most cases, these two lines can be combined by removing the Select/Selection:

```
Range("A1").Font.Bold = True
```

You will occasionally need to insert an extra object between the Select and Selection, particularly when charts or drawing objects are involved, such as changing a chart's title:

```
ActiveSheet.ChartObjects("Chart 1").Activate
ActiveChart.ChartTitle.Select
Selection.Characters.Text = "Hello"
```

Becomes:

```
ActiveSheet.ChartObjects("Chart 1").Chart.ChartTitle _
    .Characters.Text = "Hello"
```

Use Variant Arrays

Instead of reading and writing cells one by one, it is much quicker to read a range of cells into a Variant variable, then process the variable as a 2D array, or populate a Variant array then write it to a range of cells, as shown in Listing 17-12.

Listing 17-12 Reading and Writing Variant Arrays

```
Sub ReadWriteVariants()

    Dim vaData As Variant
    Dim lRow As Long
    Dim lCol As Long

    'Read the data from the sheet in one go
    vaData = ActiveSheet.Range("A1:B10").Value

    'Process the data within VBA
    For lRow = 1 To UBound(vaData)
        For lCol = 1 To UBound(vaData, 2)
            If IsNumeric(vaData(lRow, lCol)) And _
                Not IsEmpty(vaData(lRow, lCol)) Then

                vaData(lRow, lCol) = vaData(lRow, lCol) * 2
            End If
        Next
    Next
```

```
'Write the data to the sheet in one go
ActiveSheet.Range("D1:E10").Value = vaData

End Sub
```

Don't Use ActiveSheet, Selection or Worksheets() Repeatedly

Some of the more commonly used properties in the Excel object model—such as ActiveSheet, Selection or Worksheets—return the generic Object type, so all calls that use these objects will be late-bound and slow. For best performance, you should declare a variable of the specific data type and set it to be the ActiveSheet, Selection and so forth.

Test a Property Before Setting It

It is often much faster to read a property than to write it. It can save time to only update a property when it needs to change, by checking whether it is the required value first. This contradicts the general rule of reducing the amount of code you write, but it can be readily observed that reading the value of an Excel object's property (such as Range.Font.Bold) makes it much quicker to subsequently set the same property.

Use Doubles to Talk to Excel

When passing numbers to Excel—either to populate a worksheet cell or as parameters to Excel functions—it is usually most efficient to pass variables declared As Double. This is because Excel generally uses the Double data type internally and so avoids type conversions. When populating a cell, Excel will also try to apply cell formatting if other data types (such as Date or Currency) are used. Using Double's throughout avoids Excel's autoformatting and so improves performance.

Use the PAGE.SETUP XLM Function Instead of the PageSetup Object

Whenever you change any of the properties of the PageSetup object, Excel repaginates the page, to check whether the automatic zooming or automatic page breaks need to change. To do this, Excel has to communicate with the printer drivers, which is extremely slow. This can be avoided by using the PAGE.SETUP XLM function, which is fully documented in the macrofun.hlp file available from `http://support.microsoft.com/?kbid=128175`, as shown in Listing 17-13. Note that the PAGE.SETUP function always applies the settings to the active sheet.

Listing 17-13 Using PAGE.SETUP to Set a Page Header

```
Sub SetHeaders()

  'Set the header using the slow PageSetup object
  With ActiveSheet.PageSetup
    .LeftHeader = "Hello"
    .RightHeader = "World"
  End With

  'Set the header using the faster PAGE.SETUP XLM function
  ExecuteExcel4Macro "PAGE.SETUP(""&LHello &RWorld"")"

End Sub
```

Conclusion

A highly optimized VBA routine will often execute in 1/10th or 1/100th the time taken by the first version of the routine. In most cases, VBA's performance is "good enough," in that the routine executes within an acceptable time, such as 2 seconds to show a form, 0.5 seconds for elements within the form (for example, when typing into a text box) or 10 seconds to produce a report. Routines which take significantly longer than this are good candidates for optimization. The CD included with this book contains an add-in for both the Office VBE and VB6 IDE to monitor an application's performance as it runs, which can be used to assess the performance impact of changes to the code.

Macro-optimization looks at the structure of the routine, to use the most efficient algorithms and minimize the amount of code that needs to be executed. This is where most of the savings are usually found.

Micro-optimization ensures the most efficient VBA statements and data types are used within the code. These account for the final few percentage points and usually only have an impact where loops are executing thousands of times.

The trade-off is complexity. A QuickSort is much faster than a bubble sort and a binary search in a sorted array is much faster than looping through a collection, but they are also more complex and therefore slightly harder to debug and maintain.

By using the techniques suggested in this chapter when writing new routines, the knowledgeable VBA developer can write routines that are already well optimized and are likely to operate within acceptable time limits.

Controlling Other Office Applications

Excel's primary purpose is to perform calculations. It has some database-like features, but it's not a relational database. It has some text editing and formatting features, but it's not a word processor. It has presentation-quality graphics, but it's not a presentation application. It can save worksheets as Web pages, but it's not a Web authoring tool. It can send a workbook through e-mail, but it's neither an e-mail program nor personal information manager. Excel's built-in database, word processing, presentation, e-mail and Web features are sufficient for most applications, but there comes a time when we need to use a feature that is only provided by the dedicated Office application—Access, Word, PowerPoint, Outlook or FrontPage.

This chapter explains how to control those other Office applications from within Excel, suggests some best practices to use when controlling other applications and provides an introductory overview of the major objects in each application's object model.

Fundamentals

Controlling another application is only a matter of knowing how to connect to the target application and efficiently use its object model. This part of the chapter discusses the fundamentals of connecting to other applications and best practices for using third-party object models.

Automation

Automation is Microsoft's generic term for technology that allows one application to manipulate another application's objects, including allowing VBA to manipulate Excel. Automation began with a technology called OLE (Object Linking and Embedding) and has since evolved into other forms such as COM (Component Object Model), also known as ActiveX, and DCOM (Distributed Component Object Model).

The application that manipulates the objects is called the ***automation client*** or ***host application***. Applications whose objects are manipulated are called ***automation servers*** or ***target applications***.

All of the Office applications can be used as automation servers so long as they've been properly installed (registered) on the computer. Microsoft Office applications are automatically registered during installation, but can be re-registered using the /regserver command-line switch.

Referencing

The easiest way to get started is to create a reference to the object library for the application that we want to automate using the *Tools > References* menu in the VBE. In Figure 18-1, we've added a reference to the Word 2000 object library, as indicated by the 9.0 version number in the reference description.

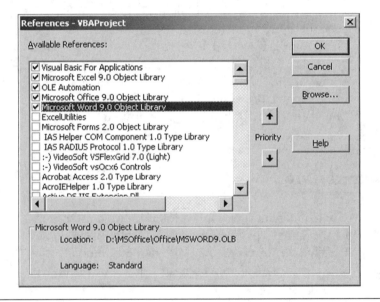

Figure 18-1 Adding a Reference to the Word Object Library

With the reference set, we can use the objects in the Word object model as if they were classes in our project, as shown in Listing 18-1, which uses the New keyword to create a new instance of the Word application.

Listing 18-1 A Simple Procedure to Control Word

```
Sub ControlWord()

    'Declare an object variable to reference
    'the Word application
    Dim wrdApp As Word.Application

    'Start a new instance of Word
    Set wrdApp = New Word.Application

    'Do something

    'Close Word and tidy up
    wrdApp.Quit savechanges:=False
    Set wrdApp = Nothing

End Sub
```

Development Best Practices

In addition to the advice given in *Chapter 3 — Excel and VBA Development Best Practices*, some additional techniques should always be used when automating other applications.

Always Include the Object Library in Variable Declarations

Whenever we declare a variable as a specific object type, such as `Dim rngData As Range`, the VBA interpreter scans through the object libraries referenced in the *Tools > References* list (in the order shown in that list) until it finds an object with the same name as specified in the variable declaration. In this case, the first object library to contain an object called Range is the Excel object library, so our variable is typed as an Excel Range object. In most cases, that's exactly what we want to happen. Problems arise, though, if we're referencing multiple object libraries that use the same name for their own objects. For example, Excel and Word both have Range objects, but they're very different. To make sure the interpreter uses the Range object from the correct library, we should always include the library name in the variable declaration, as shown in Listing 18-2.

Listing 18-2 Declaring Objects with the Correct Object Library

```
Sub GetRanges()

    'An Excel Range
    Dim rngData As Excel.Range

    'A Word Range
    Dim wrngTitle As Word.Range

End Sub
```

In addition to explicitly telling VBA which Range object we want a reference to, fully qualifying our object declarations also makes our code much easier to understand; when we see As Word.Range, we have the mental prompt that the Word object library is being used. This prompt is carried through to the variable name, where we've included a w prefix to indicate an object from the Word object library.

Always Fully Qualify Property and Method Calls

All of the Office object libraries include some global properties that we often use as shortcuts into the object model, such as Excel's ActiveSheet, ActiveCell, Selection and Word's ActiveDocument, Selection and so on. Whenever we use any such property in cross-application development, we must always provide a fully qualified object reference that can be traced back to the original variable we used to reference the application. Listing 18-3 shows the correct way to get a reference to the ActiveDocument in a Word instance that we're controlling.

Listing 18-3 Referring to the Active Document

```
Sub GetActiveDoc()

    'Declare an object variable to reference
    'the Word application
    Dim wrdApp As Word.Application
    Dim wrdDoc As Word.Document

    'Start a new instance of Word with a blank document
    Set wrdApp = New Word.Application
```

```
'Do something that opens or creates a document

'Get a reference to the active document
Set wrdDoc = wrdApp.ActiveDocument

'Close Word and tidy up
wrdApp.Quit savechanges:=False
Set wrdDoc = Nothing
Set wrdApp = Nothing

End Sub
```

If we omitted the wrdApp. in the highlighted line, the VBA interpreter will try to find a Word document in any instance of Word the user
might have open, which may not be the instance we're controlling. By providing the wrdApp. reference, we're explicitly telling the interpreter to
return the active document in the instance of Word we've created.

Develop Using the Earliest Version You'll Support

For reasons explained later, references that we declare to Office object
libraries are forward compatible but not backward compatible. This means
that if we save our workbook with a reference to the Word 2003 object
library, anyone opening the workbook on a PC with only Office 2000
installed will receive a compile error "Can't find project or library" as soon
as the code is run. If we save our workbook with a reference to the Word
2000 object library, it will work correctly on any machine with Office 2000
or any later version.

Every version of Office adds more features to each application and cor-
respondingly more objects, methods, properties and optional parameters
to the application's object library. By developing using the earliest version
that we intend to support, we stop ourselves from accidentally using any of
the more recent objects, methods, properties or parameters. If we were to
develop using the latest version of the application, we would not discover
our accidental use of the newer objects until we were well into our testing,
or even after deployment.

Group Routines in Application-Specific Modules

The VBA interpreter/compiler compiles our code on a module-by-module
basis. A module is compiled when code contained in that module is first

run. If we have a reference to an object library that isn't registered correctly, the compiler will not be able to compile the module that contains code that uses objects in that library and we'll get a compile error. This issue can be partially mitigated by ensuring that all the code that controls another application is contained in a single module dedicated to that purpose. The module should not contain any procedures used by other parts of the application. If we're automating multiple applications, the routines for each application should be in their own modules—one for Word, one for Access, one for PowerPoint and so on—with each module having a descriptive name such as MWordCode. With all the application-specific code contained in a single module, we can check whether the application is installed correctly and safely use or avoid that module, as shown later.

The vTable and Early vs. Late Binding

Every COM object has a structure called a *vTable*, or virtual function table, which lists all its properties and methods along with the memory addresses where their entry points are located and the parameters they take. When we declare a variable as a specific object data type, the compiler can look up the addresses of all the property and method calls for that object in its vTable at compile time. It can then store *jump to* instructions that identify the entry points of those property and method calls directly in our code. When the code is executed and VBA encounters one of these property or method calls, it just runs the code at the memory location specified by the stored jump to instruction. This is known as *early binding*.

Early binding requires us to set a reference to the object library through the *Tools > References* menu, so VBA can include that object library's GUIDs and other type information in our project. (A GUID is a unique 128-bit number used to identify all COM objects.) When our project is run on a different computer, VBA verifies that an object with the same GUID as the one we originally referenced is available there. If so, it means this is the *same* object as the one we originally referenced so it will have the same vTable. Therefore, all the direct memory jump instructions that were compiled into our application for that object can be trusted. If the GUID is not found on the client computer, VBA knows that the object we want to use is not available and so gives us a compile error (and marks the reference as MISSING in the *Tools > References* list). This is why MISSING object library references caused by referenced COM components not being installed on a user's computer will stop a VBA application dead in its tracks.

When we declare a variable as the generic Object data type, the compiler doesn't know which vTable to use. Therefore, it cannot determine the memory location of that object's properties and methods and it cannot compile jump to instructions for them into our code. Instead, after the generic object variable has been set to reference a specific object at runtime, VBA checks the vTable of that object every time it encounters one of the object's property or method calls in order to locate the memory address to jump to. This is known as *late binding*. The continual vTable lookups can have a significant impact on performance, but they don't require us to set a reference to the object library we're controlling. This results in any referencing problems (such as a missing object library) appearing as runtime errors (which we can handle gracefully) rather than compile errors.

The vTable also explains why Office object libraries are forward compatible, but not backward compatible. In each new version of an Office application the vTable is *extended* with new property and method entries, but the existing sections are not changed. This makes it safe to use an earlier version vTable entry to call into a later version of the same application, but not vice versa. The first section of the later version's vTable is identical to the earlier version's vTable, but it also contains additional entries that do not appear in the earlier version. If VBA attempted to execute a property or method call identified by an entry late in the Word 2003 vTable while running under Word 2000, for example, that entry wouldn't exist in the Word 2000 executable and our application would crash.

As well as controlling whether we can use early binding, adding a reference to an object library also controls whether we can use the constants and parameter names defined in the library, as shown in Listing 18-4.

Listing 18-4 Early vs. Late Binding

```
'Early-Bound
'Requires a reference to the Word object library,
'but allows us to use specific object types,
'named parameters and defined constants
'and gives us IntelliSense information
Sub EarlyBound(wrdApp As Word.Application)

    'Open a text file
    wrdApp.Documents.Open FileName:="c:\myfile.txt", _
                        Format:=wdOpenFormatText

End Sub
```

```
'Late-Bound
'Have to use the generic Object type,
'can't use named parameters or defined constants,
'don't get IntelliSense information,
'but doesn't require a reference either.
Sub LateBound(wrdApp As Object)

    'Open a text file
    wrdApp.Documents.Open "c:\myfile.txt", , , , , , , , , 4

End Sub
```

The key factor in choosing between early or late binding is the likelihood that the applications we're controlling are available and installed correctly on the users' computers. We can ensure the applications are installed correctly on our computers, so we should always use early binding during development. That allows us to use the IntelliSense information, object types, constants and named parameters which together make early-bound code much easier to develop, read, debug and maintain.

Before distributing our application to our users, we need to decide whether to switch to using late binding. This will usually depend on both the likelihood that the applications are available and the amount of code that calls the application. The fundamental advantage of using late binding is that we can easily handle a failure to link to the object we want to control (see later for an example). In the case of Excel automating Word within a company environment, it's highly likely that anyone with Excel installed will have Word installed as well, so it's probably safe to stay with early binding. The same can't be said when automating, say, FrontPage, so it would probably be best to switch to late binding for that. If we only have a few lines of code, it's safest to always use late binding. With lots of code, the inability to use named parameters and defined constants when late binding can make our applications much harder to maintain.

Handling Instances

Before we can use an application's features, we need to connect to an instance of the application. We can either hijack an instance the user might already have open or create a new instance for our dedicated use. Unless there is a specific need to link to the instance that the user is working with, we should always create our own instances, use them and close them when we're finished. This is mainly because the user may have left the instance they're using in a state that would cause errors in our application if we tried to use it, such as having a modal dialog displayed. This could either prevent our application working correctly, or worse, result in our application interfering with the work the user is doing in that instance.

Create a New Instance

We can use either the New keyword or CreateObject function to create a new instance of an application, as shown in Listing 18-5. The New keyword can only be used if we have set a reference to the *type library* (synonymous with object library), while the CreateObject function can be used either with or without a reference. The manner in which an application is started does not determine whether we're using early or late binding. Rather, the opposite is true; our choice of binding determines whether we can use New or CreateObject. Although using the New keyword is slightly faster than CreateObject, it is our opinion that CreateObject should always be used, as it is one less thing to change if we choose to switch between early and late binding.

Listing 18-5 Creating a New Instance of Word

```
Sub StartWord()

    'Early bound
    Dim wrdApp1 As Word.Application
    Set wrdApp1 = New Word.Application

    'Early bound
    Dim wrdApp2 As Word.Application
    Set wrdApp2 = CreateObject("Word.Application")

    'Late bound
    Dim wrdApp3 As Object
    Set wrdApp3 = CreateObject("Word.Application")

End Sub
```

Table 18-1 lists some of the Office application class names used by the CreateObject function.

Table 18-1 Class List for CreateObject

Application	Class
Access	Access.Application
Excel	Excel.Application
Front Page	FrontPage.Application
Internet Explorer	InternetExplorer.Application
MapPoint	MapPoint.Application
Outlook	Outlook.Application
PowerPoint	PowerPoint.Application
Project	MSProject.Application
Publisher	Publisher.Application
Visio	Visio.Application
Word	Word.Application

Properly Tidying Up

Whenever we create a new instance of an application, we must ensure that we close it correctly. In most cases, this is just a matter of calling the application's Quit method and then destroying any variables that we may be using to reference it. We must be particularly careful with error handling, to ensure that the application we're controlling is correctly shut down in the case of an error, as shown in Listing 18-6, which uses the error handling structure explained in *Chapter 12 — VBA Error Handling*.

Listing 18-6 Starting and Closing Word, with Error Handling

```
Sub ControlWord()

    Const sSOURCE As String = "ControlWord"
    Dim wrdApp As Word.Application

    On Error GoTo ErrorHandler

    'Start Word
    Set wrdApp = CreateObject("Word.Application")

    'Do something here
```

```
ErrorExit:

    'The tidy-up code is performed
    'whether or not we get an error
    If Not wrdApp Is Nothing Then

        'Close Word, ignoring any errors
        'Without On Error Resume Next, an error would
        'cause an endless loop in the error handler.
        On Error Resume Next
        wrdApp.Quit savechanges:=False
        On Error GoTo ErrorHandler

        'Tidy up
        Set wrdApp = Nothing
    End If

    Exit Sub

ErrorHandler:

    If bCentralErrorHandler(msMODULE, sSOURCE) Then
        Stop
        Resume
    Else
        Resume ErrorExit
    End If

End Sub
```

Reference an Existing Instance

It is nearly always best to create a new instance of an application for our program to use. A notable exception is when controlling Outlook, because it only allows a single instance to be running at any one time; using either the New keyword or CreateObject function to create an instance of Outlook only creates an instance if Outlook is not already running. If Outlook is already open, a reference to that instance is returned. This behavior can cause us problems when we've finished using the instance we asked for, as we won't know whether or not we should shut Outlook down. If Outlook was already running when we asked for our instance, we should leave it running. If it wasn't already running, we should close it. We can use the GetObject function to obtain a reference to an existing instance of an application, then use CreateObject if the GetObject call fails, as shown in Listing 18-7. In either case, we set a Boolean variable that we use to see whether we should close Outlook when tidying up.

Listing 18-7 Checking for, Starting and Closing Outlook, with Error Handling

```
Sub ControlOutlook()

    Const sSOURCE As String = "ControlOutlook"
    Const sOUTLOOK_APP As String = "Outlook.Application"

    Dim olkApp As Outlook.Application
    Dim bOutlookCreated As Boolean

    'Try to get a reference to Outlook
    On Error Resume Next
    Set olkApp = GetObject(, sOUTLOOK_APP)

    On Error GoTo ErrorHandler

    If olkApp Is Nothing Then
        'Start Outlook
        Set olkApp = CreateObject(sOUTLOOK_APP)
        bOutlookCreated = True
    End If

    'Do something here

ErrorExit:

    'The tidy-up code is performed
    'whether or not we get an error
    If Not olkApp Is Nothing Then

        If bOutlookCreated Then
            'Close Outlook, ignoring any errors
            On Error Resume Next
            olkApp.Quit
            On Error GoTo ErrorHandler
        End If

        'Tidy up
```

```
        Set olkApp = Nothing
    End If

    Exit Sub

ErrorHandler:

    If bCentralErrorHandler(msMODULE, sSOURCE) Then
        Stop
        Resume
    Else
        Resume ErrorExit
    End If

End Sub
```

When we use CreateObject to start a new instance of PowerPoint, we actually get a reference to an existing instance if there is one already running. The Presentations collection includes all the open presentations from all the "instances" that have been created. This is similar to Outlook's behavior, but PowerPoint also tidily handles calls to Application.Quit by closing only the presentation and not the entire application. We can therefore safely use CreateObject to start PowerPoint and Application.Quit to close it.

Multiversion Support

It is a fact of Excel application development that we can expect our users to have a variety of Office versions, typically going back as far as Office 2000. We explained previously how the vTable allows object libraries to be forward compatible but not backward compatible. This means if we save our workbook containing a reference to Word 2003, it will give a compile error when run on a machine with only Office 2000 installed.

One solution to this problem is to save our workbook with a reference to the earliest version of the object library we intend to support. When a workbook saved with a reference to Word 2000 is run on a machine with Office 2003, the reference will automatically be updated to Word 2003. Unfortunately, if that workbook is then saved, the reference to Word 2003 will remain. If the workbook is forwarded to our Office 2000 user, we'll get the compile error again. This technique is therefore only suitable for workbooks that our users won't need to save, such as add-ins and the code workbooks of dictator applications.

If we put our code and UI in separate workbooks, it is probably only the UI workbook that will need to be saved by our users, thereby avoiding this problem. The safest solution, though, is to use late binding and save our workbooks without any reference to Word. When run, we can check the availability and version of Word and run the code appropriately.

Determining the Availability of an Application

The function shown in Listing 18-8 checks whether an application is installed by simply trying to start it. If the application starts successfully, the function returns a reference to it via the objApp parameter. Note that this function can (and should) be used regardless of whether we're late binding or early binding. Even if an object library exists and is registered, there is no guarantee that the application will start correctly.

Listing 18-8 Checking for an Installed Application

```
Function bIsAppAvailable(ByVal sClass As String, _
                      ByRef objApp As Object) As Boolean

    On Error Resume Next
    Set objApp = CreateObject(sClass)
    bIsAppAvailable = (Not objApp Is Nothing)
End Function
```

Performance

VBA calls between applications, such as Excel controlling Word, are extremely slow, even if we're using early binding. To improve performance, we need to keep such calls to a minimum, using With blocks and object variables to refer to items deep in the object model. For best performance, we should move the code into the target application. For example, Listing 18-9 uses Excel to populate a number of Word bookmarks, with all the code contained in Excel. In Listing 18-10, we have moved the code that populates the document into a Word template, which is opened and called from our Excel code. Although this is a trivial example, the technique can result in a significant performance improvement in more complex situations. These examples can be found on the CD in the \Concepts\Ch18—Controlling Other Office Applications folder and comprise the following:

- **PopulateWord.xls**—An Excel workbook containing both PopulateWordDoc procedures

- **Bookmarks.dot**—A simple Word template with some bookmarked text to update
- **FillDocument.dot**—A Word template containing the code from Listing 18-10

Listing 18-9 Populating a Word Document Entirely from Excel

```
'In an Excel module, with a reference to Word
Sub PopulateWordDoc1()

    Dim wrdApp As Word.Application
    Dim wrdDoc As Word.Document
    Dim sPath As String
    Dim vaBookmarks As Variant
    Dim lBookmark As Long

    'Fill the Bookmarks array from the sheet
    vaBookmarks = wksBookmarks.Range("rngBookmarkList").Value

    'Start Word
    Set wrdApp = CreateObject("Word.Application")

    'Open the template to populate
    sPath = ThisWorkbook.Path & "\"
    Set wrdDoc = wrdApp.Documents.Add(Template:=sPath & _
                "Bookmarks.dot")

    'Populate the bookmarks in the template from the array
    For lBookmark = LBound(vaBookmarks, 1) To _
                    UBound(vaBookmarks, 1)
        wrdDoc.Bookmarks(vaBookmarks(lBookmark, _
            LBound(vaBookmarks, 2))).Range.Text = _
            vaBookmarks(lBookmark, UBound(vaBookmarks, 2))
    Next lBookmark

    'Save the filled document and close it
    wrdDoc.SaveAs sPath & "Filled1.doc"
    wrdDoc.Close
    Set wrdDoc = Nothing

    'Close Word
    wrdApp.Quit False
    Set wrdApp = Nothing

End Sub
```

Listing 18-10 Populating a Word Document Using Code in Word

```
'In a module in the Word template FillDocument.dot
Public Sub FillDocument(ByVal sTemplateName As String, _
                        ByVal sSaveName As String, _
                        ByVal vaBookmarks As Variant)

    Dim docToFill As Document
    Dim lBookmark As Long

    Set docToFill = Documents.Add(Template:=sTemplateName)

    For lBookmark = LBound(vaBookmarks, 1) To _
                    UBound(vaBookmarks, 1)
        docToFill.Bookmarks(vaBookmarks(lBookmark, _
            LBound(vaBookmarks, 2))).Range.Text = _
            vaBookmarks(lBookmark, UBound(vaBookmarks, 2))
    Next lBookmark

    docToFill.SaveAs sSaveName
    docToFill.Close

End Sub

'In an Excel module, with a reference to Word
Sub PopulateWordDoc2()

    Dim wrdApp As Word.Application
    Dim wrdDoc As Word.Document
    Dim sPath As String
    Dim vaBookmarks As Variant

    'Fill the Bookmarks array from the sheet
    vaBookmarks = wksBookmarks.Range("rngBookmarkList").Value

    'Start Word
    Set wrdApp = CreateObject("Word.Application")

    'Open the template containing our controlling code
    sPath = ThisWorkbook.Path & "\"
    Set wrdDoc = wrdApp.Documents.Open(sPath & _
                    "FillDocument.dot")
```

```
'Run the code within Word, passing all required information
wrdApp.Run "FillDocument", sPath & "Bookmarks.dot", _
          sPath & "Filled2.doc", vaBookmarks

wrdDoc.Close
Set wrdDoc = Nothing

wrdApp.Quit False
Set wrdApp = Nothing

End Sub
```

The Primary Office Application Object Models

Now that we can reliably detect, start, control and shut down other Office applications, the final piece of the puzzle is to learn each application's object model. This part of the chapter provides an introduction to the main objects within each object model, demonstrating some typical uses within Excel-based applications.

All the Office applications have a top-level Application object, which is the object we get a reference to when creating new instances of the application. From the Application object, we drill down to the other objects that provide the application's functionality.

All the examples in this section can be found on the CD in the \Concepts\Ch18—Controlling Other Office Applications folder. The workbook Ch18Examples.xls contains all the example code and a data sheet to represent the results of some analysis.

Access and Data Access Objects

It's actually quite rare to automate Access itself from an Excel application. We can easily manipulate the data in an Access (Jet) database outside of Access using ActiveX Data Objects, as described in *Chapter 13 — Programming with Databases*, and there's little reason to use Access forms instead of VBA userforms. However, Access is much better than Excel for creating continuous data-driven reports, with its sorting and grouping and separate group, page and report headers and footers.

Application

Each instance of Access has a single database, which we open using `Application.OpenCurrentDatabase` and close using `Application.CloseCurrentDatabase`. The CurrentDb object exposes a Data Access Objects (DAO) Database object, which we can use to manipulate the structure of the tables and queries in the database. Most of the other properties of the Application object provide information about the state of the application, such as which tables the user has open, and are very rarely relevant when controlling Access from Excel.

DAO.Database

The DAO Database object that we get from `Application.CurrentDb` provides programmatic access to the structure of the database, via the TableDefs, QueryDefs and Relations collections. The most commonly used of these is the TableDefs collection, through which we can access the properties of the database tables. In many situations, we may have an access table linked to a separate data source, such as an Excel workbook or SQL Server table and will need to change the table's link information prior to running a report.

DoCmd

Most automation of Access is done through the DoCmd object, which provides programmatic access to most of Access' menus, including deleting tables, importing data and running reports.

Example

The procedure in Listing 18-11 runs an Access report based on data in an Excel workbook. The Access database ReportOnExcelData.mdb contains a single table, tblExcelData, to link to the Excel workbook, a query to sort the data and a report, rptExcelData, to run. The procedure creates an instance of Access, opens the database, updates the table's connection information and runs the report, leaving it displayed onscreen.

This code can be found in the MAccess module of the Ch18Examples.xls workbook and the database containing the linked table and report is called ReportOnExcelData.mdb.

Listing 18-11 Running an Access Report Using Excel Data

```
Sub AccessRunReport()

    'Requires references to the Microsoft Access and
    'Microsoft DAO object libraries
    Dim objApp As Object
    Dim accApp As Access.Application
    Dim dbData As DAO.Database
    Dim tdExcelData As DAO.TableDef

    'Update the export range
    wksAccess.Range("tblExcelDataStart").CurrentRegion _
         .Name = "tblExcelData"

    'Save any changes to the workbook, so Access can read
    'the latest version from disk
    ThisWorkbook.Save

    'Attempt to create a new instance of Access
    Set accApp = Nothing
    Set accApp = CreateObject("Access.Application")

    With accApp
         'Set the access automation security,
         'so the database opens without prompts.
         'Use late binding and On Error Resume Next
         'to ignore version issues
         On Error Resume Next
         Set objApp = accApp
         objApp.AutomationSecurity = 2 'msoAutomationSecurityLow
         On Error GoTo 0

         'Open the database
         .OpenCurrentDatabase FilePath:=ThisWorkbook.Path & _
                                    "\ReportOnExcelData.mdb"

         'Get a reference to the DAO TableDef for the
         'tblExcelData linked table
         Set dbData = .CurrentDb
         Set tdExcelData = dbData.TableDefs("tblExcelData")

         'Update the table link to point to this workbook
```

```
    tdExcelData.Connect = "Excel 8.0;HDR=YES;IMEX=2;" & _
        "DATABASE=" & ThisWorkbook.FullName

    Set tdExcelData = Nothing
    Set dbData = Nothing

    'Open and preview the report
    .DoCmd.OpenReport ReportName:="rptExcelData", _
                      View:=acViewPreview

    'Make the App visible
    .Visible = True

End With

'Clear the variable from memory
Set accApp = Nothing

End Sub
```

Word

Word is often automated from Excel when we need to populate a Word document from data in Excel—such as a monthly report that contains some data analyzed in Excel.

Application

As well as the usual properties to control the application itself, the Word Application object has a Documents collection that we use to create, open and access Word documents.

Document

The Document object provides all the information about a Word document, akin to Excel's Workbook object.

Bookmark

Each bookmark within a document is included in the `Document.Bookmarks` collection and exposed as a Bookmark object. Bookmarks enable us to easily identify elements of text within a document.

Range

A Range is a contiguous area in a document, identified by its start and end points. Many Word objects (such as Paragraph and Bookmark) have a Range property that returns the area enclosed by the object. We can populate a bookmark by setting the text of its Range. One issue with doing this is that setting the text in a bookmark deletes the bookmark. To set a bookmark's text, we have to store the bookmark's range, set the text of the range, then re-create the bookmark, as shown in Listing 18-12.

Example

Survey results are very often analyzed in Excel and published as a Word document. This is usually achieved by creating a Word template for the survey results, identifying each insertion point as a bookmark, then copying the data from the Excel workbook to the Word document using VBA. It is quite common in corporate surveys to create a document specific to each of the respondents, where each report is essentially the same, but with that respondent's results and rankings. Listing 18-12 shows a very simple example of this, where we loop through all the divisions in a company, analyzing the data and producing a document for each.

This code can be found in the MWord module of the Ch18Examples.xls workbook and the document template is called SalaryReport.dot.

Listing 18-12 Populating a Word Template from Excel Data

```
Sub GenerateDivisionSummaries()

    Dim wrdApp As Word.Application
    Dim wrdDoc As Word.Document
    Dim wrdrngBM As Word.Range
    Dim piDiv As Excel.PivotItem
    Dim rngBookmark As Excel.Range
    Dim sPath As String
    Dim sBookmarkName As String

    'Start Word
    Set wrdApp = CreateObject("Word.Application")

    sPath = ThisWorkbook.Path & "\"
    'Create a new document based on the template
    Set wrdDoc = wrdApp.Documents.Add(Template:= _
                sPath & "SalaryReport.dot")
```

```
'Loop through each division in the pivot table
For Each piDiv In wksData.PivotTables(1) _
                  .PivotFields("Division").PivotItems

    'Populate the Division Name cell
    wksData.Range("ptrDivName") = piDiv.Value

    'Recalc the sheet to update the results
    'for the division
    wksData.Calculate

    'Populate the bookmarks from the sheet
    For Each rngBookmark In _
            wksData.Range("rngBookmarks").Rows

        'Get the name of the bookmark
        sBookmarkName = rngBookmark.Cells(1, 1).Value

        'Get the Word Range that the bookmark spans
        Set wrdrngBM = wrdDoc.Bookmarks(sBookmarkName) _
                    .Range

        'Set the text of the range
        '(which deletes the bookmark)
        wrdrngBM.Text = rngBookmark.Cells(1, 2).Text

        'Re-create the bookmark for the next iteration
        wrdDoc.Bookmarks.Add sBookmarkName, wrdrngBM
    Next rngBookmark

    'Update any fields linked to these bookmarks
    wrdDoc.Fields.Update

    'Save the filled document
    wrdDoc.SaveAs sPath & "Salary Results - " & _
                  piDiv.Value & ".doc"
Next piDiv

'Close the Word document
wrdDoc.Close
Set wrdDoc = Nothing

'Close Word
```

```
wrdApp.Quit False
Set wrdApp = Nothing

End Sub
```

PowerPoint and MSGraph

PowerPoint is usually used in a similar way to Word—populating pre-prepared presentations with data from Excel.

Application

As well as the usual properties to control the application itself, the PowerPoint Application object has a Presentations collection that we use to create, open and access PowerPoint presentations.

Presentation

The Presentation object provides all the information about a PowerPoint presentation, akin to Excel's Workbook object.

Slide

The Slide object provides the information about a slide within a presentation, akin to Excel's Worksheet object. When automating PowerPoint, it helps to give each slide a meaningful name, which can be done by selecting the slide and running the following statement from the PowerPoint VBE's Immediate window:

```
ActiveWindow.Selection.SlideRange(1).Name = "NewSlideName"
```

Shape

The Shape object is the same as Excel's Shape object and is a drawing object on a Slide, which can be a container for text boxes, lines, pictures or embedded objects such as charts. A shape can be given a meaningful name by selecting it and running the following statement from the PowerPoint VBE's Immediate window:

```
ActiveWindow.Selection.ShapeRange(1).Name = "NewShapeName"
```

Charts

PowerPoint charts are provided by the MSGraph object model, which is a version of Excel's charting engine, modified to remove the worksheet links. As such, most Excel charting code will work on a PowerPoint chart. However, it is quite common to prepare the charts within Excel, copy them to the clipboard and paste them as pictures in PowerPoint.

Example

The procedure in Listing 18-13 updates a PowerPoint presentation with data from an Excel spreadsheet. It updates both text in a bulleted list and the source data for an embedded chart.

This code can be found in the MPowerPoint module of the Ch18Examples.xls workbook and the presentation we're updating is called Salary Presentation.ppt.

Listing 18-13 Populating a PowerPoint Presentation from Excel Data

```
Sub PPTGenerateSalarySummary()

    'Powerpoint objects
    Dim pptApp As PowerPoint.Application
    Dim pptPres As PowerPoint.Presentation
    Dim pptSlide As PowerPoint.Slide
    Dim pptBullets As PowerPoint.Shape

    'MSGraph objects
    Dim gphChart As Graph.Chart
    Dim gphData As Graph.DataSheet

    'Excel objects
    Dim pfDiv As Excel.PivotField
    Dim rngDiv As Excel.Range

    'Other variables
    Dim sBulletText As String
    Dim lDiv As Long

    'Start PowerPoint
    Set pptApp = CreateObject("PowerPoint.Application")

    'Switch back to Excel
```

```
AppActivate Application.Caption

'Open the presentation
Set pptPres = pptApp.Presentations.Open(Filename:= _
    ThisWorkbook.Path & "\Salary Presentation.ppt", _
    withwindow:=False)

'Get the 'Detail' slide
Set pptSlide = pptPres.Slides("sldDetail")

'Get the shape containing the bulleted list
Set pptBullets = pptSlide.Shapes("shpBullets")

'Get the text of the first bullet in the list
sBulletText = pptBullets.TextFrame.TextRange _
    .Paragraphs(1).Text

'Update the text with the calculated total
'from the worksheet
sBulletText = Replace(sBulletText, "#SalaryTotal#", _
    wksData.Range("ptrSalaryTotal").Text)

'Update the presentation with the correct text
pptBullets.TextFrame.TextRange.Paragraphs(1) _
    .Text = sBulletText

'Get the MSGraph Chart object embedded in the slide
Set gphChart = pptSlide.Shapes("shpChart").OLEFormat _
    .Object

'Get the graph's data sheet
Set gphData = gphChart.Application.DataSheet

'Get the 'Division' pivot field in the Data worksheet
Set pfDiv = wksData.PivotTables(1).PivotFields("Division")

'Loop through the range of Divisions in the pivot table
For Each rngDiv In pfDiv.DataRange
    lDiv = lDiv + 1

    'Write the division name and total salary to the
    'graph data sheet
    gphData.Cells(1, lDiv + 1).Value = rngDiv.Text
```

```
        gphData.Cells(2, lDiv + 1).Value = rngDiv _
            .Offset(0, 1).Value
Next rngDiv

'Apply the datasheet changes
gphChart.Application.Update

'Redraw the chart object
gphChart.Refresh

'Save the presentation with a new name
pptPres.SaveAs ThisWorkbook.Path & "\Salaries 2003.ppt"

'Tidy up object variables
Set pptSlide = Nothing
Set pptBullets = Nothing
Set gphChart = Nothing
Set gphData = Nothing

'Close the presentation
pptPres.Close
Set pptPres = Nothing

'Close PowerPoint
pptApp.Quit
Set pptApp = Nothing

'Display confirmation message
MsgBox "Salary Summary Presentation Generated OK."

End Sub
```

Outlook

Outlook behaves quite differently to the rest of the Office applications. It only allows one instance to be open at any time and doesn't use the 'document' concept. Instead, it stores all its data in a single data file, represented by a Namespace object. The data file is internally structured as multiple folders that each contain a specific category of information, such as e-mails, contacts, appointments and so on.

Application

The Outlook Application object provides access to the data store through the GetNamespace property and allows us to easily create new data items (e-mails, contacts, appointments and so on) using the CreateItem method.

Namespace

The Namespace object represents an Outlook data store. Outlook was originally designed to support multiple types of data store, but only one was ever implemented. That is called the MAPI data store and is retrieved using `Application.GetNamespace("MAPI")`. The Namespace object acts as a container for all the Outlook folders, enabling us to navigate the entire folder hierarchy. It also provides the GetDefaultFolder() property to access each of the top-level folders.

MAPIFolder

The MAPIFolder object represents a single Outlook folder, such as the Inbox, Contacts or Calendar folder. It has a Folders property that returns a collection of child folders, enabling us to drill down and an Items property that returns a collection of all the individual items (e-mails, contacts and so on) contained in the folder.

AppointmentItem, ContactItem, DistributionListItem, JournalItem, MailItem, NoteItem, PostItItem and TaskItem

These objects represent the individual items within an Outlook folder. We can access them through the Items collection of a MAPIFolder and create them by using either the Add method of an Items collection or the CreateItem method of the Application object. In either case, we get an empty object of the appropriate type which we populate and save to the data store.

Example

The procedure shown in Listing 18-14 retrieves all the holidays for a specified year from the default Outlook Calendar, displaying them in an Excel worksheet.

Listing 18-14 Retrieving Holiday Dates from the Outlook Calendar

```
Sub OutlookRetrieveHolidays()

    'Outlook objects
    Dim olApp As Outlook.Application
    Dim olNS As Outlook.Namespace
    Dim olItems As Outlook.Items
    Dim olAppt As Outlook.AppointmentItem

    Dim bCreated As Boolean
    Dim lYear As Long
    Dim lRow As Long

    'Obtain a reference to Outlook
    On Error Resume Next
    Set olApp = GetObject(, "Outlook.Application")
    On Error GoTo 0

    'If Outlook isn't running, start it and remember
    If olApp Is Nothing Then
        Set olApp = CreateObject("Outlook.Application")
        bCreated = True
    End If

    'Get the MAPI namespace
    Set olNS = olApp.GetNamespace("MAPI")

    'Get the items in the Calendar
    Set olItems = olNS.GetDefaultFolder(olFolderCalendar) _
        .Items

    'Clear the destination range if previously used
    wksOutlook.Range("tblStart").CurrentRegion.ClearContents

    'Get the year criteria
    lYear = wksOutlook.Range("Year").Value

    'Set the default row counter
    lRow = 1

    'Loop through the calendar entries
    For Each olAppt In olItems

        'We only want holidays...
```

```
    If olAppt.Categories = "Holiday" Then

      '... with a title ...
      If Len(olAppt.Subject) > 0 Then

        '... that start in the given year ...
        If Year(olAppt.Start) = lYear Then
          wksOutlook.Range("tblStart") _
            .Cells(lRow, 1).Value = olAppt.Subject

          wksOutlook.Range("tblStart") _
            .Cells(lRow, 2).Value = olAppt.Start
          lRow = lRow + 1
        End If
      End If
    End If
  Next olAppt

  'Sort the holidays by date
  With wksOutlook.Range("tblStart").CurrentRegion
      .Sort key1:=.Cells(1, 2), order1:=xlAscending, _
          Header:=xlNo
  End With

  'Clear intermediate Outlook object variables
  Set olAppt = Nothing
  Set olItems = Nothing
  Set olNS = Nothing

  'Close Outlook if we started it
  If bCreated Then olApp.Quit

  'Clear the Outlook application variable
  Set olApp = Nothing

End Sub
```

Further Reading

The Office Developer Center on the MSDN Web site should be your first point of call to learn about programming the Office applications. Start at http://msdn.microsoft.com/office/understanding/ and click through to the application you're interested in. There have also been numerous books written for each application, of which the following are usually considered among the best. All have a 5-star rating at Amazon.com:

Title:	*Access 2002 Desktop Developer's Handbook*
Author:	Paul Litwin, Ken Getz, Mike Gunderloy
Publisher:	Sybex Books
ISBN:	0782140092

Title:	*Powerful PowerPoint for Educators*
Author:	David M. Marcovitz
Publisher:	Libraries Unlimited
ISBN:	1591580951

Title:	*Microsoft Outlook Programming*
Author:	Sue Mosher
Publisher:	Digital Press
ISBN:	1555582869

It seems that the publishing community has decided that books about programming Word do not sell enough to be profitable—the latest editions are for Word 2000. The best way to learn more about programming Word is to start at the Word MVP Web site at `http://www.mvps.org/word` and follow the links from there.

Practical Example

It would be too artificial to extend either the PETRAS timesheet add-in or the PETRAS reporting application to control one or more of the other Office applications. Excel's features are sufficient for our analysis and reporting requirements. If we were to do so, however, we would use the procedures shown in Listing 18-11 to Listing 18-14, which should be considered to be the practical examples for this chapter.

Conclusion

Excel is only one part of the Office suite of applications. Although its data handling, word processing and presentation features are usually sufficient for many applications, we can often add a great deal of value to our applications by controlling some of the other components of the Office suite.

The easiest way to control the other Office applications is to have a pre-prepared template database, document or presentation that we open, modify and save; all the examples in this chapter do exactly that.

This chapter has barely scratched the surface of each application's object model, only describing the object models in sufficient detail for you to understand the sample code and get started using them. We can achieve some impressive results with only a little knowledge of the objects, so learning to automate the other Office applications is not as daunting a prospect as it first appears.

XLLs and the C API

This chapter in no way attempts to provide a complete guide to programming Excel using the C API. That would be a book-length topic in its own right. A skilled C++ programmer with an in-depth knowledge of the Excel C API can create add-ins that can do anything a VBA add-in can do.

Instead, this chapter focuses on the core strength of the C API and what is arguably the most common use for it in Excel development: programming custom worksheet functions. Even this topic is too large to be covered in a single chapter, so we get you started with solid fundamentals and then point you to additional resources at the end of the chapter.

All the examples discussed in this chapter assume that you are running Microsoft Visual C++.NET 2003. The accompanying CD contains complete versions of the sample project discussed below for both VC++ 6.0 and VC++.NET 2003 in the \Concepts\Chapter 19—XLLs and the C API folder. If you are unfamiliar with C programming, you are strongly advised to open the sample files and follow along as you read. C is a very verbose programming language compared to VB/VBA, so we only have room to show the most important code contained in the sample.

Why Create an XLL-Based Worksheet Function

An XLL is a Windows DLL that is structured so Excel can recognize and open it directly. Because worksheet functions built into XLLs are compiled to machine code and treated by Excel as if they were native worksheet functions, they are extremely fast. You can create custom versions of worksheet functions that Excel doesn't get quite right as well as creating worksheet functions that Excel doesn't provide at all.

Also, Excel doesn't store hard-coded paths to XLL-based worksheet functions, so they don't suffer from broken links when files are relocated like VBA add-in based functions do.

Creating an XLL Project in Visual Studio

An XLL is just a Windows DLL with a .xll file extension and an internal structure that Excel recognizes. Prior to creating your XLL project, you need to copy the *xlcall.h* and *xlcall32.lib* from the Microsoft Excel 97 SDK into your Visual Studio include and lib directories, respectively.

We're using the SDK for Excel 97 because that was the last version of Excel for which Microsoft released an SDK. There have been no fundamental changes to the underlying Excel C API since the Excel 97 SDK was written, so this is not a problem. The Excel 97 SDK can be downloaded from `http://download.microsoft.com/download/ excel97win/Install/1.0/W9XNT4XP/EN-US/excel97sdk.exe`.

To create your XLL project, choose *File > New > Project* from the Visual Studio menu. In the New Project dialog, expand the *Visual C++ Projects* folder on the left side and select the *Win32* folder. From the *Templates* list, select *Win32 Console Project*. Enter the name for your XLL in the *Name* text box and select the location where you want the project to be saved. This is shown in Figure 19-1.

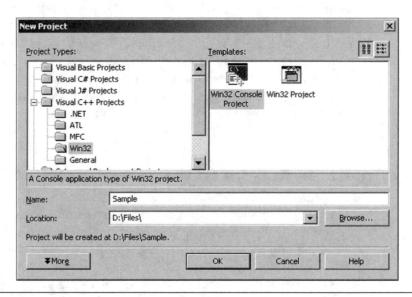

Figure 19-1 Creating the Initial XLL Project

Click the OK button and Visual Studio will display the Application Wizard dialog box shown in Figure 19-2. Select *Application Settings* on the left side and choose *DLL* as your Application type. Place a check mark in the *Empty project* check box under *Additional options* and click the Finish button. You will now have an empty Win32 DLL project.

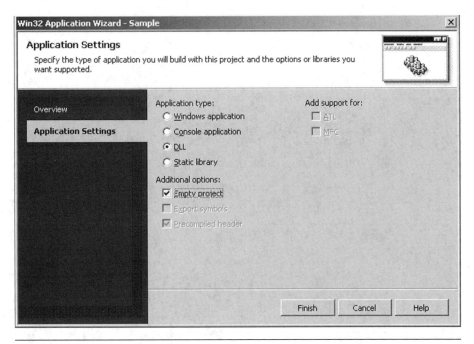

Figure 19-2 Choosing the Correct Application Wizard Settings

Next you will add two files to your project. Select *File > Add New Item* from the Visual Studio menu. In the Add New Item dialog, select *C++ File (.cpp)* from the *Templates* list. This will be the file that contains your code. Because we are creating a C project, you need to explicitly give your file a .c extension, as shown in Figure 19-3. The *Location* setting should already be pointing to your project folder. Leave this as is.

The next file you need to add to your project is a module definition file. This will enable you to export function names from your XLL that Excel can recognize. Select *File > Add New Item* from the Visual Studio menu again, but this time choose *Module-Definition File (.def)* from the list of templates. Give your module definition file the same name as the .c code file you added above, but with a .def file extension, as shown in Figure 19-4.

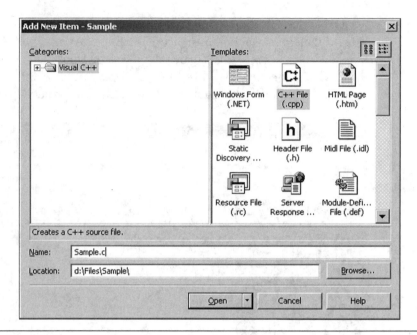

Figure 19-3 Adding a Code File to Your XLL Project

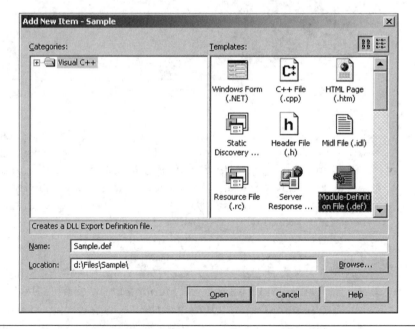

Figure 19-4 Adding a Module Definition File to Your XLL Project

You need to make several project-level settings before you're ready to start writing code. Choose *Project > Sample Properties* from the Visual Studio menu (where *Sample* is the actual name you selected for your project). In the Sample Property Pages dialog shown in Figure 19-5, select the *Debugging* folder from the tree view. Then select the *Command* option from the list of settings on the right side and browse to the location of Excel.exe on your computer. This tells Visual Studio what program to use when debugging your XLL.

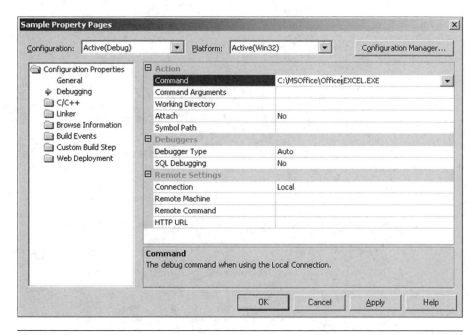

Figure 19-5 Specifying Excel.exe as the Debugging Program for Your XLL Project

Then select the *C/C++* folder, followed by the *General* subfolder from the tree view. The first setting you need to change is the *Debug Information Format* setting. The default value for this setting is *Program Database for Edit and Continue*. This value will add debug symbols to the XLL that will cause Excel not to recognize it. Change this setting to *Program Database* instead. This setting is demonstrated in Figure 19-6.

Then select the *Linker* folder, followed by the *General* subfolder from the tree view. In the *Output File* setting, manually change the file extension of the output filename from .dll to .xll, as shown in Figure 19-7.

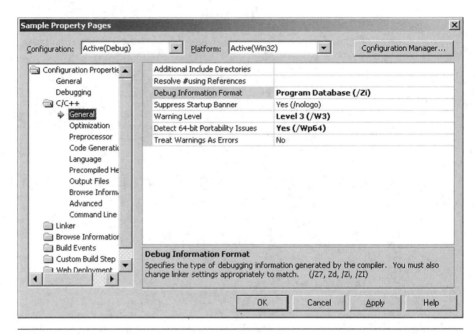

Figure 19-6 Specifying the Correct Debug Information Format Setting

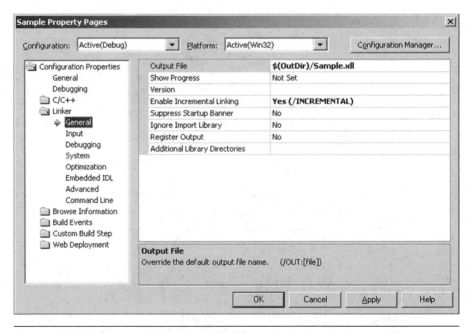

Figure 19-7 Changing the Output Filename Extension

Select the *Release* entry from the *Configurations* drop-down and repeat the file extension change for the release build. Finally, choose the *Input* folder from the Linker section of the tree view. Choose the *All Configurations* entry from the *Configurations* drop-down. Type the file-name xlcall32.lib into the *Additional Dependencies* setting as shown in Figure 19-8.

We've made all the necessary settings now, so click the OK button and we'll start writing the code for our XLL.

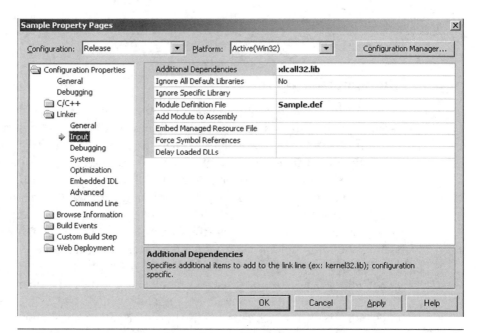

Figure 19-8 Adding xlcall32.lib to the Additional Dependencies for Your Project

The Structure of an XLL

We'll start our discussion by creating an XLL that contains two trivial custom worksheet functions. This will allow us to concentrate on the structure required to create an XLL independent of whatever worksheet functions it happens to contain. We look at an example of a real-world function later in the chapter. Listing 19-1 shows the two custom worksheet functions our first XLL will provide.

Listing 19-1 Sample Custom Worksheet Functions

```
double WINAPI AddTwo(double d1, double d2)
{
    return d1 + d2;
}

double WINAPI MultiplyTwo(double d1, double d2)
{
    return d1 * d2;
}
```

The Function Table

The first thing you need to do when creating your XLL is build a function table. This is a three-dimensional string array holding detailed descriptions of each of the custom worksheet functions that your XLL contains. The function table will be used to register each custom worksheet function with Excel when the XLL is opened. The first dimension of the table holds an entry for each custom worksheet function in the XLL. The second dimension of the table holds all of the arguments that will be passed to the Register function for a given custom worksheet function. The third dimension of the table holds the string values for each argument

The maximum allowable length of a Register function argument string is 255 characters. You must leave a blank space at the first character position of each string in the table (even unused strings). This is because Excel does not use null-terminated C strings but rather byte-counted Pascal strings. Later we will insert a byte count for each string in its first character position.

Listing 19-2 shows the function table that describes our two custom worksheet functions. Note that the NUM_REGISTER_ARGS constant must be large enough so the function table can hold all the descriptions required for the custom worksheet function in the XLL that contains the most arguments. For custom worksheet functions with fewer than the maximum number of arguments, the unused argument help topic entries at the end of the table can be left empty and Excel will ignore them. Adjustments to the NUM_REGISTER_ARGS constant must also be reflected in the HandleRegistration function described in the *Registering and Unregistering Custom Worksheet Functions* section later in the chapter.

Listing 19-2 The Sample XLL Function Table

```c
#define NUM_FUNCTIONS          2
#define NUM_REGISTER_ARGS      11
#define MAX_LENGTH             255

static char
gszWorksheetFuncs[NUM_FUNCTIONS][NUM_REGISTER_ARGS][MAX_LENGTH] =
{
    {" AddTwo",                          // procedure
     " BBB",                             // type_text
     " AddTwo",                          // function_text
     " d1, d2",                          // argument_text
     " 1",                               // macro_type
     " Sample Add-in",                   // category
     " ",                                // shortcut_text
     " ",                                // help_topic
     " Adds the two arguments.",         // function_help
     " The first number to add.",        // argument_help1
     " The second number to add."        // argument_help2
    },
    {" MultiplyTwo",
     " BBB",
     " MultiplyTwo",
     " d1, d2",
     " 1",
     " Sample Add-in",
     " ",
     " ",
     " Multiplies the two arguments.",
     " The first number to multiply.",
     " The second number to multiply."
    }
};
```

The following are brief descriptions of the purpose and usage of each entry in the function table in the order in which they appear. We describe how to actually register your functions with Excel based on this information in the *Registering and Unregistering Custom Worksheet Functions* section.

- procedure—This is the name of your custom worksheet function. It should be exactly the same as the name that appears in your function definition.
- type_text—This is a coded string that specifies the data types of all the function's arguments as well as its return value. The first letter specifies the return type of the function and all following letters specify the data types expected by each of the functions arguments, from left to right. Table 19-1 lists the codes for the most commonly used data types. For a complete list of data types, see the Microsoft Excel 97 SDK, referenced in the *Additional Resources* section at the end of the chapter.

  Excel normally recalculates worksheet functions only when they are first entered into a worksheet cell or when one of their dependencies changes. You can make a custom worksheet function volatile by appending an exclamation point character (!) to the end of that function's type_text string. Volatile functions are recalculated whenever any worksheet cell is recalculated. Therefore, you must be very careful with them, because they can cause extreme degradation in recalculation performance.
- function_text—This is the name of the function as it will appear in the Excel Function Wizard.
- argument_text—This text string enables you to display a list of arguments that your function accepts in the Excel Function Wizard.

Table 19-1 The Most Commonly Used type_text Data Types

Code	Description	Data Type
A	Boolean (TRUE = 1, FALSE = 0)	short int
B	Floating point number	double
D	Byte-counted string (max length = 255 characters)	unsigned char *
I	Signed 2-byte integer	short int
J	Signed 4-byte integer	int
K	Array	FP * (see below)
P	Excel OPER struct	OPER *
R	Excel XLOPER struct	XLOPER *

- `macro_type`—This is a numeric value indicating the type of the function. Excel worksheet functions always have a macro type of 1. We will make use of the hidden function macro type 0 to overcome a bug in unregistering custom worksheet functions. The last macro type is 2, which defines a function that can only be called from an XLM macro sheet. This function type is beyond the scope of this chapter.
- `category`—Enables you to specify the category that your function will appear in when viewed in the Function Wizard. You should always create a separate category for custom worksheet functions so you do not confuse the user about which functions are built-in and which functions require your XLL to be loaded in order to be used.
- `shortcut_text`—This is used to assign a shortcut key to command-type functions. This function type will not be covered here, so this entry can be left empty.
- `help_topic`—If you have a custom help file associated with your XLL, this will be the help topic ID for this worksheet function.
- `function_help`—This is a short descriptive help text string that will appear in the Excel Function Wizard when the user selects your function.
- `argument_help1 ... 20`—This is a short descriptive help text string that will appear in the Function Wizard when the user is entering data for each of your arguments. An Excel worksheet function can take up to 29 arguments. Unfortunately, the Register function, which we discuss later, uses the first nine of its arguments for other purposes. Therefore, you can only document the first 20 arguments of any custom worksheet function. All arguments beyond the 20th will have an argument help string that is a duplicate of that used for the 20th argument.

Note again that every function must have exactly the same number of entries in the function table, so the function with the maximum number of arguments determines the number of function table entries for all the functions in your XLL. If an argument_helpX string is not used by a function, leave it empty and Excel will ignore it.

The K data type is most frequently used as a custom worksheet function argument type because it is the nearest thing in the Excel C API to a strongly typed array data type. To use K data type arguments in your XLL, you need to add the definition for the FP struct shown in Listing 19-3 to your code.

Listing 19-3 The FP Struct

```
typedef struct _FP
{
    unsigned short int rows;
    unsigned short int columns;
    double array[1];
} FP;
```

When received as an argument, the array[] member of the FP struct will be sized such that it contains rows*columns elements.

The DLLMain Function

Because an XLL is just a variation on a standard Windows DLL, Windows will be expecting to find a DLLMain function to call when it loads the XLL. In most XLLs, this function doesn't have to do anything other than return TRUE. You may use the DLLMain function for any normal initialization operations if you want, but in an XLL it is more customary to use the xlAutoOpen callback function for this purpose.

There is one situation where use of the DLLMain function makes more sense than xlAutoOpen. This is when your XLL requires some critical internal initialization to succeed, and if that initialization fails you want to prevent Excel from loading the XLL. By returning FALSE from DLLMain, you can prevent Excel from loading your XLL. In our sample XLL, DLLMain will be empty except for a return TRUE; statement, as shown in Listing 19-4.

Listing 19-4 The DllMain Function

```
BOOL WINAPI DllMain(HINSTANCE hInstance, DWORD fdwReason, PVOID
pvReserved)
{
    return TRUE;
}
```

Standard XLL Callback Functions

Excel calls the following three functions at various times during its use of an XLL. Only the xlAutoOpen function is strictly required, but most XLLs will make use of all three of these callback functions.

xlAutoOpen

The xlAutoOpen function is the startup function of your XLL. xlAutoOpen is called whenever:

- You open the XLL file from the Excel *File* > *Open* menu.
- You load the XLL as an add-in using the *Tools* > *Add-ins* menu.
- The XLL is in the XLSTART directory and is automatically opened when Excel starts.
- Excel opens the XLL for any other reason.
- A macro calls the XLM REGISTER() function with only one argument, which is the name of the XLL.

Note that the xlAutoOpen function will not be called if your XLL is opened from a VBA macro using the Workbooks.Open method. This is consistent with the behavior of VBA add-ins. If you want to load your XLL from VBA, use the `Application.RegisterXLL` method instead.

xlAutoOpen should register all the custom worksheet functions in the XLL and perform any other initialization your XLL requires. Listing 19-5 shows the xlAutoOpen code for our sample XLL. We defer discussion of how the HandleRegistration function works until we've covered the XLOPER data type and the Excel4 function.

Listing 19-5 The xlAutoOpen Function

```
EXPORT int WINAPI xlAutoOpen(void)
{
    static XLOPER xDLL;
    int i, j;

    // In the following loop, the strings in
    // gszFunctionTable are byte-counted.
    for (i = 0; i < NUM_FUNCTIONS; ++i)
        for (j = 0; j < NUM_REGISTER_ARGS; ++j)
            gszFunctionTable[i][j][0] =
                (BYTE) lstrlen(gszFunctionTable[i][j] + 1);

    // Register the functions using our custom procedure.
    HandleRegistration(TRUE);

    return 1;
}
```

xlAutoClose

The xlAutoClose function is the shutdown function of your XLL. xlAutoClose is called whenever:

- You quit Excel.
- You unselect the XLL from the add-ins list under the *Tools > Add-ins* menu.

xlAutoClose should perform any cleanup operations required by your XLL as well as unregister the worksheet functions it contains so they no longer appear in the Function Wizard or the Paste Functions list. Note that if the user attempts to exit Excel when there is an unsaved workbook open, Excel will call the xlAutoClose function of any open XLLs before prompting the user to save changes to the unsaved workbook. If the user cancels the save prompt, Excel and your XLL will remain open. This may constrain the amount of cleanup you can safely do in the xlAutoClose function in some circumstances. Listing 19-6 shows the xlAutoClose function for our sample XLL. Again, we defer discussion of how the HandleRegistration function works until later in the chapter.

Listing 19-6 The xlAutoClose Function

```
EXPORT int WINAPI xlAutoClose(void)
{
    // Unregister the worksheet functions
    // using our custom procedure.
    HandleRegistration(FALSE);
    return 1;
}
```

xlAddInManagerInfo

The Excel Add-in Manager calls the xlAddinManagerInfo function when it loads your XLL in order to determine the descriptive string that it should display for your XLL in the list of add-ins. This function is not strictly required. If you don't provide it, the Add-in Manager will use the filename of the XLL as the descriptive text. However, providing a descriptive name for your XLL makes it much easier for users to locate. Listing 19-7 shows the xlAddinManagerInfo code for our sample XLL. We describe what most of this code is doing in the sections on the XLOPER data type and the Excel4 function.

Listing 19-7 The xlAddInManagerInfo Function

```
EXPORT LPXLOPER WINAPI xlAddInManagerInfo(LPXLOPER xlAction)
{
    static XLOPER xlReturn, xlLongName, xlTemp;

    // Coerce the argument XLOPER to an integer.
    xlTemp.xltype = xltypeInt;
    xlTemp.val.w = xltypeInt;
    Excel4(xlCoerce, &xlReturn, 2, xlAction, &xlTemp);

    // The only valid argument value is 1. In this case we
    // return the long name for the XLL. Any other value should
    // result in the return of a #VALUE! error.
    if(1 == xlReturn.val.w)
    {
        xlLongName.xltype = xltypeStr;
        xlLongName.val.str = "\021Sample XLL Add-in";
    }
    else
    {
        xlLongName.xltype = xltypeErr;
        xlLongName.val.err = xlerrValue;
    }

    return &xlLongName;
}
```

Note how we've manually byte-counted the descriptive text string for our XLL using an octal length prefix, \021. This is the format in which Excel expects to receive all string values. Rather than using the C convention of relying on the position of a null character within a string to determine its length, Excel uses the Pascal convention of a numeric prefix specifying the length of a string.

Additional XLL Callback Functions

The following functions are optional and will not be covered in detail in this chapter.

xlAutoRegister

Excel will call the xlAutoRegister function if an XLM macro tries to register one of the custom worksheet functions contained in the XLL without specifying the type_text argument. In that case, Excel passes the name of the function the XLM macro tried to register to the xlAutoRegister function and the xlAutoRegister function should fully register the function it was passed. If the function name passed by Excel is not recognized, xlAutoRegister should return a #VALUE! error. The prototype for the xlAutoRegister function is as follows:

```
LPXLOPER WINAPI xlAutoRegister(LPXLOPER);
```

xlAutoAdd

The xlAutoAdd function works exactly like the xlAutoOpen function except Excel only calls xlAutoAdd when the Excel Add-in Manager loads the XLL. The prototype for the xlAutoAdd function is as follows:

```
int WINAPI xlAutoAdd(void);
```

xlAutoRemove

The xlAutoRemove function works exactly like the xlAutoClose function except Excel only calls xlAutoRemove when the Excel Add-in Manager unloads the XLL. The prototype for the xlAutoRemove function is as follows:

```
int WINAPI xlAutoRemove(void);
```

xlAutoFree

We discuss this function in a bit more detail in the section on the XLOPER data type below. Briefly, when your XLL passes an XLOPER containing a pointer to a large amount of memory that is managed by the XLL, you can tell Excel to call the xlAutoFree function as soon as it is finished with that XLOPER so the memory it uses can be freed as soon as possible. The prototype for the xlAutoFree function is as follows:

```
void WINAPI xlAutoFree(LPXLOPER xlToFree);
```

The XLOPER and OPER Data Types

As you can see from the definitions of our two sample functions in Listing 19-1, you can write a custom Excel worksheet function using nothing but fundamental C data types. However, any time you need to communicate with Excel through its C API or create custom worksheet functions that support multiple return data types or use optional arguments, you'll need to make use of the special Excel XLOPER data type and its subset OPER. An XLOPER is a struct that provides all the storage permutations required to implement the polymorphic behavior you experience when working with cells on an Excel worksheet. The definition of the XLOPER data type is located in the xlcall.h file and is reproduced in Listing 19-8.

Listing 19-8 The XLOPER Data Type

```
typedef struct xloper
{
    union
    {
        double num;                     /* xltypeNum */
        LPSTR str;                      /* xltypeStr */
        WORD bool;                      /* xltypeBool */
        WORD err;                       /* xltypeErr */
        short int w;                    /* xltypeInt */
        struct
        {
            WORD count;                 /* always = 1 */
            XLREF ref;
        } sref;                         /* xltypeSRef */
        struct
        {
            XLMREF far *lpmref;
            DWORD idSheet;
        } mref;                         /* xltypeRef */
        struct
        {
            struct xloper far *lparray;
            WORD rows;
            WORD columns;
        } array;                        /* xltypeMulti */
        struct
        {
            union
```

```
            {
                short int level;              /* xlflowRestart */
                short int tbctrl;             /* xlflowPause */
                DWORD idSheet;                /* xlflowGoto */
            } valflow;
            WORD rw;                           /* xlflowGoto */
            BYTE col;                          /* xlflowGoto */
            BYTE xlflow;
        } flow;                               /* xltypeFlow */
        struct
        {
            union
            {
                BYTE far *lpbData;            /* data passed to XL */
                HANDLE hdata;                 /* data returned from XL */
            } h;
            long cbData;
        } bigdata;                            /* xltypeBigData */
    } val;
    WORD xltype;
} XLOPER, FAR *LPXLOPER;

// The following additional structs are used to implement
// the SRef and Ref XLOPER subtypes.

// Describes a single rectangular reference
typedef struct xlref
{
    WORD rwFirst;
    WORD rwLast;
    BYTE colFirst;
    BYTE colLast;
} XLREF, FAR *LPXLREF;

// Describes multiple rectangular references.
// This is a variable size structure.
// Its default size is 1 reference.
typedef struct xlmref
{
    WORD count;
    XLREF reftbl[1];             // actually reftbl[count]
} XLMREF, FAR *LPXLMREF;
```

At its simplest level an XLOPER contains two pieces of information: some kind of data and a flag indicating what type of data that is. There are 12 possible data types an XLOPER can hold. These are represented by the following constants defined in the xlcall.h header file:

- `xltypeNum`—Used for both integer and floating point numeric data.
- `xltypeStr`—A byte-counted string.
- `xltypeBool`—A boolean value.
- `xltypeRef`—An external cell reference or multiple area reference.
- `xltypeErr`—An error value.
- `xltypeFlow`—An XLM macro flow control command.
- `xltypeMulti`—An array of values.
- `xltypeMissing`—A missing worksheet function argument.
- `xltypeNil`—An empty XLOPER.
- `xltypeSRef`—A single rectangular cell reference on the current sheet.
- `xltypeInt`—A short int. Not commonly used.
- `xltypeBigData`—Used for persistent data storage.

Due to space limitations, we only discuss the most frequently used XLOPER types. When you receive an XLOPER from Excel, either as an argument to a custom worksheet function or as the return value from an Excel4 function call (discussed later), you query the xltype member of the XLOPER struct to determine what type of data you are receiving. When you create an XLOPER, you set the xltype member to indicate what type of data your XLOPER holds. The following are some examples of XLOPERs you might create:

Numeric data: Although the XLOPER data type has two fields that could potentially contain numeric data, only one is commonly used: xltypeNum. This is equivalent to the double data type in C. Because xltypeInt is a short int data type, its size constraints rule it out for many purposes.

```
XLOPER xlNum;
xlNum.xltype = xltypeNum;
xlNum.val.num = 5.5;
```

String data: The key thing to remember when using string data with Excel is that Excel does not use null-terminated C strings. Instead, it uses byte-counted Pascal strings. Therefore, you ***must*** byte-count any string you pass to Excel and be sure not to treat any string returned from Excel as if it were a C string. For string literals, the byte count must be provided in octal format, as shown in the following example.

```
XLOPER xlString;
xlString.xltype = xltypeStr;
xlString.val.str = "\035This is a byte-counted string";
```

Error values: One important use of XLOPERs is to provide your function with the ability to return a normal value when the function is used correctly and an error value when the function has been used outside of its expected parameters. An error value is indicated by the type xltypeErr and the `err` field is set to one of the following error value constants supplied in xlcall.h:

- `xlerrNull`—(#NULL!) Refers to the intersection of two ranges that don't intersect.
- `xlerrDiv0`—(#DIV/0!) Indicates an attempt to divide by zero or by a blank cell.
- `xlerrValue`—(#VALUE!) Indicates an argument of the wrong type.
- `xlerrRef`—(#REF!) Indicates an invalid cell reference.
- `xlerrName`—(#NAME?) Indicates a string value that cannot be recognized as a function or defined name.
- `xlerrNum`—(#NUM!) Indicates that an argument value is out of bounds.
- `xlerrNA`—(#N/A) Indicates that the function cannot calculate a valid return value based on the arguments passed to it.

In the following example we create an XLOPER containing a #VALUE! error:

```
XLOPER xlError;
xlError.xltype = xltypeErr;
xlError.val.err = xlerrValue;
```

Arrays: These are somewhat more complex XLOPERs that enable you to return arrays from your custom worksheet functions, thereby creating custom array formulas. In Listing 19-9, we create an XLOPER containing the array {1, 2, 3, 4}.

Listing 19-9 An XLOPER Containing an Array

```
XLOPER xlArray, xlValues[4];
int i;
for (i = 0; i < 4; ++i)
{
    xlValues[i].xltype = xltypeNum;
    xlValues[i].val.num = i + 1;
}
xlArray.xltype = xltypeMulti;
xlArray.val.array.lparray = &xlValues[0];
xlArray.val.array.rows = 1;
xlArray.val.array.columns = 4;
```

The most difficult part of using XLOPERs is deciding whether the XLL or Excel is responsible for the memory allocated to the XLOPER and any data it points to, as well as determining when and how this memory should be freed. The OPER data type is a struct that is a subset of an XLOPER containing only value data types, not reference data types. This makes it much simpler to work with because there is never any memory allocated to an OPER that needs to be freed by either the XLL or Excel. As a general rule, if your worksheet function accepts OPER data types as arguments and uses XLOPER data types as return values, your memory management chores will be much simplified.

The definition of the OPER struct is not included in the xlcall.h file and you are not required to define it in your application in order to accept OPER arguments to or return an OPER data type from your custom worksheet functions. You can simply declare your arguments and return values as LPXLOPER (an alias for XLOPER *) and then register your function with the code P at the appropriate positions within the type_text argument in your function table. Excel will then pass and accept OPER structs even though XLOPER structs were specified in your function definition.

If you want to declare and use OPER variables in your XLL, you will need to add the OPER struct definition shown in Listing 19-10 to your project.

Listing 19-10 The OPER Data Type

```
typedef struct _oper
{
    union
```

```
    {
        double num;
        unsigned char *str;
        unsigned short int bool;
        unsigned short int err;
        struct
        {
            struct _oper *lparray;
            unsigned short int rows;
            unsigned short int columns;
        } array;
    } val;
    unsigned short int type;
} OPER;
```

The Excel4 Function

The entire breadth of the Excel C API is accessed through a single function called Excel4. This function is declared in xlcall.h as follows:

```
int far _cdecl Excel4(int xlfn,
        LPXLOPER operRes, int count,... );
```

As you can see, the Excel4 function has three required parameters followed by a variable argument list. The required parameters and their meanings are as follows:

- xlfn—This is a constant that identifies the Excel function you are trying to call. The values for this parameter are defined in xlcall.h. There are three types of functions that can be called by the Excel4 function. C API-only functions are identified by a constant with a prefix of xl. These will be discussed in the next section. Excel4 can also call all valid Excel worksheet functions. These are identified by a constant with an xlf prefix. Finally, all valid XLM macro commands can be called from Excel4. These command-equivalent functions are identified by a constant with the prefix xlc. We do not cover command-equivalent functions in this chapter.

- `operRes`—This argument takes either the address of an XLOPER variable in which the Excel4 function will place the result of the function being called, or zero if the function being called does not have a return value. We address memory management issues related to Excel4 XLOPER return values in the *XLOPERs and Memory Management* section later in the chapter.
- `count`—This argument is used to tell Excel4 how many optional arguments follow. The number of optional arguments varies depending on the specific function being called and can vary from 0 to 30. All optional arguments passed to Excel4 must be either XLOPER or OPER data types.

You must always remember to make a distinction between the result of the function being called by Excel4 and the result of the Excel4 function call itself. The former is contained in the `operRes` parameter of the Excel4 function, whereas the latter is the `int` return value of the Excel4 function. All possible return values from Excel4 are represented by constants defined in xlcall.h. Most of these return values will not be encountered after you've debugged your XLL. Some of them are outside the scope of this chapter. A brief description of the Excel4 function return value constants follows:

- `xlretSuccess`—The Excel4 function call succeeded. This does not mean the function being called by Excel4 succeeded. You determine that by checking the `operRes` argument for an error data type.
- `xlretAbort`—An internal abort occurred. A discussion of this return value is outside the scope of this chapter.
- `xlretInvXlfn`—The function number supplied as an argument to the XLFN parameter was an invalid function number. If you use only the predefined function constants supplied by xlcall.h, you should not encounter this error.
- `xlretInvCount`—Your Excel4 function call did not supply the correct number of arguments for the function it specified in the `xlfn` argument.
- `xlretInvXloper`—An invalid XLOPER was passed to one of the Excel4 function arguments or a valid XLOPER containing an incorrect data type was passed.
- `xlretStackOvfl`—A stack overflow occurred. A discussion of this return value is outside the scope of this chapter.

- `xlretFailed`—An XLM command-equivalent function call failed. A discussion of this return value is outside the scope of this chapter.
- `xlretUncalced`—An attempt was made to dereference a cell that has not been calculated yet. If you ever encounter this error, your function must exit immediately. Excel will call your function again when the cell in question has been calculated.

Commonly Used C API Functions

The functions listed below can only be called from within an XLL using the Excel4 function. They are not available from within Excel. This is not a complete list of these functions, only those that apply most commonly to custom worksheet function projects.

xlFree

The xlFree function is used to tell Excel you are finished with the contents of an XLOPER variable Excel has allocated the memory for and that Excel is now free to reclaim that memory. The xlFree function takes one or more XLOPER variables as parameters to be freed and does not return a value to the operRes parameter of the Excel4 function. We discuss XLOPER memory management in the next section, but for now, here's the basic syntax of an xlFree function call:

```
XLOPER xlToBeFreed;
// Do something here that causes Excel to allocate
// the xlToBeFreed variable.
Excel4(xlFree, 0, 1, xlToBeFreed);
```

xlCoerce

The xlCoerce function is used to convert XLOPER structs from one data type to another. For example, you can make a custom worksheet function more robust by using xlCoerce to explicitly convert to a numeric value whatever is passed to an XLOPER parameter that expects a numeric value. The need for this would arise if the user entered something similar to the following for a function whose parameter expected a numeric data type:

```
=MYFUNC("100")
```

The default behavior of xlCoerce is to convert a cell reference to any nonreference type, in effect looking up the value of a cell that an XLOPER points to. The syntax of an xlCoerce call looks like the following:

```
XLOPER xlResult, xlType;
xlType.xltype = xltypeInt;
xlType.val.w = xltypeNum;
Excel4(xlCoerce, &xlResult, 2, pxlInput, &xlType);
```

The xlCoerce function takes two arguments:

- pxlInput—A pointer to an XLOPER (LPXLOPER) that contains the value or reference to be converted.
- xlType—A pointer to an XLOPER of type xltypeInt whose val.w member contains a bit mask of types you are willing to accept. This argument is optional. If it is not provided, xlCoerce will convert the pxlInput reference argument into the closest possible data type associated with the value in the referenced cell.

xlGetName

The xlGetName function returns the full path name and filename of your XLL. As you will see in the *Registering and Unregistering Custom Worksheet Functions* section, this information is required to register and unregister the custom worksheet functions in an XLL.

XLOPERs and Memory Management

Excel allocates and frees any arguments passed to a custom worksheet function. For most XLOPER return values, you pass Excel a static XLOPER variable. Your XLL must allocate any arguments passed to the Excel4 function. When a call to the Excel4 function returns an XLOPER containing a pointer, that memory is allocated and managed by Excel. You must call the xlFree function on that XLOPER so Excel can free its memory. You can safely call xlFree on every return value from the Excel4 function. Calling xlFree on an XLOPER that does not contain a pointer does nothing, and if xlFree is called twice on the same XLOPER Excel ignores the second call.

Excel supports two special memory management bits in the xltype field of the XLOPER data type. If you need to use an XLOPER as the return value of a worksheet function, but that XLOPER itself was returned from Excel via the Excel4 function, you set the xlbitXLFree bit in the xltype field of the XLOPER. When you do this, Excel copies out the data it needs and then frees the XLOPER for you, relieving you of the requirement to call xlFree on the XLOPER.

Similarly, if you set the xlbitDLLFree bit in the xltype field of an XLOPER, Excel copies the data it requires out of the XLOPER and then calls the xlAutoFree function in your XLL, passing it a pointer to the XLOPER. Your XLL can then free any memory it allocated for this XLOPER. This is useful for returning large amounts of data to Excel without being required to have the memory for it remain allocated indefinitely.

NOTE: Do not modify any XLOPER managed by Excel. This includes worksheet function arguments and return values from the Excel4 function. Copy the data into your own memory area if you need to work with it. Remember that Excel does not use null-terminated C strings, so if you copy a string value from an XLOPER returned by Excel you must copy it character by character into a new char array for the number of characters specified in the first byte of the XLOPER string.

Registering and Unregistering Custom Worksheet Functions

For Excel to recognize the custom worksheet functions in your XLL, you must register them. This is accomplished by using the aptly named Register function. Conversely, when your XLL is unloaded it must remove its function registrations so that Excel will no longer display them in the list of available functions.

As you saw in the xlAutoOpen and xlAutoClose functions, we've created a special-purpose function called HandleRegistration to manage the registering and unregistering of our custom worksheet functions. Pass TRUE to the function and it will register all of the custom worksheet functions specified in the function table with Excel. Pass FALSE to the function and it will unregister all the custom worksheet functions. The definition of the HandleRegistration function is shown in Listing 19-11.

Listing 19-11 The HandleRegistration Function

```
/////////////////////////////////////////////////////////////////
// Comments:     This function handles registering and
//               unregistering all of the custom worksheet
//               functions specified in our function table.
//
// Parameters:   bRegister    [in] Pass TRUE to register all the
//                            custom worksheet functions or FALSE
//                            to unregister them.
//
// Returns:      No return.
//
static void HandleRegistration(BOOL bRegister)
{
    XLOPER  xlXLLName, xlRegID, xlRegArgs[NUM_REGISTER_ARGS];
    int     i, j;

    // Get the filename of the XLL by calling xlGetName.
    Excel4(xlGetName, &xlXLLName, 0);

    // All of the XLOPER arguments passed to the Register
    // function will have the type xltypeStr.
    for (i = 0; i < NUM_REGISTER_ARGS; ++i)
        xlRegArgs[i].xltype = xltypeStr;

    for (i = 0; i < NUM_FUNCTIONS; ++i)
    {
        // Load the XLOPER arguments to the Register function.
        for(j = 0; j < NUM_REGISTER_ARGS; ++j)
            xlRegArgs[j].val.str = gszFunctionTable[i][j];

        if (TRUE == bRegister)
        {
            // Register each function.
            // NOTE: The number of xlRegArgs[] arguments passed
            // here must be equal to NUM_REGISTER_ARGS - 1.
            Excel4(xlfRegister, 0, NUM_REGISTER_ARGS + 1,
                &xlXLLName,
                &xlRegArgs[0], &xlRegArgs[1], &xlRegArgs[2],
                &xlRegArgs[3], &xlRegArgs[4], &xlRegArgs[5],
                &xlRegArgs[6], &xlRegArgs[7], &xlRegArgs[8],
                &xlRegArgs[9], &xlRegArgs[10]);
```

```
        }
        else
        {
              // Unregister each function.
              // Due to a bug in Excel's C API this is a 3-step
              // process. Thanks to Laurent Longre for discovering
              // the workaround described here.
              // Step 1: Redefine each custom worksheet function
              // as a hidden function (change the macro_type
              // argument to 0).
              xlRegArgs[4].val.str = "\0010";
              // Step 2: Re-register each function as a hidden
              // function.
              // NOTE: The number of xlRegArgs[] arguments passed
              // here must be equal to NUM_REGISTER_ARGS - 1.
              Excel4(xlfRegister, 0, NUM_REGISTER_ARGS + 1,
                    &xlXLLName,
                    &xlRegArgs[0], &xlRegArgs[1], &xlRegArgs[2],
                    &xlRegArgs[3], &xlRegArgs[4], &xlRegArgs[5],
                    &xlRegArgs[6], &xlRegArgs[7], &xlRegArgs[8],
                    &xlRegArgs[9], &xlRegArgs[10]);
              // Step 3: Unregister the now hidden function.
              // Get the Register ID for the function.
              // Since xlfRegisterId will return a non-pointer
              // type to the xlRegID XLOPER, we do not need to
              // call xlFree on it.
              Excel4(xlfRegisterId, &xlRegID, 2, &xlXLLName,
                                              &xlRegArgs[0]);
              // Unregister the function using its Register ID.
              Excel4(xlfUnregister, 0, 1, &xlRegID);
        }
    }

    // Since xlXLLName holds a pointer that is managed by Excel,
    // we must call xlFree on it.
    Excel4(xlFree, 0, 1, &xlXLLName);
}
```

Registering a custom worksheet function with Excel is very straight-forward. You just get the name of your XLL by calling the xlGetName function, and then loop the functions in the function table and call the xlfRegister function for each one, passing the XLL name as the first argument and all the function table entries as successive arguments.

Unregistering your functions requires a bit more work. Theoretically, you should simply be able to call the xlfUnregister function, passing it the Register ID of each worksheet function you want to unregister. Due to a bug in the xlfUnregister function, however, this will not remove the names of your functions from the Excel function table. They will continue to display in the Function Wizard even though they are no longer available.

XLL guru Laurent Longre (see Web site reference at the end of this chapter) discovered a workaround for this bug. It involves changing the macro_type of each function to 0, or hidden, reregistering each function as a hidden function, then unregistering the hidden functions. Because hidden functions are not displayed in the Excel UI, this has the effect of correctly removing them when your XLL exits.

Sample Application Function

For our real-world example function, we'll create a new worksheet function called IFERROR. As noted in *Chapter 5 — Function, General and Application-Specific Add-ins*, we often encounter the following worksheet function construct:

```
=IF(ISERROR(<some_long_function>), 0, <some_long_function>)
```

This is tedious and unwieldy, so we created a user-defined function in VBA that enabled us to accomplish exactly the same thing with the following:

```
=IFERROR(<some_long_function>, 0)
```

In this section we rewrite our IFERROR function in C. This will dramatically improve its performance because it will be compiled to native code and be able to communicate directly with Excel through the Excel C API. Our C IFERROR function has the definition shown in Listing 19-12.

Listing 19-12 The IFERROR Function

```
/////////////////////////////////////////////////////////////
// Comments:    This function provides a short-cut replacement
//              for the common worksheet function construct:
//              =IF(ISERROR(<some_function>),0,<some_function>)
//
```

```
// Arguments:    ToEvaluate   [in] A value, expression or cell
//                            reference to be evaluated.
//               Default      [in] A value, expression or cell
//                            reference to be returned if the
//                            ToEvaluate argument evaluates to an
//                            error condition.
//
// Returns:      ToEvaluate if not an error, Default otherwise.
//
EXPORT LPXLOPER IFERROR(LPXLOPER ToEvaluate, LPXLOPER Default)
{
    int             IsError = 0;
    XLOPER          xlResult;
    static XLOPER   xlBadArgErr;

    // This is the return value for bad or missing arguments.
    xlBadArgErr.xltype = xltypeErr;
    xlBadArgErr.val.err = xlerrValue;

    // Check for missing arguments.
    if ((xltypeMissing == ToEvaluate->xltype) ||
        (xltypeMissing == Default->xltype))
        return &xlBadArgErr;

    switch (ToEvaluate->xltype)
    {
    // The first four all indicate valid ToEvaluate types.
    // Drop out and use ToEvaluate as the return value.
    case xltypeNum:
    case xltypeStr:
    case xltypeBool:
    case xltypeInt:
        break;
    // A cell reference must be dereferenced to see what it
    // contains.
    case xltypeSRef:
    case xltypeRef:
        if (xlretUncalced == Excel4(xlCoerce, &xlResult, 1,
                                                ToEvaluate))
            // If we're looking at an uncalculateded cell,
            // return immediately. Excel will call this
            // function again once the dependency has been
            // calculated.
            return 0;
```

```
            else
            {
                if (xltypeMulti == xlResult.xltype)
                    // Multi-cell arguments are not permitted.
                    return &xlBadArgErr;
                else if (xltypeErr == xlResult.xltype)
                    // ToEvaluate is a single cell containing an
                    // error. Return Default instead.
                    IsError = 1;
            }
            // ToEvaluate is returned for all other types.
            // Always call xlFree on the return value from
            // Excel4.
            Excel4(xlFree, 0, 1, &xlResult);
            break;
        case xltypeMulti:
            // This function does not accept array arguments.
            return &xlBadArgErr;
            break;
        case xltypeErr:
            // ToEvaluate is an error. Return Default instead.
            IsError = 1;
            break;
        default:
            return &xlBadArgErr;
            break;
    }

    if (IsError)
        return Default;
    else
        return ToEvaluate;
}
```

The additional function table entry required to register this function with Excel is shown in Listing 19-13.

Listing 19-13 Function Table Entry for the IFERROR Function

```
{" IFERROR",
 " RRR",
 " IFERROR",
 " ToEvaluate, Default",
```

```
" 1",
" Sample Add-in",
" ",
" ",
" If the first argument is an error value, the second "
    "argument is returned. Otherwise the first argument "
    "is returned.",
" The argument to be checked for an error condition.",
" The value to return if the first argument is an error."
}
```

Debugging the Worksheet Functions

In the course of writing custom worksheet functions, you will need to do some debugging in order to fix errors and prove that your function is operating as intended. This is very easy to do. Because we have already specified Excel.exe as our debug executable, all that's required is to compile your XLL using the *Build > Build Solution* menu, put a break point somewhere in your function and press F5 to start debugging. Visual Studio will start Excel for you. The first time you do this you'll be prompted with the warning dialog shown in Figure 19-9.

Figure 19-9 The First-Time Excel.exe Debug Warning Dialog

This is just telling you that you won't be able to debug Excel itself because there's no debugging information available. Because that's not what we're trying to do here, you can safely check the *Do not prompt in the future* check box and click OK to continue.

When Excel is open, you will have to make sure your XLL is also open inside Excel. This does not happen automatically. You can open your XLL in one of two ways. Either use the *File > Open* menu to open the XLL directly, or add the XLL to the list of add-ins that Excel loads automatically on startup. The second method is the preferred method for use over multiple debugging sessions.

To do this, choose *Tools > Add-ins* from the Excel menu to display the Add-ins dialog. Click the Browse button on the Add-ins dialog and use the Browse window to point Excel at your XLL. If you have both debug and release versions of your XLL, be sure to point Excel at the debug version. Click OK twice and your XLL will be loaded.

Now all you need to do is enter your custom worksheet function into a worksheet cell. As soon as code execution reaches your break point it will stop and you can begin debugging your code.

Miscellaneous Topics

A Caution for Users of COM Automation

A function that is defined in an XLL can be called in three situations:

1. During the recalculation of a workbook
2. As a result of Excel's Function Wizard being called to help with the XLL function
3. As a result of a VBA macro calling Excel's `Application.Run` method

Under the first two circumstances, Excel's object model does not expect and is not prepared for incoming Automation calls. Unexpected results or crashes may occur if you use COM Automation under these circumstances.

C++ Keyword Clash with the XLOPER Definition

To compile xlcall.h in a C++ project (as opposed to the C project demonstrated here) using a standards-compliant C++ compiler (such as VC.NET), you must add the following wrapper around the xlcall.h include. This is because the bool variable name used in the XLOPER struct definition is now a C++ keyword.

```
#define bool boolean
#include "xlcall.h"
#undef bool
```

Additional Resources

The Excel 97 SDK on MSDN

An extensive resource on creating XLLs using plain C code, the Excel 97 SDK covers a much wider variety of topics than this chapter. In addition, the source files that go with it include a handy framework for easing some of the repetitive chores involved in building an XLL. Just note that in a number of places, this framework attempts to directly modify string literal values. This is undefined behavior in C++ and therefore you must modify these instances to use char arrays instead. The text of the Excel 97 SDK can be found in the MSDN library at `http://msdn.microsoft.com/library/`.

Under:

> Office Solutions Development
> > Microsoft Office
> > > Microsoft Office 97
> > > > Product Documentation
> > > > > Excel
> > > > > > Microsoft Excel 97 Developer's Kit

You can find the files that go with the SDK at `http://download.microsoft.com/download/excel97win/Install/1.0/W9XNT4XP/EN-US/excel97sdk.exe`.

Excel Add-in Development in C/C++: Applications in Finance

Authored by Steve Dalton
ISBN 0470024690—Wiley
An excellent book-length discussion on creating XLLs in C and C++, this title is highly recommended for anyone who wants to pursue this topic further.

William Hooper's Web Site

`http://www.whooper.co.uk/excelstuff.htm`
Excellent discussion and examples on various advanced XLL topics.

Laurent Longre's Web Site (French Only)

http://longre.free.fr/
More excellent discussion of XLL creation for those who can read French.

The Microsoft Excel Public Newsgroups

Point your newsreader to msnews.microsoft.com. You'll find experts in a wide array of topics willing to answer your questions for no charge. Most discussions related to XLL development will be found in the microsoft.public.excel.programming and microsoft.public. excel.sdk newsgroups. The microsoft.public.vc.language newsgroup is the best choice for C/C++ specific questions.

Planatech XLL+

http://www.as-ltd.co.uk/main/
If you develop any significant number of XLLs, you owe it to yourself to buy a copy of XLL+. This is absolutely the best object-oriented XLL development framework available. It eliminates all the grunt work involved in creating XLLs and provides many advanced features in an easily accessible format. In addition, the help file for XLL+, although specific to the XLL+ development framework, is probably the best basic XLL development tutorial available. (Note: The authors have no financial incentive for this recommendation, it is based purely on the merits of the product.)

Keith Lewis' Freeware Object-Oriented C++ Wrapper for the Excel C API

http://sourceforge.net/projects/xll
An open source implementation of an object-oriented wrapper for the Excel C API.

ManagedXLL

http://managedxll.net
Similar to Planatech XLL+ but designed to work specifically with the .NET programming languages.

Conclusion

After you've written a few user-defined functions in VBA, you cannot help but notice that they do awful things to your calculation performance. Converting your VBA user-defined functions into C or C++ based XLLs will solve this performance problem. Well-written XLL functions exhibit calculation performance that is indistinguishable from native Excel worksheet functions. If you need user-defined functions and calculation speed is important, take the time to learn how to program XLLs. The results will be well worth the effort.

Combining Excel and Visual Basic 6

Before we begin this chapter, we must note that Visual Basic 6 is no longer sold by Microsoft. Its place has been taken by VB.NET, which is a very different programming language despite the similarity of its name to VB6. However, VB6 is still widely used by working programmers all over the world. VBA is the primary programming language for all current versions of Excel and it will continue to be so for some time to come. VBA and VB6 are very closely related and work very well together, so the case for using VB6 to extend the powers of VBA is still a strong one.

If you do not already have a copy of VB6, it may be difficult to locate one. Check online auction sites such as E-bay. Many used bookstores also sell used software, so those may be another good place to find a copy of VB6.

You can think of VB6 as the more powerful big brother to VBA. It has a number of capabilities that VBA does not, including the ability to generate truly compiled code in the form of DLLs or stand-alone executable files, a more powerful forms package, superior object-oriented programming capabilities, support for resource libraries, and Clipboard, Printer and Screen objects among others. All of these features can be easily and tightly integrated with your VBA projects with no loss of performance. In fact you will see a gain in performance in some cases due to the fact that VB6 code is truly compiled, rather than being interpreted like VBA.

In this chapter we show you how to get started combining VB6 and Excel and cover the most common reasons why you would want to extend your VBA projects with VB6. Keep in mind that VB6 is yet another topic that would require an entire book to cover properly, so we focus very narrowly on just the VB6 features you would be most likely to use in conjunction with your Excel applications.

A Hello World ActiveX DLL

VB6 can be used to create more than half a dozen different types of application, but the only two that are typically used in conjunction with Excel are ActiveX DLLs and Standard EXEs. In this section we introduce you to using VB6 ActiveX DLLs from Excel with a simple Hello World application. We cover the basics of combining Excel and VB6 EXEs in the *Automating Excel from a VB6 EXE* section later in the chapter.

The first iteration of our Hello World ActiveX DLL demonstrates one-way communication only, from Excel to the DLL. We then extend the example in the second iteration to demonstrate two-way communication. Excel will communicate with the DLL and the DLL will communicate back to Excel. In the third iteration we demonstrate how to show a VB6 form in Excel as if it were a native userform. In this way, without complicating the example with any advanced features, you will see just how easy it is to create and use all the basic features of a VB6 ActiveX DLL from Excel. Later sections of the chapter show how to add nontrivial VB6 features to the base that we build in our Hello World application. The complete set of files for this example is located on the CD in the *\Concepts\Ch20—Combining Excel and Visual Basic 6\HelloWorld* folder.

Creating an ActiveX DLL Project

When you first open VB6 you are presented with the New Project dialog shown in Figure 20-1. If you have used VB6 in the past and configured it not to display this dialog on startup, you can access it from the *File > New Project* menu.

As shown in Figure 20-1, we will be selecting the ActiveX DLL project type. After you have selected this project type, click the Open button and VB6 will create a new ActiveX DLL project for you.

In its simplest form, which is the form we will be using in the first iteration of our Hello World application, an ActiveX DLL consists of only two parts: a project and a class module. The project determines the application name of your DLL, and the class module exposes the features of your DLL to other programs. Figure 20-2 shows the structure of a newly created ActiveX DLL project as seen in the Project window.

If this Project window appears familiar, it's no accident. You will find that the VB6 development environment and the VBA development environment are so similar that it's easy to confuse them. This also makes it very easy to work with VB6 if you already have experience with VBA.

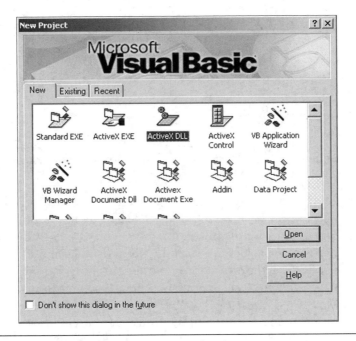

Figure 20-1 The VB6 New Project Dialog

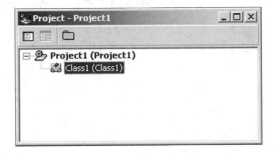

Figure 20-2 A Newly Created ActiveX DLL Project

We'll use the Properties window in VB6 to provide friendly names for our project and class module in exactly the same way we would do it in VBA. Instead of Project1, we'll give our project the name AFirstProject. Instead of Class1, we'll give our class module the name CHelloWorld. We then save the project. The result is shown in Figure 20-3.

Figure 20-3 The Component Names for the Hello World Project

Notice that after we have saved the VB6 project, a filename appears in parenthesis beside each of the friendly names of our components. This is one example of the difference between VBA and VB6. In VBA, all components of a project are stored within a single file. In the case of an Excel application they are stored within the file structure of the workbook in which they're located. In VB6, all components are stored as separate text files in the directory in which you saved the project. (Certain objects such as forms and resource files have binary files associated with them, but this detail isn't important for the purposes of our discussion.)

The Simplest Case—One-Way Communication

Now that we have the skeleton of an ActiveX DLL project completed, let's add some code to make it do something. For the first iteration of our Hello World project the DLL will do nothing more than display a message box with the caption "Hello World!" when prompted. This is accomplished by adding a method to our class module that displays the message box when called.

Adding a method to a VB6 class module is done in exactly the same way as adding a method to a VBA class module. Just open the class module and add the code shown in Listing 20-1.

Listing 20-1 The ShowMessage Method

```
Public Sub ShowMessage()
    MsgBox "Hello World!"
End Sub
```

That's it! Wasn't that easy? Now all we need to do is compile our ActiveX DLL and call it from an Excel application to display its message.

Before you can use a VB6 project you must compile it. This is accomplished through the use of the *File > Make AFirstProject.dll* menu, as shown in Figure 20-4. The AFirstProject.dll portion of this menu name will differ depending on the name and type of the project you are compiling.

Figure 20-4 Using the File > Make Menu to Compile the DLL

After you have compiled your DLL you will find a file named AFirstProject.dll in the directory in which you saved your project. This is the compiled, executable form of all the files in the project combined.

So how do we use this from Excel? It's so easy that if you have never done it before you will be amazed. The first step is to create a new workbook and save it as Book1.xls to the same directory as your VB6 project. Saving the workbook to this location is not a requirement; it just makes things simpler by keeping all the files for the example in one place. In reality, the DLL could be used by any Excel application anywhere on your computer.

Next, open the VBE from Excel and insert one standard code module. Before we can start adding code to call our DLL we need to tell VBA where to find it. This is done using the *Tools > References* menu in the VBE. As mentioned previously, the name of your project serves as its application name. Therefore, the name of the reference you need to add is the same as the name of your VB6 project, in this case, AFirstProject.

Figure 20-5 shows the VBA References dialog with the AFirstProject DLL reference selected. Note that the path shown in the Location listing at the bottom of the References dialog will reflect the location where the DLL was compiled on your computer, so it will be different from the path shown in the figure.

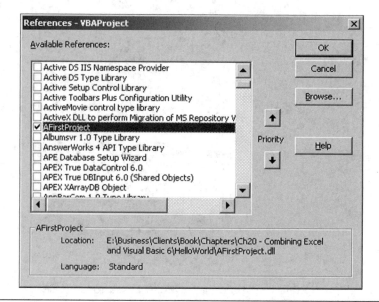

Figure 20-5 Referencing the AFirstProject DLL from Excel

After you have set a reference to the DLL, you can use it exactly like you would use any other outside object referenced from Excel. To demonstrate our DLL, we create a simple ShowDLLMessage procedure in the standard module of our Excel workbook. The complete code for this procedure is shown in Listing 20-2.

Listing 20-2 The ShowDLLMessage Procedure

```
Public Sub ShowDLLMessage()
    Dim clsHelloWorld As AFirstProject.CHelloWorld
```

```
    Set clsHelloWorld = New AFirstProject.CHelloWorld
    clsHelloWorld.ShowMessage
    Set clsHelloWorld = Nothing
End Sub
```

That's all there is to it! Notice that like we have done in several previous chapters, we referenced our DLL class here using a two-part notation: ApplicationName.ClassName. This uniquely identifies the class we want to use and prevents any confusion that might arise from two referenced applications sharing the same class name. When you run the ShowDLLMessage procedure, the message box in Figure 20-6 will display.

Figure 20-6 The Hello World! Message from Our ActiveX DLL

An interesting side note demonstrated by Figure 20-6 is the text displayed in the title bar of the message box. If you don't supply a title of your own, the text displayed in the title bar of a message box by default will be the name of the application that displayed it. For example, if you displayed a message box from Excel without specifying a title, the title text would be set to "Microsoft Excel" by default. Similarly, because we didn't specify a title for the message box shown by our ActiveX DLL its title defaults to the application name of the DLL, which is AFirstProject. This proves that the message box indeed originated from within the DLL and not from within the Excel project that called it.

The More Complex Case—Two-Way Communication

The first iteration of our Hello World application demonstrated in an uncomplicated fashion how to create an ActiveX DLL and a corresponding Excel project that could communicate with the DLL. But the example was significantly limited by the fact that all communication was one-way, Excel calling the DLL.

To take advantage of the full power afforded by combining Excel with a VB6 ActiveX DLL, we must create a structure that allows communication to flow in both directions. In the second iteration of our Hello World application, we extend the previous example to allow two-way communication.

A DLL is fundamentally a dependent component. A DLL cannot take any action by itself, it can only respond to requests from applications that are making use of its code. After a request is made, however, a DLL can communicate directly with the application that called it. The first thing we must do to enable two-way communication between Excel and the DLL is provide the DLL with a way of knowing who called it.

The first step required to accomplish this is to set a reference from the DLL to the Excel object library, which provides the DLL with the all information about Excel that it needs in order to communicate directly with Excel. The process of setting a reference in VB6 is virtually identical to the process of setting a reference in VBA. The only difference is the location of the menu item. To set a reference to Excel from our VB6 ActiveX DLL we select *Project > References* from the VB6 menu. Figure 20-7 shows a reference created from our VB6 project to the Microsoft Excel 9.0 Object Library. This is the object library for Excel 2000 and it will work correctly for all versions of Excel from 2000 forward.

As discussed in *Chapter 18 — Controlling Other Office Applications*, because of potential backward-compatibility problems you should always set a reference to the earliest version of the application you expect to be using. In this case, the earliest version of Excel that we expect to use is Excel 2000.

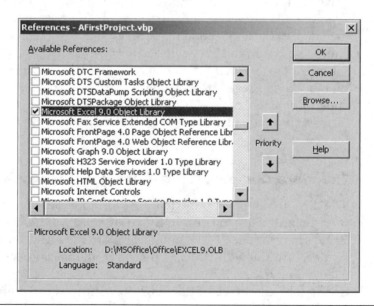

Figure 20-7 Setting a Reference to Excel From VB6

Now that our DLL has a reference to the Excel object library, we add the code to allow the DLL to communicate with the instance of the Excel application that loaded it. Because, as mentioned earlier, a DLL is a fundamentally dependent component, it is up to the VBA code running in the Excel application to establish two-way communication by providing the DLL with a reference to the Excel Application object. The DLL must simply be prepared to accept and store this reference.

To demonstrate this process in our Hello World application, we will create a second method that when called by Excel will enter the string "Hello World!" into the currently selected cell on the active worksheet. As we implied earlier, the first thing our DLL needs in order to accomplish this is a reference to the Excel application that called it. We will create a module-level variable to store the reference to the calling Excel Application object and a new Property procedure that Excel can use to pass a reference to itself into the DLL.

Because our DLL is now holding a reference to an outside application we must also be sure this reference is destroyed when the DLL is unloaded from memory. We use the Class_Terminate event procedure to accomplish this. The complete code for the new version of our CHelloWorld class module is shown in Listing 20-3. Note that we have used good code commenting techniques to visually separate the various sections of this new, more complex class module code.

Listing 20-3 The Complete Updated CHelloWorld Code Module

```
Option Explicit

' ***********************************************************
' Class Variable Declarations Follow
' ***********************************************************
' Object reference to the calling Excel Application.
Private mxlApp As Excel.Application

' ***********************************************************
' Class Property Procedures Follow
' ***********************************************************
Public Property Set ExcelApp(ByRef xlApp As Excel.Application)
    Set mxlApp = xlApp
End Property

' ***********************************************************
```

```
' Class Event Procedures Follow
' ************************************************************
Private Sub Class_Terminate()
    Set mxlApp = Nothing
End Sub


' ************************************************************
' Class Method Procedures Follow
' ************************************************************
Public Sub ShowMessage()
    MsgBox "Hello World!"
End Sub

Public Sub WriteMessage()
    mxlApp.ActiveCell.Value = "Hello World!"
End Sub
```

We have added the following additional code to our DLL class module:

- An mxlApp module-level variable that will hold a reference to the Excel Application object that called the DLL. The DLL will communicate with Excel through this object reference.
- An ExcelApp property procedure that will be used by the Excel Application calling the DLL to provide a reference to itself.
- A Class_Terminate event procedure that ensures the module-level reference to the Excel Application object is destroyed when the class is destroyed.
- A WriteMessage method that will place the text string "Hello World!" into the currently selected cell in the currently active worksheet in the currently active workbook in the Excel Application that called the method.

It is now time to recompile our DLL. If you are following along on your own computer and you still have Excel open from testing the previous version of the DLL, you will notice that VB6 will not allow you to recompile the DLL until you have closed Excel. The symptoms of this are a "Permission denied:" error message when you attempt to compile. After an Excel application has loaded a DLL, the DLL will not be released from memory until Excel is closed. Closing the workbook that references the DLL will not do the trick. You must close Excel completely.

After you have closed Excel you just select the *File > Make AFirstProject.dll* menu, as in the previous example, to recompile your DLL so that it includes the features we have added in this section. Because you already have a previous version of AFirstProject.dll located in your project directory, VB6 will warn you and ask if you want to replace it with a new version. Select Yes and the new version of your DLL will be compiled.

Now that you have a newly compiled version of your DLL, you need to add a procedure to your Excel workbook that takes advantage of the new WriteMessage method. Open the Book1.xls workbook that you saved to the VB6 project directory and add the procedure shown in Listing 20-4 to its code module:

Listing 20-4 The WriteDLLMessage Procedure

```
Public Sub WriteDLLMessage()
    Dim clsHelloWorld As AFirstProject.CHelloWorld
    Set clsHelloWorld = New AFirstProject.CHelloWorld
    Set clsHelloWorld.ExcelApp = Application
    clsHelloWorld.WriteMessage
    Set clsHelloWorld = Nothing
End Sub
```

The only fundamental difference between the WriteDLLMessage procedure and the previous ShowDLLMessage procedure is that we use the new ExcelApp property of our CHelloWorld class to pass a reference to the Excel Application object into the class. This tells the class what application called it and therefore what application its communications should be directed back to.

Because the new WriteMessage method operates on a cell on the active worksheet, we have added two Forms toolbar Button controls to the first (and only) worksheet in Book1.xls and assigned their OnAction properties to each of the two procedures in Book1.xls. If you select a cell on the worksheet and click the Write DLL Message button, the WriteDLLMessage procedure assigned to that button will be run. This procedure asks the DLL to enter a message string into the currently selected cell of that Excel Application object. The DLL uses its reference to the Excel Application object to enter the string "Hello World!" into the currently selected cell. The result of this call is shown in our newly constructed Excel user interface in Figure 20-8.

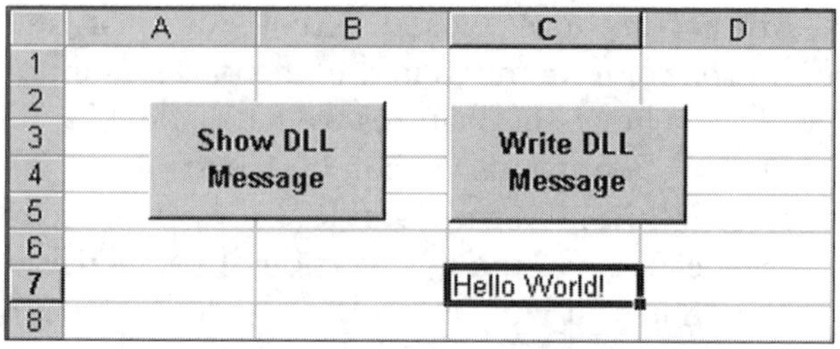

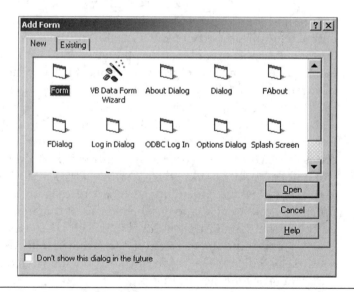

Figure 20-8 Two-Way Communication Between Excel and an ActiveX DLL

Displaying a VB6 Form in Excel

For the next iteration of our VB6 Hello World application we perform an even more complex task: displaying a VB6 form in Excel exactly as if it were a VBA userform. There are a number of reasons you might want to do this, and we discuss them at length in the *Taking Advantage of VB6 Forms* section later in the chapter. For now let's leave the complications aside and look at the bare minimum requirements for displaying a VB6 form in Excel.

The first step is to add a form to our Hello World project by choosing *Project > Add Form* from the VB6 menu. This displays the Add Form dialog shown in Figure 20-9.

Figure 20-9 The Add Form Dialog

Select the Form icon in the upper-left corner and click the Open button. A new form object will be added to your project. Before we save our project with the new form object in it, we need to change a few properties of the form. The properties to be changed and the values they should be changed to are shown in Table 20-1.

Table 20-1 The Property Settings for Our New Form

Property Name	Property Setting
(Name)	FHelloWorld
BorderStyle	3—Fixed Dialog
Caption	Hello From VB6
Icon	(None)—Select and delete the default value
StartupPosition	1—Center Owner

After you have made these property changes, save your project. Because the form has never been saved before, VB6 will prompt you with a Save File As dialog asking you where to save the form. Make sure you save it in the same directory where the rest of the project is saved. Your project should now look like the one shown in the Project window in Figure 20-10.

Next we add a CommandButton and a Label control to our new form. Name the CommandButton cmdOK and give it the caption OK. Give the Label the caption "Hello World!", change the Alignment property to 1—Center and increase the Font size to 24 points. Your completed form should resemble the one shown in Figure 20-11, but don't worry if yours looks a little different.

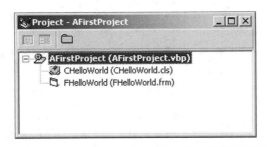

Figure 20-10 The Project with a Form Added

Figure 20-11 The VB6 Hello World! Form

The only code that we'll need to put behind the form is a line in the cmdOK_Click event procedure that hides the form when the OK button is clicked. This event procedure is shown in Listing 20-5.

Listing 20-5 The cmdOK_Click Event Procedure

```
Private Sub cmdOK_Click()
    Me.Hide
End Sub
```

A form object in a VB6 ActiveX DLL is not directly accessible to outside applications. Therefore we need to add code to our class module that will allow our Excel application to display the form. We also need to make one additional tweak to the form so that it behaves like a native Excel userform. The complete code for the new version of our CHelloWorld class is shown in Listing 20-6 with the new code for this version shaded.

Listing 20-6 The CHelloWorld Code Module Updated to Support the Form

```
Option Explicit

' ***************************************************************
' Class Constant Declarations Follow
' ***************************************************************
' SetWindowLongA API constant.
Private Const GWL_HWNDPARENT As Long = -8

' ***************************************************************
' Class Variable Declarations Follow
' ***************************************************************
```

```
' Object reference to the calling Excel Application.
Private mxlApp As Excel.Application
' Window handle of the calling Excel Application.
Private mlXLhWnd As Long


' *************************************************************
' Class DLL Declaractions Follow
' *************************************************************
Private Declare Function FindWindowA Lib "user32" _
                    (ByVal lpClassName As String, _
                    ByVal lpWindowName As String) As Long
Private Declare Function SetWindowLongA Lib "user32" _
                    (ByVal hWnd As Long, _
                    ByVal nIndex As Long, _
                    ByVal dwNewLong As Long) As Long


' *************************************************************
' Class Property Procedures Follow
' *************************************************************
Public Property Set ExcelApp(ByRef xlApp As Excel.Application)
    Set mxlApp = xlApp
    ' Get the window handle of the Excel Application object
    ' as soon as it is passed to us.
    mlXLhWnd = FindWindowA(vbNullString, mxlApp.Caption)
End Property


' *************************************************************
' Class Event Procedures Follow
' *************************************************************
Private Sub Class_Terminate()
    Set mxlApp = Nothing
End Sub


' *************************************************************
' Class Method Procedures Follow
' *************************************************************
Public Sub ShowMessage()
    MsgBox "Hello World!"
End Sub

Public Sub WriteMessage()
    mxlApp.ActiveCell.Value = "Hello World!"
End Sub
```

```
Public Sub ShowVB6Form()
    Dim frmHelloWorld As FHelloWorld
    Set frmHelloWorld = New FHelloWorld
    Load frmHelloWorld
    ' Parent the Form window to the Excel Application window.
    SetWindowLongA frmHelloWorld.hWnd, GWL_HWNDPARENT, mlXLhWnd
    frmHelloWorld.Show vbModal
    Unload frmHelloWorld
    Set frmHelloWorld = Nothing
End Sub
```

A VB6 form is a top-level window by default. That is to say it is a child window only of the desktop. To make a VB6 form behave like a native userform in Excel, we need to use the Windows API to change the parent window of the VB6 form from the desktop to the window of the Excel Application object that called it. Changing the parent window of a form involves two steps:

1. Retrieving the window handle of the window we want to use as the form's parent window.
2. Changing the form's parent window by putting the window handle we retrieved into the storage area of the form's window structure that is used to specify the parent window of the form.

Implementing this in our code requires us to make a number of additions, all of which are highlighted in Listing 20-6 above. We have declared a new module-level variable, mlXLhWnd, to hold the window handle of the Excel Application object that called our class. We have added two Windows API function declarations: FindWindowA to locate the window handle of the Excel Application window and SetWindowLongA to change the parent window of our form. The new GWL_HWNDPARENT constant identifies the location in our form's window structure where the window handle of the new parent window will be placed. We have added a line of code to the ExcelApp property procedure to extract the Excel Application object's window handle as soon as the property is set.

We have also created a new ShowVB6Form method that is responsible for displaying the form in Excel in response to a call from the Excel application. This method uses the following steps to accomplish its task:

- It creates a new instance of the FHelloWorld form.
- It loads that instance of the FHelloWorld form into memory.

- It changes the form's parent window from the desktop window to the Excel Application window using the SetWindowLongA API.
- It shows the form using the vbModal flag. Unlike userforms, VB6 forms will show modeless by default. Because this is not what we want for this example we add the vbModal flag to the form's Show method to force the form to be modal.
- When the user has closed the form the method unloads it from memory and destroys the object variable that refers to it.

After you have added the new code to your VB6 project, close Excel and recompile your DLL using the *File > Make AFirstProject* menu. On the Excel application side you just need to add a new procedure in the code module to call the DLL and have it display the VB6 form and add a new button on the worksheet assigned to this procedure. The code for the new DisplayDLLForm procedure is shown in Listing 20-7.

Listing 20-7 The DisplayDLLForm Procedure

```
Public Sub DisplayDLLForm()
    Dim clsHelloWorld As AFirstProject.CHelloWorld
    Set clsHelloWorld = New AFirstProject.CHelloWorld
    Set clsHelloWorld.ExcelApp = Application
    clsHelloWorld.ShowVB6Form
    Set clsHelloWorld = Nothing
End Sub
```

As you can see, the code for the DisplayDLLForm procedure is virtually identical to the code for the WriteDLLMessage procedure shown back in Listing 20-4. The only difference is that one calls the ShowVB6Form method of our CHelloWorld class while the other calls the WriteMessage method of our CHelloWorld class. The Excel user interface with the VB6 form displayed over it is shown in Figure 20-12.

Notice how our VB6 form looks and behaves exactly like a userform in Excel. You may be asking yourself why we would go through all this trouble when we could have spent five minutes creating an identical userform in VBA. In the *Taking Advantage of VB6 Forms* section later in this chapter you will see that VB6 forms have a number of features that userforms don't, and the simple structure for displaying a VB6 form in Excel that we have developed here is the first step in allowing us to take advantage of these features.

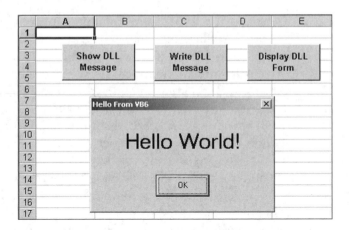

Figure 20-12 The VB6 Form Displayed in Excel

Why Use VB6 ActiveX DLLs in Excel VBA Projects

Although the core VBA language contained in VB6 is exactly the same as that used by Excel, VB6 supports a number of additional features that are not available in a pure Excel application. These features include very strong code protection due to its fully compiled nature and a more powerful forms package with the ability to use third-party ActiveX controls, control arrays and with enhanced data-binding capabilities. VB6 also provides better support for object-oriented programming, the ability to create resource files and other useful features, including the Clipboard, Printer and Screen objects.

Code Protection

A frequent problem that comes up in the context of Excel applications is the complete inability of VBA to protect your code from prying eyes. Sure you can protect your VBA project with a password. But VBA project password breaking programs that can remove this password instantaneously are widely available. Because VBA code is never truly compiled, it will never be possible to prevent other people from gaining access to it.

For run-of-the-mill applications this is not a very significant problem. There are a number of applications, however, that rely on valuable proprietary algorithms. The only way to protect this proprietary code is to store it in a truly compiled state like that provided by a VB6 DLL. Note that the compiled machine code produced by VB6 can be decompiled to a very limited extent. The result of decompiling a VB6 DLL, however, is little more than assembly language, which so few people understand that code compiled in VB6 is effectively invulnerable.

Taking Advantage of VB6 Forms

The forms package used by VB6 is very different from the one used by VBA. As mentioned in *Chapter 10 — Userform Design and Best Practices*, the forms package used to create userform objects in Excel applications is called MSForms. The forms package used to create form objects in VB6 is known as Ruby Forms.

There are superficial similarities between the two. Both provide a blank canvas onto which you can drag and drop controls to visually construct your form. Both types of form have event models and both allow you to program controls by responding to events raised by those controls.

There are also differences between the two forms packages and those differences range from the subtle to the significant. For example, there are minor differences in the set of properties, methods and events exposed by the two types of forms and their built-in controls. There are also significant differences in the capabilities of the two.

For example, in *Chapter 10 — Userform Design and Best Practices* we showed in detail how to modify the window styles of userforms using API calls to achieve effects that were not directly supported by userforms. All of these window styles are directly supported by VB6 forms and it requires nothing more than setting the appropriate form properties in the Properties window to implement them. VB6 forms also provide a wide variety of built-in shapes and drawing methods that allow you to create sophisticated form designs without ever having to resort to the Windows API.

Where API techniques are still required to achieve a certain effect, they are much easier to implement in VB6 forms because VB6 forms expose their window handles and device contexts as native properties, obviating the need for API calls to obtain them. And in contrast to the lightweight, windowless controls provided with VBA userforms, VB6 form controls all have windows and they all expose their window handles as native properties. This allows them to be manipulated in ways that are simply impossible with windowless userform controls. We discuss additional differences between VBA userforms and VB6 forms that are of particular interest to the Excel programmer in the sections that follow.

Better ActiveX Control Support

Not only do VB6 forms provide better support than userforms for a wide variety of built-in Windows controls, they can also host hundreds of third-party ActiveX controls that are completely unavailable to userforms. The reason for this is that almost all third-party ActiveX controls come in two versions. When building your project the version you use is called the *design-time version* of the control. When your project is distributed and running in a compiled state it uses the *runtime version* of the control.

When you purchase a third-party ActiveX control, what you are really buying is a license to build your VB6 forms using the design-time version of the control. The runtime version of the control, required by your VB6 form after it is compiled, can be redistributed without restrictions in most cases. This is because it cannot be used in the design-time environment and therefore cannot be used to build new projects.

By contrast, VBA userforms *always* operate in design mode, so runtime versions of ActiveX controls will not work with them. If you were to distribute the design-time version of a control to get it to run on an uncompiled VBA userform, you would essentially be giving that control away to other users for free. Anyone who has the design-time version of a control installed on their computer can use it in their own projects, whether they purchased it or not.

As you can imagine, there are very few ActiveX control vendors who will allow you to redistribute the design-time versions of their controls. This makes the use of those controls effectively off-limits to all VBA userform-based projects.

NOTE: It is possible to wrap a third-party ActiveX control inside a custom VB6 ActiveX control project. The wrapper project would need to duplicate all the required properties, methods and events of the control it wraps. Once compiled, however, it uses the runtime version of the third-party control. Userforms can host custom VB6 ActiveX controls, so this is a way to get around the limitation described above. However, this is difficult and time-consuming to implement, probably a violation of the license agreements of most third-party controls and, anyway, beyond the scope of this chapter.

Control Arrays

Control arrays are one of the most useful features provided by VB6 forms. There is simply nothing like them supported by VBA userforms. Using control arrays, you can declare a set of controls to be an array. Each control in the array is given the same name but a unique Index property value.

VB6 then treats all the controls in the array almost as if they were a single control. For example, a single event procedure of each type is fired in response to activity from any of the controls within the array. This event procedure passes the Index value of the specific control that fired the event, allowing you to respond appropriately.

Not only are all controls in a control array treated as a single control, but you can easily add or remove controls dynamically from the array as required at runtime. Adding or removing controls from the array physically adds or removes actual controls on the form, a capability that greatly simplifies the creation of dynamically configured forms.

We demonstrate a very simple example of a control array below. This example is available on the CD in the *\Concepts\Ch20—Combining Excel and Visual Basic 6\ControlArrays* folder. The plumbing required to display the VB6 form in Excel is identical to that shown in the third iteration of our Hello World example above, so we do not rehash any of that material. Instead we concentrate on how to create and program a control array on a VB6 form.

Our control array demo will consist of a VB6 form that will eventually contain six OptionButton controls along with a ListBox control. The option button selected by the user will determine the contents of the ListBox control. Rather than having to respond to a separate Click event from each option button, we create the six option buttons as a control array so that we can manage them from a single Click event.

The initial form containing a list box and a single nonarray option button is displayed side by side with the Properties window showing the properties for the option button in Figure 20-13. The Properties window is shown with its Categorized tab active and all categories except Misc collapsed. The Misc properties are the ones we want to focus on when it comes to creating control arrays.

Note that we have given our option button the name optType and that the Index property selected in the Properties window is empty. This identifies optType as a standard control. The next step is to add the five additional option buttons to our form. Because we have already drawn one OptionButton control on our form that we want to duplicate, there's no reason to add five more option buttons from scratch. Instead we'll just copy our first option button and paste new copies of it back on to the form.

To do this, we just select our existing option button, right-click over it and choose *Copy* from the shortcut menu. We then select an empty area on our form, right-click over it and choose *Paste* from the shortcut menu. As soon as we attempt to paste a copy of our existing option button onto the same form where it originated, VB6 displays the message shown in Figure 20-14.

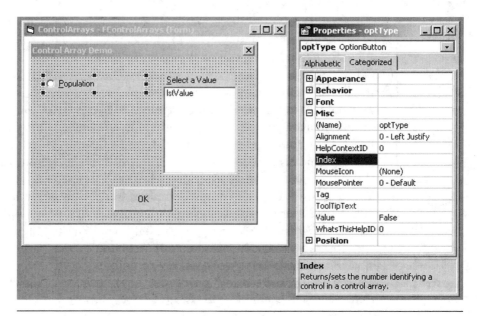

Figure 20-13 The Initial Control Array Demo Form

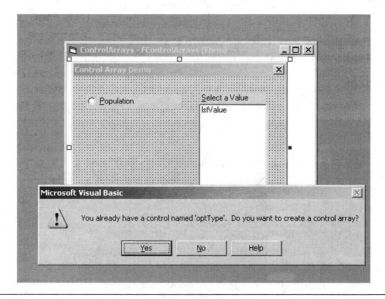

Figure 20-14 VB6 Helps us Create a Control Array

When you attempt to paste a control that has the same name as an existing control onto a form, VB6 assumes you want to create a control array and it offers to help you do so. Click the Yes button in the message box and let's see what happens. We have reselected our original option button and displayed the result in Figure 20-15.

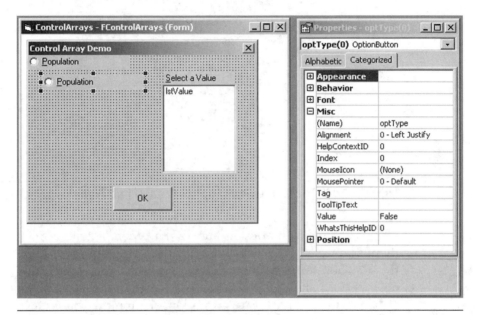

Figure 20-15 A Control Array Created by the Copy/Paste Method

The copy of the option button that we pasted appears in the upper left corner of the form. What is intriguing is to compare the previous property values for our first option button from Figure 20-13 with its new property values shown in Figure 20-15. The first thing to note is that the name of our original option button is now optType(0) instead of optType. We allowed VBA to create a control array for us when we pasted the copy of this option button onto our form, and the original option button is now the first element in the array. Control arrays begin at zero by default.

The second thing to notice is that the formerly empty Index property now also has a value of zero. This property is what really determines whether a control is part of an array or not. If the Index property is blank, the control is not part of an array. If the Index property contains a number, the control is part of an array and the Index property value is its position within the array.

We now position the copied option button control (which has an Index of 1) below the original option button and set its caption. Then we'll paste four more copies of the original option button onto the form and do the same. The results are shown in Figure 20-16.

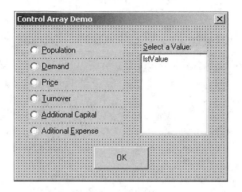

Figure 20-16 The Completed Control Array Demo Form

Even though the option buttons have completely different captions, they have exactly the same name with a unique Index value to identify them. Therefore we now have option buttons optType(0) through optType(5). Note that when you paste a control that is already part of a control array onto a form, VB no longer prompts you with the question shown in Figure 20-16. It just adds the control to the next available index position within the existing control array.

Now that we have completed the visible part of our Control Array Demo form, let's have a look at the code required to manage it. Our form requires only two properties and three event procedures to perform all of its operations:

- One property to expose the option selected and another to expose the list item selected for that option.
- A Click event procedure that handles all the option buttons in the control array.
- A Click event procedure for the cmdOK button that validates the user's selections.
- A QueryUnload event for the form that reroutes clicks on the X-Close button to the cmdOK_Click event procedure.

The code behind our Control Array Demo form is shown in Listing 20-8.

Listing 20-8 The Control Array Demo Form-Specific Code

```
Option Explicit

' ************************************************************
' Form Property Procedures Follow
' ************************************************************
Public Property Get OptionSelected() As Long
    Dim lIndex As Long
    Dim sOption As String
    For lIndex = optType.LBound To optType.UBound
        If optType(lIndex).Value Then Exit For
    Next lIndex
    Select Case lIndex
        Case 0
            sOption = "Population"
        Case 1
            sOption = "Demand"
        Case 2
            sOption = "Price"
        Case 3
            sOption = "Turnover"
        Case 4
            sOption = "Additional Capital"
        Case 5
            sOption = "Additional Expense"
    End Select
    OptionSelected = sOption
End Property

Public Property Get ListSelection() As Double
    ListSelection = CDbl(lstValue.Text)
End Property

' ************************************************************
' Form Event Procedures Follow
' ************************************************************
Private Sub optType_Click(Index As Integer)
    Dim vItem As Variant
    Dim vaList As Variant
    lstValue.Clear
    Select Case Index
        Case 0   ' Population
            vaList = Array(500, 1000, 100000, 100000)
```

```
        Case 1  ' Demand
            vaList = Array(50, 100, 1000, 10000)
        Case 2  ' Price
            vaList = Array(9.99, 19.99, 29.99, 39.99)
        Case 3  ' Turnover
            vaList = Array(0.01, 0.015, 0.02, 0.025, 0.03)
        Case 4  ' Additional Capital
            vaList = Array(1000, 2000, 3000, 4000)
        Case 5  ' Additional Expense
            vaList = Array(500, 1000, 1500, 2000)
    End Select
    For Each vItem In vaList
        lstValue.AddItem vItem
    Next vItem
    lstValue.ListIndex = -1
End Sub


Private Sub cmdOK_Click()
    Dim bOptionSelected As Boolean
    Dim lIndex As Long
    ' Do not allow the user to continue unless an option button
    ' has been selected and a list item has been selected
    For lIndex = optType.LBound To optType.UBound
        If optType(lIndex).Value Then
            bOptionSelected = True
            Exit For
        End If
    Next lIndex
    If Not bOptionSelected Or lstValue.ListIndex = -1 Then
        MsgBox "You must select an option and a list item."
    Else
        Me.Hide
    End If
End Sub


Private Sub Form_QueryUnload(Cancel As Integer, _
                                        UnloadMode As Integer)
    ' Route the x-close button through the
    ' cmdOK_Click event procedure.
    If UnloadMode = vbFormControlMenu Then
        Cancel = True
        cmdOK_Click
    End If
End Sub
```

The OptionSelected property procedure returns a string identifying the option button within the control array that the user selected. It does this by just looping the control array until a control with a value of True is located. After this control is located, the loop is exited and the index value converted into its corresponding string description. The ListSelection property does nothing more than return the Text property of the list box (whose values are constrained by the option button selection).

The optType_Click event procedure is something that we have never seen before. This event procedure behaves exactly like the Click event for any option button except that it fires when any option button in the control array is clicked. This is why it has an Index argument. The Index argument will contain the value of the Index property of the option button that fired the event. We use this event procedure to load the list box with values that correspond to the options selected. Look at the structure of this procedure and imagine how easy it would be to add or remove options.

The cmdOK_Click event demonstrates some very simple validation code. When the form is first displayed, no option button is selected and there is nothing in the list. If this were a real application we would write code to disable the cmdOK button until all the appropriate selections had been made. For the purposes of this demo, however, we just check the status of the option button array and the list when the cmdOK button is clicked. If everything is in order, we hide the form and continue. Otherwise we display a message to the user indicating what they need to do.

The Form_QueryUnload event is used to trap cases where the user tries to close the form with the X-Close button rather than the OK button. In a real application, we would have cancel logic coded into the form that would be activated by this button, but because the only route out of the form that we have provided for this example is through the cmdOK button, we cancel any clicks on the X-Close button and reroute them through the cmdOK_Click event procedure.

As mentioned in the final section of our Hello World example, VB6 forms cannot be accessed directly by outside applications. Therefore we have created a public CDialogHandler class module to expose the Control Array Demo form and the selections the user has made in it to our Excel application. The method used to expose the form is shown in Listing 20-9.

Listing 20-9 The CDialogHandler ShowVB6Form Method

```
Public Sub ShowVB6Form(ByRef sOption As String, _
                                   ByRef dValue As Double)
    Dim frmCtrlArrays As FControlArrays
```

```
      Set frmCtrlArrays = New FControlArrays
      Load frmCtrlArrays
      ' Parent the Form window to the Excel Application window.
      SetWindowLongA frmCtrlArrays.hWnd, GWL_HWNDPARENT, mlXLhWnd
      frmCtrlArrays.Show vbModal
      sOption = frmCtrlArrays.OptionSelected
      dValue = frmCtrlArrays.ListSelection
      Unload frmCtrlArrays
      Set frmCtrlArrays = Nothing
End Sub
```

This ShowVB6Form method procedure is almost identical to the method we used to display the form in our Hello World application. The only difference is that in the Hello World application the form did not return any value to the calling procedure, while in this example the form returns the option selected by the user and the item they selected in the list box. The additional code you see in this procedure is used to retrieve these two values and pass them back to the calling Excel application. This is accomplished by the two ByRef arguments to the ShowVB6Form method

In a real-world application, we would typically have much more data to transfer back to Excel and therefore we would design a much more efficient method for doing so, creating a global user-defined type to hold all the information transferred out of the form and passing this UDT directly from the DLL to the Excel application for example. We have not done so here so as not to draw attention away from the main point, which is to demonstrate the use of control arrays.

Better Support for Object-Oriented Programming

More Class Instancing Types

The Instancing property of a class determines its visibility with respect to the application within which it is located. Excel VBA classes are limited to the Instancing types Private and PublicNotCreatable. A class with its Instancing property set to Private is invisible to all outside applications. A class with its Instancing property set to PublicNotCreatable can be seen by outside applications but it can only be used by an outside application if your project creates and exposes an instance of the class through a publicly accessible property, method or procedure first.

What this means for Excel VBA projects is that no outside applications (or even other VBA projects within the same instance of Excel) can create instances of classes that exist within an Excel VBA project. As shown in Figure 20-17, however, a VB6 ActiveX DLL has two additional Instancing types, both of which allow classes of those types to be created and used directly by other applications.

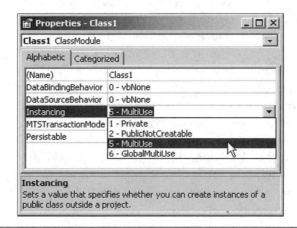

Figure 20-17 VB6 ActiveX DLL Class Types

MultiUse

MultiUse is the default instancing type for class modules added to a VB6 ActiveX DLL project. This is the instancing type that has been used by all the class modules that we have used in this chapter so far. After you have created a class with the MultiUse instancing type, any application that references your DLL can create and use new instances of that class.

The MultiUse instancing type is the one you want to use in cases where it is important for you to require that your public classes are explicitly created before their features are used. This is most frequently the case when your VB6 ActiveX DLL contains an object model that implements the business logic layer of an application, for example.

GlobalMultiUse

Class modules with the instancing type GlobalMultiUse don't need to be explicitly created. Sometimes referred to as auto-instancing classes, this type of class module will be instantiated automatically as soon as any reference is made to one of its publicly exposed components. This type of class is most frequently used for creating libraries of user-defined types, enumeration constants and functions that will be used by multiple files in an application. They are also a good place to define interfaces that you will be implementing in multiple files.

For example, if the code for your data access tier resides in a VB6 ActiveX DLL and the code for your business logic tier resides in an Excel workbook but they both need to share the same user-defined type in order to pass data between them, you can define that UDT in a GlobalMultiUse class in a separate ActiveX DLL that both projects reference. Both projects will then be able to "see" the declaration of the UDT and they can pass variables of that type between themselves even though the UDT is not declared in either one of them. This same technique can be used to expose common enumerations as well.

GlobalMultiUse classes also provide an excellent container for library procedures. Library procedures are generically designed custom subroutines and functions that you find yourself using in most of your projects. If you store these procedures in a GlobalMultiUse class compiled into an ActiveX DLL, all of them can be made available to any project by just referencing that DLL. There is no need to create any object in order to use these library procedures, because public procedures of GlobalMultiUse classes effectively become part of the global namespace in any project that references their DLL. This means you can use your custom bSheetExists() function exactly the same way you use the built-in VBA Replace() function. A working example of a VB6 ActiveX DLL containing a GlobalMultiUseClass can be found on the CD in the *Concepts\Ch20— Combining Excel and Visual Basic 6\GlobalMultiUse* folder.

Better Support for Custom Collections through Direct Support of NewEnum

As explained in *Chapter 7 — Using Class Modules to Create Objects*, VB6 has two significant advantages over VBA when it comes to creating custom Collection objects. It supports default procedures and it has a user interface that can give the required NewEnum method the "magic number" procedure attribute of –4.

For example, the Item property and NewEnum method from the CCells collection introduced in Chapter 7 are shown in Listing 20-10.

Listing 20-10 The Item Property and NewEnum Method from the CCells Collection

```
Property Get Item(ByVal vID As Variant) As CCell
    Set Item = mcolCells(vID)
End Property
```

```
Public Function NewEnum() As IUnknown
    Set NewEnum = mcolCells.[_NewEnum]
End Function
```

If this code were located in a custom collection class in VB6, you would make the Item property the default procedure of the class by placing your mouse cursor anywhere within the procedure and selecting the *Tools > Procedure Attributes* menu. This would display the Procedure Attributes dialog. In the Procedure Attributes dialog you would click the Advanced button and select (Default) from the Procedure ID dropdown. The result of this is shown in Figure 20-18.

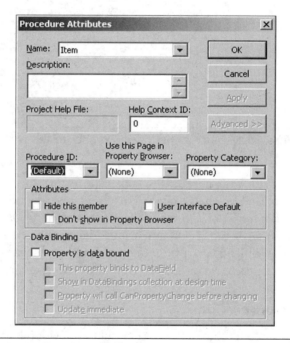

Figure 20-18 Creating a Default Procedure in VB6

Similarly, to give the NewEnum procedure the magic number procedure attribute of –4, you would place your cursor anywhere inside the NewEnum procedure and select *Tools > Procedure Attributes* from the VB6 menu. You would again click the Advanced button, but instead of selecting a preexisting item from the Procedure ID dropdown you would type in the number –4. The result of this is shown in Figure 20-19.

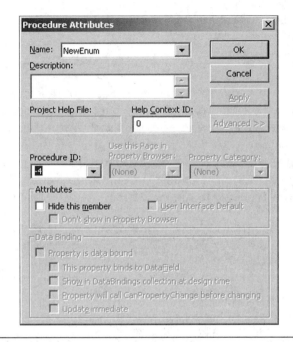

Figure 20-19 Adding the Magic Number to the NewEnum Method

With VB6 it requires very little effort to create a custom collection object that behaves exactly like a built-in collection object. As we described in *Chapter 7 — Using Class Modules to Create Objects*, you can accomplish this in VBA but it is a much more laborious process. Because custom collection objects are a fundamental building block in creating custom object models, the ease of creating them in VB6 is a very significant advantage.

Resource Files

Resource files are a type of container provided by VB6 to store string tables and a wide variety of binary objects. These resources, as they are called, are compiled into your VB6 DLL and made available through the use of specialized VB6 functions. In traditional VB6 projects, the most common use of a resource file is to hold a string table that is used to translate the application into multiple languages. A separate string table is provided for each language under which the application needs to run, and all text displayed by the application is loaded dynamically from the string table that corresponds to the language setting on the user's computer.

Excel applications have the advantage of being able to use worksheets for this type of data storage. What Excel applications lack is an easy way to store binary resources such as icons and bitmaps. You can store these types of resources on worksheets either directly as shapes or as picture objects within a large number of Image controls, or you can distribute them as separate files with the rest of the application. All of these methods have significant problems associated with them that VB6 resource files do not. We show an example of how to use a resource file to store command bar control icons in the *Practical Examples* section later in the chapter.

Other VB6 Features

- **The Clipboard object**—The MSForms object library provides text-only access to the clipboard through the DataObject. VB6 has a clipboard object that supports a complete range of operations for both text and graphics.
- **The Printer object**—The VB6 Printer object enables you to communicate directly with the printer installed on the user's computer. This in no way replaces the built-in printing capabilities of an application like Excel, but it opens up a wide variety of additional printing options that are not available from VBA.
- **The Screen object**—The VB6 Screen object, among other useful features, has two methods that allow you to convert from pixels to twips in both the horizontal and vertical directions, obviating the need for a series of API calls required to determine that information with VBA alone.

In-Process versus Out-of-Process

When you connect two different applications, in this case an Excel VBA application and an application written in VB6, there are two different methods by which the two applications can communicate. These two methods are known as in-process and out-of-process communication.

In-Process Communication

In-process communication occurs when two applications run in the same virtual memory area allocated by Windows. ActiveX DLLs are the type of VB6 application that will run in process with Excel VBA applications.

When an Excel VBA application calls a VB6 ActiveX DLL, Windows loads the DLL into the same memory area it has allocated for the Excel VBA application. (All Excel VBA applications running within a given instance of Excel always run in the same memory area as each other and Excel.)

This has important practical implications. When two applications share the same memory area, communication between them is very fast. In fact communication between an Excel VBA application and a VB6 ActiveX DLL operates at more or less exactly the same speed as communication within an Excel VBA application. Therefore, you do not sacrifice any performance due to communication overhead when using VB6 DLLs with Excel VBA applications and you potentially gain performance due to the fact that unlike VBA, a VB6 DLL is truly compiled and runs more efficiently as a result.

Out-of-Process Communication

Out-of-process communication occurs when two applications run in different memory areas allocated by Windows. This is always the case for communications between two EXE applications. Windows loads all EXE applications into separate memory areas. It is not possible for two EXE applications to share the same memory area.

Therefore, when you use a VB6 EXE together with an Excel VBA application, the VB6 EXE and the Excel VBA application will run in separate memory areas. This results in a significant performance degradation caused by the overhead of communicating between the two memory areas (technically termed inter-process communication). Out-of-process communication runs several orders of magnitude more slowly than in-process communication. One of the obvious implications of this is that you should not choose an out-of-process architecture for highly performance-intensive applications. If, for some reason, you must use an out-of-process architecture for a performance-intensive application, put as much code as possible in the Excel workbook so that it is run in-process by VBA.

Automating Excel From a VB6 EXE

In the most common types of application that combine a VB6 EXE with Excel, the VB6 EXE is the initiating application. The VB6 EXE may either be the primary application automating Excel, or just a front loader for an

Excel application yet to be started. In this section, we demonstrate a stripped-down example of a VB6 EXE application automating Excel. We then describe one of the most common real-world examples of a VB6 EXE combined with an Excel application, the front loader.

An Excel Automation Primer

Automating Excel from a VB6 EXE application is much simpler than using a VB6 ActiveX DLL from an Excel application. In fact we have already covered all of the points required to automate one application from another in *Chapter 18 — Controlling Other Office Applications.* The process of controlling Excel from VB6 is no different from controlling an outside application from Excel.

We now demonstrate a very basic example of a VB6 EXE that automates Excel. The files for this example can be found on the CD in the *Concepts\Ch20—Combining Excel and Visual Basic 6\AutomatingExcel* folder. Creating an elaborate example using Excel would be time consuming and would tend to obscure the fundamentals. Instead we create a somewhat lighthearted example that uses an obscure function provided by Excel to convert whole numbers into Roman numerals. This is not as far from reality as it may seem at first. One of the primary reasons for automating Excel from VB6 is to utilize the powerful capabilities of Excel's calculation engine in a VB6 application.

To begin the project, start VB6 and select Standard EXE as the project type in the New Project dialog. In addition to the project itself, you will get a single VB6 form by default. This is all we need for this example. Rename your project ConvertToRoman, rename your form FRoman and then save your project. In the VB6 Project window, your project should now look like Figure 20-20.

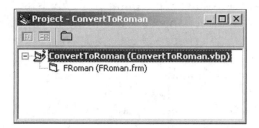

Figure 20-20 The ConvertToRoman Project

The first step required in any project that intends to automate Excel is to set a reference to the Excel object library. Choose *Project > References* from the VB6 menu and select the Microsoft Excel X.0 Object Library, as shown in Figure 20-21, where X is the version number of the earliest version of Excel that you expect to automate with your VB6 application.

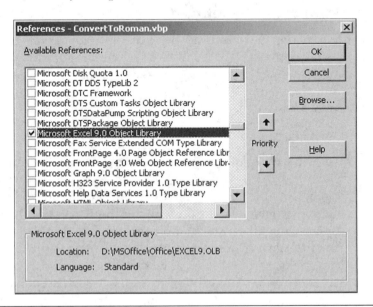

Figure 20-21 Referencing the Excel Object Library

The default form will be the only VB6 class we use in this example. Add three controls to the form: a TextBox control in which to enter the number to be converted to Roman numeral format, a CommandButton control to run the code that performs the conversion and a Label control in which to display the results. Our completed form is shown in Figure 20-22.

We have not changed any of the default properties of our form or its controls. For a change of pace, we show how easy this is to do in code when the form loads. We do need to give our controls reasonable names, however, so we name the CommandButton cmdConvert, the TextBox txtConvert and the Label lblResult.

Now let's look at the code behind our form. All of this code will consist of event procedures for the form object and its controls. The first event procedure we'll examine is the Form_Load event shown in Listing 20-11.

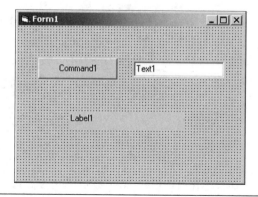

Figure 20-22 The Initial FRoman Form

Listing 20-11 The Form_Load Event Procedure

```
Private Sub Form_Load()
    ' Form properties
    Me.BorderStyle = vbFixedDouble
    Me.Caption = "Convert to Roman Numerals"
    ' CommandButton properties
    cmdConvert.Caption = "Convert To Roman"
    ' TextBox properties
    txtConvert.Alignment = vbRightJustify
    txtConvert.MaxLength = 4
    txtConvert.Text = ""
    ' Label properties
    lblResult.Alignment = vbCenter
    lblResult.BackColor = &HE0E0E0
    lblResult.BorderStyle = vbFixedSingle
    lblResult.Caption = ""
    lblResult.Font.Name = "Courier"
End Sub
```

In this procedure we set all the properties of the form and its controls that are required to make the form user friendly. The result of displaying the form with only this procedure in place is shown in Figure 20-23. Compare this picture with the design-time version of the form shown in Figure 20-22.

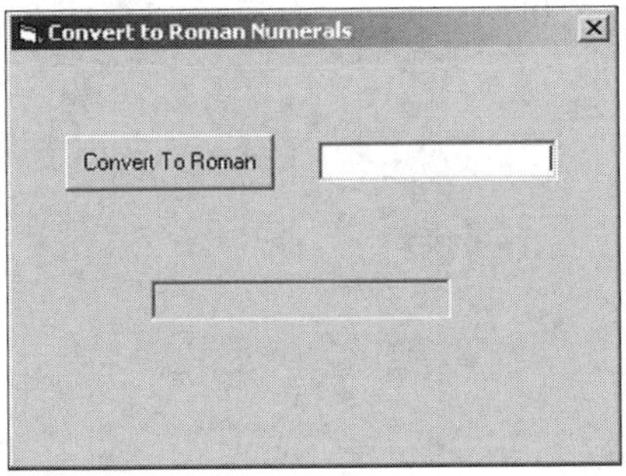

Figure 20-23 The Display Appearance of the Form

The next thing we need to account for is the fact we can only convert whole numbers to Roman numerals. This means we need to prevent the user from entering anything into the txtConvert TextBox control other than the numerals 0 through 9. We accomplish this using the txtConvert_KeyPress event.

The KeyPress event allows you to examine each character the user tries to enter into a control before it actually gets there. This enables you to alter the character, for example by converting lowercase characters to uppercase characters, or cancel the character entirely, as we do for any character other than 0 through 9 in our example. The code for our txtConvert_KeyPress event is shown in Listing 20-12.

Listing 20-12 The txtConvert_KeyPress Event Procedure

```
Private Sub txtConvert_KeyPress(KeyAscii As Integer)
    Select Case KeyAscii
        Case 8, 48 To 57
            ' Backspace and numerals 0 through 9
            ' these are all OK. Take no action.
        Case Else
            ' No other characters are permitted.
            KeyAscii = 0
    End Select
End Sub
```

The KeyPress event passes us a KeyAscii argument that is the ASCII value of the character the user is trying to enter. You can modify that character by changing the value of the KeyAscii argument with the KeyPress event. To cancel a character you just change the KeyAscii argument to zero, which is the equivalent of Chr$(0) or vbNullChar, and therefore has the effect of entering nothing.

In our txtConvert_KeyPress event we use a Select Case statement to handle the incoming characters. This construct makes it easier to enable one whole series of characters and disable all others. We enable the Backspace character (to allow editing) and the numerals 0 through 9 by including their ASCII values in a Case expression that takes no action. All other characters are caught by the Case Else clause, which cancels them by setting the KeyAscii argument to 0. In this manner the KeyPress event ensures the value in the txtConvert TextBox will always be within the domain of values convertible to a Roman numeral.

Speaking of Excel, didn't we say the point of this exercise was to demonstrate how to automate Excel? Well now we have created everything required by our CommandButton's Click event procedure to use Excel to convert the contents of the txtConvert TextBox into an equivalent Roman numeral. The cmdConvert_Click event that accomplishes this feat is shown in Listing 20-13.

Listing 20-13 The cmdConvert_Click Event Procedure

```
Private Sub cmdConvert_Click()

    Dim bError As Boolean
    Dim xlApp As Excel.Application
    Dim lConvert As Long
    Dim sErrMsg As String

    ' Coerce the text box value into a long.
    ' Val is required in case it is empty.
    lConvert = CLng(Val(txtConvert.Text))

    ' Don't do anything unless txtConvert contains
    ' a number greater than zero.
    If lConvert > 0 Then

        ' The maximum number that can be converted
        ' to Roman numeral is 3999.
        If lConvert <= 3999 Then

            Set xlApp = New Excel.Application
            lblResult.Caption = _
                xlApp.WorksheetFunction.Roman(lConvert)
```

```
            xlApp.Quit
            Set xlApp = Nothing

        Else
            sErrMsg = "The maximum number that can be converted"
            sErrMsg = sErrMsg & " to a Roman numeral is 3999."
            bError = True
        End If

    Else
        sErrMsg = "The minimum number that can be converted"
        sErrMsg = sErrMsg & " to a Roman numeral is 1."
        bError = True
    End If

    If bError Then
        MsgBox sErrMsg, vbCritical, "Error"
        txtConvert.SetFocus
        txtConvert.SelStart = 0
        txtConvert.SelLength = Len(txtConvert.Text)
    End If

End Sub
```

Before we go into a detailed discussion of the cmdConvert_Click event procedure we present a working example of the form in Figure 20-24. If you have been following along with the example in your own copy of VB6, just press F5 to start the application. Because the form is the only object in the project it will display automatically. If you select the *File > Make ConvertToRoman.exe* menu you will generate a standalone executable file that can be run by just double-clicking it from Windows Explorer.

One of the first things you'll notice about the cmdConvert_Click event procedure is the vast majority of it has nothing to do with automating Excel. This is a very important point. It often requires a significant amount of preparation on the part of the automating application to ensure Excel will run without error when it is finally started.

The first thing the cmdConvert_Click event procedure does is to verify that the input from the txtConvert TextBox is within the bounds that can be handled by the Excel Roman function. The number to be converted to a Roman numeral must be greater than 0 and less than or equal to 3999. If the number that has been entered is out of bounds, an error message is displayed to the user and they are sent back to the txtConvert TextBox to try again.

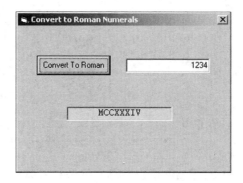

Figure 20-24 The Completed Convert to Roman Numerals Dialog

If the number to be converted is within bounds, the event procedure creates an instance of Excel and goes to work. Using Excel to convert a whole number into a Roman numeral requires merely four lines of code (not counting variable declarations), but it illustrates several of the most important points to follow when automating Excel from VB6:

1. Wherever possible, start your own instance of Excel using the `Set xlApp = New Excel.Application` syntax. Hijacking an existing instance of Excel using GetObject should be avoided at all costs. You have no idea what the user is doing in any existing instance of Excel and therefore you cannot be sure you won't cause them to lose data. Excel will allow you to run multiple instances of itself on the same machine without any trouble at all, so design your applications to create and use their own private instance of Excel.

2. Always fully qualify all references to Excel objects you use, ultimately tying all of them back to the Excel Application object you created. If you don't do this you will often create separate implicit global references to objects within the instance of Excel you are automating. This will make it difficult or impossible to close your instance of Excel when you are finished with it.

3. When you are finished with your instance of Excel be sure to explicitly call the `xlApp.Quit` method on the Excel Application object. Setting the Excel Application object variable to Nothing is not good enough. If you do not explicitly quit the instance of Excel you started, you cannot be sure it is not still running, even after your VB6 application has exited.

In addition, you cannot help but notice that you never saw Excel when running this example. This is because when an instance of Excel is created via automation it is invisible by default. In the *Standard EXE—Creating a Front Loader for Your Excel Application* section below, we demonstrate not only how to make an automated instance of Excel visible, but how to turn it over to the user and exit the VB6 application that started it completely, leaving the created instance of Excel running for the user.

Lastly, if you are expecting any add-ins or other auto-loaded files to be open when you create an instance of Excel via automation you will be disappointed. An instance of Excel created via automation does not load any add-ins that are selected in the *Tools > Add-ins* list nor does it load any files located in auto-start directories like XLStart. If your application depends on these files being loaded you will need to write the code to open them yourself.

Using a VB6 EXE Front Loader for Your Excel Application

A VB6 EXE front loader has the unique ability to examine the configuration of a user's computer without committing itself to any specific version of Excel or any other application. If your Excel application will be distributed widely and/or run on hardware and software over which you have no control, the front loader can verify that everything required to run your application is in place prior to starting Excel, running your application and exiting.

A VB6 EXE front loader can also create an instance of Excel and start your application in it without triggering any of Excel's macro security features. With a VB6 EXE front loader, you never need to be concerned about the user disabling your application by setting macro security to high.

A VB6 EXE front loader can also be used as a security mechanism for your application. The Excel *File > Open* password is the only truly strong password Excel has to offer. But you need to allow your users to open your Excel application in order to use it. A VB6 EXE front loader neatly solves this problem by allowing you to compile all of the *File > Open* passwords required to run your application into a VB6 EXE. This VB6 EXE can then open the Excel files required by your application without ever exposing their passwords to VBA's weak project protection.

NOTE: Any password stored as a literal string in any application is vulnerable to an experienced programmer with a good hex editor. Therefore, if you want your passwords to be truly secure you must store them in an encrypted format and use a procedure to decrypt them just before they are required by your code. But keep in mind that just compiling your passwords into a VB6 EXE front loader will eliminate the ability of at least 99 percent of hackers to break into your application. Adding an encryption layer might increase this to 99.9 percent. For the vast majority of real-world applications, adding an encryption layer is simply not worth the effort.

Practical Examples

ActiveX DLL—Using a Resource File to Load Icons

Adding a Resource File to Your Project

To use resource files in VB6, you must have the *VB6 Resource Editor* add-in loaded in the VB6 IDE. If this add-in is loaded you will see a *Project > Add New Resource File* menu item on the VB6 menu bar. If you do not see this menu, choose *Add-ins > Add-in Manager* from the VB6 menu. This will display the Add-in Manager dialog shown in Figure 20-25.

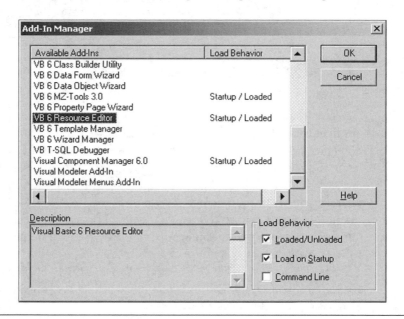

Figure 20-25 The Add-in Manager Dialog

The list of available add-ins will likely be different on your system, but locate the VB6 Resource Editor add-in as shown and under the *Load Behavior* section of the Add-in Manager dialog check the *Loaded/Unloaded* and *Load on Startup* check boxes.

After the Resource Editor add-in is installed, make sure your project has been saved and then choose *Project > Add New Resource File* from the VB6 menu to add a resource file to your project. You will be prompted with the rather confusingly named Open a Resource File dialog shown in Figure 20-26.

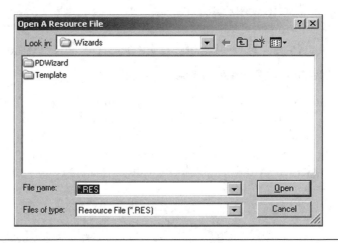

Figure 20-26 The Open a Resource File Dialog

This dialog can be used to either add an existing resource file to your application or create a new resource file. We'll create a new resource file. Navigate to the folder where your project is saved and type the name you want to give your resource file, without the .RES extension, into the *File name* box. When you click the Open button, the Resource Editor will prompt you with the message shown in Figure 20-27. (We have chosen the filename Icons because that is what we will be storing in this resource file.) Click the Yes button and an empty resource file will be created and added to your project.

The Project window view of our ActiveX DLL project containing the Icons.res resource file is shown in Figure 20-28. As you will see later in this example, the CResourceProvider class will be used to expose the bitmaps contained in the resource file to outside callers as StdPicture objects. This is the object type required to set the Picture and Mask properties for Excel 2002 and later command bar controls.

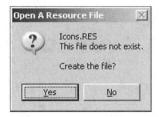

Figure 20-27 Creating a New Resource File

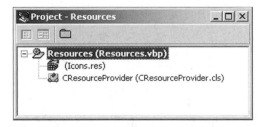

Figure 20-28 The Resources ActiveX DLL Project

Adding Bitmaps to the Resource File

You can add icons, bitmaps or custom binary resources to your resource file. Because the ultimate target for our resources are command bar control icons, we load them as bitmaps. Bitmaps have the advantage of being very simple. They can be created using nothing more than the Paint program that ships with every copy of Windows. The only restriction is that bitmaps designed to be command bar button icons must be 16 pixels by 16 pixels in size in order to provide the optimal appearance.

In this section, we load two bitmaps into our resource file: a command bar button icon and its corresponding mask. We use the custom arrow icon and mask we saw in *Chapter 8 — Advanced Command Bar Handing* for demonstration purposes. To begin the process, double-click the resource file in the VB6 Project window in order to open it in the Resource Editor. The currently empty resource file will open in the Resource Editor as shown in Figure 20-29. The top line in the Resource Editor displays the full path and filename of the resource file being edited.

To add a bitmap to the resource file, click the *Add Bitmap* toolbar button on the Resource Editor toolbar. This is the third button from the right in Figure 20-29. The Resource Editor will display the Open a Bitmap File dialog shown in Figure 20-30.

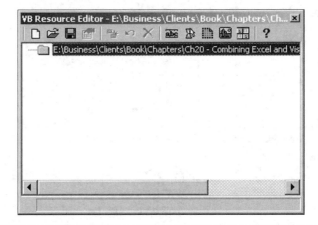

Figure 20-29 The Empty Icons.res File Opened in the Resource Editor

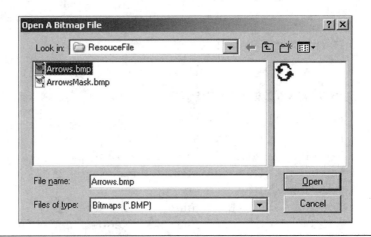

Figure 20-30 The Open a Bitmap File Dialog

We have already navigated to the folder containing the two bitmaps we want to load and selected the first one. As you can see, the Open a Bitmap File dialog displays a preview of the selected bitmap in its right pane. Click the Open button to add the selected Arrows.bmp bitmap to the resource file. The result is shown in Figure 20-31.

The Resource Editor has given our bitmap the default ID property value 101. You can modify this value by selecting the bitmap resource and clicking the *Edit Properties* toolbar button. In the next section we'll use an enumeration to map these numeric IDs onto something more recognizable.

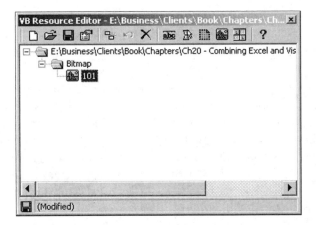

Figure 20-31 The Icons.res Resource File Containing One Bitmap

Repeat the steps above to load the ArrowsMask.bmp resource into the resource file. This will be given the default ID property value 102. Click the *Save* icon to save the resource file and then close the Resource Editor using the X-Close button in the upper right corner. An important point to note is that adding bitmaps to your resource file copies them into it. The original bitmap files you selected are still in their original location and they are not connected to the copies contained in the resource file in any way.

Using Bitmaps Located in the Resource File

A simple, one-line property procedure in the CResourceProvider class module will return any of the bitmap resources stored in our resource file. All that will be required is to pass this property procedure the enumeration value (discussed below) identifying the resource you want to retrieve. The property procedure will return a reference to the specified resource as an StdPicture object. The entire contents of the CResourceProvider class module are shown in Listing 20-14.

Listing 20-14 The Icon Property Procedure

```
Public Enum resIcon
    resIconArrows = 101
    resIconArrowsMask = 102
End Enum
```

```
Public Property Get Icon(ByVal uName As resIcon) As StdPicture
    Set Icon = LoadResPicture(uName, vbResBitmap)
End Property
```

As you can see, we have used an enumeration to provide readable names for the numeric ID property values that identify the bitmap resources in our resource file. Inside the property procedure the VB LoadResPicture function is used to retrieve the specified resource from the resource file. The first argument to this function specifies which resource should be returned. The second argument specifies the type of the resource to be returned using a built-in VB constant, in this case vbResBitmap.

After you have compiled the Resources ActiveX DLL, any program capable of consuming a StdPicture object can use the resources it contains. To demonstrate the use of this DLL, we rework the Load Picture and Mask example from *Chapter 8 — Advanced Command Bar Handling* to retrieve its icons from the Resource DLL rather than loading them from individual bitmap files on disk. The procedures shown in Listing 20-15 build a command bar with a single button that uses our custom arrow icon and mask loaded from the Resources DLL.

Listing 20-15 Loading a Custom Icon from a Resource File into a Command Bar Button

```
Public Sub CreateBar()

    Dim cbrBar As CommandBar
    Dim ctlControl As CommandBarButton
    Dim objRes As Resources.CResourceProvider

    ' Make sure any previously created version of our demo
    ' command bar is deleted.
    RemoveBar

    ' Create an instance of the resource provider.
    Set objRes = New Resources.CResourceProvider

    ' Create a toolbar-type command bar.
    Set cbrBar = CommandBars.Add("Demo", msoBarTop, False, True)
    cbrBar.Visible = True

    ' Add the command bar button control.
```

```
    Set ctlControl = cbrBar.Controls.Add(msoControlButton)
    ' Load the foreground bitmap file.
    ctlControl.Picture = objRes.Icon(resIconArrows)
    ' Load the mask bitmap file.
    ctlControl.Mask = objRes.Icon(resIconArrowsMask)

End Sub

Public Sub RemoveBar()
    On Error Resume Next
    CommandBars("Demo").Delete
End Sub
```

The complete code for this example can be found in the LoadPictureAndMask.xls workbook located on the CD in the *\Concepts\Ch20—Combining Excel and Visual Basic 6* folder. Note that this example will only work in Excel 2002 or later and you must have registered the Resources ActiveX DLL on your computer. Notice how the Picture and Mask properties of our command bar button in this example are now retrieving their contents from the custom resource file in our DLL rather than from bitmap files stored on disk.

Standard EXE—Creating a Front Loader for Your Excel Application

An application utilizing a VB6 front loader begins with the execution of a VB6 application rather than an Excel application. The corresponding Excel application is only executed if the conditions being verified by the front-loader application are met by the system on which the application is executing.

We covered the reasons for using a VB6 EXE front loader in your Excel application in the *Using a VB6 EXE Front Loader for Your Excel Application* section above. In this section we focus on how to build a VB6 EXE front loader. In this example, we assume that the task of our front loader is to verify Word and Outlook are correctly installed on the user's computer before running our PETRAS timesheet application.

Start by opening VB6 and choosing Standard EXE as the project type in the New Project dialog. In addition to the default form object that VB6 provides with this project type add one standard code module to your project using the *Project > Add Module* menu. Rename your default objects to the names shown in Table 20-2.

Table 20-2 Front Loader Application Object Names

Default Object Name	New Object Name
Project1	FrontLoader
Form1	FWarning
Module1	MEntryPoints

Next, set a reference to the Microsoft Excel Object Library using the *Project > References* menu. Finally, save your project's files to a common folder. The end result as displayed in the Project window should look like Figure 20-32.

When you create a Standard EXE project, the default startup object is the form object that is added by default when the project is first created. This is not how we want our front loader application to work. Instead, we add a special procedure to the MEntryPoints module called Sub Main. We then modify our project's properties so that Sub Main is run on startup rather than the default form.

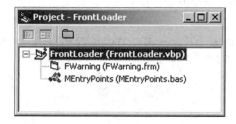

Figure 20-32 The Structure of the Front Loader Application

Open the MEntryPoints module and create the Sub Main stub procedure shown in Listing 20-16.

Listing 20-16 The Sub Main Stub Procedure

```
Public Sub Main()
    ' Code goes here later.
End Sub
```

We must now tell the project that we want our Sub Main procedure to be executed when our VB6 EXE is first run. This is accomplished using the *Project > FrontLoader Properties…* menu. As shown in Figure 20-33, we have changed the *Startup Object* setting in the upper right corner of the Project Properties dialog *General* tab from FWarning (the default) to Sub Main.

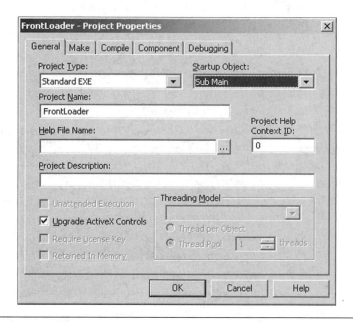

Figure 20-33 Changing the Startup Object to Sub Main

Next we build the FWarning form. This form is relatively uncomplicated. Its only purpose is to notify the user that the validation check failed prior to the front loader exiting without starting the Excel application. First we'll set the properties of the form object itself as shown in Table 20-3.

Table 20-3 FWarning Property Settings

Property Name	Setting
BorderStyle	3—Fixed Dialog
Caption	Startup Validation Failed
Icon	PetrasIcon.ico (supplied on the CD)
StartupPosition	2—Center Screen

Rather than displaying the bland, default VB6 icon for our final FrontLoader.exe application, we want to use the same branded PETRAS icon that we used in our FWarning form. To accomplish this, select the *Project > FrontLoader Properties* menu and then select the *Make* tab in the Project Properties dialog. As shown in Figure 20-34, select FWarning from the *Icon* dropdown in the upper-right corner. This will make the icon defined for the FWarning dialog be the icon displayed for our FrontLoader.exe file in Windows Explorer and by any shortcuts we create to it.

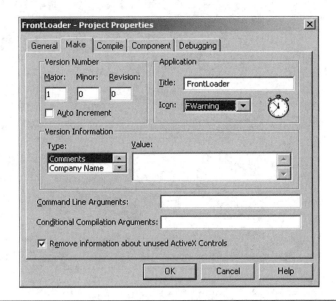

Figure 20-34 Modifying the Icon Displayed by Our FrontLoader.exe File

The FWarning form itself will contain only two controls: a cmdOK CommandButton to dismiss the form and a static Label control to display the validation failure message to the user. The form should look similar to the one displayed in Figure 20-35.

The click event of the cmdOK button is displayed in Listing 20-17. It just unloads the form after the user has read the message.

Listing 20-17 The cmdOK_Click Event Procedure

```
Private Sub cmdOK_Click()
    Unload Me
End Sub
```

Figure 20-35 The Layout of the FWarning Dialog

The decision whether to run the Excel application or display the FWarning message will be made by the code logic controlled by the Sub Main procedure. Our Word and Outlook validation logic will be encapsulated in two separate functions. One will determine whether Word is installed and operating correctly and the other will do the same for Outlook.

Two functions are required because the two applications behave differently when automated. When your application creates an instance of Word via automation you always get a brand new hidden instance of Word, regardless of whether the user is currently running Word. With Outlook, the result of creating an instance via automation depends on whether the user already has Outlook open. If Outlook is already open, you get a reference to the currently open instance. If Outlook is not open, you get a new hidden instance.

For our validation logic we use the most rigorous test possible, whether or not we can actually get a reference to running instances of Word and Outlook. The functions that will perform the validation for the status of Word and Outlook are shown in Listing 20-18.

Listing 20-18 The bWordAvailable and bOutlookAvailable Functions

```
Private Function bWordAvailable() As Boolean
    Dim wdApp As Object
    ' Attempt to start an instance of Word.
    On Error Resume Next
        Set wdApp = CreateObject("Word.Application")
    On Error GoTo 0
    ' Return the result of the test.
    If Not wdApp Is Nothing Then
        ' If we started Word we need to close it.
```

```
        wdApp.Quit
        Set wdApp = Nothing
        bWordAvailable = True
    Else
        bWordAvailable = False
    End If
End Function

Private Function bOutlookAvailable() As Boolean
    Dim bWasRunning As Boolean
    Dim olApp As Object
    On Error Resume Next
        ' Attempt to get a reference to a currently open
        ' instance of Outlook.
        Set olApp = GetObject(, "Outlook.Application")
        If olApp Is Nothing Then
            ' If this fails, attempt to start a new instance.
            Set olApp = CreateObject("Outlook.Application")
        Else
            ' Otherwise flag that Outlook was already running
            ' so that we don't try to close it.
            bWasRunning = True
        End If
    On Error GoTo 0
    ' Return the result of the test.
    If Not olApp Is Nothing Then
        ' If we started Outlook we need to close it.
        If Not bWasRunning Then olApp.Quit
        Set olApp = Nothing
        bOutlookAvailable = True
    Else
        bOutlookAvailable = False
    End If
End Function
```

The first thing to notice is that we're using late binding in both of these validation functions. If we didn't use late binding and tried to run our front loader on a computer that didn't have Word or Outlook installed, the front loader would fail before it ever got the chance to run the validation functions.

This is the result of using a compiled vs. an interpreted programming language. When you run an Excel VBA application, its code is validated by the VBA runtime on a module-by-module basis. The code in any given module is only validated when some code in that module is called or referenced by the application. This means, for example, that if you had a reference to an invalid component in your Excel VBA project, but the code making use of this reference was confined to one module and no code in that module was ever called or referenced by your application, that module would never be loaded by the VBA runtime, its code would never be validated and your application would not experience a runtime error.

In a fully compiled application, all references are validated on startup. Therefore, if you reference a component that doesn't exist on the machine where your fully compiled application is run, the application fails immediately.

The second thing to notice is the difference between the bWordAvailable and bOutlookAvailable functions. Because automating Word is very straightforward, we just attempt to create a new instance of Word and the result of the function is determined by whether we succeed or fail. The logic of the Outlook validation function is exactly the same, but due to the different behavior of Outlook the implementation is different.

Rather than just attempting to create a new instance of Outlook we first need to try the GetObject function. This will return a reference to any instance of Outlook the user is currently running. If this succeeds, it satisfies our validation test. If the user can successfully run Outlook we can be reasonably sure that our application can as well. If we are not able to locate a currently running instance of Outlook, we then try to create a new one using the CreateObject function. If this succeeds we have validated the availability of Outlook, but we have also started a new instance of Outlook that needs to be closed before our function exits.

This is the point where the logic of the bWordAvailable and bOutlookAvailable functions diverge. If the bWordAvailable function succeeds then we know we have started a new instance of Word that we must close before the function exits. If the bOutlookAvailable function succeeds, whether or not we need to close Outlook on exit depends on whether or not our function actually started the instance of Outlook that validated its availability or whether we simply attached to an instance of Outlook the user was already running. If the GetObject function retrieved our reference to Outlook then we leave it alone. If CreateObject retrieved our reference to Outlook then we must close that instance of Outlook before we exit. This is the purpose of the bWasRunning variable in the bOutlookAvailable function. It tells us whether we need to close Outlook at the end of the function.

Now that we have seen all the pieces of the front-loader application, let's look at the procedure that brings them all together. As we stated earlier, the Sub Main procedure is the controlling procedure in our front-loader application. It calls the validation functions, examines their results, and based on those results it determines whether to run our Excel application or display a warning message and exit. The Sub Main procedure is shown in Listing 20-19.

Listing 20-19 The Sub Main Procedure

```
Public Sub Main()

    Dim bHasWord As Boolean
    Dim bHasOutlook As Boolean
    Dim xlApp As Excel.Application
    Dim wkbPetras As Excel.Workbook
    Dim frmWarning As FWarning

    ' Verify that we can automate both Word and Outlook on
    ' this computer.
    bHasWord = bWordAvailable()
    bHasOutlook = bOutlookAvailable()

    If bHasWord And bHasOutlook Then
        ' If we successfully automated both Word and Outlook,
        ' load our Excel app and turn it over to the user.
        Set xlApp = New Excel.Application
        xlApp.Visible = True
        xlApp.UserControl = True
        Set wkbPetras = xlApp.Workbooks.Open(App.Path & _
                                    "\PetrasAddin.xla")
        wkbPetras.RunAutoMacros xlAutoOpen
        Set wkbPetras = Nothing
        Set xlApp = Nothing
    Else
        ' If we failed to get a reference to either Word or
        ' Outlook, display a warning message to the user and
        ' exit without taking further action.
        Set frmWarning = New FWarning
        frmWarning.Show
        Set frmWarning = Nothing
    End If

End Sub
```

There are two things in particular to note about the way the Sub Main procedure handles Excel. First, after creating an instance of Excel and making it Visible, it sets the Excel Application object's UserControl property to True. This makes the Excel Application behave as if it had been started directly by the user rather than via automation.

Second, after opening the PETRAS application workbook, it runs the RunAutoMacros method of the Workbook object. This is because the Auto_Open procedure will not run automatically when an Excel workbook is opened via automation. Therefore, we need to run it ourselves.

As mentioned previously in the *An Excel Automation Primer* section, an Excel Application object created via automation will also not open any add-ins specified in the *Tools > Add-ins* list nor any workbooks located in startup folders like XLStart. If your application relies on any secondary workbooks of this nature, you will have to add code to your front loader to open these workbooks (and run their startup procedures if required).

Conclusion

There are many good reasons to take advantage of the additional power afforded by VB6 in your Excel VBA applications. VB6 ActiveX DLLs provide code protection, the ability to use the more powerful VB6 forms in your Excel projects, excellent support for object-oriented programming, support for resource files and a number of miscellaneous features not available in VBA, including the Clipboard, Printer and Screen objects. VB6 EXE applications enable you to automate Excel, initiating your application from VB6 rather than Excel. This allows you to create components such as front loaders. These can scan the operating environment for you prior to start up to ensure that your application has the required resources available, allow you an extra level of VBA code protection by compiling your *File > Open* passwords in an EXE file, and let you start Excel and run your VBA application without triggering any VBA macro security features.

Writing Add-ins with Visual Basic 6

Ever since VBA was added to Excel 5.0, we've been able to add features to Excel by creating add-in workbooks, as discussed in *Chapter 5 — Function, General and Application-Specific Add-ins*. Word, Access and PowerPoint had their own application-specific add-in architectures. In Office 2000, Microsoft created a new add-in architecture, called a COM Add-in, which was common to all the Office applications and the VBIDE. This chapter explains how to create COM Add-ins using Visual Basic 6. *Chapter 22 — Using VB.NET and the Visual Studio Tools for Office* explains how to achieve similar results using Visual Basic.NET.

A Hello World Add-in

At its most fundamental level, an add-in architecture has four basic requirements:

- A mechanism for telling the host application that the add-in exists.
- A mechanism for the host application to call a procedure in the add-in when the add-in is loaded, usually during the application's startup processing. At this point, the add-in sets up its menu items, toolbar buttons and/or shortcut keys
- A mechanism for raising events that the add-in can respond to.
- A mechanism for the host application to call a procedure in the add-in when the add-in is unloaded, usually during the application's shutdown processing.

For Excel add-ins, we can either put the add-in file in the XLStart folder (so it's always installed for all users) or use the *Tools > Add-ins* dialog to select the add-in file and mark it as installed (on a per-user basis).

When Excel starts up, it sees the add-in, opens the file and runs the start-up procedure. When Excel 5 had loaded the add-in, it called the special Auto_Open procedure and prior to shutting down, it called the special Auto_Close procedure. Both procedures were placed in a standard VBA module (the only module type that existed at the time!). A Hello World add-in looked like Listing 21-1.

Listing 21-1 A Hello World Add-in Using Auto_Open in a Standard Module

```
'Run when the add-in is loaded
Sub Auto_Open()
    MsgBox "Hello World"
End Sub

'Run when the add-in is closed
Sub Auto_Close()
    MsgBox "Goodbye World"
End Sub
```

When the VBIDE was introduced in Excel 97, every workbook was given a ThisWorkbook class module, within which we could write code to respond to a number of workbook-related events, including Workbook_Open and Workbook_BeforeClose. These procedures were also called when Excel 97 opened and closed an add-in workbook. Listing 21-2 shows a Hello World add-in that uses workbook events.

Listing 21-2 A Hello World Add-in Using Workbook Events in the ThisWorkbook Module

```
'Run when the add-in is loaded
Private Sub Workbook_Open()
    MsgBox "Hello World"
End Sub

'Run when the add-in is closed
Private Sub Workbook_BeforeClose(Cancel As Boolean)
    MsgBox "Goodbye World"
End Sub
```

Both the Auto_Open and Workbook_Open methods continue to work in all recent versions of Excel and which one to use is a matter of personal preference.

So let's do the same with Visual Basic 6. Start VB and select the Addin project type from the New Project dialog. This creates a new COM Add-in project called MyAddin, with a default form and Designer class called Connect. We prefer to always start with a clean project, so change the project name to HelloWorld, remove the default form and delete all the existing code from the Connect class. The Add-in Designer is the COM Add-in equivalent of Excel's ThisWorkbook class and handles all the communication between Excel and the COM Add-in. It has a simple UI for us to set the add-in's properties, such as its title, description and which Office application it targets, as shown in Figure 21-1, where we've completed it for our Hello World example. We cover the dialog's options in more detail later.

Excel's ThisWorkbook class gives us a Workbook object that has the Open and BeforeClose events that we use for our startup and shutdown code. The equivalent in the Add-in Designer class is the AddinInstance object and OnConnection and OnDisconnection events, shown in Figure 21-2.

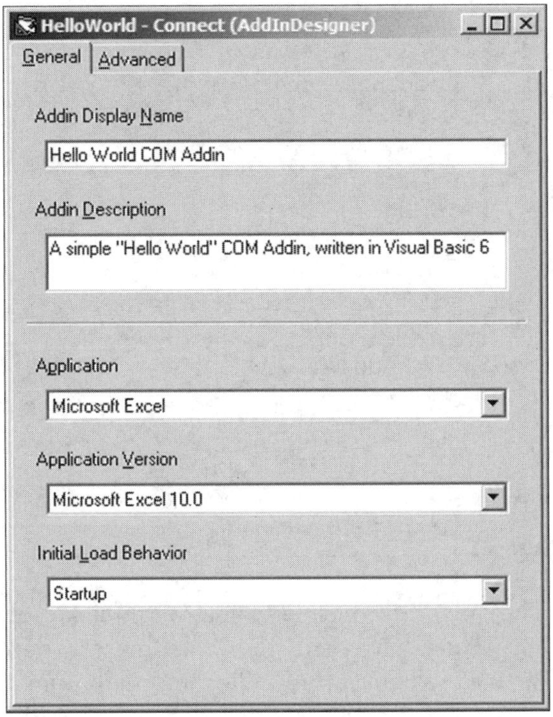

Figure 21-1 The Completed Add-in Designer Dialog

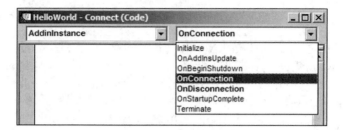

Figure 21-2 The AddinInstance Object and Events

Listing 21-3 uses these two events for our Hello World COM Add-in.

Listing 21-3 A Hello World COM Add-in

```
'Run when the add-in is loaded
Private Sub AddinInstance_OnConnection( _
          ByVal Application As Object, _
          ByVal ConnectMode As _
               AddInDesignerObjects.ext_ConnectMode, _
          ByVal AddInInst As Object, _
          custom() As Variant)

    MsgBox "Hello World"
End Sub

'Run when the add-in is unloaded
Private Sub AddinInstance_OnDisconnection( _
          ByVal RemoveMode As _
               AddInDesignerObjects.ext_DisconnectMode, _
          custom() As Variant)

    MsgBox "Goodbye World"
End Sub
```

The only difference between this code and the workbook add-in is that the two events have many more parameters (described later). To build the add-in, save all the project files and click *File > Make HelloWorld.DLL*. Now start Excel 2000 or above and you should see the Hello World message box appear. Close Excel and the Goodbye World message box pops up. Congratulations, you've created a COM Add-in!

The first thing you'll want to do now is switch it off! All the Office applications have a *COM Add-ins* dialog to enable or disable COM Add-ins, but it is not included on the default set of menus. To add it, right-click a toolbar, choose *Customize*, select the *Commands* tab and find COM Add-ins... halfway down the list for the Tools category. Drag it to Excel's Tools menu. Figure 21-3 shows the COM Add-ins dialog with our add-in selected. The add-in can be disabled by unticking it or removed from the list by clicking the Remove button.

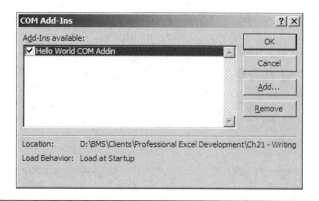

Figure 21-3 The COM Add-ins Dialog

The Add-in Designer

Excel's *Tools > Add-ins* dialog is actually a simple UI that handles the following two registry keys (where the 10.0 indicates the version of Office):

- HKEY_CURRENT_USER\Software\Microsoft\Office\10.0\ Excel\Add-in Manager
-
  HKEY_CURRENT_USER\Software\Microsoft\Office\10.0\Excel\ Options

The first key lists the full path of any add-in workbooks that are not in Excel's Library folder (that is, where we've used the Browse button to locate the add-in) and are not installed—they just appear unticked in the *Tools > Add-ins* list. The second key contains a number of OPENx values, listing the full path for all add-in workbooks that are installed—that is, ticked in the *Tools > Add-ins* list. These registry entries are covered in more detail in *Chapter 24 — Providing Help, Securing, Packaging and Distributing*. To check for installed add-ins when Excel starts up, it looks for the OPENx entries in the Excel\Options key, opens those workbooks and calls the Auto_Open and/or Workbook_Open procedures therein.

To check for installed COM Add-ins, Excel looks in the registry to see whether there are any keys below HKEY_CURRENT_USER\Software\ Microsoft\Office\Excel\Addins. Each COM Add-in adds a key below that with the ProgID of its Add-in Designer class, having the form <Project Name>.<Designer Name>. In our case, the key is called HelloWorld.Connect. Within that key are a number of registry entries that directly correspond to the options on the Designer form, shown in Figure 21-1 earlier. When the project is built and the DLL is registered, the Designer writes the registry values into the HKEY_CURRENT_USER key (commonly referred to using its acronym HKCU) to install the add-in for the current user. These values and options are detailed below.

General Tab

For convenience, the General tab of the Add-in Designer is repeated in Figure 21-4.

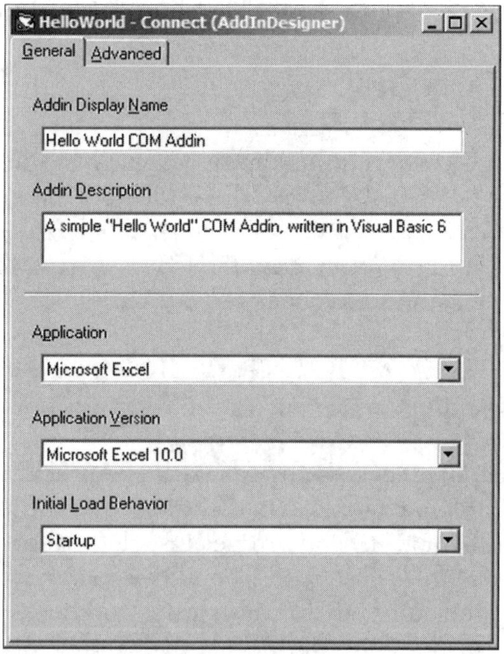

Figure 21-4 The General Tab of the Designer Dialog

Add-in Display Name

This is the name displayed in Excel's *Tools > COM Add-ins* dialog box. It is stored in the registry in the *FriendlyName* value.

Add-in Description

Excel does not display the description anywhere. If writing a COM Add-in that targets the VBIDE, the description is shown in the VBE's Add-in Manager dialog when the add-in is selected. It is stored in the registry in the *Description* value.

Application

A drop-down list of all the installed applications that can be extended using COM Add-ins. Selecting this list determines which key is used for the registry entries, such as:

Excel: HKCU\Software\Microsoft\Office\Excel\Addins

Word: HKCU \Software\Microsoft\Office\Word\Addins

VBIDE: HKCU \Software\Microsoft\VBA\VBE\6.0\Addins

Application Version

A drop-down list of all the installed versions of the selected application. The observant reader might have noticed that when we built our Hello World COM Add-in above, it was immediately working in Excel 2000, 2002 and 2003. This is because the Application Version is ignored for Excel COM Add-ins; the details always get written to the same registry key of HKCU\Software\Microsoft\Office\Excel\Addins. When writing COM Add-ins that target the VBIDE, the version (6.0) is included in the registry key. Of course, we've yet to see anything other than version 6.0 of the VBIDE!

Initial Load Behavior

A set of four choices that control whether and how Excel loads our add-in. The choice is stored in the *LoadBehavior* value and can be one of the following:

- *Startup*, value = 3: The add-in is loaded every time Excel starts. This is the most common load behavior setting.

- *None*, value = 0: The add-in is not loaded and does not appear in the *Tools > COM Add-ins* dialog. This option would be selected if the COM Add-in is to be installed for all users. See *Installation Considerations* later for more details.
- *Load on Demand*, value = 9: The add-in is loaded the first time one of its menu items is clicked. It is highly unusual for this value to be set within the Designer.
- *Load at Next Startup Only*, value = 16: The add-in is loaded the first time Excel is started after the add-in is installed, so it can add its menu items permanently to Excel's command bars. Once loaded, Excel changes this value to 9 (Load on Demand), so it is loaded the first time one of its menu items is clicked. See *Command Bar Handling* later for more details.

Advanced Tab

The Advanced tab of the Add-in Designer is shown in Figure 21-5.

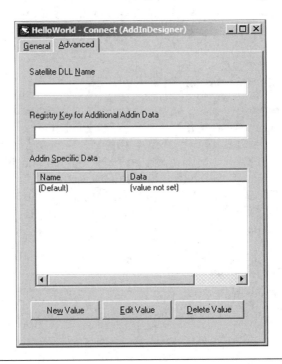

Figure 21-5 The Advanced Tab of the Designer Dialog

Satellite DLL Name

The COM Add-in architecture has been designed to allow easy localization. This means that instead of storing the text of the add-in's name and description in the registry, we can store those strings in a resource table in a separate DLL. We can then use a standard Windows resource editor to translate the text into localized versions of the DLL. In the Designer form, we type in the resource IDs instead of the name and description and provide the name of the DLL containing the resource table in this field (stored as *SatelliteDLLName* in the registry). When Excel needs to show the Display Name in the *Tools > COM Add-ins* dialog, it should recognize that a resource DLL is being used and extract the display name from the resource table. Unfortunately, however, Excel doesn't check for the resource DLL and always displays the meaningless resource ID instead! The use of a satellite DLL in this way works correctly for add-ins targeting the VBIDE.

Registry Key for Additional Add-in Data and Add-in-Specific Data

When the COM Add-in is installed, we have the option of writing additional entries in the registry. These fields specify the entries to write and the registry key where those entries will be written. They are most often used if the COM Add-in is to be installed for all users. See *Installation Considerations* below for more details.

Installation Considerations

A COM Add-in is an ActiveX DLL that needs to be registered on the computer before it can be used. The registration is done by a program called regsvr32.exe, usually found in the *C:\Windows\System32* directory. The easiest way to do it manually is to right-click the DLL, choose *Open With...* and browse to the regsvr32.exe file. You can also use the *Add...* button on Excel's COM Add-ins dialog and browse to the DLL. A final alternative is to use a setup program, which should automatically register any ActiveX DLLs it installs.

All of these methods call a special function within the DLL, telling it to write whatever registry entries it requires to work. For COM Add-ins, the Designer ensures this includes the registry entries required to get it working with Excel. The Designer, however, only writes the entries required to install the add-in for the current user (that is, under the HKEY_CURRENT_USER section of the registry).

Excel also allows add-ins to be installed for all users of the machine. As well as looking within the HKCU section, it also looks in the same path of the HKEY_LOCAL_MACHINE section (often referred to as HKLM). If we want our add-in to be installed for all users, we have to set the Designer's *Initial Load Behavior* to None and use the Advanced tab to add our own registry entries, as shown in Figure 21-6. Note that the *LoadBehavior* value is a DWORD type, whereas the other two are strings.

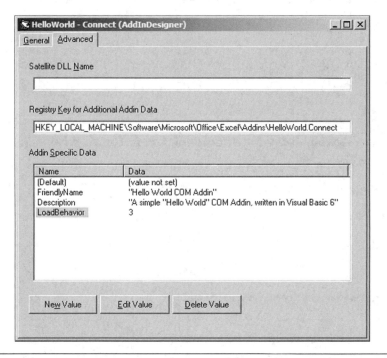

Figure 21-6 The Advanced Tab of the Designer Dialog, Showing the Entries for an All-User Installation

COM Add-ins that are installed in this way do not show up in the COM Add-ins dialog and can only be uninstalled by deleting the registry entries using regedit (which you might want to do right now!). They will also obviously require access to the HKLM section of the registry, which is usually only granted to people in the Power Users or Administrators network groups. Members of the basic Users group will not be able to install (or uninstall) the add-in.

The AddinInstance Events

Now that we've created, installed and tested a simple Hello World COM Add-in, it's time to take a more detailed look at how Excel interacts with the COM Add-in, using the Designer's code module. During the life of a session, Excel tells us what's going on by raising events through the Designer's AddinInstance object, in exactly the same way that it raises events through the Workbook object of a workbook's ThisWorkbook code module. These events are listed below, in the order in which they're fired during a typical Excel session.

Initialize

```
Private Sub AddinInstance_Initialize()
```

The Initialize event is fired when the class is first instantiated and is exactly the same as the Class_Initialize event of a class module. It's rare to see this event used.

OnConnection

```
Private Sub AddinInstance_OnConnection( _
    ByVal Application As Object, _
    ByVal ConnectMode As _
        AddInDesignerObjects.ext_ConnectMode, _
    ByVal AddInInst As Object, _
    custom() As Variant)
```

Every COM Add-in uses the OnConnection event, which is raised by Excel during its startup processing, when a demand-loaded add-in is loaded (see the *Command Bar Handling* section later) or when the add-in is enabled in the COM Add-ins dialog. This is the equivalent of the VBA Auto_Open or Workbook_Open procedures and should be used to initialize the project, set up menu items and so on. This procedure should not display any forms or show any message boxes.

The Application parameter is a reference to the host's Application object (Excel.Application in our case). Most add-ins will assign this to a global variable, to provide access to the application's properties, methods and events.

The ConnectMode tells us when the add-in was started, either ext_cm_Startup (as Excel started) or ext_cm_AfterStartup (when a demand-loaded add-in is loaded, or from the COM Add-in dialog).

The `AddInInst` parameter is Excel's COMAddin object that refers to this COM Add-in. We use this object to get the add-in's ProgID to use when setting up our menu items (see the *Command Bar Handling* section later). The AddInInst object also enables us to expose the functions in our add-in to VBA, by including the following line:

```
AddInInst.Object = Me
```

in the OnConnection procedure. Any Public properties and methods we include in the Designer class can then be called from VBA using code like this:

```
'Run the SomeSub() procedure in the Hello World COM Addin
Application.COMAddins("HelloWorld.Connect").Object.SomeSub
```

The `custom()` parameter allows the COM Add-in host application to send extra information to a COM Add-in. For Excel, the first element of the custom() array is used to tell us how Excel was started: 1 = Opened from the user interface, 2 = Opened as an embedded object, 3 = Opened through automation.

OnStartupComplete

```
Private Sub AddinInstance_OnStartupComplete( _
    custom() As Variant)
```

Excel raises the OnConnection event within its startup processing, as it encounters a COM Add-in to open. The OnStartupComplete event is raised after Excel has completed its startup processing, just before returning control to the user. This is the place to display any forms you want to show on startup, such as "Thanks for Installing" or "Did You Know?" dialogs. In practice, it is rarely used.

OnAddInsUpdate

```
Private Sub AddinInstance_OnAddInsUpdate( _
    custom() As Variant)
```

The OnAddInsUpdate event is raised whenever another COM Add-in is loaded or unloaded (although we're not told which, or whether it's just been loaded or unloaded). We've never seen it used.

OnBeginShutdown

```
Private Sub AddinInstance_OnBeginShutdown( _
    custom() As Variant)
```

The OnBeginShutdown event is raised when Excel starts its shutdown processing, if the add-in is loaded at the time. It is not called if the add-in is unloaded using the COM Add-ins dialog. We've never seen it used.

OnDisconnection

```
Private Sub AddinInstance_OnDisconnection( _
    ByVal RemoveMode As _
        AddInDesignerObjects.ext_DisconnectMode, _
    custom() As Variant)
```

The OnDisconnection event is raised when Excel shuts down or when the add-in is unloaded using the COM Add-ins dialog. This procedure is where you should put your add-in's shutdown code, such as tidying up menus and so forth.

The RemoveMode parameter tells us why the add-in is being unloaded, either ext_dm_UserClosed (unloaded using the COM Add-ins dialog) or ext_dm_HostShutdown (Excel is shutting down). We would use this to decide whether or not to delete our menu items, if using a permanent-menu design (see the *Command Bar Handling* section later).

Terminate

```
Private Sub AddinInstance_Terminate()
```

The Terminate event is fired when the class is destroyed and is exactly the same as the Class_Terminate event of a class module. It's rare to see this event used.

Command Bar Handling

Using Command Bar Event Hooks

Toward the end of *Chapter 8 — Advanced Command Bar Handling*, we explained the difference between using the CommandBarControl's OnAction property to call our procedures and using class modules to hook the CommandBarButton's Click event or the CommandBarComboBox's Change event. When creating COM Add-ins, we have to use the event-hook method for all our controls. It would be a good idea to reread that section of Chapter 8, but to summarize it we need to do the following:

- Give all our menu items the same Tag property, to uniquely identify them as belonging to our add-in.
- Give each menu item a unique Parameter property, to identify them in code.
- Have a class module containing a With Events declaration for a CommandBarButton (and/or CommandBarComboBox).
- In the class's CommandBarButton_Click event procedure, confirm that the Tag is set to ours then call the procedure appropriate to the Parameter value.
- When setting up our menus, create a new instance of the class for each combination of ID and Tag that we use. If we're not using any built-in menu items, we would only need a single instance of the class.

Permanent vs. Temporary Menu Items

In an Excel add-in, we can respond to the AddInInstall event to permanently add our menu items to Excel (by setting the `temporary` parameter to False when adding them) and respond to the AddInUninstall event to remove them. In the meantime, they will always be available to the user, will feature in their usage counting (if they've elected to show partial menus) and can be moved around, copied to other toolbars and so on. This is the preferred method for general-purpose add-ins that might be expected to always be installed.

Alternatively, we could choose to add our menu items on a temporary basis, in which case we would add them in the Workbook_Open event and remove them in the Workbook_BeforeClose event. This is the preferred method for application-specific add-ins, where the menu items would typically be contained in their own command bar and we wouldn't want the user to move them around.

COM Add-ins differ from normal Excel add-ins in that we aren't told when the add-in is installed or uninstalled (particularly uninstalled); we can only infer it from the value we gave the Initial Load Behavior setting and the parameters passed to the OnConnection and OnDisconnection events.

A Permanent-Menu Architecture

When using permanent menus with COM Add-ins, we set the *Initial Load Behavior* in the Designer to *Load at next startup only*. This means Excel will load the add-in the next time it starts, run the OnConnection procedure, then set the load behavior to *Load on demand*.

In the OnConnection procedure, we need to check the ConnectMode parameter. If it is ext_cm_Startup, we create our command bars and menu items then set up the event hooks for them. If the ConnectMode is ext_cm_AfterStartup, our menu items should already be there, so we only need to set up the event hooks. We should include some code to check whether any of our menu items have been removed and add them back.

In the OnDisconnection procedure, we need to check the RemoveMode parameter. If it is ext_dm_UserClosed, the user has unticked the add-in in the COM Add-ins dialog, so we should delete our menu items. If the RemoveMode is ext_dm_HostShutdown, we don't need to do anything.

When creating our menu items, we need to tell Excel that the menu belongs to our COM Add-in. We do that by setting the command bar control's OnAction property to !<ProgID>, where the ProgID can be obtained from the AddInInst object passed to the event. This tells Excel which add-in owns the control so it loads the add-in and calls the OnConnection event (if necessary), allowing the add-in to set up the event hooks, then raises the Click or Change event.

The code for a permanent-menu architecture is shown in Listing 21-4.

Listing 21-4 A Permanent-Menu Architecture

```
'Run when the add-in is loaded
Private Sub AddinInstance_OnConnection( _
    ByVal Application As Object, _
    ByVal ConnectMode As _
        AddInDesignerObjects.ext_ConnectMode, _
    ByVal AddInInst As Object, _
    custom() As Variant)

    Dim sOnAction As String

    'Store a reference to the application object
    Set gxlApp = Application

    'If we're starting up, it must be the first time,
```

```
'so create our menu items permanently
If ConnectMode = ext_cm_Startup Then

    'Get the ProgID from the AddInInst object
    sOnAction = "!<" & AddInInst.ProgId & ">"

    'Create our menus, passing the OnAction string
    CreateMenus sOnAction
End If

'Whether at startup or after startup,
'we have to set up our event hooks
HookMenus

End Sub

'Run when the add-in is unloaded
Private Sub AddinInstance_OnDisconnection( _
    ByVal RemoveMode As _
        AddInDesignerObjects.ext_DisconnectMode, _
    custom() As Variant)

    'If the user chose to uninstall the add-in,
    'remove our menus
    If RemoveMode = ext_dm_UserClosed Then
        RemoveMenus
    End If

    'Tidy up our application reference
    Set gxlApp = Nothing

End Sub
```

The problem with using a permanent-menu design with COM Add-ins is that it is quite likely the add-in would be uninstalled while Excel is closed. As COM Add-in DLLs need to be registered on the user's computer, it is common practice to distribute them using a proper setup file. The setup file will usually include an Uninstall option and/or include the add-in in the user's Add/Remove Programs list. If our users were to use this option to uninstall the add-in, the add-in's menu items would remain, orphaned. This risk has to be weighed against the benefit of allowing the user to move the menus around, create copies and so on. In practice, temporary menu architectures are the most common.

A Temporary-Menu Architecture

A temporary-menu architecture is much simpler. We set the *Initial Load Behavior* in the Designer to *StartUp*, so the add-in is loaded every time Excel starts. In the OnConnection event, we always re-create our menus and set up the event hooks. In the OnDisconnection event, we always remove them. If we're creating our own command bars, we need to store their visibility, docked state and position before removing them and make sure they're added back in the same state. Because the add-in will always be open, we do not need to set the OnAction property. Even though we're removing our menu items in the OnDisconnection event, it is good practice to add them with the `temporary` parameter set to True. The code for a temporary-menu architecture is shown in Listing 21-5.

Listing 21-5 A Temporary-Menu Architecture

```
'Run when the add-in is loaded
Private Sub AddinInstance_OnConnection( _
    ByVal Application As Object, _
    ByVal ConnectMode As _
        AddInDesignerObjects.ext_ConnectMode, _
    ByVal AddInInst As Object, _
    custom() As Variant)

    'Store a reference to the application object
    Set gxlApp = Application

    'Always create our menu items
    CreateMenus

    'Set up our event hooks
    HookMenus

End Sub

'Run when the add-in is unloaded
Private Sub AddinInstance_OnDisconnection( _
    ByVal RemoveMode As _
        AddInDesignerObjects.ext_DisconnectMode, _
    custom() As Variant)

    'Always remove our menus
    RemoveMenus
```

```
'Tidy up our application reference
Set gxlApp = Nothing

End Sub
```

Custom Toolbar Faces

A COM Add-in does not have a worksheet handy to store the pictures and masks that we need for custom toolbar faces. Instead, we store the bitmaps in a resource file within the COM Add-in project and use LoadResPicture to retrieve the image when needed. For more information about the use of resource files in VB6, see *Chapter 20 — Combining Excel and Visual Basic 6*. For Excel 2002 and 2003, we set the Picture and Mask directly, but Excel 2000 gives us more of a problem. When stored in resource files, the bitmaps lose the transparency that we could give them when they were stored in a worksheet. When we Copy/PasteFace the picture onto an Excel 2000 toolbar and disable the button, the image usually turns into an unidentifiable gray blob. This can be worked around by using API calls to create a transparent bitmap during the Copy/Paste procedure and is documented in Microsoft KB article 288771 at `http://support.microsoft.com/?kbid=288771`.

The Paste Special Bar COM Add-in

In *Chapter 8 — Advanced Command Bar Handling*, we used a Paste Special command bar to demonstrate the concept of hooking command bar button events. The workbook is called PasteSpecialBar.xls and is located on the CD in the *\Concepts\Ch08—Advanced Command Bar Handling* folder. To demonstrate a working temporary-menu architecture in a COM Add-in and the use of custom toolbar faces, we have converted the workbook to a COM Add-in. The code for it can found in the *\Concepts\Ch21—Writing Add-ins with Visual Basic 6\PasteSpecialBarVB6* folder. The READ_ME module lists the changes that were made to convert the Excel add-in to a COM Add-in, while each module lists the changes that were required in the module header. The changes are summarized below:

- Use the Designer and OnConnection / OnDisconnection instead of Auto_Open / Auto_Close.
- Add a global variable to store a reference to the Excel.Application object and use that variable whenever referring to any of Excel's global objects.

- Remove all the code for the table-driven command bar builder, replacing it with a simpler procedure to add the toolbar buttons individually.
- Copy the custom toolbar images to a resource file and use them instead of the PastePicture module.
- Add the MCopyTransparent module, to handle copying transparent bitmaps for Excel 2000.
- Change the values of a few of the global variables, so the Excel add-in and COM Add-in can coexist in Excel.
- Tidy up a few minor references to ThisWorkbook.

It is interesting to note that the only change required to the add-in's payload of performing the Paste Special was to prefix CommandBars and Selection by our global Application object variable. If you're still unsure of the differences and similarities between Excel and COM Add-ins, open both versions of the Paste Special Bar and compare them. Both add-ins do exactly the same things in exactly the same ways, using the same module and procedure names, except where noted in the comments. Familiarizing yourself with both versions of the add-in will also prepare you for the next chapter, in which we convert it to a Visual Studio Tools for Office (VSTO) solution, using Visual Basic.NET.

Why Use a COM Add-in?

By now, you've hopefully realized that while the details are slightly different between COM Add-ins and Excel add-ins, the concepts are the same and the code in them can be almost identical. That begs the question "Why bother?"

Improved Code Security

The code contained in Excel workbooks is notoriously easy to break into; tools are readily available on the Internet that can crack (or simply remove) the VBProject protection password. If your add-in contains sensitive information or intellectual property that you would prefer remained hidden, you should consider creating it as a COM Add-in. COM Add-ins are distributed as DLLs compiled to machine code; the source code is never included. Although it is theoretically possible to decompile an add-in, it is extremely difficult and impractical to do.

Multi-Application Add-ins

A COM Add-in can contain multiple Designer classes, each handling the connection to a different Office application. Imagine an Insert Customer Details add-in, which displayed a form enabling you to select a customer from a central database and then inserted their name, address and/or telephone number in the current place in the document. By including multiple Designer classes in the add-in, we could easily make the add-in available to all the Office applications. Each class's OnConnection event would be used to add a standard menu item to the host application's command bars, with the Click event handled by a single class. When clicked, it would display the form and would only branch into application-specific code when the Insert button was clicked to insert the selected details into the cell, paragraph, field, presentation or Web page.

Exploiting Separate Threading

One of the more interesting things about COM Add-ins is that each one is given its own execution thread. The vast majority of Excel and VBA is single-threaded, meaning that VBA code stops when Excel is working (such as showing one of its dialogs) and vice versa. COM Add-ins don't have this limitation. A COM Add-in can initialize a Windows timer callback, tell Excel to display a dialog (or Print Preview or whatever), then continue processing (in the callback function) while Excel is still displaying the dialog. This enables us to (a) prepopulate the dialog, (b) watch what the user is doing within the dialog (and respond to it) and even (c) change the layout of the dialog itself!

It should be noted that Excel is not designed to be used like this and these techniques are in no way supported by Microsoft. Attempting to call into Excel's object model while it is displaying a form may or may not work (but if it works in one case, it will always work in that case), often depending on whether we're simply reading properties (usually reliable) or trying to get Excel to do something (which usually fails).

As an example, the \Concepts\Ch21—Writing Add-ins with Visual Basic 6\ToolsRefSize folder on the CD contains a COM Add-in which uses this technique to modify the labels at the bottom of the VBE's Tools > References dialog, to display the filename of the referenced project using two lines with word wrap. Figure 21-7 shows the modifications made by the COM Add-in, enabling us to see the full path of the referenced project.

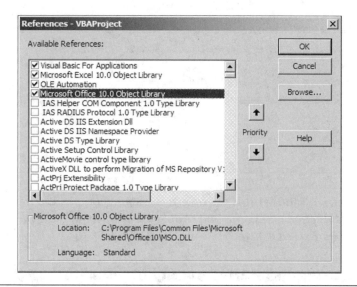

Figure 21-7 The VBE's Tools > References Dialog, Modified by the ToolsRefSize COM Add-in to Show the Full Location of the Selected Project

Automation Add-ins

When initially introduced in Excel 2000, the functions contained in COM Add-ins could not be called directly from a worksheet. In Excel 2002, Microsoft added ***Automation Add-ins*** to solve that problem. An automation add-in is nothing more than an ActiveX DLL that contains a public function.

Creating the IfError Automation Add-in

Chapter 5 — Function, General and Application-Specific Add-ins introduced the IFERROR() function, written as a VBA user-defined function. In *Chapter 19 — XLLs and the C API*, it was rewritten in C, for best performance. We can re-create this as an automation add-in to improve on the performance of the VBA version, although not as much as the C version. This can be thought of as a compromise, improving the performance but keeping the simplicity of the Visual Basic code. To create the add-in, start a new empty ActiveX DLL project in VB6, change the project name to ProExcel and the class name to Functions, then copy in the code shown in Listing 21-6.

Listing 21-6 The IFERROR User-Defined Function

```
Public Function IFERROR(ByRef ToEvaluate As Variant, _
                        ByRef Default As Variant) As Variant
    If IsError(ToEvaluate) Then
        IFERROR = Default
    Else
        IFERROR = ToEvaluate
    End If
End Function
```

Note that this is *exactly* the same code as Listing 5-3 in *Chapter 5 — Function, General and Application-Specific Add-ins*. Click *File > Make ProExcel.DLL* to build the DLL.

Using the IfError Automation Add-in

Open Excel 2002, click the *Tools > Add-ins* menu and click the *Automation* button. The Automation Servers dialog lists every registered ActiveX DLL on the PC, including the one we just created. Select the entry for ProExcel.Functions and click OK. It should now be listed in the normal *Tools > Add-ins* dialog. Click OK to return to the worksheet. The function can now be called directly from the worksheet just like any other function:

```
=IFERROR(A1/B1,0)
```

Accessing the Excel Application Object from an Automation Add-in

When creating anything more than a trivial function, we will usually want to use some of Excel's worksheet functions within the procedure. Alternatively, we may need to mark our function as volatile, so it is called every time the sheet is recalculated. Both of these situations require us to interact with the Excel Application object.

If we add one of the same Add-in Designer classes to our project that we used for COM Add-ins, Excel will call the OnConnection event when the DLL is first loaded, giving us the opportunity to store a reference to the Application object. We can then use that object within our functions. The following steps explain how to set it up:

1. Within the ProExcel project, click *Project > Add Add-in Class* to add a new Add-in Designer to the project. If that menu isn't available, click *Project > Components* and put a tick next to the *Add-in Class* item on the *Designers* tab to make it available.

2. In the Designer dialog, set the *Application* to Microsoft Excel and the *Initial Load Behavior* to None.

3. We don't need to provide a name or description, but change the Designer's class name in the Properties window from AddInDesigner1 to AppFunctions and set *Public* to True (ignoring the warning).

4. Click *Project > References*, select Microsoft Excel from the list to create a reference to the Excel object library, then copy in the code shown in Listing 21-7.

Listing 21-7 The AppFunctions Code, Using the Excel Application Within Automation Add-ins

```
Option Explicit

'Reference to the Excel application
Dim mxlApp As Excel.Application

'Called when the automation add-in is loaded
Private Sub AddinInstance_OnConnection( _
    ByVal Application As Object, _
    ByVal ConnectMode As _
        AddInDesignerObjects.ext_ConnectMode, _
    ByVal AddInInst As Object, _
    custom() As Variant)

    'Store away a reference to the Application object
    Set mxlApp = Application
End Sub

'Volatile function to return VB's Timer value
Public Function VBTimer() As Double
    mxlApp.Volatile True
    VBTimer = Timer
End Function
```

```
'Function to count how many items in Source lie between
'Min and Max
Public Function CountBetween(ByRef Source As Range, _
        ByVal Min As Double, ByVal Max As Double) As Double

    'If we get an error, return zero
    On Error GoTo ErrHandler

    'Count the items bigger than Min
    CountBetween = mxlApp.WorksheetFunction _
                .CountIf(Source, ">" & Min)

    'Subtract the items bigger than Max, giving the number
    'of items in between
    CountBetween = CountBetween - mxlApp.WorksheetFunction _
                .CountIf(Source, ">=" & Max)

Exit Function

ErrHandler:
    CountBetween = 0
End Function
```

5. Close Excel, compile the DLL and install the ProExcel.AppFunctions add-in by selecting it from the *Tools > Add-ins > Automation* list.

The first time any of the functions in the add-in is used, Excel loads the add-in, calls the OnConnection procedure, then calls the function. In the OnConnection procedure, we store a reference to the Excel Application object, which we use within the functions contained in the class.

Practical Example

COM Add-ins are most applicable to creating general-purpose add-ins, often working across many of the Office applications. There is very little benefit to be gained from using them for application-specific add-ins, such as the PETRAS timesheet add-in we've been developing through the book.

Therefore, neither the PETRAS timesheet add-in nor the PETRAS reporting application have been modified for this chapter. However, the Paste Special Bar add-in demonstrates a practical example of a COM Add-in, and the IfError add-in demonstrates a practical example of an automation add-in.

Conclusion

The COM Add-in architecture enables us to create a single add-in that can target any (or many, or all) of the applications in the Office suite and any third-party applications that license the VBA6 development environment.

The code contained within a COM Add-in is virtually impossible to decompile, making it a much more secure medium than standard Excel add-ins, in terms of protecting intellectual property.

There is very little difference between the code contained in a COM Add-in and an Excel add-in; in many cases, the code can be copied from Excel and run virtually unchanged in the COM Add-in.

Because COM Add-ins are typically written using Visual Basic 6, all the best practices described in *Chapter 20 — Combining Excel and Visual Basic 6* apply.

Both the Paste Special Bar and the IFERROR function examples have demonstrated that an Excel add-in can be converted to a COM Add-in relatively easily.

Using VB.NET and the Visual Studio Tools for Office

Relatively late in the planning process for Office 2003, the irresistible force of .NET crashed into the immovable object of Office. The Visual Studio Tools for Office was crafted from the debris. This chapter explains the concepts behind VSTO, how it works, what it can do (and cannot do) and discusses other ways of leveraging the .NET framework within Excel solutions. Note that this chapter applies to Visual Studio 2003, Office 2003 and VSTO 1.0, and all code samples are in Visual Basic.NET. You need to have these applications installed to be able to run the examples for this chapter.

The sample files for this chapter need some modification to adjust their security configuration before you will be able to run them. We suggest you read through the entire chapter to understand how to do this, before trying out the samples.

Overview

Target Audience

Visual Studio.NET and the .NET languages are the responsibility of the Visual Tools division of Microsoft. The Office applications and their object models are the responsibility of the Office division. Office programmability lives in the no man's land between the two. At the time of this writing, the VBA language and the integrated VBIDE are owned by the Visual Tools division, but its ownership has flipped back and forth a few times since Excel 5. It's possible that ownership of VBA and the VBIDE may switch back to the Office division, to allow the Visual Tools division to concentrate on .NET technologies, which includes the Visual Studio Tools for Office (VSTO) added for Office 2003.

The distinction is very important because the two divisions have radically different types of customers, and it's the customers' requirements that drive the development of new tools and technologies.

The primary focus in the Office division is that of end-user productivity, providing tools that enable end users to create, access, manipulate and share their documents and data quickly, easily and reliably. For this group, Office programmability ranges from using VBA to automate repetitive tasks (at the low end of the scale) to creating standalone line-of-business applications using one or more of the Office applications to provide the core features (at the top end of the scale).

The primary focus of the Visual Tools division is the professional developer who creates enterprise-wide and/or Web-based applications using the most up-to-date tools available. It is for this group that the .NET technologies were developed and continue to be enhanced. For them, Office programmability has typically been an afterthought, maybe adding a final feature to their application to export their data or reports as an Excel spreadsheet or Word document. The Visual Studio Tools for Office has been created to allow this group to apply their skills to Office development.

What Is VSTO?

The Visual Studio Tools for Office is a set of Visual Studio.NET project templates that bring Office-based application development to the .NET developer, allowing them to consider Excel and Word as first-class citizens of the .NET framework, alongside Windows Forms, Web Forms, ASP.NET and the rest.

VSTO allows those developers who have embraced the .NET initiative to link code to Excel workbooks and Word documents that will be executed when the workbook or document is opened (in much the same way we do with VBA), subject to security constraints. A key distinction is that the code does not form part of the workbook file. Instead, the code is contained in an assembly (the .NET term for a DLL) placed in a central location, such as a network share, and a link to the assembly is added to the workbook as a custom document property. When Excel 2003 opens a workbook, it checks whether the custom document property exists, reads where to download the assembly from, downloads the assembly, checks the security configuration and calls some standard entry points to run the code. This new process is referred to as the VSTO Loader and is the *only* change that has been made to Excel 2003 for it to support .NET.

How Does .NET Interact with Office?

At the risk of stating the obvious, VBA interacts with the Office applications through their object models. The object models are exposed as COM interfaces which VBA can call to access the underlying application code. To enable the .NET languages to interact with Office, Microsoft has created a Primary Interop Assembly (PIA) for each application. The PIA is an extra layer on top of the COM interfaces that exposes (almost) the same objects with the same properties, methods and events that we know from VBA, allowing them to be used by .NET code.

Is This the End for VBA?

No, no, no, no and no. VSTO is a toolset to allow .NET developers to link VB.NET or C# code to Office documents, typically to add features to the workbooks and documents produced by their enterprise-wide applications. It does little to address the needs of the typical VBA user community. VBA and the VBA IDE will continue to be included within Office for the foreseeable future, and all new features added to Office will be exposed via the object models to both VBA and .NET. To do otherwise would be financial suicide for Microsoft, because all their corporate customers that have significant investments in VBA solutions would simply refuse to upgrade to a version of Office that does not support VBA and allow it to be maintained.

The situation is very similar to the XLM functions used to program Excel 4. Although VBA was introduced in Excel 5, some ten years ago, XLM macros are still supported and can be maintained in Excel 2003; indeed there are still some things that can only be done using XLM function calls, such as finding the coordinates of chart elements as discussed in *Chapter 15 — Advanced Charting Techniques*.

At the time of writing, VSTO is just another tool for creating Excel applications.

Terminology

.NET introduced some new terminology that we use throughout this chapter:

- *Assembly* is the .NET term for a DLL or EXE, being a file containing .NET code.
- *Code behind* is the term given to a linked VSTO assembly; that is, the assembly that is pointed to by the custom document property, downloaded and run when the document is opened. Don't be confused by this term; it does not imply that the code is contained within the document in the same manner as VBA.

- *Managed* means something written using a .NET language, usually VB.NET or C#, and executed by the .NET runtime, so *managed code* means code written using VB.NET, C# or one of the other .NET languages, and a *managed workbook* is a workbook which has managed code behind it.

How to Leverage the .NET Framework

We can use five different mechanisms (at least) to include some managed code in our Excel-based applications, all of which have their pros and cons. They are summarized below, and the last three are explored in greater detail later in the chapter:

- *Managed COM DLLs* are assemblies that include special attributes to expose the classes, methods and properties as standard COM objects. To create a Managed COM DLL, we start with a project of type Class Library and add a class of type COM Class. That class will be exposed as a COM object and any public procedures we add to the class will be exposed as the object's methods and properties, in exactly the same way that we explain in *Chapter 20 — Combining Excel and Visual Basic 6*.
- *Managed COM add-ins* are COM DLLs that implement the IDTExtensibility2 interface. To create a Managed COM Add-in, we start with a Managed COM DLL and add a reference to the Microsoft Add-in Designer library. We then implement the interface by adding

```
Implements AddInDesignerObjects.IDTExtensibility2
```

at the top of the class module and adding our code for all the interface procedures. In *Chapter 21 — Writing Add-ins with Visual Basic 6*, we used the Add-in Designer class instead, which is a wrapper for the IDTExtenxibility2 interface. When writing managed COM Add-ins, we have to implement the interface directly and also write the registry entries to install the add-in. As we explain in *Chapter 24 — Providing Help, Securing, Packaging and Distributing*, if the user doesn't have the *Trust all Installed Add-ins and Templates* setting ticked in the *Tools > Macro > Security* dialog, Excel will only automatically load a COM Add-in if it is digitally signed with a trusted digital signature. Unfortunately, Excel ignores any digital signatures we apply to managed assemblies, so will not automatically load managed COM Add-ins. The workaround for this issue is explained at `http://msdn.microsoft.com/library/en-us/dnoxpta/html/odc_shim.asp` and involves using C++ to create an unmanaged shim that can satisfy Excel's security checks.

■ ***Managed workbooks*** are the pure document-centric VSTO design philosophy. With this mechanism, a workbook is linked to an assembly created using the VSTO tools. The assembly contains a standard ***OfficeCodeBehind*** class that Excel calls and provides ThisWorkbook and ThisApplication objects. The ThisWorkbook object is a reference to the workbook the assembly is linked to, and ThisApplication is a reference to the Excel Application object. The code contained in the assembly is used to automate the single document it is linked to. If you have multiple copies of the same workbook open, each one gets its own instance of the linked assembly, so the code contained in the assembly has to take that into account. We explain some ways of doing this later in the chapter.

■ A ***Managed Excel add-in*** is a managed workbook that has been saved as an Excel add-in, but does not contain any VBA code. When Excel starts, it loads the add-in as normal, but instead of running the Auto_Open or Workbook_Open routine, it uses the VSTO Loader to run the linked assembly. The code in the assembly can act as either a general-purpose or application-specific add-in, as described in *Chapter 5 — Function, General and Application-Specific Add-ins.*

■ ***Hybrid VBA/VSTO Solutions*** are workbooks that both contain VBA and have linked VSTO assemblies interoperating with each other. This usage is officially untested and unsupported by Microsoft but in our opinion provides by far the best mechanism for a gradual migration from VBA to a managed (VSTO) solution, should we want to do so.

Managed Workbooks

Concept

Managed workbooks are at the core of the VSTO design. The basic principle is to completely separate code from data—a principle that has been stressed many times in this book. In VBA, our code is always embedded within a workbook and we achieve code/data separation by using multiple workbooks—one for the code and one for the data. In a VSTO solution, our VB.NET or C# code is compiled into a .NET assembly and the workbook is linked to the code by the two custom document properties **_AssemblyLocation0** and **_AssemblyName0**, giving the directory and filename of the assembly respectively.

To deploy the application, the assembly is copied to a network share (with the appropriate security permissions set—see later) and the _AssemblyLocation0 property is updated with the URL of the share, in *server\share* form. The workbook is then distributed to the end users. When they open it, Excel checks the custom properties, downloads the assembly, checks the user's security settings and runs it (via the .NET runtime) if the security settings are configured to allow it to run.

This concept brings a number of benefits:

- We can update everyone's code by copying a new version of the assembly to the network share—we no longer need to track who the document has been sent to in order to distribute updates.
- As the assembly is always downloaded before being run, it doesn't matter whether someone has the workbook open when we update the assembly—they'll automatically start using the new assembly the next time they open the workbook.
- We never have to distribute the source code, so there is better protection for our intellectual property.
- If each user has his .NET security settings configured to allow VSTO solutions to run only if they have come from a specific URL, opening managed workbooks from other (untrusted) sources will not run the code, thereby preventing viruses and improving security.

Unfortunately, it also introduces a few issues:

- It's much harder to have different groups of people running different versions of the application, such as during a phased rollout or region-specific updates—we would have to distribute new versions of the document that point to different assemblies, negating the benefit of the "automatic" updates.
- Everyone must be able to access the network share in order to download and run the assembly, which makes it **much** harder to use the document outside the corporate network, such as taking it home to work on, or sharing it with partner companies.

- Every computer has to have its .NET security permissions set to allow VSTO solutions to run from the network share. In a corporate environment, this could be administered centrally by including the configuration with a login script. A small company or home user would have to configure the settings manually, requiring detailed knowledge of the .NET and VSTO security model (see later).

A Hello World Managed Workbook

Let's start by creating a simple Hello World VSTO solution. Fire up Visual Studio.NET 2003, select *New Project* and choose a new Excel workbook, as shown in Figure 22-1.

After clicking OK through the dialogs, we end up with a VSTO OfficeCodeBehind class template, including a collapsed region called Generated initialization code and some stubs for the Workbook_Open and Workbook_BeforeClose events. Adding a MsgBox call to each stub gives us our Hello World VSTO solution, shown in Listing 22-1, where the code we've added has been highlighted and the collapsed section expanded to show its contents.

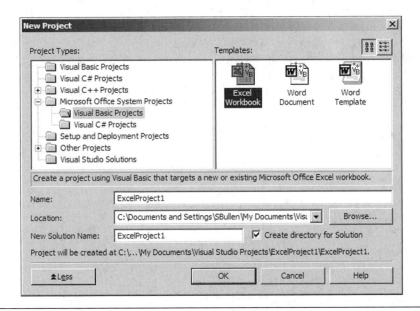

Figure 22-1 The Visual Studio.NET NewProject Dialog

Listing 22-1 VSTO Solution

```vbnet
Imports System.Windows.Forms
Imports Office = Microsoft.Office.Core
Imports Excel = Microsoft.Office.Interop.Excel
Imports MSForms = Microsoft.Vbe.Interop.Forms


' Office integration attribute. Identifies the startup
' class for the workbook. Do not modify.
<Assembly: System.ComponentModel.DescriptionAttribute( _
           "OfficeStartupClass, Version=1.0, " & _
           "Class=ExcelProject1.OfficeCodeBehind")>

Public Class OfficeCodeBehind

   Friend WithEvents ThisWorkbook As Excel.Workbook
   Friend WithEvents ThisApplication As Excel.Application

#Region "Generated initialization code"

   ' Default constructor.
   Public Sub New()
   End Sub

   ' Required procedure. Do not modify.
   Public Sub _Startup(ByVal application As Object, _
           ByVal workbook As Object)
     ThisApplication = CType(application, Excel.Application)
     ThisWorkbook = CType(workbook, Excel.Workbook)


   End Sub

   ' Required procedure. Do not modify.
   Public Sub _Shutdown()
     ThisApplication = Nothing
     ThisWorkbook = Nothing
   End Sub

   ' Returns the control with the specified name on
   ' ThisWorkbook's active worksheet.
   Overloads Function FindControl(ByVal name As String) _
           As Object
```

```vb
        Return FindControl(name, CType(ThisWorkbook.ActiveSheet, _
                        Excel.Worksheet))
    End Function


    ' Returns the control with the specified name on the _
    ' specified worksheet.
    Overloads Function FindControl(ByVal name As String, _
            ByVal sheet As Excel.Worksheet) As Object

        Dim theObject As Excel.OLEObject
        Try
            theObject = CType(sheet.OLEObjects(name), _
                        Excel.OLEObject)

            Return theObject.Object
        Catch Ex As Exception
            ' Returns Nothing if the control is not found.
        End Try
        Return Nothing
    End Function
#End Region

    ' Called when the workbook is opened.
    Private Sub ThisWorkbook_Open() Handles ThisWorkbook.Open
        MsgBox("Hello World")
    End Sub

    ' Called before the workbook is closed. Note that this
    ' method  might be called multiple times and the value
    ' assigned to Cancel might be ignored if other code or
    ' the user intervenes. Cancel is False when the event
    ' occurs. If the event procedure sets this to True, the
    ' document does not close when the procedure is finished.
    Private Sub ThisWorkbook_BeforeClose( _
            ByRef Cancel As Boolean) _
            Handles ThisWorkbook.BeforeClose

        MsgBox("Goodbye World")
        Cancel = False
    End Sub

End Class
```

When you press F5 to run the project, Visual Studio builds the assembly and starts Excel, passing in the workbook to open. Excel opens the workbook, checks the _AssemblyLocation0 and _AssemblyName0 custom properties, loads the assembly, reads the OfficeStartupClass assembly attribute to find the class to start and calls the _Startup procedure in that class. Excel passes in a reference to itself and a reference to the workbook it opened, which the _Startup procedure assigns to two module-level WithEvent variables, ThisApplication and ThisWorkbook. That gives us both application-level and workbook-level events by default. Excel then raises the workbook's Open event, which we handle in the ThisWorkbook_Open procedure to show our "Hello World" message.

The Default VSTO Template

The default Excel workbook VSTO class shown in Listing 22-1 includes procedure and variable names that have been chosen to mimic those found in Excel—such as ThisWorkbook—to make it a little easier for those with some experience of VBA to get started. Note that these are nothing more than normal variable and procedure names and do not have the intrinsic meaning they do in VBA.

For some reason, the template also includes two versions of a FindControl function, used to locate MSForms controls on worksheets. Presumably, this is because the designers thought most VSTO solutions would include MSForms controls in the worksheet, which would need to have event hooks configured.

In practice, the default template really doesn't work well for people used to working in VBA. We're used to having global objects such as Application and ThisWorkbook and being able to refer to worksheets by the code name. It also mixes up the procedures required for the communication with Excel, the event handling code for the workbook and some standard functions. Our best practice recommendation would be to separate out these functional areas into their own modules.

The ProExcel VSTO Template

When we create VSTO projects, the first thing we do is remove the default ThisWorkbook module and use our own template instead. The template files are located on the CD in the *\Concepts\Ch22—Using VB.NET and the Visual Studio Tools for Office\ProExcelTemplate* folder and comprise the following:

- VSTOHooks.vb contains the procedures that Excel calls to start up and shut down the VSTO project.
- CExcelApp.vb contains procedures to set up and handle the Excel Application's events
- CThisWorkbook.vb contains procedures to set up and handle the workbook's events.
- CSheet1.vb, CSheet2.vb and CSheet3.vb contain procedures to set up and handle the worksheet events for each worksheet in a default three-sheet workbook.
- MGlobals contains global variable definitions to refer to the application class, the workbook class and each of the three sheet classes.
- MStandardCode contains standard functions to identify a worksheet from its CodeName property and the FindControl function to find an ActiveX control on a worksheet.

MGlobals

Listing 22-2 shows the code contained in the MGlobals.vb file, which just defines some global variables to refer to the Excel Application object, the workbook event handler class and the worksheet event handler classes.

Listing 22-2 The MGlobals Code

```
Option Explicit On

Module MGlobals

    'The Excel Application event-handler class
    Friend ExcelApp As CExcelApp

    'The workbook event-handler class
    Friend ThisWorkbook As CThisWorkbook

    'The worksheet event-handler classes
    Friend Sheet1 As CSheet1
    Friend Sheet2 As CSheet2
    Friend Sheet3 As CSheet3

End Module
```

VSTOHooks

Listing 22-3 shows the code contained in the VSTOHooks.vb file.

Listing 22-3 The VSTOHooks Code

```
Option Explicit On

'Define aliases for commonly-used libraries
Imports Excel = Microsoft.Office.Interop.Excel
Imports Forms = System.Windows.Forms

' Office integration attribute. Identifies the startup class
' for the workbook. Do not modify.
<Assembly: System.ComponentModel.DescriptionAttribute( _
    "OfficeStartupClass, Version=1.0, " & _
    "Class=" & VSTOHooks.msAssemblyName & ".VSTOHooks")>

Public Class VSTOHooks

  'TODO: Change this to be the name of the Assembly
  Friend Const msAssemblyName As String = "ProExcelTemplate"

  ' Default constructor. Do not remove
  Public Sub New()
  End Sub

  ' Required procedure. Do not remove.
  ' Called by Excel when it loads the workbook.
  ' Used to check the environment and set up event hooks.
  ' DO NOT DO ANYTHING WITH THE EXCEL OBJECT MODEL IN HERE!
  Public Sub _Startup(ByVal application As Object, _
                      ByVal workbook As Object)

    'Initialise global variables to refer to classes that
    'handle the events for the Excel application class...
    ExcelApp = New CExcelApp(CType(application, _
            Excel.Application))

    '... and the workbook that this assembly is linked to
    ThisWorkbook = New CThisWorkbook(CType(workbook, _
            Excel.Workbook))

  End Sub
```

```
' Required procedure. Do not remove.
' Called when Excel closes the workbook
'(after any prompts/confirmation etc.)
Public Sub _Shutdown()

    'Tell the CThisWorkbook class to shut down
    ThisWorkbook.ShutDown

    'Tear down the global variables
    ExcelApp = Nothing
    ThisWorkbook = Nothing
    Sheet1 = Nothing
    Sheet2 = Nothing
    Sheet3 = Nothing

End Sub

End Class
```

The line that starts <Assembly: tells Excel which class in the assembly contains the _Startup and _Shutdown procedures for it to call. Modifying this line is likely to stop Excel being able to load and start the assembly. It uses the constant msAssemblyName to identify the class; the definition of that constant **must** be changed to match the name of the assembly created by the VSTO New Project Wizard.

The _Startup procedure is called by Excel when the workbook and assembly are first loaded. It is used to set up event handlers for the application and workbook events, with the worksheet events being set up within the Workbook_Open event in the CThisWorkbook class (shown later). If Excel is started from the command line with a VSTO workbook to open, the assembly's _Startup procedure is called before Excel fully initializes its object model. If you add anything to the _Startup procedure that uses the object model, Excel may become unpredictable. We recommend only using the _Startup procedure to set up the plumbing for the application and workbook event hooks and perhaps including .NET-only code. All other initialization tasks should be done within the Workbook_Open event, which occurs after Excel has loaded the object model.

After checking it's okay to start the code, we create new instances of each of our event handling classes, passing in the Excel Application or Workbook. In .NET, every class has a Sub New() procedure, which can be modified to include extra parameters used in initializing the class.

The _Shutdown procedure is called immediately prior to Excel unloading the workbook. Note that this occurs after the user has had an opportunity to cancel the close, so can be safely used for cleanup routines, such as tearing down command bars and so forth. To improve encapsulation, we've included a public ShutDown procedure in the CThisWorkbook class (shown later), where we can place our cleanup code, rather than include it here.

CExcelApp

Listing 22-4 shows the code contained in the CExcelApp class:

Listing 22-4 The CExcelApp Code

```
'Class to handle events for the Excel Application object
Option Explicit On

'Define aliases for commonly-used libraries
Imports Office = Microsoft.Office.Core
Imports Excel = Microsoft.Office.Interop.Excel

Public Class CExcelApp

  Friend WithEvents Application As Excel.Application

  'Called when we create an instance of the class
  Public Sub New(ByVal appExcel As Excel.Application)
    Application = appExcel
  End Sub

End Class
```

The CExcelApp class contains the code required to set up the plumbing to handle application events. We first declare a variable to handle the application-level events, then use the Sub New() procedure to set it to the application object Excel gives us in the VSTOHooks _Startup procedure. We can then add procedures to handle any of the Excel application events by selecting from the object and event dropdowns in the normal way, as shown in Figure 22-2.

Note that the ExcelApp global variable holds a reference to the instance of this class, not to the Excel Application object itself. The Excel

Application object is exposed by declaring the Application variable as Friend, which makes it appear as a property of the class. All our other classes and modules can access the Excel Application object using `ExcelApp.Application`. By using this mechanism, the ExcelApp variable will also expose any properties we add to the class, thereby enabling us to encapsulate the Application object, its event handling and any custom properties we might add to control those events. The same mechanism is used for the workbook and worksheet classes below, so we can use `ThisWorkbook.Workbook` to refer to the Excel workbook we're linked to and `Sheet1.Worksheet` to refer to the worksheet handled by the Sheet1 variable.

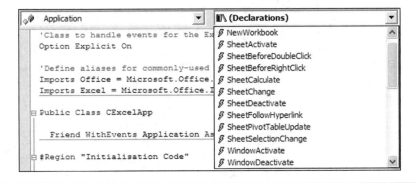

Figure 22-2 The Object and Event Drop-Downs, Used to Add New Application Event Procedures

CThisWorkbook

The CThisWorkbook class shown in Listing 22-5 contains code very similar to the CExcelApp class, with the only difference being the variable names and object types. The Workbook_Open event should be used for any startup checks, command bar configuration and so on.

Listing 22-5 The CThisWorkbook Code

```
'Class to handle events for the Workbook
Option Explicit On

'Define aliases for commonly-used libraries
Imports Office = Microsoft.Office.Core
Imports Excel = Microsoft.Office.Interop.Excel
```

```
Public Class CThisWorkbook

  Friend WithEvents Workbook As Excel.Workbook

  'Called when we create an instance of the class
  Public Sub New(ByVal wkbWorkbook As Excel.Workbook)
    Workbook = wkbWorkbook
  End Sub

  'The standard Workbook_Open event, used to set up the
  'worksheet event-handler classes, command bars etc.
  Private Sub Workbook_Open() Handles Workbook.Open

    'Make sure we can read the code names in the VBProject,
    'so we can identify each worksheet accurately.
    Try
      Dim bSaved As Boolean = workbook.VBProject.Saved
    Catch
      MsgBox("Access to the Visual Basic Project must " & _
             "be trusted for this workbook." & vbLf & _
             "Please tick the 'Trust access to Visual " & _
             "Basic Project' box in the " & vbLf & _
             "Tools > Macro > Security dialog, then " & _
             "close and reopen this workbook.")
      Exit Sub
    End Try

    'Create event handlers for each sheet in the workbook.
    Sheet1 = New CSheet1(FindWorksheetByCodeName("Sheet1"))
    Sheet2 = New CSheet2(FindWorksheetByCodeName("Sheet2"))
    Sheet3 = New CSheet3(FindWorksheetByCodeName("Sheet3"))

  End Sub

  'Called by the _Shutdown procedure in VSTOHooks
  'Used to destroy commandbars etc, akin to an
  'After_Close event
  Public Sub ShutDown()

  End Sub

End Class
```

Within the Workbook_Open event, we set up the worksheet event handler classes, using the FindWorksheetByCodeName function (from the MStandardCode module) to identify a worksheet based on its VBA code name. Fortunately, the code name is still available to us, as long as we have access to the VBProject and force it to be initialized. Checking the `Workbook.VBProject.Saved` property both forces Excel to initialize the VBProject and tests whether we have access to it. If the test causes an error, we ask the user to allow access to the VBProject and reopen the workbook. Note that trying to do this code within the Startup processing (as opposed to Workbook_Open) corrupts the VBProject! Most VSTO solutions would also include code in the Workbook_Open procedure to set up command bars and so forth.

The ShutDown procedure is called from the _Shutdown procedure in the VSTOHooks class when Excel shuts down the workbook and is a good place to clean up command bars and so forth because it occurs after the user has had a chance to cancel the close.

CSheet1

The template code modules for each of the worksheets follow the same structure as the CExcelApp and CThisWorkbook classes, so won't be repeated here. When setting up the VSTO project, you will need to add a worksheet class for each of the worksheets in your solution, adding global variables to refer to them and adding code to Workbook_Open to initialize them. If the worksheet has any ActiveX controls (including controls from the Control Toolbox), the `Sub New()` procedure should be used to set up their event hooks, as shown in Listing 22-6, for a worksheet that contains a command button btnShow.

Listing 22-6 A Worksheet Class with a CommandButton Event Handler

```
'Class to handle events for a worksheet
Option Explicit On

'Define aliases for commonly-used libraries
Imports Office = Microsoft.Office.Core
Imports Excel = Microsoft.Office.Interop.Excel
Imports MSForms = Microsoft.Vbe.Interop.Forms

Public Class CSheet1

  Friend WithEvents Worksheet As Excel.Worksheet
```

```
'An event handler for the button
Dim WithEvents btnShow As MSForms.CommandButton

'Called when we create an instance of the class
'Use this procedure to set up event hooks for any
'controls on the sheet
Public Sub New(ByVal wks As Excel.Worksheet)
   Worksheet = wks

   'Hook up the button's event handler
   btnShow = FindControl("btnShow", Worksheet)
End Sub

'The Click event for the button
Private Sub btnShow_Click() Handles btnShow.Click
   MsgBox("Clicked me!")
End Sub

End Class
```

MStandardCode

The MStandardCode module shown in Listing 22-7 contains two simple functions to locate a control on a worksheet (so we can set up event hooks for it) and to locate a worksheet in the workbook, from its VBA code name.

Listing 22-7 The MStandardCode Module

```
'Module containing standard procedures, copied between projects
Option Explicit On

'Define aliases for commonly-used libraries
Imports Office = Microsoft.Office.Core
Imports Excel = Microsoft.Office.Interop.Excel

Module MStandardCode

   ' Returns the control with the specified name on the
   ' specified worksheet.
   Function FindControl(ByVal name As String, _
         ByVal sheet As Excel.Worksheet) As Object
```

```
   Dim theObject As Excel.OLEObject
   Try
      theObject = CType(sheet.OLEObjects(name), _
                     Excel.OLEObject)

      Return theObject.Object
   Catch Ex As Exception
      ' Returns Nothing if the control is not found.
   End Try
   Return Nothing
End Function

'Identify a worksheet in the workbook, by matching the
'CodeName
Function FindWorksheetByCodeName( _
     ByVal sCodeName As String) As Excel.Worksheet

   Dim wksSheet As Excel.Worksheet

   'Find the sheet with the matching codename
   For Each wksSheet In ThisWorkbook.Workbook.Worksheets
     If wksSheet.CodeName = sCodeName Then
        Return wksSheet
     End If
   Next

End Function

End Module
```

Sharing Command Bars

Like VB6 COM Add-ins, VSTO solutions use event hooks to trap the Click event of command bar buttons and the Change event of command bar combo boxes. Instead of repeating here how command bar events are handled, you should review the relevant section of *Chapter 8 — Advanced Command Bar Handling*, but to summarize it we need to do the following:

- Give all our menu items the same Tag property, to uniquely identify them as belonging to our add-in.

- Give each menu item a unique Parameter property, to identify them in code.
- Have a class module containing a With Events declaration for a CommandBarButton (and/or CommandBarCombobox).
- In the CommandBarButton_Click event procedure, confirm that the Tag is set to ours then call the procedure appropriate to the Parameter value.
- When setting up our menus, create a new instance of the class for each combination of ID and Tag that we use. If we're not using any built-in menu items, we would only need a single instance of the class.

We show some examples of this later in this section.

The basic operation of a VSTO workbook involves Excel loading and running the linked VSTO assembly, which sets up event hooks for application, workbook, worksheet and control events and responds to the events being raised. The principle is that each VSTO assembly is self-contained, works only with the workbook it's linked to and doesn't interact with any other VSTO workbooks that might be open. How, then, should we handle the situation of a workbook having some custom menu items and the user having multiple instances of the workbook open? The easiest solution is to design our VSTO workbook to neatly collaborate with any other instances that might be open.

When starting up, we should first test for the existence of our menu items and only add them if they don't already exist (because they might have been added by another copy of the workbook). Either way, we set up event hooks for them. This means we will have one set of menu items shared by all open copies of the workbook, which each have their own instance of the VSTO assembly. When a menu item is clicked, the Click event is raised in all the assemblies, so within the Click event handler, we should only respond if that assembly's workbook is the active workbook. When closing down, we should see whether there are any other workbooks open which use the shared menu items. The easiest way to do this is to check whether there are any other workbooks open that link to the same VSTO assembly. If we find one, we leave the menus for it to use; if we don't find one, we delete the menus. Example code for collaborative menu sharing between VSTO projects is shown in Listing 22-8 and can be found on the CD in the \Concepts\Ch22—Using VB.NET and the Visual Studio Tools for Office/SharedMenus folder.

Listing 22-8 Collaborative Use of Command Bars

```
'
'   In Module MGlobals
'

'Command bar constants
Public Const gsMENU_NAME As String = "Shared Menus"
Public Const gsMENU_TAG As String = "tgSharedMenus"
Public Const gsMENU_TOGGLE As String = "ToggleCase"

'Command bar event handler
Public gclsControlEvents As CControlEvents


'
'   In Class CThisWorkbook
'

'The standard Workbook_Open event, used to set up the
'worksheet event-handler classes, command bars etc.
Private Sub Workbook_Open() Handles Workbook.Open

  'Check for and create the menus
  SetUpMenus()

  'Set up the command bar button hooks
  gclsControlEvents = New CControlEvents

End Sub

'Restore the menus when shutting down
Public Sub ShutDown()
  RestoreMenus()
End Sub


'
'   In Module MCommandBars
'

'Check for and set up our menus
Public Sub SetUpMenus()

  Dim cbBar As Office.CommandBar
  Dim btnCaps As Office.CommandBarButton
```

```
    Try
       'Does the commandbar exist?
       cbBar = ExcelApp.Application.CommandBars(gsMENU_NAME)

    Catch ex As Exception
       'No, so create it...
       cbBar = ExcelApp.Application.CommandBars.Add( _
                  gsMENU_NAME, temporary:=True)
       cbBar.Visible = True

       '... And add our button to it
       btnCaps = cbBar.Controls.Add( _
           Office.MsoControlType.msoControlButton, _
           temporary:=True)

       With btnCaps
          .Parameter = gsMENU_TOGGLE
          .Tag = gsMENU_TAG
          .Caption = "Toggle Case"
          .Style = Office.MsoButtonStyle.msoButtonCaption
       End With
    End Try
End Sub

'Tidily clean up
Public Sub RestoreMenus()

    Dim sThisAssembly As String
    Dim wkbWorkbook As Excel.Workbook

    'Get which assembly we link to
    sThisAssembly = AssemblyLocation(ThisWorkbook.Workbook)

    'Check if any other workbooks link to the same assembly
    'we do and quit the routine if we find one
    For Each wkbWorkbook In ExcelApp.Application.Workbooks
       If Not wkbWorkbook Is ThisWorkbook.Workbook Then
          If AssemblyLocation(wkbWorkbook) = sThisAssembly Then
             Exit Sub
          End If
       End If
    Next

    'No others, so delete the commandbar
```

```
      Try
          ExcelApp.Application.CommandBars(gsMENU_NAME).Delete()
      Catch ex As Exception
      End Try
  End Sub


  '
  '   In Module MStandardCode
  '
  'Read the location of a linked VSTO assembly from a
  'workbook's custom document properties
  Function AssemblyLocation( _
        ByVal wkbBook As Excel.Workbook) As String

      Dim iProp As Integer
      Dim sPath As String
      Dim sName As String

      'Read the assembly location and name, allowing for long
      'entries to spill into multiple properties
      For iProp = 0 To 3
        Try
          sPath = sPath & _
                  CType(wkbWorkbook.CustomDocumentProperties( _
                  "_AssemblyLocation" & iProp), _
                  Office.DocumentProperty).Value
        Catch ex As Exception
        End Try

        Try
          sName = sName & _
                  CType(wkbWorkbook.CustomDocumentProperties( _
                  "_AssemblyName" & iProp), _
                  Office.DocumentProperty).Value
        Catch ex As Exception
        End Try
      Next

      Return sPath & "\" & sName

  End Function

'Class CControlEvents
'Class to handle command bar button events
```

```vbnet
Option Explicit On

'Define aliases for commonly-used libraries
Imports Office = Microsoft.Office.Core
Imports Excel = Microsoft.Office.Interop.Excel

Public Class CControlEvents

  'Variable to hook the buttons' events
  Dim WithEvents btnButton As Office.CommandBarButton

  'Hook the events for our buttons
  Public Sub New()
    btnButton = ExcelApp.Application.CommandBars _
                .FindControl(tag:=gsMENU_TAG)
  End Sub

  'Handle the Click event
  Private Sub btnButton_Click( _
      ByVal Ctrl As Office.CommandBarButton, _
      ByRef CancelDefault As Boolean) _
      Handles btnButton.Click

    'Only process this event if it's our tag
    If Ctrl.Tag = gsMENU_TAG Then

      'Only process this event if our workbook is active
      If ExcelApp.Application.ActiveWorkbook Is _
        ThisWorkbook.Workbook Then

        'What to do?
        Select Case Ctrl.Parameter
          Case gsMENU_TOGGLE
            Try
              'Toggle the case of the active cell
              With ExcelApp.Application.ActiveCell
                If .Value = UCase$(.Value) Then
                  .Value = LCase$(.Value)
                Else
                  .Value = UCase$(.Value)
                End If
              End With
```

```
            Catch ex As Exception
            End Try
        End Select
      End If
    End If
  End Sub
End Class
```

Managed Excel Add-ins

The Visual Studio Tools for Office provides a document-centric mechanism for automating Excel. By that, we mean the code is linked to workbooks and not the application itself. In contrast, COM Add-ins are application-centric, because they link to the application directly. It is somewhat complicated (but possible and beyond the scope of this book) to create COM Add-ins using VB.NET, but we can achieve the goal of application-centric code much easier by saving a managed workbook as a normal Excel add-in. Unfortunately, the VSTO template does not enable us to create an Excel add-in solution directly and only enables us to launch xls files during debugging, but everything works as expected if we just save the xls as an add-in after we've finished development.

The Paste Special Bar VSTO Add-in

In *Chapter 8 — Advanced Command Bar Handling*, we created a Paste Special Bar Excel add-in that added command bar buttons for each of the Paste Special options. In *Chapter 21 — Writing Add-ins with Visual Basic 6*, we converted the example to a COM Add-in. We have also converted it to a VSTO add-in, which can be found on the CD in the *\Concepts\Ch22—Using VB.NET and the Visual Studio Tools for Office\PasteSpecialBarVSTO* folder. The VSTO solution was created by starting with a standard VSTO workbook, copying the code from the VB6 COM Add-in, then getting it to work in VB.NET. There were very few changes required, all of which are documented in the READ_ME module contained in the project and each procedure header. The only complicated part of the conversion was the code required to obtain an IPicture interface for an image contained in a

.NET resource file, which is documented in an MSKB article at `http://support.microsoft.com/?824017`. You might like to open all three versions of the add-in to compare their differences and note that most of the code is exactly the same in each.

Hybrid VBA/VSTO Solutions

If you want to convert an existing VBA application to a VSTO solution, the only ***supported*** way is to do it all in one go, as we did to create the Paste Special Bar VSTO add-in. For any nontrivial application, that is a huge undertaking and is certain to introduce bugs, with very little clearly identifiable benefit. If all you want to do is to make use of some VB.NET features (such as consuming Web services), a lower-risk and more manageable approach is to expose the .NET classes as COM objects and reference them from VBA.

If you still want to press ahead and convert your VBA application to VSTO, it can be done on a piecemeal basis by creating a hybrid VBA/VSTO solution. Hybrid solutions are officially unsupported by Microsoft, but we believe they provide by far the best approach to migrating existing VBA applications to VB.NET.

In a hybrid solution, a workbook both contains some VBA code and links to a VSTO assembly. In the VSTO assembly's Workbook_Open event, we use `Application.Run` to call a procedure in the VBA project, passing in a reference to a VB.NET class, which the VBA procedure stores in a global variable. Any procedures added to the VB.NET class can then be called directly from VBA, and any procedures added to VBA modules can be called from VB.NET using `Application.Run`. Listing 22-9 shows a simple example that displays messages to show where code is being executed. The sample can be found on the CD in the *Concepts\Ch22—Using VB.NET and the Visual Studio Tools for Office\HybridWorkbook* folder. When adding the CMigratedCode module to the project, we chose to add it as a ***COM Class***. That enables us to add a reference to it in our VBA Project and make use of early binding and the IntelliSense lists.

Listing 22-9 A Hybrid VBA/VSTO Workbook

```
'
'VB.NET Module MGlobals
'
```

```vb
'Module containing declarations of global variables
Option Explicit On

Module MGlobals

   'The Excel Application event-handler class
   Friend ExcelApp As CExcelApp

   'The workbook event-handler class
   Friend ThisWorkbook As CThisWorkbook

   'Hold open the MigratedCode class
   Public gclsMigratedCode As CMigratedCode

End Module

'
'In the CThisWorkbook VB.NET Class
'
   Private Sub Workbook_Open() Handles Workbook.Open

     MsgBox("VSTO Workbook_Open Start")

     'Create a new instance of the MigratedCode class
     gclsMigratedCode = New CMigratedCode

     'Call a VBA procedure, passing a reference to the
     'class containing the migrated code
     Try
       ExcelApp.Application.Run("'" & Workbook.Name & _
           "'!SetVSTOClass", gclsMigratedCode)

     Catch ex As Exception
     End Try

     MsgBox("VSTO Workbook_Open End")

   End Sub

'
'The CMigratedCode VB.NET Class
'
<ComClass(CMigratedCode.ClassId, _
         CMigratedCode.InterfaceId, _
```

```vbnet
            CMigratedCode.EventsId)> _
Public Class CMigratedCode

#Region "COM GUIDs"
    ' These  GUIDs provide the COM identity for this class
    ' and its COM interfaces. If you change them, existing
    ' clients will no longer be able to access the class.
    Public Const ClassId As String = _
        "AB1B282E-F015-4FF4-B4C7-DAC57A318867"

    Public Const InterfaceId As String = _
        "CEBA2C5D-D286-43E0-B8D5-A5C4525C6301"

    Public Const EventsId As String = _
        "856AE29A-455C-4693-93CB-C51D5CBDA2CE"
#End Region

    ' A creatable COM class must have a Public Sub New()
    ' with no parameters, otherwise, the class will not be
    ' registered in the COM registry and cannot be created
    ' via CreateObject.
    Public Sub New()
        MyBase.New()
    End Sub


  'Example procedure called from VBA
  Public Sub VSTOProc(ByVal sText As String)
    MsgBox("In VSTO Procedure. Message is:" & vbLf & sText)
  End Sub

End Class

'
'In a standard VBA module, with a project reference set to
'HybridWorkbook
'
'Reference to the class containing the migrated code
Dim gclsMigrated As HybridWorkbook.CMigratedCode

'Called by VSTO, giving us the class containing the
'migrated code
Public Sub SetVSTOClass(clsMigrated As Object)
```

```
'Store a reference to the VSTO class
Set gclsMigrated = clsMigrated

MsgBox "Now in VBA!"

'Call a procedure in the VSTO class
gclsMigrated.VSTOProc "Passed from VBA"

MsgBox "Back in VBA!"

End Sub
```

When the workbook is opened, we get the following messages displayed:

VSTO Workbook_Open Start
Now in VBA!
In VSTO Procedure. Message is: Passed from VBA
Back in VBA!
VSTO Workbook_Open End

After the plumbing for a hybrid VBA/VSTO application has been set up using this mechanism, we can migrate our applications at our own pace, on a gradual procedure-by-procedure basis, starting with the simplest procedures and those with most to gain from being converted. As our experience and confidence increases, we can migrate larger and more complex procedures until our entire application is in managed code.

It is a shame that Microsoft has decided to not support this method. We believe that it is the only sensible way for nontrivial VBA applications to be migrated to managed code. We can only hope that it is officially supported (and indeed promoted) in future releases.

The VSTO Security Model

The Visual Studio Tools for Office uses the .NET framework's ***code access security*** mechanism to decide whether an assembly can execute instead of building on VBA's "trusted sources" approach. A key element of this model is that the user has to specifically allow managed code to run prior to opening the workbook in Excel. This is known as making a ***trust decision*** and requires a much more conscious decision than just clicking an *Enable macros* button. In a corporate environment, the trust decision could be made centrally and deployed to users through Group Policy and so on.

The essence of a trust decision is for users to ask themselves "What do I need to know about this assembly before I will allow it to run?" It might be sufficient that the assembly is in a specific directory, such as a network share, or maybe it has to have a specific filename as well. Trust decisions that are based solely on location are somewhat dangerous, because the user could be easily fooled into copying malicious assemblies into the same location. A better trust decision is one based on both location and identity—that is, the person who created the assembly.

Strong Names

In an identity-based trust decision, we use one of the Visual Studio tools (sn.exe) to create a cryptographic public/private key pair for ourselves, known as a ***strong name***, which is stored in a file on our computer. When creating an assembly, we add an assembly attribute to the project which tells the .NET compiler to include the public key within the assembly file. When we distribute the assembly to the end user, we can talk them through the one-time process of telling the .NET framework to trust that key, which of course assumes that the end user trusts us! When Excel opens the workbook and loads the assembly, it asks the .NET framework "Is this assembly OK to run?" The framework sees that it has been stamped with our strong name key, sees that the end user has specified a trust relationship for that key and answers "Yes, the assembly is OK to run." Any other assemblies that we stamp with our strong name key and distribute to the same end user will also be allowed to run—regardless of where it's copied to (as long as it's somewhere on their computer) and without any extra configuration. This scenario is quite similar to trusting VBA code signed with a specific digital signature, but has the distinct advantage of not requiring us to purchase a signature.

Strong Name Risks

Basing our .NET security policy exclusively around strong names does not eliminate risk, because it permits bugs in our code to be exploited by malicious people. Imagine that our assembly contained a cleanup routine whereby we maintained a list of filenames in a worksheet and deleted those files when the workbook was closed. We strong-named and released that assembly. One of our users finds a way to gain access to that list, so he could type in any filename he wanted and our code would delete it when closing. We release a bug-fix assembly that includes extra checks on the files to be deleted (such as only deleting those in the Temp folder), or an entirely different mechanism, and replace all known copies of our original assembly with the fixed one.

Unknown to us, a malicious user gets a copy of our original assembly and creates a workbook to exploit the vulnerability and delete some key system files. He then sends the document to people who have trusted our strong name, .NET allows the assembly to run when the document is opened and the end users' machines are destroyed! This risk also exists in VBA's reliance on digital signatures as the evidence used to decide whether to trust code.

In .NET (but not in VBA), the risk can (and should) be mitigated by adding extra restrictions based on where the assembly is located, such as "on my computer" or "on a specific network share." The ability to add these restrictions is the main reason why VSTO solutions are deemed to be more secure than VBA—but only if the restrictions are set up!

Creating and Using Strong Names

Strong name key files are generated using the sn.exe command-line utility, usually found at *C:\Program Files\Microsoft Visual Studio .NET 2003\SDK\v1.1\Bin\sn.exe*. To generate the key file, use the –k switch and provide the name of the key file to create:

```
sn -k "c:\MyPath\MyStrongName.snk"
```

To stamp an assembly with the strong name key, add the following code to the AssemblyInfo.vb module:

```
'Add a strong name for the assembly
<Assembly: AssemblyKeyFile("c:\MyPath\MyStrongName.snk")>
```

In each case, use a sensible name for the key file! All of the VSTO example assemblies for this chapter have been stamped with a strong name generated specifically for this book, which will need to be replaced with your own before they can be run.

The main issue to remember when using strong names is that when Excel opens a workbook with a linked assembly, it copies the assembly file to a local store, usually located somewhere under *C:\Documents and Settings\<Username>\Local Settings\Application Data\assembly\dl2*. However, if a strong named version of the assembly already exists at the temporary location, the assembly will only be copied if it is a newer version. This means that when debugging our strong-named VSTO assemblies, we can do one of four things to ensure we're always using the latest version:

- Don't strong-name the assembly until debugging is complete.
- Each time the assembly is rebuilt, copy the DLL to the temporary location.
- Each time the assembly is rebuilt, delete the old version from the temporary location, so Excel copies the new version there for us.
- Each time the assembly is rebuilt, edit the `<Assembly:` `AssemblyVersion("1.001.*")>` line in the AssemblyInfo.vb file, to increment the minor version number (the 001 in this example).

Trusting a Strong Name

Before our assemblies will be allowed to run on our end user's computer, the .NET framework has to be told to trust our strong name. If all we're doing is copying the workbook and assembly to another computer (such as taking the workbook home), we can configure the security to allow any assembly that contains our strong name and is run from the computer (that is, not from the network), using the following manual process. You will need to do this on your computer to get the example assemblies for this chapter working.

1. Open the *Microsoft .NET Framework 1.1 Configuration* utility, found under *Control Panel > Administrative Tools*.
2. Expand the tree to show the *Runtime Security Policy > User > Code Groups > All_Code* node and select it, as shown in Figure 22-3.
3. In the right-hand pane, click the Add a Child Code Group link.
4. In the Create Code Group dialog, give the group a name, such as "ProExcel VSTO Projects" and a description, such as "VSTO Projects stamped with the ProExcel strong name key." Click the Next > button.

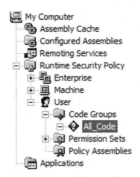

Figure 22-3 Selecting the User's All_Code Group in the Security Policy Editor

5. Choose Strong Name from the Condition Type drop-down, to create a trust condition based on a strong name key, then click the Import button and select any assembly that has been stamped with the key. Click the Next > button.

6. Choose the Full Trust permission set, which tells the .NET framework that assemblies stamped with that strong name can do anything. Click the Next > button and then the Finish button on the confirmation dialog.

The .NET framework has now been configured to allow any assembly stamped with the same strong name key to run from that machine.

Adding the code group to the User level means that .NET will only run assemblies that are physically located on the local machine and only for that user. In most cases when working on documents at home or sending them to people outside the network, that is exactly what we'd like to happen, as it's an extra layer of security that won't impede our ability to use the document. We could allow the assembly to be run for all users from that computer and/or from the local network by adding the code group at the machine level, within the My_Computer_Zone and/or the LocalIntranet_Zone, as shown in Figure 22-4.

Adding code groups at the Machine level requires Admin rights, but is a good place for network administrators to add groups that allow specific strong names to run. If we do that, we **must** (from a security point of view) add extra conditions that restrict the assembly to only run from specific network shares, to prevent the attack described in *Strong Name Risks* earlier.

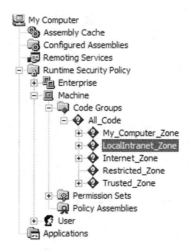

Figure 22-4 Selecting the Machine's LocalIntranet_Zone Group in the Security Policy Editor

We have walked you through the steps that need to be taken to trust a strong name using the Security Policy Editor mainly so you understand what is going on, and can modify it to suit your requirements. The .NET *Trust an Assembly* Wizard (found under *Control Panel > Administrative Tools > Microsoft .NET Framework 1.1 Wizards*) can also be used to trust a strong name and provides a much simpler end-user experience. It must not, however, be used to trust a strong name at the machine level, because doing so explicitly enables the type of attack we've described.

Caspol

Providing instructions for the end user to formally establish a trust relationship is a good way to ensure they understand what they're allowing, but is very dangerous if they do it wrong. It is quite easy for them to inadvertently open up their security and allow any .NET code to run on their machine!

An alternative is to provide a batch file or other installation script to set the .NET policy for them; the trust decision is then whether or not to run the script. The framework security policy can be set using the caspol command line utility, usually found at *C:\WINDOWS\Microsoft.NET\ Framework\v1.1.4322*. The command line to do the same as the previous manual steps is shown below, where the CD is drive E:

```
caspol -q -u -ag All_Code -strong -file "E:\Concepts\Ch22 - Using VB.NET
and the Visual Studio Tools for Office\SharedMenus\SharedMenus\bin\
SharedMenus.DLL" -noname -noversion FullTrust -n "ProExcel VSTO
Projects" -d "VSTO Projects stamped with the ProExcel strong name key."
```

The caspol command line switches we've used are as follows:

Switch	Description
-q	Quiet mode, doesn't ask for confirmation.
-u	Add this to the User node.
-ag All_Code	Add a code group below the All_Code group.
-strong -file "E:\...\SharedMenus.DLL"	Using a strong name key as evidence, extracted from that file.
-noname	Don't use the assembly name as evidence.
-noversion	Don't use the assembly version as evidence.
FullTrust	Give Full Trust to any assemblies with a matching set of evidence (that is, stamped with the same strong name).
-n "ProExcel VSTO Project"	Create the code group with this name.
-d "VSTO Projects…"	Create the code group with this description.

To add the strong name to the machine's LocalIntranet_Zone, but only allowing assemblies stored on the network at *Server\Share\Folder* or below, the caspol command line would start:

```
caspol -q -m -ag LocalIntranet_Zone -url \\Server\Share\Folder\*
-strong -file ...
```

The Big Issues

The Visual Studio Tools for Office is a v1.0 product, so we don't expect perfection. This section identifies what we consider to be the major issues with v1.0, in the hope they will be addressed in future releases. We imagine that most of these issues are a result of the Office team not having sufficient time to modify their applications to fully support VSTO solutions. Some of the issues may be improved by the use of creative workarounds in VSTO 2005, but we expect most of them to remain until changes can be made to the Office applications, in Office 12 or later.

Functional Gaps

A few things that can be done with VBA cannot be achieved using VSTO workbooks, the main ones being these:

- User-defined functions callable from a worksheet
- Calling VSTO code from OnKey, OnTime, OnData and so on
- Calling VSTO code from the OnAction property of drawing objects
- Uniquely identifying worksheets (without relying on the sheet tab)

Application Links

The only change made to Excel 2003 to support VSTO was to add the VSTO Loader, used to open and start VSTO assemblies. There are numerous links between Excel and VBA that we take for granted, but are missing in VSTO, including the following:

- Automatically having classes in VBA to handle the events for the workbook and each worksheet.
- Adding a worksheet to a workbook doesn't add an event handler class to the VSTO project.
- Adding a control to a worksheet doesn't add an event handler to the VSTO worksheet class.
- With VBA, as soon as we add a control to the worksheet, we can add code to its events. With VSTO, we have to stop and restart the project.
- In VBA, the worksheet's properties and methods and any properties and methods we add to its class module are exposed through the same object; in VSTO solutions we have to use separate objects, resulting in the awkward `ExcelApp.Application` and `ThisWorkbook.Workbook` syntax.
- In VBA, the code for multiple workbooks is handled by the same IDE, enabling us to easily copy code between them (such as being able to drag/drop a form or class between projects). VSTO solutions have one solution per instance of the Visual Studio IDE.

Global Solutions

Consider the following line of code, placed in the ThisWorkbook_Open procedure of a standard VSTO workbook (that is, created with the normal VSTO template, not our ProExcelTemplate classes):

```
ThisWorkbook.ActiveSheet.Range("A1").Value = 2000
```

Assuming that the active sheet is a worksheet (and not a chart), that code can be relied upon to always put the value 2000 in cell A1, right? Wrong! Assuming you have a standard U.S. English installation of Office 2003 and Windows, use the *Control Panel > Regional Settings* applet to switch to French (France) number formats and start the VSTO workbook. Instead of putting 2000 in A1, we get a runtime error with the helpful message of "Exception from HRESULT," which roughly translates as "Something went wrong in Excel." But what?

Within the low-level communication that occurs when we call into an object model, there is a field called the Locale Identifier (lcid for short). The lcid specifies which locale (that is, regional settings) to use if the program needs to interpret the data being passed to it. For example, if we pass the string "2,000" to Excel, is that two thousand (U.S. locale) or two point zero (most European locales)? The VBA runtime *always* sets the lcid field to U.S. English, which is why we always have to use U.S. formats when sending strings containing dates or numbers to Excel. Although it takes a little getting used to, that has the clear advantage of predictability; as long as we ensure our communication with Excel is done using U.S. formats, our VBA applications will work worldwide. The *International Issues* chapter of our *Excel 2002 VBA Programmers Reference* explains this in detail and can be read online at `www.oaltd.co.uk/ExcelProgRef/Ch22`.

The .NET runtime, however, passes the lcid of the thread the assembly is running on, which by default is the locale that Windows is set to— French in our example. The first thing many of Excel's properties and methods do is check the lcid and raise an error if it isn't recognized. Unfortunately, the default installation of Office 2003 only recognizes English lcids, which is why we got the error. All other lcids require the Mulitlingual User Interface (MUI) Pack to be installed, which is only available to customers on Microsoft's volume licensing programs.

In our experience, it is extremely rare for customers to install the language packs throughout an organization. The usual situation is to install the U.S. English version, but allow the end users to set their own regional settings—exactly the situation that breaks our code.

Another nasty issue arises from .NET passing the lcid to Excel. There are many properties in the Excel object model that have both a U.S. and local version, such as the Formula and FormulaLocal properties of a Range. Both properties call the same underlying routine and the only difference between them is the lcid passed to that routine. Using the Formula property tells VBA to pass an lcid of U.S. English, while using FormulaLocal tells VBA to pass the lcid used by Windows. From .NET, however, the lcid of the thread is passed to them both, so they both behave like FormulaLocal!

Even if the MUI Pack is installed, we can still get rather more subtle bugs in our code if the user has customized his Windows regional settings and is not using the default for the locale. Consider the code in Listing 22-10.

Listing 22-10 Demonstrating Bugs with Customized Locales

```
Private Sub ThisWorkbook_Open() Handles ThisWorkbook.Open
  Dim sValue As String

  sValue = InputBox("Enter a number according to your " & _
                    "regional settings.")

  With CType(ThisWorkbook.ActiveSheet, Excel.Worksheet)
    'Allow Excel to do the conversion, using the lcid
    .Range("A1").Value = sValue

    'Get .NET to do the conversion, using the full set of
    'regional settings
    .Range("A2").Value = CType(sValue, Double)
  End With
End Sub
```

Now set the Windows regional settings back to English, but customize it to use a comma for the decimal symbol and a period for the thousand separator—which is a number format used widely in Europe. This sort of customization is often done by people in the UK who want to print reports using English date formats, month names and so on, but European number formats. Run the code and type 2,000 in the input box. You will discover that A1 has the (wrong) value 2000, but A2 has the (correct) value 2. This happens because Excel is only using the lcid—English—and assuming that the standard number formats are being used (where comma is the thousand separator), but .NET is using the full set of regional settings, including the customization of using a comma for the decimal separator.

So we cannot rely on the users having the MUI Pack installed, and even with it installed, we have to handle the problem of Formula behaving like FormulaLocal and so on, and we cannot rely on them not customizing the Windows regional settings. The only thing we can do is force .NET to communicate with Excel in U.S. English. To do this, we have to change the *culture* (.NET's term for regional settings) that .NET is using to U.S. before every call into the Excel object model and change it back to the Windows default before every interaction with the user, as shown in Listing 22-11.

Listing 22-11 Toggling the .NET Culture

```
'Global variables used to handling culture switching

'This thread
Public gThread As System.Threading.Thread = _
    System.Threading.Thread.CurrentThread

'The Windows culture information
Public gCultureWin As System.Globalization.CultureInfo = _
    gThread.CurrentCulture

'The US culture information
Public gCultureUS As System.Globalization.CultureInfo = _
    New System.Globalization.CultureInfo("en-US")


' Called when the workbook is opened.
Private Sub ThisWorkbook_Open() Handles ThisWorkbook.Open

  Dim sValue As String
  Dim dValue As Double
  Dim dResult As Double

  'Interacting with user, so switch to Windows culture
  gThread.CurrentCulture = gCultureWin

  'Get the value and convert to a double, using Windows
  'culture
  sValue = InputBox("Enter a number according to your " & _
                    "regional settings.")
```

```
dValue = CType(sValue, Double)

'Always use exception handling, so the culture gets
'switched back in case of a run-time error
Try

   'About to talk to Excel, so switch to US
   gThread.CurrentCulture = gCultureUS

   'Do the Excel stuff...
   With CType(ThisWorkbook.ActiveSheet, Excel.Worksheet)

      'Send the data to Excel
      .Range("A1").Value = dValue

      'Enter a formula
      .Range("A2").Formula = "=A1*A1"

      'Read the result. We can't display it until we
      'switched the culture back
      dResult = .Range("A2").Value
   End With
Finally

   'Finished with Excel, so switch back to Windows
   gThread.CurrentCulture = gCultureWin
End Try

'Show the result to the user
MsgBox("Your value squared is " & dResult.ToString)

End Sub
```

Other than being a ton of extra code, we have to be extremely careful that we have the correct culture set for every line, which becomes increasingly unwieldy as we call functions and subprocedures which also have to switch cultures. In the example in Listing 22-11, we had to use the dResult variable to temporarily hold the result while we switched cultures back to the Windows default, prior to displaying it to the user.

The problem doesn't stop there. Excel runs all VSTO assemblies on the same thread, so when we switch cultures, that affects every loaded VSTO assembly. If a separate VSTO assembly is responding to application events, that assembly could easily switch the culture back, causing our assembly to fail.

Correcting this issue will require changes to both Excel and the VSTO template, so it's extremely unlikely to be fixed before Office 12. One solution would be to have a new Office-specific assembly attribute (such as the ones that VSTO introduced) for the ExcelAutomationCulture. If omitted or set to Default, the behavior would be the same as now, but if set to a specific lcid, such as en-US, Excel would use that culture ID regardless of the lcid sent with the object model calls. By making it an assembly attribute (instead of, say, a property of the Excel Application object), different VSTO workbooks would be able to work side by side with different settings. We would be able to set the ExcelAutomationCulture to en-US and from then on rely on the predictability that we are accustomed to with VBA.

Security and Sharing Managed Workbooks

Office users share their files; often by e-mailing the files to each other, but also by copying them to disk or memory sticks. The linked nature and stringent security requirements of VSTO solutions make this much more difficult than at present, particularly when sending the workbook outside of the corporate network. As well as copying the document file, we now need to copy the assembly too, modify the _AssemblyLocation0 custom document property (so Excel finds the assembly on the target machine) and configure the .NET security policy to trust the assembly (so Excel will run it). And when we get it back to the office, we have to modify the _AssemblyLocation0 again to point back to the server. Do we really think the average low-end Excel users will be able to do all that without error every time they want to share a document?

Migrating from VBA

At the start of this chapter, we explained that the Visual Studio Tools for Office was primarily created to bring Office development into the realm of professional .NET developers. Consequently, the emphasis has been on making Office behave in a similar way to the other .NET technologies, rather than making VSTO behave in a similar way to VBA. The result is that those of us with VBA experience have a long uphill struggle to migrate both our knowledge and our applications to managed code; we have neither the conversion wizard nor the supported Interop option enjoyed (if that's the right word) by our VB6 colleagues. If Microsoft wants to see significant numbers of Office developers moving to managed code, Office 12 *must* make it much more approachable for those with a VBA background.

Office Versions

VSTO workbooks are only supported in the Professional version of Office 2003 and the standalone version of Excel 2003. They are not supported in either the Standard or Student versions of Office, nor in any previous version. As application developers, that means we simply can't predict whether our applications will run when we send them to our users. That uncertainty alone might be sufficient reason to stay with VBA. We can only hope that Office 12 will enable VSTO workbooks in all its versions and provide sufficient incentive for the majority of users to upgrade.

Further Reading

At the time of writing, no books have been written about the Visual Studio Tools for Office. To find out more about VSTO, we suggest you start with the following:

- For general information about VSTO, start at the Microsoft Web site, at `http://msdn.microsoft.com/office/understanding/vsto`
- For information about the VSTO security model, we recommend Peter Torr's blog, at `http://weblogs.asp.net/ptorr/category/2391.aspx?Show=All`
- If you encounter any problems while developing VSTO projects, ask for help in the Microsoft support newsgroup, `microsoft.public.vsnet.vstools.offfice`

Practical Example

The PETRAS application files for this chapter can be found on the CD in the folder *Application\Ch22—Using VB.NET and the Visual Studio Tools for Office* and includes the following files:

- **PetrasTemplate.xlt**—The timesheet template
- **PetrasAddin.dll**—The timesheet data-entry support add-in, rewritten as a VSTO assembly and linked to from the PetrasTemplate.xlt template
- **PetrasReporting.xla**—The main reporting application
- **PetrasConsolidation.xlt**—A template to use for new results workbooks
- **Petras.mdb**—A database file to store timesheet data
- **Debug.ini**—A dummy file that tells the application to run in debug mode
- **PetrasIcon.ico**—An icon file, to use for Excel's main window

PETRAS Timesheet Add-in

The PETRAS timesheet is an ideal example of the type of workbook for which the Visual Studio Tools for Office was designed. Instead of creating an Excel add-in and distributing it to all our users, the VSTO solution uses a single assembly deployed to a network share and a linked Excel template. The PetrasTemplate.xlt links to the assembly using the custom document properties. To test this example, you will need to copy the PetrasAddin.DLL to a folder of your choice, go through the steps described in *Trusting a Strong Name* earlier in this chapter and change the template's custom document property to point to the folder containing the PetrasAddin.dll (using the full folder name). The PetrasTemplate.xlt file should be saved to your Templates folder, usually located at *C:\Documents and Settings\ <Username>\Application Data\Microsoft\Templates*. The PetrasAddin VSTO project contains the following modules:

- **AssemblyInfo.vb**—The .NET attributes for this assembly.
- **MGlobals.vb**—Global constants and variables.
- **VSTOHooks.vb**—Procedures to handle the communication between Excel and the assembly.
- **CThisWorkbook**—Class to handle workbook events, most of which were handled at the application level in previous versions of the add-in.
- **MCommandBars.vb**—Module to create and remove our command bar buttons. Rewritten to create and destroy them individually instead of using the table-driven command bar builder.

- **CControlEvents.vb**—Class to hook the events for our command bar buttons.
- **MEntryPoints.vb**—Module containing the procedures called by the command bar buttons.
- **MBrowseForFolder.vb**—Module to display a Browse for Folder dialog, rewritten to use the standard .NET dialog.
- **MDataAccess.vb**—Module containing the ADO data layer.
- **MErrorHandler.vb**—The common error handler routine.
- **MStandardCode.vb**—Standard routines, copied between projects.

In this version of the add-in, we've moved from an application-centric add-in to a document-centric one, so each timesheet workbook gets its own instance of the VSTO code. The most noticeable change with this is that new timesheets are created using Excel's normal *File > New* menu instead of a *New Time sheet* button on our command bar. The code is unloaded when the timesheet document is closed, so we no longer need an *Exit PETRAS* button either. The major changes required to convert the PetrasAddin from an Excel add-in to a managed VTSO template workbook are listed in Table 22-1.

PETRAS Reporting Application

The PETRAS reporting application has not been updated for this chapter.

Table 22-1 Changes to the PETRAS Timesheet Add-in for Chapter 22

Module	Procedure	Change
All	All	Converted syntax, object references etc. to VB.NET style.
Multiple	Multiple	Where the Excel add-in code used the ActiveWorkbook in previous chapters, we're now only interested in the workbook linked to the assembly, given by ThisWorkbook.Workbook.
CAppEventHandler		Removed the class, as each workbook has its own instance of the code, so can handle its own events at workbook level. Moved much of the code to the ThisWorkbook class.

Table 22-1 Changes to the PETRAS Timesheet Add-in for Chapter 22 (*cont.*)

Module	Procedure	Change
MGlobals		Added global variables from standard ProExcel VSTO template. Changed ThisWorkbook.Path to use the assembly's path.
MEntryPoints		Removed the procedures for New Timesheet and Exit PETRAS. As this is now an automated timesheet, we'll use Excel's *File > New* to create new ones and the code is automatically unloaded when the timesheet is closed. Removed calls to bInitGlobals as they can now be trusted to remain set.
MBrowseForFolder		Rewritten to use the .NET Browse for Folder dialog.
MCommandBars		Rewritten to create our command bar buttons individually, instead of using the table-driven command bar builder.
CControlEvents (new class)		New class to handle the command bar button Click events.
MErrorHandler	bCentralErrorHandler	Changed ThisWorkbook.Path to use the assembly's path.
CThisWorkbook	bMakeWorksheetSettings	Rewritten to configure our worksheets individually instead of using a table-driven approach.
PetrasTemplate.xlt		Added setHideRows and setHideCols named ranges to allow the rows and columns to be hidden directly. Added the _AssemblyLocation0 and _AssemblyName0 custom document properties, to launch the VSTO assembly. Saved the template in its ready-to-edit state.

Conclusion

Office 2003 and the Visual Studio Tools for Office should be thought of as a typical Microsoft "version 1.0" product; it does exactly what it has been designed to do, but you might not be the kind of person it was designed for and the design may be too limited for practical use in most common situations. It also lacks many of the ease-of-use features that we take for granted in our VBA projects, such as automatically having class modules for each of our worksheets and automatically having events for any controls we add to them.

You might consider a VSTO solution if *all* of the following apply:

- This is a new application which won't make much use of any VBA code libraries you might have, and
- You already have some experience with VB.NET or C# and the .NET framework, and
- The .NET framework 1.1 is installed for all users, and
- You can administer .NET security policy centrally and roll it out to all users, and
- All users have Office 2003 Professional installed, running with U.S. English regional settings, and
- You don't need to use any of the features that VSTO doesn't support, such as user-defined functions, OnKey, OnTime and so on, and
- You have a central server to host the VSTO assemblies, and
- All users will be connected to the central server when using the document; it will not be used outside the company or offline, such as taken home or being shared with a third party.

If you can't tick all those boxes, but still want to use the facilities provided by the .NET framework, consider exposing the managed code as a COM DLL and calling it from VBA.

VSTO 1.0 was designed to bring Office development into the realm of the professional Visual Studio.NET developer. It was not designed to bring managed code development into the realm of the Office power user or VBA developer and doesn't attempt to do so. It is in no way a replacement for VBA, which will continue to be supported for many years to come.

VSTO 2.0 (a.k.a. VSTO 2005) takes a further step away from the average Office user by hosting the Excel window inside Visual Studio.NET and making it behave just like the Windows Forms drawing surface, allowing the .NET developer to drag and drop Windows Forms controls onto worksheets. By forcing Excel to behave in the same manner as other Visual Studio.NET elements, such as Windows Forms and ASP.NET, VSTO 2.0 makes it much easier for the VS.NET developer to embrace Office development, but at the cost of many of the ease-of-use features that Excel end users have come to expect. On the plus side, VSTO 2.0 includes many of the automatic features we take for granted in VBA, such as automatically getting a new event handler class module when we add a worksheet and so forth. It also includes a number of new programming elements, in which the existing Excel events have been wrapped and combined in innovative ways.

This chapter started with the statement that the collision between .NET and Office came relatively late in the Office 2003 planning process—far too late for major changes to be considered. With the planning for Office 12 well under way, it is incumbent upon both the Visual Tools and Office divisions at Microsoft to work hand in hand to bring managed code development within the realm of the traditional Office power user and VBA developer. This must include the ability for the owners of existing VBA applications to migrate their code, their skills and their knowledge to .NET in a gradual manner at their own pace, which only a seamless hybrid VBA/VB.NET environment would allow.

Excel, XML and Web Services

With every version of Excel since Office 97, Microsoft has gradually added features that enable Excel applications to work with Internet-based solutions. Starting with the ability to open and save HTML pages and perform rudimentary Web queries in Excel 97, this has progressed through much improved Web queries in Excel 2000, saving a workbook as XML in Excel 2002 and culminating with Excel 2003's ability to read and write arbitrary XML schemas. Along the way, Microsoft released the Web Services Toolkit, which allows our VBA code to communicate with Web services.

This chapter explains why we might want to use XML and Web services within our Excel applications, how to use them effectively in Excel 2003 and how they can be used in versions prior to Excel 2003.

XML

Unless you've been living in a vacuum for the past few years, you will have heard the acronym **XML** thrown around with increasing regularity. If you're primarily an Excel developer, you're probably also wondering what all the fuss is about. XML is a format used for the textual expression of data. In that respect, it's no different from the fixed-width, comma-separated or tab-delimited text formats we've been using for years. There are, however, a number of key factors that differentiate XML from all the other text formats that have come before it and make it much more appealing to developers:

- XML is a **structured** format, which means that we can define exactly how the data is to be arranged, organized and expressed within the file. When we are given a file, we can validate that it conforms to a specific structure, prior to importing the data. As we know the structure of the file in advance, we know what it contains and how to process each item. Prior to XML, the only structure in a text file was positional—we knew the bit of text after the fourth comma should be a date of birth—and we had no way to validate whether it was a date of birth, or even a date, or whether it was in day/month/year or month/day/year order.

- XML is a **described** format, which means that within the text file, every item of data has a name that is both human- and machine-readable as well as being uniquely identifiable. We can open these files, read their contents and understand the data they contain, without having to refer back to another document to find out what the text after the fourth comma represents (and was that comma a separator, or part of the text of the second item?). Similarly, we can edit these documents with a fairly high level of confidence that we're making the correct changes.

- XML can easily describe **hierarchical** data and the **relationships** between data. If we want to import and export a list of authors, with their names, addresses and the books they've written, deciding on a reasonable format for a CSV file is by no means straightforward. Using XML, we can define what an Author item is and that it has a name, address and multiple Book items. We can also define what a Book item is and that it has a title, a publisher and an ISBN. The hierarchy and relationships are a natural consequence of the definition.

- XML can be **validated**, which means we can provide a second XML file—an XML schema definition file—that describes exactly how the XML data file should be structured. Before processing an XML file, we can compare it with the schema to ensure it conforms to the structure we expect to receive.

- XML is a **discoverable** format, which means programs (including Excel 2003) can parse an XML data file and infer the structure and relationships between the items. This means we can read an XML file, infer its structure and generate new XML data files that conform to the same structure, with a high degree of confidence the new XML data files will pass validation.

- XML is a **strongly typed** format, which means the schema definition file specifies the data type of each element. When importing the data, the application can check the schema definition to identify the data type to import it as. We no longer run the risk of the product code 01-03 being imported as a date.

- XML is a *global* format. There is only one way to express a number in an XML file (with U.S. number formats) and only one way to express a date. We no longer have to check whether a CSV file was created with U.S. or French settings and adjust our processing of it accordingly.
- XML is a *standard* format. The way in which the content of an XML file is defined has been specified by the World Wide Web Consortium (W3C). This allows applications (including Excel 2003) to read, understand and validate the structure of an XML file and create files that conform to the specified structure. It also allows *different* applications to read, write, understand and validate the *same* XML files, enabling us to share data between applications in an extremely robust manner.

So is there anything we can do with XML we couldn't do using technologies we already know? No, not really. But then, there's nothing we can do with a spreadsheet we couldn't also do with a pen and paper (and maybe a basic calculator!). Since the earliest computers, we've been storing data and sharing it between applications. If we control both ends of the dialogue, it doesn't matter what's passed between them, so long as each end knows what to supply and what to expect and nothing goes wrong. If the format of a file is documented, any application could (in theory) be programmed to read and write the same data files. With XML files, an application can read (or infer) the structure definition and join in any conversation without extra programming. Using XML just makes some things a whole lot easier and more reliable.

An Example XML File

Listing 23-1 shows an example XML file for an author, including his name, e-mail address and some of the books he has been involved with.

Listing 23-1 An Example XML File

```
<?XML version="1.0" encoding="utf-8" ?>
<Author>
  <Name>Stephen Bullen</Name>
  <Email>stephen@oaltd.co.uk</Email>
  <Book>
    <Title>Professional Excel Development</Title>
```

```
   <Publisher>Addison Wesley</Publisher>
   <ISBN>0321262506</ISBN>
 </Book>
 <Book>
   <Title>Excel 2002 VBA Programmer's Reference</Title>
   <Publisher>Wrox Press</Publisher>
   <ISBN>1861005709</ISBN>
 </Book>
</Author>
```

If XML lives up to its hype, you should have been able to read and understand all the items of data in that file and understand the relationships between the elements. Just in case, we'll highlight the main items:

- The first line identifies the contents of the file as XML. Every XML file starts with this line.
- The file consists of both data and pairs of tags surrounding the data, which are together called an **element**. Our file consists of Author, Name, Email, Book, Title, Publisher and ISBN elements. A tag is identified by text enclosed within angle brackets, like <Tag>. All the tags come in pairs, with an opening tag like <Tag> and a closing tag like </Tag>; all the text between the opening and closing tags in some way "belongs" to the tag. However, if there is nothing contained within the opening and closing tags, they can be combined so that <Tag></Tag> can be shown as <Tag/>. This is often used when the data for an element is provided as an **attribute** of the element, using a syntax like <Publisher name="Addison Wesley"/>. There is little difference between using elements or attributes, though our preference is to use elements. Note that tags and attributes are case-sensitive, so <Author> will not match with </author>.
- The second line identifies a **root element**, which in this file represents an Author. Every XML file must have one and only one root element; all other elements in the file belong to the root element.
- The third and fourth lines identify the author's name and e-mail address; we know it's the author's name and e-mail address because they're both within the same <Author> element.
- The fifth line is the start of a Book element, with the next three lines giving the book's details (because they're contained within the Book element). The ninth line closes the Book element, telling us we've finished with that book.

- Lines 10 to 14 show a second Book element, with the book's details.
- Line 15 closes the Author element, telling us we've finished with that author.

That example hopefully demonstrates the main attributes of an XML file. It is structured, described, hierarchical and relational, but how is it validated?

An Example XSD file

The structure of an XML file is specified using an XML schema definition file, which usually has the extension .xsd and contains sets of XML tags that have been defined by the W3C. The XSD file for the Author XML data is shown in Listing 23-2.

Listing 23-2 An Example XSD File

```
<?XML version="1.0" ?>
<xs:schema xmlns:xs="http://www.w3.org/2001/XMLSchema">
 <xs:element name="Author">
  <xs:complexType>
   <xs:sequence>
    <xs:element name="Name" type="xs:string"/>
    <xs:element name="Email" type="xs:string"
                minOccurs="0" maxOccurs="unbounded"/>
    <xs:element name="Book"
                minOccurs="0" maxOccurs="unbounded">
     <xs:complexType>
      <xs:sequence>
       <xs:element name="Title" type="xs:string"/>
       <xs:element name="Publisher" type="xs:string"/>
       <xs:element name="ISBN" type="xs:string"/>
      </xs:sequence>
     </xs:complexType>
    </xs:element>
   </xs:sequence>
  </xs:complexType>
 </xs:element>
</xs:schema>
```

This is slightly less readable XML! We explain how to create an XSD file later in the chapter, but it's helpful to understand how this file describes the structure of the XML data file shown in Listing 23-1:

- Like all XML files, the first line identifies the contents as XML.
- The second line identifies the namespace `http://www.w3.org/2001/XMLSchema` and gives it the alias, xs. This is the namespace defined by the W3C that contains all the XML tags used in XML schema definition files. When we need to use a tag from that namespace, we precede it with the xs: alias identifier so the XML processor can correctly identify it. This mechanism of using namespace aliases is often encountered in XML files that contain elements from multiple namespaces (such as Excel workbook files, which contain tags from both the Excel and Office namespaces).
- The third line defines an Author element which must occur once and only once in the file (unless otherwise specified, the default occurrence of a tag is 'must occur once and only once'), so our XML data file can only be for one author.
- The fourth line states that the Author element is a complexType, which means it contains other elements.
- The fifth line states that all the items within the Author element must be listed in the sequence shown in the XSD file (that is, Name, then Email, then Book).
- The sixth line defines an element within Author called Name, of type string and there must be one and only one of them. The use of the `/>` at the end of the element tag is a shorthand for creating a self-closing tag, so `<Tag/>` is equivalent to `<Tag></Tag>`.
- The seventh and eighth lines define an element within Author called Email, of type string, which doesn't have to occur (`minOccurs="0"`) or there can be any number of them (`maxOccurs="unbounded"`).
- Lines 9–15 define an element within Author called Book, of which there can be any number. If provided, each Book element must contain a single Title, Publisher and ISBN string element in that order.
- Lines 16–22 close out the tags.

Before we import any data files, we can check that they conform to these rules (assuming we have the XSD file to check them against) and reject any files that can't be validated.

Overview of Excel 2003's XML Features

NOTE: The XML features added to Excel 2003 are only available in the Professional version of Office and Standalone version of Excel; they have been disabled in the Standard and Student versions of Office. In practice, this means that if we want to utilize the new XML features, we and all our users must be running Office 2003 Professional.

Throughout this book, we've been stressing the importance of physically separating our data from our code, so we can easily update our code without affecting the data; our PETRAS timesheet add-in has undergone some major changes, but our timesheet template file has stayed (pretty much) the same throughout. We've been a little quiet, though, about what we should consider our "code" to be, and hence where to put the break between application and data. That is because the only real choice we've had is to put the break at the boundary between VBA and our Excel workbooks and templates. Whenever we've had a new set of data to store, we've stored it inside a copy of our template.

That leaves us a little concerned and hopeful that we don't have to change anything in the template. If we discovered a bug in the data validation settings, we would have to open and update every copy of every timesheet submitted using that template (or just ignore it for archived files!). We haven't really separated our data from our logic. Within each of our data files, we're storing lots of formatting, validation and ancillary information as well as the data entered into the timesheet.

What we would really like to do is to completely separate the raw data from the formatting and data validation, so we would only need one copy of the data-entry workbook on each machine which could import and export the raw data. That's exactly what Excel 2003's XML features enable us to do!

Using Excel 2003's new *XML Source* task pane, we can import an XML schema definition file into a workbook and link the elements defined in that file to cells (for the single elements) or Lists (for the multiple-occurring elements) in the workbook.

We can then import any XML data file that conforms to the schema into our workbook. Excel will parse the XML data file, check that it conforms to the schema, read the data from all the elements and populate the linked cells and lists. Figure 23-1 shows an Excel 2003 workbook containing the XSD from Listing 23-2 and having imported the XML data from Listing 23-1.

We can also type data into the linked cells and lists and export the data as an XML file. Excel will create an XML data file that conforms to the schema and contains the data from the linked cells and lists.

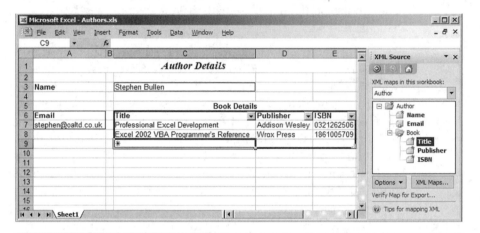

Figure 23-1 An Excel Workbook Linked to an XML Schema

Excel's XML features can greatly help with the maintenance of our financial models as well. Until Excel 2003, if we wanted to use our model to analyze different data sets, we would have to use a separate copy of the model workbook for each set. If we subsequently found an error in our model, we would have to open and update all the copies. In Excel 2003, we can create a schema for our model's input variables and another schema for its results, include them both in the workbook and link them to the relevant cells or Lists. We can then use a single copy of the model workbook to import the input variables, calculate the model and export the results.

The new XML features are, of course, all exposed to VBA, so we can easily identify which cells are linked to which elements of which schemas (and vice versa), read and write the XML to/from strings as well as (or instead of) importing and exporting files and respond to events raised both before and after XML data is imported or exported.

A Simple Financial Model

To demonstrate how Excel 2003 uses XML, we'll create a simple financial model that calculates the net present value of a list of cash flows, giving us the number of flows, the total cash flow and the net present value. We'll also record the model's version number and the date and time the model was calculated. Figure 23-2 shows the spreadsheet for the model, which can also be found in the Model1.xls workbook on the CD in the \Concepts\Ch23—Excel, XML and Web Services folder.

	A	B	C	D	E
1		Net Present Value Calculation Model			
2					
3		Control Information		Processing Details	
4	Submitted by:	Stephen Bullen		Version:	1.0
5	Email:	stephen@oaltd.co.uk		Date:	30 Jun 2004
6	Comment:	Fee Fi Fo Fum			
7					
8		Input Data		Results	
9	Rate	Flows		Flows:	4
10	5%		10	Total:	100.00
11			20	NPV:	86.49
12			30		
13			40		
14					
15					

Figure 23-2 The Net Present Value Calculation Model

Note that the Flows data in B9:B13 is in an Excel 2003 List, so as data is typed into it, the references used in the functions in cells E9:E11 are automatically updated. This is obviously a very simple financial model to demonstrate the principles. In practice, there may be many sets of input data, many worksheets of calculations, pivot tables and so forth, and a large set of results.

Let's assume for now we want to analyze many sets of data—in this case, different combinations of rates and cash flows, and we want to store each set of data somewhere, so we can come back to it at a later date. Let's also imagine this is a large and complex model, so we would prefer not to have multiple copies of it to keep in sync.

What we'd really like to do is tell Excel what bits of the file are the raw data and be able to import and export just that data in a form we could edit and maybe even create offline. With Excel 2003, we can do exactly that.

Creating an XML Schema Definition

The first step is to create an XML schema definition (XSD) file to define our raw data. If we already have an XML file containing some data we want to import, Excel can infer an XSD from it. Excel generally does quite a good job at inferring the structure, but we have more control over the details if we define it ourselves. For example, in the Authors XML file in Listing 23-1, the data file included a single e-mail address. Excel will infer the schema only allows one address, but the real schema allows multiples. Excel also always assumes data is optional, while we've made the author name mandatory.

All the input data is shown with a light shading in Figure 23-2, from which we can see the structure we would like to emulate:

- There is a single block of control information, which must exist.
- Within the control information, we have a name, e-mail address and comment. For this example, we'll make the name and e-mail required, but the comment optional. Each item can only occur once (if at all) and they're all strings.
- We then have a single block of data information, which must exist.
- The data information contains a single Rate figure and multiple Flows figures, all of which are Doubles. Although not required by the NPV function, we'll require a minimum of two cash flow amounts.

The XSD for this data is shown in Listing 23-3, which includes a root NPVModelData element to contain our data types.

Listing 23-3 The XSD File for the NPV Model Data

```
<?XML version="1.0" ?>
<XSD:schema xmlns:XSD="http://www.w3.org/2001/XMLSchema">
 <XSD:element name="NPVModelData">
  <XSD:complexType>
   <XSD:sequence>
    <XSD:element name="ControlInformation">
     <XSD:complexType>
      <XSD:sequence>
       <XSD:element name="SubmittedBy" type="XSD:string" />
       <XSD:element name="Email" type="XSD:string" />
```

```
        <XSD:element name="Comment" type="XSD:string"
                        minOccurs="0" maxOccurs="1" />
      </XSD:sequence>
     </XSD:complexType>
    </XSD:element>
    <XSD:element name="InputData">
     <XSD:complexType>
      <XSD:sequence>
       <XSD:element name="Rate" type="XSD:double" />
       <XSD:element name="Flows" type="XSD:double"
                        minOccurs="2" maxOccurs="unbounded" />
      </XSD:sequence>
     </XSD:complexType>
    </XSD:element>
   </XSD:sequence>
  </XSD:complexType>
 </XSD:element>
</XSD:schema>
```

As this is XML, you should be able to read Listing 23-3 and see the direct correlation to the data in our worksheet and the previous statements about the structure we want to emulate. A few noteworthy points are as follows:

- We always start an XSD file with the same first two lines.
- Every element that is a container of other elements must be followed by the <XSD:complexType> tag and a tag to identify how the elements are contained. In this example (and in most cases), we use the <XSD:sequence> tag to say that the elements are contained in the sequence shown.
- The Comment element includes the attributes minOccurs="0" maxOccurs="1", which is how we specify an optional item; it doesn't have to occur (minOccurs="0"), but if it does occur, there can only be one of them (maxOccurs="1").
- The Flows element includes the attributes minOccurs="2" maxOccurs="unbounded", which is how we specify that there must be at least two cash flows, but there can be any number. Theoretically, we should put maxOccurs="65527", as that is the maximum number of flows that will fit on our model worksheet.

XML Maps

Now that we have an XSD file describing our data, we need to tell Excel to use it and to link each element in the XSD file to a worksheet cell or range. Importing the schema and linking it to cells is known as *mapping* and Excel refers to these as *XML Maps* (which is Excel's terminology, not an industry-wide one).

So let's map our XSD to our model. Open the Model1.xls file, click *View > Task Pane* and select the XML Source task pane from the drop-down in the task pane title bar, shown in Figure 23-3.

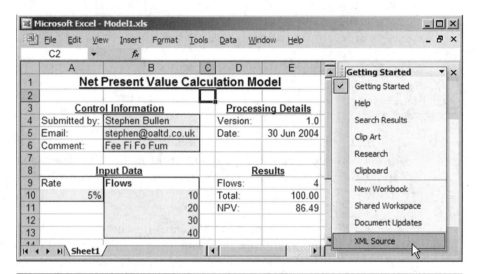

Figure 23-3 Selecting the XML Source Task Pane

Click the XML Maps… button at the bottom of the XML Source task pane to bring up the XML Maps dialog, click the Add button on the dialog and browse to the XSD file. If the XSD is valid, Excel will import the schema and create an XML map using it, as shown in Figure 23-4. If there is an error in the XSD, Excel will show you where it thinks the error is. Note that if we selected an XML data file instead of the XSD, Excel would infer a schema from the XML data. It is definitely best practice, though, to create and use an XSD file.

When we click OK on the XML Map dialog, Excel examines the schema and displays it in the XML Source task pane, as shown in Figure 23-5.

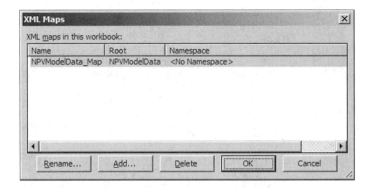

Figure 23-4 The XML Map Dialog After Adding the NPVModelData Schema

Figure 23-5 The XML Source Task Pane, Showing the NPVModelData Schema

Note that Excel has identified the hierarchical structure of the schema, the elements that are required (shown with an asterisk in the icon) and the elements that are repeating (shown by the arrow at the bottom of the Flows icon).

The final step is to associate the elements in the schema with the data-entry cells in our model worksheet. We do this by selecting each element from the tree in the task pane, dragging it to the worksheet and dropping it on the cell that we want to link it to. In Figure 23-6, we're dragging the SubmittedBy element and dropping it on cell B4.

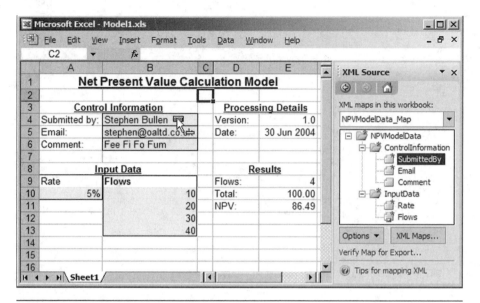

Figure 23-6 Drag and Drop the Elements from the Task Pane to the Worksheet

Similarly, we'll map the rest of the schema to our worksheet by dropping the Email element to B5, the Comment element to B6, the Rate element to A10 and the Flows element to B10 (or anywhere inside the Flows list). As we do that, Excel annoyingly adjusts the column widths of each cell to fit the data it contains. We would much prefer the default behavior to not do that, but we can switch it off by right-clicking one of the mapped cells and choosing *XML > XML Map Properties* from the popup menu to display the XML Map Properties dialog shown in Figure 23-7, in which we've set the properties that we recommend using. We should be able to access this dialog from the XML Maps dialog we used to select a map, but for some reason, we can't!

The first check box *Validate data against schema for import and export* defaults to off, but in our opinion is the most important setting in the whole of Excel's XML support. With it turned on, Excel will verify that the XML data files we import conform to the format defined in the schema and that the data we type into cells conforms to the schema before allowing us to export it. Turning off those checks seems to us to invalidate the whole point of using XML in the first place—that of reliable and robust data transfer.

Figure 23-7 The Recommended Settings for XML Map Properties

That's it! We've defined the raw data our financial model uses, created an XSD file to formally specify it, added the schema to the model and linked the elements in the schema to the model's data entry cells. The completed workbook can be found in the Model2.xls workbook.

Exporting and Importing XML Data

The menu items to import and export our XML data can be found on the *Data > XML* menu, with toolbar buttons also located on the List toolbar. Using the *Export XML* menu results in the XML data file for our model shown in Listing 23-4.

Listing 23-4 The XML Data File Produced from Our Model

```
<?XML version="1.0" encoding="UTF-8" standalone="yes"?>
<NPVModelData>
  <ControlInformation>
    <SubmittedBy>Stephen Bullen</SubmittedBy>
    <Email>stephen@oaltd.co.uk</Email>
    <Comment>Fee Fi Fo Fum</Comment>
  </ControlInformation>
  <InputData>
```

```
    <Rate>0.05</Rate>
    <Flows>10</Flows>
    <Flows>20</Flows>
    <Flows>30</Flows>
    <Flows>40</Flows>
  </InputData>
</NPVModelData>
```

Hopefully, everything in the file makes sense by now, particularly the multiple `<Flows>` elements. If we delete the `<Comment>` element, add a few more `<Flows>` elements to the bottom, save it with a different name and use the *Import XML* menu to import it into our model, we get the worksheet shown in Figure 23-8. Remember that our XSD file specified the `<Comment>` tag as optional, so our file passes the schema validation even though the comment data is missing. The extra `<Flows>` elements have been included in the List, which has automatically extended to accommodate them, and the formulas in cells `E9:E11` have also automatically been adjusted to suit!

We have achieved our goal of being able to totally separate our data from our model, importing and exporting the data as we choose, with the model automatically updating to use the new data as we import it.

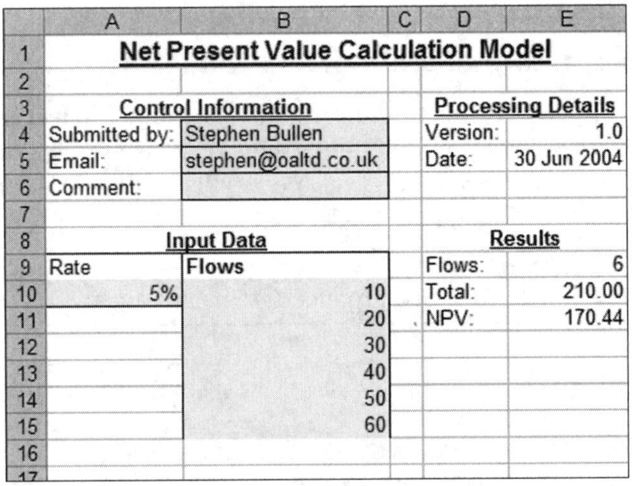

	A	B	C	D	E
1	**Net Present Value Calculation Model**				
2					
3	**Control Information**			**Processing Details**	
4	Submitted by:	Stephen Bullen		Version:	1.0
5	Email:	stephen@oaltd.co.uk		Date:	30 Jun 2004
6	Comment:				
7					
8	**Input Data**			**Results**	
9	Rate	Flows		Flows:	6
10	5%	10		Total:	210.00
11		20		NPV:	170.44
12		30			
13		40			
14		50			
15		60			
16					
17					

Figure 23-8 Importing an XML Data File Adjusts the Ranges

The XML Object Model and Events

Now that we can import and export the raw data for the model, we'll probably want to import the data and then export the results, with the export file containing a copy of the input data, details about the model itself, such as the version number and when the calculation was done, and the model's results. Listing 23-5 shows the XSD file for the full set of our NPVModel data, which can be found on the CD in the NPVModel.XSD file. The definition for the NPVModelData schema from Listing 23-5 has been included inside the new root NPVModel tag and we've added elements for the model details and results. It looks complicated, but isn't really—just remember that when we want to nest one element inside another, we have to include a pair of `<XSD:complexType>` and `<XSD:sequence>` tags between them.

Listing 23-5 The Full XSD File for Our Model

```
<?XML version="1.0" ?>
<XSD:schema xmlns:XSD="http://www.w3.org/2001/XMLSchema">
 <XSD:element name="NPVModel">
  <XSD:complexType>
   <XSD:sequence>
    <XSD:element name="NPVModelData">
     <XSD:complexType>
      <XSD:sequence>
       <XSD:element name="ControlInformation">
        <XSD:complexType>
         <XSD:sequence>
          <XSD:element name="SubmittedBy"
                       type="XSD:string" />
          <XSD:element name="Email" type="XSD:string" />
          <XSD:element name="Comment" type="XSD:string"
                       minOccurs="0" maxOccurs="1" />
         </XSD:sequence>
        </XSD:complexType>
       </XSD:element>
       <XSD:element name="InputData">
        <XSD:complexType>
         <XSD:sequence>
          <XSD:element name="Rate" type="XSD:double" />
          <XSD:element name="Flows" type="XSD:double"
                       minOccurs="2" maxOccurs="unbounded" />
```

```
      </XSD:sequence>
       </XSD:complexType>
      </XSD:element>
     </XSD:sequence>
    </XSD:complexType>
   </XSD:element>
   <XSD:element name="NPVModelDetails">
    <XSD:complexType>
     <XSD:sequence>
      <XSD:element name="ModelVersion" type="XSD:string" />
      <XSD:element name="CalcDate" type="XSD:dateTime" />
     </XSD:sequence>
    </XSD:complexType>
   </XSD:element>
   <XSD:element name="NPVModelResults">
    <XSD:complexType>
     <XSD:sequence>
      <XSD:element name="FlowCount" type="XSD:double" />
      <XSD:element name="FlowTotal" type="XSD:double" />
      <XSD:element name="FlowNPV" type="XSD:double" />
     </XSD:sequence>
    </XSD:complexType>
   </XSD:element>
  </XSD:sequence>
 </XSD:complexType>
 </XSD:element>
</XSD:schema>
```

We can add this schema to our model as a second XML map and map the NPVModelDetails and NPVModelResults elements to the appropriate cells in column E. When we try to map the ControlInformation elements to the cells in column B, however, Excel displays an error message "The operation cannot be completed because the result would overlap an existing XML mapping" and prevents us from doing the mapping. This is because Excel limits us to a one-to-one relationship between cells and XML elements; any one cell can only map to one element from one XML map and vice versa. We want all our input data to map to both the NVPModelData map (so we can import it) and the NVPModel map (so we can include it in the export). The only way we can achieve our objective is to have a copy of the input data that we include in our NPVModel map, as shown in Figure 23-9. All the single items, such as the e-mail address and rate, can be linked using standard worksheet formulae, but the lists will have to be synchronized through VBA.

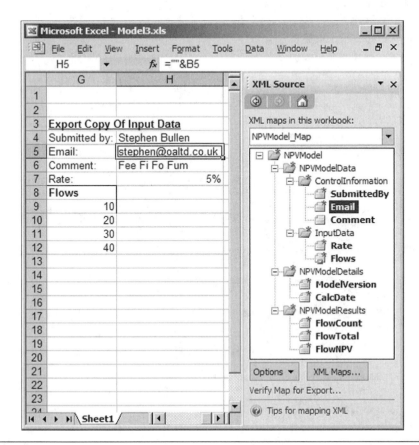

Figure 23-9 Mapping the NPVModel Elements to a Copy of the Input Data

Fortunately, Excel 2003 includes a rich object model and event model for working with XML maps. We can use the Workbook_BeforeXMLExport event to copy the Flow data from the input range (B9 and below) to the export range (G8 and below), using the mapping to identify the ranges in each case, as shown in Listing 23-6.

Listing 23-6 Copying the Input Flows List to the Export Copy

```
'Run before any XML is exported
Private Sub Workbook_BeforeXMLExport(ByVal Map As XMLMap, _
    ByVal Url As String, Cancel As Boolean)

  Dim rngSource As Range
  Dim rngTarget As Range
```

```
'Are we exporting the full Model data?
If Map.RootElementName = "NPVModel" Then

   'Find the data part of the target list
   Set rngTarget = Sheet1.XMLDataQuery( _
       "/NPVModel/NPVModelData/InputData/Flows")

   'If there is any existing data in the target list,
   'remove it.
   If Not rngTarget Is Nothing Then rngTarget.Delete

   'Find the data part of the source list
   Set rngSource = Sheet1.XMLDataQuery( _
       "/NPVModelData/InputData/Flows")

   'Is there any source data to copy?
   If Not rngSource Is Nothing Then

      'Find the header part of the target list
      Set rngTarget = Sheet1.XMLMapQuery( _
          "/NPVModel/NPVModelData/InputData/Flows")

      'Copy the data to the cell below the target list header
      rngSource.Copy
      rngTarget.Cells(1).Offset(1, 0).PasteSpecial xlValues
   End If
End If

End Sub
```

Within the object model, the linking between ranges and XML schema elements is done using XPaths. The XPath is a concatenated string of all the element names in an element's hierarchy, so to get to the Flows element in the NPVModelData map, we start at the root NPVModelData, go down to the InputData element and then to the Flows element, so the XPath for the Flows element in that map is `/NPVModelData/InputData/Flows`. This is stored in the XPath property of the Range object, so we can directly find out which element a range is mapped to. To find the range mapped to a given element, we use the XMLMapQuery and XMLDataQuery methods, passing the XPath of the element. It's a curiosity of the object model that while XML maps are workbook-level items and an element can be mapped to any range in any sheet in the workbook, the XMLMapQuery and XMLDataQuery methods are worksheet-level methods. If we didn't know which sheet the range was on, we would have to scan through them all, repeating the XMLMapQuery for each.

Both XMLMapQuery and XMLDataQuery return the range that is mapped to a given XPath string. The only difference between them is when the mapped range is a List; the XMLMapQuery returns the full range of the List, including the header row, whereas the XMLDataQuery returns only the data in the List, or Nothing if the List is empty.

With just a few mouse clicks, we can now import some raw data for our financial model, recalculate it and export the results, giving an XML data file like the one shown in Listing 23-7.

Listing 23-7 The XML Data File from Our NPV Model

```xml
<?XML version="1.0" encoding="UTF-8" standalone="yes"?>
<NPVModel>
  <NPVModelData>
    <ControlInformation>
      <SubmittedBy>Stephen Bullen</SubmittedBy>
      <Email>stephen@oaltd.co.uk</Email>
      <Comment>Fee Fi Fo Fum</Comment>
    </ControlInformation>
    <InputData>
      <Rate>0.05</Rate>
      <Flows>10</Flows>
      <Flows>20</Flows>
      <Flows>30</Flows>
      <Flows>40</Flows>
    </InputData>
  </NPVModelData>
  <NPVModelDetails>
    <ModelVersion>1.0</ModelVersion>
    <CalcDate>2004-07-01T13:44:04.430</CalcDate>
  </NPVModelDetails>
  <NPVModelResults>
    <FlowCount>4</FlowCount>
    <FlowTotal>100</FlowTotal>
    <FlowNPV>86.49</FlowNPV>
  </NPVModelResults>
</NPVModel>
```

It's not hard to envisage our financial model being used as a "black box" service, whereby individuals (or other applications) submit XML files containing the raw data for the model, we import it, calculate and export the results and send them back.

Notice the very specific format used for the date and time in the CalcDate element, which is how XML avoids the issues of identifying different date formats. It doesn't, however, account for different time zones!

By adding the ability to export results directly from our model, we've also created a vulnerability. Users could import data into that map as well, which would overwrite our formulas! We can prevent this using the Workbook_BeforeXMLImport event, as shown in Listing 23-8.

Listing 23-8 Prevent Importing of the Results XML

```
'Run before any XML is imported
Private Sub Workbook_BeforeXMLImport(ByVal Map As XMLMap, _
      ByVal Url As String, ByVal IsRefresh As Boolean, _
      Cancel As Boolean)

   'Are we importing to the full Model data?
   If Map.RootElementName = "NPVModel" Then

      'Yes, so disallow it
      MsgBox "The XML file you selected contains the " & _
             "results for this model, and can not be imported."

      'Cancel the import
      Cancel = True
   End If

End Sub
```

XML Support in Earlier Versions

Excel 2003 has made the handling of arbitrary XML files extremely easy, but we don't **have** to upgrade to Excel 2003 to use XML. As mentioned at the start of the chapter, XML is just another text file format, so in theory we can read and write XML files using standard VBA text handling and file

I/O code. When Excel 2003 imports an XML data file, it uses the MSXML library to do the validation and parsing of the file, and there's nothing stopping us referencing the same library from VBA. Of course, we also have to write our own routines to import the data from the MSXML structure to the worksheet and export the data from the sheet to an XML file. Multiple-version compatibility is one of the key design goals for our PETRAS timesheet application, so we show the VBA technique in the *Practical Example* section at the end of this chapter.

The VBA technique is also required in Excel 2003 if the structure of the XML data is too complex to be handled by Excel's fairly simplistic mapping abilities. For example, our PETRAS timesheet workbook includes a table of clients and projects, with the client names across the top and the projects listed below each client (to feed the data validation drop-downs). It is not possible to map an XML schema to that layout, so the import of that section of the XML data file has to be done with VBA in all versions of Excel.

Using Namespaces

All of the examples shown so far in this chapter have ignored the use of namespaces. This means the XML files we use and produce are only identified by the root elements of NPVModel and NPVModelData. There is nothing in the file to identify them as the data for **our** NPV model. This means that, in theory, someone else could create an XML file that uses a very similar structure to ours and we could import it without knowing it was not intended for our application. To avoid this, we can include a namespace identifier both in the XSD and XML files, which is used to uniquely identify all the tags in the file, and hence the data they contain. When the file is processed, the namespace is prepended to all the tags, allowing the parser to distinguish between, say, the Name element in this file denoting the author's name and the Name element in a workbook file denoting an Excel Defined Name. The text of the namespace can be any string, but should be globally unique. It is general practice to use a URL, which has the advantage that the viewer of the file could browse to the URL in the hope of finding a description of the namespace.

We tell Excel the namespace to use by including it within the <XSD:schema> tag at the top of our XSD file, as shown in Listing 23-9 and included on the CD in the file NPVModelData - NS.xsd.

Listing 23-9 Providing Excel with a Namespace

```
<?XML version="1.0" ?>
<XSD:schema xmlns:XSD="http://www.w3.org/2001/XMLSchema"
  targetNamespace="http://www.oaltd.co.uk/ProExcelDev/NPVModelData"
  xmlns:md="http://www.oaltd.co.uk/ProExcelDev/NPVModelData"
  elementFormDefault="qualified" >
  <XSD:element name="NPVModelData">
...
```

When that schema is added to a workbook, Excel will remember the namespace, create an alias for it, such as ns0, ns1, ns2 and so on, and add that alias to the front of all the elements in the file, as shown in Figure 23-10.

Figure 23-10 All the XML Elements are Prefixed with the Namespace Alias

When the XML is exported, Excel includes the namespace in the file and qualifies all the elements with the namespace alias, as shown in Listing 23-10.

Listing 23-10 Providing Excel with a Namespace

```
<?XML version="1.0" encoding="UTF-8" standalone="yes"?>
<ns1:NPVModelData
 xmlns:ns1="http://www.oaltd.co.uk/ProExcelDev/NPVModelData">
```

```
<ns1:ControlInformation>
   <ns1:SubmittedBy>Stephen Bullen</ns1:SubmittedBy>
   <ns1:Email>stephen@oaltd.co.uk</ns1:Email>
   <ns1:Comment>Fee Fi Fo Fum</ns1:Comment>
</ns1:ControlInformation>
<ns1:InputData>
   <ns1:Rate>0.05</ns1:Rate>
   <ns1:Flows>10</ns1:Flows>
   <ns1:Flows>20</ns1:Flows>
   <ns1:Flows>30</ns1:Flows>
   <ns1:Flows>40</ns1:Flows>
</ns1:InputData>
</ns1:NPVModelData>
```

It is definitely a good practice to use namespaces in our XML files, to avoid any chance of Excel importing erroneous data into our applications. The only reason we haven't used them so far in this chapter is to avoid overcomplicating our explanation of Excel's XML features.

Web Services

Like XML, **Web services** is another term you've probably heard about with mild curiosity, but ultimately rejected as being irrelevant to Excel. This section aims to explain what Web services are, how to create them (using Visual Basic.NET) and how they can play an important role in our applications. What we will **not** do is explain how they work, because that **is** largely irrelevant to us as Excel developers.

A Web service is a piece of code running on a computer somewhere that we can find, connect to and use from anywhere in the world (as long as we have an Internet connection). The computer on which the Web service is running can be very tightly controlled, monitored and secured, forcing the clients to treat the code as a "black box"—the user of the Web service can only see its input and outputs and cannot access the program itself. This makes Web services ideal for providing information in a very controlled and regulated manner by running applications on the server instead of distributing applications which might include sensitive information (such as database IDs and passwords) and/or intellectual property (such as a proprietary financial model) and run the risk of them being hacked. Additionally, we only need to manage one copy of the code, running on the server, so as soon as we modify the code and copy it to the server, all users immediately start using the new version.

Any application that exposes its functionality to such a wide audience is going to have the problem of how to specify and validate the data it accepts and the results it produces, which is where XML comes into the picture. All the communication between the Web service and its client is done using XML.

But haven't we just been discussing how Excel 2003 can read and write arbitrary XML data files? So shouldn't we be able to point the XML export/import to a Web service somewhere and be able to call the proprietary financial model directly from the worksheet? In theory, yes we should, but the final step is missing from Excel 2003; we have to glue the ends together using VBA.

And haven't we just been demonstrating how to create a proprietary financial model in Excel 2003 that accepts XML for its inputs and writes its results as XML too? So we could put that on the server and, hey presto, we have a Web service? Again, in theory, yes. Unfortunately, Excel is not designed to run on a server, doesn't scale at all and Microsoft strongly discourages us from using Excel in that way. Nor does Excel 2003 include the glue to expose an Excel workbook as a Web service.

So we can't connect directly to a Web service from Excel and we can't use Excel as a Web service, but we can use VBA to connect to a Web service, either to make use of proprietary calculations or to access data from and send data to a central database, over the Internet. Being able to do this means we can take our Excel applications out of the office, but still allow them to connect to the corporate data.

In this part of the chapter, we explain how to create a simple Web service for a financial model and connect to it from VBA, so we can call it directly from the worksheet. In the *Practical Example* section, we modify the PETRAS timesheet add-in to retrieve data from and send data to a Web service. Instead of the timesheet add-in connecting directly to a database on the network, the Web service will handle the database connection. In both cases, we focus on using the Web service, rather than creating one with all the scalability and security considerations. For this example we use a local Web server (`http://localhost`) to run the Web service. To run the examples in this section, you will need a computer running Internet Information Services and have Visual Studio.NET 2003 to create the Web service. The Excel part of the example works in any version from Excel 2000 forward.

Creating a Web Service with VB.NET

To demonstrate how to connect to and use a Web service from Excel, we'll create a very simple one to reproduce the AddTwo and MultiplyTwo functions seen in *Chapter 19 — XLLs and the C API*. Start Visual Studio.NET 2003, start a new project, choose the ASP.NET Web Service Visual Basic project and rename the location to http://localhost/ProExcelDev, as shown in Figure 23-11.

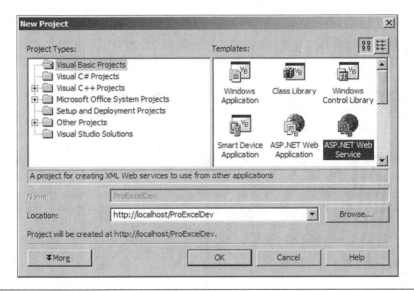

Figure 23-11 Creating a New Visual Basic Web Service

Click OK to let Visual Studio create a new Web service project. This project includes a class called Service1 that we want to rename to be Maths. The name needs to be changed in both the filename (by editing the filename in the Solution Explorer tree) and the class name (by editing the code module). In Listing 23-11 we've changed the class name in both lines three and four and added the two functions we want to make available to users of our Web service.

Listing 23-11 The ProExcelDev Maths Web Service

```
'The Professional Excel Development Maths Web Service
Imports System.Web.Services

<System.Web.Services.WebService( _
  Namespace:="http://tempuri.org/ProExcelDev/Maths", _
  Description:="Pro Excel Dev Maths Functions")> _
Public Class Maths
    Inherits System.Web.Services.WebService

    [Web Services Designer Generated Code]

    'Add two numbers
    <WebMethod(Description:="Adds two numbers")> _
    Public Function AddTwo(ByVal d1 As Double, _
            ByVal d2 As Double) As Double

        Return d1 + d2
    End Function

    'Multiply two numbers
    <WebMethod(Description:="Multiplies two numbers")> _
    Public Function MultiplyTwo(ByVal d1 As Double, _
            ByVal d2 As Double) As Double

        Return d1 * d2
    End Function

End Class
```

That's all there is to it; we've created a Web service! The key bit is the <WebMethod()> attribute that we add to any functions we want to expose. In this example, we're only passing simple data types—doubles—but in the PETRAS Web service, we'll be passing and returning more complex data sets, using XML. Build the solution, close Visual Studio and let's get on with the interesting bit—using the Web service from Excel.

Using a Web Service

Excel's Web Service connectivity is provided by the Microsoft Office Soap Type Library, mssoap30.dll, included in the Office Web Services Toolkit. The toolkit is an optional install in Office 2003 Professional and can be downloaded by following the *Office 2003: Web Services Toolkit*

2.01 link from `http://msdn.microsoft.com/office/downloads/ toolsutils/default.aspx`. When deploying applications that use Web services, our users will also need to have the Web Services Toolkit installed, to provide them with the mssoap30 DLL and its dependencies. As well as containing the type library, the toolkit includes an add-in to the VBIDE that enables us to find and select Web services, then adds classes to our VBProjects to wrap the calls into the Soap Type Library and expose the Web service as a standard VBA class (or set of classes). Despite its name, the Web Services Toolkit is not dependent on Excel 2003 and works fine in all versions from Excel 2000 forward.

Download and install the toolkit, switch to the Excel VBE and click on *Tools > Web Service References...* to bring up the Microsoft Office Web Services Toolkit dialog. This dialog provides the capability to search for a Web service by keyword (by linking to a Microsoft Web site for that information), but we'll provide it with the location of the ProExcelDev Maths Web service we created above. When we built the Web service, Visual Studio compiled our source code into a file called Maths.asmx, which is the Web service equivalent of an EXE or DLL. Because we know which file to connect to, we can tell the Web Services Toolkit to connect directly to it and search for the Web services it contains, as shown in Figure 23-12.

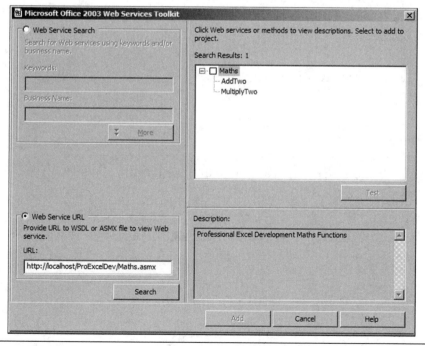

Figure 23-12 Connecting to the ProExcelDev Maths Web Service

When we click the Add button, the toolkit will create class modules for each of the Web services we've ticked in the top-right box. So tick the Maths Web service, click Add and look at the generated code in the new clsws_Maths class the toolkit just created. An extract of the generated code is shown in Listing 23-12 (where we've removed the error handling and changed a few comments for clarity).

Listing 23-12 The Generated Class to Connect to the Maths Web Service

```
'Dimensioning private class variables.

'The sc_Maths object handles all the communication
Private sc_Maths As SoapClient30

'These constants reflect the selections in the dialog,
'and tell the class where to connect to
Private Const c_WSDL_URL As String = _
    "http://localhost/ProExcelDev/Maths.asmx?wsdl"

Private Const c_SERVICE As String = "Maths"
Private Const c_PORT As String = "MathsSoap"
Private Const c_SERVICE_NAMESPACE As String = _
    "http://tempuri.org/ProExcelDev/Maths"

Private Sub Class_Initialize()

  Dim str_WSML As String
  str_WSML = ""

  Set sc_Maths = New SoapClient30

  'Initialize the connection to the Web service
  sc_Maths.MSSoapInit2 c_WSDL_URL, str_WSML, c_SERVICE, _
      c_PORT, c_SERVICE_NAMESPACE

  sc_Maths.ConnectorProperty("ProxyServer") = "<CURRENT_USER>"
  sc_Maths.ConnectorProperty("EnableAutoProxy") = True

End Sub

Private Sub Class_Terminate()
  Set sc_Maths = Nothing
End Sub
```

```
'Wrapper for the AddTwo function in our Web service
Public Function wsm_AddTwo(ByVal dbl_d1 As Double, _
    ByVal dbl_d2 As Double) As Double

  wsm_AddTwo = sc_Maths.AddTwo(dbl_d1, dbl_d2)

End Function

'Wrapper for the MultipleTwo function in our Web service
Public Function wsm_MultiplyTwo(ByVal dbl_d1 As Double, _
    ByVal dbl_d2 As Double) As Double

  wsm_MultiplyTwo = sc_Maths.MultiplyTwo(dbl_d1, dbl_d2)

End Function
```

The class module is generated from the selections we made in the Web Services Toolkit dialog. The class uses a module-level variable called sc_Maths to hold a reference to a SoapClient30 object, which does all the communication with the Web service for us. The constants at the top of the module specify the location of the Web service, its name and so on, which are used in the Class_Initialize event to connect to the service. The rest of the class contains wrappers for each function exposed by our Web service, each of them having the prefix wsm_, for Web service method. As this is just a normal class module, we can, of course, change the names to anything we want, add more properties, and so forth.

To use the Web service from our VB code, we create an instance of the class and call the wrapper functions, as shown in Listing 23-13.

Listing 23-13 Using the Maths Web Service

```
Sub Add1And2()

  Dim clsMaths As clsws_Maths

  Set clsMaths = New clsws_Maths

  MsgBox "1 + 2 = " & clsMaths.wsm_AddTwo(1, 2)

End Sub
```

We could, of course, put the same code in a standard VBA user-defined function and call it from the worksheet, so if, say, a proprietary pricing function has been exposed as a Web service, we can now use it within our worksheets!

Practical Example

The examples used to explain XML and Web services were obviously very simple so we could focus on the technology and how to use it, particularly with the explanation of Web services. In the practical example for this chapter, we create a rather more complex Web service to act as an interface between our PETRAS timesheet add-in and the central database used to store the static information of consultants, clients and projects and submitted timesheet data. By using the Web service, our consultants can now access the time sheet information over the Internet, enabling them to submit their timesheets from anywhere in the world.

The data sent between the Web service and the add-in will be done using XML, which makes it extremely easy to connect to the database and enables us to validate the data structure at each end of the communication. Specifically, the following data will be passed between the Web service and the add-in:

- At startup, the add-in will retrieve some XML containing the static lists of consultants, clients, projects and activities, by calling the Web service's GetStaticData function.
- When the user clicks the *Post Timesheet Data* button, the add-in will generate some XML to contain the timesheet data and send it to the Web service, which will store it in the central database.

PETRAS Web Service

The new PETRAS Web service has been written using Visual Basic.NET, connecting to the same Access database we introduced in *Chapter 13 — Programming with Databases*, but this time using ADO.NET. Visual Studio.NET creates numerous files for a Web service. The interesting files are:

- **StaticData.XSD**, containing the XSD file for the XML returned by the GetStaticData function

- **TimeSheet.XSD**, containing the XSD file for the XML passed to the StoreTimeSheet function
- **PETRAS.asmx**, containing the code for the Web service

The Web service provides the following two functions:

- **GetStaticData**, which returns an XML data set containing all the lists of consultants, activities, clients and projects. An example of the XML returned is shown in Listing 23-14. Notice that the Project elements for a client are nested inside the Client element.
- **StoreTimeSheet**, which is passed an XML data set containing the timesheet data entered into the Excel sheet, writes the data to the BillableHours table of the Access database and returns a confirmation message that includes the number of rows inserted. An example of the XML passed is shown in Listing 23-15.

Listing 23-14 Example XML Output from the GetStaticData Function

```
<StaticData xmlns="http://www.oaltd.co.uk/PETRASWeb/StaticData">
  <Consultant>
    <ID>1</ID>
    <Name>Rob Bovey</Name>
  </Consultant>
  <Consultant>
    <ID>2</ID>
    <Name>Stephen Bullen</Name>
  </Consultant>
  <Activity>
    <ID>1</ID>
    <Name>General Programming</Name>
  </Activity>
  <Activity>
    <ID>2</ID>
    <Name>Phone Conference</Name>
  </Activity>
  <Client>
    <ID>1</ID>
    <Name>Big Auto Corp.</Name>
    <Project>
      <ID>1</ID>
      <Name>BAC 1</Name>
```

```
    </Project>
    <Project>
      <ID>2</ID>
      <Name>BAC 2</Name>
    </Project>
  </Client>
</StaticData>
```

Listing 23-15 Example XML Passed to the StoreTimeSheet Function

```
<TimeSheet xmlns="http://www.oaltd.co.uk/PETRASWeb/TimeSheet">
  <Consultant>
    <ID>2</ID>
    <Name>Stephen Bullen</Name>
  </Consultant>
  <WeekEnding>2004-07-04</WeekEnding>
  <BillableHours>
    <DateWorked>2004-07-01</DateWorked>
    <ProjectID>2</ProjectID>
    <ActivityID>1</ActivityID>
    <Hours>6.75</Hours>
  </BillableHours>
  <BillableHours>
    <DateWorked>2004-07-02</DateWorked>
    <ProjectID>2</ProjectID>
    <ActivityID>1</ActivityID>
    <Hours>7.5</Hours>
  </BillableHours>
</TimeSheet>
```

All of the data connectivity for the Web service is set up using Visual Studio's wizards, resulting in the following objects that can be seen on the Web service's "Design" page:

- **conPETRASDbConnection**—An OleDbConnection used to define the connection to the Access database.
- **daConsultants, daActivities, daClients and daProjects**— OleDbDataAdapters, used to retrieve the list of consultants, activities, clients and projects from the database.

- **cmDeleteTime**—An OleDbCommand to delete timesheet records from the database. When a timesheet is submitted, any previous records for the same consultant and period are deleted.
- **cmInsertTime**—An OleDbCommand to insert timesheet records into the database.

When we include an XSD file in a Visual Studio.NET project, we have the option of automatically creating a DataSet from the schema. After we've done that, we can map the elements in our schema to fields in a DataAdapter, in much the same way that Excel 2003 enables us to map elements to worksheet cells. In our Web service, each section of the schema is mapped to its own DataAdapter. (For example, the <ID> and <Name> in the <Consultant> elements in the XSD are mapped to the ConsultantID and Name fields in the daConsultants DataAdapter.) Having mapped everything in our StaticData schema to the DataAdapters, we can retrieve the XML for all our static lists by telling each of the DataAdapters to fill their part of the schema, then reading the XML from the data set, as shown in the code for the GetStaticData function in Listing 23-16.

Listing 23-16 The GetStaticText Function

```
<WebMethod(Description:="Provides all the static data " & _
    for the PETRAS Time Sheet")> _
Public Function GetStaticData() As String

  'Declare an instance of our StaticData data set,
  'which was generated by .NET from the XSD
  Dim dsStatic As New StaticData

  'Set the connection string of our connection object
  Me.conPETRASDbConnection.ConnectionString = _
    "Provider=""Microsoft.Jet.OLEDB.4.0"";Data Source=""" & _
    msDATABASE & """;User ID=Admin;Password=;"

  'Clear the data set
  dsStatic.Clear()

  'Fill each section of the data set
  daConsultants.Fill(dsStatic)
  daActivities.Fill(dsStatic)
  daClients.Fill(dsStatic)
```

```
daProjects.Fill(dsStatic)

'Return the resulting XML
Return dsStatic.GetXML

End Function
```

The DataSet created from our XSD is a strongly typed object that enables us to treat our data as if it were a full object model—so each of our XML complexType elements become objects, our repeating elements become collections and our simple element types become properties. We are then able to use the names of our data types directly in our code, such as iterating through all the <BillableHours> elements of the timesheet table:

```
Dim bhRow As PETRASTimeSheet.BillableHoursRow
For Each bhRow In dsTimeSheet.BillableHours.Rows
```

Listing 23-17 shows the code for the StoreTimeSheet function, with the error handling removed for clarity.

Listing 23-17 The StoreTimeSheet Function

```
<WebMethod(Description:="Writes time sheet data to the " & _
    "central database")> _
Public Function StoreTimeSheet(ByVal sTimesheet As String) _
    As String

  Dim dsTimeSheet As New PETRASTimeSheet
  Dim iConsultant As Integer
  Dim dtWeekEnd As Date
  Dim bhRow As PETRASTimeSheet.BillableHoursRow

  'Read the text into the data set and validate it
  dsTimeSheet.ReadXML(New System.IO.StringReader(sTimesheet))

  'Get the consultant ID and week ending
  iConsultant = dsTimeSheet.Consultant(0).ID
  dtWeekEnd = dsTimeSheet.TimeSheet(0).WeekEnding

  'Open the database connection
  conPETRASDbConnection.ConnectionString = _
```

```
      "Provider=""Microsoft.Jet.OLEDB.4.0"";Data Source=""" _
      & msDATABASE & """;User ID=Admin;Password=;"

conPETRASDbConnection.Open()

'Clear any existing data for this consultant and week
With cmDeleteTime
   .Parameters("prmConsultantID").Value = iConsultant
   .Parameters("prmWeekStart").Value = dtWeekEnd.AddDays(-6)
   .Parameters("prmWeekEnd").Value = dtWeekEnd
   .ExecuteNonQuery()
End With

'Loop through the billable hours, adding them to the table
With cmInsertTime
   .Parameters("prmConsultantID").Value = iConsultant

   'We can treat our data like objects!
   For Each bhRow In dsTimeSheet.BillableHours.Rows
      .Parameters("prmDateWorked").Value = bhRow.DateWorked
      .Parameters("prmProjectID").Value = bhRow.ProjectID
      .Parameters("prmActivityID").Value = bhRow.ActivityID
      .Parameters("prmHours").Value = bhRow.Hours
      .ExecuteNonQuery()
   Next
End With

'Close the connection when we're done
conPETRASDbConnection.Close()

'Return an OK message, with the number of rows inserted
Return "OK:" & dsTimeSheet.BillableHours.Rows.Count & _
   " row(s) inserted for " & dsTimeSheet.Consultant(0).Name

End Function
```

Note that the Web service we have created for this book is for demonstration purposes only and should not be used in a production environment. We have not included any security checks in our connectivity, nor any data validation checks (other than that provided by the XML schema), so anyone who can connect to the Web service could insert records into our timesheet database (assuming they can work out the XML schema we're using).

PETRAS Timesheet

The PETRAS timesheet add-in has been changed for this chapter to receive data from and send data to the new Web service, instead of connecting directly to the central database across the network. To maintain compatibility with Excel 2000 onward, we do not use Excel 2003's XML handling features, instead using the MSXML object library directly to do the validating and parsing of the XML data we receive from the Web service. Similarly, we construct the XML containing our timesheet information using VBA. The communication between the add-in and the Web service is done using classes generated using the Web Services Toolkit.

Because we're no longer connecting directly to the database, we no longer need the Browse for Database feature, which has been replaced by a simple input box to provide the URL of the PETRAS Web service (in case we have to deploy it to a different server).

Table 23-1 details the changes required to use the Web service.

Table 23-1 Changes to the PETRAS Timesheet Add-in for Chapter 23

Module	Procedure	Change
wksCommandBars		Renamed menu items to refer to the Web service instead of the database.
MEntryPoints	PostTimeEntriesToWebService	Renamed to refer to Web service. Modified to create XML string instead of UDT and submit to Web service.
MEntryPoints	SpecifyWebServiceLocation	Renamed to refer to Web service. Modified to use an input box to specify the Web service URL instead of a folder.
MBrowseForFolder		Removed module as it is no longer required.
CPetrasWeb (new class)		Class created by the Web Service Toolkit to handle the connection to the PETRAS Web service.

Table 23-1 Changes to the PETRAS Timesheet Add-in for Chapter 23 (*cont.*)

Module	Procedure	Change
MOpenClose		Remove calls to create and destroy the database connection.
MDataAccess		Modified to communicate with the Web service (via the CPetrasWeb class) instead of the database, importing the XML using VBA.
MDataAccess	bLoadInitialData	Rewritten to retrieve the data from the XML obtained from the Web service and populate the static data worksheet.

The most interesting changes to the PETRAS timesheet add-in are in the MDataAccess.bLoadInitialData and MEntryPoints.PostTimeEntries ToWebService procedures. Part of the bLoadInitialData routine is shown in Listing 23-18, showing the VBA to extract the Consultant data from the XML and populate the static data sheet. Using the MSXML library to parse the XML enables us to navigate through our data using syntax very similar to navigating an object library:

Listing 23-18 Populating the Consultant List from GetStaticData

```
'An object to parse the XML from GetStaticData
Dim xmlParser As MSXML2.DOMDocument40

'Objects use to navigate around the XML
Dim xeParent As MSXML2.IXMLDOMElement

'Create an instance of the Web service connection
Set clsPetrasWeb = New CPetrasWeb

'Initialise the URL
clsPetrasWeb.WebServiceURL = GetSetting(gsREG_APP, _
    gsREG_SECTION, gsREG_KEY, clsPetrasWeb.WebServiceURL)
```

```
'Connect to the Web service
clsPetrasWeb.Connect

'Get the XML representing the static lists
sXML = clsPetrasWeb.GetStaticData

'Load the XML into the MSXML parser
Set xmlParser = New MSXML2.DOMDocument30
xmlParser.LoadXml sXML

'Use XPath expressions to find our elements
xmlParser.SetProperty "SelectionLanguage", "XPath"

'Specify the default namespace to look for, giving it
'the alias 'sd' to use in our element names
xmlParser.SetProperty "SelectionNamespaces", _
    "xmlns:sd=""http://www.oaltd.co.uk/PETRASWeb/StaticData"""

' Load each of the program data lists.
' Consultants
With wksProgData.Range(gsRNG_CONSULT_TOP)

  'Remove any existing consultants
  .CurrentRegion.Offset(1, 0).ClearContents
  lItem = 1

  'Loop through all the Consultant elements in the XML
  'Equivalent to:  For Each oConsultant in Consultants
  For Each xeParent In xmlParser.selectNodes( _
      "sd:StaticData/sd:Consultant")

    lItem = lItem + 1

    'Store the consultant name and ID
    'Equivalent to:  Cell.Value = oConsultant.Name
    .Cells(lItem, 1).Value = xeParent.selectSingleNode( _
        "sd:Name").nodeTypedValue

    .Cells(lItem, 2).Value = CLng(xeParent.selectSingleNode( _
        "sd:ID").nodeTypedValue)
  Next
End With
```

We also use the MSXML library to create our XML in the PostTimeEntriesToWebService procedure, as shown in Listing 23-19.

Listing 23-19 Building the XML to Submit to the Web Service

```
Public Sub PostTimeEntriesToWebService()

  Dim rngCell As Range
  Dim rngTable As Range
  Dim domXML As MSXML2.DOMDocument

  Set rngTable = wksSheet.Range(gsRNG_BILLABLE_HOURS)

  'Create a new XML document
  Set domXML = New MSXML2.DOMDocument

  'Create the root element <TimeSheet>
  Set domXML.documentElement = _
      NewElement(domXML, "TimeSheet")

  With domXML.documentElement

    'Add the <Consultant> element
    With .appendChild(NewElement(domXML, "Consultant"))

      'Add the Consultant's ID and Name elements and values
      .appendChild(NewElement(domXML, "ID")) _
        .nodeTypedValue = rngTable.Cells(1, 1).Value

      .appendChild(NewElement(domXML, "Name")) _
        .nodeTypedValue = wksSheet.Range("inpEmployee").Value
    End With

    'Add the WeekEnding element and value
    .appendChild(NewElement(domXML, "WeekEnding")) _
      .nodeTypedValue = Format( _
      wksSheet.Range("inpWeekEnding").Value, "yyyy-mm-dd")

    ' Loop each entry in the time sheet and add it to the XML
    For Each rngCell In rngTable

      'Add a <BillableHours> element
```

```
        With .appendChild(NewElement(domXML, "BillableHours"))

            'Add the elements for a BillableHours record
            .appendChild(NewElement(domXML, "DateWorked")) _
                  .nodeTypedValue = Format(_
                  rngCell.Offset(0, 1).Value, "yyyy-mm-dd")

            .appendChild(NewElement(domXML, "ProjectID")) _
                  .nodeTypedValue = rngCell.Offset(0, 2).Value

            .appendChild(NewElement(domXML, "ActivityID")) _
                  .nodeTypedValue = rngCell.Offset(0, 3).Value

            .appendChild(NewElement(domXML, "Hours")) _
                  .nodeTypedValue = _
                  Trim$(Str$(rngCell.Offset(0, 4).Value))
        End With
    Next rngCell
  End With

  'Submit the XML to the Web service
  bSubmitXML domXML.XML

  'etc.

End Sub


' Create a new element with our namespace
Private Function NewElement( _
      ByRef domXML As MSXML2.DOMDocument, _
      ByVal sElementName As String) As IXMLDOMNode

  Const sNS As String = _
        "http://www.oaltd.co.uk/PETRASWeb/TimeSheet"

  Set NewElement = domXML.createNode(NODE_ELEMENT, _
      sElementName, sNS)

End Function
```

PETRAS Reporting

The PETRAS reporting application has not changed for this chapter, because it is still retrieving its data from the same database as before.

Conclusion

By representing our data as XML, we are able to define its structure, content, data types and other rules and validate any data file against those rules before we attempt to process it. This can greatly increase the robustness of our data processing code, while also reducing its complexity and thereby making it much easier to maintain.

XML adds names, data types and hierarchies to our data, enabling us to think of our data in terms of individual elements and the data they contain, in the same way that class modules allow us to think of our application in terms of objects and their properties and methods. Indeed, Visual Studio.NET displays XML data in IntelliSense lists and so on, in almost the same way as it does the content of object libraries.

Excel 2003's XML-handling features can perform most of the processing we would otherwise have to code, including checking for completeness and consistency and removing unwanted data such as header and footer records (by simply not mapping that data to worksheet cells).

Web services are programs running on Web servers that expose the functions they contain for use over the Internet. They can be used to provide access to proprietary financial models, company data and so forth without having to expose the code for the model, the database connection information or any other details that should be kept secret. By using the Office Web Services Toolkit, we can use the features provided by Web services from within our VBA code and from within our worksheets (via VBA user-defined functions).

We can combine Excel 2003's use of XML with the ability to connect to Web services to create an entirely new breed of Excel application—that of the rich client of a distributed, Web-based application, such as this final iteration of our Professional Excel Timesheet Reporting and Analysis System.

Unfortunately, we cannot use Web services directly from our worksheets (we need some VBA to glue them together), nor can we expose the financial models in our worksheets as Web services for others to use (because Excel is not designed as a server product). Excel 2003 is so close to achieving both those, it wouldn't surprise us to see a *Web Services* button on the *Tools > Add-ins* dialog and a *File > Save as Web Service* menu in a future version.

Providing Help, Securing, Packaging and Distributing

The final step in developing an Excel-based application is preparing it for release to our users. This includes creating a help file and adding code to display it from our application, securing the application to prevent accidental and/or malicious changes, limiting access to features by checking the user's network group memberships and avoiding the display of the macro security warning dialogs. Finally, we need to decide upon a mechanism for installing the application on our users' machines. We might also want to include features within our application to easily deploy updates.

Providing Help

From the very start of our project, we should be thinking about how to provide assistance to our users. For simple add-ins, this can take the form of a set of instructions displayed at the bottom of an About dialog, or a separate text file or Word document distributed with the add-in. For more complex add-ins and dictator applications, we should consider providing a help file. Doing so requires us to add code throughout the application to display pages from the help file as well as writing the help text.

To demonstrate how to create a help file and display it from our application, we use the Microsoft HTML Help Workshop to create a very simple help file for our PETRAS reporting application. The HTML Help Workshop is a fairly rudimentary tool, best used for simple help files. For large and/or complex help files, we recommend you use a third-party application, such as Macromedia's RoboHelp (www.robohelp.com) or Component One's Doc-to-Help (http://www.doctohelp.com/products.aspx?ProductCode=1&ProductID=122).

Overview

We create each page of an HTML help file as a separate HTML file and give it a code word, known as a *topic*. We can give it any name we like, but it's good practice to use a naming convention to help us quickly and easily identify each topic. For example, we might use the name htFrmActivities to denote the help topic for a userform used to maintain a list of activities. The HTML Help Workshop is used to create and maintain a *help project* file, which contains configuration information and a list of the topics to include in the help file. After all the help content has been written, the HTML Help Workshop is used to compile the individual HTML files into a single HTML help file (with an extension of *.chm*) that we distribute with our application. To display help pages from Excel, we have to give each topic a unique number. The mapping between topic names and numbers is also stored in the help project file.

Getting Started

If you don't already have the HTML Help Workshop installed, you can download it from http://go.microsoft.com/fwlink/?LinkId=14188. To produce a compiled skeleton help file, you need to follow a number of steps:

1. Create a help project file.
2. Update the project options.
3. Create an introductory HTML file.
4. Create a simple HTML file to display "Sorry, there is no help available for this topic."
5. Create a list of topics, with each topic initially referring to the above file.
6. Create a list that maps each topic to a numeric ID.
7. Compile the project.

Create a Help Project File

To create a new help project, start the HTML Help Workshop, click *File > New*, select *Project* from the list and click OK to launch the New Project Wizard. We're not converting an old help project, so skip over Step 1. In Step 2, type in or select a location and name for the help project file, such as *C:\PETRAS\Help\PETRAS.hhp* (where the *C:\PETRAS\Help* directory must already exist). Ideally, this should be in an empty directory, because we'll be adding lots of files later. By default, the name we give to the help project file will be used for the compiled help file, but we can change it later if we want. We don't have any existing files to include, so skip Step 3 and click Finish. We end up with a help project similar to Figure 24-1.

Figure 24-1 The HTML Help Project Window

Update the Project Options

Click the *Change project options* button shown in Figure 24-2 to set the initial project options.

In the *General* tab of the Options dialog, give our help file the title of PETRAS Reporting Application. In the *Files* tab, type in a Contents filename of Contents.hhc, an Index filename of Index.hhk and tick both check boxes. By doing this, the Help Workshop will automatically populate a table of contents and an index file for us when the project is compiled. Set the *Maximum head level* to 1, which tells the compiler to create TOC entries from all the <H1> header tags we include in our HTML files. In the Compiler tab, tick the *Compile full-text search information*, to add a Search tab to the help file. Click OK to close the Options dialog.

To create the table of contents and index files, click the *Contents* and *Index* tabs. With each tab, ignore the error message that the file can't be found and let the Help Workshop create new files. Give them the names Contents.hhc and Index.hhk.

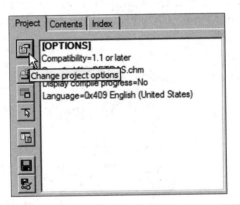

Figure 24-2 The Change Project Options Button

Create an Introductory HTML File

To create the pages of the help file, we can use any application that will generate HTML files, such as FrontPage, Word, Notepad or the HTML Workshop itself. We can create a simple introductory page within the HTML Workshop, so click *File > New > HTML File* and give it a title of Introduction. Just below the <BODY> tag, type in the following:

```
<H1>Introduction</H1>
```

```
This is the help file for the PETRAS reporting application.
```

Save the file as *C:\PETRAS\Help\htIntro.htm*. After creating the file, we need to include it in our help project. Click the *Add/Remove topic files* button shown in Figure 24-3, click the *Add* button and select the htIntro.htm file.

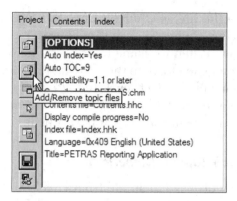

Figure 24-3 The Add/Remove Topic Files Button

Create a "No Help Available" Topic File

When we first set up the help file, we'll point every topic to the same help page, which will display a simple "No Help Available" message. To create the page, add a new HTML file and type the following text after the <BODY> tag:

```
Sorry, there is no help available for this topic.
```

Save the file as htNoHelp.htm and use the *Add/Remove topic files* button to add it to our project.

Create a List of Topics

We can create a skeleton help file containing just a few topics and add to it as we develop our application. Click *File > New > Text* to create a blank text file and type in the list of topics shown in Listing 24-1, with each one referring to the htNoHelp.htm file.

Listing 24-1 The PETRAS Help File Topic List

```
htNoHelp=htNoHelp.htm            ;The No Help page
htFrmActivities=htNoHelp.htm     ;The Activities userform
htFrmConsultants=htNoHelp.htm    ;The Consultants userform
htFrmClients=htNoHelp.htm        ;The Clients/Projects userform
htFrmExtractData=htNoHelp.htm    ;The Extract Data userform
```

Save the file as *C:\PETRAS\Help\TopicToFile.h*. Each time we add a form to our application, we should give it a topic name and add the topic to this list. When we come to write the help file content, we can edit this list to point each topic to the correct HTML file. To include the list of topics in our help project, click the *HtmlHelp API information* button (the fourth of the Project buttons), select the *Alias* tab, click the *Include* button and type in the filename of TopicToFile.h.

Give Each Topic a Numeric ID

When we display a help file from Excel, we have to use numeric IDs for our help topics. We map each topic to an ID in the same way we map them to HTML files. Click *File > New > Text* to create another text file and type in the list of mappings shown in Listing 24-2.

Listing 24-2 The PETRAS Help File Topic IDs

```
#define htNoHelp          100   //The No Help page
#define htFrmActivities   101   //The Activities userform
#define htFrmConsultants  102   //The Consultants userform
#define htFrmClients      103   //The Clients/Projects userform
#define htFrmExtractData  104   //The Extract Data userform
```

We're actually creating a C-style header file, defining these topic names as constants using the #define directive. The // is used to indicate the start of a comment. Save the file as *C:\PETRAS\Help\TopicToID.h*. Again, each time we add a new feature to our application we should give it a topic ID and add the topic name and ID to this list. We also need to include this file in our help project, by clicking the *HtmlHelp API information* button, selecting the *Map* tab, clicking the *Header file* button and typing in the filename of TopicToID.h.

Compile the Project

Click *File > Compile* to create the PETRAS.chm help file and then click *View > Compiled File* to display it. If all went well, you should see a window similar to Figure 24-4.

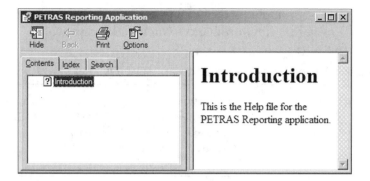

Figure 24-4 The PETRAS Reporting Skeleton Help File

Writing Content

The best recommendation we can give about writing help content is this: ***Don't write it yourself***. As the developer of the application, you know far too much about its inner workings to be able to explain it at a level that an average user can understand. The best person to write the help content is a user representative, if you have one. He will be able to explain the application in business terms, including how it should be used within the business environment. When writing the content, there are two things a user representative needs to do to allow the Help Workshop to automatically generate the Table of Contents and Index files.

Table of Contents

In the *Files* tab of the project's Options dialog, we can specify the *Maximum head level* to use when automatically creating the table of contents. That number corresponds to the <Hn> heading styles used in the HTML files. If Word is being used to write the help content, the number corresponds to Word's heading styles. If these tags are used consistently throughout all the help files, the table of contents can be generated without any effort on our part.

Index

In the *Files* tab of the project's Options dialog, we can tick the *Include keywords from HTML files* box. The content author can then include the keywords for the index within the source HTML file. To do so, the author needs to include the <Object> tag shown in Listing 24-3, replacing Keyword1, Keyword2 and so on with his own words.

Listing 24-3 Adding Index Keywords to an HTML File

```
<Object type="application/x-oleobject"
        classid="clsid:1e2a7bd0-dab9-11d0-b93a-00c04fc99f9e">
        <param name="Keyword" value="Keyword1">
        <param name="Keyword" value="Keyword2">
</Object>
```

Displaying Help from VBA

When we display a help topic from VBA, we have to use the numeric topic IDs rather than the names. Instead of scattering these "magic numbers" throughout our code, it is a very good idea to expose them in an enumeration, such as the one shown in Listing 24-4.

Listing 24-4 Enumeration for the Help Topic IDs

```
Public Enum pxlHelpTopics
      htNoHelp = 100                 'Generic 'No Help Available'
      htFrmActivities = 101          'The Activities userform
      htFrmConsultants = 102         'The Consultants userform
      htFrmClients = 103             'The Clients/Projects userform
      htFrmExtractData = 104         'The Extract Data userform
End Enum
```

We can then use the enumeration members instead of the topic IDs. For example, the code in Listing 24-5 can be used to display a message box with a Help button that will show our help file when clicked.

Listing 24-5 Displaying a Help File from a MsgBox

```
Sub ShowAMessage()

    Dim sMessage As String
    Dim sHelpFile As String

    sHelpFile = ThisWorkbook.Path & "\petras.chm"
```

```
sMessage = "The activity name is already being used."

MsgBox sMessage, vbOKOnly + vbMsgBoxHelpButton, _
        "Add Activity", sHelpFile, htFrmActivities

End Sub
```

Other than using the MsgBox's additional arguments, the best way to display a help file from VBA is to call directly into the HHCtrl.ocx file, using the HtmlHelp API function. Although it is possible to use Application.Help to display a custom help file, it usually mixes our help file with Excel's. In Listing 24-6, we've wrapped the call in a generic ShowHelp procedure, to verify that the help file exists and tidily handle missing topic IDs.

Listing 24-6 Displaying a Help File by Calling the HHCtrl.ocx

```
Declare Function HtmlHelp Lib "HHCtrl.ocx" _
    Alias "HtmlHelpA" (ByVal hwndCaller As Long, _
    ByVal pszFile As String, ByVal uCommand As Long, _
    ByVal dwData As Long) As Long

Const HH_DISPLAY_TOPIC = &H0
Const HH_HELP_CONTEXT = &HF

'Show a topic of a help file
Sub ShowHelp(ByVal uTopicID As pxlHelpTopics)

    Dim sHelpFile As String
    Dim sCheckFile As String
    Dim lResult As Long

    'Locate the help file
    sHelpFile = ThisWorkbook.Path & "\PETRAS.chm"

    'Check the help file exists
    On Error Resume Next
    sCheckFile = Dir(sHelpFile)
    On Error GoTo 0

    If Len(sCheckFile) > 0 Then
```

```
            'Try to show the requested help topic
            lResult = HtmlHelp(0, sHelpFile, HH_HELP_CONTEXT, _
                                uTopicID)

            If lResult = 0 Then
                'If it failed, try to show the 'No Help' topic
                lResult = HtmlHelp(0, sHelpFile, HH_HELP_CONTEXT, _
                                    htNoHelp)
            End If
        End If

        'If we couldn't find the help file, or failed to show it,
        'display a message in VBA.
        If lResult = 0 Then
            MsgBox "No help is available at this time.", _
                    vbOKOnly, "PETRAS Reporting"
        End If

End Sub
```

We should call this procedure whenever we want to display a help topic, such as in the Click event handler of a form's Help button, shown in Listing 24-7. Using the enumeration member helps to ensure we're showing the correct topic for the form.

Listing 24-7 Using the ShowHelp Procedure from a Form's Help Button

```
Private Sub cmdHelp_Click()
    ShowHelp htFrmActivities
End Sub
```

Securing

Excel Security

Excel is not secure and cannot be made totally secure. In other words, there is no way to prevent the determined hacker from gaining access to our worksheets, formulas and VBA code. Worksheets can be unprotected with a two-character password. VBProject passwords can be removed by modifying the binary file. The only aspect of Excel's security that can be considered secure is the workbook file password, but we can't use that in our applications because our users need to be able to open our workbooks to use them! Even if we could use them, the determined hacker can use GetObject to get a reference to the instance of Excel running our application and use automation to save all our workbooks without passwords.

The best we can do with Excel's security is prevent accidental damage and discourage the casual hacker, which we do by password-protecting our worksheets, workbook structure, workbook files and the VBA Projects.

We can improve the security of our application through the use of a "front-loader" workbook. This is the only workbook file that we do not password-protect and is therefore the only workbook that our users can open. The front-loader workbook then opens the rest of the workbooks used in our application, supplying the passwords. If the user holds down the Shift key while opening the front-loader workbook, the code contained within it won't run so our application won't be loaded and cannot be hacked. The only way in is to break into the front-loader's VB Project, read the passwords from there and then open our application workbooks. Unfortunately, tools to do exactly that are readily available on the Internet.

The only way to really secure our code is to move it outside of Excel, typically into Visual Basic 6, as described in *Chapter 20 — Combining Excel and Visual Basic 6*. We can use a front-loader VB6 EXE to start Excel and open our password-protected application workbooks, keeping the passwords hidden within the compiled VB6 code. For strongest security, the passwords should not be stored as plain text in the program, but in an encoded form that is run through a decoding function when used. Once started, we can use VB6 DLLs for most of our application's features, so our workbooks contain only enough VBA to instantiate the DLL and call its procedures.

Checking Network Groups

It's a common requirement for us to restrict access to parts of our applications depending on the user's network group membership. For example, we might want to allow only people in the Auditors group to be able to run certain reports. We can find this information from the Windows Script Networking and Active Directory Service Interfaces object libraries, as shown in Listing 24-8. We need to set references to these object libraries, which are listed in the *Tools > References* dialog as "Windows Script Host Object Model" and "Active DS Type Library."

Listing 24-8 Checking Network Group Membership

```
'Define a UDT to hold user login information
Public Type LOGON_INFO
  ComputerName As String
  UserName As String
  Domain As String
  Groups As String
End Type

'Retrieve user's login information
'Suggested by Jake Marx, Excel MVP
Public Function GetUserInfo() As LOGON_INFO

  'Use a static variable, so we only retrieve the
  'information once
  Static uLogonInfo As LOGON_INFO

  'Requires a reference to
  '"Windows Script Host Object Model"
  Dim wshNetwork As IWshRuntimeLibrary.wshNetwork

  'Requires a reference to "Active DS Type Library"
  Dim adsUser As ActiveDs.IADsUser
  Dim adsGroup As ActiveDs.IADsGroup

  'Fill the logon info UDT if not already set
  If Len(uLogonInfo.UserName) = 0 Then

    'Get the username and domain from Windows Scripting
    Set wshNetwork = New IWshRuntimeLibrary.wshNetwork
    With wshNetwork
      uLogonInfo.ComputerName = .ComputerName
      uLogonInfo.UserName = .UserName
      uLogonInfo.Domain = .UserDomain
    End With

    'Use the domain/username to get a list of groups from
    'Windows Active Directory Services
    Set adsUser = GetObject("WinNT://" & uLogonInfo.Domain & _
                   "/" & uLogonInfo.UserName & ",user")

    'Create a concatenated string of groups,
```

```
    'separated by commas
    For Each adsGroup In adsUser.Groups
      uLogonInfo.Groups = uLogonInfo.Groups & _
                            adsGroup.ADsPath & ","
    Next
  End If

  'Return the login information
  GetUserInfo = uLogonInfo

End Function

'Function to check if the current user is in the
'Auditors group
Function IsAuditor() As Boolean
  IsAuditor = InStr(1, GetUserInfo.Groups, _
    "/Domain/Auditors,", vbTextCompare) > 0
End Function
```

Note that we're storing the fully qualified ADsPath for the group, which includes both the domain name and the group name, then checking for the domain and group in the IsAuditor function. This prevents a malicious user creating a bogus Auditors group on their machine, which would have passed a test based on just the group name. Even using the domain/group style leaves a possible security hole, because our user could rename his computer to be the same as the domain name. To be totally sure, we should store and check the groups' GUIDs instead of their names.

Macro Security and Digital Signatures

Whenever we manually open a workbook that contains VBA code, Excel checks the macro security settings (set under the *Tools > Macro > Security* menu) and either enables or disables any VBA code contained within the workbook, depending on the security level, the way in which the file is opened, whether the VBA code has been digitally signed and whether the signature has been trusted, summarized in Table 24-1.

Some of the details are a little different if the code has been signed, but the signature is invalid or has expired, or if the add-in is being opened using *Tools > Add-ins* instead of *File > Open* and the *Trust all installed add-ins and templates* option in the Macro Security dialog has been ticked. The exact details can be found by searching for "macro security levels" in Excel's help.

Table 24-1 Summary of Excel's Macro Security Behavior

Security Level	Unsigned	Signed, but Untrusted	Signed and Trusted
Low	Allows code to run without prompting	Allows code to run without prompting	Allows code to run without prompting
Medium	Prompts us whether to run the code	Prompts us whether to run the code and allows us to trust the signature	Allows code to run without prompting
High	Does not run the code	Prompts us whether to trust the signature and only runs the code if we choose to trust it	Allows code to run without prompting
Very High (*new to Excel 2003*)	Does not run the code	Does not run the code	Only runs code in installed add-ins and templates, and only if that option is enabled

So if we want our code to run with the strictest settings, we have to sign it with a digital signature, purchased from a certificate authority such as VeriSign (www.verisign.com) or Thawte (www.thawte.com). Digital signatures are not cheap and have to be renewed annually. At the time of writing, they cost $200 per annum from Thawte.

If our workbook is opened after the certificate has expired (usually one year), Excel will treat it as if it were unsigned (although the prompts differ slightly). This can be avoided by telling Excel to time stamp the signing of the file. When a signed-and-time-stamped file is opened, Excel can see that the file was signed while the digital signature was valid, so will allow the code to run. We tell Excel to time stamp the signature by adding the following registry entries to *HKEY_CURRENT_USER\Software\ Microsoft\VBA\Security* (creating that key if it doesn't exist):

```
TimeStampURL =
http://timestamp.verisign.com/scripts/timstamp.dll
TimeStampRetryCount = 1
TimeStampRetryDelay = 2
```

Digital signatures also provide a level of assurance to the developer. The signature is applied whenever the VBA code is changed and the file is saved. If the digital signature private key is not installed, the signature will be removed from the file. This gives us a foolproof way of identifying whether our code has been tampered with—it won't be signed with our digital signature.

Microsoft has released a very good white paper about digital signatures and macro security, which can be downloaded from the following site:

```
http://www.microsoft.com/downloads/details.aspx?FamilyID=7e3eab1f-b313-
44f4-8900-3399abb2001d
```

Alternatives to Digital Signatures

In practice, very few Excel developers digitally sign their workbooks. Most users have the *Trust all installed add-ins and templates* check box ticked in the Macro Security dialog, which means that add-ins opened using the *Tools > Add-ins* dialog will run without being signed (unless Macro Security is set to Very High in Excel 2003). Workbooks and add-ins opened using *File > Open* will still display the macro security warnings.

For dictator applications, we can make use of the fact that the macro security checks are not done when workbooks are opened through the object model. *Chapter 20 — Combining Excel and Visual Basic 6* shows how to create and use a front-loader VB6 EXE to start Excel and open our workbooks without triggering the macro security checks.

Ultimately, the need to digitally sign our code depends on the users' security settings, the client's security policies and our own professionalism. Using a digital signature is the only sure way to have our code run without displaying a macro security prompt.

Packaging

For simple single-workbook applications, we can just e-mail the workbook to our users and ask them to open it. For more complex applications, we may need to install templates, add-ins or other files in specific directories for Excel to pick up and write specific registry entries to ensure our add-ins are listed and/or installed correctly.

Installation Location

When thinking about how to install our application, we need to consider how the user will start it, create new files and so on. Dictator applications are almost always started by opening one of the workbooks, or starting a VB6 EXE front loader. As such, dictator applications should be installed to a single folder and run from there.

Add-ins can be installed either by copying them to one of two specific locations, or by writing registry entries to include them in the *Tools > Add-ins* list (see later for details). Copying the xla to the user's AddIns folder is the easiest way to manually install add-ins, but is only appropriate for single-file add-ins. If our add-ins use other supporting files (such as templates, databases and so forth), all the files should be installed to their own folder, with the registry entries written for the *Tools > Add-ins* list.

When installing application-specific add-ins, we need to consider whether the user should be able to use the *File > New* menu to create new instances of our data-entry workbooks. If we want them to use that mechanism, the template workbook needs to be copied to the user's templates folder. For this to work properly, the corresponding add-in must be installed and using Application events to detect the user creating the new workbook (see *Chapter 7 — Using Class Modules to Create Objects*). The main problem with this approach is that the only way to ensure the corresponding add-in is installed is to include code in the template file to check that, which breaks the principle of not including code in our templates. Instead, we can use the AddIn_Install event to copy the template file to the user's templates folder and the AddIn_Uninstall event to remove it.

Many application-specific add-ins (including our PETRAS example) ignore the *File > New* menu and provide their own menu or toolbar button for creating new instances of their data-entry workbooks. By doing this, we don't need to copy files to different locations for Excel to use them. We can simply install all our files to a single folder and write registry entries to install our add-ins.

Installation Requirements

Templates

Templates that are intended to appear in the *File > New* dialog are installed on a per-user basis by copying them to the following folder:

C:\Documents and Settings\<UserName>\
```
Application Data\Microsoft\Templates
```

If our templates are opened under program control (such as the New Timesheet button in our PETRAS timesheet example), they should be kept with the add-in in their own folder.

Add-ins

Single-file, general-purpose add-ins can be installed on a per-user basis by copying them to the following folder:

C:\Documents and Settings\<UserName>\
```
Application Data\Microsoft\AddIns
```

or for all users by copying them to the following folder:

C:\Program Files\Microsoft Office\Office\Library

where Microsoft Office is the folder in which Office has been installed.

When add-ins are copied to either of these folders, they automatically appear in the *Tools > Add-ins* list, but are not installed by default. To have them installed as well as listed requires us to write some registry entries.

For more complex add-ins that may have other support files, it is better to install all the files to their own directory and write registry entries to add them to the *Tools > Add-ins* list. To do that, we add a string value in the registry key:

```
HKEY_CURRENT_USER\Software\Microsoft\Office\10.0\Excel
\Add-in Manager
```

where the name of the value is the full path and name of the add-in. The 10.0 in the registry key refers to the version of Excel:

- 9.0 = Excel 2000
- 10.0 = Excel 2002
- 11.0 = Excel 2003

When we add entries to the Add-in Manager key, the add-in is listed in the *Tools > Add-ins* dialog, but is not installed (that is, active). To have the add-in automatically installed, we have to write an entry to the registry key:

```
HKEY_CURRENT_USER\Software\Microsoft\Office\10.0\Excel\Options
```

instead of the Add-in Manager key. The entry must be a string value where the name is the next available item in the sequence OPEN, OPEN1,

OPEN2, OPEN3 and so on, and the value is the full path and name of the add-in, surrounded by quotation marks. This means that when writing registry entries to have our add-ins automatically installed, we have to first check whether there is a value called OPEN, then check whether there is a value called OPEN1, then check for OPEN2 and so forth until we find one that isn't used. If we precede the add-in name with a /R switch, Excel will open the add-in read-only. Figure 24-5 shows two OPEN registry entries, for the analysis toolpack and the IfError automation add-in.

Name	Type	Data
OPEN	REG_SZ	/R "C:\Program Files\Office 2002\Office 10\Library\Analysis\ANALYS32.XLL"
OPEN1	REG_SZ	/A "ProExcel.Functions"

Figure 24-5 The OPEN Registry Entries for an Excel and an Automation Add-in

COM Add-ins

The registry entries required to install COM Add-ins are covered in detail in *Chapter 21 — Writing Add-ins with Visual Basic 6*. The registry entries can be written by the Add-in Designer object, under either:

```
HKEY_CURRENT_USER\Software\Microsoft\Office\Excel\Addins
```

for per-user installation, or:

```
HKEY_LOCAL_MACHINE\SOFTWARE\Microsoft\Office\Excel\Addins
```

to install the COM add-in for all users. The Designer will write the registry entries when the COM Add-in DLL is registered on the user's machine, which is done using the regsvr32.exe program:

```
regsvr32 c:\mypath\myCOMAddin.dll
```

Automation Add-ins

Automation add-ins must also be registered on the user's machine using regsvr32, but they do not write their own registry entries. Instead, we have to write the same entries that we would for normal add-ins, but using the ProgID (that is, ProjectName.ClassName) instead of the file path and

name. For example, to install the IfError function from *Chapter 21 —
Writing Add-ins with Visual Basic 6* so it is listed in the *Tools > Add-ins* list
but not installed, we would add a new string value with the name
ProExcel.Functions within the registry key:

```
HKEY_CURRENT_USER\Software\Microsoft\Office\10.0\Excel
\Add-in Manager
```

To have the same add-in automatically installed, we would instead write a
new value in:

```
HKEY_CURRENT_USER\Software\Microsoft\Office\10.0\Excel\Options
```

where the name is OPEN, OPEN1 or OPEN2 and so forth, and the value is:

```
/A "ProExcel.Functions"
```

The /A identifies it as an automation add-in, and the "ProExcel.
Functions" is the ProgID of the class containing the IfError function, as
shown in Figure 24-5.

Installation Mechanisms

Manual

If our application consists of just a template and associated add-in, we
could provide instructions telling the users where to copy the files to, and
hope they do it correctly. As the number of files increases, so does the likelihood of failure.

An Installation Workbook

A very common method of installing Excel-based applications is to zip all
our files together and tell our users to unzip the file to a new directory and
open the Setup.xls workbook. The Setup.xls workbook performs the following tasks, then closes itself. These tasks could also be performed by a
VB6 front loader, as described in *Chapter 20 — Combining Excel and
Visual Basic 6*:

■ Registers any DLLs, using:

```
Shell "regsvr32 /s """ & ThisWorkbook.Path &"\MyDLL.DLL"""
```

- Moves add-ins and/or templates to the correct directories using `Application.LibraryPath` and/or `Application.TemplatesPath` to identify where to move them to.
- Uses the Excel object model to install add-ins (instead of writing registry entries), as shown in Listing 24-9.

Listing 24-9 Installing Add-ins Using the Object Model

```
Sub InstallAddins()

  'Install an Excel Addin
  Application.AddIns.Add(ThisWorkbook.Path & _
      "\MyAddin.xla").Installed = True

  'Silently register an Automation Addin
  Shell "regsvr32 /s """ & ThisWorkbook.Path & _
      "\ProExcel.dll"""

  'Install an Automation Addin
  Application.AddIns.Add("ProExcel.Functions") _
      .Installed = True

End Sub
```

Windows Installer

The biggest problems with the Manual or Workbook installs is that they do not provide an easy uninstall mechanism and they aren't really "professional." Doing it properly requires us to write an installation routine using InstallShield, WISE or similar application. Unfortunately, they are both expensive purchases and it is beyond the scope of this book to describe how to create installation routines using them. If you intend to use one of these packages, we suggest you refer to the product documentation, specifically to write the registry entries we detailed above.

Distributing

Originals

Excel-based applications are usually extremely easy to distribute—just zip up the files and e-mail them to the users. There are no runtimes that must be installed before our application (other than Excel itself, of course), so the user can just unzip and go.

Some companies prefer to administer the installation of applications centrally, rolling them out during the user's login scripts. For that case, we will need to create a proper installation package that will install our application without displaying any prompts (such as asking for file locations).

Updates

When distributing updates, we need to take a little more care to preserve our users' data and application settings. If we have followed the advice to always physically separate the code from the data, the only thing we need to be careful about is to not overwrite the users' data files with the empty templates we might include. If we didn't follow the advice to separate data from code, this is the time that we realize why we should have!

We should never distribute patches that attempt to modify the VBA code contained within another workbook. For us to be able to modify the code, the user must have ticked the Trust Access to Visual Basic Project box in the *Tools > Macro > Security* dialog, the project cannot be protected and saving the modified project will remove any digital signature we've applied. If the split between data and code has been planned in advance, we will always be able to simply overwrite files with the new versions.

Phone Home

If we have included a front-loader workbook or VB6 exe to start our application, we could include "phone home" distribution of updates. Every time the application starts, it connects to a central Web site (or Web service) to see whether any of the application files have been updated. If they have, the new files are downloaded, then opened and run. This mechanism is built in to the Visual Studio Tools for Office (see *Chapter 22 — Using VB.NET and the Visual Studio Tools for Office*), but can easily be built in to a front-loader workbook by using a Web service to check for updates (see *Chapter 23 — Excel, XML and Web Services*), then using Workbooks.Open and Workbook.SaveAs to open the new file from the server and save it to the local machine.

Conclusion

As developers of applications, it's all too easy for us to assume our user interfaces are so intuitive and easy to use there's no need to provide a help file. In reality, we can only achieve that level of simplicity with the most trivial features. Including a well-written help file with our application can provide the explanations our users require to effectively use the features we provide. The increase in confidence that brings will often lead to an improved perception of the entire application.

While developing Excel applications, we usually don't include any security restrictions, because they tend to get in the way of our work. We must, however, consider the security implications of everything we do, both in terms of whether our application could be misused and whether our application can be broken into.

Excel is not a secure environment; a malicious hacker can access any worksheet or VBProject in any workbook using tools readily available on the Internet. If we want to protect our code from the determined hacker (rather than accidental change), we must move it outside of Excel VBA, usually into VB6 DLLs.

When distributing our applications to end users, we usually need to provide an installation routine to ensure all our files are copied to the correct folders and write any registry entries that may be required. This is most often done using a separate setup.xls workbook, which can use the Excel object model to copy the files, install add-ins and so on. For a professional look, however, we should be creating proper installation routines using a commercial installer package such as WISE or InstallShield that can also be used to uninstall our applications.

Index

informIT

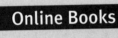

Register
Your Book
at www.awprofessional.com/register

You may be eligible to receive:

- Advance notice of forthcoming editions of the book
- Related book recommendations
- Chapter excerpts and supplements of forthcoming titles
- Information about special contests and promotions throughout the year
- Notices and reminders about author appearances, tradeshows, and online chats with special guests

Contact us

If you are interested in writing a book or reviewing manuscripts prior to publication, please write to us at:

Editorial Department
Addison-Wesley Professional
75 Arlington Street, Suite 300
Boston, MA 02116 USA
Email: AWPro@aw.com

Visit us on the Web: http://www.awprofessional.com

PQ7982341